Operations Management:
PROBLEMS AND MODELS

THE WILEY SERIES IN MANAGEMENT AND ADMINISTRATION

Elwood S. Buffa, Advisory Editor

University of California, Los Angeles

MANAGEMENT SYSTEMS, Second Edition
Peter P. Schoderbek

OPERATIONS MANAGEMENT: PROBLEMS AND MODELS, Third Edition
Elwood S. Buffa

PROBABILITY FOR MANAGEMENT DECISIONS
William R. King

PRINCIPLES OF MANAGEMENT: A MODERN APPROACH, Third Edition
Henry H. Albers

MODERN PRODUCTION MANAGEMENT, Third Edition
Elwood S. Buffa

CASES IN OPERATIONS MANAGEMENT: A SYSTEMS APPROACH
James L. McKenney and Richard S. Rosenbloom

ORGANIZATIONS: STRUCTURE AND BEHAVIOR, Volume I, Second Edition
Joseph A. Litterer

ORGANIZATIONS: SYSTEMS, CONTROL AND ADAPTATION, Volume II
Joseph A. Litterer

MANAGEMENT AND ORGANIZATIONAL BEHAVIOR:
A MULTIDIMENSIONAL APPROACH
Billy J. Hodge and Herbert J. Johnson

MATHEMATICAL PROGRAMMING: AN INTRODUCTION TO THE
DESIGN AND APPLICATION OF OPTIMAL DECISION MACHINES
Claude McMillan

DECISION MAKING THROUGH OPERATIONS RESEARCH
Robert J. Thierauf and Richard A. Grosse

QUALITY CONTROL FOR MANAGERS & ENGINEERS
Elwood G. Kirkpatrick

PRODUCTION SYSTEMS: PLANNING, ANALYSIS AND CONTROL
James L. Riggs

SIMULATION MODELING: A GUIDE TO USING SIMSCRIPT
Forrest P. Wyman

BASIC STATISTICS FOR BUSINESS AND ECONOMICS
Paul G. Hoel and Raymond J. Jessen

BUSINESS AND ADMINISTRATIVE POLICY
Richard H. Buskirk

INTRODUCTION TO ELECTRONIC COMPUTING: A MANAGEMENT APPROACH
Rodney L. Boyes, Robert W. Shields and Larry G. Greenwell

COMPUTER SIMULATION OF HUMAN BEHAVIOR
John M. Dutton and William H. Starbuck

INTRODUCTION TO GAMING: MANAGEMENT DECISION SIMULATIONS
John G. H. Carlson and Michael J. Misshauk

Operations Management:

PROBLEMS AND MODELS

Third Edition

ELWOOD S. BUFFA
University of California
Los Angeles

JOHN WILEY & SONS

New York • Chichester • Brisbane • Toronto

Library of Congress Catalog Card Number: 78-37167

ISBN 0-471-11867-2

Printed in the United States of America.

10 9 8 7

TO
E.E.B.
C.M.B.
J.C.B.
L.C.B.

PREFACE

The objective of this book is to present basic material for courses in production and operations management in the general context of the analytical methods. To establish a frame of reference for the student, the basic chapter outline of the third edition is organized around the problems associated with productive systems. Specific analytical methodologies are discussed in connection with the problems to which they are applicable. Thus, the CRAFT algorithm and line balance models are discussed in Chapter 6. Inventory models are discussed in relation to the general managerial problems of forecasting and item inventories. Linear programming as a solution technique is discussed prior to the problems of aggregate planning and scheduling where the technique is of particular importance in the problems of product mix and production programming. Waiting line and simulation models are discussed not only as a description of certain kinds of micro-productive systems but are arranged in sequence prior to the discussion of job shop scheduling because of the importance of queuing concepts in understanding the job shop system. Thus, the book is organized (1) in relation to the nature of the problems in operations management, and (2) in terms of the analytical models found most useful in approaching the problems. Therefore, the subtitle, *Problems and Models,* is descriptive of the overall content. The book is written in a relatively non-mathematical style and attempts to give concepts and ideas without indulging in naive over-simplification.

My intention is to develop a basic comprehension of both problems and methods so that in operations situations we can make intelligent decisions based on the results of analyses performed by staff specialists. This, of course, requires a keen understanding of the problem and how the basic model in question is constructed and functions. However, it does not require any deep understanding of underlying mathematical derivations and manipulations. For students who wish to develop into staff specialists in operations analysis, this book should serve as an introduction which may be followed by deeper penetration into many of the individual topics in subsequent courses.

Operations Management: Problems and Models should be of help to the growing number of instructors who feel that the concepts and methods of production and operations analysis need to be strongly tied to the appropriate analytical methods. Although emphasis has been placed on some of the more recent developments, such as mathematical and simulation models, I have not ignored either the breadth of present day conceptions of operations management or the traditional models for approaching the analyses of problems such as work measurement and methods analysis. In many instances I have utilized traditional analysis in discussing the nature of problems because of the straightforward graphic character of many of these traditional models.

The third edition involves a very substantial reorganization of the sequencing and grouping of materials in order to achieve improved flow and integration. In addition, there are substantial deletions, additions, and general updating. The former chapter dealing with a review of fundamental statistical concepts has been deleted, since it appears that virtually all students taking courses based on the book have a basic course in statistics in their backgrounds. New materials appear in Chapters 2, 7, 13, 19, and 21. Some new problems have been added in these as well as other chapters.

As in the previous editions, I assume that the student has had a basic course in statistics and, therefore, that he understands something about distributions, measures of central value and variability, and statistical inference. In general, only the basic mathematical skills are required since we do not go beyond rudimentary operations without direct explanation of the techniques. Derivation is kept to a minimum and occurs mainly in Part III in order to develop basic economic lot size models and in Part V to develop the simple waiting line models.

ACKNOWLEDGEMENTS

I wish to thank particularly the many graduate students in my seminar who made specific contributions to various sections of the book through discussions and class papers. Outstanding in this regard were Drs. Jack Alcalay, Andrew Grindlay, Arnold Reisman, William Taubert, and Tom Sikes, and Mr. George McFadden. I should also like to acknowledge the contributory effects of the environment at UCLA and my colleagues who helped create that environment.

The book has benefited a great deal by critical comment by colleagues around the country. The second edition was reviewed by Professors Trevor Sainsbury of the University of Pittsburgh, Robert D. Smith and Michael P.

Hottenstein of the Pennsylvania State University, William Thompson of the University of Houston, and Billy Goetz of the Massachusetts Institute of Technology. The present third edition benefited greatly by the thoughtful review of Professor Gene K. Groff of Indiana University.

Where specific ideas, illustrations, or quotations are used I have directly acknowledged them in footnotes or references. The book could not have been written without the use of or reference to these materials. I acknowledge with pride the fact that the general subject matter of this book is based on the works of many individual researchers who have created a field study worthy of careful attention.

Pacific Palisades, California   ELWOOD S. BUFFA

CONTENTS

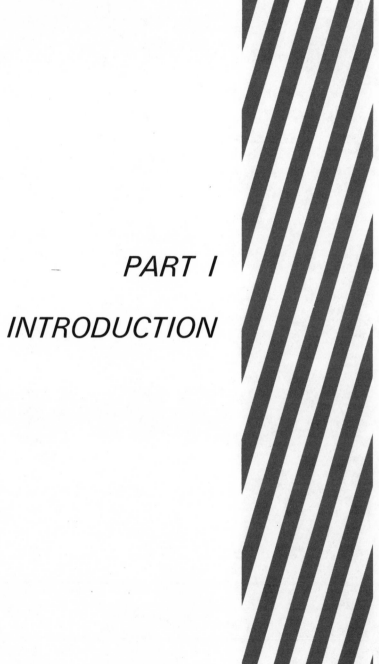

PART I

INTRODUCTION

chapter 1

SCIENCE IN MANAGEMENT

The growth of science in management since the end of World War II is one of the most exciting developments ever to come on the business and industrial scene. It has produced managerial obsolescence in many functions of business, and at a minimum has created a feeling of uneasiness in the hearts of men who see the developing power of analytical techniques applied to management problems. It has hastened the development of professionalism in management.

The seeds that would grow into the branching treelike applied science were planted originally by Frederick W. Taylor [9],* at the turn of the century. Taylor, who was trained as an engineer, applied his fertile mind to the reduction of the worker's art and trade knowledge to a set of empirically derived work rules which improved productivity in such skills or trades as metals machining, pig iron handling, shoveling, and others. In developing these improved working procedures, tools, and systems, Taylor resorted to careful experimentation as a basis for the development of his improved systems. More important than the improvement of specific management work systems was the general philosophy of "scientific management" which Taylor expounded. Taylor believed that management could be reduced to an applied science in many of its aspects and became the zealous proponent of scientific management, devoting much of his later life to the preaching of this philosophy. Taylor did not envision or predict the course of events by which the applied science and methodology would develop, or the character of science in management at its current stage of development.

*Numbers in brackets refer to references at the end of chapters.

Following the great impetus given by war operations research during World War II, there was a rapid development of the application of mathematical and statistical models to business and industrial problems. Although the greatest proportion of these applications have occurred in the production or operations functions of business, marketing, financial, and general management, functions have also benefited. During the same war and postwar period, technology produced concepts of automatic control and data processing undreamed of by the pioneers of scientific management. The pace of automation of operations and computation quickened, and many people spoke of the effects on our economy and society as being comparable to a second industrial revolution. One of the outstanding developments of this trend for management science has been computer simulation. Problems of incredible complexity which could not be approached by mathematical methods could be approached through simulation. Simulation provided a laboratory for management to test the ultimate effects of policies without actually disrupting operations. Also, the computer provided the basis for rapid integrated management controls. The end results of this latter technological trend may well become the most important from a social and economic point of view.

Meanwhile, other branches of management science which focus on the human being as an individual and as a member of work groups have also developed rapidly. These disciplines have their roots in experimental psychology and physiology, sociology, and the behavioral sciences in general. One main stem of this activity has to do with the organization of work (job design), the measurement of work, and human engineering. Other main stems have dealt with communications and organization, motivation, leadership, and many other questions of great significance to large and small organizations.

Management and Management Science

Management has always been practiced mainly as an art. As an art, management teaches through experience. To be sure, the art has progressed tremendously, but usually these experiences represent special cases, and very little of what was learned is transmitted. Forrester [5] states:

> The advancement of an "art" eventually reaches a plateau. The human lifetime limits the knowledge that can be gained from personal experience. In an art, experiences are poorly transferred from one location to another or from the past to the present. Historical experiences lack a framework for relating them to current problems. One company's experiences cannot be directly and meaningfully used by another.

If management art has indeed reached a plateau, further development may be paced by the rate at which managerial experience can be generalized into a common frame of reference that is applicable to different companies in different industries, managed by different men. This might be stated as a general objective of management science; that is, to develop a body of knowledge which is transferable.

Without doubt, the general area of usefulness that we must allot to the art in management far exceeds the area for management science today. Perhaps a more unfortunate observation is that practicing art, and management science, have a very small area in which there is an overlap—that is, much too small a proportion of the knowledge of the embryonic science of management has trickled into active use. It would be easy to shrug off this unhappy result by assigning the cause to the inertia of thought of practicing managers. Although inertia undoubtedly accounts for some of the lag, equally important reasons may be that management scientists have preferred to talk to each other about management problems they have concocted rather than the real problems the manager faces. Too often, the management scientist feels that his task has been completed when a paper (often exhibiting mathematical elegance) has been published in an academically oriented journal (which the practicing manager does not, and cannot read, because it is written in a language that is foreign to him). Usually the same ideas and results can be translated into the English language with the help of charts and graphs, but there is an apparent hesitancy to do this because such a paper may be misjudged by academic colleagues as work of "low power." We face a breakdown of communications.

The criticism that management scientists too often work on problems that they themselves construct, rather than the real problems, has less long-run significance than the failure of communications, in this author's view. We must all agree that management science is embryonic. Early models in any science are usually highly idealized. They may assume linear relationships where known nonlinearity exists. They may ignore factors which enter the problem but which are not the major factors. They may ignore some interactions between factors. Nevertheless, models which ignore some known factors often have good enough predictive value, and their relative simplicity makes solutions possible. On the other hand, the more realistic and complex models may not be solvable. At a minimum, these early models have value as stepping stones to more realistic models that may ultimately have enough predictive accuracy to be of value as practical working models.

A good example of the point that early models, which may in themselves be inadequate, lead ultimately to more realistic models is in the original development of the Linear Decision Rule (LDR). The LDR was a relatively early proposal (1955) for the broad planning and scheduling of production rates and employment levels in aggregate terms. The model made it possible for higher management to retain the power of decision over the key variables guiding the levels and use of enterprise resources in broad terms. These decisions each period, in aggregate terms, then became constraints under which the plant developed detailed schedules for hiring and layoff, how much to produce of each item, inventories to build or draw down, and so on. The LDR was a stroke of genius in that it conceptualized in a simple end use package some of the broad key variables of interest to management, yielding specific instructions on aggregate production rate, employment, and inventory levels which were optimal *for the model*. The difficulty was, however, that to achieve this optimality in the mathematical model required a warping of the company cost structure into a series of quadratic cost functions. The LDR was not used a great deal because the quadratic cost functions did not fit well enough the few cost components represented and mathematical complexity restrained us from attempting to include additional cost components. But the fundamental objective of the LDR was recognized and a number of different approaches to the same problem have been developed, namely, heuristic and computer search methods, both of which are free from constraints on the mathematical nature of the cost functions and the overall complexity of the cost structure. Though the final answer to the aggregate planning problem is still not clear, there has been a great deal of progress in building on the original LDR model. We will discuss these aggregate planning models in Chapters 12 and 13.

Management and Decision Making

Management's primary function is to make the decisions that determine the future course of action for the organization over the short and the long term. These decisions have to do with every conceivable physical and organizational problem; they may deal with markets and marketing channels, financial planning, personnel procurement policies, alternate plans for expanding production facilities, policies for material procurement, labor control, and so on. More often than not the decisions involved cut across functional lines.

Decision theory is directed toward determining how rational decisions ought to be made. It attempts to establish a logical framework for decisions that correlates science and the world of models with the real world for various alternative lines of action. These decisions are concerned with everything that goes on in the organization. For day-to-day operating or repetitive decisions, a set of decision rules makes possible continuity and smooth operation, for example, the decision rules which determine the amount of raw materials to be ordered at one time. Larger-scale decisions, such as the determination of an overall plan for expansion, or the decision to float a new bond issue, employ the same general concepts of decision theory but occur only occasionally.

As new managerial problems occur, they are usually faced by management with the only tools available—managerial experience, judgment, and intuition. Decisions are made on this basis because they must be made; however, the decisions may become formalized into policies and procedures to guide future decisions. These decisions may be classified as almost semi-automatic and are normally the domain of middle management. In some instances a problem may lend itself to the refinement of formal decision models, thus providing automatic decision rules. This flow is diagramed in Figure 1, and the relative areas seem to represent the importance of each of these areas in management decisions today. We should not assume that management science is working only at the automatic decision rule level. It is certainly true that the objectives of management scientists are to

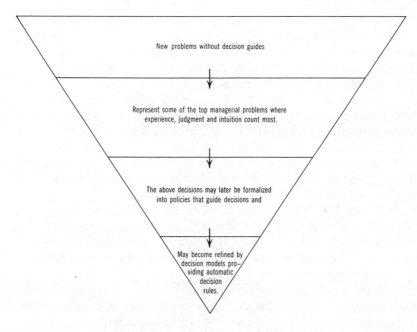

FIGURE 1. The refinement of new problems into policies and automatic decision rules. The relative areas may represent the approximate position of judgment, policy, and automatic decision making today.

move as many problem areas as possible to the most automatic level possible; however, management science is working at all of the levels. Where highly realistic working models can be developed, decisions may be reduced to automatic decision rules, thus expanding the scope of the smallest triangle in Figure 1. In addition, management science may help to formalize policies and questions which previously had been decided only on the basis of experience, judgment, and intuition. Where the real world problems are too complex for present-day models to handle effectively, management science may be able to formalize part of the problem so that intuitive decisions can be made more effectively. Finally, management science may be able to help define more effectively some of the new problems. We wish to expand progressively the relative size and scope of each of the areas representing the application of management science at the expense of any of the areas representing a lesser application of scientific methodology.

An example of the process diagramed in Figure 1 is in the inventory problem. At the turn of the century when Frederick Taylor was preaching his principles of scientific management the inventory problem was virtually without decision guides other than the general recognition that inventories were necessary for doing business and that they cost money and should be minimized. As total business volume increased the total of inventories increased. Inventories became a top managerial problem, and a great deal of emphasis was placed on them. A manager with the experience and judgment to manage the inventory problem was a valued executive. He may have sensed that as business volume expanded the inventories necessary to sustain the entire production-distribution process did not need to increase in direct proportion. Later he probably established definite and formal policies for inventory levels and set up procedures for how much of each item or class of items to order at one time to have some degree of control, recognizing that there was some sort of balance between having too much or too little inventory.

In 1915 these developing guidelines were first placed into the rigorous format of a mathematical model by F. W. Harris. He proposed the first economic lot size model. It was a deterministic model and fell short in many respects of describing total inventory reality, but it defined the major cost variables and gave a definite answer to the question of the quantity of an item to be ordered at one time. This economic order quantity (EOQ) formula also gave the first clue that some components of inventory levels might logically vary as the square root of sales, rather than in direct proportion. Guidelines for ordering now became more formalized as EOQ systems with order points stated precisely when to order and how much to order at one time.

In the years that intervened, the small beginning by Harris developed with the efforts of many people into first formal policies and decision guides and finally into models providing automatic decision rules. Before the latter became a reality a great deal of research effort was expended in evolving the original inventory model into one which took account of uncertainty of demand and greater sophistication in terms of the recognition and measurement of additional, more realistic cost structures. The result is that today automatic decision rules can be programmed to handle the inventory problem and in many instances the entire material procedure has been computerized. Today it is no particular novelty to recognize that cycle stocks (to sustain the production-distribution process) should vary as the square root of sales, buffer stocks (to absorb the random fluctuations in demand) may also vary as the square root of sales, and that transit inventories (an equivalent amount of stock always in motion) should vary directly with changes in sales. We will discuss the entire question of inventory models and systems in Chapters 8 and 9, and inventories in context with overall production-distribution systems in Chapter 13.

In decision making, management selects from a set of alternatives what is considered to be the best course of action. To judge which of the alternatives is best, however, we must have criteria and values that measure the relative worth of the alternatives, and a system for forecasting the performance of the alternative courses of action. These elements, taken together, form the basis for a decision criterion which balances off the desirable and undesirable characteristics of the alternatives. The difficulties come in establishing the comparability of the various criteria that may conflict and in determining the future performance of the alternatives. Much of what we will discuss has to do with these forecasting systems, for they are models of the operating mechanisms with which we are dealing. Figure 2 shows the structure of this decision-making process.

In Figure 2 we have indicated that we wish to select the alternative that maximizes desirability. Since we are dealing with future values, what is the meaning of this term? What is the probability of attaining the results forecasted, or conversely, what is the risk of not attaining these results? Actually, the final net desirability is weighted by the probability of attainment so that for decision purposes we are dealing with *expected values*.

Let us illustrate this point briefly. If we were placing bets at the track, a "long shot" might pay $150 on a $2 ticket whereas a "favorite" might pay only $3. If the long shot had only a 1.5 percent chance of winning, and the favorite had an 80 percent chance, we should choose the favorite, because the probability weighted value is $2.40 versus $2.25 for the long shot. To be sure, if the long shot wins, our actual profit is much more, but the probability of winning is so small that a rational decision maker would

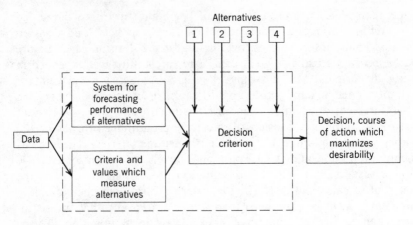

FIGURE 2.   *Structure of decision making.*

choose the favorite. In a more typical business situation, we may want to select the best method for performing a given task. Perhaps one alternative involves a manual system which has been proven practical so that we are quite sure of attaining the forecasted result. The second alternative involves the design and perfection of a machine to perform the operation. In this latter situation we are breaking new ground, and this involves some risks. These risks are, for example, that a practical machine may cost somewhat more than expected initially and that the maintenance and operating costs of the system may be somewhat greater than anticipated. The risks mean that the probability of attaining the forecasted benefits of the machine system are sometimes less than 100 percent, perhaps 75 percent. For decision purposes then, the potential measured benefits of the machine system over the manual system need to be scaled down by the factor 0.75.

Although we are always dealing with expected values in decision-making problems, we will note that in the majority of instances no apparent account has been taken of attainment probabilities in the models with which we deal. This does not mean that the probabilities have been ignored. Rather, it means that the probabilities of attainment of the various alternatives are all equal, or that we have no basis for saying that they are not equal, or the payoffs and probability distributions are symmetrical.

Models

In the decision-making structure of Figure 2, models are the bases of the prediction systems and are vital to the formal decision-making process.

Indeed, they are vital to an intellectual attack on any problem. Models come to us from scientific methods. The scientist attempts to duplicate in some kind of model the behavior of the system or subsystem with which he is working. Once he has achieved this parallelism between the real world situation and his model, it is usually easier to manipulate the model to study the characteristics in which he is interested than it is to try to work with the real world system.

Models are invariably abstractions to some degree of the actual systems for which we wish to predict performance. A prominent example is the aerodynamicist's model used in conjunction with wind tunnels. Since he is primarily interested in aerodynamic performance, shape is the main characteristic of concern, and other factors in flight, such as weight, strength of individual parts, etc., are ignored. Therefore the characteristic of shape is carefully duplicated in the model and the other factors are ignored. By abstracting only the characteristic of shape, such a study is much more economical, and considerably more economical than attempting to study aerodynamic performance on actual aircraft. Using the model, the aerodynamicist can make measurements more easily and manipulate variables at will, and all at fairly low cost. By abstracting from the real world system he can focus his attention on a much simpler system without great loss because some details have been ignored.

A model is useful in a practical sense when it accurately duplicates the behavior of the real world system. If a model does not accomplish this, it is useful only insofar as it provides information and insight into the development of a new model. Models must be validated, sometimes repeatedly. Certainly the first planetariums did not predict the movement of planets and stars perfectly, but by correlating the predictions of the model with actual observed data, corrections could be introduced into the model which improved predictions. Also, as technology and science advance, new situations develop that require the revision and updating of models (such as the discovery of new stars in the case of the planetarium, or the development of supersonic flight in the case of wind tunnel models). Figure 3 shows the structure of successive steps in the development of an acceptable model with intermediate validations of models with data from the real world.

Kinds of Models. Models may be classified as iconic, analogue, and symbolic. *Iconic* models retain some of the physical relationships of the things they represent, that is, they look like the real thing, but they are usually scaled up or down. Good examples are the aerodynamicists' models, planetariums, engineering blueprints, globes of the world, photographs, and of course, the three-dimensional models of physical facilities often used in architecture and factory planning. Iconic models preserve physical relationships, although not necessarily all physical relationships. As with

World of models

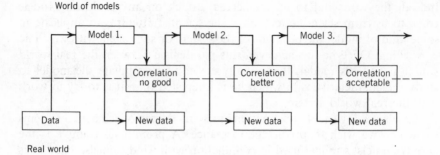

FIGURE 3. *Steps toward the development of an acceptable model.*

other kinds of models, only those characteristics of interest to the study are retained, which results in both economy and relative simplicity. Iconic models are useful to study conditions that prevail at a given time, much as a photograph freezes action. They are not particularly useful for the study of dynamic situations, nor helpful in discovering relationships between variables in a system.

Analogue models establish a relationship between a variable in the system and an analogous variable in the model. Thus a graph of sales by months uses the length of lines as analogous to the magnitude of sales and time. An electrician's schematic diagram uses lines to show electrical connections. Various kinds of flow charts use lines as analogous to material or information flow. One of the most useful analogues found in technological work has been the electrical analogue. Analogue computers establish a relationship between variables in a real world problem and an electrical system. Analogue models are often useful for the study of dynamic situations. Usually, changes in an analogue model can be made more easily than in an iconic model, so they can fit more different situations, and thus have greater generality.

Symbolic models substitute symbols for components or variables in the real world system, and the symbols are generally related mathematically. The symbolic system then is a model of some aspect of the real situation. For example, Newton's second law of motion, $F = ma$, states a relationship between three variables; force, mass, and acceleration. The great advantage of symbolic models is that interrelationships between variables can be uncovered through manipulation of the model, and these interrelationships might not be made obvious by less powerful means. The symbolic model is often the most difficult and expensive to construct, yet it is usually more general in application and yields the most information. Symbolic models have been used most commonly in the sciences. Today, however, the business world is becoming aware of the power of symbolic models in many organization and management problems.

Models in This Book. The models useful in operations management are of several kinds and generally seem to run the gamut of all kinds of models. *Physical* models are sometimes used in the development of facility layouts in order to clearly visualize the effects of alternate arrangements on physical flow, in-process storage, machine and work place layout, and so on. *Graphical* models of various types have been extremely useful, particularly in studying flow on a macro basis and in studying micro flow at an operation in attempting to optimize man-machine systems. In recent years network flow models in the form of PERT-CPM charts have been the basis for planning and control of large-scale one-time projects such as those which occur in research and development and in the aerospace industry in particular. These network flow concepts have also been of value in sequencing models for production line balancing and for the job shop scheduling problem.

Statistical models were some of the earliest models used in operations management which had a rigorous mathematical basis. The general field of statistical quality control has developed models for controlling the output quality of processes and, through sampling procedures, models to determine whether or not to accept a large lot of items based on a relatively small sample. The problem of the measurement of human work in a reliable way is also in essence a statistical sampling problem.

With the advent of modern computing capabilities *simulation models* have shown great power where mathematical models might be too complex to solve. Where stochastic processes enter complex production models (and they usually do) simulation incorporating Monte Carlo techniques has made it possible to represent stochastic elements in a process, thereby retaining realism in large-scale system simulations of entire producing plants. Simulation models often incorporate heuristic decision rules (logical rules which provide clear and definite decisions though the rules themselves may not be optimal). *Waiting line or queuing* models are mathematical models which have been developed to describe the basic processes involved in a situation where some kind of service center processes something which may arrive for service by some random schedule. For example, machines may break down and need to be repaired. Basic waiting line models have been useful in examining the maintenance problem and in the inventory problem. Coupled with the simulation methodology, waiting line models have been useful in examining the production line balancing problem and the sequencing of orders in a job shop.

Inventory models are mathematically based and describe the cost consequences of alternate ordering policies. Production-inventory models embed the inventory problem in the overall decisions to set production rates, hire and fire labor, accumulate inventories, and so on. Such problems have been approached by linear programming, quadratic programming, heuristic programming, and computer search methods. *Linear programming* models are broadly useful in resource allocation problems which might be involved in the scheduling of men and facilities as well as other resources.

Advantages and Disadvantages of Models. Models provide the most effective means yet developed for predicting performance. Indeed, it is hard to conceive of a prediction system which is not finally a model. To construct a model of a real process or system, careful consideration of just which elements of the system need to be abstracted is required. This in itself is usually a profitable activity, for it develops insights into the problem. When building a model, we are immediately struck with the magnitude of our ignorance. What do we really know? Where are the gaps in available data? It is often impractical, or impossible, to manipulate the real world system to determine the effect of certain variables. Business systems are typical, for to use the business system itself as a laboratory could be disastrous, and at a minimum, very costly.

The dangers in using predictive models lie in the possibility of oversimplifying problems to keep models in workable form. The decision maker may place too much faith in a seemingly rigorous and complete analysis. Even though the quantitative analysis makes no pretense at accounting for some factors and does not include intangible and human values, it is often true that an executive is drawn to the decision indicated by a limited model without a careful weighing of the total problem, including the factors not reduced in the model. Presumably, the formal decision-making process has as its ultimate objective the reduction of as many decisions as possible to the automatic region of Figure 1, where the model is so complete that its performance as a predictor is entirely satisfactory.

MODELS AND THE PRODUCTION FUNCTION /

Although management science is in general applicable to the entire organization, the majority of the work done to date has been done in the setting of the production or operations function. The result is that the area of overlap between managerial art and management science is somewhat greater for operations than for general management and the management of other functions. This book deals with the methodologies of many different kinds of models as applied to production and operations systems. The models discussed are some that have proved to be of value in the analysis of certain phases of operational systems. We shall now define what we mean by production, attempt to place it in an overall setting, develop generalized descriptive models of production systems, and finally describe the general nature of problems encountered. We will use the terms "production" and "operations," or the terms "production systems" and "operations systems" as being synonymous.

What is Production?

Production is the process by which goods and services are created. Production systems combine materials, labor, and capital resources in an organized way with the objective of producing some good or service. Production systems may occur in factories, banks, offices, retail stores, hospitals, etc. In all instances, some input to the system is being processed within the system to produce a good or service as an output. We are, in fact, dealing with the operations phase of any enterprise.

Boundaries of the Production System

Let us first attempt to subdivide the entire organization into functional subsystems. One subsystem will describe a single function or a component of a function, which may be executed by many persons or machines in different geographic locations. In attempting to apply the definition of production given earlier, we shall assign the *single* function of "creation" of goods and services to production. To perform this function, the production system requires inputs from other subsystems of the organization, such as service inputs (for example, maintenance, supervision, plant layout design, etc.) and control inputs (for example, measurement, data processing, planning, control, order and sales information processing, forecasting, etc.). Although the other subsystems and their functions in an organization could be subdivided in other ways, it is convenient for our purposes to define the following subsystems in addition to the production subsystem just described:

1. *Policy-formulating system.* The function of this system is to adapt basic organization policies to information reflecting present and forecasted future conditions. Conceivably, we could have incorporated this function in the general control function described in 2. In both subsystems, the basic function is the gathering and data processing of information with the purpose of planning and of

control. The only reason for the separate definition of our policy-formulating system is that it has a line authority characteristic which is not a necessary part of the control system.

2. *Control system.* The basic function of the control system is the transformation of information. As we shall see, this function may be subdivided into component functions. It is entirely conceivable that the transformation of information can ultimately be handled completely by machines and computers.

3. *Intermediate organization systems.* For convenience, we shall define intermediate organization systems with functions to provide the necessary *service* to other subsystems of the organization or to some subsystems of the environment which directly affect the organization subsystems. We are including here such services as supervision, delegation of authority, the transmitting of decisions, as well as the other kinds of service which we have already mentioned.

Figure 4 places the production system in context with the other subsystems, showing the broad scheme of information flow and physical flow between the various subsystems and between the enterprise system as a whole and the environment. Here, the environment represents the broad economic, social, and physical factors which have an effect on the enterprise system. Figure 5 shows the production system in relation to control subsystems. Here we see that measurements taken from within the production system (for example, time requirements for operations, costs, raw material, and in-process inventory levels, etc.) together with information from other organization subsystems are fed into the data-processing system. The data-processing system in turn feeds transformed information on operations to the two subsystems for day-to-day control of operations and for forecasting and planning. Higher-level, longer-term control represents an integration and transformation of information from the other subsystems as shown.

Ideally, we would like to construct a single mathematical model of the production system, within the framework indicated by Figures 4 and 5, which would forecast the operation of any production system, given the characteristics of the production system and the various related subsystems. This is much too ambitious at the present stage of development of models of production and operations systems. Currently, we must be satisfied with models that tend to account only for small parts of the problems we shall define later in this chapter. Nevertheless, it is important to maintain the "system's" point of view just described and summarized by Figures 4 and 5. The basic reason for this is that there are inevitably interactions between the various subsystems of the enterprise and local solution of local problems

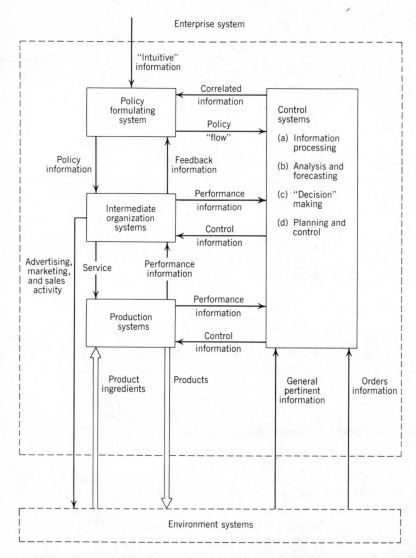

FIGURE 4. Interaction between production subsystem, other organizational subsystems, and environment systems. From J. A. Alcalay and E. S. Buffa, "Conceptual Framework for a General Model of a Production System," International Journal of Production Research, *March, 1963.*

often results in "suboptimization," that is, the best solution viewed from within the subsystem, but not the best solution when viewed within the system as a whole. In general, our present capability does not permit the

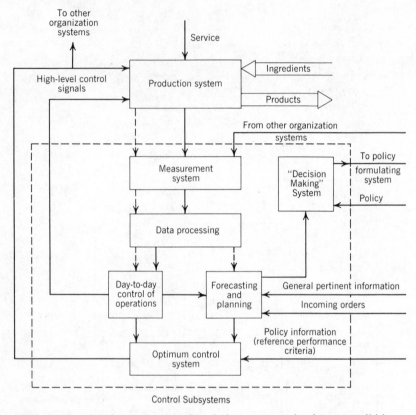

FIGURE 5. Production system in relation to control subsystems. Ibid.

strict adherence to this systems point of view. In attempting to approach it, however, we shall endeavor to apply this principle: Models of operations should be as broad as practicable, taking account insofar as is feasible, with the power of existing technique, of interactions between various subsystems; whenever a reasonably validated model indicates incremental gains which exceed incremental costs, we assume that the systems view has been approached.

A Generalized Descriptive Model of Production

Let us now attempt to describe the generalized nature of production or operations activity. According to our definition, the factory, the office, the supermarket, the hospital, etc., all represent special cases with special characteristics: Our production system has inputs that represent the material, parts, paper work forms, and the customers or patients, as the case may be. The input will be processed in some way by a series of operations, whose sequence and number are specified for each input. The operations may vary from one only, to any number, and may take on any desired characteristics; they may be mechanical, chemical, assembly, inspection and control, dispatching to the next operation, receiving, shipping, personal contact (such as an interview), and paper work operations. The outputs of our system are completed parts, products, chemicals, service to customers or patients, or completed paper work. There is provision for storage in our system after the receipt of the input and between each operation in the system. The time and storage may vary from zero to any finite value. Inputs are transported among all operations in the system. Any means of transportation may be supplied, including self-transportation in the case of clients and customers. Our model also has an information system and a decision maker. The information system interconnects all the physical activities and provides a basis for management decision. The information system may provide continuous feedback of information regarding the progress of work, its quality, and other factors for control purposes, or it may provide data for special studies to revise and improve operations. These functions provide the equivalent of a "nervous system" for the model. Figure 6 represents our production system.

Production systems may occur in series; for example, when completed products are shipped from the factory to a warehouse, they are leaving the factory system only to arrive at a second production system, called a warehouse. In this way the two systems may be considered as parts of one large system. Systems may also occur in parallel, such as when a number of factories produce similar products and supply several market areas. For solving some problems these factories may be considered one large production system. The nature of the problem under study will usually determine the boundaries of the production system.

Now let us consider what would happen to an input to the system. After being received, the input goes into storage to take its turn in the processing. By some set of priority rules, it is drawn from storage to begin processing. These rules might be: first in–first out, time or date required for completion or delivery, urgency, or some other system of priority rules. The input is then processed according to a predetermined sequence. Let us assume the sequence b, d, c. From initial storage the input goes to operation b and is placed in temporary storage to await processing there. We assume that operation b has already some assigned work or load, and, therefore, our input takes its place in line (in storage) and will be processed at b according to the priority decision rules established. After being pro-

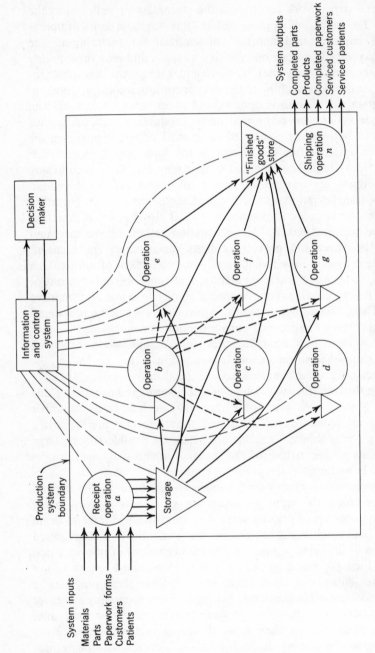

FIGURE 6. *Diagram of a generalized production system. Inputs may be processed in any specified sequence of operations and are transported between operations. The number of operations may vary from one to any finite number. Storage occurs between all operations, and the time in storage may vary from essentially zero to any finite amount. Note: There are interconnections between all combinations of operations b through f, although only those originating at b are shown. The information system interconnects all activities and provides the basis for management decision.*

cessed at b it is transported to d, placed in storage, drawn out according to priority rules, processed, and so on through the entire sequence of operations. One of the operations may be an inspection. The operation just preceding shipment may be a packaging operation, preparing the item for shipment.

If we are speaking of a high-volume, standardized, fabricated part, the operations may be placed in sequence and may be interconnected by conveying equipment. The storages would take place on the conveyors themselves, and the decision rules are first in–first out. If we are speaking of a hospital, the storages may take place in waiting rooms or in hospital beds. The priority rules may be first in–first out, with urgency exceptions. Many of the tasks are mobile as in the instance of the hospital, for example, when nurses give shots or medication. In a supermarket, products are received and stored on display shelves. Customer receiving is practically nonexistent as an operation. A customer picks the desired items from the shelves, transports them, and takes his place in line for the single operation of checkout. In soap manufacturing by the continuous process, materials are received and stored. They are then taken from storage in a large quantity, dissolved, and pumped through a series of chemical operations, so that transportation and storage between operations occurs in the pipes. The material is chemically processed while it moves and emerges as soap. It is then packaged and shipped. The operations of a bank may be considered in a parallel way. Consider the handling of a check presented for payment at a cashier's window. Customers take their place in line and are normally served on a first come–first served basis. The sequence of operations which follows may take the form of an inspection of cash balances for a certain account, a comparison of signatures, a stamping of the check as paid, counting of money, etc. Later, the check goes through a sequence of operations which adjusts the appropriate account balances, prepares daily and monthly reports, and so on.

The job shop manufacturing situation, where custom products are fabricated and assembled, is undoubtedly the most complex type of production system. Take a space satellite and its propulsion system, for example. Thousands of individual parts must be fabricated and assembled into subassemblies, and thence, into final assemblies. This activity must be dovetailed to fit a complex schedule, so that operation time is available when it is needed to provide parts for subassemblies and final assemblies. The pattern or flow of the multitude of parts from operation to operation is so complex that it can only be visualized by some abstract means of representation. Many of the parts require operation time on the same machines, but the operations occur at different times in the overall manufacturing cycle. The problem of loading the operations in such a way that they can be utilized effectively is obviously a difficult one. Table I summarizes inputs, processes, and outputs for different kinds of production systems.

TABLE I. Inputs, processes, and outputs for different kinds of systems which create a good or service

Facility	Input	Conversion Process	Output
Bank:			
teller window	Customers	Cash checks, make deposits	Serviced customers
accounting office	Canceled checks, deposit slips, etc.	Adjust balances of accounts	Status of accounts, reports
Supermarket:			
store and display shelves	Merchandise	Receive, unpack and store on shelves	Merchandise ready for sale
check-out counters	Customer with purchases	Checkout, add up bill, receive payment and make change; package	Customer with purchases, less cash
Factory	Raw material, parts and supplies	Change shape or form by fabrication and assembly; package	Completed parts and products
Hospital:			
patients' rooms, operating rooms, laboratories, etc.	Patients	Examinations, shots, tests, operations, etc.	Serviced patients

Continuous versus Intermittent Models

Continuous flow production systems are those where the facilities are standardized as to routings and flow, since inputs are standardized. Therefore, a standard set of processes and sequence of processes can be adopted. Continuous models are represented in practice by production and assembly lines, large-scale office operations processing forms by a standard procedure, continuous flow of chemical operations, and many others. Intermittent production situations are those where the facilities must be flexible enough to handle a wide variety of products and sizes, or where the basic nature of the activity imposes change of important characteristics of the input (change in product design). In instances such as these, no single sequence pattern of the operations is appropriate, so the relative location of the operations must be a compromise that is best for all inputs considered together. Transportation facilities between operations must be flexible to accommodate the wide variety of input characteristics as well as the wide variety of routes that the inputs may require. These conditions commonly define an intermittent production system—intermittent because the flow is intermittent. Considerable storage between operations is required so the individual operations can be carried on somewhat independently, resulting in ease of scheduling and in fuller utilization of men and machines. In practice, intermittent production is represented by custom- or job-order machine shops, hospitals, general offices, batch chemical operations, and many others.

As we have shown, our generalized descriptive model in Figure 6 can be made to fit both the intermittent and continuous flow situations by the specification of some of the detailed characteristics. We have assumed intermittent flow in our model and defined it in general enough terms that the specification of a fixed operation sequence, the specification of continuous flow transportation facilities, the assumption of low-storage times between operations, and a first in–first out set of priority decision rules would all determine continuous flow conditions. The continuous flow situation is common enough today, however, that we tend to think in terms of the dichotomy of continuous and intermittent flow models. Therefore, we have constructed the special case of continuous flow as a separate model in Figure 7.

Basic layout types fit into this intermittent-continuous classification of production systems. When a system is designed for the intermittent conditions, equipment of the same type is grouped together according to the functions performed, such as in Figure 8. Here we see a layout for a machine shop that is process oriented, and this type of layout is commonly called process layout or, sometimes, functional layout. The continuous flow model that we have discussed results in a layout illustrated by Figure 9, where the location of equipment is determined by the sequence of operations to be performed on the product. This type of design is commonly called product layout because the layout is oriented around the product produced. An equally common name for this type of design is line layout. If similar equipment is required for both parts *A* and *B* in Figure 9, it would normally be duplicated in the two lines, even though the equipment was not fully utilized for either part. Actually, most layouts are a combination of process and product in manufacturing activity, with fabrication operations generally following process layout and assembly operations generally following product layout.

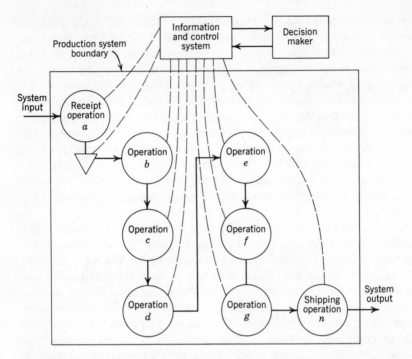

FIGURE 7. Diagram of a continuous flow production system. Input-output characteristics are standardized, allowing standardization of operations and their sequence. Minor storage of inputs occurs after receipt. Once on the transportation system, any storage between operations is combined with transportation. In the ideal situation the operations are also combined with transportation so that the inputs are processed while they are being moved.

Process layout is commonly employed when the same facilities must be used to process a wide variety of items for which the processing sequence varies and perhaps is changing. Quite often the volume of individual items is quite low, even though the total volume may be high for the entire system. The prime requirement of process layout is for flexibility of operation sequence, flexibility of part or product design, and flexibility of the volume of individual items being processed.

When the conditions for a product or line layout are met, the result is a low-cost system of production. There is no one volume that we can point to as being "adequate." Instead, economic analysis determines the break-even volume between process and product layout for a given situation. Stable demand is required to justify the special layout and tools necessary so that at least a minimum run can be foreseen. This is also related to

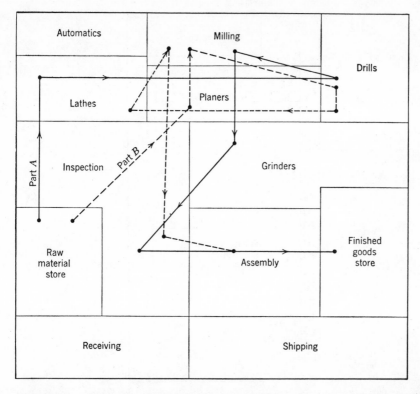

FIGURE 8. Process or functional layout. Machines are arranged in functional groups. Parts take various routings as dictated by their design requirements. Illustrative routes for two parts A and B are shown. Parts are moved from operation to operation in batches or lots and stored temporarily at each work station to await their turn.

product standardization, since changes in product design have the same general effect on the system as on stable demand. In manufacturing, parts interchangeability is required so that no special reworking or fitting is needed on the line, since this condition disrupts the flow of work resulting in line imbalance.

The Problems of Production and Operations Management

Using our generalized model as a background, let us outline the nature of problems generated in a production system. These problems require two major types of decisions, one that relates to the design of the system

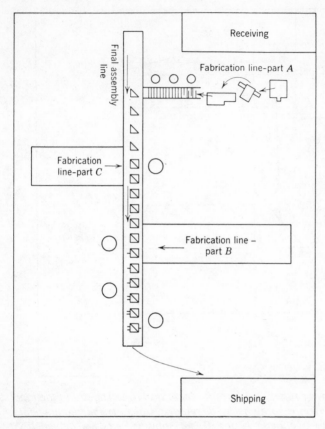

FIGURE 9. Product or line layout. Machines and equipment are arranged according to the sequence of operations required to fabricate and assemble. Machines and workers are specialized in the performance of specific operations, and parts approach continuous movement.

and one that relates to the operation and control of the system (that is, both long-run and short-run decisions). The relative balance of the emphasis on such factors as cost, service, and reliability of both functional and time performance depends on the basic purposes of the total enterprise or institution and on the general nature of the goods or service being produced. In general, economic enterprises will probably emphasize cost, consistent with quality and delivery commitments. Hospitals may emphasize reliability and service, consistent with cost objectives, etc. A classification of problems follows.

A. Long-run decisions related to the design of production and operations systems:

1. *Long-range forecasting and planning* for capacities and locations.

2. *Selection of equipment and processes.* Usually alternate equipment and processes are available for a given need. Operations management must make decisions that commit capital of the enterprise and its basic approach to production.

3. *Production design of items processed.* Production costs interact strongly with the design of parts, products, paper work forms, and so on. Design decisions often set the limiting characteristics of the cost and processing for the system.

4. *Job design and the measurement of work.* Job design is an integral part of the total system design involving the basic organization of work as well as the integration of human engineering data to produce optimally designed jobs. The measurement of the time requirements to perform work is a significant problem which provides basic data which enter many of the decision models we will discuss. Job design is being recognized as a problem embedded in a broader context called socio-technical systems.

5. *Location of the system.* Location decisions can in some cases be important where the balance of cost factors determined by nearness to markets and to raw material supply are critical.

6. *Physical facility layout.* Decisions must be made related to design capacity, basic modes of production, number of shifts, use of overtime, and subcontracting. In addition, operations and equipment must be located in relation to each other in a pattern that minimizes overall material handling cost or some equivalent criterion. The latter requirement is most difficult for the complex intermittent model of production where routes vary.

B. Decisions related to the design of operation and control systems:

1. *Forecasting* in order to make decisions for day-to-day operations and for a reasonable planning time horizon.

2. *Inventory control.* Policies, procedures, and decisions designed to maintain inventories at levels which will provide the necessary service at reasonable cost.

3. *Aggregate planning and scheduling* decisions which set basic production rates and employment levels in the short run and for a reasonable time horizon in the future.

4. *Scheduling and production control.* Feasible schedules must be worked out which are compatible with the aggregate planning decisions already made and which make the best use of available men and equipment. Once scheduled, the progress and flow of work must be controlled through information feedback and appropriate action.

5. *Maintenance and reliability of the system.* Decisions must be made regarding maintenance effort, recognizing the random nature of equipment breakdowns and that machine downtime may itself be associated with important costs or possible loss of sales.

6. *Quality control.* Decisions must be made to set the permissible levels of risk that bad items are produced and shipped, or that errors are made, as well as the risk that good parts are scrapped. Control costs must be balanced against the probable losses due to passing defective material or services.

7. *Labor and cost control.* Labor is still the major cost element in most products and services. Planning requires an appraisal of the labor component. Day-to-day decisions must be made which involve the balance of labor, material, and certain overhead costs.

Different Emphasis for Different Systems

The relative importance of these problems in operations management varies considerably, depending on the nature of individual production systems. Nevertheless, every system has these problems to some degree. For example, replacement policy may occupy a dominant position in production systems where the capital investment per worker is very large, as in the steel industry. On the other hand, replacement policy may occupy a minor role in a system that is represented by a large labor component or a large material cost component. Part of the art of operations management involves the sensing of the relative importance of these various components in a given situation.

Analytical Methods for Problem Areas

The various analytical methods we shall discuss find application in many of the problem areas outlined. For example, any of the physical and schematic models discussed are of great importance in job design, layout, production control, labor control, and cost improvement. Flow charts and assembly charts have been used with good effect in analyzing overall product flow so that the components of a production system could be related properly. Physical models of systems aid in visualizing the overall interacting effects of each component of the system and in allocating space to activities in the most effective way. Other kinds of flow charts aid in the design of specific activities involving labor, or the design of a man-machine system. Symbolic models find rather different fields of application. For example, statistical methods have been found to be of great value in product quality control, work measurement, a determination of the optimal combination of control factors (such as in the chemical industries), and in the design of experiments to determine the effects of variables in the operation of production systems. Of course, inventory and production control models have direct application in those areas. Waiting line models have been found to be valuable as aids to job design, the determination of capacities of facilities like unloading docks, check-out counters, storage facilities, and tool cribs, as well as the analysis of inventory systems, labor requirements for multiple machine operation, and for maintenance systems.

Programming models have been found to be of value in the analysis of distribution systems, plant location, production programming, waste control, and so on. Replacement models have been found to be of value in the selection of equipment and processes, and in general where comparisons of alternate systems or subsystems of production are to be made. Competitive models have future significance in the analysis of bidding procedures and for the development of basic strategies that an organization should follow to maximize its position with respect to competitors. Simulation models have already found application in a wide variety of problems that deal with both the design of production systems and with the operation and control of systems. Simulation models may be used in practically all situations where mathematical models have application; however, their field of advantage is where the complexity required by the problem makes mathematical analysis difficult or impossible. In these situations, simulation can be used where mathematical methods fail.

The Need for a System Point of View

Many of the problems of production interact with each other. For example, job design may interact with the material handling system used, the design of the thing being processed, the equipment or process being used, and the overall facility layout. An optimal inventory policy to follow is partially dependent on the means by which production levels are controlled. The best process (in instances where alternatives exist) may depend on whether idle labor or equipment is available. Thus if we were to study inventory problems in isolation, ignoring the effects of changes in production level, we would develop a suboptimal solution to the problem, because the solution that minimizes inventory costs might result in very high costs associated with production fluctuations. The policy we wish to determine is one that would minimize all costs affected. Therefore, the broader the point of view taken in attempting to solve the problem, the less likely it is that factors will be ignored which bear significantly on the final result. This, then, is the guide to the determination of the limits of the production system under study.

Achieving this systems concept in practical application is difficult for two important reasons: first, as we mentioned earlier, present-day models fall short of this ideal, and second, it requires crossing established functional lines of authority within organizations. This latter factor is of great practical significance because of the human relations problems involved in gaining support for proposals that may tear down personal empires or threaten individuals within organization structures.

SUMMARY

Science in management is growing rapidly, yet poor communication between the management scientist and the operating manager tends to introduce a lag in the actual use of known methods. One strong branch of management science views management in its decision-making function, attempting to reduce as many decisions as possible to a set of automatic decision rules. This development is directed toward the determination of how decisions ought to be made. Another branch of management science which is based in the behavioral sciences emphasizes human values and is directed toward the study of how decisions are actually made in the living organization. Other books deal with this branch of management science, but the present volume does not attempt to deal with the behavioral sciences [4, 6].

Models and model building are an integral part of formal decision theory, and they are the focus of this book. Models are the mechanism by which predictions of performance of a process or system are made, and they may be the basis of valuable control mechanisms. When criteria and values tend to be objective and when models are good predictors, decisions based on them seem scientific, almost automatic. On the other hand, when criteria and values are vague and where quantitative aspects of models can account for only a portion of the problem, decisions rest heavily on judgment and experience.

REVIEW QUESTIONS

1. Define the term *production*.

2. What is meant by the term *operations*? How does it differ from the term production?

3. Describe the nature of interactions between the production subsystem and other organizational subsystems within the total enterprise system.

4. Discuss the nature of interactions between the enterprise system and the environment systems.

5. How do we define intermediate organization systems? What are the comparable functions performed by organizational units in a factory system?

6. What control subsystems are common in a manufacturing organization?

7. Using the diagram of Figure 2 as a background, outline a system for labor cost control, quality control, and inventory control.

8. Using the generalized descriptive model of production as a background, select an activity which you know and show that the general model is applicable to it.

9. Differentiate between intermittent and continuous models of production. What kinds of facility layout are applicable to each?

10. Name and discuss the short- and long-run problems of operations management.

REFERENCES

1. Albers, H. H., *Principles of Organization and Management*, John Wiley & Sons, New York, 3rd ed., 1969.
2. Boulden, J. B., and E. S. Buffa, "The Strategy of Interdependent Decisions," *California Management Review*, Vol. I, No. 4, 1959, pp. 94–100.
3. Bross, I. D. F., *Design for Decision*, The Macmillan Company, New York, 1959.
4. Dalton, M., *Men Who Manage*, John Wiley & Sons, New York, 1959.
5. Forrester, J., *Industrial Dynamics*, MIT Press, Cambridge, Mass., 1961.
6. Litterer, J. A., *The Analysis of Organizations*, John Wiley & Sons, New York, 1965.
7. Schoderbek, P., *Management Systems*, John Wiley & Sons, New York, 2nd ed., 1971.
8. Starr, M. K., *Systems Management of Operations*, Prentice-Hall, Inc., Englewood Cliffs, N.J., 1971.
9. Taylor, F. W., *Scientific Management*, Harper and Brothers, New York, 1947.

chapter 2

COSTS

An understanding of the behavior and structures of costs is essential in dealing with the problems of operations management. It is important to know about both the conventional accounting construction of costs (so that proper interpretations can be made of them) and a construction of costs for decision purposes. These two viewpoints are sometimes the same, but sometimes average costs and arbitrary allocations of fixed cost elements mask the behavior in which we are interested and may not include some components of great importance, for example, opportunity costs or sunk costs. Also, the concepts of incremental costs are of great importance to operations management. For model building purposes, we may wish to express a continuous or discrete cost relationship as a mathematical function.

Cost-Volume Relationships

One of the useful and interesting aspects of cost analysis is the relationship of overall costs with changes in volume. For a manufacturing concern, the basic picture of costs we wish to discuss is shown in Figure 1. What happens to total costs as volume increases is of the greatest interest especially near or at the sharp changes in the organization of resources which occur with the addition or deletion of second and third shifts. Following the conventional accounting definition of fixed, semifixed, and variable costs, the interesting factors which dominate the shape taken by the total cost curve are in the semifixed and variable cost categories.

To put on a second shift would require a reorganization of the supervisory structure and other managerial functions such as

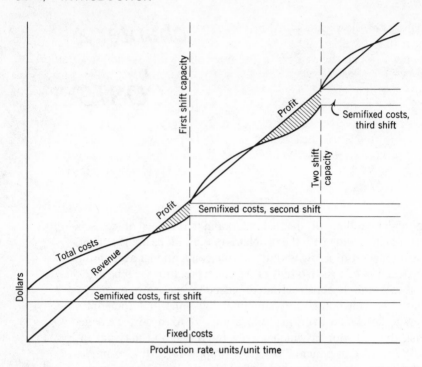

FIGURE 1. General structure of costs for a manufacturing company over a wide range of volume. From E. S. Buffa and W. H. Taubert, "Evaluation of Direct Computer Search Methods for the Aggregate Planning Problem," Industrial Management Review, Fall, 1967.

maintenance and quality control, thus causing a quantum step-up in costs. In addition, there may be required some physical changes in the reorganization of facilities to maintain two-shift operation. Thus, we observe the discontinuities in the total cost curve at the limits of one- and two-shift capacity.

But why should we not expect the variable costs to be linear? There are a variety of reasons, and we illustrate some of them in Figure 2. First, it is important to recognize that we must look at the system as something dynamic, changing in response to changes in demand quantity, product mix, and technology, as well as changing organizational and social patterns. To regard the enterprise as being static, thus reflecting a static view of costs, is to miss the entire flavor and character of the problems of operations management. In Figure 2a the payroll costs may be close to being linear, though even this assumption could be attacked on the basis of the supply and demand for labor as indicated by the dashed line in Figure 2a.

In any case, the productivity of labor in relation to volume of activities shown in Figure 2*b* makes the labor cost per unit a nonlinear function. Viewing labor in the aggregate and not considering substantial changes in basic technology, we would expect the toe of the productivity curve to exhibit the start-up difficulties which would be reflected in low output per man hour. In the middle range of one-shift operations, the curve may be approximately linear. But as we approach the limits of one-shift capacity, productivity falls off because of increased congestion, cramped quarters, interference, and delays. There is a logical tendency to try to achieve the

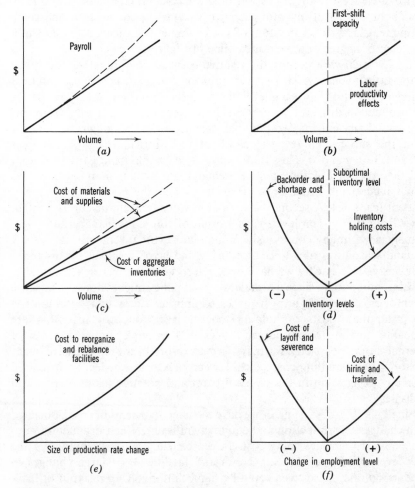

FIGURE 2. Selected cost behavior patterns.

increased output near the limits of one-shift capacity through the use of overtime with the existing work force and its higher cost of marginal productivity. Changes in technology might change the level and contour of the curve but the general nonlinearities would remain.

In Figure 2c we see two cost components related to materials. We assume that the cost of materials could be linear with volume (dashed line) but quantity discounts and an aggressive procurement staff should produce economies at higher volumes (solid line). As volume goes up, however, the size of aggregate inventory necessary to maintain the production-distribution process increases also but not in direct proportion. As we shall see in our discussion of inventories in Chapters 7, 8, and 9, some components of inventory tend to vary as the square root and some components as a direct function of sales volume, and this effect is shown in the "cost of aggregate inventories" line in Figure 2c.

In Figure 2d we examine the relative costs of holding either too much or too little inventory. This presupposes that there exists some suboptimal aggregate inventory for each level of operation which is necessary to sustain the production-distribution process. But inventories might vary from this suboptimal amount for two possible reasons. First, they might be different from the suboptimal levels because of the capriciousness of customer demand. If demand was less than expected, we would incur extra inventory and the costs of holding them. If demand was greater than expected, we would incur back order or shortage costs and the possible opportunity costs of lost sales. A second basic reason why aggregate inventories might differ from suboptimal levels is as a result of conscious managerial design. Management might consciously accumulate extra inventories in a slack demand season in order to reduce hiring and layoff costs, as we discussed previously. This is why we have been referring to the base inventory level as being suboptimal, since a broader horizon policy might choose to increase inventories above this level in order to approach a system optimum. At any rate, these costs of holding too much or too little inventory are probably not linear over larger ranges. For example, as we run out of internal storage capacity we may need to resort to more expensive space and/or higher handling cost space. Larger back orders reflect an increased degree of congestion in the physical plant and possibly losses of goodwill and sales.

Finally, in Figures 2e and 2f we have included two items of cost associated with changes of production and employment levels. When production rates are changed there are some costs in reorganizing and replanning for the new level and in rebalancing crews and facilities. For large changes in production rate, these costs could be significant involving relayout of facilities and rebalancing of production lines for the new rate. In addition, there are the costs of hiring and training or layoff and severance, depending on the direction of the change. Union rules may have an effect on both but particularly on layoff and severance costs. Large layoff and/or severance programs are likely to be progressively more expensive and in the limiting situations may involve the cost of labor disturbances and slowdowns, as well as the costs to process the personnel changes plus fringe benefit costs. Large recruitment and training programs will be relatively more expensive than small ones.

Now back to Figure 1. Cost-volume patterns will not be linear for many of the reasons discussed, and therefore profit appears in a "pocket" beyond a break-even point. Profit increases to a point where the diseconomies discussed become effective at which point it is reduced as volume continues to increase and *may* disappear as we approach the limits of one-shift capacity as shown. The reasons for the relative increases in costs and decline in profit we have already discussed in some of the cost components, but generally the profit decline is associated with the decline in labor productivity, the increased use of overtime, the relative inefficiency of newly hired labor which may now be a larger fraction of the total labor force. These cost increases normally are somewhat greater than the savings in material and inventory costs. When the decision to add the second shift is made, there will be the much heavier cost input as a semifixed cost to put on the second shift. As we progress into the volume range which includes the second shift, labor productivity will be relatively low reflecting start-up conditions as shown in Figure 2b, and a pattern similar to the first-shift cost-volume relationships will be repeated. The quantitative relationships will be different for different organizations, but the general relationships described are pertinent. For example, profit may not entirely disappear at the point of adding a second shift for a specific organization because of the relative profit margins and cost factors. In some of the analyses of operations management problems, we shall assume linear approximations to cost functions in order to simplify and conceptualize problems. In many instances the assumption of linearity is an excellent one, but near the limits of a defined capacity it may be dangerous. Break-even analysis is a technique which assumes linearity of costs and provides some important decision criteria and broad managerial concepts.

Break-Even Analysis

Break-even analysis idealizes the cost volume relationship described in Figure 1 by assuming linear costs. Semivariable costs are reduced to a fixed and variable component so that all costs are separated into an equiv-

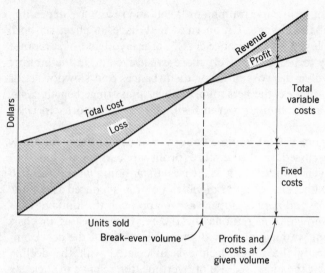

FIGURE 3. Typical break-even chart.

alent fixed and variable cost effect. Conceptually, then, we can consider fixed costs as a total pool of costs which must be recovered by net revenue over and above variable costs before any profit is to be made. This point, or volume of sales, where total net revenue after variable costs just equals the total pool of fixed costs is called the break-even point. Figure 3 shows an example of a simple break-even chart. The sales line begins at the origin and is linear. The total cost line intersects the vertical axis at a value equal to the pool of fixed costs and increases in proportion to the number of units sold. Beyond the break-even point, the ratio of profits to sales increases with each unit sold. This is because of the broadened base for the absorption of fixed costs. Contribution to fixed costs and profit is a fixed ratio, however.

Contribution. The concept of contribution to fixed costs and profit is a valuable one, and it is used in a number of cost models. Contribution is the difference between sales and variable costs, that is,

$$C = S - V \tag{1}$$

and

$$S = F + V + P \tag{2}$$

where

$$C = \text{Contribution}$$
$$S = \text{Sales}$$
$$V = \text{Variable costs}$$
$$F = \text{Fixed costs}$$
$$P = \text{Profit}$$

Since both S and V vary with volume, C varies with volume also. This idealized property is useful because it is a linear measure in the model which is proportional to profit. C can be calculated by knowing the percentage of the sales dollar that is V. Suppose, for example, that variable cost is 75 percent of the sales dollar and fixed costs are $5,000,000, then from equation (1) C is 25 percent. The only costs which have not been deducted are the fixed costs, therefore, substituting the expression for S from equation (2) into equation (1) we have

$$C = F + P \qquad (3)$$

or

$$P = C - F$$

Profit can now be computed at any level of sales. If total sales are $16,000,000, then C is 25 percent or $4,000,000 and

$$P = C - F = \$4,000,000 - \$5,000,000 = -\$1,000,000 \quad \text{(loss)}$$

If total sales are $24,000,000, C is $6,000,000 and

$$P = C - F = \$6,000,000 - \$5,000,000 = \$1,000,000$$

Break-even takes place at the sales volume where $C = F = \$5,000,000$. Since in this case C is 25 percent of the sales dollar, sales required to break even are,

$$S = 4 \times 5,000,000 = \$20,000,000$$

Usefulness of Break-Even Analysis. From a managerial point of view break-even analysis is useful in appraising the general effects of a number of changes as well as managerial decisions. For example, a change in volume of business should have a direct effect on profits. Changes in product mix, labor performance, material utilization, or selling prices will have complex effects on profits, the break-even point, and contribution. Changes in fixed costs alone, however, will not affect contribution.

A variety of managerial decisions, such as plans to increase plant capacity, to replace obsolete plant and equipment, to subcontract, and the scheduling of overtime can all be placed into the break-even analysis format to estimate effects on the break-even point, profits, and contribution.

While it is a valuable concept, break-even analysis has important limitations both because of the linear assumptions and because of problems of cost measurement. An exact break-even point is hard to find because of the inherent difficulties in obtaining exact data on the ratio of fixed and variable costs and because day-to-day managerial decisions are constantly changing the break-even point. The break-even point is probably more logically described as a break-even "zone." In multiproduct integrated organizations the meaning of the figures is not clear, since excellent performance in one product line or department may mask poor performance in others. This often leads to break-even charts by product line, but this involves a difficult problem of allocating certain joint costs. In spite of the difficulties, break-even analysis is important in forming a conceptual framework for budgetary controls and profit planning, and the technique becomes much sharper for more limited decisions such as those found in process selection. For example, a clear-cut and logical break-even chart could be developed which would show the volume at which a turret lathe would be more economical as a process than an engine lathe. Certainly, the concept of contribution as a linear measure is a useful one.

Incremental Costs

The concepts of incremental costs are important for operations management and form the basis for many of the day-to-day decision problems. The terms marginal costs, out-of-pocket costs, and differential costs are often used to mean the same thing as incremental costs. These costs vary with alternative courses of action, varying with the nature of the situation. A common example is in the "make versus buy" decision. If we are currently manufacturing an item and are considering the possibility of purchasing or subcontracting it instead, it will be important to consider exactly which costs are saved by ceasing manufacture. Presumably the machinery, building, and supervisory staff will continue, so most of the allocated fixed and semi-variable costs will remain. The incremental costs actually eliminated ordinarily will be far less than the average manufacturing cost. Conversely, if we are currently subcontracting an item and are now considering internal manufacture, it will be important to determine if we have the existing capacity to do so. If we do, the incremental costs of internal manufacture will be only the direct costs of labor and materials plus any net additions to other costs, such as utilities and supplies. The usual overhead costs already exist and will not change by the addition of the subcontracted item. If the available capacity does not exist, however, the net incremental costs for internal manufacture will have to include the costs of providing the needed capacity. The existence of idle capacity changes the character of the decision drastically.

Opportunity Costs and Investment Criteria

The physical aspects of an operational system presents some special problems of analysis. The building and its productive equipment are normally quite expensive in first cost and in maintenance, and they commonly account for the largest share of the assets of an enterprise. Yet the fact that they have enduring use and value is part of the problem. Machines do not wear out in the same sense that a light bulb burns out. By maintenance and the replacement of components, the physical useful life of a machine may be extended indefinitely. This raises questions such as: When should an existing asset be replaced? How do we compare the desirability of two or more alternate machines and are any of them justified from an economic point of view? Part of the answer lies in a recognition of opportunity costs and sunk costs.

To see the nature of some of the analytical and practical problems involved, let us consider a simple example. We have just installed a machine that performs a highly specialized operation. Because of our particular physical facilities a custom installation was required. The result of the specialized nature of the equipment and the custom installation is that the equipment is of no value to anyone else; therefore, its salvage value is zero as soon as it is installed. The installed cost of the equipment was $12,000 and this is a *sunk* cost, meaning simply that it is gone forever regardless of what we may list as the "book value" of the equipment. Since the $12,000 is "sunk," it is completely irrelevant to any future decisions since no future decision can affect it. In general, book values are meaningless in the decisions we shall discuss, since they are ordinarily derived by arbitrary means for other purposes. Instead we shall always be concerned with salvage value, that is, the actual recoverable value of an asset at any point in time.

Opportunity costs represent another concept which enters capital investment problems. Suppose we are considering an asset which is used for more general purposes than the preceding example, such as an over-the-road semitrailer truck. Let us assume that we own such a truck. How much does it cost just to own the truck? The cost of owning the truck for one more year depends on its current value. If the truck can be sold on the secondhand market for $5000, this is a measure of its economic value. Since it has value we have two basic alternatives: we can sell it for $5000 or we can retain it. If we sell, the $5000 can earn interest or a return on an alternative investment. If we keep the truck, we forgo the return which then becomes an *opportunity cost*. Similarly, if we keep the truck, it will be worth less one year hence resulting in a second component of opportunity cost measured by the fall in salvage value during the year.

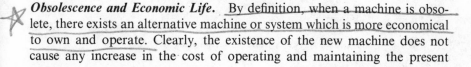

Obsolescence and Economic Life. By definition, when a machine is obsolete, there exists an alternative machine or system which is more economical to own and operate. Clearly, the existence of the new machine does not cause any increase in the cost of operating and maintaining the present machine. These costs are already determined by the design, installation, and condition of the present machine. The existence of the new machine causes the value of the present machine to fall, however, and therefore induces an increased capital cost due to the opportunity cost in the fall in value. Thus for assets in technological dynamic classifications the salvage value schedule falls rapidly in anticipation of typical obsolescence rates, and economic lives are very short. On the other hand, where the rate of innovation is relatively slow, salvage values hold up fairly well. Economic life, then, is the length of time a given machine holds its superiority compared to alternate machines or systems in terms of the combined costs of owning and operation. Since the comparison invariably involves a projection of future values, we need to be able to place all of the future expenditures on some common time base so that they can be compared rationally. Present value concepts achieve this.

Present Values. Since money has a time value, future expenditures and opportunity costs will have different present or current values to us. What do we mean by the time value of money? Since money can earn interest, $1000 in hand now is equivalent to $1100 a year from now if the present sum can earn interest at 10 percent. Similarly, if we must wait a year to receive $1000 due now, we should expect not $1000 a year hence, but $1100. When the time spans involved are extended, the appropriate interest is compounded and its effect becomes much larger. The timing of payments and receipts can make an important difference in the value of various alternatives.

Let us illustrate this point briefly and more precisely before returning to the example of the two machines. We know that if a principal sum P is invested at an interest rate i, it will yield a future total sum S in n years hence, if all of the earnings are retained and compounded. Therefore, P, in the present is entirely equivalent to S in the future by virtue of the compound amount factor:

$$S = P(1 + i)^n$$

where $(1 + i)^n$ = the compound amount factor for interest rate i and n years

Similarly, we can solve for P to determine the present worth of a sum to be paid n years hence:

$$P = \frac{S}{(1 + i)^n} = S \times PV_{sp}$$

where $PV_{sp} = 1/(1 + i)^n$ = the present value of a single payment of $1 to be made n years hence, with interest rate i

Therefore, if we were to receive a payment of $10,000 in 10 years, we should be willing to accept a smaller but equivalent sum now. If interest at 10 percent were considered fair and adequate, that smaller but equivalent sum would be:

$$P = 10{,}000 \times 0.3855 = \$3855$$

since

$$\frac{1}{(1 + 0.10)^{10}} = PV_{sp} = 0.3855$$

At some point in the life of machines it becomes economical to replace them with identical models. Therefore, a chain of identical machines should be considered for comparative purposes. Most of the common criteria for comparing alternate capital investments attempt to circumvent these problems by (*a*) assuming an economic life, and (*b*) assuming some standard schedule for the decline in value of the asset. We shall now consider some of these criteria.

Common Criteria for Comparing Investment Alternatives

Some of the common criteria used for evaluating proposals for capital expenditures and for comparing alternatives involving capital assets are: (*a*) present values; (*b*) uniform equivalent annual cost; (*c*) rate of return; and, (*d*) payoff period.

Present Value Criterion. Present value methods for comparing alternatives determine the sum of present values of all future out-of-pocket expenditures and credits over the economic life of the asset. This figure is compared for each alternative. If differences in revenue are involved, their present values are also accounted for. Table VII in the Appendix gives the present values for single future payments or credits, and Table VIII gives present values for annuities for various years and interest rates. An annuity is a sum that is received or paid annually. The factors in Table VIII (Appendix) convert the entire series of annual sums to a single sum in the present, for various interest rates and years. We shall use the notation PV_a for the present value factor of an annuity and PV_{sp} for the present value of a future single payment.

As an example, let us consider the present values of a machine which costs $12,000 installed. The economic life of the machine is estimated as 10 years, at which time the salvage value is forecasted to be $2000. The average operating and maintenance cost is estimated as $6000 per year. With interest at 8 percent, the present value of the expenditures and credits is as follows:

$$\frac{1}{(1+.08)^0} = 1$$

Initial investment,

$$B = \$12,000 \times PV_{sp} = 12,000 \times 1.000 = 12,000$$

Annual operating and maintenance expenses, SUM: 10 yrs, 8% int

$$E = \$6000 \times PV_a = 6000 \times 6.710 = 40,260$$

Less credit of present value of salvage to be received (PMT, at 10 yrs, 8%) in 10 years,

$$S = \$2000 \times PV_{sp} = 2000 \times 0.463 = -926$$

Total present value $= \$51,334$

The net total of $51,334 is the present value of the expenditures and credits over the 10-year expected life of the machine. The initial investment is already at present value, that is, the present value factor is 1.000. The annual costs of operation and maintenance are a 10-year annuity so the entire stream of annual costs can be adjusted to the present value by the multiplication of PV_a from Table VIII. Finally, the present value of the salvage is deducted. This total could be compared with comparable figures for other alternatives over the same 10-year period. If another alternate machine was estimated to have a different economic life, perhaps 5 years, to make the present value totals comparable, two cycles of the 5-year machine would be compared with one cycle of the 10-year machine. Let us continue this example with such a comparison.

Suppose we have another alternate machine with an estimated economic life of 5 years. This machine will do the same job as the previous machine; however, its characteristics and costs are somewhat different. The installed price of the machine is $13,000 and its salvage value at the end of 5 years is expected to be $1000. This machine, however, is completely automatic, fitting into a production line in such a way that parts are fed to it automatically on a conveyor system and leave the machine automatically by way of the conveyor system to proceed to the next operation. The result is that there is no direct labor cost. The only operating costs are costs of maintenance which increase rapidly for the first five years by the following schedule:

$2000, $2200, $5000, $2600, $3000

The $5000 estimated maintenance charge for the third year is particularly heavy because of the need for the replacement of major components. The present values of expenditures and credits for a 10-year period comparable to the life of the first machine are as follows:

First cycle,

$$B_1 = 13,000 \times PV_{sp} = 13,000$$

$$E = E_i \times PV_{sp}$$

$$
\begin{aligned}
E_1 &= 2000 \times 0.926 = 1,852 \\
E_2 &= 2200 \times 0.857 = 1,885 \\
E_3 &= 5000 \times 0.794 = 3,970 \\
E_4 &= 2600 \times 0.735 = 1,911 \\
E_5 &= 3000 \times 0.681 = \underline{2,043} \\
&\qquad\qquad E_{total} \quad 11,661
\end{aligned}
$$

$$S_1 = -1000 \times PV_{sp} = -1000 \times 0.681 = -681$$

Second cycle,

$$B_2 = 13,000 \times PV_{sp} = 13,000 \times 0.681 = 8853$$
$$E = E_i \times PV_{sp}$$

$$
\begin{aligned}
E_6 &= 2000 \times 0.630 = 1260 \\
E_7 &= 2200 \times 0.583 = 1283 \\
E_8 &= 5000 \times 0.540 = 2700 \\
E_9 &= 2600 \times 0.500 = 1300 \\
E_{10} &= 3000 \times 0.463 = \underline{1389} \\
&\qquad\qquad E_{total} \quad 7932
\end{aligned}
$$

$$S_2 = -1000 \times PV_{sp} = -1000 \times 0.463 = -463$$

Total present value for 10 years = \$40,302

Note in the foregoing analysis that for 10 years of useful life it was necessary to have a net investment of \$26,000; however, the timing of the second investment reduces its present value considerably. Also note that since the expenditures for maintenance were not represented by a uniform annual cost, but by a rising cost function, the expenditure in each year must be reduced to present value separately through the factor PV_{sp}. The comparison between the basic alternatives is shown by the total present values for the equivalent span of time of 10 years, or \$51,334 for the first alternative and \$40,302 for the second. On the basis of the cost figures, the second alternative involving a purchase of two machines at 5-year intervals would be chosen. Normally, of course, there would be intangible values which might influence the decision, especially if the economic comparison was very close.

Uniform Equivalent Annual Cost. Instead of converting all figures to present value as we have done in the previous illustration, we can just as easily convert all figures to an equivalent annuity. Since we are commonly talking about cost figures, this annuity is usually referred to as the "uniform equivalent annual cost." The technique is a simple variant of the present value methods just described. Table VIII (Appendix) gives values for PV_a, the present value of an annuity of $1.00 for interest rate i and n years. Knowing the amount of the annuity, we then determine the present value by

$$P = A \times PV_a$$

With the same general relationship, we could, of course, determine the equivalent annuity of a present value, thus,

$$A = \frac{P}{PV_a}$$

For example, the equivalent annuities for the two alternate machines discussed under "present value criterion" would be:

First machine:

$$P = \$51{,}334$$

$$PV_a = 6.710 \text{ (for 10 years at 8 percent)}$$

$$A = 51{,}334/6.710 = \$7650 \text{ per year for 10 years}$$

Second group of two machines:

$$P = \$40{,}302$$

$$PV_a = 6.710$$

$$A = 40{,}302/6.710 = \$6020 \text{ per year for 10 years}$$

In other words, the equivalent average annual cost, including capital costs, operating and maintenance costs, for the first machine is $7650 and $6020 for the second group of two machines. As before, the second alternative is the cheaper of the two. We see that the present value criterion and the annual cost criterion are entirely equivalent. The only real difference is in the expression of the answer in terms of present values, or in terms of an equivalent annuity.

There are some instances where the uniform equivalent annual cost criterion can be expressed with slightly less computation. For example, the illustration used previously required that we consider two cycles of the second machine to compare the results to the 10-year life of the first machine. This required the separate calculation of present values for each cost item for two cycles of the machine over a 10-year period. We could have avoided this by determining the annuity from the first cycle as follows:

The present values are

$$
\begin{aligned}
B &= \$13,000 \\
E &= 11,661 \\
S &= -681 \\
\hline
P &= \$23,980
\end{aligned}
$$

The equivalent annuity for five years is

$$
A = \frac{P}{PV_a} = \frac{\$23,980}{3.993} = \$6020
$$

This is, of course, the same figure we obtained by calculating the annuity based upon the 10-year period. The only difference is that one is an annuity for 5 years, the other for 10 years. Since the cost performance of the two cycles is identical, we could have used this shortcut to calculate the 10-year present value figure of $40,302 obtained under "present value criterion." We could have done so by determining the equivalent annuity for 5 years, as we have just shown. Then from Table VIII (Appendix), we obtain for 10 years, 8 percent, $PV_a = 6.710$. The present value for the two identical cycles over a 10-year period is then:

$$
P = 6020 \times 6.710 = \$40,302
$$

Whether we express answers for comparison as present values or uniform equivalent annuities is then a matter of preference. In either case, we are dealing with the *present value criterion* as a basic method for comparing economic alternatives. As we shall see later when we discuss the general model for equipment investment, expressing everything in terms of present values has an advantage in the simplicity of the mathematics involved. The businessmen, however, who are used to thinking in terms of annual costs often prefer the uniform equivalent annual cost concept as a mode of expression.

Rate of Return Criterion. One of the most common methods of evaluating new projects or comparing alternative courses of action is to calculate a percent rate of return, which is then judged for adequacy. Usually, no attempt is made to take account of interest costs, so the resulting figure is referred to as the "unadjusted" rate of return, that is, unadjusted for interest values. It is computed as follows:

Unadjusted rate of return

$$= \frac{100 \ (\text{net operating advantage} - \text{amortization})}{\text{average investment to be recovered}}$$

The net monetary advantage reflects the algebraic sum of incremental costs of operation and maintenance plus possible differences in revenue for the new investment as compared to some existing situation. If the rate of return sought is a "before-tax" rate, then

$$\text{Amortization} = \frac{\text{Incremental investment}}{\text{Economic life}}$$

is subtracted and the result is divided by average investment and multiplied by 100 to obtain a percentage return. If an "after-tax" rate is sought, the net increase in income taxes due to the project is subtracted from the net monetary advantage, and the balance of the calculation is as before. Obviously, the adequacy of a given rate of return changes drastically if it is being judged as an after-tax return.

Let us develop an example to demonstrate the use of the rate of return criterion. A company is contemplating the installation of a large-scale conveyorized material-handling system that will inter-connect a series of production operations with a unified flow system. A consideration of the new handling system is particularly appropriate, since some of the presently used trucks need replacement, and this would result in a net investment of $20,000 to continue using the present system. The new conveyorized handling system would require an investment of $150,000 for the basic system plus $80,000 for auxiliary equipment needed to implement the system. The terminal salvage value of the new system is set at zero with an economic life of 15 years. There are numerous operating advantages in the new system, including lower material-handling labor costs, lower costs due to damaged product, and considerably less handling by the direct labor operators at the individual machines and operations. Increased operating costs as a result of the new system are in maintenance, property taxes, and insurance. The pertinent operating cost figures are as follows for the new and old material-handling systems:

Cost Item	New System	Old System
Material handling labor	$ 1,000	$20,000
Cost of damaged product	500	4,000
Cost of material handling at machines	2,000	15,000
Maintenance	4,000	500
Property tax and insurance	3,000	500
Total	$10,500	$40,000

Since the net investment required to install the new system is $210,000 and the net operating advantage is $29,500, the unadjusted before-tax rate of return is:

$$\frac{29,500 - (210,000/15)}{210,000/2} \times 100 = 14.8\%$$

The after-tax rate of return requires that incremental taxes be deducted from the net operating advantage. Incremental taxable income will be the operating advantage less increased allowable tax depreciation. Assuming straight-line depreciation and an allowed depreciation term of 20 years, incremental taxable income is $29,500 less $210,000/20, or $19,000. Assuming an income tax rate of 50 percent, the incremental tax due to the installation of a new system is $9500. Therefore, the after-tax return is:

$$\frac{29,500 - 14,000 - 9500}{105,000} \times 100 = 5.72\%$$

Whether or not either the before- or after-tax rates calculated in the example are adequate is a matter to be judged in relation to the risk involved in the particular venture and the returns possible through alternate uses of the capital.

Payoff Period Criterion. The payoff period is the time required for an investment to "pay for itself" through the net operating advantage or revenues which would result from its installation. It is calculated as follows:

$$\text{Payoff period, years} = \frac{\text{net investment}}{\text{net annual operating advantage after taxes}}$$

The payoff period for the conveyorized handling system we were discussing previously is:

$$\frac{\$210,000}{\$29,500 - \$9500} = 10.5 \text{ years}$$

It is the period of time for the net after-tax advantage to just equal the net total investment. Presumably, at the end of that period the after-tax advantage of $20,000 per year is all profit or return, since the invested amount has been recovered. The question might be raised: "If the economic life of the equipment is 15 years and 10 percent is regarded as an appropriate rate of after-tax return for the project, what should the payoff period be?" Obviously, the period for both capital recovery and return is the 15-year economic life. The period of time which recovers capital only, but which also allows enough equivalent time left in the economic life to provide the return on investment, will be somewhat shorter, and will depend on the required rate of return. Let us note now that the payoff period is another interpretation that can be given to the present value factors for annuities, PV_a, given in Table VIII (Appendix). As an example, for an economic life of 15 years and a rate of return required of 10 percent, $PV_a = 7.606$, from Table VIII. This indicates that capital recovery takes place in 7.6 years. The equivalent of 10 percent compound interest takes place in $15.0 - 7.6 = 7.4$ years. Therefore, any of the PV_a values in Table VIII, for a given economic life in years and a given rate of return, indicate the shorter period in years required to return just the investment, or, more simply, they give directly the maximum payoff period that would generate at least the rate of return specified for the project.

The proper procedure would be to estimate economic life and determine the applicable rate of return. From the present value tables, determine the payoff period associated with these conditions. Then compute the actual payoff period of the project in question and compare it to the standard period from the tables. If the computed payoff period is less than, or equal to, the standard period from the tables, the project meets the payoff and risk requirements imposed. If the computed value is greater than the table value, the project would earn less than the required rate.

We are now in a position to see rather easily what the *adjusted rate of return* would be for the project we have been discussing. The investment we propose to make is, of course, already at present value without further adjustment. Therefore, the actual rate of return that it will earn is determined by the rate of interest that discounts the future earnings generated over the economic life to a present value total that exactly equals the net investment.

Recall the simple formula stated previously:

$$P = A \times PV_a$$

where P = a sum at present value (net investment), A = an annuity (future earnings due to operating advantage), and PV_a = the present value factor for an annuity. Therefore, when we calculate the payoff period by dividing net investment by after-tax operating advantage, we are computing the PV_a which would discount the future earnings to equal the net investment. Recall that the value was 10.5 in the previous payoff period calculation. To determine the adjusted rate of return that the project would earn, we simply search Table VIII (Appendix) for the number 10.5 in the 15-year row. By interpolating in the tables, we find that $PV_a = 10.5$ is associated with an interest rate of 4.88 percent. This rate may be compared now with the value of 5.72 percent obtained by the unadjusted rate of return methods and indicates the margin of error in that calculation.

A before-tax adjusted rate of return could also be calculated for comparative purposes. It is calculated as follows:

$$PV_a = \frac{210,000}{29,500} = 7.12$$

By interpolating in Table VIII for $n = 15$ years, we obtain an adjusted rate of return of 11.2 percent. This rate may be compared with the unadjusted rate obtained previously of 14.8 percent. The error in using the simpler unadjusted rate of return method is of course greater when we are dealing with longer economic lives and larger future values.

A GENERAL MODEL FOR EQUIPMENT INVESTMENT /

We have studied the common criteria for comparing economic alternatives, or judging the adequacy of an investment in equipment. They are all slightly different in form and some more approximate than others. Let us now generalize and develop a model which regards the common models we have discussed, as well as many other models, as special cases. We can then see the basic relationships between them.

The General Investment Problem

When we make an investment for a profit of any kind, we are expecting the discounted future net income to at least equal the investment. The rate of discount which returns the stream of future net income payments to a present value equal to the original net investment is the rate of return. Recall the relationship, $P = A \times PV_a$, where P is the present sum (net investment in this context), A is an annuity (annual net income from the investment), and PV_a is the present value factor of an annuity of $1.00 for the number of years of the expected annuity and at the interest rate which makes $A \times PV_a$ just equal the original investment P. The term of the annuity could be any number of years, including an infinite stream of income payments, and the interest rate could be any value. A direct parallel to the situation we have just stated is the investment in a $1000 bond which produces annual income payments of $150 for 10 years. The rate of return which makes the present value of the 10-year stream of interest payments just equal to the original $1000 investment is easily determined by the PV_a,

$$PV_a = \tfrac{1000}{150} = 6.67$$

What interest rate is associated with a 10-year PV_a of 6.67? Looking in Table VIII (Appendix), for 10 years, we see that it is approximately 8 percent. The PV_a is in essence the fulcrum determining a balance between the original investment and the future stream of income payments (see Figure 4). Any investment problem can be reduced to this equivalent simple form.

Of course, instead of determining the actual rate of return produced, we could establish a rate of return minimum based on the earning rate of other comparable investment opportunities. Then, to determine if the investment in question meets the minimum standard, we determine PV_a, given n and the minimum return r, and compute the present value of the

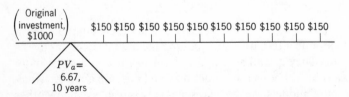

FIGURE 4. The rate of return is determined by the PV_a which reduces the ten annual income payments of $150 to the present value of the original investment of $1000.

income stream. If the present value of the income stream is equal to or greater than the investment amount, the investment earns the minimum rate of return or greater. If the present value of the income stream is less than the investment amount, the rate of return is less than the requirement. Comparing alternate investments in this way, we would select the alternative which maximizes $A(PV_a) - P$; PV_a is now the value determined by the required rate of return and the term of the investment.

Relative Rates of Return. The earning rates of individual pieces of equipment in a production system are often difficult to establish because their contributions to the total earning power of the system and of the enterprise as a whole are not clear. Normally then, absolute rates of return cannot be determined so that we are forced to consider relative rates of return, or a cost minimizing model. In the case of investment in equipment, the proposed new equipment is usually replacing some existing equipment or method of operation. Even though it may not be possible to assign any direct revenue to either the old or proposed systems, the equivalent of revenue may be produced by reductions in operating costs compared to present methods, if the new equipment is installed. Thus, regarding the potential operating cost reductions as the equivalent of income, we can compute a rate of return as we did with the bond, but this rate of return is relative to continuing operation with the existing equipment. Also, we can establish a minimum rate of return and compute the present value of the future operating cost advantage to see if it is larger than the required investment. Alternate equipment design could then be compared, selecting the one which maximized the net difference between the present value of future operating advantage and net investment.

Cost minimizing models are commonly used in equipment investment policy because revenues assignable to the installation of new equipment are usually of minor significance in comparison to the outlays for initial investment and operating expenses. For each alternative, then, the sum of the present values of expenditures, less any offsetting revenues yields a positive net cost which we wish to minimize when comparing various alternatives. The general model which we shall develop uses this convention of signs.

The Equipment Investment Problem

To maximize return on investment, or minimize overall costs for the non-profit enterprise, capital equipment must be used which provides the capacity needed in the most economical way. Since technology is continually developing new machines and systems, we must look not only at what equipment is available, but what may become available. If, for example, we had a machine in operation for some time and a new and improved design became available, part of our problem is in assessing not only the relative merits of the new machine but in deciding if even better equipment might be available in the near future. Should the present machine be replaced now, or should we wait for the future equipment which will be even better? Should replacement take place now followed by a second replacement with the even better machine at a later date? If so, at what future date? Part of the problem, then, is the consideration of a *chain* of machines rather than the isolated case of the new machine now available.

Also, because of the dynamics of technology, we find that a machine may be succeeded by a better, perhaps more automatic, machine, or that a group of machines and operations may be replaced by a new system which changes the concept of production entirely.

The General Model*

The general model which we shall develop reduces to present value all disbursements and receipts involved in the possession and operation of a succession of equipment having *varying* initial costs, life spans, salvage values, expense, and revenue functions. It will be convenient to adopt the following symbols:

C = the consideration of a chain or succession of equipment in the model.

E = the present value of operating expenses or disbursements for each individual piece of equipment in the chain.

R = the present value of revenues which result from the possession or use of each individual piece of equipment in the chain.

B = the present value of the purchase price of each individual piece of equipment in the chain.

S = the present value of the salvage of each individual piece of equipment in the chain.

Thus, the investment case involving C, E, R, B, and S, ($CERBS$), is the most general situation. It considers a chain of machines, each item in the chain having its own individual purchase price and salvage value, revenue and expense functions, and individual economic life spans. The comparison for the various functionally equivalent chains of equipment would then be made on the basis of the total present value P for *each chain*, or,

---

*Based on A. Reisman and E. S. Buffa, "A General Model for Investment Policy," *Management Science*, Vol. VIII, No. 3, April 1962.

$$P\dagger = B - S + E - R$$

The great majority of management investment decisions can be based on a comparison of cases less complicated than *CERBS*, but from this most general case all the others may be derived by simply dropping or simplifying certain terms in the general model expression. For example, if the decision rests with the alternate items of equipment which are not to be succeeded, a comparison of *ERBS* is called for. If the equipment involves no revenue function or if all alternatives have the same revenue, only *EBS* need be considered. Thus, the entire field of equipment investment comparisons may be covered in a systematic way.

Development of the Terms of the General Model

Now let us take up the development of the individual four terms in the general model. We shall begin with the implications of the purchase of a chain of machines, followed by the consideration of salvage values, expense functions, and revenue functions. Recall that for each term we will be reducing all monetary values to the present value. Perhaps the simplest device for achieving this discounting is to multiply the value by the general factor, $PV = e^{-rt}$, where e is the base of natural logarithms (2.71828), r is the rate of return which can be earned, and t is the elapsed time. Of course $f(t) = e^{-rt}$ is simply the negative exponential distribution which is tabulated in the Appendix as Table VI. Thus the discounting process obtained by e^{-rt} is just an exponential decay function where $e^{-rt_o} = 1$, that is, the discounting factor at time zero is 1 as we would expect. We will use this factor in our discounting process.

Purchase Price. The price of each generation of items of equipment in the chain will have its own characteristic value. We do not conceive that each generation is simply a new version of the same piece of equipment. Succeeding generations could be rather different in design, degree of automation, etc. Therefore, the first item will cost B_0, the first replacement B_1, the second replacement B_2, and, in general, the jth replacement will cost B_j. Beginning at time zero when the initial item of equipment is purchased, its present value is B_0. But the present value of the first replacement is less than its purchase price B_1, since the time T_1, equal to the economic life of the initial piece of equipment has elapsed. The present

---

†Note that this is for a cost minimizing model, and the signs for the terms have been assigned to produce a net positive value of P. For an investment dominated by revenue figures, such as a stock or bond, the opposite sign convention makes better sense, that is, $P = R - E - B + S$.

value of B_1 is, therefore, $B_1 e^{-rT_1}$, where e^{-rT_1} is the present value factor. The present value of the money required to purchase B_2 is $B_2 e^{-rT_2}$, where $T_2 - T_1$ is the economic life of the first replacement. Similarly, the jth replacement will take place T_j time units from the present. Hence, the present value of the money required to buy the jth replacement which will take place at the time specified is:

$$B_j e^{-rT_j} \tag{1}$$

Finally, the present value of the chain of investments to be made for purchasing the initial item of equipment plus n generations of replacement is:

$$B = B_0 + B_1 e^{-rT_1} + B_2 e^{-rT_2} + \cdots + B_j e^{-rT_j} + \cdots + B_n e^{-rT_n}$$

$$= \sum_{j=0}^{n} B_j e^{-rT_j} \tag{2}$$

This is simply a sum of the product of purchase price times the appropriate present value factor for the entire chain of investments. The present value factor for each separate generation, of course, depends on the interest rate and the elapsed time from the present. Figure 5 diagrams the time relationships of our chain of investments.

Salvage Value. The value of each generation of equipment at the time of its retirement from service may, in general, vary from one to the next succeeding item in the chain. This value may be positive, negative, as when

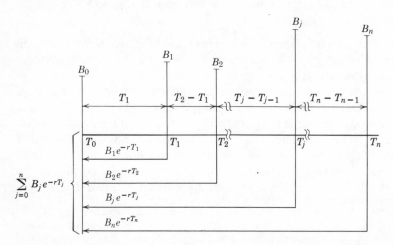

FIGURE 5. Timing of the purchases of a chain of machines, discounted to present values.

it has no market value and requires an expenditure to get rid of it, or zero. The salvage value can only be realized at the end of the life period T of the particular generation. Therefore, the present value of the salvage of the first piece of equipment in the chain, S_{1,T_0} (read, salvage value of the initial item, at time zero), is

$$S_{1,T_0} = S_1 e^{-rT_1}$$

The present value of the first replacement is:

$$S_{2,T_0} = S_2 e^{-rT_2}$$

and the present value of the jth replacement is:

$$S_{j,T_0} = S_j e^{-rT_j}$$

The total present value of the salvage of the entire chain is, therefore:

$$S = \sum_{j=0}^{n} S_j e^{-rT_j} \tag{3}$$

Again, this expression is simply the sum of the product of salvage value times the appropriate present value factor, for the entire chain of investments. The notation takes account of the fact that the initial equipment is salvaged at the time of purchase of the first replacement, the first replacement salvaged at the time of purchase of the second replacement, etc. Figure 6 shows the salvage values of the equipment chain in relation to time.

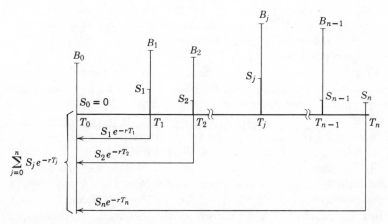

FIGURE 6.   Timing of salvage values of a chain of machines.

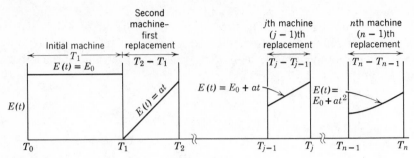

FIGURE 7. Typical expense functions.

Expense Function. The expense function describes the total of all expenses required to operate and maintain the equipment. The expense function can take many different forms, typical cases being shown in Figure 7. With simple machines requiring little maintenance, it is possible that the average operating and maintenance expense could be constant as shown for the initial machine in Figure 7. An asset requiring no operating expense, only maintenance, may begin its life with zero maintenance cost, but increase as time passes, shown by the first replacement in Figure 7. Operating and maintenance expense may begin with some finite value and increase linearly, or increase at some increasing rate, as shown by the jth and nth replacements respectively in Figure 7. Many other forms for the expense function are, of course, possible, including decreasing curves and more complex forms.

We will use the notation $E(t)$, read E of t, to represent the mathematical expression for any expense function in relation to time. For example, $E(t) = E_0$, where E_0 is a constant representing the initial operating expenses, describes the expense function for the initial machine in Figure 7. For the first replacement, $E(t) = at$, describes the expense function where a is the slope of the straight line. The jth replacement in Figure 7 has an expense function described by $E(t) = E_0 + at$.

Now, $E(t)$ represents the rate of expenditure for any point in time t in the life of the machine, so that the area under the curve $E(t)$ between any two lines t_1 and t_2 yields the total expenditure during that time period, as shown in Figure 8. The gross expenditure over the life of the equipment is then represented by the area under the curve $E(t)$ between the times 0 and the end of its life T. This area may be determined either graphically or analytically by summing the areas of all thin rectangles such as $abcd$, shown in Figure 8. $E(t)dt$ is the undiscounted area of the rectangle which may be discounted back to time zero by $E(t)dt(e^{-rt})$. The accuracy of such a procedure varies inversely with the size of the increment Δt, that is, the smaller the increment of time, Δt, the greater the accuracy. In the limiting

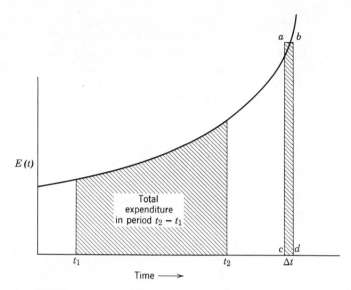

FIGURE 8. *Total expenditure in period* $t_2 - t_1$ *is area under curve of* E(t) *between* t_1 *and* t_2. *Areas under the curve may be determined graphically by summing the areas of all thin rectangles under curve of width* Δt, *such as* abcd, *or by the integral calculus.*

situation where Δt is made infinitely small, we can obtain the exact solution by means of the integral calculus. Therefore, using the calculus notation, the summation of all infinitely thin rectangles may be expressed as

$$E(T) = \int_0^{T_1} E(t)\, dt$$

where $E(t)$ is some function of time describing the expected rate of expense.

Since the expenses are accumulated continuously, they must be discounted to present value continuously; therefore, the present value of $E(t)$ for the initial machine is

$$E_1 = \int_0^{T_1} E_1(t)e^{-rt}\, dt \qquad (4)$$

The present value of expenses incurred by the first replacement (second machine), for example, is

$$E_2 = \int_0^{T_2} E_2(t)e^{-rt}\, dt \qquad (5)$$

The limits of integration of equation (5) are from 0 to T_2 in order that the expenses are discounted back to the present. Actually expenses for the second machine are zero from time 0 to T_1. The effective zone where the expense function of the second machine is contributing positive present values is, of course, from time T_1 to T_2. Finally, the present value of all expenses incurred by all items in a chain of machines is

$$E = \int_0^{T_j} E_j(t)e^{-rt}\,dt \tag{6}$$

Revenue Function. The meaning and derivation of the revenue function parallels exactly that of the expense function. Expected revenue functions $R(t)$ may vary with time, as with expense functions. The revenue function is then

$$R = \int_0^{T_j} R_j(t)e^{-rt}\,dt \tag{7}$$

The General Model Restated. The present value of all receipts and disbursements attributable to the possession as well as operation of a chain of investments in equipment is

$$P = B - S + E - R = \sum_{j=0}^{n} (B_j - S_j)e^{-rT_j} - \int_{T_0}^{T_j} (R_j - E_j)e^{-rt}\,dt \tag{8}$$

Equation (8) is solvable by the methods of the difference and differential calculus.

Note that in the development of the general model, each item in the succession of machines could have its own characteristic purchase price, salvage value, revenue and expense function, and economic life. Since any of the five elements B, S, E, R, and T may enter the model as constants, or as variables from one item in the chain of machines to the next. For example, in the most general case, *CERBS*, B, S, E, R, or T may be constants from item to item in the chain, or they may be variable as was true in the derivation of the general model. Therefore, one special case might be a model where a chain of machines is considered, and each machine has an expense function, a revenue function, initial purchase price and salvage value. But suppose that only the expense and revenue functions vary from item to item in the chain, the purchase price, salvage value and economic life being identical for each item in the chain. We have then the *er* subcase of *CERBS*, using lower-case letters to indicate which items appear as variables from item to item. If all five factors are identical from item to item in the chain, we have the zero subcase of *CERBS*.

We are now in a position to classify any model in relation to the general model. First, we may classify models by which of the elements C, E, R, B, and S are accounted for. Second, we may classify models involving C, that is, a chain of machines, by determining whether or not the factors B, S, E, R, and T are variable or constant in the model.

Classifying Models

Now that we have developed the general model, we are in a position to see how the common criteria discussed previously fit into the structure of the general model.

Present Value and Annual Cost Methods. The usual conceptual framework of these models involves the $ERBS$ subcase of $CERBS$. If a chain of machines is considered, usually only nonvarying parameters are involved so we would have the zero subcase. Because the method is quite flexible in application, however, almost any situation may be correctly analyzed though it may be tedious.

Rate of Return Methods. These methods commonly consider E, R, B, and S, that is, the $ERBS$ subcase of $CERBS$. Since a chain of machines is not considered, none of the factors are variable. In addition, expense and revenue functions are usually taken as a constant over the life of the equipment.

Payoff Period Methods. If it is assumed that the payoff period means the time at which all costs have been recovered, this period is obtained by determining the time in the life of the equipment when P, the present worth of the sum of all receipts and disbursements, is zero in any of the $CERBS$ subcases. The usual applications of this technique, however, involve only E, R, B, and S, so that none of the factors are variable. In addition, expense and revenue functions are usually taken as constant over the life of the equipment.

Classifying Other Models

A large number of other models of equipment investment have been developed which are somewhat more sophisticated than the common criteria. The characteristics of many of these models are summarized in reference [1], and many of them have been classified in $CERBS$ framework in reference [15].

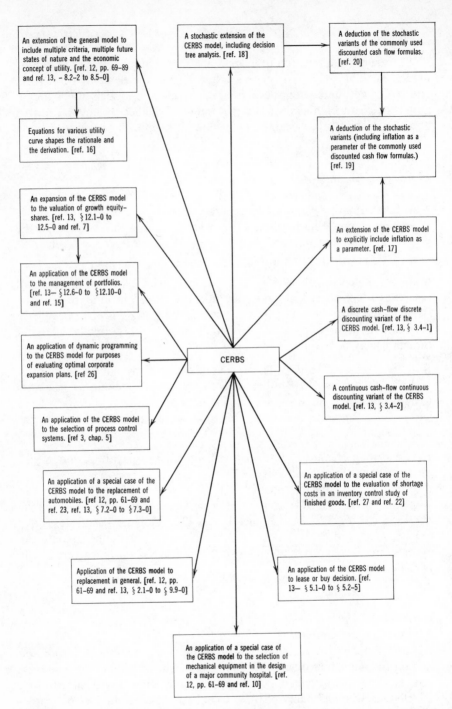

FIGURE 9. Guide to applications and extensions of the general CERBS model. Courtesy of Professor Arnold Reisman, Case Western Reserve University.

APPLICATIONS
AND EXTENSIONS
OF THE GENERAL MODEL /

Since 1962 the *CERBS* general model has been applied to a wide variety of situations and has been extended in concept. The applications have ranged from the typical replacement decisions to evaluations of lease-buy decisions, of portfolios, and of corporate expansion plans. The conceptual extensions have been in the directions of representing the variables as being stochastic in nature, including multiple criteria, and including inflation as a parameter. Figure 9 is a summary guide to the various applications and extensions with references indicated for those interested in further information.

SUMMARY

We have attempted in this chapter to embrace a very broad spectrum in our discussion of costs and cost models. In order to develop the criterion functions by which we shall judge the effects of alternate courses of action in the models which we shall develop throughout this book, we have focused our attention on the structure of costs. In Figures 1 and 2 we developed the reality of how many of the cost functions in operations management systems might actually behave. In the development of cost models we shall often idealize the shape of cost functions in order to simplify problems and make them solvable.

An extremely important problem in cost models centers on the way of handling capital costs and monetary values and flows which occur in the future. Thus it has been necessary to focus attention on present value concepts as a basis for placing all future values on a common base. Associated with these kinds of cost problems, and others, are the concepts of incremental, sunk, and opportunity costs. These cost concepts are often elusive and we should gain a clear understanding of them.

Remarks on the General Model

One of the important objectives of the general model presented is to place in perspective the dozens of other models, most of which are special cases of the general model. One of the real difficulties in dealing with equipment investment policy in the past has been the fact that a large number of different models has been developed to deal with special cases. Each new model had characteristics that were common with some others, with perhaps some variation in methodology or an addition to generality. The result has been considerable confusion about the applicability of the various methods. The general model presented here seems applicable to most situations, as complex as a merger of two enterprises or as simple as the evaluation of a fixed term bond.

REVIEW QUESTIONS

1. Using Figures 1 and 2 as a background, defend the assumption of linear costs.

2. Define the break-even point.

3. Why is it that a sunk cost is irrelevant in models for investment?

4. How are book values of equipment handled in investment analysis?

5. What is an opportunity cost?

6. What are capital costs?

7. What is the structure of capital costs incurred by retaining ownership of an asset one more year?

8. What are the meanings of the terms, Economic Life? Physical Life?

9. How is obsolescence reflected in the actual costs of owning and operating an asset?

10. What is the compound amount factor? How is it computed?

11. What is the meaning of the reciprocal of the compound amount factor?

12. What is an annuity?

13. Define the factor PV_a. What is the meaning of its reciprocal?

14. Why is it that most of the common criteria for comparing alternate capital investments assume an economic life and some standard schedule for the decline in value of the asset?

15. Outline the methodology for comparing alternate investments by the present value criterion. Compare the present value criterion with the uniform equivalent annual cost criterion and show that they are directly equivalent.

16. Compare the calculations required for the before- and after-tax rate of return.

17. Outline the payoff period criterion methodology: With what standard payoff period should the computed value be compared to determine if the investment is justified? How is the standard payoff period determined?

18. Compare and evaluate the four criteria for investment analysis discussed. Under what conditions might we use each of them?

19. What future income stream for 20 years with interest at 10 percent just equals a present value of $1000?

20. Why is it that absolute rates of return ordinarily cannot be determined for a specific equipment investment?

21. What is the meaning of a relative rate of return?

22. Why is it that cost minimizing models are most commonly used in equipment investment problems?

23. Why is it necessary, conceptually, to consider a chain of machines rather than the isolated case of the new machine now available?

24. Define each of the terms in the most general situation for an investment model, *CERBS*. Derive each of the terms in the general model.

25. What kinds of expense and revenue functions are permitted in the general model?

26. As normally used, how would you classify within the *CERBS* framework the four common criteria for comparing investments?

PROBLEMS

1. A company is considering the purchase of a new grinder which will cost $20,000. The economic life of this machine is expected to be 6 years, at which time the salvage value will be $2000. The average operating and maintenance costs are estimated to be $5000 per year.

 a. Assuming an interest rate of 10 percent, determine the present value of the future costs of the proposed grinder.

 b. Compare this machine to a presently owned grinder that has annual operating costs of $4000 per year and expected maintenance costs of $2000 in the next year with an annual increase of $1000 thereafter.

 c. What is the effect of using an interest rate of 6 percent rather than 10 percent?

 d. Express the 6 percent and 10 percent results as equivalent annual costs.

2. A company owns a 5-year old turret lathe with a book value of $10,000 and a present market value of $8000. The average loss in salvage value is expected to be $1000 per year until a scrap price of $1000 is reached. Maintenance costs are expected to average $700 per year. A new turret lathe would decrease direct labor and fringe benefits by $1500 per year. Such a machine costs $20,000 and could be expected to have an economic life of 12 years at which time the salvage value will be $3000. Annual maintenance is expected to average $600. Incremental property taxes will average $100 per year if the proposed machine is purchased. Interest is at 10 percent.

Evaluate the feasibility of acquiring the proposed machine on the basis of the present value criterion.

3. A large research and development company is considering the purchase of a numerically controlled jig borer. If such a machine is purchased, four jig borer operators can be eliminated at an annual savings of $28,000. In addition, two tool makers can be eliminated at a savings of $16,500 per year since complex fixtures will not be

required. The maintenance on the proposed machine is estimated to be $1000 per year. The maintenance on the five jig borers that would be replaced by the numerically controlled machine totals $2000 per year. If the proposed machine is purchased, a programmer must be hired at $9000 per year. The cost of the proposed machine is $110,000 on the floor and running. In addition, a controlled atmosphere room must be built around the machine at a cost of $10,000. It is anticipated that training costs for this equipment will be $5000. The machine is expected to have an economic life of 10 years with a salvage value of $15,000.

    a. Calculate the unadjusted before-tax rate of return.

    b. Calculate the after-tax rate of return assuming a 12-year depreciation life, $20,000 salvage value, straight-line method, and an incremental tax rate of 45 percent.

    4. The question is often raised, "Should you rent or buy a car?" The car in question can be purchased for $4500 or rented for $130 per month payable in advance in one-year increments for a three-year period. After consulting the automobile blue book and other sources, you estimate that a reasonable value for this type of car at the end of a three-year period is $2000. In light of bank interest charges, opportunities, etc., an interest rate of 10 percent seems appropriate. Also the following factors may influence the decision.

    a. If you rent, the lessor requires more comprehensive insurance costing $60 more per year than you would carry if you bought.

    b. If you buy, ready cash balances will be depleted and you will have to borrow $1000 at a net cost of $50.

    c. Your present garage is not long enough to fit the proposed car; alterations will cost $1000.

    d. If you rent the car you will spend less on preventive maintenance. You anticipate that you could save $50 in the second year and $75 in the third year.

Determine the least cost alternative and the potential savings. Would your answer change if you believed a more appropriate salvage value to be $1000?

    5. The management of a job shop has been asked to bid on a one-lot manufacture of 1000 frying pans. The estimating and engineering departments have proposed three alternatives as manufacturing plans for the pans as follows:

    a. Using minimal tooling. The pans could be made on existing equipment with 0.40 direct labor hour each.

    b. Constructing a draw die. The pans could be made with 0.32 direct labor hour each. It has been estimated that a suitable drawing die would require 70 hours to construct.

    c. A special spinning lathe can be purchased that would make the pans with 0.20 direct labor hour each. Such a lathe would cost $2500 installed, would have a useful life of 10 years, and would have no salvage value because of its specialized nature.

Material is expected to cost $0.20 per unit. The company has an average direct labor rate of $2.60 per hour, a factory burden rate of 150 percent of direct labor, a general and administrative expense rate of 20 percent of factory cost, and a target profit rate of 10 percent on total cost. It has been estimated that 10 percent of the burden items (e.g., direct supplies, power, etc.) vary in proportion to factory activity. The company uses an interest rate of 15 percent for evaluation purposes.

Determine the least cost method of manufacture and the lowest unit price that could be accepted stating any necessary assumptions.

How would the analysis change if the company was operating at full capacity and the frying pan job could be accepted only if run entirely on overtime?

REFERENCES

1. Ackoff, R. L., Editor, *Progress in Operations Research (Vol. 1)*, John Wiley & Sons, Inc., New York, 1961.

2. Alchian, A., *Economic Replacement Policy*, Report R-224, RAND Corporation, Santa Monica, Calif., 1952.

3. Bowman, E. H., and R. B. Fetter, *Analysis for Production and Operations Management*, Richard D. Irwin, Homewood, Ill., 3rd ed., 1967.

4. Clapham, J. C. R., "Economic Life of Equipment," *Operational Research Quarterly*, Vol. 8, pp. 181–190, 1957.

5. Dean, J., "Replacement Investments," Chapter VI in *Capital Budgeting*, Columbia University Press, New York, 1951.

6. Dreyfus, S. E., "A Generalized Equipment Replacement Study," *Journal of the Society of Industrial and Applied Mathematics*, Vol. 8, Number 3, pp. 425–435, 1960.

7. Fleischer, G. A., and A. Reisman, "Investment Decisions Under Conditions of Inflation," *International Journal of Production Research*, VI:87–95, 1967. A paper presented at the 14th International Meeting of the Institute of Management Sciences, Mexico City, August 1967.

8. Grant, E. L., and W. G. Ireson *Principles of Engineering Economy,* Ronald Press Company, New York, 5th ed., 1970.

9. Kramerich, G. L., "Economics of Process Control Systems," Ph.D. Dissertation, Division of Systems Engineering, Case Western Reserve University, Cleveland, Ohio, 1970.

10. Oral, M., M. S. Salvador, A. Reisman, and B. V. Dean, "On the Evaluation of Shortage Costs for Inventory Control," Technical Memorandum No. 205, Department of Operations Research, Case Western Reserve University, October, 1970.

11. Orenstein, R. D., "Topics on the MAPI Formula," *Journal of Industrial Engineering*, pp. 283–294, 1956.

12. Reisman, A., *Engineering Economics: A Unified Approach*, Reinhold Publishing Co., Chicago, 1969.

13. Reisman, A., *Managerial and Engineering Economy: A Unified Approach*, Allyn & Bacon Publishing Company, Boston, 1971.

14. Reisman, A., "Unification of Engineering Economics: The Need and a Suggested Approach," *Engineering Economist*, Vol. 14, No. 1, Fall 1968.

15. Reisman, A., and E. S. Buffa, "A General Model for Investment Policy," *Management Science*, Vol. 8, No. 3, April, 1962, pp. 304–310. Also reprinted in *Models and Analysis for Production Management*, International Textbook Co., Scranton, Pa., 1968, pp. 53–60, M. P. Hottenstein, Editor.

16. Reisman, A., E. Kondylis, and M. S. Salvador, "On Utility Curves," Technical Memorandum No. 213, Department of Operations Research, Case Western Reserve University, March, 1970.

17. Reisman, A., and J. Pill, "Investment Decisions under Conditions of Inflation," Technical Memorandum No. 199, Department of Operations Research, Case Western Reserve University, August, 1970.

18. Reisman, A., and A. K. Rao, "A General Model for Investment Decisions: A Stochastic Extension," Technical Memorandum No. 179, Department of Operations Research, Case Western Reserve University, March, 1970.

19. Reisman, A., and A. K. Rao, "Stochastic Cash Flow Formulae under Conditions of Inflation," Technical Memorandum No. 206, Department of Operations Research, Case Western Reserve University, December, 1970.

20. Reisman, A., and A. K. Rao, "Stochastic Variations of Common Discounted Cash Flow Formulae," Technical Memorandum No. 187, Department of Operations Research, Case Western Reserve University, July, 1970. A paper presented at the Annual Meeting, American Institute of Industrial Engineers, Boston, May, 1971.

21. Rifas, B. E., "Replacement Models," Chapter 17 in *Introduction to Operations Research*, edited by C. W. Churchman, R. L. Ackoff, and E. L. Arnoff, John Wiley & Sons, New York, 1957.

22. Sloane, W. R., "Capital Decision Theory: Review, Restatement and Reconciliation through Organization," Ph.D. dissertation, Department of Finance, University of Wisconsin, Madison, 1968.

23. Sloane, W. R., and A. Reisman, "Stock Evaluation Theory: Classification, Reconciliation and General Model," *The Journal of Finance and Quantitative Methods*, III: 171–2–4, 1968.

24. Smith, V. L., "Economic Equipment Policies: an Evaluation," *Management Science*, Vol. 4, pp. 20–37, 1957.

25. Terborgh, G., *Business Investment Policy*, Machinery and Allied Products Institute, Washington, D.C., 1958.

26. Watson, H. P., R. A. Wolfson, and A. M. Emyanitoff, "Source Energy Study," for the proposed Rock Island Franciscan Hospital, Rock Island, Illinois, February, 1967.

27. White, J. M., "A Dynamic Model for the Analysis of Expansion," *Journal of Industrial Engineering*, May, 1966. Also reprinted in *Models and Analysis for Production Management*, International Textbook Co., Scranton, Pa., 1968, M. P. Hottenstein, Editor.

PART II

DESIGN OF OPERATIONAL SYSTEMS

chapter 3

PRODUCTS
AND PROCESSES

Operational systems are not often designed in total, emerging "full-blown" as we see them in existence, but they are usually a product of design, development, modification, and redesign, as conditions evolve and change. Figure 1 is a schematic diagram of the process in broad terms where management must make critical plans and forecasts of a longer term nature to project trends and goals. These trends and goals concern the future of product designs and the mixture of the demand for those products or services based on their evaluation and forecast of the size and location of markets. The projections, goals, and plans are critical since it is on the basis of them that the enterprise makes longer range commitments. These commitments are in three major areas, often involving huge expenditures: products, their design, emphasis, and quality levels; markets and possibly therefore plant and warehouse locations; and, production system design. Though these commitments are not usually irrevocable in an absolute sense, they are not revocable without cost. Though the commitments to product designs, market quality levels, market locations, and production system design must be discussed separately to an extent, the crucial thing to recognize is that they are really inseparable and interdependent; as we have attempted to show in Figure 1 by the feedback loops between the product design and production system design blocks and the feedback loop from both blocks back to the managerial long-range planning process.

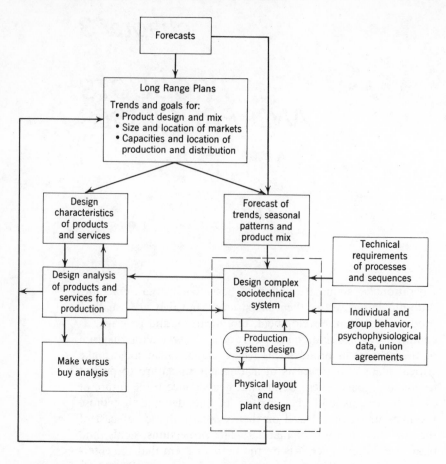

FIGURE 1.   Overall schematic diagram for the design of operational systems.

Markets, Product Designs, and Production Systems

The market quality levels selected will influence product designs which in turn have a strong influence on the design of the processes required to produce the products. Process engineering data and the relative quality and economy of alternate processes, in turn, have an impact on how the product is finally designed for production. Some parts or components in resulting production designs of products may be more economically purchased outside or subcontracted, thus again having an impact on the production system design, its capacity, and capability.

The production system design itself is a complex internal process which takes as basic inputs the final production design of products and forecasts of trends, seasonal patterns and product mixes, as well as technical requirements for processes and their sequences, human behavior, and location. As already noted, however, the production design of products is not simply a direct input but has been derived by an iterative process where the production system and product designs have had an influence on each other. In designing production systems, we are in reality attempting to bring together technology and people in the most effective way. We are designing a sociotechnical system, both aspects of which impose limitations, hopefully leaving a compatible common solution space. It has been the practice in the past for production engineers to ignore the human values other than the more mechanistic ones (i.e., strength, reach, visual acuity, etc.). The result has been progressive division of labor to the point where labor has been only a link in a giant machine. Today, a crucial social and economic issue is centered on how work should be organized, with job satisfaction being recognized as one of the major criteria.

Capacity Decisions

But the job of designing the system cannot end with the evolution of a compatible sociotechnical system. A major decision having important economic and social significance is centered on the capacity decision. The forecasts of trends, seasonals, and product mix raise nagging questions about the pattern of production rates. Should we attempt to gear production to the sales pattern, hiring and laying off personnel to absorb the fluctuations? If so, then plant capacity must accommodate the *peak* requirements. As an alternative extreme, we can gear production levels to average demand, accumulating inventory during slack periods. There are possibly large differences in both capital expenditure requirements as well as risk in the investment of inventories. But from a social, labor relations, and public relations point of view, the extreme alternatives may be just as divergent because if the sales curve is followed, hiring and firing will be costly both directly and indirectly in terms of labor and public reaction. What good will it do to design an internal sociotechnical system which yields job satisfaction only for short periods after which the worker may be laid off? Alternately, if all sales fluctuations are absorbed through inventories, then the enterprise must take a possibly substantial risk of heavy loss either because the total annual market was misjudged or because of inventory spoilage, obsolescence, or other losses. So here is another feedback loop involving the capacity decision, planning and scheduling system, and the sociotechnical system design.

Modes of Production

Finally, there remains an important element in the forecasts which has an impact on the particular mode of production (or sociotechnical system) chosen. It is in the general relationships of product mix, the volumes of each item, and the time stability of product designs. If volumes of items are large and designs stable over time, there will be an economic pressure toward production systems characterized by the high volume standardized products of our society (autos, appliances, chemicals, etc.) with attendant job specialization and relatively low skills in jobs. If the complex of variables involving product mix, volume, and time stability of design is in the reverse direction, that is, either low volume of standardized products or custom designs, then there will be an economic pressure toward production systems which are flexible. These systems produce an economic pressure toward job enlargement and relatively high skills in jobs. The production systems associated with these two extreme situations are the classic production line and job shop models. There are, of course, continuous variations between the extremes. Obviously, there is involved an important interaction of the character of the demand process, the basic economic characteristics of alternate production modes, and the sociotechnical system.

In a sense, the output of the entire process is the physical layout and plant design, since the physical arrangements are an expression of the final result. The design of the system as a whole, characterized by the facility layout and plant design, establishes limitations of flexibility, capacity, and how the enterprise can operate and be controlled. But it is important to remember that the design of a production or operational system is more than that. It is an expression of organized technology, a social system, a reaction to the market, a philosophy of management, and a plan for processing and scheduling. But, it looks like a layout and plant design.

Production Design and Process Planning

The limiting minimum production cost of an item is determined by its design. If the product design and process planning for producing the item go on independently the likelihood of the occurrence of a joint optimum for both is considerably lessened. When a conscious effort is made to bring the two processes together, the process is referred to as *production design* as distinct from functional design of products. Obviously the dominant design task is to create something which functions according to requirements set, but once this has been accomplished there are usually alternatives of design which meet functional requirements. The remaining question then is, which alternative will minimize production cost?

Processes Involve Transformation. Production, or processing, takes place through some kind of transformation, that is, something is happening which in some way transforms the thing being worked on. In general, transformations may effect a chemical change, alter the basic shape or form, add or subtract parts as in assembly, change the location of the thing being processed as in transportation operations, provide or alter information systems as in clerical operations, or check the accuracy of any other process as in inspection operations. We shall not go into the details of any of these individual kinds of processes, but, in general, there are experts or professions in the processes or technology in a wide variety of fields. For example, the chemical engineer is the expert on chemical processing, the industrial engineer or production engineer in the mechanical industries, and the data processing systems man for information transformation processes. In many instances, knowledge about alternate ways of accomplishing a given end is well known and codified.

Examples in the Mechanical Industries

In the mechanical industries the primary forming operations may take place at the steel mill where basic shapes, such as bars, sheets, billets, I-beams, and many other shapes are produced. Designers can often take advantage of these standard shapes, using them to advantage for further processing. Alternately some parts and products might require beginning with some molding process, such as sand casting or die casting, to establish the basic shape or form which may or may not require further processing. Other basic forming processes are powder metallurgy, drop forging, and stamping.

Metal machining is accomplished through basic machine tool processes which involve the generation of cylindrical surfaces, flat surfaces, complex curves, and holes. There are a number of different types of machine tools to accomplish these various generalized tasks, depending on the size and shape of the part to be machined, the quality of finish required, accuracy demands, and the differences in output rate demanded in various manufacturing situations. Thus, a shaper and a planer are both used to generate flat surfaces. For the planer, however, the work reciprocates instead of the tool, and its reciprocating table accommodates large pieces better than does the shaper. Similarly, a grinder can produce cylindrical surfaces as does the lathe or flat surfaces like the mill, but the big difference in application is in resulting accuracy and finish. The grinder, therefore, is largely a finishing machine tool used only after other machine tools have made the rough cuts which produce the basic dimensions. Many of the machine tool operations have been automated through a process which combines computer instructions to the machine and are known as numerically controlled processes.

General versus Special Purpose Machines. General purpose machines are those that have general use capability in their field. For example, a typewriter is a general purpose machine. It can be used for various kinds of copy: letters, manuscripts, some kinds of charts, and figures. On the other hand, a typewriter can be made special purpose by adapting it to the special uses of accounting. The accounting machines do the accounting tasks very well but perform poorly on many of the tasks demanded by a general typewriter. In the machine shop we find a similar dichotomy. There are general purpose lathes, drill presses, milling machines, and planers which are capable of performing their functions on a wide variety of parts and materials. These kinds of machine tools are commonly found in machine shops more generally termed job shops. Yet where the situation warrants it, we find special designs of these same types of machines which are meant to produce some one part or group of parts efficiently. An example might be a special lathe to produce proper outside diameters for an automotive piston. It has special quick clamping devices and special cutters, is of the right size, and runs at the proper spindle speed to machine the outside diameter surface in minimum time. Yet its capability would be restricted in the machining of other parts. Since the volume of pistons is so great, this specialization of equipment design is warranted. This general concept of special versus general purpose equipment extends fairly uniformly throughout industry.

Basic Alternatives. Much of the designer's latitude lies in the selection of materials and, often thereby, the selection of basic kinds of processes. Each material and associated process may be appropriate under certain combinations of conditions of functional requirements and manufacturing cost. Manufacturing cost will be drastically affected by the contemplated volume.

There is ample evidence of the interaction between design and production cost, but Figure 2 (based on a study at Lockheed Aircraft Corporation) shows how pervasive the influence of design can be. The shaded areas of Figure 2 indicate the relative amount of each cost category under the direct control of the design engineer. The shaded areas were determined by studies at Lockheed of detailed cost estimates over a period of years. Hundreds of designs were analyzed by taking the difference in cost between two or more designs which were functionally acceptable, the shaded area representing the difference in cost between the least and most expensive

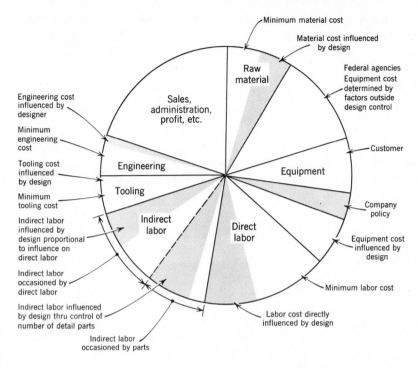

FIGURE 2. Cost breakdown of a transport airplane, showing the effect of design alternatives on various major components of cost. From G. W. Papen, "Minimizing Manufacturing Costs Through Effective Design [12].

designs. Note that the influence extends to the raw material, direct labor, indirect labor, tooling, and engineering cost categories. It is not surprising that the direct labor and materials cost components should be affected by design, but the effects on equipment cost, tooling cost, indirect labor cost, and the nonmanufacturing costs of engineering are not so obvious. Indirect costs tend to be hidden, but suppose that one design required 30 different parts whereas another required only 15. This would mean differences in indirect costs due to the greater paper work and cost of ordering, storing, and controlling 30 parts instead of 15 for each completed assembly. In general, the basic alternatives of design are expressed in terms of alternate processes and materials, ways of joining parts, appraisal of alternatives in tolerances, simplified designs involving fewer parts, and designs that may require less processing to the finished item or easier less time-consuming processing.

PROCESS PLANNING /

It is difficult to state precisely where production design ends and process planning begins, but in engineered products the dividing line may be taken as the point where detailed specifications and drawings of *what to make* become available. At this point, the most basic processing decisions have already been made in the production design phase, as we have commented, so this dividing line refers to process planning in the organizational sense rather than in the functional sense. Our real interest is in the overall view of process planning, however, so Figure 3 is presented to unify the entire process. Process planning also phases into the facilities planning stage as we have shown in Figure 3. Some of the process planning will take place as a part of the actual plant layout in order to accommodate physical and sequential limitations, to take advantage of available space, or to improve methods or sequence. The organizational dividing line between process planning and the layout phase is ordinarily taken at the point where *route sheets* and *operation sheets* become available. These documents summarize the operations required, the preferred sequence of operations, auxiliary tools required, estimated operation times, etc.

Process planning, then, takes as inputs the drawings or other specifications which indicate what is to be made, together with forecasts, orders, or contracts which indicate the number to be made. The drawings and specifications are then analyzed to determine first the overall scope of the project. If it is a complex assembled product, considerable effort may go into "exploding" the product into its component parts and assemblies. This overall planning takes the form of special drawings that show the relationship of parts, cutaway models, and assembly diagrams. Preliminary decisions about subassembly groupings to determine which parts to make and which to buy may be made at this point as well as to determine the general level of tooling expenditure that should be considered. Then for each part a detailed routing of required operations is developed. Here technical knowledge of processes and machines and their capability is required, but of almost equal importance is a knowledge of production economics as discussed in Chapter 2.

The graphic and schematic models useful in process analysis are such things as assembly charts, operation process charts, product flow process

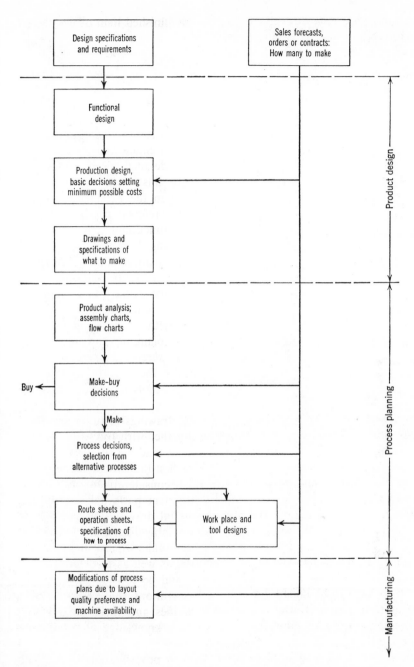

FIGURE 3.   Diagram of the overall development of processing plans.

charts, and procedure flow charts. The following section discusses the use of these types of graphic and schematic models, giving examples.

Models of Product Flow

Assembly Charts. An assembly chart shows the relationship of parts for an assembled product. It shows the make-up of subassemblies, their relationship to the product as a whole, and to the assembly operations required. Figure 4 shows a capacitor assembled and partially assembled. Although the capacitor is a fairly simple assembled product with only eleven different parts plus the impregnating material, inerteen, the assembly chart in Figure 5 yields a great deal of information about the way the product is assembled. We see that there are two subassemblies and note the sequence of assembly and inspections or tests. For example, the first subassembly, SA-1, is made up of two parts, part number 4, aluminum foil, and part number 6, flat leads. Analysis of the chart could deal with alternate sequences of assembly or the advisability of more or fewer subassemblies.

The actual usefulness of an assembly chart is a function of the complexity of the product. For a product as simple as the capacitor, its value is limited because the same level of analysis could probably be carried on without the chart. For a complex product such as an airplane, missile, or a piece of electronic equipment, however, an assembly chart would be of great assistance in planning the gross features of a production system for the product.

Operation Process Charts. The operation process chart is developed from the structure of the assembly chart, but simply adds more information concerning the actual fabrication of the parts which make up the assembled product. Assuming that the product is already engineered, we have available complete drawings and specifications of the parts, their dimensions, tolerances, and materials to be used. From the data on "what to make" (drawings and specifications) and "how many to make" (contracts or sales forecasts), we must develop a plan for "how to make." This means that decisions will have to be made concerning which parts to manufacture and which to purchase. The engineering drawings and specifications will indicate the materials to be used, the location and size of holes to be drilled, surfaces to be finished, etc. With this information (a knowledge of the quantities required, and a knowledge of the appropriate production processes) the most economical processes and sequences of processes can be specified.

The result of all of this effort to specify "how to make" can be summarized in the form of the operation process chart, an example of which is

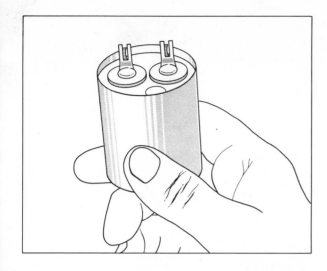

FIGURE 4.   A capacitor, showing its several parts.

shown in Figure 6 for the capacitor. Note that a great deal of information in addition to operation sequences is summarized on the chart. Raw material is specified, and purchased parts labeled B.O., "bought outside," are indicated as horizontal lines flowing into assembly operations (parts 3, 5, 11, and inerteen). The numbers to the left of symbols for operations and inspections are estimates of the per piece time standards for performance

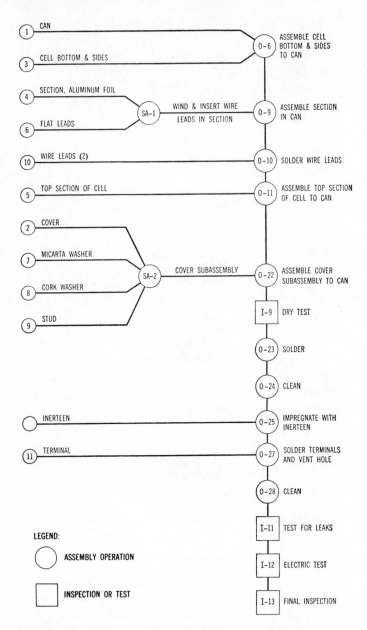

FIGURE 5. *Assembly chart for capacitor of Figure 4.*

of the activities, or where D.W. is indicated the work is performed on a "day work" basis with no time standard available.

Notice how the operation process chart appears as a schematic diagram for the flow and manufacture of the product. It indicates the basic flow from machine to machine as well as the structure of how parts are related in the subassembly and assembly processes. In the development of the design of a production system to produce the product, basic questions can be raised regarding the necessity of certain operations, as well as possibilities for combining and rearranging operation and inspection sequences to improve physical flow.

Product Flow Process Charts. The flow process chart is similar in concept to the operation process chart except that it adds more detail and has a slightly different field of application. The flow process chart adds transportation and storage activity to the information already recorded in an operation process chart. Thus, whereas the latter focuses only on the productive activity, the flow process chart focuses on nonproductive activities as well.

The nonproductive activities of moving the material from place to place and storing it (while it waits for men and equipment to become available) actually represent by far the major amount of the total time spent in the overall cycle for many of the production systems which occur in business and industry today. These nonproductive activities require labor and equipment for transportation, loading, and unloading; capital investment for the plant storage space; and carrying charges on the inventory. Naturally, management is strongly motivated to focus attention on these activities so that their expenditures can be minimized within the framework of minimum overall production cost. It is obvious that decreasing in-process inventories by reducing lot sizes to an extremely low level might result in much higher material handling costs and idle direct labor at machines.

In general, the operation process chart would be used at the broadest level dealing with entire complex products, and the flow process chart would be used with a smaller segment of the product. There is overlap, however, in the areas of their actual use. As an example let us take the manufacture of a potentiometer shaft. (A potentiometer shaft is commonly used in radios, TV sets, and other electronic devices as a part of the volume control. The control knob fits on one end and the potentiometer, or volume control, fits on the other end.) The product flow process chart for the potentiometer shaft is shown in Figure 7. Additional symbols have been adopted to code the activities of transport and storage. Note how clearly the chart shows the occurrence of the various operations, transports, storages, and inspections.

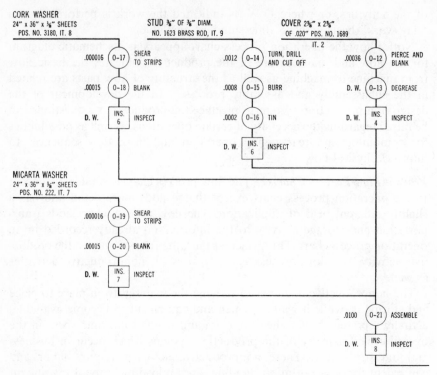

FIGURE 6. Operation process chart for a capacitor showing the productive operations and inspections and their sequence relationships. Courtesy Westinghouse Electric Corporation.

In the use of such a chart, every detail of the process is questioned, first with the objective of completely eliminating steps that cannot be justified, and second with the objective of combining operations. Let us see what sort of questions might be raised about the manufacture of the potentiometer shafts. First, we see that the shafts travel a total of 725 feet before they are ready to be assembled into the final product. This in itself seems excessive for such a simple part. Analysis of this flow shows that the raw material starts on the first floor, moves to the second floor, moves back to the first floor for inspection, then to the basement for storage, and finally to the seventh floor assembly area when the shafts are actually needed. Reference to the flow diagram of Figure 8 which relates the movement to the physical layout of the plant emphasizes this excessive movement. The improvement of this flow pattern depends on the possibility of relocating one or more of the departmental areas, and this depends on the flow patterns of other products as well. Another question to be raised is, "Is it

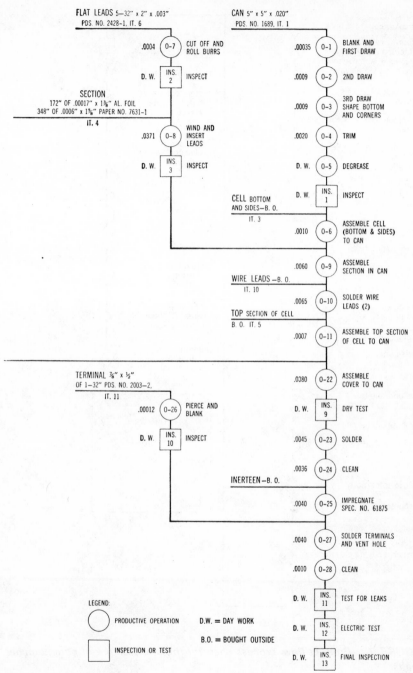

FLAT LEADS 5—32" x 2" x .003"
PDS. NO. 2428-1, IT. 6

.0004   O-7   CUT OFF AND ROLL BURRS

D. W.   INS. 2   INSPECT

SECTION
172" OF .00017" x 1⅜" AL. FOIL
348" OF .0006" x 1⅝" PAPER NO. 7631-1
IT. 4

.0371   O-8   WIND AND INSERT LEADS

D. W.   INS. 3   INSPECT

TERMINAL ⅜" x ½"
OF 1—32" PDS. NO. 2003—2,
IT. 11

.00012   O-26   PIERCE AND BLANK

D. W.   INS. 10   INSPECT

CAN 5" x 5" x .020"
PDS. NO. 1689, IT. 1

.00035   O-1   BLANK AND FIRST DRAW

.0009   O-2   2ND DRAW

.0009   O-3   3RD DRAW SHAPE BOTTOM AND CORNERS

.0020   O-4   TRIM

D. W.   O-5   DEGREASE

D. W.   INS. 1   INSPECT

CELL BOTTOM
AND SIDES—B. O.
IT. 3

.0010   O-6   ASSEMBLE CELL (BOTTOM & SIDES) TO CAN

.0060   O-9   ASSEMBLE SECTION IN CAN

WIRE LEADS —B. O.
IT. 10

.0065   O-10   SOLDER WIRE LEADS (2)

TOP SECTION OF CELL
B. O. IT. 5

.0007   O-11   ASSEMBLE TOP SECTION OF CELL TO CAN

.0080   O-22   ASSEMBLE COVER TO CAN

D. W.   INS. 9   DRY TEST

.0045   O-23   SOLDER

.0036   O-24   CLEAN

INERTEEN—B. O.

.0040   O-25   IMPREGNATE SPEC. NO. 61875

.0040   O-27   SOLDER TERMINALS AND VENT HOLE

.0010   O-28   CLEAN

D. W.   INS. 11   TEST FOR LEAKS

D. W.   INS. 12   ELECTRIC TEST

D. W.   INS. 13   FINAL INSPECTION

LEGEND:

◯ PRODUCTIVE OPERATION

▢ INSPECTION OR TEST

D.W. = DAY WORK

B.O. = BOUGHT OUTSIDE

FIGURE 6 (Continued)

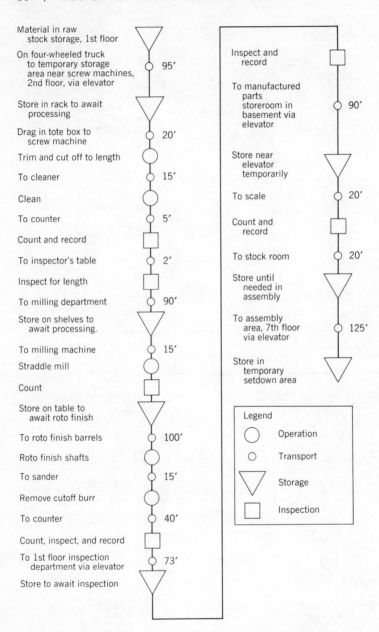

Material in raw stock storage, 1st floor

On four-wheeled truck to temporary storage area near screw machines, 2nd floor, via elevator — 95'

Store in rack to await processing

Drag in tote box to screw machine — 20'

Trim and cut off to length

To cleaner — 15'

Clean

To counter — 5'

Count and record

To inspector's table — 2'

Inspect for length

To milling department — 90'

Store on shelves to await processing.

To milling machine — 15'

Straddle mill

Count

Store on table to await roto finish

To roto finish barrels — 100'

Roto finish shafts

To sander — 15'

Remove cutoff burr

To counter — 40'

Count, inspect, and record

To 1st floor inspection department via elevator — 73'

Store to await inspection

Inspect and record

To manufactured parts storeroom in basement via elevator — 90'

Store near elevator temporarily

To scale — 20'

Count and record

To stock room — 20'

Store until needed in assembly

To assembly area, 7th floor via elevator — 125'

Store in temporary setdown area

Legend

○ Operation

○ Transport

▽ Storage

□ Inspection

FIGURE 7. Product flow process chart for the manufacture of potentiometer shafts.

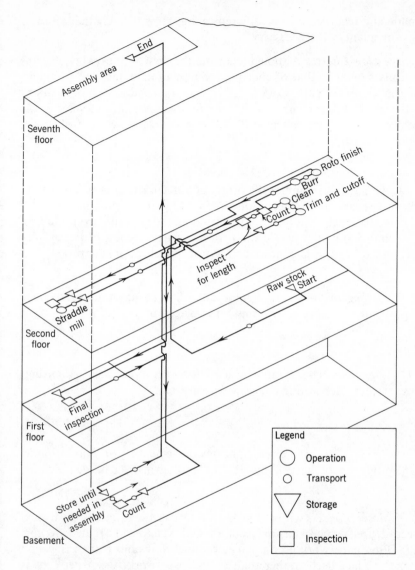

FIGURE 8. *Flow diagram for manufacture of potentiometer shafts.*

necessary for these parts to go to the manufactured parts storeroom, since they are always used in the assembly area"? The parts are small, and a large quantity of them could be stored at the point of use in the assembly area. Another question to be raised relates to the preoccupation with counting the number of parts at various stages in the process. Part counts are made and recorded at four different points. It is unlikely that all these checks for quantity are necessary.

Procedure Flow Chart. Although charting the flow of paperwork systems is basically similar to that of charting the flow of manufactured products, the characteristics of paperwork flow problems demand some modifications from the product flow charts which were discussed previously. Some of the differences required are indicated by the modified set of symbols which are commonly used:

◎ 1. *Origin*. This signifies the origin of a document or a record and is similar in concept to the operation symbol used in product flow charts. It indicates the beginning of the flow of the record resulting from the *first* information of any kind placed on a form, a single record, or a multiple-part record, whether it is handwritten, typed, punched, or stamped.

◍ 2. *Adding to the record*. This symbol is used any time subsequent writing or other additional information is placed on the form.

◯ 3. *Handling*. This symbol is used for operations such as sorting, folding, stapling, separating copies, matching, etc.

o 4. *Move*. The small circle indicates movement or transportation as with the product flow chart. The word, "to" is often inserted inside the circle.

☐ 5. *Inspection*. As with the product flow chart, a square is used when the record itself is checked for accuracy and when errors found are corrected. Often paperwork accompanies product flow, and if the inspection is of the product itself, rather than of the paperwork, the paperwork is usually indicated to be in a state of delay.

▽ 6. *Delay*. The triangle symbol is used as with the product flow process chart. It is used when a record is filed, held at a desk, is awaiting pickup, is destroyed, etc.

$\bigwedge$ 7. *Relationship.* This symbol is used when one form *causes* something to happen to another form. The form being charted then is said to have an effect, or a "relationship" to the other document.

Because of the common necessity for multiple copies to accomplish the needed control, procedure flow charts are often complex and long. Such a chart can be subjected to the same kind of questioning applied to a product flow chart to determine the necessity of various copies as well as the necessity of some of the operations in the sequence. The existence of multiple copies often results in duplication of checks and balances as well as in duplication of permanent files. A schematic model of the entire system makes it possible to study the needs of the system as a whole.

Route Sheets and Operation Sheets. At each stage of its processing, every part is analyzed in order to determine the operations required and to select and specify the processes that will perform the functions required. Thus, the *routing* of the part is determined. This information is commonly summarized on *route sheets.* Here we see the specification of how the part is to be made. The route sheet (*a*) shows the operations required and the preferred sequence of these operations, (*b*) specifies the machine or equipment to be used, and (*c*) gives the estimated setup time and run time per piece. When a part is a standard part, which is run and rerun periodically to fill needs, the standard routing sheets are maintained as the accepted manufacturing methods. More precise specifications of manufacturing methods are often developed in the form of *operation sheets*, which tell in greater detail how the operation is to be accomplished, giving the standard method.

The route sheet together with operation sheets specify how the part or product is to be manufactured. These documents are basic to the manufacturing organization and take the same relative position to the design of a production system as the blueprint or drawing does to the design of a part or product. The drawing specifies *what is to be made* and the route and operations sheets specify *how to make it.*

REVIEW QUESTIONS

1. Describe the overall problem of the design of production systems in terms of the broad elements and interactions involved.

2. Distinguish between functional and production design of products.

3. Describe the major information feedback loops in the overall design of operational systems.

4. Using the term "process planning" in its functional sense, develop a definition.

5. What is a sociotechnical system?

6. Distinguish between general and special purpose machines. What are the conditions which make a special purpose machine economical?

7. Distinguish between functional and organizational definitions of process planning.

8. What is the difference between assembly charts, operation process charts, and flow process charts? What sorts of problems might call for the use of each?

9. Why does the charting of paper work flow as opposed to the flow of a manufactured part call for a modification of flow process charting procedures?

10. In what ways do flow charts oversimplify the representation of the flow problem?

PROBLEMS

1. Construct an assembly chart for the caster shown in Figure 9, assuming that parts 2, 3, 4, and 5 form a subassembly. The subassembly is later joined to the shaft and the end of the shaft is staked (flattened). The wheel and axle are then assembled to the housing and joined permanently by staking one end of the axle.

Assume that the plastic wheel and the ball bearings are purchased outside and that the other parts are fabricated in-plant. Lead times required for the purchase of

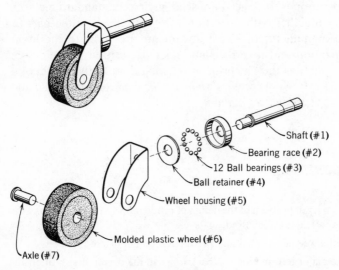

FIGURE 9. Drawing of a caster showing the assembly relationship of its parts.

materials (overall time to prepare orders, transmit them to vendors, and receive them in plant ready for use) are as follows:

Wheels	5 days
Bearings	10 days
Sheet metal for housing and retainer	3 days
Bar stock for bearing race, shaft and axle	3 days

Fabrication and assembly times (overall flow times) for an order of 500 casters are estimated as follows:

Shaft	4 days
Bearing race	10 days
Wheel housing	3 days
Ball retainer	2 days
Axle	2 days
Subassembly	7 days
Assembly and pack	5 days

Construct a schedule diagram to indicate minimum total lead time required for an order of 500 casters.

2. Given the following additional information about the processes for the fabricated parts and assembly operations of the caster described in Problem 1 develop an operation process chart.

	Operations	Machine	Production Rate, Parts per Hour
Part No. 1,			
Shaft	1. Cut to length	Cutoff lathe	100
	2. Turn finished shape	Lathe	40
	3. Inspect	Bench	40
Part No. 2,			
Bearing race	1. Turn and drill	Lathe	50
	2. Deburr	Tumble barrel	250
	3. Inspect	Bench	50
	4. Heat treat (outside operation)		5 days required
	5. Inspect	Bench	50
Part No. 4,			
Retainer	1. Shear stock	Press	250
	2. Pierce hole	Press	250
	3. Blank and form	Press	100
	4. Deburr	Tumble barrel	500

	Operations	Machine	Production Rate, Parts per Hour
Part No. 5,			
Wheel housing	1. Shear stock	Press	250
	2. Pierce 3 holes	Press	100
	3. Blank and form	Press	100
	4. Deburr	Tumble barrel	250
Part No. 7,			
Axle	1. Cut to length	Cutoff lathe	100
	2. Form head	Swaging press	100
Subassembly,	1. Subassembly	Bench	20
assembly and	2. Assemble and pack	Bench	30
packing			

REFERENCES

1. Barnes, R. M., *Motion and Time Study: Design and Measurement of Work*, John Wiley & Sons, New York, 6th ed., 1968.
2. Begeman, M. L., and B. H. Amstead, *Manufacturing Processes*, John Wiley & Sons, New York, 5th ed., 1963.
3. Buffa, E. S., *Modern Production Management*, John Wiley & Sons, New York, 3rd ed., 1969.
4. Close, G., *Work Improvement*, John Wiley & Sons, New York, 1960.
5. Eary, D. F., and G. E. Johnson, *Process Engineering for Manufacturing*, Prentice-Hall, Englewood Cliffs, N.J., 1962.
6. Krick, E. V., *Methods Engineering*, John Wiley & Sons, New York, 1962.
7. Lehrer, R. N., *Work Simplification*, Prentice-Hall, Englewood Cliffs, N. J., 1957.
8. Nadler, G., *Motion and Time Study*, McGraw-Hill Book Company, New York, 1955.
9. Nadler, G., *Work Design: A Systems Concept*, Richard D. Irwin, Homewood, Ill., Rev. ed., 1970.
10. Niebel, B. W., and E. N. Baldwin, *Designing for Production*, Richard D. Irwin, Homewood, Ill., 5th ed., 1972.
11. *Operations Analysis*, Westinghouse Electric Corporation, Pittsburgh, Pa., 1948.
12. Papen, G. W., "Minimizing Manufacturing Costs through Effective Design," *Proceedings, Sixth Annual Industrial Engineering Institute*, University of California, Berkeley-Los Angeles, 1954.
13. Starr, M. K., *Systems Management of Operations*, Prentice-Hall, Inc., Englewood Cliffs, N.J., 1971.

chapter 4

DESIGN AND MEASUREMENT OF JOBS

Job Design

In spite of the great advances in computer and automation technology, manual labor at various levels is predominant today. This situation will be in effect for a long time, and, therefore, we should expect that the design of jobs and of the methods used will continue to be emphasized in operations management. Even in an automated system today, labor is very necessary in a surveillance capacity. In such situations, an operator of an automated system may be seated in front of a control board which continually flashes information about the progress of the process. It is important, then, that these display panels be designed to transmit the essential information to the operator with minimum error. Under such conditions of automation, the effect of errors may be more serious than before because the operator is dealing with very expensive equipment and with a high-volume processing system. Wrong decisions could result in tons of scrap. At any rate the broad process planning which we have been discussing in Chapter 3, together with the graphical and schematic models used, states the operations to be performed. To accomplish these operations normally requires people in some way, so that jobs must be designed. The effectiveness of these job designs is an important factor in the overall effectiveness of the system design.

93

Perhaps the majority of business and industrial manual jobs today consist of some combination of man and machine or at least of man and mechanical aids. Where there is a fixed machine cycle, such as exists in most machine tool processes, the design of the machine in relation to the operator is of great importance. The location and design of controls, working heights, information displays, the flow of work, safety features, and the relative utilization of both the man and the machine in the cycle are all important determinants of quality, productivity, and worker acceptance of the job situation. Many jobs are strictly manual, such as assembly, maintenance, and heavy labor. Here mechanical aids or tools are common, and we need to consider the design of those tools from the point of view of the user; in addition, we must consider layout of the workplace, the flow of work, and physical and mental fatigue produced by these job conditions. In all types of jobs there is an interaction between the worker and his physical environment. In some situations environmental factors of heat, humidity, light, noise, and hazards can produce serious effects on measures of fatigue, productivity, quality, health, and worker acceptance of the job.

Models of man-machine systems need to take account of all of these physical, physiological, and psychological factors.

Man

Man is the dominant element in job design. He has certain physiological, psychological, and sociological characteristics which define both his capabilities and his limitations in the work situation. These characteristics are not fixed quantities but vary from individual to individual. This does not mean, however, that we cannot make predictions about human behavior; rather, it means that predictive models of human behavior must reflect this variation. To take a physical factor as an example, the distribution of the arm strengths of men indicates the percent of the male population that can exert a given force. This distribution also indicates the limitations in demand for arm strength. The average man can exert a right-hand pull of 120 pounds. If we designed a machine lever that required the operator to exert this force, approximately half the male population would be unable to operate the machine. On the other hand, the distribution also tells us that about 95 percent of the male population can exert a right-hand pull of 52 pounds. A lever designed to take this fact into account will accommodate a large proportion of the male population.

In performing work, man's functions fall into three general classifications:

1. *Receiving information* through the various sense organs, that is, eyes, ears, touch, etc.

2. *Making decisions* based on information received and information stored in the memory of the individual.

3. *Taking action based on decisions.* In some instances the decision phase may be virtually automatic because of learned responses, as in a highly repetitive task. In others the decision may involve a high order of reasoning, and the resulting action may also be complex.

The general structure of a closed-loop automated system is parallel to the foregoing concept. Wherein lies the difference? Are automatic machines like men? Yes they are in certain important respects. Both have sensors, stored information, comparators, decision makers, effectors, and feedback loops. The differences are in man's tremendous range of capabilities and in the limitations imposed on him by his psychological and sociological characteristics. Thus machines are much more specialized in the kinds and range of tasks that they can perform. On the other hand, machines perform tasks as faithful servants, reacting mainly to physical factors; for example, bearings may wear out because of a dusty environment. But man reacts to his psychological and sociological environment as well as to his physical environment. The latter fact requires that one of the measures of effectiveness of job design be worker acceptance, or job satisfaction.

Man's effectiveness as an element in the production process depends on a number of factors which include: matching job requirements to his physiological and psychological limitations, layout and work flow, overall organization of his part in relation to the broad plan of manufacture, the design of his tools and processes, and his motivation and job satisfaction.

Where Man Surpasses Machines. Although there are few really objective guides to the allocation of tasks to men and machines on other than an economic basis, a subjective list of the kinds of tasks most appropriate for men and for machines is given by McCormick [6].

Human beings appear to surpass existing machines in their ability to do the following:

- Sense very low levels of certain kinds of stimuli: visual, auditory, tactual, olfactory, and taste.
- Detect stimuli against high-"noise"-level background, such as blips on cathode-ray-tube (CRT) displays with poor reception.
- Recognize patterns of complex stimuli which may vary from situation to situation, such as objects in aerial photographs and speech sounds.
- Sense unusual and unexpected events in the environment.
- Store (remember) large amounts of information over long periods of time (better for remembering principles and strategies than masses of detailed information).

- Retrieve pertinent information from storage (recall), frequently retrieving many related items of information; but reliability of recall is low.
- Draw upon varied experience in making decisions; adapt decisions to situational requirements; act in emergencies. (Does not require previous "programming" for all situations.)
- Select alternative modes of operation, if certain modes fail.
- Reason inductively, generalizing from observations.
- Apply principles to solutions of varied problems.
- Make subjective estimates and evaluations.
- Develop entirely new solutions.
- Concentrate on most important activities, when overload conditions require.
- Adapt physical response (within reason) to variations in operational requirements.

Existing machines appear to surpass humans in their ability to do the following:

- Sense stimuli that are outside man's normal range of sensitivity, such as x-rays, radar wavelengths, and ultrasonic vibrations.
- Apply deductive reasoning, such as recognizing stimuli as belonging to a general class (but the characteristics of the class need to be specified).
- Monitor for prespecified events, especially when infrequent (but machines cannot improvise in case of unanticipated types of events).
- Store coded information quickly and in substantial quantity (for example, large sets of numerical values can be stored very quickly).
- Retrieve coded information quickly and accurately when specifically requested (although specific instructions need to be provided on the type of information that is to be recalled).
- Process quantitative information following specified programs.
- Make rapid and consistent responses to input signals.
- Perform repetitive activities reliably.
- Exert considerable physical force in a highly controlled manner.
- Maintain performance over extended periods of time (machines typically do not "fatigue" as rapidly as humans).
- Count or measure physical quantities.
- Perform several programmed activities simultaneously.
- Maintain efficient operations under conditions of heavy load (men have relatively limited channel capacity).
- Maintain efficient operations under distractions.

Such a list raises the question: Why do not business, industry, and government use men and machines according to these guides? Certainly we have all observed that man is used extensively for tasks given in the list for machines. The answer lies in the balance of costs for a given situation. Both labor and machines cost money; when the balance of costs favors machines, conversions are normally made. In many foreign countries low-cost labor in relation to the cost of capital dictates an economic decision to use manual labor in many tasks for which man is not well suited. Because of relatively high wages in the United States, machines are used much more extensively.

The Design of Jobs

When we speak of the *design of jobs*, we are thinking of two broad areas: job content and work methods. Given the job content, the work methods design is meant to develop the optimal combination of all variables of the job. We shall discuss in a moment the measures of effectiveness in these situations. If we accept a given job content and then try to arrive at some optimal combination of the remaining variables, however, we run the risk of suboptimization, because job content is also a major determinant of effectiveness.

Thus in a typical case we may have taken an entire complex assembly process and broken it down into a series of operations so that the product could be produced on an assembly line. The line was designed to meet certain capacity-demand requirements, such as an output of 480 units per 8-hour shift, or 1 per minute. Output, then, dictates the maximum content of each of the operations, which can take no longer than one minute each. What is more, there is a certain required sequence of assembly, so that operation 1 takes the elements that come first which require 1 minute or less, operation 2 the second 1-minute group, etc. Of course there is usually some flexibility as to sequence, so that by rearranging the sequences we end up with the job content in each operation that seems to make the most sense.

In other situations, the process, the machine, the physical layout, time requirements, and traditions are likely to play a dominant role in determining job content. Each resulting job or operation can be analyzed from the several points of view, which are presented in Chapters 3, 4, 5, and 6, in order to produce an optimally designed job. *But how would this optimal design compare with other basic alternatives of job content?* We can see that if we were to consider as a part of the problem all possible alternatives of job content, there would be a baffling number. Unfortunately there is very little information available to guide us here, and the result in practice is that such considerations as the machines, layouts, production quotas, and machine and conveyor pacing, often dictate job content [3, 7].

Since the time of Adam Smith, the main guide for determining job content has been *division of labor*. We have accepted this idea almost completely. Adam Smith specified no limit to division of labor, and the principle has been applied as a one-way mechanism to achieve the maximum benefits of job design. Jobs have been broken down to the point where the worker finds little satisfaction in performing his tasks. In recent years there has been a reaction against excessive job specialization; a few investigators found that combinations of operations to create jobs of greater scope recaptured the worker's interest, and increases in productivity, quality level, etc., were reported. A new term, *job enlargement*, appeared, and practical applications of job enlargement described in the literature verified the findings of the investigators. Unfortunately, although proponents of job enlargement recognize that division of labor can be carried too far, they have not been able to specify any principles or guides on how far to go in the other direction. Job enlargement, too, is a one-way mechanism. It does, however, provide a balancing force through the inclusion of job satisfaction as a major criterion of successful job design. The ultimate answer lies in research attempts to isolate the factors that determine an optimal combination of tasks to make up jobs. This effort has been called *job design* [3].

Management Objectives in Job and Methods Design.   Lehrer stated succinctly the objectives of job design in profit-making organizations as: "To make money," and "to make money" [4]. He says, "Although these appear to be identical objectives, they differ considerably. The first 'to make money' is a short-range objective. It implies immediate survival and the short-range prosperity of the organization. The second 'to make money' deals with the long-run objectives of the organization. It is concerned with survival over a prolonged period, and the proper relationship of the organization with society and the economy as a whole."

This quotation summarizes fairly well the past and present point of view of American business and industry. It emphasizes the economic criterion as the controlling factor of the organization, and considers other criteria as effective mainly insofar as they meet economic requirements. Thus a quality criterion often reduces to an economic criterion when the job design that improves quality levels also improves productivity. For example, removing fatiguing elements of a job commonly improves productivity; eliminating hazards may reduce insurance premium rates, as well as improve overall productivity; designing tasks that increase employee satisfaction often also improves productivity. There certainly are instances where the various subcriteria do not correlate with the economic criterion, however. To obtain higher-quality levels often demands increased costs, and the value of the reduced scrap may not counterbalance the higher labor costs. To reduce the risk of hazards to extremely low levels might be very costly.

In Taylor's time the noneconomic criteria would have been shrugged off. Today, however, jobs and methods are frequently designed or altered to meet noneconomic needs. It is true that the economic criterion is dominant, and job and methods designs are seldom set or altered without reference to the effects on costs. Most often, costs are regarded as the "quantitative" measure, with noneconomic criteria being considered in the list of "intangible" advantages or disadvantages.

What Is Involved in the Design of Jobs? Conceptually the design of jobs can be divided into the determination of job content and the determination of the actual methods of execution. As we have already noted, there is very little in the way of guides or principles to help us determine optimal job content. In general, job content is not consciously designed, but, rather, is the result of limitations of product designs, machine designs, layouts, production quotas, pacing effects, and of the desire to make skill requirements uniform within jobs. Within these limitations, the scope of jobs is determined, on the one hand, by a desire to gain the advantages inherent in division of labor, and on the other hand, by a desire to design jobs that meet worker satisfaction needs. Whether an organization tends toward finely divided jobs or enlarged jobs depends on its managerial philosophy, traditions, and degree of investment committed in existing systems.

The design of job methods has received much attention since the time of Taylor. Over the years, considerable handbook data has been compiled which may be drawn on to develop method designs which tend to optimize productivity and other measures of effectiveness for a given set of conditions. These data pertain to control of the work environment, physiological measures of body strength and sizing, psychological factors related to the various sensory inputs to the human operator, principles of the arrangement and flow of work, and fatigue and work schedules. These data are applied within a framework of physical and economic limitations. Figure 1 shows the relation of these factors in determining job content and job methods. Physical limitations may relate to existing products, machines, and layouts. Economic limitations refer both to the economic resources of the organization and to the justifiable expenditures on a given project; the latter depend to a great extent on the volume and market stability of the products. Thus the work methods design for a high-volume automotive part, such as a spark plug, will justify careful study from all points of view, and will also

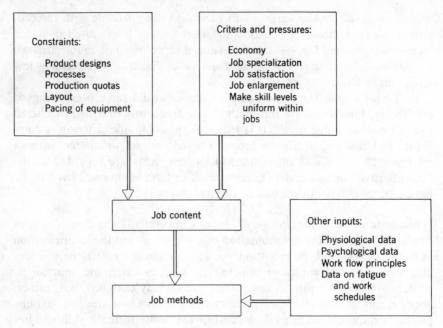

FIGURE 1. *Relationship of constraints, criteria, and other pressures in determining job content. Inputs to job methods design.*

justify expenditures of funds for machines, jigs, fixtures, and other special tools. On the other hand, job designs to produce a novelty toy, which may cease to exist in six months, might be quite crude. Here again, we see the dominant position of the economic criterion. Thus, a given job design is likely to be a temporary thing which may change with gross changes in the volume and market stability of the part or product.

Who Designs Jobs and Work Methods? In industrial organizations the professional designer of jobs and work methods is the industrial engineer. In many less formalized organizations, however, foremen and managers at various levels design jobs. In most nonmanufacturing organizations, managers and supervisors are responsible for determining job content and methods design. The wide variety of organizations and of people holding responsibility for job design makes dissemination of the known data a difficult problem. Since, for most of these people, job design is only a part of their responsibility, they have tended to rely on existing standard workplace designs and on basic equipment (such as office desks, type-writers, benches, and standard machine tools) to fix many of the characteristics of the job, and actual details of method are often left to the workers themselves.

Psychophysiological Data

In the post-World War II era there has been an increasing acceptance and recognition of the need to design workplaces and machines to fit the human operator better. This has reversed a previous trend of trying to select the few people from the working population who had certain special abilities or characteristics that made it possible for them to operate monster machines. During this earlier era there was an emphasis on finding people who could perform as if they had six fingers per hand or three hands, eyes in the backs of their heads, swivel hips, or legs that were double jointed at the knee. There was a need to find business and industrial freaks because the emphasis in machine design was on functional performance. The successful design engineer accomplished miracles of functional design. Indeed, he had solved the limiting part of the total engineering problem.

During this era, industrial engineers worked feverishly to patch up functional designs by relocating controls, putting extensions on levers to multiply the effect of workers' muscles, etc., but they were limited by the original design of the machine. In this same period, industrial engineers began to develop some of the necessary psychophysiological data that helped them establish the limits of normal working areas, design foot pedals, scales and information displays, and establish principles of the effective use of the human hands and body. Psychologists and physiologists were busy with other activities and, in general, were not interested in the practical problems of business and industry. From the safe distance of the laboratory, a few psychologists and physiologists offered criticism of what was being done in industry, but they did not offer their special knowledge and skills in any great degree until the postwar period.

Since World War II the picture has been different. Experimental psychologists and physiologists, largely subsidized by government projects, have been working to compile a large store of data on the human operator and his relation to machines. Many of these data are applicable to business and industry, as well as to the military. But unfortunately most data take the form of scattered experimental results in learned journals, which are read by other psychologists and physiologists and which seldom reach the people who actually design jobs in any form that they can use. Much effort is needed to integrate these data into an overall framework. Nevertheless, a great deal of data is available on man's physical size and strength, work area limits, chair and table heights, the speed and accuracy of various motor responses, information displays, controls coding, fatigue and work schedules, and the working environment [1, 6, 7]. These data can be useful adjuncts to job design.

Much of the analysis of jobs is accomplished through the use of the following graphic and schematic models.

GRAPHIC AND SCHEMATIC MODELS FOR ARRANGE- MENT AND FLOW OF WORK /

The psychophysiological data we have discussed consider various phases of human activity and attempt to give guides for job design—information such as recommended working heights, force to be applied by the hands and arms, placement of positioning elements, and display of information and code controls. All these data must be integrated into a logical pattern of work performance which uses the man, his machine, and mechanical aids to the best advantage. Here the principles of arrangement and work flow come into play.

Flow Charts. Since jobs occur in such great variation, the activities of each one must be analyzed separately to see if efforts go to accomplish the job, or are wasted. Here is where the general schematic and graphic methods of analysis known as flow charts, operation charts, activity charts, man-machine charts, etc., are used to help design and improve the job.

Before any of the methods of analysis described here are used, the need for performing the activity at all should have been established. As previously discussed in Chapter 3 under product flow process charts, specific operations can often be eliminated, combined with other operations, or placed in a different sequential position to advantage. The general areas of application of the several analysis methods of this chapter are summarized in Table I.

Repetitive Short-Cycle Tasks. *Operation charts* are appropriate when the

TABLE I. *Summary of areas of application of different man and man-machine analysis methods*

Nature of Activity	Analysis Method
Repetitive short-cycle task, low to moderate production volume	Operation chart, or operation chart supplemented by motion-time standard data
Repetitive short-cycle task, high production volume	Micromotion analysis chart, motion-time standard data
Repetitive long-cycle tasks	Man flow process charts, activity charts
Repetitive tasks involving a crew and/or a machine	Activity charts
Jobs involving tasks occurring at irregular intervals	Activity classification

task has a fairly short cycle and the production volume is low to moderate. The operation chart analyzes the motions of the right and left hands into components of reach, grasp, transport, position, assemble, etc., and places the activities for each hand in parallel columns so that it can readily be seen how the two hands work together. Sometimes symbols are added, as in Figure 2, usually with large circles to indicate manipulative activity, small circles to indicate reaches and transports of material, and a simple connective line to indicate that the hand is idle. Using the symbols, Figure 2 shows a completed operation chart for opening a corrugated case.

Sometimes the data of the operation chart are displayed against a time scale so that the relative value of the activities can be appraised. These time data may come from standard time values for motions such as reach, grasp, move, and position, or from detailed time studies of the operation being analyzed. The motion-time standard data discussed later in this

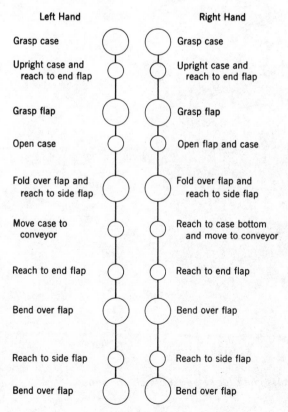

Left Hand	Right Hand
Grasp case	Grasp case
Upright case and reach to end flap	Upright case and reach to end flap
Grasp flap	Grasp flap
Open case	Open flap and case
Fold over flap and reach to side flap	Fold over flap and reach to side flap
Move case to conveyor	Reach to case bottom and move to conveyor
Reach to end flap	Reach to end flap
Bend over flap	Bend over flap
Reach to side flap	Reach to side flap
Bend over flap	Bend over flap

FIGURE 2.   Operation chart for opening and forming a corrugated case.

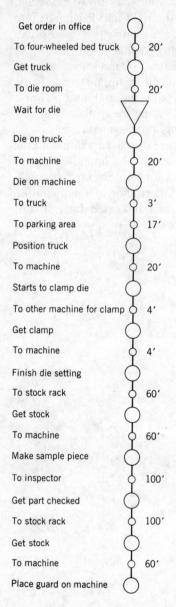

Get order in office

To four-wheeled bed truck   20'

Get truck

To die room   20'

Wait for die

Die on truck

To machine   20'

Die on machine

To truck   3'

To parking area   17'

Position truck

To machine   20'

Starts to clamp die

To other machine for clamp   4'

Get clamp

To machine   4'

Finish die setting

To stock rack   60'

Get stock

To machine   60'

Make sample piece

To inspector   100'

Get part checked

To stock rack   100'

Get stock

To machine   60'

Place guard on machine

FIGURE 3.   Man flow process chart for setting a punch press die.

chapter may be helpful particularly in evaluating the estimated effect of proposed changes.

Micromotion analysis breaks an operation down into elements called therbligs, which represent a finer breakdown than do the elements for the operation chart, and the results are plotted against a time scale so that the exact simultaneity of the two hands working together can be examined. The resulting chart is often called a "simo chart" because it shows this relationship. The data for the chart are gathered by means of motion pictures taken of a qualified operator. Time is measured either by placing a clock in the camera field that reads to a thousandth of a minute, or by using a synchronous motor drive on the camera so that each frame of the film represents one thousandth of a minute. (Faster camera speeds are sometimes used.) In either case, a special movie projector is used to analyze the film. This type of projector allows the analyst to advance the film one frame at a time to obtain the elapsed times for the therblig elements by the clock readings or from the frame counter on the projector.

Owing to the extra time and cost required to use micromotion analysis, a simo chart is commonly limited to situations where a large number of workers are performing the same repetitive task, so the total saving may be great, even though the percent reduction might be fairly small. It has also been found valuable in the design and development of new special production equipment. Here, a motion analyst and a machine designer working together often produce a superior design.

Repetitive Tasks Involving Long Cycles. *Man flow process charts* are commonly used to analyze long-cycle tasks in which the worker moves about considerably from place to place in the performance of his work. The same general type of analysis of the product flow process chart is used except that the analyst follows the worker, instead of a part, and classifies his activities sequentially into operations, transports (walking unloaded as well as when transporting material), storages (idleness), and inspections. Analysis of the resulting chart parallels product flow process charts, in that activities are examined with the objectives (*a*) of elimination, (*b*) of combination, and (*c*) of improved sequence, etc. Figure 3 is a man flow process chart for the task of setting a die in a punch press. Figure 4 shows the flow diagram of the activities of the die setter and emphasizes the amount of backtracking involved in the task as it was actually done. A common-sense analysis of the activity based on the process chart and flow diagram indicates that preplanning and maintaining a set of standard tools on the truck (such as the clamps) would reduce the amount of walking involved. Gang process charts are used where activities of a crew are studied, by using one column of symbols for each man in the crew.

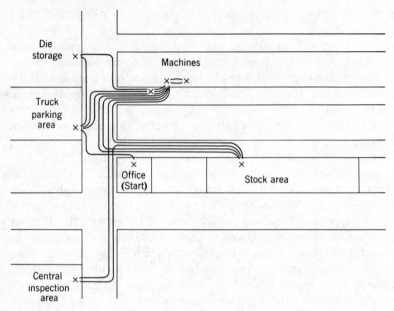

FIGURE 4. Flow diagram for setting a punch press die.

Repetitive Tasks Involving Crews or Machines. *Activity charts* analyze operations into the time required to perform major manual and machine elements, or activities, and plot the elements on a time scale. Relationships between man and machine or between crew members can then be examined. Let us take the milling of a slot in a bracket as an example. Figure 5 shows a bracket and the activity chart for the milling of the slot. Here the major elements of the repetitive work of the man and the machine have been plotted side by side on a time scale, and the times are recorded in decimal hours. In this type of analysis the major objectives are commonly to maximize man and machine utilization. In the example of the milling of the bracket slot, we see that the machine is 100 percent utilized, since it is either being loaded, unloaded, or actually taking a cut, and at no time is it idle. Nevertheless, machine effectiveness could be increased by improving the manual methods of loading and unloading, thus improving machine output per unit of time. The techniques for accomplishing this require a detailed study of the manual activity by means of the operation chart, etc., already discussed. On the other hand, the man is idle 73 percent of the cycle while he waits for the milling machine to complete its cut. This general situation is common in many kinds of machine and process operations.

The question is, what to do with idle man time in such a situation.

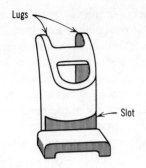

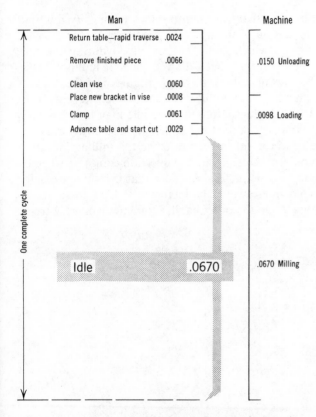

FIGURE 5. Activity chart of "mill slot in bracket." Courtesy Westinghouse Electric Corporation [9].

Perhaps the first consideration is whether the operator is really idle; some types of machine operations require operator vigilance and surveillance during the machine cycle, and an attempt to utilize such time could affect quality adversely. But it is often true that this is purely idle time. When such is the case on repetitive operations of considerable volume, it may be possible to have the man operate two or more machines. For the bracket slot milling operation, the operator could handle three machines doing the identical operation without introducing any idle machine time. Beyond that number, idle machine time develops, and an economy study would be required to determine whether idle man or machine time would be preferable.

Where the volume on the activity in question does not justify multiple machine operation, examination of the operator process chart for the part might reveal other elements which could be performed during the idle time. As an example, the operation that followed the slot milling on the bracket happened to be one of milling the lugs. Figure 6 is the activity chart for lug milling, and Figure 7 is the resulting composite operation of milling both the slot and the lugs. Note that the idle man time has now been reduced to about 40 percent of the total cycle, but in so structuring the job, idle machine time has been introduced into the lug milling machine, amounting to about 45 percent. Here again, the question comes up whether idle man or idle machine time is preferable. Note that if milling capacity were greater than demand, there would be incremental labor costs to do the two activities separately. On the other hand, if milling demand were at

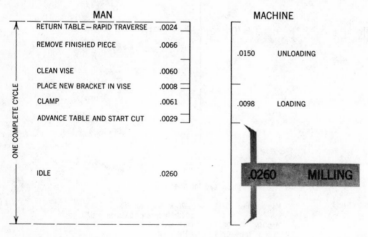

FIGURE 6. Activity chart for "mill lugs of bracket." Courtesy Westinghouse Electric Corporation [9].

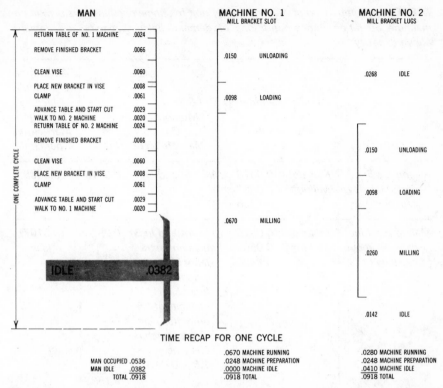

FIGURE 7. *Activity chart for the composite operation, "mill slot and lugs of bracket." Courtesy Westinghouse Electric Corporation* [9].

capacity or exceeded it, there would be created additional demand equal to the new machine idle time and there would be incremental labor costs equal to the extra hours at overtime rates. But since the two operations are being performed in the labor time of the slot milling operation, there may still be a net gain from combining the two operations. Table II summarizes the comparison for the conditions of demand below milling capacity and demand above milling capacity (forcing additional overtime). We see that multiple machine operation is advantageous only when demand is below capacity. When demand is above capacity the induced idle *machine* time requires a net additional labor cost which makes single machine operation advantageous.

Where it is impractical to combine two or more machining operations, it may be that other kinds of activity can be incorporated to reduce the idle time, for example, the removal of burrs produced by machining, or stacking

TABLE II. Comparison of man-hours per unit for single machine versus multiple machine operation under conditions of demand below capacity and demand above capacity

Condition	Single Machine Operation, Man-Hours per Unit	Multiple Machine Operation, Man-Hours per Unit	Advantage of Multiple Machine Operation Man-Hours per Unit
Milling machine demand below capacity	Mill slot 0.0918 Mill lugs 0.0508 $\overline{0.1426}$	Mill slot and lugs 0.0918	0.0508
Milling machine demand above capacity	Mill slot 0.0918 Mill lugs 0.0508 $\overline{0.1426}$	Mill slot and lugs 0.0918 Equivalent extra labor hours due to induced demand for milling capacity of 1.5 times the incremental machine idle time = $1.5 \times 0.0410 =$ 0.0615 $\overline{0.1533}$	(0.0107) loss

otherwise jumbled parts so that they may be procured more easily in the following operation. Any useful work that can be accomplished during such idle times, of course, incurs no incremental labor cost.

Sometimes skilled workers object to running more than one machine, but where these idle times are long, workers often become bored and may welcome a more even distribution of load. It is common that other workers, such as inspectors, assemblers, and many who operate machines that do not have automatic or semiautomatic cycles, are loaded fairly steadily throughout the work day.

Crew or team activities which often appear complex to the observer are considerably simplified by activity charts. Because of the difficulty in observing the simultaneity of the operations, the motion picture camera is an excellent means for gathering the basic data.

Analysis of Tasks Occurring at Irregular Intervals. *Activity classification* often provides valuable data for the analysis of jobs that have tasks (usually of wide variety) which occur at irregular intervals. An initial step in analysis is to determine the average proportion of time spent in each of several categories of activity. There are two valuable methods for gathering pertinent data for activity classification: work sampling and time-lapse movie camera techniques.

Work sampling involves a random sampling of activities so that the proportion of time spent in each activity can be estimated. Time-lapse movie cameras also can be used to obtain similar data. The camera, which takes pictures at slow speed intervals—one per second or slower, is set up to view the field of activity; it is driven by a synchronous motor so that each film frame represents a definite time unit. Since camera speeds can be slow, it is possible to obtain half-day or full-day records with a fairly modest film consumption. We will cover work sampling in greater detail in Chapter 5 as a statistical model.

Principles of Motion Economy. Over the years, industrial engineers have developed a set of general statements, called principles of motion economy, which concern work arrangement, the use of the human hands and body, and the design and use of tools. These guides to job design have general applicability and are supplemented, and in some cases corroborated, by some of the research into the speed and accuracy of motor activities.

Universal Standard Times. An extremely useful tool, from the job designer's point of view, is a set of universal time values for fundamental types of motions that he can use to predict total cycle time for as many alternative structures of jobs as he may wish to consider. Fundamental time values of this nature could be used as building blocks to forecast the all-important time criterion, provided that the time values were properly gathered and that the various minute motion elements required by the tasks were perfectly analyzed. Taylor envisioned something comparable to this, and many alternative proposals have been made by management consultants who sell services consisting of installing systems based on their data. Some of these alternate time-value systems are known by the trade names: Methods-Time-Measurement (MTM), Work Factor, and Basic Motion Time Study.

Although we have discussed standard time data systems as a means of helping to develop job designs, they also serve to forecast expected output. This forecast is of considerable importance, for business and industrial management are always interested in the labor content of a given job design, and, therefore, an estimate of the work standard is desirable. These work standards, however, usually involve appraisals of work time, rest time, delay allowances, and allowances for personal time. The universal standard times for fundamental motions discussed give estimates for the *work time* only.

Other kinds of standard time data exist as handbook data for common operations. These data can be very accurate in specifying machining or process time if all of the variables can be stated. The worker handling time is of course subject to the usual difficulties of measuring human work. Nevertheless, knowing an estimate of the time required to perform operations is an important input to many of the models we will discuss elsewhere in the book. The following section on work measurement states the special problems in attempting to measure human work and discusses some of the alternate methods used for accomplishing work measurement.

PRODUCTION STANDARDS AND WORK MEASUREMENT /

What is a "fair day's work"? A production standard is an answer to the question, and the field of work measurement provides a methodology and rationale for determining a fair day's work for different jobs. Production standards state either how many parts, assemblies, etc., should be produced per minute, hour, or day, or they may indicate the amount of time allowed as standard for producing a unit of work. Whether standards are expressed in terms of pieces per unit of time or time per piece is quite irrelevant; however, they are often called "time standards" when expressed in time units. Although production standards are designed to determine how much output is expected of an employee, they include more than just work. Actually, production standards include standard allowances for rest, delays that occur as part of the job, time for personal needs, and, where the work is heavy, an allowance for physical fatigue. You can see that the problems of measuring work and setting up good standards of performance that are consistent from job to job are going to be difficult. They are indeed, so why go to the trouble of setting them up? Why are standards important?

Standards Provide Basic Data.   Production standards provide data that is basic to many decision making problems in production. The production standard is of critical importance because labor cost is a predominant factor influencing many of the decisions that must be made. For example, decisions to make or buy, to replace equipment, or to select certain manufacturing processes require estimates of labor costs, as well as estimates of other costs, and these decisions necessarily require an estimate of how much output can be expected per unit of time.

Production standards also provide basic data for use in the day-to-day operation of a plant. For example, to schedule or load machines demands a knowledge of the projected time requirements for the various orders. For custom manufacture we must be able to give potential customers a bid price and delivery date. The price is ordinarily based on expected costs for labor, materials, and overhead, plus profit. Labor cost is commonly the largest single component in such situations. To estimate labor cost requires an estimate of how long it will take to perform the various operations.

Finally, production standards provide the basis for labor cost control. By measuring worker performance in comparison to standard performance, indexes can be computed for individual workers, whole departments, divisions, or even plants. These indexes make it possible to compare performance on completely different kinds of jobs. Standard labor costing systems and incentive wage payment systems are based on production standards. Production standards are useful in so many ways in both the design and in the operation and control of production systems that we must regard them as truly basic data.

Informal Standards. The plain fact is that every organization has production standards of sorts. Even when they seem not to exist formally, foremen and supervisors have a standard in mind for the various jobs that come under their supervision based on their knowledge of the work and past performances. These types of standards are informal. They can be formalized merely by writing them down and recognizing them as being the standards of performance expected. Standards based on foremen's estimates and past performance data have weaknesses, however. First of all, in most all such situations, methods of work performance have not been standardized, so that it is difficult to state what production rate, based on past records, is appropriate, because past performance may have been based on various methods. Since it has been well demonstrated that production rates depend heavily on job methods, standards based on past performance records might not be too dependable. A second major defect in standards based on estimates and past performance records is that they are likely to be too strongly influenced by the working speeds of the individuals who held the jobs during the periods of the available records. Were those workers high or low performers?

The Core of the Work Measurement Problem

We wish to set up production standards which are applicable to the industrial population, not just to a few selected people within that population. Our production standards problem is comparable in some ways to that of designing a lever with the proper mechanical advantage to match the capabilities of man. But not just any man; the force required to pull the lever should accommodate perhaps 95 to 99 percent of the population, so that anyone who comes to the job will have the necessary arm strength. If the lever required a man with superhuman strength, we would have to seek out only these kinds of people for the job.

The production standard that we wish to set up actually requires a knowledge of the distribution of performance times (or production rates) for the entire working population doing the job for which we are setting up a standard. Suppose that we have 500 people all doing an identical task, and make sample studies on all of them and plot the data. Figure 8 shows the results of just such a study. The distribution shows that average performance time varies from 0.28 minutes to 0.63 minutes per piece. Obviously, if our past records reflected data from one or more individuals taken at random from our population of 500 for this task, a standard based on their performance might not fit the whole population very well. On the other hand, if we know the entire distribution, as in Figure 8, we can set up standards that we are fairly sure would accommodate everyone who might come to the job. One way to do this is to follow a procedure similar to that used in job design when drawing on anthropometric data. Set the standard so that it accommodates about 95 percent of the popula-

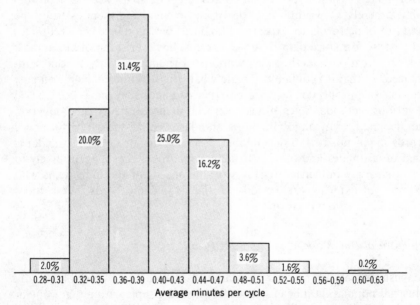

FIGURE 8. Distribution of the performance of 500 people performing a wood block positioning task, in percent. About 5.4 percent pf the people averaged 0.48 minute per cycle or longer, Adapted from R. M. Barnes [2].

tion. For Figure 8, a standard performance time of about 0.48 minutes is one which about 95 percent of the individuals exceeded. If we pegged the standard at this level, we would expect that practically all employees on the job should be able to meet or exceed the standard.

Some industrial managers feel that it is not good to quote minimum performance standards such as these for fear that they will encourage relatively poor performance as acceptable. These people prefer to say that the standard performance is about the average of the distribution (0.395 minute for Figure 8) and expect that most workers will produce about standard, that some will fall below, and some will exceed standard. Both systems of quoting standards are used, although the practice of quoting *minimum acceptable values* is more common than that of quoting average values.

To this point we have been discussing only the work time. The distribution of Figure 8 shows how long it took on the average to perform the task. Using the minimum acceptable level as our basic standard of performance, we will call the actual work time at that level the *normal time*. The normal time for the data of Figure 8 is 0.48 minute, and the total standard time is then:

> Normal time + standard allowance for personal time
> + allowance for measured delays normal to the job
> + fatigue allowance

We shall discuss the several allowances later, but the central question now is: "How do we determine normal time in the usual situation when only one or a few workers are on the job?" Very seldom would we find a large number of workers doing the same job, so that usually we cannot build up a distribution. Without a knowledge of the distribution, how can we pick out the level which about 95 percent of the workers could meet or exceed, that is, normal time? The approach to this problem used in industry is called performance rating.

Performance Rating

Performance rating is a critically important part of any formal means of work measurement. To be able to rate accurately requires considerable experience. It works something like this. A pace or performance level is selected as standard. An analyst observes this pace and compares it with various other paces and learns to judge pace level in percent of the standard pace. For Figure 8 we have called the cycle time of 0.48 minute "normal," and the pace or rate of output associated with this time is normal pace. A pace of work that was 25 percent faster would require proportionately less time per cycle, or $0.48/1.25 = 0.384$ minute. Then if a skilled analyst observed a worker performing the task on which Figure 8 is based and rated performance at 125 percent of normal, while simultaneously measuring the actual average performance time as 0.384 minute, he would have to add 25 percent to his observed time to adjust it to the normal level. In this instance, his performance rating is perfect, according to our distribution, since $0.384 \times 1.25 = 0.48$. Other perfect combinations of rating and actual observed time are 150 percent and 0.32 minute, 175 percent and 0.274 minute, 90 percent and 0.533 minute, etc. In an actual work measurement situation, of course, the analyst does not have the answer beforehand, so he simultaneously observes the actual time taken to do the task and rates the performance. The normal time is then computed as:

$$\text{Normal time} = \text{actual observed time} \times \frac{\text{performance rating}}{100}$$

All of the several formal work measurement systems involve this rating or judgment of working pace or some equivalent procedure. Alternate methods of actually measuring time and determining normal time will be considered later in the chapter.

Rating as a System of Measurement. What do we need in order to be able to measure something, whether it be the length of a line, the pressure inside a vessel, or the pace at which a man is working? It is really quite simple. We need basically two things: (*a*) a standard for comparison which is accepted, and (*b*) a unit of measurement, or a scale. Both may be set arbitrarily. For example, in linear measurement (the measurement of length) our basic standard has been a platinum-iridium bar held in the Bureau of Standards in Washington, D.C., which, in turn, is based on the international standard. Two scales are commonly used, based on two different ways of dividing up the bar. One is the English system (yards, feet, inches), and the other the metric system (meters, centimeters, millimeters). Any number of other scales could be based on the same basic standard. Also, any number of other bar lengths could have served as basic standards of length on which to base the scales. The thing that makes our present basic standard and the two common scales valuable measurement systems is that they have received general acceptance.

Does the use of these systems of measure then involve judgment? Yes, even the use of the best precision measuring instruments involves some judgment. In using a micrometer, for example, one must judge how tightly to turn down the spindle, and the importance of this "feel" cannot be minimized.

Let us consider performance rating in the same general light. Are there basic standards of reference which have general acceptance? Yes there are motion picture films of operations in many types of occupations which show "normal paces" for those tasks, as well as both faster and slower paces. One set of such films was made by the Society for Advancement of Management (SAM) and consists of 24 factory and clerical operations, which have been rated by thousands of experienced time study analysts throughout the country. Walking at 3 miles per hour has been selected as "normal pace." Many organizations, such as Deere and Company, General Motors, and Caterpillar Tractor Company, have their own standards in the form of films of various operations throughout their plants, which exhibit normal and other paces of work. These film standards do not enjoy the same degree of acceptance as do the physical standards of weights and measures, but the fact is that they exist. Analysts can use them to recalibrate their judgment and to train people in performance rating.

Now to the question of scales. There are, unfortunately, three scales in common use, and this fact is often the source of some confusion. Figure 9 shows these scales in relation to the basic standards of walking at 3 miles per hour, etc. Scale A is the most common and it is the scale which we shall assume throughout this book where work standards are mentioned. It labels "normal pace" as 100 percent. Scale B provides maximum confusion by labeling a much higher level of performance as 100 percent. We can convert easily between the two scales by recognizing that 125 percent on scale A is the same performance level as 100 percent on scale B. Scale B is used by organizations who wish to quote standards at a higher level. Scale C is in points instead of percent and it is often called the Bedaux scale. On the Bedaux scale, 60 points is equivalent to 100 percent performance on scale A.

How Accurate Is Performance Rating? In the actual work measurement situation, it is necessary to compare our mental image of "normal performance" with what is observed and record our rating of the performance. This rating enters the computation of production standards as a factor, and the final standard can be no more accurate than the rating. How accurately can experienced people rate? Commonly accepted figures would be ± 5 percent. Controlled studies in which films have been rated, indicated a standard deviation of 7 to 10 percent. In other words, experienced people probably hold these limits about 68 percent of the time. Therefore, the effect of the element of judgment in current work measurement practice is considerable. This fact is important in all of the uses of production

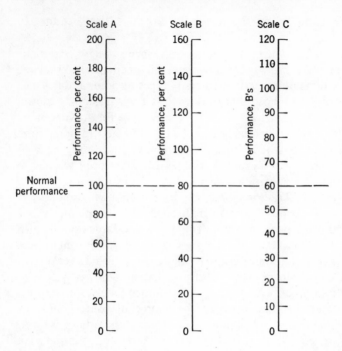

FIGURE 9. Three alternate performance rating scales in relation to normal performance.

standards which we discussed at the beginning of this chapter. None the less, standards developed by measurement (including the rating) are better than standards based simply on past records, because they specify a given work method and they correct for the working pace of the employee observed. A standard based on past records only could easily be off 200 to 300 percent for these reasons, and therefore ±7 to 10 percent is modest by comparison.

WORK
MEASUREMENT SYSTEMS /

All practical work measurement systems involve (a) the measurement of actual observed time, and (b) the adjustment of observed time to obtain "normal time" by means of performance rating.

The alternate systems which we shall discuss combine these factors in somewhat different ways.

Stop-watch Methods.   By far the most prevalent approach to work measurement currently used involves a stop-watch time study and simultaneous performance rating of the operation to determine normal time. The general procedure is as follows:

1. Standardize methods for the operation, that is, determine the standard method, specifying workplace layout, tools, sequence of elements, etc. Record resulting standard practice.

2. Select operator for study, experienced and trained in the standard methods.

3. Determine elemental structure of operation for timing purposes. This may involve a breakdown of the operation into subelements and the separation of the elements that occur each cycle from those that occur only periodically or even randomly. For example, tool sharpening might be required each 100 cycles to maintain quality limits. Machine adjustments might occur at random intervals.

4. Observe and record the actual time required for the elements, making simultaneous performance ratings.

5. Determine the number of observations required to yield the desired precision of the result based on the sample data obtained in step 4. Obtain more data as required.

6. Compute normal time = average observed actual time × average rating factor/100.

7. Determine allowances for personal time, delays, and fatigue.

8. Determine standard time = normal times for elements + time for allowances.

There are important statistical problems involved in the determination of adequate sample sizes, and we shall touch on them in Chapter 5.

Work Sampling Methods.   Work sampling is an alternate procedure used commonly both to determine allowances for other work measurement techniques and to make a complete determination of standards. Work sampling will be covered in Chapter 5.

Universal Standard Times.   These methods referred to in connection with our discussion of job design are quite often used in connection with other methods of measurement.

REVIEW QUESTIONS

1. What kinds of functions can man perform in work situations?

2. Compare man's capability with that of known machines.

3. How is job content determined?

5. What is the area of usefulness of the assembly chart? The operation process chart? The man flow process chart?

6. How can a flow diagram help to visualize the information shown on a flow process chart?

7. What sort of analytical tool might be used to show working relationships between an operator and the machine he is using?

8. What information is necessary for the development of such an analytical tool discussed in question 7?

9. What are the general conditions under which one worker might operate more than one machine?

10. What modes of analysis are appropriate for activities which have no set repetitive pattern? How can the data be gathered?

11. Why are labor standards important? How are they used?

12. Relate the problem of the determination of production standards to the problem of designing a lever that requires arm strength available in 95 percent of the working population.

13. Define the terms normal time, performance rating, allowances, standard time.

14. Discuss the function of performance rating in the determination of production standards.

15. Discuss performance rating as a system of measurement. How accurate is performance rating?

16. What is the general procedure for determining standards by stop watch methods?

17. Why is it general practice to divide a job into elements for stop watch study?

18. What is the current basis for fatigue allowances used in work measurement?

19. Discuss the possible range of application of work measurement technique in manufacturing and nonmanufacturing activity.

PROBLEMS

1. Construct an operation chart for the assembly of some simple device such as a ball-point pen, a chair caster, or a pair of scissors.

2. A custom machining company has received an order for a lot of 10,000 parts which requires a simple milling operation for which the company has available

capacity. Plans are now being made for the method of operation to be used, and work will begin next week, the promised delivery date being 13 weeks from the first of next week. The plant works one shift, 40 hours per week, with up to 20 percent overtime possible. The company normally attempts to obtain better labor utilization on relatively large orders like this one by having one worker operate more than one machine when it is feasible, with established layout, and by investing in special jigs and fixtures to speed up unloading and loading of the machine.

The layout of the milling machine area and the automatic machining cycle make it possible for an operator to unload and load a machine, start the machine on its automatic cycle, and then proceed to the next machine, giving it the required attention when it has completed its machining cycle and so on. The machines will automatically turn off when the normal machining cycle has been completed. From previous records of similar orders and from standard data on machining times for specified materials and length of cut, the following estimates of times for the job elements have been assembled:

Load part in machine	1.00 minute
Machine part (automatic)	5.00 minutes
Unload part from machine	0.50 minute
Inspect part	0.75 minute
Walk from machine to machine	0.25 minute

After feasible man-machine cycles have been assembled using the foregoing data, the company follows the practice of adding 10 percent to the total cycle to obtain a standard time for the job to be used in cost calculations. The 10 percent allowance is for rest and delay and for other personal needs. The following cost data have also been assembled:

Milling machine operator's rate	$3.00/hour
Machine variable cost (power, cutting fluids, etc.)	1.00/hour
Material	1.50/piece
Tooling (special holding fixtures)	300/set up
Labor cost to set up machine	100/set up

There are up to four machines available, and the department supervisor says that he could assign as many as three men to the job.

(a) Determine the method of operation which would minimize costs by developing a table of pertinent costs for the lot of 10,000 parts for systems where a worker operates one, two, three, and four machines. Which mode of operation would you choose and why?

(b) What kinds of costs do you think may have been ignored in the statement of the problem? Are any of the costs given as irrevelant data?

3. A young couple has started a laundrette. Their business, The Blue Monday Laundrette, offers the following services:

(a) Washers for use by customers

(b) Drying service for customer's washes

(c) Dry cleaning and finished laundry

(d) Washing and fluff drying

The husband performs the "fluff dry" work (washing, extracting, and fluff drying). The wife handles all other matters such as dealing with customers, aiding people who do their own washing, etc. She also folds and bundles the "fluff dry" work during slack periods in the day.

The "fluff dry" business has been unusually heavy and the couple has been forced to work evenings to get work out on time. It is their contention that five washers, if kept busy, can do the "fluff dry" work, but there are so many other things to be done such as semidrying the wet clothes in the extractor and loading and unloading the dryer that one person simply cannot keep the washers loaded. The wife does not have time to assist the husband during normal working hours.

The following times are required to perform the various tasks:

	Time (minutes)
Washer (5 available for "fluff dry")	
(1) Load soiled clothes and soap, set water temperature, start machine	2
(2) Running time (automatically stops)	40
(3) Unload wet clothes into cart	2
Extractor (1 available for "fluff dry"; each holds one washer load only)	
(1) Load wet clothes and start machine	2
(2) Running time (automatically stops)	5
(3) Unload semidry clothes into cart	2
Dryer (2 available for "fluff dry"; each holds one washer load only)	
(1) Untangle and load clothes, start machine	3
(2) Running time (automatically stops)	20
(3) Unload dry clothes into cart	2
Miscellaneous	
Travel times between equipment	Negligible

(a) With the data given, construct an activity chart for the best method of coordinating the work of one man, five washers, one extractor, and two dryers.

(b) What is the overall cycle time (time difference between identical points in the process such as loading washer No. 1 on consecutive loads)?

4. A company is constructing a parking lot for which dump trucks and a power shovel are the primary equipment being used. Time studies reveal the following average times:

Time to load a truck	7.50 minutes
Travel time to dump point	9.00 minutes
Dumping time	2.00 minutes
Return time	7.00 minutes

(a) How many trucks are required to move dirt as rapidly as possible?

(b) If it costs $19 per hour for the shovel and operator and $12 per hour for each truck and driver, what number of trucks will minimize idle equipment cost?

(c) Construct a multiple-activity chart for the answer to (b).

5. A company has decided to plate its own bushings rather than have them done elsewhere. Under their newly developed process a single operator performs the entire process as follows:

(1) A tumbler to remove burrs, etc.

(2) A degreasing tank to remove oil.

(3) Two plating tanks.

Loads consist of 250 bushings each with all equipment starting by the operator's push of a button and shutting off automatically. Therefore, the equipment does not require the operator's attention while running. The times required to perform the various operations are as follows:

Load tumbler	5 minutes
Running time for tumbler	24 minutes
Unload tumbler	6 minutes
Load degreaser	3 minutes
Degreaser running time	36 minutes
Unload degreaser	6 minutes
Load plating tank	6 minutes
Plating process time	60 minutes
Unload plating tank	6 minutes

(a) How many minutes does it take to complete one full cycle?

(b) How much of the total idle time of each plating tank is unnecessary?

(c) If the running time of the limiting process is reduced 25 percent by equipment redesign what is the new cycle time in minutes?

6. A moonshine company utilizes one man and several pieces of automated equipment (blender, ager, and bottler) to produce their product. The process and associated times are as follows:

Blending:	
Put in ingredients	6 minutes
Blending cycle	25 minutes
Remove blend, put in crock	4 minutes
Aging:	
Put blend in aging tank	2 minutes
Aging cycle	26 minutes
Remove and filter into crock	10 minutes
Bottling:	
Filter blend into bottling machine	7 minutes
Bottling cycle	15 minutes
Remove cans and pack in case	12 minutes

(a) What is the cycle time?

(b) What percentage of the time is the blender idle?

7. A one-man washing operation consists of the following process:

Washing cycle

Load clothes and soak	2 minutes
Run (automatic)	25 minutes
Unload	2 minutes

Extracting cycle:

Load clothes into extractor	1 minute
Run (automatic)	6 minutes
Unload	1 minute

Drying cycle:

Load clothes into dryer	2 minutes
Run (automatic)	40 minutes
Unload and fold clothes	12 minutes

The present set-up utilizes one washer, one extractor, and two dryers.

(*a*) What is the cycle time?

(*b*) What reduction in the extractor's unnecessary idle time would occur if a second washing machine were purchased?

8. Select a simple assembled product for which parts can be obtained. Determine a time study elemental breakdown for the assembly of the product and time 12 cycles.

9. Lay out a 100-foot walking course in such a way that the total time for walking the course can be measured. Using the standard 3 mile per hour pace as 100 percent performance, one should walk the course in 0.3785 minute. Figure 10 shows a chart

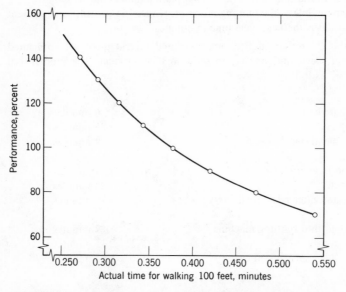

FIGURE 10. Actual time for walking 100 feet versus performance in percent with 3 miles per hour used as a standard walking pace.

which relates measured time for walking 100 feet versus percent performance using the three mile per hour pace as a standard. Working in groups, have subjects walk the 100-foot course while one individual measures elapsed time. Others in the group should rate the walking pace in percent. After a series of observing several different walking paces, compare actual pace (from Figure 10) with rated pace. Plot the results on a graph of actual pace in percent versus rated pace.

10. A time study is made of a punch press operator the results of which yield an average actual time per piece of 0.30 minute. The punch press operator's performance during the study was rated at 120 percent. If total allowances are 10 percent of standard time, what is the standard time in minutes for this operation?

11. A continuous time study was made on a collating job in an office with the following results:

Element	Cycle, minutes						Perform-ance Rating Percent
	1	2	3	4	5	6	
(1) Apply glycerin to fingers.	0.04	—	0.46	—	3.10	—	120
(2) Get four pages with each hand.	0.16	0.35	0.63	2.99	3.24	3.45	105
(3) Jog eight sheets.	0.19	0.39	2.83*	3.04	3.28	3.49	110
(4) Staple and put aside.	0.22	0.41	2.86	3.07	3.30	3.52	90

*Operator dropped the eight sheets on the floor.

(*a*) Calculate the normal time per collated set.

(*b*) If the allowances for this type of work total 15 percent, what would be the standard time per set?

(*c*) Should the set of papers dropped be considered as a part of the study or should this data be thrown out? What are the implications of not considering this data in the study?

REFERENCES

1. Barnes, R. M., *Motion and Time Study: Design and Measurement of Work*, John Wiley & Sons, New York, 6th ed., 1968.
2. Buffa, E. S., *Modern Production Management*, John Wiley & Sons, New York, 3rd ed., 1969.
3. Davis, L. E., "Toward a Theory of Job Design," *Journal of Industrial Engineering*, Vol. VIII, No. 5, September–October, 1957, pp. 305–309.
4. Lehrer, R. N., "Job Design," *The Journal of Industrial Engineering*, Vol. IX, No. 5, September–October 1958, pp. 439–446.
5. Lehrer, R. N., *Work Simplification*, Prentice-Hall, Englewood Cliffs, N.J., 1957.

6. McCormick, E. J., *Human Factors Engineering*, McGraw-Hill Book Company, New York, 3rd ed., 1970.
7. Nadler, G., *Work Design: A Systems Concept*, Richard D. Irwin, Homewood, Ill., Rev. ed., 1970.
8. Niebel, B. W., *Motion and Time Study*, Richard D. Irwin, Homewood, Ill., 5th ed., 1972.
9. *Operations Analysis*, Westinghouse Electric Corp., Pittsburgh, Pa., 1948.

chapter 5

STATISTICAL MODELS IN WORK MEASUREMENT

The unique problems of work measurement utilize some of the same general methodology found useful in statistical quality control (see Chapters 19 and 20) but with a different emphasis and objective. In work measurement, we are dealing first with the problem of estimating the mean and standard deviation of a highly variable distribution. The techniques of process control, commonly used in quality control, can help in establishing whether or not the data taken were being generated by a system under statistical control. The second statistical problem in work measurement is in estimating a data sample size large enough to establish a predetermined confidence level and precision for the resulting standards. The models and procedures take different forms for the two work measurement methodologies which we will discuss: stop-watch time study and work sampling.

Stop-Watch Methods

In Chapter 4 we presented a general outline of stop-watch work measurement procedure. Our present interest is in steps 3, 4, and 5 of that procedure. We shall amplify on the procedures for breaking down jobs into measureable elements, taking and recording data, determining sample sizes, and insuring the consistency of sample data.

Breakdown of Elements.   Common practice is to divide the total operation into elements, rather than to measure the entire cycle as a whole. There are several reasons why this practice is followed:

1. The element breakdown helps to describe the operation in some detail, indicating the step-by-step procedure followed during the study.

2. More information is obtained which may have valuable use in comparing times for like elements on different jobs and to build up a handbook of standard-data times for common elements in job families. With standard data for elements, cycle times for new sizes can be forecast without additional study.

3. A worker's performance level may vary in different parts of the cycle. With an element breakdown, different performance ratings can be assigned to different elements where the overall cycle is long enough to permit separate evaluation of performance.

In breaking an operation into elements, it is common practice to make elements a logical component of the overall cycle, as illustrated in Figure 1. For example, element 1, "pick up piece and place in jig," is a fairly homogeneous task. Note that element 4, "drill ¼-inch hole," is the machining element, following the general practice to separate machining time from handling time. Finally, constant elements are usually separated from elements whose times might vary with size, weight, or some other parameter.

Taking and Recording Data.   Figure 1 is a sample study where 20 cycles have been timed by the continuous method, that is, the stop watch is allowed to run continuously, being read at the breakpoints between elements. Elapsed times for elements are then obtained by successive subtraction. *Repetitive* or "snap-back" methods of reading the watch are also common. In repetitive timing, the observer reads the watch at the end of each element and snaps the hand back to zero so that each reading gives the actual element time without the necessity of subtraction. Comparative studies indicate that the two methods are equally accurate. Note the other data recorded in Figure 1 which identifies the part, operation, operator, material, etc., as well as check data of elapsed time of the study, and the number of completed units. The "selected times" represent averages of the element times, and the cycle "selected time" is merely the sum of the element averages. A single performance rating of 100 percent was made for the study and a 5 percent allowance added to obtain the standard time of 1.17 minutes per piece.

Adequacy of Sample Size.   Considering the work measurement problem from the viewpoint of statistics, we are attempting to estimate, from the

OBSERVATION SHEET

SHEET 1 OF 1 SHEETS | DATE

OPERATION Drill ¼"Hole | OP. NO. D-20

PART NAME Motor Shaft | PART NO. MS-267

MACHINE NAME Avey | MACH. NO. 2174

OPERATOR'S NAME & NO. S.K. Adams 1347 | MALE ✓ FEMALE ☐

EXPERIENCE ON JOB 18 Mo. on Sens. Drill | MATERIAL S.A.E. 2315

FOREMAN H. Miller | DEPT. NO. DL 21

BEGIN 10:15 | FINISH 10:38 | ELAPSED 23 | UNITS FINISHED 20 | ACTUAL TIME PER 100 115 | NO. MACHINES OPERATED 1

ELEMENTS	SPEED	FEED	T/R	1	2	3	4	5	6	7	8	9	10	SELECTED TIME
1. Pick Up Piece and Place in Jig			T	.12	.11	.12	.13	.12	.10	.12	.12	.14	.12	
			R	.12	.29	.39	.54	.66	.77	.92	8.01	14	.32	
2. Tighten Set Screw			T	.13	.12	.12	.14	.11	.12	.12	.13	.12	.11	
			R	.25	.41	.51	.68	.77	.89	7.04	.14	.26	.43	
3. Advance Drill to Work			T	.05	.04	.04	.04	.05	.04	.04	.04	.03	.04	
			R	.30	.45	.55	.72	.82	.93	.08	.18	.29	.47	
4. DRILL ¼ Inch Hole	980	H	T	.67	.64	.66	.61	.64	.68	.52	.63	.69	.56	
			R	.87	.99	3.11	4.23	5.36	6.51	.60	.71	.88	11.03	
5. Raise Drill from Hole			T	.04	.03	.03	.03	.03	.03	.03	.03	.04	.03	
			R	.91	2.02	.14	.26	.39	.54	.63	.74	.92	.06	
6. Loosen Set Screw			T	.06	.06	.07	.06	.06	.06	.06	.06	.07	.08	
			R	.97	.08	.21	.32	.45	.60	.69	.80	.99	.14	
7. Remove Piece from Jig			T	.08	.09	.08	.08	.09	.08	.07	.08	.09	.07	
			R	1.05	.17	.29	.40	.54	.68	.76	.88	10.08	.21	
8. Blow Out Chips			T	.13	.10	.12	.14	.13	.12	.13	.12	.12	.11	
			R	.18	.27	.41	.54	.67	.80	.89	9.00	.20	.32	
9.			T											
			R											
10. (1)			T	.12	.11	.13	.14	.12	.12	.11	.13	.12	.12	.12
			R	11.44	.56	.69	.82	.87	17.01	18.09	.21	.31	.42	
11. (2)			T	.12	.14	.12	.11	.12	.10	.13	.15	.12	.11	.12
			R	.56	.70	.81	.93	.99	.11	.22	.36	.43	.53	
12. (3)			T	.04	.04	.04	.03	.04	.04	.04	.04	.04	.04	.04
			R	.60	.74	.85	.96	16.03	.15	.26	.40	.47	.57	
13. (4)			T	.54	.53	.55	.52	.57	.54	.50	.53	.55	.54	.54
			R	12.14	13.27	14.40	15.48	.60	.69	.76	.93	21.02	22.11	
14. (5)			T	.03	.03	.03	.03	.03	.03	.03	.03	.03	.03	.03
			R	.17	.30	.43	.51	.63	.72	.79	.96	.05	.14	
15. (6)			T	.06	.06	.06	.07	.06	.05	.06	.06	.05	.06	.06
			R	.23	.36	.49	.58	.69	.77	.85	20.02	.10	.20	
16. (7)			T	.08	.08	.09	.08	.08	.07	.08	.06	.08	.08	.08
			R	.31	.44	.58	.66	.77	.84	.93	.08	.18	.28	
17. (8)			T	.14	.12	.10	.09	.12	.14	.15	.11	.12	12	.12
			R	.45	.56	.68	.75	.89	.98	19.08	.19	.30	22.40	
18.			T											1.11
			R											

SELECTED TIME 1.11 | RATING 100% | NORMAL TIME 1.11 | TOTAL ALLOWANCES 5% | STANDARD TIME 1.17

Overall Length 12" / Drill ¼" Hole — 1" — ¾" — 1½"

TOOLS, JIGS, GAUGES: Jig No. D-12-33
Use H.S. Drill ¼" Diam.
Hand Feed
Use Oil - S4

TIMED BY J.B.M.

FIGURE 1. Stop-watch time study of a drilling operation made by the continuous method. From R. M. Barnes, Motion and Time Study [3].

sample times and performance ratings observed, a normal time of performance. The precision desired will determine how many observations will be required. For example, if we wanted to be 95 percent sure that the resulting answer, based on the sample, was within ± 5 percent, we would calculate the sample size n required from a knowledge of the mean and standard deviation of our sample data. If we wanted greater confidence, or closer precision, the sample size would have to be larger.

Assume, for example, that we have made a sample study based on 20 observations and have computed preliminary values of $\bar{x}$ and s as 1.0 minute and 0.20 minutes, respectively. ($\bar{x}$ and s are estimates of the population mean and standard deviation, respectively.) If we wished to be sure that $\bar{x}$ was within ± 5 percent 95 percent of the time then the 95 percent confidence interval would be:

$$0.95 \leqq \bar{x} \leqq 1.05$$

In other words, we want $2s_{\bar{x}}$ set equal to the permissible variation in $\bar{x}$, or

$$2s_{\bar{x}} = 2 \frac{s}{\sqrt{n}} = 0.05$$

and since s is 0.20

$$\frac{2 \times 0.20}{\sqrt{n}} = 0.05$$

Solving for n

$$n = \left(\frac{2 \times 0.20}{0.05} \right)^2 = (8)^2 = 64$$

Obviously we need at least $64 - 20 = 44$ additional observations for the requirements we have established.

Figure 2 is a convenient chart for estimating required sample sizes to maintain a ± 5 percent precision in the answer, for 95 and 99 percent confidence levels. To use the chart, we merely calculate the mean value $\bar{x}$ and the standard deviation based on the sample data. The "coefficient of variation" is simply the percentage variation, $(s/\bar{x})100$. The chart is entered with the calculated coefficient of variation, and the sample size is read off for the confidence level desired. The most common confidence level is 95 percent in work measurement.

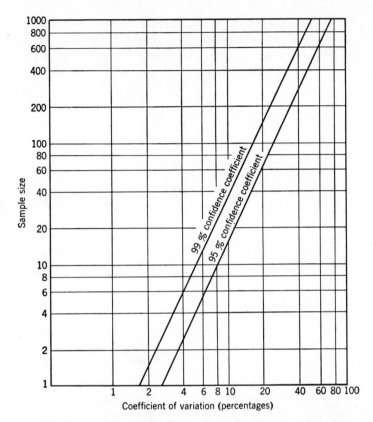

FIGURE 2. Chart for estimating the sample size required to obtain maximum confidence intervals of ±5 percent for given coefficient of variation values. From A. Abruzzi [1].

Let us test the adequacy of the sample taken in the study of Figure 1. First, was $n = 20$ adequate for estimating the overall cycle within a precision of ±5 percent and a confidence level of 95 percent? Table I shows the calculation of the coefficient of variation for the cycle times as about 5 percent, that is, the standard deviation 0.057 minute is about 5 percent of the mean cycle time of 1.12 minutes. From Figure 2 we see that a sample of $n = 4$ would be adequate to maintain a precision within ±5 percent of the correct mean cycle time, 95 percent of the time, or $n = 10$ for a confidence level of 99 percent. Our actual sample of 20 was more than adequate. The reason that the small sample sizes were adequate is easy to see. The variability of the readings is small in relation to the mean cycle time, so that a good estimate of cycle time is obtained by only a few observations.

TABLE I. Cycle times from Figure 1, and calculated mean value, standard deviation, coefficient of variation and required sample sizes from Figure 2

Cycle Number	Cycle Time, minutes	Cycle Time, squared	Cycle Number	Cycle Time, minutes	Cycle Time, squared
1	1.18	1.395	11	1.13	1.280
2	1.09	1.190	12	1.11	1.235
3	1.14	1.300	13	1.12	1.255
4	1.13	1.280	14	1.07	1.145
5	1.13	1.280	15	1.14	1.300
6	1.13	1.280	16	1.09	1.190
7	1.09	1.190	17	1.10	1.215
8	1.11	1.235	18	1.11	1.235
9	1.20	1.440	19	1.11	1.235
10	1.12	1.255	20	1.10	1.215
			Sum	22.40	25.150

$$\bar{x} = \frac{22.40}{20} = 1.12$$

$$s = \sqrt{\frac{\Sigma x_i^2 - \frac{(\Sigma x_i)^2}{n}}{n - 1}} = \sqrt{\frac{25.150 - \frac{(22.40)^2}{20}}{19}} = 0.057$$

$$\text{Coefficient of variation} = \frac{0.057 \times 100}{1.12} = 5.09\%$$

From Figure 2:

$$n \approx \ \ 4 \ @ \ 95\% \ \text{confidence level.}$$

$$n \approx 10 \ @ \ 99\% \ \text{confidence level.}$$

Incidentally, this is commonly true of operations dominated by a machine cycle. In this case, the actual drill time is almost half of the total cycle, and the machining time itself does not vary much.

If all we wanted was an estimate of cycle time, we could stop at this point. Suppose, however, that we want our estimates of each of the average element times to be adequate for future use as elemental standard data. Was the sample size of $n = 20$ adequate for each of these elements?

Let us take element 1, as an example. The mean element time is $\bar{x} = 0.121$ minute, the standard deviation is $s = 0.0097$ minute, and the coefficient of variation is 8 percent. From Figure 2 we see that we should have taken a sample of $n = 10$ for a 95 percent confidence level and $n = 20$ for a 99 percent confidence level. The reason why a larger sample is needed on element 1 than for the entire cycle is that element 1 is somewhat more variable than is the total cycle (coefficient of variation of 8 percent compared with only 5 percent for the cycle).Therefore, if data on each of the elements are needed, the element for which the largest sample size is indicated, from Figure 2, dictates the minimum sample size for the study. This procedure insures the precision and confidence requirements for the limiting element and yields better results than this on all other elements.

Procedures for Insuring Consistency of Sample Data. A single study such as that illustrated in the preceding section always leaves open the question: "Were the data representative of usual operating conditions?" If a similar study were made on some other day of the week or some other hour of the day, would the results have been different? This question suggests the possibility of dividing the total sample into smaller subsamples taken at random times. Then, by setting up control limits based on an initial sample, we can determine if the subsequent data taken are consistent; that is, did all of the data come from a common universe? Obviously this situation is comparable to that found in quality control. If a point falls outside of the established control limits, we know that the probability is high that some assignable cause of variation is present which has resulted in an abnormally high or low set of sample readings. These assignable causes could be anything that could have an effect on the time of production, for example, material variations from standard, changes in tools, workplace, or methods of work, as well as changes in the working environment. As with quality control, we would attempt to determine the nature of these assignable causes and eliminate data where abnormal readings have an explanation.

The general procedure is as follows:

1. Standardize methods, select operator, and determine elemental breakdown as before.

2. Take an initial sample study. (*a*) Compute preliminary estimates of $\bar{x}$ and s. (*b*) Determine estimate of total sample needed from Figure 2. (*c*) Set up control limits for balance of study based on preliminary estimates of $\bar{x}$ and s.

3. Program and execute balance of study. (*a*) Divide total sample by subsample size to obtain the number of separate subsamples to obtain. Subsample sizes are commonly 4 or 5. (*b*) Randomize the

time when these subsamples will be taken. A random number table is useful for this purpose. (c) At the random times indicated obtain subsample readings and plot points on control chart. If points fall outside limits, investigate immediately to determine the cause. Eliminate data from computations for standards where causes can be assigned. (d) When study is complete, make final check to be sure that the precision and confidence level of the result is at least as good as desired.

4. Compute normal time, determine allowances, and compute standard time as before.

Work Sampling

The unique thing about work sampling is that it accomplishes the results of stop-watch study without the need for a stop watch. Although this statement does not summarize, by any means, the net advantage or disadvantage of work sampling, it indicates that there is something startlingly different about work sampling, and indeed there is.

Work sampling was first introduced to industry by L. H. C. Tippett in 1934. However, it has been in common use only since about 1950. We can illustrate the basic idea of work sampling by a simple example. Suppose we wish to estimate the proportion of time that a worker, or a group of workers, spends working and the proportion of time spent not working. We can do this by long-term stop-watch studies in which we measure the work time, the idle time, or both. This will take a long time, perhaps a day or longer, and when we are done with measuring we will not be sure that the term of the study covered representative periods of work and idleness. Instead, suppose that we make a large number of *random* observations in which we simply determine whether the operator is working or idle and tally the result, similar to that shown in Figure 3. The percentage of the

	Tally	Number	Per cent
Working	THL THL THL THL THL THL THL THL THL THL THL THL THL THL THL THL THL THL THL I	96	88.9
Idle	THL THL II	12	11.1
Total		108	100.0

FIGURE 3. Work sampling tally of working and idle time. When observations occur at random times, the percentages estimate the percent of time that the worker was in the working or idle state. The accuracy of the estimate increases with the number of observations.

tallies that are recorded in the "working" and "idle" classifications are estimates of the actual percent of time that the worker was working and idle. Herein lies the fundamental principle behind work sampling: *the number of observations is proportional to the amount of time spent in the working or idle state.* The accuracy of the estimate depends on the number of observations, and we can preset precision limits and confidence levels.

Number of Observations Required. The statistical methods of work sampling depend on the distributions for proportions, as do control charts and sampling by attributes in quality control. Recall that

$$\bar{p} = \frac{x}{n} = \frac{\text{number observed in classification}}{\text{total number of observations}} \qquad (1)$$

and

$$s_p = \sqrt{\frac{\bar{p}(1 - \bar{p})}{n}} \qquad (2)$$

To determine the sample size required we must state the precision and confidence level desired in the final answer. Suppose, for example, that we wished to determine the number of observations required to estimate the proportion of idle time in an operation within ± 5 percent and be sure of this estimate at the 95 percent confidence level. A preliminary study involving 200 observations shows that the operator was idle at the time of observation 60 times, giving a preliminary estimate of:

$$\bar{p} = \frac{60}{200} = 0.30$$

The 95 percent confidence interval then states that $\bar{p}$ must fall within the limits of $\pm 2s_p$ of p', the population mean (from the normal distribution, Table I, Appendix), or

$$p' - 2s_p \leqq \bar{p} \leqq p' + 2s_p$$

Introducing the numbers from our example, since we wish to hold $\bar{p}$ within ± 5 percent of p', 95 percent of the time, $\bar{p}$ must be within the limits of $\pm(0.30 \times 0.05 = 0.015)$ and the 95 percent confidence interval becomes:

$$0.285 \leqq \bar{p} \leqq 0.315$$

We want $2s_p$ to be set equal to 0.015 when $\bar{p} = 0.30$. What sample size will produce this precision? Using equation (2) we may solve for n as follows:

$$2s_p = 0.015 = 2 \sqrt{\frac{0.30 \times 0.70}{n}}$$

squaring both sides,

$$0.000225 = \frac{4 \times 0.21}{n}$$

and

$$n = \frac{4 \times 0.21}{0.000225} = 3735 \text{ observations}$$

Given the preliminary sample of 200 and the resulting estimate $\bar{p}$, a total of 3735 observations will be required, or 3535 additional observations. When the study has been completed, a final check on the adequacy of the sample may be obtained by repeating the above calculations based on the new estimate $\bar{p}$. We may find that even more observations are required if the refined estimate $\bar{p}$ is greater than the original estimate $\bar{p} = 0.30$, given the error limits in percent of p'.

From the simple formulas for mean proportion and the standard deviation of a proportion given by equations (1) and (2), charts and tables have been developed which give directly the number of observations required for a given value of $\bar{p}$, precision limits, and the 95 percent confidence level. Figure 4 is a chart from which estimates of sample sizes can be obtained.* Note that the number of observations required is fairly large. For example, to maintain a precision in the estimate $\bar{p}$ of ± 1.0 percentage points at 95 percent confidence, 10,000 observations are required if $\bar{p}$ is in the neighborhood of 50 percent, that is, to be sure that, if an estimate $\bar{p} = 50$ percent, then p' is between 49 and 51 percent. For an estimate of $\bar{p} = 10$ percent, about 3600 observations are required to be sure that p' is between 9 and 11 percent. Smaller samples are required for looser limits. Although these numbers of observations seem huge, we must remember that the nature of the observation required is merely a recognition of whether or not the employee is working or possibly a classification of his activity into various reasons for idleness.

Work Sampling to Measure Delays and Allowances. One of the most common uses of work sampling is to determine the percent of time that workers are actually spending for personal time and delays that are a part of the job. The resulting information could then be used as the basis for the percentage allowances that enter into the calculation of standard time.

Let us consider, as an example, the determination of delay and personal allowances in a lathe department of a machine shop. There are 10 workers

---

*More complete information on sample sizes is available in R. M. Barnes, [4].

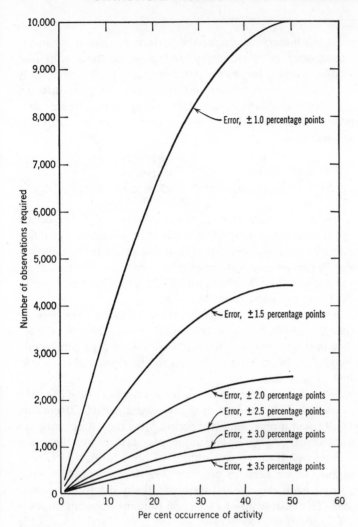

FIGURE 4. Curves for determining the number of observations required to maintain precision within the percentage points indicated, at 95 percent confidence.

involved. The delays of which we are speaking are a part of the job, such as, waiting for tools, materials and instructions, machine clean up, securing an inspector's approval, change of jobs, minor mechanical difficulties, etc. We wish to determine the extent of the delays and to determine how much time workers are spending for personal time. Our procedure is as follows:

1. *Design work sampling study.*

    a. *Estimate preliminary values* for the percent of time spent in the three categories of work, delay, and personal time from past knowledge, studies, foremen's estimates, or a preliminary study of the jobs. These preliminary estimates are necessary in order to gage the magnitude of the data-taking phase. Based on a composite of past information and foremen's estimates, our best guesses are:

working	85 percent
delays	10 percent
personal time	5 percent

    b. *Set desired precision limits* of estimates to be obtained. We decide that ± 1.0 percentage point at 95 percent confidence on our delay estimate will be controlling; that is, if our estimate for delays is actually 10 percent, we want to be 95 percent sure that the actual delay is not less than 9 percent or more than 11 percent, with 10 percent being the most probable value.

    c. *Estimate total number of readings* from Figure 4. For $\bar{p} = 10$ percent, $N = 3600$, for ± 1.0 percentage point error. Note from Figure 4 that our precision for personal time of 5 percent would then be slightly better than ± 1.0 percentage point and for working time slightly worse.

    d. *Program total number of readings over desired time span of study.* We decide that 3600 readings over a two-week period (10 working days) will cover a representative period, therefore, we propose to obtain $3600/10 = 360$ observations per day. Since there are 10 workers involved we will obtain 10 observations each time we sample, so we need to program $360/10 = 36$ random sampling times each day for 10 days to obtain the total of 3600 readings. The easiest way to select 36 random sampling times is to use a random number table.

    e. *Plan the physical aspects of the study.* This includes an appropriate data sheet, as well as a determination of the physical path, observation points, etc., so that the results are not biased because workers see the observer coming and change activities accordingly.

2. *Take the data* as planned. Table II shows a summary of the actual data taken in this instance with a breakdown between morning and afternoon observations. The percentages for "working," "delay," and "personal time" have been computed for each half-day and for the total sample.

TABLE II. Summary of work sampling data for lathe department study

Date		Total Obser- vations	Working		Delay		Personal	
			Obs.	Per- cent	Obs.	Per- cent	Obs.	Per- cent
10–2	a.m.	190	152	80.0	24	12.6	14	7.4
	p.m.	170	145	85.3	14	8.2	11	6.5
10–3	a.m.	160	144	90.0	10	6.3	6	3.7
	p.m.	200	158	79.0	19	9.5	23	11.5
10–4	a.m.	150	127	84.7	15	10.0	8	5.3
	p.m.	210	182	86.6	23	11.0	5	2.4
10–5	a.m.	180	142	78.9	24	13.3	14	7.8
	p.m.	180	148	82.2	20	11.1	12	6.7
10–6	a.m.	220	189	85.9	24	10.9	7	3.2
	p.m.	140	114	81.4	17	12.1	9	6.5
10–9	a.m.	210	185	88.2	14	6.6	11	5.2
	p.m.	150	135	90.0	9	6.0	6	4.0
10–10	a.m.	190	155	81.6	25	13.2	10	5.2
	p.m.	170	146	85.9	14	8.2	10	5.9
10–11	a.m.	200	166	83.0	22	11.0	12	6.0
	p.m.	160	136	85.0	14	8.8	10	6.2
10–12	a.m.	140	118	84.3	15	10.7	7	5.0
	p.m.	220	185	84.1	25	11.4	10	4.5
10–13	a.m.	210	181	86.2	19	9.1	10	4.7
	p.m.	150	130	86.7	12	8.0	8	5.3
		3600	3038	84.4	359	9.97	203	5.63

3. *Recheck precision of results and consistency of data.* A final check of the delay percentage of 9.97 percent shows that the number of readings taken was adequate to maintain the ± 1.0 percentage point precision on the delay time. The consistency of the data could be checked by setting up a control chart for proportions to see if any of the subsample points fell outside of limits. Other statistical tests comparing A.M. observations with P.M. observations could also be carried through.

Based on the work sampling study, we could then conclude that the delay part of the work in the lathe department was about 10 percent. We are 95 percent sure that the sampling error has been held to no more than ± 1.0 percentage point, and it is probable that it is less. We have based these conclusions on a study which covered two weeks time, with any time of the day being equally likely as a sampling time. The personal time of 5.6 percent is slightly greater than the company standard practice of allowing 5 percent for personal time; however, 5 percent is within the probable range of error of estimate.

Work Sampling to Determine Production Standards. The previous example showed the use of work sampling to determine percentage allowances for noncyclical elements such as delays and for personal time. Why not carry the idea forward one more step and utilize the observations on percent work time to establish production standards? What additional data do we need? If we knew (a) how many pieces were produced during the total time of the study and (b) the performance rating for each observation of work time we could compute normal time as follows:

$$\text{Normal time} = \frac{\left(\begin{array}{c}\text{total}\\\text{time of}\\\text{study in}\\\text{minutes}\end{array}\right) \times \left(\begin{array}{c}\text{work time}\\\text{in decimals}\\\text{from work}\\\text{sampling study}\end{array}\right) \times \left(\begin{array}{c}\text{average}\\\text{performance}\\\text{rating in}\\\text{decimals}\end{array}\right)}{\text{total number of pieces produced}}$$

Standard time is then computed as before:

Standard time =

normal time + allowances for delays, fatigue, and personal time

We have already seen how the allowances for delays and personal time can be determined from work sampling. Here we see the complete determination of a production standard without the use of a precise timing device. All that was needed that a timing device could furnish was a rather ordinary calendar from which we might calculate the total available time.

Although work sampling approaches to work measurement can be used in most situations, its most outstanding field of application is in the measurement of noncyclical types of work where many different tasks are performed, but where there is no set pattern of cycle or regularity. In many jobs, the frequency of tasks within the job is based on a random demand function. For example, a storeroom clerk may fill requisitions, unpack and put away stock, deliver material to production departments, clean up the storeroom, etc. The frequency and time requirements of some of these tasks depend on things outside the control of the clerk himself. To determine production standards by stop-watch methods would be difficult or impossible. Work sampling fits this situation quite ideally because, through its random sampling approach, reliable estimates of time and performance for these randomly occurring tasks can be obtained.

An Example

As an example, let us consider the determination of standards for a warehouse handling group, reported by George H. Gustat of Eastman Kodak Company. [6, 7]. In this study 30 people were engaged in the following nine groups of activities: packing, shipping, receiving, small orders, reoperating (opening and repacking for tests, etc.), sort and stack, inventory, wait for equipment, personal and lost time.

Two separate work sampling studies were made in which the observer classified the activities of the workers and rated their performance using IBM cards and mark sensing lead so that computations could be carried out on card tabulating equipment. The combined overall results of these studies, which involved 6601 observations, are shown in Table III. Here we see the distribution of time spent by the group of 30

TABLE III. Combined results of two work sampling studies of warehouse handling group covering a total of 14 days and 6601 observations

Operation	Number of Observations	Percent of Total
Packing	2223	33.7
Shipping	1141	17.3
Receiving	912	13.8
Small orders	462	7.0
Reoperating	213	3.2
Sort and stack	361	5.5
Inventory	246	3.7
Wait for equipment	194	2.9
Personal and lost time	849	12.9
	6601	100.0

men. Figures 5 and 6 show the summary of data for the packing operation only and the control chart for the operation, both being based on the second of the two work sampling studies. Figure 7 shows sample calculations of standard time for the packing operation. (Allowances were added to the total of all operations.) Before the study was made, there were few sound data on which to base estimates for labor needs to perform the tasks in the warehouse. Based on the work sampling standards, a wage incentive payment plan was established, which increased output per man to the extent that 16 men could perform all of the work formerly done by 30 men. It is unlikely that such a program could have been attempted in the absence of work sampling.

Stop-Watch Study and Work Sampling Compared. Perhaps the final major question to be raised is: "Are stop-watch study and work sampling interchangeable?" So far as general accuracy of results is concerned, apparently they are. Figure 8 shows the results of a comparative study in which both

	Packing operation, summary		
Day	Total observations	Total packing observations	Daily per cent p
M	450	142	31
T	467	152	32
W	477	125	26
T	470	160	34
F	470	177	38
M	464	155	33
T	465	159	34
W	475	142	30
T	470	153	33
F	466	169	36
	4674	1534	327

Average subsample size
= 4674 ÷ 10 = 467

$\bar{p} = 33\%$

FIGURE 5. *Daily summary of sampling data for the packing operation. From G. H. Gustat [6, 7].*

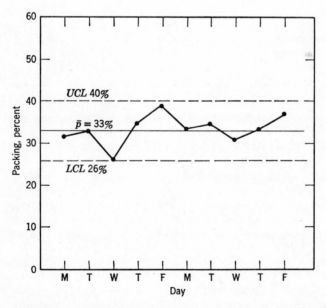

FIGURE 6. *Work sampling control chart. From G. H. Gustat [6, 7].*

Packing operation—calculation of standard time			
Employee:	J. Green	R. Smith	M. O'Riley _____etc.
a. Total hours	78	80	65 _____
b. Total observations	134	157	142 _____
Packing operation:			
c. Observations	42	53	61 _____
d. Per cent of total *(c ÷ b)*	31.3	33.8	43.0 _____
e. Packing time, hours *(d × a)*	24.4	27.1	28.0 _____
f. Average rating	105	90	95 _____
g. Standard time packing, hours *(f × e)*	25.6 +	24.4 +	26.6 + _____= 386 Total standard packing hours
h. Total footage of film shipped = 11,309,529			
i. Standard unit time = 386 ÷ 11,309,529			
j. Standard hours per 1000 feet = 0.034			

FIGURE 7. Calculation of the standard time for packing operation. From G. H. Gustat [6, 7].

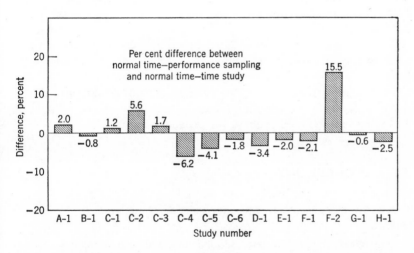

FIGURE 8. Results of a comparison between work sampling and stop-watch study of 14 operations. Bars represent positive and negative deviations from work sampling. From R. M. Barnes and R. B. Andrews [5].

stop-watch studies and work sampling studies were made on 14 different operations to estimate normal time. The differences between the two techniques are within the limits of rating error. This does not mean that both techniques have the same field of application, however. We cannot overestimate the importance of the work sampling advantage of not requiring the use of a stop watch. The psychological impact of using a stop watch on personnel being measured has never been determined, but many people feel that it is significant. If for no other reason than this, it is likely that the practical use of work sampling will grow.

SUMMARY

Statistical models in work measurement provide management with a basis for knowing a stated degree of confidence which they should have in the data on which production standards are based. First, standard statistical techniques make it possible to determine the sample sizes required in order that we might have a predetermined degree of confidence in the computed mean values. Second, by using statistical control techniques when taking the data we can have confidence that the data were taken from a stable, common universe. This is an important consideration for it helps insure that the data were representative of standard operating conditions.

The work sampling technique found its first field of application in the measurement of idle time, delays and allowances. The fact that these kinds of factors in a job are non-repetitive made their measurement difficult prior to the development of work sampling. Even long-term time studies were often not long enough to include an adequate sample of some non-repetitive activities. While it is not yet common to determine production standards solely by work sampling methods, the significant advantages of the technique seem to hold promise for expanded future use.

REVIEW QUESTIONS

1. What is the general procedure for determining standards by stop-watch methods?

2. Why is it general practice to divide a job into elements for a stop-watch study?

3. Discuss the problem of determining the adequacy of sample sizes for various elements in a stop-watch time study.

4. Outline the procedures necessary for insuring that sample data are consistent and representative of usual operating conditions.

5. What is the fundamental principle on which work sampling is based?

6. Outline the general procedure for a work sampling study to determine the extent of delays and personal time.

7. What additional information is necessary in order to determine production standards completely by work sampling?

8. Compare stop-watch study and work sampling in terms of the cost to make studies, representativeness of samples taken, field of application, comparative accuracy.

REFERENCES

1. Abruzzi, A., *Work Measurement*, Columbia University Press, New York, 1952.
2. Allderige, J. M., "Statistical Procedures in Stop-Watch Work Measurement," *Journal of Industrial Engineering*, Vol. VII, No. 4, July–Aug., 1956, pp. 154–163.
3. Barnes, R. M., *Motion and Time Study: Design and Measurement of Work*, John Wiley & Sons, New York, 6th ed., 1968.
4. Barnes, R. M., *Work Sampling*, John Wiley & Sons, New York, 2nd ed., 1957.
5. Barnes, R. M., and R. B. Andrews, "Performance Sampling in Work Measurement," *Journal of Industrial Engineering*, Vol. 6, No. 6, Nov.–Dec., 1955, pp. 8–18.
6. Gustat, G. H., "Applications of Work Sampling Analysis," *Proceedings of Tenth Time Study and Methods Conference*, SAM—ASME, New York, April, 1955.
7. Gustat, G. H., "Incentives for Indirect Labor," *Proceedings, Fifth Industrial Engineering Institute*, University of California, Berkeley–Los Angeles, 1953.
8. Heiland, R. E., and W. J. Richardson, *Work Sampling*, McGraw-Hill Book Co., New York, 1957.
9. Mundell, M. E., *Motion and Time Study*, Prentice-Hall, Englewood Cliffs, N.J., 3rd ed., 1960.
10. Nadler, G., *Work Design: A System Concept*, Richard D. Irwin, Homewood, Ill., Rev. ed., 1970.
11. Niebel, B. W., *Motion and Time Study*, Richard D. Irwin, Homewood, Ill., 5th ed., 1972.

chapter 6

LOCATION AND LAYOUT OF PRODUCTIVE SYSTEMS

LOCATION /

The geographic location of a productive system has an impact on the design of the production system, because there are certain physical factors which will have an impact on both layout and building design, and because location will partially determine operating and capital costs. There are some purely physical factors in plant design which stem from location. For example, the availability locally of subcontractors may have an impact on in-plant capacity, whether or not we purchase power, the extent of heating and ventilating requirements, the types of common carriers available for shipping and receiving, and so on. There are also differences in operating and capital costs for different locations, largely centered in the costs of labor, taxes, land, construction, and fuel. The combination of fixed and variable costs for different locations when subjected to rigorous cost analysis may reveal cost-volume relationships which favor certain locations depending on the volumes involved.

There are, of course, a wide variety of subjective factors which might enter into plant location, not the least of which is the owners' or managers' personal preference for location. Labor unrest in a particular location may be sufficient to rule it out. Other factors such as local attitudes toward industry, the quality of local transportation, the amount of labor available, and the availability of schools cannot be quantified in an economic sense yet may have a significant influence on location decisions.

Multiplant Location. Location analysis for the multiplant situation is particularly interesting since each alternate location considered has a dynamic relationship to every other existing plant and warehouse location. The addition of a new plant, then, must consider the interdependencies between existing plants and markets so that a solution from the economic point of view is one which minimizes combined production and distribution costs for the entire network of plants (including the proposed plant or warehouse) and is not necessarily the minimum cost location taken independently. Consider, for example, a company which has two existing plants in Detroit and Chicago and five existing warehouse distribution

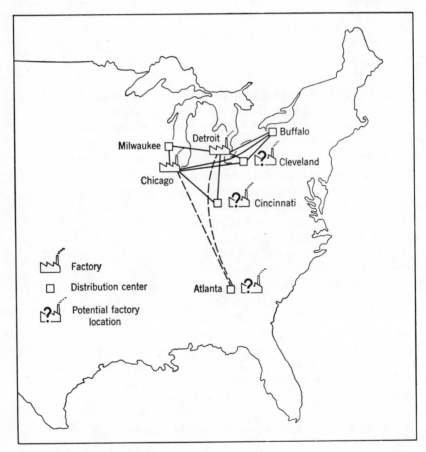

FIGURE 1. *Geographical locations of factories, distribution centers, and potential new factory locations.*

centers in Milwaukee, Cleveland, Cincinnati, Buffalo, and Atlanta. In order to meet increased demand the company has decided to build a new plant with a capacity of 25,000 units per week and general surveys have narrowed the choice to three locations, Cincinnati, Cleveland, and Atlanta. Figure 1 shows the geographical locations of the existing factories and distribution centers as well as the proposed locations for the new plants. Table I shows a summary of the distribution costs per unit between all combinations of distribution centers and existing plants as well as proposed plant locations. Weekly market forecasts are indicated by market areas together with plant capacities and estimated unit production costs in each of the existing and proposed plant locations.

Although we are tempted to grasp the Atlanta location because of its slightly smaller estimated unit production cost, it would be hazardous to do so without a careful analysis of the optimum production-distribution system for each of the alternatives. The pattern of capacity used in each location will change with each alternative because of the dynamic inter-relationships of the costs. These interdependencies may be represented in a linear programming matrix and solved by distribution methods of linear programming according to the methods we shall cover in Chapter 11.

TABLE I. *Production costs, distribution costs, plant capacities, and market demands, for the location problem*

From plants / To distribution centers	Distribution costs per unit: handling, warehousing, and freight					Forecast weekly market demand, units
	Existing plants		Proposed plant locations			
	Detroit	Chicago	Cincinnati	Cleveland	Atlanta	
Milwaukee	$0.42	$0.32	$0.46	$0.44	$0.48	10,000
Cleveland	0.36	0.44	0.37	0.30	0.46	15,000
Cincinnati	0.41	0.42	0.30	0.37	0.43	16,000
Buffalo	0.38	0.48	0.42	0.38	0.47	19,000
Atlanta	0.50	0.49	0.43	0.45	0.28	12,000
Normal weekly plant capacity, units	27,000	20,000	25,000	25,000	25,000	
Unit production cost	$2.70	$2.68	$2.64	$2.69	$2.62	

Locational Dynamics for Multiplants. Another interesting aspect of the multiple plant-multiple distribution center problem is in the continuing assessment concerning which plants to operate and at what levels as the balance of economic factors and markets change over time. If these factors do change, then the optimum allocation of capacity to markets should also change. In such situations, production capacity on overtime must be considered to be an additional supply source, and data concerning fixed costs when each plant is operating and when it is shut down are important. Linear programming as a basic model can then be used to determine the optimum production program for the complex of plants. When the contrast of fixed costs for each plant are considered, when operating and when shut down, an optimum solution might dictate the operation of some plants at overtime while shutting down an existing plant. Again, the linear programming methods appropriate for looking at this kind of problem will be covered in Chapter 11.

FACILITY LAYOUT /

The development of a layout or physical plan for the design of a production system represents an integration of all of the kinds of analysis which we have discussed in the preceding two chapters. Again, the activities involved tend to merge with some of the other problems we have discussed, such as production design of products, process analysis and planning, job design, and location. They are all in a sense interdependent and going on simultaneously. Nevertheless, at some point the other plans become frozen to the extent that they can be put into a physical relationship and this is the layout phase.

The key decision problems beyond the details of physical layout are the *capacity decision* and the determination of the *basic mode of production*. We referred earlier in Chapter 3 to the capacity decision in connection with our general discussion of the design of production systems. Will we design for peak requirements or some average level? How will we balance the costs of extra plant investment versus inventory costs and the costs of production fluctuation? We have again an allocation problem where production capacity is allocated to operating periods minimizing combined plant investment costs, inventory, and the costs of production fluctuation, where investment costs are some nonlinear function of capacity.

In order to analyze the other key decision problems, for example, the determination of the basic mode of production, let us consider basic layout types.

Physical Models of Facility Layout. Layouts and models using two- and three-dimensional templates have a wide area of application in the development and planning of new facilities, as well as in the relayout of existing facilities. These graphic aids are important in visualizing the development of the design of a complex production system. The resulting layout expresses the designer's specification of the location of all equipment, storage areas, aisle space, utilities, etc., and the relationships between machines and departments. It is important, however, not to mistake the activity of preparing and locating templates on a layout board for the broader activity of facility layout. The templates themselves are tools.

Other kinds of analyses must supplement the facilities design project; that is, economic analysis helps to determine the location, the design capacity, whether the plant represented by the layout is to operate on one, two, or three shifts, which parts to buy and which to manufacture, and what equipment to select. Analyses of work methods and relationships of parts and products help to determine work areas required and relative locations of activities. Studies of "balance" will determine what the basic design of an assembly line should be. These are typical of supporting analyses and indicate that the two- and three-dimensional layouts cannot stand alone. Two-dimensional templates are by far the most commonly used. They can successfully represent the plan view of a layout and can show floor utilization fairly well.

Basic Layout Types

Production systems can be classified into two basic types depending on whether or not the layout is *process oriented* or *product oriented*. The constrast is illustrated by Figures 2 and 3. In Figure 2, a process-oriented functional, or job shop layout, the machines and work centers are grouped according to the function they perform. Since Figure 2 represents a machine shop, the generic types of equipment are lathes, mills, drills, etc. Process-oriented layout is commonly used where item volumes are low and there is a high value placed on flexibility of operation sequences and of the specific operations to be performed. In process layout we expect to find general purpose equipment to facilitate the flexibility of operations to be performed.

Another related reason for using process layout is to gain relatively high equipment utilization. Since the machine hours volume is small for any particular order on the milling machines, for example, it would be uneconomical to allocate the use of the mill only for the order in question or subsequent orders like it. Thus by grouping all milling machines together we can route all milling work to that work center, and by time sharing the use of the men and equipment for all kinds of milling work we can obtain good utilization.

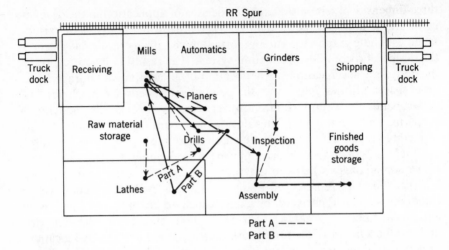

FIGURE 2. *Process or functional layout with machines arranged in functional groupings.*

In contrast, Figure 3 shows a *product-oriented layout* the name of which comes from the fact that equipment is arranged or laid out according to the needs of the product (or part). Product layout is also often called line layout. In the fabrication line for part *A*, each piece of equipment is placed in the sequence in which it will be used to process part *A*. If similar equipment is used for both parts *A* and *B*, the equipment would not normally be time shared, and possibly identical pieces of equipment would be placed in both lines. The layout follows the needs of the product. Product-oriented layout would be considered in situations where volume warranted the intensive use of equipment allocated to one part or product. In product layout we expect to find much more special purpose equipment designed to do some particular operation very effectively. Assembly work is commonly arranged in line fashion because of the ease in balancing the line and the fact that relatively low investment per worker is required so that equipment utilization is not as important. Product or line layout is often used when the following conditions prevail:

1. An adequate volume that makes possible reasonable equipment utilization.

2. Reasonably stable product demand.

3. Product standardization.

4. Parts interchangeability.

5. Continuous supply of raw material.

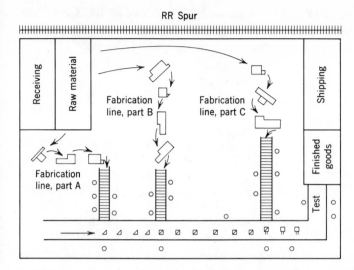

FIGURE 3. Product or line layout where equipment is located according to the sequence of fabrication and assembly operations.

Most layouts are actually a combination of the process and product modes. Quite often fabrication facilities are laid out by process and assembly operations by product.

Continuous versus intermittent systems. Another common way of classifying production systems is by the terms "continuous" and "intermittent." Continuous systems are those where the part or product approaches continuous movement as is common in line layouts. Intermittent systems are those where the parts or products move intermittently as in process layouts, where each order is moved to a department, waits until a man and machine are available, is processed, waits to be moved, is moved to the next work center, etc. Using the continuous-intermittent basis of classification, we might elaborate the classification as follows:

A. Continuous systems
    1. Distribution (pure inventory systems).
    2. Production-distribution system for high volume standardized products, usually produced for inventory.

B. Intermittent Systems
    1. Closed job shops, i.e., shops laid out by process layout but which manufacture a set line of products, often produced for inventory.
    2. Open job shops, i.e., open to custom job order.
    3. Large-scale one-time project systems.

While the layouts of the five systems classified may be divided by the continuous-intermittent classification, many of the problems of operating the five different systems are unique, as we shall see in Chapter 12.

PROCESS LAYOUT
FOR INTERMITTENT SYSTEMS /

The major problem of a strictly "layout" nature in process layout is the determination of the most economical relative location of the various process areas. This fact is emphasized by the realization that for only six process areas arranged in a simple grid, as in Figure 4, there are 6! (six factorial) or $6 \cdot 5 \cdot 4 \cdot 3 \cdot 2 \cdot 1 = 720$ arrangements possible. Fortunately, only 45 of them are really different in terms of their effects on idealized measures of material-handling cost. The number of combinations goes up very rapidly as we increase the number of process areas. Let us consider the nature of an objective function in this situation. The major criterion for selecting an arrangement is usually material-handling cost. Thus we want an arrangement that places the process areas in locations relative to each other, such that material-handling cost for all parts is minimized. Therefore, if we examined the required material-handling activity between departments A and C of Figure 4 and found that it was heavy compared to AB, we would want to consider switching the locations of departments B and C. But before concluding that this switch would be advantageous, we want to see if this advantage would be wiped out by an increase in the relative material-handling activity between DB and DC. We might take as our measure of material-handling cost the product of the distance times the number of loads that must be moved in

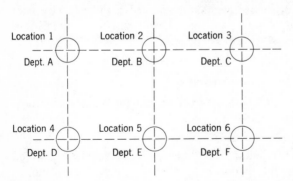

FIGURE 4. There are 6! = 720 arrangements of the six process areas in the six locations of the grid.

some period of time. For each combination of arrangements, then, we could simply add up the load-distance products between all combinations of departments. The combination with the smallest total is the basic arrangement that we are looking for. To formalize this statement of our objective, the measure of effectiveness, E is;

$$E = \sum_i \sum_j A_{ij}X_{ij} = \text{minimum}$$

where A_{ij} = number of loads per week, month, or period required, to be transported between departments i and j, and X_{ij} = distance between departments i and j.

This measure of effectiveness closely approximates material-handling costs. Each material-handling operation requires certain fixed times associated with picking up the load, positioning it to set down, etc. These costs, mainly labor costs, would be about the same for large or small loads, and need not be considered unless alternate handling systems are a part of the analysis. The variable costs associated with a material-handling operation (mainly labor plus power) are related to distance.

Operation Sequence Analysis [4]. The data we need are the number of loads that must be transported between all combinations of work centers. This type of data can be summarized from routing sheets which indicate operation sequences, and from engineering drawings. The route sheets indicate sequences; from the drawings of the parts themselves and the production rates, we can determine the number of parts transported at one time, and, therefore, the number of loads.

Table II shows a summary of the number of loads per month for all combinations of work centers for a typical small production situation. We idealize our problem by assuming a structure similar to Figure 4, with circles representing the functional groupings of equipment. We regard departments as being adjacent if they are either next to each other, as are A and B, or diagonally across from each other, as are A and E, in Figure 4. Nonadjacent locations are those that are more than one grid unit away from each other, horizontally, vertically, or diagonally, represented by AC, AF, DC, and DF in Figure 4. We can see now that for the idealized layout the measure of effectiveness reduces to minimizing the sum of the nonadjacent (unit distance) × (loads).

For problems of reasonable size, the minimum non-adjacent (distance) × (load) solution is fairly readily seen by graphical methods. We have an initial solution which may be improved by inspecting the effect of changes in location. When an advantageous change is found, the diagram is altered.

This graphical approach to the solution is accomplished by placing the information contained in the load summary, Table II, in an equivalent

TABLE II. Load summary*

From		Rec. 1	Stores 2	Saw 3	Eng. Lathe 4	Turret Lathe 5	Drill 6	Mill 7	Grinder 8	Ass'y 9	F.G. 10	Ship 11
Departments												
Receiving	1		600									
Stores	2			400	100			100				
Saw	3				350	50						
Engine Lathe	4						100	450				
Turret Lathe	5							50				
Drill	6				100					150	100	
Mill	7						50		450	100		
Grinder	8						200			250		
Assembly	9										500	
Finished Goods	10											600
Shipping	11											

*Number of loads per month between all combinations of work centers.

schematic diagram in which circles represent work centers (functional groups of machines), and labeled connecting lines indicate the number of loads transported between work centers. A first solution is obtained merely by placing the work centers on the grid, following the logic from the pattern indicated by Table II. When all lines are on the diagram and labeled we have an initial solution which may be improved by inspecting the effect of changes in location. When an advantageous change is found, the diagram is changed accordingly. Figure 5 shows the diagram which results.

Further inspection reveals no further advantageous shifts of location, so we adopt Figure 5 as the ideal schematic layout, which has a 2 × 100 = 200 load-distance rating. For larger problems, the grid distance becomes an important part of the measure of effectiveness, because work centers might be separated by two, three, or four grid units. Figure 5 is not a provable optimum solution, because we have no test of optimality. The ideal schematic diagram is now the basis for developing a physical layout in which the work centers or department locations are specified.

The block diagram. Now that we know how the work centers should be located in relation to each other in the idealized layout, we can use the idealized schematic diagram as a basis for developing a block diagram in which the physical areas required by the work centers take the same relative locations. Estimates of the areas required by each work center can be developed from the number of machines required in each center, and the floor area required by each machine. Commonly, the machine areas are multiplied by a factor of 3 or 4 to obtain an estimate, or first approxima-

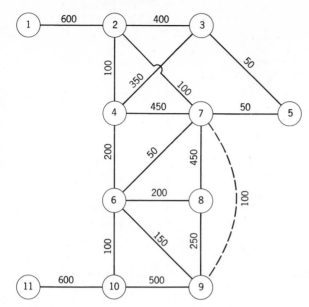

FIGURE 5. Ideal schematic diagram.

tion, of the total area required, including working space for the operator, material storage, and pro rata aisle space.

The block diagram is developed by substituting estimated areas for the small circles in the idealized schematic layout. Initially this can be done with block templates, in order to find an arrangement compatible with both the flow pattern of the ideal schematic diagram and the various size requirements for work centers. Slight variation of the shapes of work areas will make it possible to fit the system into a rectangular configuration and meet the possible shape and dimension restrictions that may be imposed by the site, or by an existing building if we are dealing with re-layout. Figure 6 shows such a block diagram.

The block diagram represented by Figure 6 presents a frame of reference for the development of the details of layout. Now we can proceed with aisle layout, machine arrangement within work centers, work place layout, the design of plant and personnel areas, the selection of specific material-handling equipment, etc., knowing that the work centers are located relative to each other in an economical way.

When the block diagram is complete, combinations of work centers can be made for practical departmentalization. These combinations can be based on work center sizes, the number of workers involved, similarity of work, and other criteria important to the particular application.

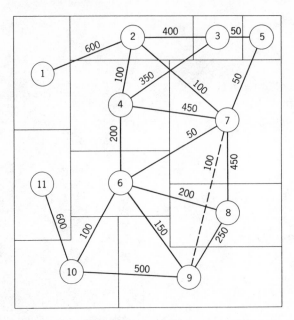

FIGURE 6. Block diagram which takes account of rectangular building shape and other possible restrictions of shape and dimension imposed by site but still retains approximate work center area requirements and Figure 5 flow pattern.

The detailed layout phase will undoubtedly require minor shifts in space allocation and shape. Here, the templates and physical models discussed later become valuable aids in visualizing the developing details. Standards for minimum machine spacing, aisle widths for different uses, and column spacings for different building designs all exist in handbook form [21, 22].

Computerized Relative Allocation of Facilities Technique [CRAFT, 2]

Operation sequence analysis is a graphical approach to the determination of the relative location of physical facilities. Recall that the graphical solution worked reasonably well for problems where the number of departments was relatively small and the flow patterns between departments not too complex. When the problem becomes complex, the graphical solution breaks down rapidly because of the difficulty of seeing which changes in location will result in net improvement. In addition, the graphical solution neither accounts for differences in material-handling cost between different departments because of different handling systems, nor of different area requirements for departments in the best way.

A computer program has been developed called CRAFT, Computerized Relative Allocation of Facilities Technique, which simulates the cost of

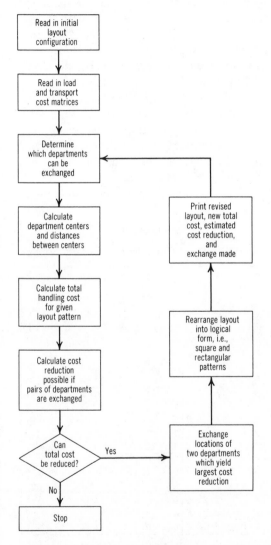

FIGURE 7. *Basic flow diagram for simulating the location of facilities and selecting only alternative layouts which represent improved material handling costs. Figures 7–12 are based on G. C. Armour and E. S. Buffa* [2].

alternative layouts and progressively selects only layouts that represent improved total material-handling cost. Figure 7 shows a vastly simplified flow diagram which describes the basic structure of the program.

Input Data Required. The program requires three types of input data: an initial layout configuration, a load matrix, and a material-handling cost matrix. Figure 8 represents an initial layout for a plant with twenty departments, with physical dimensions of 200 feet by 300 feet. The initial solution may be completely arbitrary, any suggested layout felt to be good, or perhaps the existing layout. It is arranged so that each line is represented by one punched card. The card is punched with the sequence of letters, for example, line 1 would be punched, *AAAAAABBBLLLLLLL*, etc. When this sequence of cards is printed, it takes on the configuration of a block layout as shown in Figure 8. The lines separating the various groupings of letters in Figure 8 have been added to show more clearly the relative sizes and shapes of departmental areas. Each character represents 100 square feet for the particular problem of Figure 8.

Figure 9 shows the load matrix. This is simply a tabulation of the number

Location Pattern Iteration 0

	1	2	3	4	5	6	7	8	9	10	11	12	13	14	15	16	17	18	19	20	21	22	23	24	25	26	27	28	29	30
1	A	A	A	A	A	A	B	B	B	L	L	L	L	L	L	L	S	S	S	S	S	S	S	S	W	W	W	W	W	W
2	A				A	A	B		B	L						L	S							S	W					W
3	A					A	B	B		B	L						L	S						S	W					W
4	A					A	B			B	L						L	S						S	W					W
5	A	A	A	A	A	B	B	B	B	L						L	S						S	W					W
6	C	C	C	C	C	C	D	D	D	L					L	L	S	S	S					S	W					W
7	C					C	C	D		D	L					L	G	G	G	S				S	W					W
8	C					C	D	D		D	L					L	G		G	S				S	W					W
9	C					C	D			D	L	L	L	L	L	L	G	G	G	S	S	S	S	S	W	W	W	W	W	W
10	C	C	C	C	C	D	D	D	D	N	N	N	N	N	N	H	H	H	T	T	T	T	T	T	T	T	T	T	T	T
11	E	E	E	E	E	E	F	F	F	N					N	H		H	T											T
12	E					E	F		F	N	N	N	N	N	N	H	H	H	T											T
13	E	E	E	E	E	E	F		F	P	P	P	P	P	P	J	J	J	T											T
14	K	K	K	K	K	K	F		F	P						P	J		J	T	T	T	T	T	T	T			T	T	T
15	K					K	F		F	P						P	J	J	J	U	U	U	U	U	U	T	T	T	T	V	V
16	K					K	F	F	F	P	P	P	P	P	P	R	R	R	U				U	U	V	V	V	V	V
17	K	K	K	K	K	K	M	M	M	M	M	M	R	R	R	R	R	U							U		V	V	V	V
18	M	M	M	M	M	M	M						M	R				R	U							U		V			V
19	M						M						M	R				R	U							U		V			V
20	M	M	M	M	M	M	M	M	M	M	M	M	R	R	R	R	R	U	U	U	U	U	U	U	V	V	V	V	V	V

Total cost $10,164.34   Estimated cost reduction 0   MOVEA   MOVEB

FIGURE 8. Initial relative location pattern, iteration O. Scale: one matrix element equals 100 square feet. Each row and column equals 10 feet.

	A	B	C	D	E	F	G	H	J	K	L	M	N	P	R	S	T	U	V	W
A	0.	120.0	80.0	0.	0.	0.	0.	0.	0.	40.0	80.0	0.	0.	80.0	0.	0.	0.	0.	0.	0.
B	120.0	0.	80.0	1630.0	30.0	0.	930.0	0.	80.0	90.0	0.	0.	0.	0.	0.	0.	0.	0.	460.0	0.
C	80.0	80.0	0.	0.	0.	0.	0.	0.	210.0	260.0	0.	0.	0.	870.0	0.	0.	0.	100.0	910.0	0.
D	0.	1630.0	0.	0.	60.0	380.0	500.0	0.	130.0	0.	0.	70.0	0.	0.	0.	0.	0.	0.	1050.0	0.
E	0.	30.0	0.	60.0	0.	0.	150.0	90.0	0.	0.	0.	0.	0.	0.	90.0	0.	0.	70.0	0.	0.
F	0.	0.	0.	380.0	0.	0.	410.0	0.	0.	0.	0.	0.	0.	0.	0.	0.	0.	0.	0.	0.
G	0.	930.0	0.	500.0	150.0	410.0	0.	1600.0	0.	110.0	0.	0.	0.	0.	0.	0.	0.	110.0	0.	250.0
H	0.	0.	0.	0.	90.0	0.	1600.0	0.	0.	0.	0.	0.	0.	0.	0.	0.	0.	0.	0.	2230.0
J	0.	80.0	210.0	130.0	0.	0.	0.	0.	0.	0.	0.	0.	0.	0.	0.	0.	0.	0.	0.	0.
K	40.0	90.0	260.0	0.	0.	0.	110.0	0.	0.	0.	30.0	800.0	0.	1240.0	160.0	0.	0.	0.	350.0	0.
L	80.0	0.	0.	0.	0.	0.	0.	0.	0.	30.0	0.	150.0	0.	200.0	80.0	1500.0	350.0	90.0	0.	0.
M	0.	0.	0.	70.0	0.	0.	0.	0.	0.	800.0	150.0	0.	0.	500.0	110.0	0.	1000.0	0.	560.0	0.
N	0.	0.	0.	0.	0.	0.	0.	0.	0.	0.	0.	0.	0.	650.0	40.0	500.0	0.	0.	0.	0.
P	80.0	0.	870.0	0.	0.	0.	0.	0.	0.	1240.0	200.0	500.0	650.0	0.	0.	0.	0.	60.0	0.	0.
R	0.	0.	0.	0.	90.0	0.	0.	0.	0.	160.0	80.0	110.0	40.0	0.	0.	0.	350.0	0.	0.	0.
S	0.	0.	0.	0.	0.	0.	0.	0.	0.	0.	1500.0	0.	500.0	0.	0.	0.	1000.0	0.	0.	0.
T	0.	0.	0.	0.	0.	0.	0.	0.	0.	0.	350.0	1000.0	0.	0.	350.0	1000.0	0.	0.	500.0	0.
U	0.	0.	100.0	0.	70.0	0.	110.0	0.	0.	0.	90.0	0.	0.	60.0	0.	0.	0.	0.	310.0	0.
V	0.	460.0	910.0	1050.0	0.	0.	0.	0.	0.	350.0	0.	560.0	0.	0.	0.	0.	500.0	310.0	0.	0.
W	0.	0.	0.	0.	0.	0.	250.0	2230.0	0.	0.	0.	0.	0.	0.	0.	0.	0.	0.	0.	0.

FIGURE 9. Interdepartment product flow in tens of unit loads per annum.

of loads which flow between all combinations of departments. The matrix is symmetrical on its main diagonal; for example, the flow from A to B is shown as 120.0 and this is also shown as the flow from B to A, though the reverse flow may be unusual. This information could be summarized from records of past orders, and for very large plants it would probably represent a random sample of orders.

Figure 10 shows the interdepartmental material-handling cost per unit load per each 100 feet moved. For this particular example, three methods of material handling were used: manual truck, fork-lift truck, and low-bed lift truck, with respective costs of $0.026, $0.015, and $0.012 per unit load per 100 feet. In some instances, figures other than these appear in Figure 10, and these are weighted averages of the base figures and indicate that more than one method of material handling is in use between the departments concerned.

The Simulation. With the three items of basic data available, the program uses the following rationale (see the flow diagram of Figure 7):

1. The program determines which of the departments can be exchanged. A limitation in the program specifies that the only candidates for exchange are departments of equal size, or departments adjacent to each other even though they may not be equal in size. Although it appears that this may limit the exchanges which can be made, actually it does not, because through a sequence of exchanges of departments any pair of departments may finally be exchanged.

2. The program calculates the physical centers of the various departments and then determines the distances between all combinations of departments.

3. Data is now available to calculate the total handling cost for a given layout pattern. This is computed from the input data on loads and unit transport costs between departments and the matrix of distances calculated in 2 above. Of course the first layout pattern for which total material-handling costs are calculated will be the initial pattern.

4. The program now evaluates what changes in total cost would occur if each department was exchanged with all other departments in location. It does this by exchanging temporarily the two departments in question and recalculating total material-handling cost. This requires $(n^2 - n)/2 = 190$ evaluations for the example problem.

	A	B	C	D	E	F	G	H	J	K	L	M	N	P	R	S	T	U	V	W
A	0.	0.015	0.015	0.	0.	0.	0.	0.	0.	0.026	0.014	0.	0.	0.015	0.	0.	0.	0.	0.	0.
B	0.015	0.	0.012	0.015	0.026	0.	0.015	0.	0.015	0.015	0.	0.	0.	0.	0.	0.	0.	0.	0.015	0.
C	0.015	0.012	0.	0.	0.	0.017	0.	0.	0.015	0.015	0.	0.	0.	0.015	0.	0.	0.	0.	0.015	0.
D	0.	0.015	0.	0.	0.018	0.015	0.015	0.015	0.018	0.026	0.	0.020	0.	0.	0.015	0.	0.	0.015	0.015	0.
E	0.	0.026	0.	0.018	0.	0.	0.015	0.015	0.	0.026	0.	0.	0.	0.	0.	0.	0.	0.015	0.	0.
F	0.	0.	0.017	0.	0.	0.	0.015	0.	0.	0.	0.	0.015	0.	0.	0.	0.	0.	0.015	0.	0.
G	0.	0.015	0.	0.015	0.015	0.015	0.	0.015	0.	0.017	0.	0.	0.	0.016	0.	0.	0.	0.015	0.	0.015
H	0.	0.	0.	0.015	0.015	0.	0.015	0.	0.	0.	0.	0.	0.015	0.	0.	0.	0.	0.	0.015	0.015
J	0.	0.015	0.015	0.	0.	0.	0.	0.	0.	0.	0.	0.	0.	0.015	0.	0.	0.015	0.	0.	0.
K	0.026	0.015	0.015	0.018	0.026	0.	0.017	0.	0.	0.	0.012	0.015	0.	0.015	0.012	0.015	0.	0.	0.015	0.
L	0.014	0.015	0.015	0.	0.	0.015	0.	0.	0.012	0.015	0.	0.015	0.	0.015	0.012	0.	0.	0.	0.015	0.
M	0.	0.	0.	0.020	0.026	0.	0.	0.015	0.	0.015	0.015	0.	0.	0.015	0.015	0.015	0.	0.	0.015	0.
N	0.	0.	0.	0.	0.	0.015	0.016	0.	0.	0.015	0.015	0.	0.	0.016	0.026	0.012	0.016	0.015	0.	0.
P	0.015	0.015	0.015	0.	0.	0.	0.016	0.	0.015	0.015	0.015	0.015	0.016	0.	0.015	0.	0.	0.	0.	0.
R	0.	0.	0.	0.015	0.015	0.	0.015	0.	0.	0.012	0.012	0.015	0.026	0.015	0.	0.	0.015	0.	0.	0.
S	0.	0.	0.	0.	0.	0.	0.	0.	0.	0.	0.	0.	0.012	0.	0.	0.	0.012	0.	0.	0.
T	0.	0.	0.	0.	0.	0.015	0.	0.	0.015	0.	0.	0.015	0.	0.015	0.015	0.012	0.	0.	0.015	0.
U	0.	0.	0.	0.015	0.	0.	0.015	0.015	0.	0.015	0.015	0.015	0.	0.015	0.	0.	0.015	0.	0.015	0.
V	0.	0.015	0.015	0.015	0.	0.	0.	0.015	0.	0.015	0.015	0.015	0.	0.	0.	0.	0.015	0.015	0.	0.
W	0.	0.	0.	0.	0.	0.	0.015	0.015	0.	0.	0.	0.	0.	0.	0.	0.	0.	0.	0.	0.

FIGURE 10. Interdepartment material handling cost per unit load per 100 feet moved in dollars.

5. If any of the changes in location produce a reduction in material-handling cost, the program proceeds. If not, the program stops, for the best possible solution is the one for which computations have just been made.

6. If there are exchanges that produce cost reduction, the program selects the exchange of the two departments that yields the largest cost reduction and effects their exchange in the layout pattern.

7. Since some of the exchanges will be for departments of unequal size, program subroutines are required to rearrange the layout into a logical form, that is, square or rectangular patterns.

8. The program now calls for the printing of the revised layout, the new total cost, the estimated cost reduction, and the record of the exchanges just made. Figure 11 shows the print-out for the first iteration of the example problem. It shows that by exchanging the locations of departments A and V, a net improvement in material-handling cost of almost 12 percent has been obtained.

9. The program now repeats the basic steps until no further cost reduction can be achieved, the last iteration representing the best

```
                    Location Pattern                          Iteration 1

   1  2  3  4  5  6  7  8  9 10 11 12 13 14 15 16 17 18 19 20 21 22 23 24 25 26 27 28 29 30
 1 V  V  V  V  V  V  B  B  B  L  L  L  L  L  L  L  S  S  S  S  S  S  S  S  S  W  W  W  W  W
 2 V           V     B     B  L              L  S                       S  W           W
 3 V           V  B  B     B  L              L  S                       S  W           W
 4 V           V     B     B  L              L  S                       S  W           W
 5 V  V  V  V  V  B  B  B  B  L              L  S                       S  W           W
 6 C  C  C  C  C  C  D     D  L           L  L  S  S  S                 S  W           W
 7 C              C  D     D  L           L  G  G  G     S              S  W           W
 8 C           C  D  D     D  L           L  G     G  S                 S  W           W
 9 C              C  D     D  L  L  L  L  L  L  G  G  G  S  S  S  S  S  S  W  W  W  W  W
10 C  C  C  C  C  D  D  D  D  D  N  N  N  N  N  N  H  H  H  T  T  T  T  T  T  T  T  T  T  T
11 E  E  E  E  E  E  F  F  F  N     N  H        H  T                             T
12 E              E  F        F  N  N  N  N  N  H  H  H  T
13 E  E  E  E  E  E  F        F  P  P  P  P  P  P  P  J  J  J  T                          T
14 K              K  F        F  P              P  J     J  T  T  T  T  T  T  T  T     T  T
15 K              K  F        F  P  P  P        P  J  J  J  U  U  U  U  U  U  T  T  T  T  T  A  A
16 K  K  K  K  K  K  F  F  F  F  F  P  P  P  P  R  R  R  U              U  U  A  A  A     A
17 K  K  K  K  K  K  M  M  M  M  M  M  R  R  R  R     R  U              U  A              A
18 M  M  M  M  M  M  M        M  R              R  U              U  A              A
19 M                       M  R              R  U              U  A              A
20 M  M  M  M  M  M  M  M  M  M  M  M  R  R  R  R  R  R  U  U  U  U  U  U  U  A  A  A  A  A
```

Total cost $8,979.26   Estimated cost reduction $1,185.08   MOVEA A   MOVEB V

FIGURE 11.   First improved relative location pattern.

Location Pattern   Iteration 7

```
    1  2  3  4  5  6  7  8  9 10 11 12 13 14 15 16 17 18 19 20 21 22 23 24 25 26 27 28 29 30
 1  E  E  E  E  E  E  F  F  F  L  L  L  L  L  L  L  L  S  S  S  S  S  S  S  S  S  U  U  U  U  U
 2  E           E  F     F  L                   L  S                   S     U              U
 3  E  E  E  E  E  F  F     F  L                L  S                   S     U              U
 4  E  C  C  C  C  F        F  L                L  S                   S     U              U
 5  C  C        C  F  F  F  F  L                L  S                   S     U              U
 6  C           C  C  D  D  D  L             L  L  S  S  S             S     U              U
 7  C           C  C  D     D  L          L  G  G  G  G  S             S     U              U
 8  C  C  C  C  C  D        D  L          L  G        G  S             S     U  U  U  U  U  U
 9  C  V  V  V  V  D        D  L  L  L  L  L  L  L  G  G  G  G  S  S  S  S  S  S  S  W  W  W  W  W  U
10  V  V           V  D  D  D  D  N  N  N  N  N  N  N  H  H  H  T  T  T  T  W  W  W  W           W  W
11  V              V  V  B  B  B  N                   H     H  T        T  W  W              W
12  V              V  B        B  N  N  N  N  N  N  N  H  H  H  T        T  T  W              W
13  V  V  V  V  V  V  B        B  P  P  P  P  P  P  P  J  J  J  J  T        T  W              W
14  K  K  K  K  K  K  B        B  P                P  J     J  T        T  W              W  W
15  K              K  B        B  P  P  P  P  P  P  P  J  J  J  J  T        T  T  W  W  W  W  A  A
16  K              K  B  B  B  P  P  P  P  P  P  R  R  R  R  T           T  A  A  A  A  A  A
17  K  K  K  K  K  K  K  M  M  M  M  M  M  M  R  R  R  R     R  T           T  A              A
18  M  M  M  M  M  M  M              M  R              R  T              T  A              A
19  M                                M  R              R  T              T  A              A
20  M  M  M  M  M  M  M  M  M  M  M  M  R  R  R  R  R  R  R  T  T  T  T  T  T  T  A  A  A  A  A  A
```

Total cost $7,862.09   Estimated cost reduction $213.54   MOVEA E   MOVEB C

FIGURE 12. Suboptimum relative location pattern. Exchanging any two departments from their locations above here would increase the objective function, annual material handling expense.

possible solution. Figure 12 shows the seventh and final iteration for the sample problem. The final solution shows a 23 percent reduction in material-handling cost, as compared to the initial layout configuration, and the entire solution required 0.62 minute to execute on an IBM 7090 computer. The final block diagram of Figure 12 would be used as a basis for the development of a more detailed template layout.

The most recent version of the computer program (at the time of the publication of this book) allows for a maximum of forty departments and makes it possible to fix the location of any number of the departments. This latter feature is often important as a practical matter since it is sometimes true that not all departments can be changed in location. For example, the existing location of a railroad spur or road may determine the desirable location for receiving and shipping facilities. In such an instance, we wish to determine the best location of the other departments, given the location of the receiving and shipping departments. The present version of the program also considers candidates for exchange three at a time, rather than two at a time. The more powerful version of the CRAFT program is now available through the IBM SHARE Library under number SDA 3391.

PRODUCT LAYOUT /

Balance is the central problem in designing a production or assembly line. This is not to minimize the other problems of physical positioning of equipment, the design of material-handling devices and special tools, and work place layout, for in many instances solutions to these problems will contribute to the balance of the line. Balance refers to the equality of output of each of the successive operations in the sequence of a line. If they are all equal, we say that we have perfect balance, and we expect smooth flow. If they are unequal, we know that the maximum possible output for the line as a whole will be dictated by the slowest operation in the sequence. This slow operation, often called the bottleneck operation, restricts the flow of parts on the line in much the same way that a half-closed valve restricts the flow of water, even though the pipes in the system might be capable of carrying twice as much water. Thus where imbalance exists in a line, we have wasted capacity in all operations, except the bottleneck operation.

To achieve balance to the best of our ability, we need to know the performance times for the smallest possible whole units of activity, such as tightening a bolt, making a solder joint, etc., and the knowledge of the flexibility that we have in the sequence of these tasks or activities. There are, of course, certain limitations on the sequence of the tasks. For example, a washer must go on before the nut, wires must be joined physically before they can be soldered, a hole must be drilled before it can be reamed, and reamed before it can be tapped. On the other hand the sequence may be irrelevant in some situations, as the order in which a series of nuts is put on. This sequence flexibility is important in helping us specify the groups of tasks making up operations or stations for the line which achieves the best balance.

An Example

Let us see the nature of the problem through an example. Figure 13 shows the cylinder subassembly for a typical small air compressor with the parts named and numbered. By examining the assembly, we can readily see the sequence restrictions that we would have to observe. In assembling the cylinder head to the cylinder, the cylinder head gasket (part No. 8) would have to be positioned first. Also, in assembling the discharge valve unit, the valve itself (part No. 3) must go in first, followed by a valve spring (part No. 6), and finally by a discharge valve fitting (part No. 4). A similar procedure for the suction valve unit would be followed, but the sequence of the valve and spring

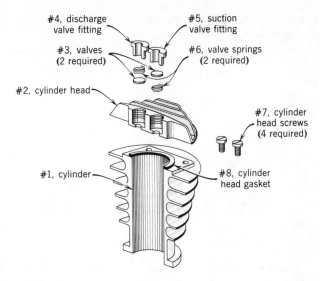

FIGURE 13.   Cylinder subassembly for a typical air compressor.

would be reversed. These are the sequences that must be observed, because the cylinder subassembly cannot be assembled correctly any other way. On the other hand, it makes no difference whether the valve units are assembled to the cylinder head before or after the cylinder head is assembled to a cylinder. Similarly, which valve unit is assembled first is irrelevant. The cylinder head is joined to the cylinder by four screws. All four of them need not be assembled at the same time, and there is no required sequence for their assembly.

These task sequence restrictions are summarized in Table III so that we can use the result to advantage. The assembly tasks listed in Table III are, in general, broken down into the smallest whole activity. Note, for example, that the screws and the valve fittings are first positioned and the threads engaged so that tightening can take place separately, perhaps as a part of the next station or some subsequent station. In addition, for each task, we note in the far right-hand column the task or tasks which must precede it. Thus tasks a, e, and i can take any sequence, because no tasks need precede them. Task d, position cylinder head on cyclinder, however, must be preceded by task a, position cylinder head gasket on cylinder. Task c-1 must be preceded by tasks a and b. The repetition of a is not absolutely necessary, since we know that b must be preceded by a. With this information, together with the task times also given in Table III, we can construct the diagram shown in Figure 14.

Figure 14 merely reflects in a graphical way the sequence requirements that we have determined. For convenience, the performance times are indicated beside the tasks. Now we can proceed with the grouping of tasks to obtain balance. But balance at what level? What is to be the capacity of our line? This is an important point and one which makes a balancing problem difficult. With no restriction on capacity, the problem would be simple; we could take the lowest common multiple approach. For

TABLE III. List of assembly tasks showing sequence restrictions and performance times for the cylinder subassembly of figure 13

Task	Performance Time, Seconds	Task Description	Task Must Follow Task Listed Below
a	1.5	Position cylinder head gasket (No. 8) on cylinder (No. 1)	—
b	2.0	Position cylinder head (No. 2) on cylinder (No. 1)	a
c-1	3.2	Position a cylinder head screw (No. 7) in hole and engage threads	ab
c-2	3.2	Repeat	ab
c-3	3.2	Repeat	ab
c-4	3.2	Repeat	ab
d-1	1.5	Tighten a cylinder head screw	abc-1
d-2	1.5	Repeat	abc-2
d-3	1.5	Repeat	abc-3
d-4	1.5	Repeat	abc-4
e	3.7	Position valve (No. 3) in bottom of discharge hole	—
f	2.6	Position valve spring (No. 6) on top of valve in discharge hole	e
g	3.2	Position discharge valve fitting (No. 4) in hole and engage threads	ef
h	2.0	Tighten discharge valve fitting	efg
i	3.1	Position 2nd valve spring (No. 6) in bottom of suction hole	—
j	3.7	Position 2nd valve (No. 3) on top of spring in suction hole	i
k	3.2	Position suction valve fitting (No. 5) in hole and engage threads	ij
l	2.0	Tighten suction valve fitting	ijk

example, if we had three operations that required 3.2, 2.0, and 4.0 minutes respectively, we could provide eight work places of the first, five of the second, and ten of the third, so that the capacity of the line would be 150 units per hour at each of the operations, all in balance. But capacity has been specified by balance, rather than by considerations of product demand and economics.

We must take the capacity of the line as given and develop good balance within that restriction. For illustrative purposes, let us assume that we must balance our line for a 10-second cycle. A completed unit would be produced by the line each 10 seconds,

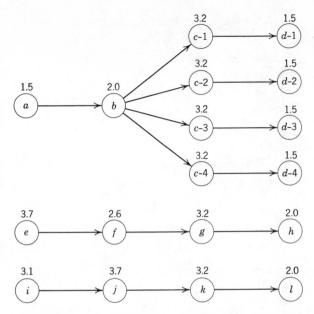

FIGURE 14. *Diagrammatic representation of the sequence requirements shown in Table III. Numbers indicate performance times of elements.*

and to meet this capacity requirement no station could be assigned to more than 10 seconds worth of the tasks shown on the diagram of Figure 14. Proceeding, then, we could group the tasks into station assignments. The total of all task times is 45.8 seconds; therefore, with a 10-second cycle, five stations would be the minimum possible. Any solution that required more than five stations would increase direct labor costs. Figure 15 shows one solution that yields five stations.

The line balance or sequencing problem is of considerable importance not only for product layout but for rebalancing to obtain the desired output for a given schedule requirement.

LINE BALANCE MODELS /

The line balance problem is essentially a combinatorial one where we are seeking a combination of task times which will maximize labor utilization on the line or in an equivalent sense minimize labor idle time. But, a 40-task line balance problem would be considered a fairly small one and there are 40! different sequences or approximately 8.16×10^{47}. Of course the technological sequencing requirements reduce the number of *feasible* sequences, but we are still

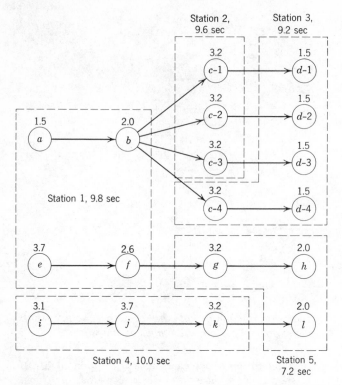

FIGURE 15. A solution to the cylinder subassembly line balancing problem which requires no more than 10 seconds per station and does not violate the element sequence requirements.

faced with a problem where it is not possible to consider enumerating the feasible solutions in order to select an optimal solution. Another factor which helps make the problem a manageable one is that normally there are a number of equivalent solutions which will produce the minimum number of work stations for a given output rate requirement.

A task or work element is defined as the smallest unit of productive work which is separable from another activity such that it can be performed relatively independently and possibly in different sequences. Recall that Figure 14, often called a precedence diagram, was a way of summarizing the technological sequence restrictions. Thus a large number of possible task sequences are eliminated. The problem becomes one of finding a grouping of tasks into work stations which is feasible in terms of the technological sequence restrictions and minimizes the number of work stations, given a specification of the required output rate or cycle time.

The foregoing statement is a statement of the problem in its simplest form. But in fact there are constraints which may make the problem somewhat more complex. First there may be physical constraints, such as the following: Should the work station where an automotive engine is mounted be located on the front or backside of the line, or above or below the line? A careful examination of the auto may be required to see how the work station should be oriented with respect to the line in order to accomplish the work to be done. In some instances, physical restrictions of this kind might require a reorientation of the product being assembled or alternately a change in sequence of tasks could possibly eliminate the need to reorient, and thus we may have a new kind of sequence restriction.

Other problems may occur if one or more of the task times exceed the stated cycle time. Sometimes flexibility of worker position up and down the line may help solve this kind of problem, or sometimes it may be necessary to simply assign more manpower to the station involved. Sometimes, however, it may be impossible to solve such a problem with more manpower simply because of lack of working room. Another complexity might be the reverse of the one just stated. Perhaps the nature of a task requires more than one man, another man being in a supporting role to help lift or guide a part. If the second man is not fully utilized, then he becomes part of the overall balance and sequencing problem in an attempt to find other useful work for him by sequencing tasks which he can do at the same work station.

Cycle Time

The choice of a cycle time to be used can set limitations on the possible quality of the final solution. First, we must recognize that the choice of cycle time is related to the demand for the product and to the aggregate planning function which sets production requirements for some period into the future. Thus, balance does not specify output rate, but instead output rate places limitations on the problem of balance. Within the limited range of output rates which might satisfy decisions made by the aggregate plan, there are certain choices for cycle time which might be superior. We can determine these superior choices by an examination of the balance delay function [14]. The balance delay function shows for a given situation the percent idle time inherent in a range of cycle times which might be selected.

An Example

Let us take as an example a line balance problem, where the sum of all task times is 450 seconds, and plot the balance delay function over a range of cycle times from

30 to 90 seconds (equivalent to output rates from 40 to 120 units per hour). Under these conditions, we can obtain perfect balance theoretically with certain combinations of cycle time and numbers of stations on the line, such as $c = 30$, $n = 15$; $c = 45$, $n = 10$; $c = 50$, $n = 9$; $c = 75$, $n = 6$; and, $c = 90$, $n = 5$. Other feasible combinations of c and n will have a positive balance delay, d, defined by

$$d = \frac{100(nc - \Sigma t_i)}{nc} \qquad (1)$$

where n and c are respectively the number of stations on the line and the cycle time, the t_i are task times, and n, c, and the t_i are integer numbers. Figure 16 shows the graph of the balance delay function for the case we have described. We can see from Figure 16 that some cycle times are potentially much better than others, for example, the values of $c = 30, 45, 50, 75$, and 90. Also we can see that low values of percent balance delay occur for cycle times just over the ideal values. On the other hand, cycle times just below the ideal values produce maximum percent balance delay. We also note in Figure 16 that perfect balance is not attainable for a line composed of 7, 8, 11, 12, 13, and 14 stations.

The balance delay function is then one input or guide to the process of developing good solutions for sequencing tasks. It is not sufficient, however, to have selected a potentially good cycle time because we must be able to assign the task times to the corresponding number of work stations. The following discussion of sequencing models to solve the line balance problem presents proposed solutions to the problem.

Sequencing Models for Line Balance

There have been a very large number of both theoretical and practical proposals for solving the sequencing problem for line balancing, a large number of which are cited in the reference list at the end of the chapter. While the theoretical proposals may not have offered immediate solutions to large-scale problems, they have provided deeper understanding of the problem [9, 10]. Others have been less interested in the theoretical optimum solution for small-scale problems but have focused attention on the practical solution of actual large-scale complex problems [1, 13]. The characteristics of the more realistic practical problem include the capability of handling situations involving 75 to 100 tasks or more, line lengths of 10 to 15 stations or more, as well as some of the physical constraints which we discussed previously. One technique which develops excellent solutions for the larger scale complex problem is known as COMSOAL (*Computer Method of Sequencing Operations for Assembly Lines*). COMSOAL is a computerized technique which simulates feasible sequences of tasks through a system of biased sampling. Some of the other approaches to the problem of sequencing for line balance have been heuristic [13], dynamic program-

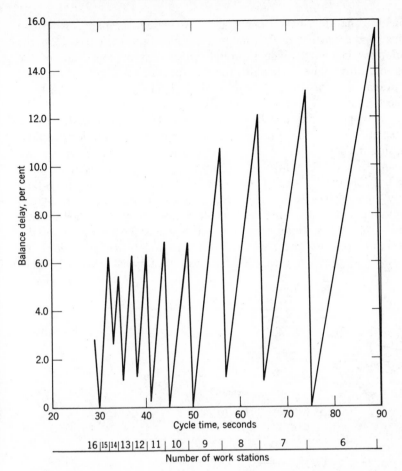

FIGURE 16. Graph of balance delay function for a task time total of 450 seconds.

ming [9], linear programming [23], and others. We shall discuss the COMSOAL technique in some detail followed by a comparative simulation study by Mastor [19] which evaluates the effectiveness of a number of the proposed techniques.

COMSOAL (Computer Method of Sequencing Operations for Assembly Lines)

The basic methodology of COMSOAL, which was developed by A. L. Arcus, is based on the generation of a fairly large number of feasible solutions to the line balance problem by biased sampling. Alternate solutions to the particular line balance problem are then based on the best solutions generated. The sampling universe is of course all of the feasible solutions to the particular problem, there being a finite probability that optimal solutions will be generated, a slightly larger probability of "next best solutions," and so on. Of course, the sample size governs the probability of generating excellent solutions and the economic feasibility of the technique is in the process of generating feasible solutions rapidly and biasing the generation of these solutions toward the better ones.

The simple example shown in Figure 17 illustrates the theory behind COMSOAL. Figure 17a shows a precedence diagram for an 8-task assembly job which is to be balanced for a 10-minute cycle time. Arcus manually enumerated all of the 112 feasible combinations of the tasks which involved 4, 5, or 6 stations and Figure 17b shows the histogram of the distribution of results. There were 25 solutions which used 4 stations, 84 which used 5 stations, and only 3 which used 6 stations. Obviously there

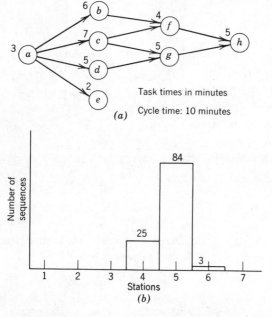

FIGURE 17. (a) *Eight task precedence diagram, and* (b) *histogram of 112 feasible solutions for a 10 minute cycle time. From A. L. Arcus, "COMSOAL: A Computer Method of Sequencing Operations for Assembly Lines," in* Readings in Production and Operations Management, *E. S. Buffa, ed., John Wiley & Sons, New York, 1966.*

are additional feasible solutions involving 7 and 8 stations but they are not very interesting.

COMSOAL generates feasible solutions by the following general procedure:

Step I. First, by scanning precedence information, list *A* is formed which simply tabulates the total number of tasks which immediately precede each given task. For the example of Figure 17*a* we have

| | *Total number of immediately* |
| | *preceding tasks* |

List A Task	*preceding tasks*
a	0
b	1
c	1
d	1
e	1
f	2
g	2
h	2

Step II. The computing routine then scans list *A* to identify all tasks which have no preceding tasks and places them in list *B*, the "available list." For our simple example, only task *a* meets these requirements so list *B* is

(Available) *List B*	*Task*
	a

Step III. The available list *B* is then partitioned by placing in list *C* those tasks which have times no greater than the time left available at the station being assigned work. List *C* is called the "fit list" since only elements that fit the time left to be assigned within a station are listed. In our example, the available time at station 1 is ten since no assignments have yet been made, and the time for task *a* in list *B* is only three, so it is transferred to list *C*

(Fit) *List C*	*Task*
	a

Step IV. In the simplest form of COMSOAL, assignment is now made by selecting at random from the fit list a task to be assigned to station 1. Since only task *a* is in the fit list at this point, it is selected and assigned to station 1.

Step V. Eliminate task *a* from lists *B* and *C* (leaving them empty at this point of our example).

Step VI. Update list A by scanning the immediate followers of task a and deduct 1 from the tally of the "total number of preceding tasks" as follows:

	Total number of immediately
List A Task	preceding tasks
a	0
b	$1 - 1 = 0$
c	$1 - 1 = 0$
d	$1 - 1 = 0$
e	$1 - 1 = 0$
f	2
g	2
h	2

Step VII. Update the tasks available in list B by transferring from list A all tasks now listed as having no preceding tasks. List B becomes:

(Available) List B	Task
	b
	c
	d
	e

Step VIII. Transfer from list B to list C those tasks which *fit* the remaining time to be assigned to station 1, or $10 - 3 = 7$. Since in this instance all of the task times in list B are 7 or less, the fit list becomes

(Fit) List C	Task
	b
	c
	d
	e

Step IX. Select at random from list C a task to assign to station 1.

Step X. Eliminate the selected task from lists B and C. Repeat Steps VI through X until station 1 has been as fully assigned as it can be, and continue the procedure, station by station, until all elements are assigned. As a solution is completed its station count is compared to the station count of the previous best sequence. If there is an improvement, the new solution is stored in memory and the old one discarded. The result is that the computer memory holds no more than two solutions at any one time.

As mentioned, the COMSOAL procedure just outlined was simplified to facilitate the explanation. Actually, instead of selecting a task at random from the fit list, C, as mentioned in both Steps IV and IX, the program biases the selection of the element by weighting the tasks in the fit list. A second variation from the procedure outlined provides for aborting a solution as soon as it becomes apparent that the accumulated idle time of the incomplete solution exceeds the total idle time of the previous best solution, since the solution being generated cannot be an improvement. The result of the aborting procedure is to save computer time and have that time spent in examining potentially better solutions.

The weighting procedure for biasing the selection of tasks from the fit list developed by Arcus is a product of the weights computed by the following five rules:

Rule 1 Weight tasks that fit in proportion to task time. The effect of this weighting is to give large tasks a greater probability of being assigned than small ones.

Rule 2 Weight tasks that fit by $1/X'$, where X' is equal to the total number of unassigned tasks minus 1, less the number of all of the tasks that follow the task being considered. The effect of Rule 2 is to give those tasks that have a large number of followers a greater probability of being assigned than tasks with a small number of followers.

Rule 3 Weight tasks that fit by the total number of all following tasks plus 1. The effect of this rule is to prefer tasks which, when selected, will be replaced and therefore expand the available list.

Rule 4 Weight tasks that fit by the times of the task and of all following tasks. The effect of this rule is to combine the advantages of Rules 1 and 3 by selecting large tasks early at each station in the entire sequence or, alternatively, by preferring tasks which, although small, tend to expand the available list.

Rule 5 Weight tasks that fit by the total number of following tasks plus 1, divided by the number of levels which those following tasks occupy plus 1. The effect of this weight is to give tasks in the longest chains the greatest probability of being assigned first.

Results. The computer program designed to operate in the form just described, with the weighting and aborting procedures, is described by Arcus as being applicable to the sequencing and assembly line balance problem in simple form. Arcus applied the program to the 45 task example used by Wester and Kilbridge [30] and produced optimal assignments in an average of 32 seconds of IBM 7090 computer time. Arcus also applied the program to Tonge's [27, 28] 70 task example (22 stations) in 0.7 seconds and to a 111 task industrial example (27 stations) in 0.7 seconds.

COMSOAL for the Balance Problem in Complex Form. Having found a computing procedure that produced optimal or near optimal solutions for basic line balance problems, Arcus proceeded to provide for a series of other more realistic constraints on the program. In essence, these constraints affect the fit list which must satisfy the new constraints in addition to those stated earlier. We shall not attempt to describe these additional constraints in detail, but the following list should serve to describe their general nature:

1. Tasks larger than the cycle time.

2. Tasks that require two men.

3. Tasks fixed in location.

4. Space for parts.

5. Time to obtain a tool.

6. Time for the worker to change position.

7. Time to change the position of a unit. (Orientation of the unit being worked on.)

8. Grouping tasks by criteria.

9. Wages related to tasks.

10. Worker movement between units being assembled.

11. Mixed production on the same line.

12. Stochastic task performance times.

Arcus states that the earlier model of COMSOAL has already been implemented by Chrysler Corporation and that a hypothetical line with 1000 tasks and a known optimum of 200 stations with zero idle time has been run. In addition, a sequence requiring 203 stations resulting in 1.48 percent idle time was computed in about 2 minutes of IBM 7094 time, and, a line has been run with 111 tasks, 5 mixed products, and all of the complexities just listed.

One of the obvious advantages of a program like COMSOAL for the production scheduling function in an enterprise is the rapidity with which we can call for alternate balance solutions in an attempt to provide the best possible way to adjust to changes in the employment level called for by aggregate plans. COMSOAL can also help in building the cost model required for the aggregate plan. It can evaluate the realistic cost effects of decisions for different production levels. Since the employment levels are not a continuous function of production rate, we need the actual number of employees required so we can determine the actual hiring and layoff costs which would be associated with decisions to change levels.

Comparative Evaluation of Line Balance Models

Mastor [19] made a comparative investigation of some of the proposed line balancing models. In the past 10 years or so there have been at least sixteen different proposals in the literature as can be seen by scanning the reference list at the end of this chapter. Thus, a comparative study such as that performed by Mastor should help considerably in evaluating the relative power of some of the proposals and in pointing out some of their outstanding strengths and weaknesses. Three factors were systematically varied; problem size as measured by the number of tasks to be assigned, line length as measured by the number of stations, and order strength of the precedence diagram as measured by the ratio of the number of ordering relations present to the possible number of ordering relations. Computations were made for 20 and 40 task problems at three different order strengths (0.25, 0.50, and 0.75), and several line lengths. Mastor established a *lower bound* cycle time for each problem so that the measured average cycle times for each model represented idle time for the solution, and comparisons between techniques were made on this basis.

Either special computer programs were written for a given model or programs were obtained from their original authors. In establishing bases for comparison, certain benchmark rules for assigning tasks to stations were constructed. We shall discuss briefly both the nature of the benchmark rules and the other models for line balancing which were the focus of the investigation.

Bench-Mark Rules

1. *Lexicographic order rule.* In the lexicographic order rule tasks are placed in the available list in the order in which they become available. The first task in the available list is assigned to a station first unless the task time exceeds the remaining time in the station. If the task time exceeds the remaining time an attempt is made to assign the next task in the list, and so on. The lexicographic order rule does not attempt to determine the best tasks for an initial assignment to stations or to adjust or to improve

any of the assignments made. The rule is similar to a rule which randomly assigns tasks from the available list. Mastor included the lexicographic rule as a bench mark representing the type of production line that might result if no attempt were made to obtain good results.

2. *Number of immediate follower tasks rule.* This rule assigns a task to a station according to the number of tasks that immediately follow it. For each task, the number of immediate follower tasks is recorded in the order of assignments. Assignments are then made from the available list, the task with the largest number of follower tasks being assigned first. The use of the number of immediate followers rule is based on the concept that a large number of available tasks makes it possible to utilize more fully the available time in a station.

3. *Random sampling rule.* The random sampling rule was first proposed by Arcus [1] and the main difference between this rule and the other Arcus rule described previously in this chapter is that the random rule does not attempt to include a bias into the selection of feasible sequences.

4. *Work element time ordered rule.* This rule assigns tasks to stations based on the time required to perform the task. The task with the largest time in the available list is assigned first. If the task time exceeds the remaining time in the station an attempt is made to assign the task with the next largest time. If all of the tasks in the available list exceed the remaining station time the number of stations is increased by one and the process repeated. The work element time ordered rule is based on the concept that the early assignment of large work elements to stations gives greater flexibility in the assignment of smaller work elements as the remaining station time decreases.

Description of Line Balance Models to Be Evaluated. In addition to the bench-mark rules just discussed, comparative studies were made for several models proposed in the literature which are briefly described as follows:

1. *Helgeson and Birnie* [10]. This line balance model establishes the order for assigning tasks to stations by summing the task times for a given task plus all of the tasks which follow. Tasks with the largest sum are assigned first.

2. *Hoffman* [11]. The Hoffman model enumerates every feasible combination of tasks that may be assigned to a station and selects the combination of tasks that minimizes idle time for the station. The model uses a precedence matrix to indicate the ordering relations among tasks. At the beginning of each station, a task that does not have any unassigned preceding tasks is tentatively assigned. The

ordering relations in the matrix are adjusted to show that this task has been tentatively assigned. The process is continued until it is not possible to assign a task without exceeding the remaining station time. At this point, a task is deleted from the list of tentative assignments, the ordering relations in the matrix readjusted, and an attempt is made to assign another task that does not have any unassigned preceding tasks. This process is continued until a combination of tasks that equals the cycle time is found, or all feasible combinations of tasks have been enumerated. If all feasible combinations have been enumerated, the combination that minimizes idle time for the station is assigned, and the precedence matrix is adjusted accordingly. The line length is then increased by one, and the process repeated for the next station.

3. *Column rule* (based on Heuristic Line Balancing by Kilbridge and Wester [13]). Mastor states that "The Kilbridge and Wester technique was developed primarily to balance line production systems without the aid of a computer. The main feature of this technique is the grouping of tasks into columns to guide in their selection. Each task is identified by two column numbers. One column number denotes the first column in which the task may be selected for assignment to a station while the second column number denotes the last column in which the task may be selected." Mastor developed the following procedure to calculate the column numbers for each task. All tasks with no predecessors are placed in column 1. Tasks that immediately follow tasks in column 1 are placed in column 2. This is repeated until all tasks are identified by at least one column number. If a task is identified by two or more column numbers, the largest column number is used as the final identification for the first column in which the work element may be selected for assignment to a station. The second column number is calculated in a similar way. Tasks with no follower tasks are identified by the largest column number obtained in the first series of calculations, and immediately preceding tasks are identified by the next to the last column number. This procedure is continued until all tasks have been identified. If a task is identified by two or more column numbers, the smallest column number is used as the final identification for the last column in which a task can be selected for assignment to a station. The Kilbridge and Wester assignment procedure begins by assigning tasks in the first column in the order of size. If an optimum solution is not achieved, tasks within columns are permuted in an attempt to obtain an optimum solution.

In addition, tasks are laterally transferred into subsequent columns up to but not exceeding their second column number identification. During this process a record of ordering relations among work elements is maintained to insure that these relations are not violated. Kilbridge and Wester state that judgment and intuition should be used in permuting tasks within columns and in laterally transferring tasks. It was not possible to program this feature of the Kilbridge-Wester technique.

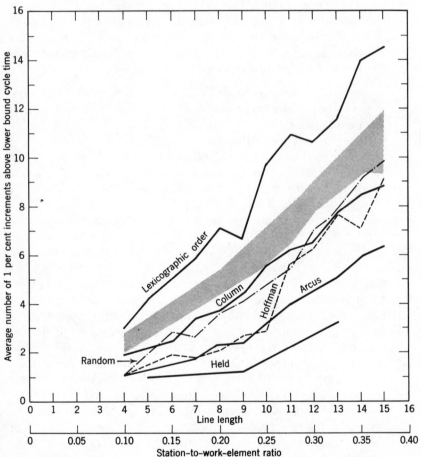

FIGURE 18. Idle time curves for forty-element problems, order strength 0.50. (Figure 18 and 19 are from A. A. Mastor, An Experimental Investigation and Comparative Evaluation of Production Line Balancing Techniques, *Unpublished Ph.D. Dissertation, UCLA, 1966. See also* Management Science, *Vol. XVI, No. 11, July 1970, pp. 728–746.)*

4. *COMSOAL*, the Arcus biased sampling technique [1]. The Arcus methodology was described previously in this chapter.

5. *Held, Karp, and Sharesian* [9]. This model is based on a dynamic programming formulation and a heuristic incorporating dynamic programming for solving subsections of problems.

Comparative Results. Since the results for the 40 task problems were representative of the entire set of experiments, we shall restrict our discussion to the results obtained there. Figures 18 and 19 summarize the results in terms of comparative idle time. While Figure 18 is for the results of the 0.50 order strength only, it is typical in general form of the results for all order strengths. In Figure 18 considerable overlapping occurs among the results obtained for several of the models, so that they are not shown individually but as a shaded area to indicate the boundaries within which they were all located. Similar results are indicated in both Figures 18 and 19 in terms of the relative ranking of the different models. The Held, et al., and Arcus models consistently require the least idle time for any line length and for all order strengths. The Held model seems to have limitations in terms of the size of problem to which it is applicable, but otherwise it con-

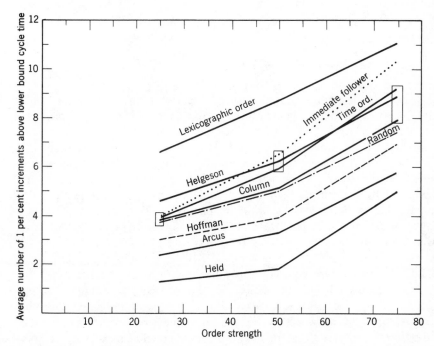

FIGURE 19.   *Idle time curves for forty-element problems, all order strengths.*

sistently performs best. The best results for the Arcus model involved sample sizes of 80 feasible sequences. Even larger sample sizes probably would have improved the results. The lexicographic order rule was consistently the worst performer as we would suspect. The relatively poor showing of the column rule based on the heuristic line balancing method of Kilbridge and Wester is without doubt affected by the fact that the computer program could not include the intuition of the analyst.

Computing Time. The Held model required about 10 times as much computing time as did the Arcus model on the 40 element problem. Nevertheless, the computing time for the Held model was not excessive, ranging from 1.8 seconds for the high order strength problem to 32.4 seconds for low order strength problems. The comparable figures for the Arcus model were 0.8 to 2.7 seconds.

Industrial Problems. Mastor also compared performance on five actual industrial problems ranging in size from 21 to 111 tasks. For the large problems (involving 70, 92, and 111 tasks) the Held and Arcus models performed almost identically when the Arcus sample size was run to 999 sequences. Still the Arcus computing time was less, being 20 seconds compared to 34.2 seconds for the 70 task problem, and 56 seconds compared to 94.3 seconds for the 111 task problem.

Conclusions on Line Balancing Models

The results of Mastor's comparative investigation point to the Held, et al., and the Arcus models as being most effective over a wide range of problem sizes, order strengths, and line lengths. The performance of the Arcus model improved with sample size and seemed to match the performance of the Held model with less computer time for large problems, when 999 sequences were used as the sample size. All of the problems computed by Mastor were described by the simple definition of balance problems, rather than the more complex definition discussed on page 171. Most of the techniques were not designed to handle the more complex problem definition. Analysis of the various models indicates that only the COMSOAL program by Arcus and Heuristic Line Balancing by Kilbridge and Wester permit the handling of the more complex problem definition. By not including the intuition furnished by the analyst in the heuristic technique, Mastor effectively cut the heart out of it. Previous studies indicated that the heuristic method worked very well on large and small problems for both simple and complex problem definition. Our conclusion is that for very large complex problems COMSOAL and Heuristic Line Balancing methods are probably best. For moderate sized and small problems involving the simple problem definition, the Held model will produce a near optimum solution and is therefore a logical alternate model.

Auxiliary Balancing Techniques. Certainly the general methods for balance just discussed are the most important, but there are auxiliary balancing techniques which can be used effectively also. These techniques involve careful methods study, selection of operators, artificial subdivision of tasks, and an examination of layout. The limiting work station can often be subjected to careful methods study which can reduce the overall station time. Since the station involved is the limiting one, these improvements increase the output for the line as a whole. Also, by careful selection and assignment of operators, compensations for imbalance can be accomplished. By assigning operators with high manual skills to the limiting operations, an additional degree of balance can be obtained. Still another technique is to place banks of material ahead of the limiting station so that the operator never has to incur idle time because of lack of material supply.

SUMMARY

In general, the physical layout of production systems can be classified into two types: product or process. Although it is true that most actual production systems might combine some features of both, analytical technique has developed around the two classic types. The central problem of process layout is the determination of the relative location of departments or facilities, but the central problem of product layout is line balance. In situations where a combination of the two types of layout exist, such as when fabrication operations are appropriately laid out by process while assembly operations are carried out on lines, a broad two-stage analysis is appropriate. In the first stage of analysis the assembly line would be regarded as one of the process areas and a block diagram of the layout determined on the basis of the relative location techniques. The assembly line department thus located within the plant as a whole, by CRAFT or some other technique, then becomes a subject for line balance study.

REVIEW QUESTIONS

1. Discuss the nature of the multiplant location problem. What kinds of analyses are appropriate?

2. In the multiplant location problem, how could it happen that the proposed

plant location with the lowest estimated manufacturing cost was not the optimal choice?

3. Discuss the problem of locational dynamics for multiple plants. What are the general circumstances under which one plant might be closed down while the remaining plants are operated on overtime schedules?

4. Define the terms process-oriented and product-oriented layout.

5. What are the general conditions which foster the use of line layout?

6. How are production systems classified in the text?

7. Describe the relative location of facilities for process layout. What is a logical objective function for this problem?

8. Outline a graphical approach to determining the best relative location of facilities in a process layout.

9. State the nature of the line balance problem.

10. Relate line balance sequencing models and job shop sequencing models to the general model structure for waiting lines.

11. How is the term "task" defined for purposes of line balance sequencing models?

12. Describe the line balance problem in simple form. In complex form.

13. Define the balance delay function. Why are some choices for cycle time superior to others?

14. Describe the biased sampling procedure developed by Arcus. Why is the procedure efficient as compared to enumerating all possible feasible solutions?

15. Mastor established a lower bound cycle time for each problem used in his comparative experiments. Outline the basis for computing a lower bound cycle time.

16. Describe the comparative results obtained by Mastor. Account for the relatively poor showing of the column rule.

17. After balancing a line with one of the formal models described, are there additional methods for refining balance even more?

PROBLEMS

1. An organization does job machining and assembly and wishes to relayout its production facilities so that the relative location of departments better reflects the average flow of parts through the plant. Following is shown an operation sequence summary for a sample of seven parts, with approximate area requirements for each of the thirteen machine or work centers. The numbers in the columns headed by each of the parts indicate the number of the work center to which the part goes next. Just

below the sequence summary is shown a summary of production per month and the number of pieces handled at one time through the shop for each part.

a. Develop a load summary showing the number of loads per month going between all combinations of work centers.

b. Develop an ideal schematic layout.

c. Develop a block diagram that reflects the approximate area requirements given and results in an overall rectangular shape.

Machine or Work Center	Area, Square Feet	Work Center Number	A	B	C	D	E	F	G
Saw	50	1		2	2				2
Centering	100	2		4	3				3
Milling machines	500	3	5	9	5	5		4	4
Lathes	600	4		5, 7	7		5	10	5
Drills	300	5	8	3	4	11	7		6
Arbor press	100	6					11		7
Grinders	200	7		12	12		6		8
Shapers	200	8	9			3			9
Heat treat	150	9	11	4					10
Paint	100	10						11	11
Assembly bench	100	11	12	13	13	13	13	13	12
Inspection	50	12	13	11	11				13
Pack	100	13							

Production Summary

			A	B	C	D	E	F	G
Pieces per month			500	500	1600	1200	400	800	400
Pieces per load			3	100	40	40	100	100	2
Loads per month			250	5	40	30	4	8	200

2. Examine the ideal schematic diagram of Figure 5 in the text. Find an improved diagram with no nonadjacent loads.

3. Following is a list of assembly tasks showing sequence restrictions and performance times. Develop a diagram showing the sequence requirements and determine a task grouping that minimizes the number of stations (groups of tasks), does not violate sequence restrictions, and produces 10 units per hour.

Task	Performance Time, Minutes	Task Must Follow Task Listed Below
a	4	—
b	3	a
c	5	ab
d	2	—
e	4	abc
f	6	abcd
g	2	—
h	3	dg
j	5	dgh
k	2	—
l	3	k
m	4	kl

REFERENCES

1. Arcus, A. L., "COMSOAL: A Computer Method of Sequencing Operations for Assembly Lines, I—The Problem in Simple Form, II—The Problem in Complex Form," in *Readings in Production and Operations Management*, E. S. Buffa, ed., John Wiley & Sons, New York, 1966. Also published in slightly different form as, "COMSOAL: A Computer Method of Sequencing Operations for Assembly Lines," *International Journal of Production Research*, Vol. 4, No. 4, 1966.

2. Armour, G. C., and E. S. Buffa, "A Heuristic Algorithm and Computer Simulation Approach to the Relative Location of Facilities," *Management Science*, Vol. 9, No. 2, January, 1963.

3. Buffa, E. S., "Pacing Effects in Production Lines," *Journal of Industrial Engineering*, Vol. XII, No. 6, November-December, 1961.

4. Buffa, E. S., "Sequence Analysis for Functional Layouts," *Journal of Industrial Engineering*, Vol. VI, No. 2, March–April, 1955.

5. Buffa, E. S., and W. H. Taubert, *Production-Inventory Systems: Planning and Control*, Richard D. Irwin, Inc., Homewood, Ill., Rev. ed., 1972.

6. Burgeson, J. W., and T. E. Daum, "Production Line Balancing," 650 Program Library, File 10.3.002, International Business Machines, Inc., Akron, Ohio, 1958.

7. Dillon, J. D., "The Geographical Distribution of Production in Multiple Plant Operations," *Management Science*, Vol. 2, No. 4, July, 1956.

8. Gutjahar, L., and G. L. Nemhauser, "An Algorithm for the Line Balancing Problem," *Management Science*, Vol. II, No. 2, November, 1964.

9. Held, M., R. M. Karp, and R. Sharesian, "Assembly-Line Balancing—Dynamic Programming with Precedance Constraints," *Operations Research*, Vol. 11, No. 3, May–June, 1963.

10. Helgeson, W. B., and D. P. Birnie, "Assembly Line Balancing Using the Ranked Positional Weight Technique," *Journal of Industrial Engineering*, Vol. XII, No. 6, November–December, 1961.

11. Hoffman, R., "Permutations and Precedence Matrices with Automatic Computer Applications to Industrial Problems," Ph.D. Dissertation, University of Wisconsin, Madison, June, 1959. Also, "Assembly Line Balancing with a Precedence Matrix," *Management Science*, Vol. 9, No. 4, July, 1963.

12. Jackson, J. R., "A Computing Procedure for a Line Balancing Problem," *Management Science*, Vol. 2, No. 3, April, 1956.

13. Kilbridge, M. D., and L. Wester, "A Heuristic Method of Assembly Line Balancing," *Journal of Industrial Engineering*, Vol. XII, No. 4, July–August, 1961.

14. Kilbridge, M. D., and L. Wester, "The Balance Delay Problem," *Management Science*, Vol. 8, No. 1, October, 1961.

15. Kilbridge, M. D., and L. Wester, "A Review of Analytical Systems of Line Balancing," *Operations Research*, Vol. 10, No. 5, September–October, 1962.

16. Klein, M., "On Assembly Line Balancing," *Operations Research*, Vol. 11, No. 2, March–April, 1963.

17. "Location Analysis and Site Selection," *Industrial Development*, Vol. 131, No. 5, May 1962, pp. 5–14.

18. Mansoor, E. M., "Assembly Line Balancing—An Improvement on the Ranked Positional Weight Technique," *Journal of Industrial Engineering*, Vol. XV, No. 2, March–April, 1964.

19. Mastor, A. A., *An Experimental Investigation and Comparative Evaluation of Production Line Balancing Techniques*, Unpublished Ph.D. Dissertation, UCLA, 1966. Also *Management Science*, Vol. 16, No. 11, July 1970, pp. 728–746.

20. Moodie, C. L., and H. H. Young, "A Heuristic Method of Assembly Line Balancing for Assumptions of Constant or Variable Work Element Times," *Journal of Industrial Engineering*, Vol. XVI, No. 1, January–February, 1965.

21. Moore, J. M., *Plant Layout and Design*, The Macmillan Company, New York, 1962.

22. Reed, R., *Plant Layout*, Richard D. Irwin, Homewood, Ill., 1961.

23. Salveson, M. E., "The Assembly Line Balancing Problem," *Journal of Industrial Engineering*, Vol. VI, No. 3, May–June, 1955.

24. Smith, W. P., "Travel Charting," *Journal of Industrial Engineering*, Vol. VI, No. 1, January, 1955.

25. *Techniques of Plant Location, Studies in Business Policy, No. 61*, National Industrial Conference Board, New York, 1953.

26. Thomopoulos, N. T., "Mixed Model Line Balancing With Smoothed Station Assignments," *Management Science*, Vol. 16, No. 9, May 1970, pp. 593–603.

27. Tonge, F. M., *A Heuristic Program for Assembly Line Balancing*, Prentice-Hall, Inc., Englewood Cliffs, N.J., 1961. Also, "Summary of a Heuristic Line Balancing Procedure," *Management Science*, Vol. 7, No. 1, October, 1960.

28. Tonge, F. M., "Assembly Line Balancing Using Probabilistic Combinations of Heuristics," *Management Science*, Vol. 11, No. 7, May, 1965.

29. Vazsonyi, A., *Scientific Programming in Business and Industry*, John Wiley & Sons, New York, 1958.
30. Wester, L., and M. Kilbridge, "Heuristic Line Balancing: A Case," *Journal of Industrial Engineering*, Vol. XIII, No. 3, May–June, 1962.
31. Yaseen, L. C., *Plant Location*, American Research Council, New York, 1960.
32. Young, H. H., "Optimization Models for Production Lines," *Journal of Industrial Engineering*, Vol. XIII, No. 1, January, 1967, pp. 70–78.

PART III

OPERATIONS PLANNING AND CONTROL —FORECASTING AND INVENTORIES

chapter 7

PROBLEMS OF FORECASTING AND INVENTORIES

The design of an operational system as discussed in Chapters 3, 4, 5, and 6 involves a careful specification of the product or whatever is being processed, the specification of the sequence and nature of the processes themselves, and a physical design of the relationships of the processes. To accomplish these objectives we had to consider the design and measurement of jobs and the location problem. We have discussed the design of the production system in the physical sense; however, we recognize that we have not included the *design* of the information and planning system and the extremely important controls necessary to operate productive systems, up to this point. This is not to deny that designing the information, planning, and control aspects are a part of the total operational system design but is merely a way of partitioning the problem into physical aspects, and information, planning, and control aspects. Our present objective then will be to deal with and state the problem of operating productive systems and the design of the necessary information, planning, and control aspects. Let us note that there are immense problems in operating productive systems, which are related to human values, supervision, personnel selection, organization, etc. These are behaviorally oriented problems and are not the focus of this book. We do not deny their impact and importance but simply accept the more limited definition of operating problems and direct the student to seek other books and courses for the behavioral orientation.

Boundaries of the System

Let us first recall how we subdivided the entire organization into functional subsystems in our discussion in Chapter 1. One subsystem described a single function, or a component of a function, which may be executed by many persons or machines in different geographic locations. In attempting to apply the definition of production given earlier, we assigned the *single* function of "creation" of goods and services to production. To perform this function, the production system requires inputs from other subsystems of the organization, such as service inputs (for example, maintenance, supervision, plant layout design, etc.) and control inputs (for example, measurement, data processing, planning, control, order and sales information processing, forecasting, etc.). Although the other subsystems and their functions in an organization could be subdivided in other ways, it is convenient for our purposes to define the following subsystems in addition to the production subsystem just described:

1. *Planning and policy-formulating system.* The function of this system is to adapt basic organization policies to information reflecting present and forecasted future conditions. Conceivably, we could have incorporated this function in the general control function described in 2. In both subsystems, the basic function is the gathering and processing of information with the purpose of planning and control. The only reason for the separate definition of the planning and policy-formulating system is that it has a line authority characteristic which is not a necessary part of the control system.

2. *Control system.* The basic function of the control system is the transformation of information. This function may be subdivided into component functions.

3. *Intermediate organization systems.* For convenience, we defined intermediate organization systems with functions to provide the necessary *service* to other subsystems of the organization or to some subsystems of the environment which directly affect the organization subsystems. We included here such services as supervision, delegation of authority, the transmitting of decisions, as well as the other kinds of service which we have already mentioned.

Figure 1 places the production system in context with the other subsystems, showing the broad scheme of information flow and physical flow between the various subsystems and between the enterprise system as a whole and the environment. Here, the environment represents the broad economic, social, and physical factors, which have an effect on the enterprise system. Figure 2 shows the production system in relation to control subsystems. Here we see that measurements taken from within the production

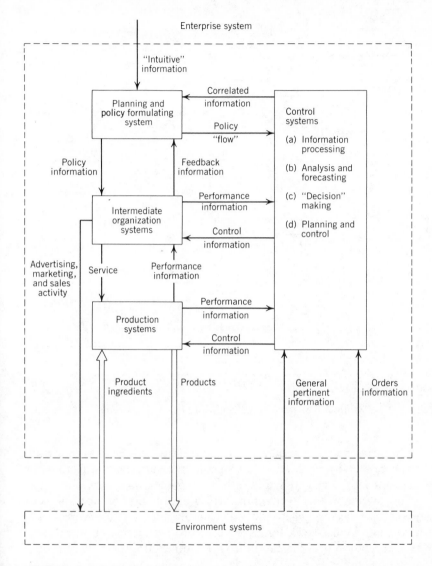

FIGURE 1. Interaction between production subsystem, other organizational subsystems, and environment systems. (Figures 1, 2, and 3 are from J. A. Alcalay and E. S. Buffa, "Conceptual Framework for a General Model of a Production System," International Journal of Production Research, March, 1963.)

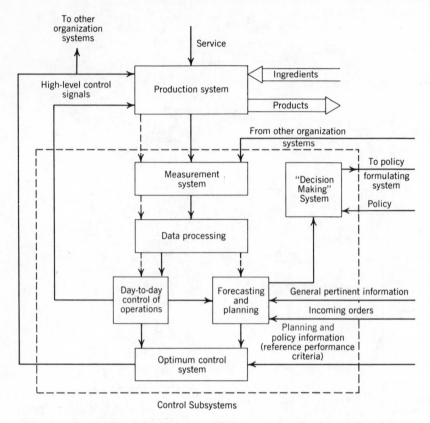

FIGURE 2. Production system in relation to control subsystems.

system (for example, time requirements for operations, costs, raw material, and in-process inventory levels, etc.) together with information from other organization subsystems are fed into the data-processing system. The data-processing system in turn feeds transformed information on operations to the two subsystems for day-to-day control of operations and for forecasting and planning. Higher-level, longer-term control represents an integration and transformation of information from the other subsystems as shown.

A Systems Point of View

The operations phase of the organization is our focus of interest yet we must constantly maintain a systems viewpoint with regard to the interdependence of the operations functions and the other major functions, such as marketing, finance, personnel, purchasing, and general organization service. If, contrary to accepted terminology in management literature, supervision and transfer of decisions are incorporated into a generalized meaning of "service" (the service of supervising or the service of delegating authority and transferring decisions), the single function of the intermediate organization systems could be formulated as structured in Figure 3 as follows: To provide the necessary service to other subsystems of the organization or to some subsystems of the environment which directly affect organization subsystems.

Note in Figure 3 the dotted line enclosing the environment systems of the several reservoirs of materials and equipment, manpower, finance, demand, and the interaction of our enterprise (and the production system) with the competitive enterprises in drawing on these reservoirs.

In attempting to structure the various problems of operations management, reality demands that we consider not only the complex interactions of the factors internal to the operations phase but, where appropriate, the interactions between the operations phase and other functions, as well as their interactions with the environment systems. Thus, the aggregate planning and scheduling problem demands a model that accounts for some of these "between subsystems" interactions in setting production rates and employment levels for the upcoming period.

The first, and perhaps most obvious, environment factor is the consumer demand reservoir where we are in direct competition with other enterprises. Part of the aggregate planning model must include a forecast (represented symbolically by the "level gage") as well as the feedback of information on our actual orders flow (represented symbolically by the orders flow gage). The production rate and employment level decisions also are dependent on interactions with the manpower reservoir (since the decisions may call for either hiring or layoff), on the raw materials and equipment reservoirs to facilitate the production rate decisions, and on the finance reservoir (since the decisions may call for the accumulation or drawing down of inventories). The coordination with other functional subsystems is parallel, that is, marketing in the forecast problem, purchasing in the equipment and raw material problem, personnel in the manpower problem, and finance in the inventory, payroll, and purchasing problems.

The foregoing may sound like, "Everybody is involved with everything, so where are we?" But this is not true if we utilize the power of systems analysis. To develop an effective model for aggregate planning, for example, we do not have to develop a detailed model for all of the coordinating subfunctions. We need only to represent the resulting interacting effects. Thus we do not need a detailed model of the personnel-manpower reservoir complex to reflect their effects on the aggregate planning problem just

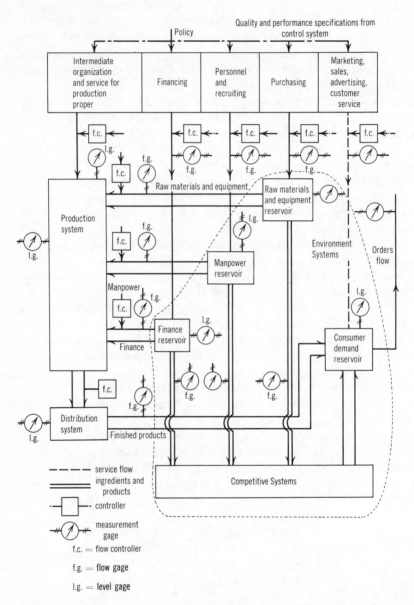

FIGURE 3. Relation among production system, service systems, and some environment systems.

because we may hire or lay off. We can abstract just the parts that are meaningful to the problem at hand. For example, because of union agreements perhaps the layoff rate is limited to a certain percent. Or, because of the competition for labor in the manpower reservoir, wages have gone up. This needs to be reflected in the aggregate planning model since that model will be attempting to balance certain kinds of costs. So a structural relationship similar to Figure 3 is valid for our purposes, since it makes the production system the "center of the world" and relates everything else to it. As long as we, in fact, do relate the interdependencies of the various organizational functions (as we just discussed), we will be utilizing a true systems point of view. Retaining the systems viewpoint is difficult in complex organizational problems, but it is important to attempt to do so to the greatest extent possible.

Ideally, we might like to construct a single mathematical model of the production system within the framework indicated by Figures 1, 2, and 3, which would forecast the operation of any production system given the characteristics of the system and the various related subsystems. This is much too ambitious at the present stage of development of models of operational systems. Currently, we must be satisfied with models that tend to account only for small parts of the problem, which we shall define later on. Maintaining the systems point of view which we discussed helps to minimize the effects of *suboptimization*, that is, the best solution viewed from within the subsystem, but not the best solution when viewed within the system as a whole. In general, our present capability does not permit the strict adherence to this systems point of view. In attempting to approach it, however, we shall endeavor to apply this principle: Models of operations should be as broad as practicable, taking into account (insofar as is feasible by means of existing techniques) interactions between various subsystems. The result is that whenever a reasonably validated model indicates incremental gains which exceed incremental costs we shall assume that the systems view has been approached.

Suboptimization. Because of its importance, let us expand a little on suboptimization. It can and does occur in many ways. We could easily suboptimize by taking a short-range view of maximizing profits or an organizational narrow-gage view. A short-range view might cause a production manager to produce according to the rise and fall of the sales curve, but a broader horizon would look for trends and seasonal variations and develop a production program to meet requirements. The latter view might stabilize production levels, causing higher total inventory costs but substantially lower hiring and layoff costs. The short-range view would be a suboptimization, since it focused only on the payroll cost but ignored the longer time effects and costs of production fluctuation and inventories. The usual economic order quantity model is a suboptimization when it considers the inventory problem in isolation rather than as a part of the production-distribution system as a whole, where costs other than those associated directly with inventories may be important also.

Organizational suboptimization is common where the production function and the distribution function are operated essentially as two separate businesses. The factory, then, will try to minimize its costs independently, as will the sales and distribution function. Thus, sales and distribution will be faced mainly with an inventory management, shipping, and customer service problem and will try to minimize the associated costs. On the other hand, the factory will be faced with minimizing production cost. Each suborganization optimizing separately will likely result in a combined cost somewhat larger than if the attempt were made to optimize the combined system as a whole. The reasons are fairly obvious, since in minimizing the costs of inventories the sales function transmits directly to the factory most of the effects of sales fluctuation instead of absorbing these fluctuations through buffer inventories, and suboptimization is the result. By coordinating their plans and efforts, however, it may be possible to achieve some balance between inventory costs and production fluctuation costs.

The Control Subsystem

The policy and intermediate organization subsystems in Figure 1 are highly aggregated for our purposes, since we wish to focus our attention on the operational control subsystems in relation to the production system. To do this let us examine the block diagram shown in Figure 2 where the broad nature of the control subsystem is shown. We are considering all kinds of controls on the production system at this point, so the block diagram is generalized in terms of a measurement system, data processing, day-to-day control, forecasting and planning, etc. All kinds of controls fit generally into this scheme, but let us discuss the generalized structure in terms of an example, the control of quality.

Quality Control as an Example. Quality refers to specific measurable properties of the product or service, for example, the dimension of a part in relation to standards or the length of time a customer must stand in line waiting. Thus a control system always involves some kind of measurement of what is actually happening. This information is fed into a data processing system where the measurements are compared with standards which have been derived. These standards are based on managerial policies directly or indirectly. For example, there may be a policy in a bank which states that we want to offer customer service at the windows such that the average waiting time is only 1 minute. The standards for a part dimension are indirectly based on a managerial policy for a certain quality level which when translated by engineering design states that a certain dimension must be held to a tolerance of ± 0.0001 inch. Based on the measurements taken and their comparisons to the desired measurements, the day-to-day controls interpret the difference and take corrective action to change the performance of the productive system. For example, if the waiting time exceeds the 1 minute standard by more than say 10 percent, then additional tellers' windows are opened. Or, if the dimension is outside standard limits, perhaps the machine is stopped, the settings checked and reset, and so on.

The simple day-to-day control process is shown in Figure 4 as a control feedback loop, involving sensing or measurement, comparison with standards, interpretation, and control action or correction of performance. The basic control loop shown in Figure 4 then represents the generalized loop in Figure 2, through the measurement system, data processing, and day-to-day control of operations fed back to the production system.

While the day-to-day control process is going on, however, there is a broader "optimum" control system also in operation. We use the term optimum advisedly here and perhaps "optimum seeking" is a better term. This optimum control system is taking as inputs information from the day-to-day control system (short range), forecasting and planning, and policy information to create a broader range (perhaps broader horizon time) criterion of performance. In terms of the bank service example, it may involve studies of future demand for banking service and the planning for needed capacity with the same standard of service, or studies of the service standard itself with the object of revising the standard. In terms of the part

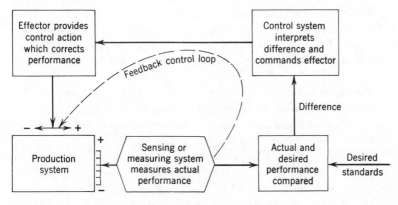

FIGURE 4.   Elements of a simple feedback control loop.

dimension example, studies of actual product performance and of competitive products may produce revised dimensional standards. These corrections of standards involve the additional feedback control loop in Figure 2 of forecasting and planning, the planning and policy formulating system, and a correction of standards.

There is another type of function for the optimum control system however, where optimum operations possibly might not be defined on a day-to-day basis. Production scheduling might be an example where a broader time horizon and broader criterion function are required to develop an optimum control system for production programs. These programs may involve complex models which balance the costs of inventories and the costs of changing production levels in anticipation of forecasted sales. The day-to-day schedule then must fit into the constraints established by the period schedule. The day-to-day schedule in itself may be far from optimum, but the longer range production programs may approach optimality.

Interfunctional and Environment Relationships. The production or operations phase of an enterprise cannot exist in isolation, so we must see how this function relates to other organizational functions and to the environment. This we have done in Figure 3. The dotted line in Figure 3 encloses the environment systems which involve the pools of available resources, such as raw materials, manpower, external finance, the consumer demand reservoir, and competitive systems. The other major functional units of finance, personnel, purchasing, and marketing are also shown in their general relationships to the production system and the environment systems. We have also shown in two ways likely measurement points for use by the control subsystems. These measurements involve determinations of level (shown as level gages in Figure 3), such as might be necessary in determining inventory levels, demand levels, or manpower levels. Measurements for control might also involve determinations of rates of flow (shown as flow gages in Figure 3), such as manpower hiring rates of flow and raw materials flow. We have also indicated likely control points by the insertion of "controllers" without tying these controllers back into the control system as a whole.

The relationships indicated by Figure 3 are meant to show the broad nature of the interdependencies of the production system, the other major functions, and the environment. These interdependencies are of critical importance to an understanding of the operations, planning, and control of productive systems, and we will try to emphasize these interactions throughout the discussion of the problems involved in operating and controlling such systems. As a general example of the interactive nature of problems, let us discuss briefly the construction of a production program for an inventoriable item, such as a small appliance. Stated simply, we wish to develop a production program over the next 12 months, that is, a statement of how much to produce each period. One of the major inputs will be the measurement and projection of demand and its seasonal pattern. This involves the marketing and sales function in forecasting consumer demand level and our share of it (influence of competitive systems). Other inputs are productive capacity and the possibility of expanding or contracting it (availability of manpower and raw material from the reservoirs and coordination with personnel and purchasing) and the financing of the program.

All three of these reservoirs of resources can have interacting effects with competitive systems which may be bidding for the same resources. In addition, we have as inputs to the production programming problem the relative costs of the several resources. In arriving at a production program, we must weigh the relative costs of programs which follow the expected demand curve, thereby minimizing inventory costs but incurring high costs of fluctuating production levels, such as hiring and layoff and the costs of reorganizing production facilities and rebalancing them for new levels. Such a program would require extensive coordination with the personnel and purchasing functions. The opposite extreme, level production, would stabilize employment levels but require an investment in inventories during the slack sales season to provide for the demands of the peak selling season. This program would require extensive coordination with the finance function to provide for the extra inventories, a possibly risky investment due to inventory spoilage and obsolescence.

The models which we shall develop later in the book for the production programming problem deeply involve these interfunctional dependencies, though they may not be explicit in the models. The cost data, policies limiting hiring and layoff rates, union contract limitations, demand levels, and so on are incorporated in such models. As we discuss the operating and control problems of operations management in the following sections, we shall try to maintain this system viewpoint, both in terms of interfunctional dependencies between operations, finance, personnel, marketing, and so on and in terms of the interaction between variables which define the system.

Five Kinds of Productive Systems—Seven Major Problem Areas

Let us now establish a format for discussing the operations, planning, and control problems. Recall in our Chapter 6 discussion we developed the two-part classification of types of physical layouts for productive systems, such as product-process, line-functional, or continuous-intermittent. Later we pointed out that most systems were actually combinations of these two extremes and that there were typical subclassifications possible which resulted in five kinds of productive systems as follows:

- A. Continuous Systems
  1. Distribution systems for inventoriable products
  2. Production-distribution systems for high volume standardized products
- B. Intermittent Systems
  3. Closed job shops for inventoriable items
  4. Open job shops for custom items
  5. Large-scale one-time projects

Recall that the continuous-intermittent dichotomy results in two fundamentally different kinds of layouts. Within the two classifications, however, the basis for further classification is different.

Systems 1 and 2 under the continuous classification both deal with inventoriable items, but system 1 (the distribution system) is just a part of the larger production-distribution system listed as number 2. The difference is solely one of the boundaries of the system which are under managerial control. Some enterprises are simply distributors of products—they do not manufacture. They buy finished goods, store them, and distribute them. The manufacturing phase is outside their managerial control. The reason for segregating system 1 as being separate and distinct is that it commonly occurs in business, the military establishment, and in government as pure inventory or distributing activities.

System 2 includes both manufacturing and distribution within the same organization and involves all of the problems of system 1 plus the problems of manufacturing. System 2, however, has more managerial degrees of freedom since a greater range of activities are under managerial control. For example, the inventories throughout the system can be used as trade-offs for other objectives such as smoothing production. The large automotive and appliance manufacturers are examples of system 2.

Systems 3, 4, and 5 are all intermittent systems, but beyond that the reason for listing the three as separate and distinct is that each occurs fairly commonly and has distinct characteristics and problems. System 3, for example, the closed job shop, is characterized by functional physical layout but produces inventoriable items. The design of the products themselves may be stable, but the volume demands on equipment will not justify producing the items continuously. Most machine shops we know of are examples of system 3 since they are captive shops of large concerns or manufacture a restricted line of products for inventory. System 4, the open job shop, is the custom shop in its field that takes job orders, being the classic concept of the job shop. Its products are not inventoriable since they are produced to custom order, and the orders may never be repeated. Job printers and jobbing machine shops are examples of system 4.

System 5, the large-scale one-time project, is in many ways similar to the open job shop since the product is of custom design. The thing which distinguishes system 5 is its large scale and complexity, being representative of large construction projects or large research and development projects such as missile systems.

Let us emphasize again that the five systems which we have isolated may not occur in their "pure" forms but more commonly as mixtures of systems. The pure forms are more easily analyzed and are typical of at least segments of organizations. Therefore, it is worthwhile to discuss their problems and talk about the solutions which result.

Seven Major problems. All of the five kinds of productive systems have the seven major problem areas to deal with in some degree, varying from near zero levels in some instances to very strongly in others. The seven major problem areas in the operation and control of productive systems are the ones to which we referred near the end of Chapter 1. They are as follows.

1. Forecasting
2. Inventories
3. Aggregate planning and scheduling
4. Day-to-day scheduling and production control
5. Maintenance of the physical system
6. Quality control
7. Labor and cost control

The balance of our discussion on operations planning and control will consider the five kinds of production systems for each of the seven major problem areas. We note again that there are other important problem areas in the operation of productive systems which we shall not attempt to cover, such as organization and other behaviorally related problems. Also, we do not suggest that the list of seven problems in an exhaustive list.

FORECASTING /

Forecasting is a critical input for some of the most important decision models in operations management, particularly those related to inventories, aggregate planning and scheduling, and production control. As we noted in Chapter 3, forecasts are also a critical input to the design of productive systems for they are a direct factor in the determination of the most economical production design of products, processes, equipment, tooling, capacities, and layouts.

Forecasts, then, may be needed for roughly three different time spans: the immediate future on which plans for current operations may be based; the next 3 to 5 years for plans to provide for capacity adjustments; and long-range forecasts on which to base long-range plans for plant and warehouse locations and capacities, and changes in the balance of product lines or services. The intermediate and long-range forecasts involve the study of consumer preferences and trends, the economy, technological development and trends, and so on.

Our interest is in forecasting for current operations and for a reasonable planning horizon time into the future. A reasonable horizon time depends on the incremental value of additional periods of forecast information, and we shall have more to say on this subject when we discuss computer search methods of aggregate planning and scheduling in Chapter 13. Ordinarily if there is a seasonal aspect to demand, a reasonable planning horizon would include one full cycle. Before considering methodology, let us discuss the needs and role of forecasting for current operations in each of the five types of productive systems.

System 1, Distribution Systems. Since the boundaries of the system under managerial control exclude manufacturing in system 1, the function of forecasting is direct in determining the extent of inventories to be held in readiness to meet demand. These inventories must be adequate to meet the expected demand, pipeline or transit stock, and have an amount held as a buffer to provide service in case demand is greater than expected. Thus, demand forecasting is critical since it provides the basis for important managerial decisions related to the entire operation. It is not, however, catastrophic if the forecast is not perfectly accurate (and it never is), because inventory policy can provide for forecasting errors and supplies can be replenished on relatively short notice or be expedited in delivery.

System 2, Production-Distribution Systems. When a production system is added to the head end of a distribution system, the functions of forecasts become more important because the operating decisions based on forecasts as a major input may involve major commitments in the form of investments in raw material, in-process inventories, finished goods inventories, and also commitments to labor.

There are considerable time lags in effecting decisions in a complex production-distribution chain so that a decision to build up the labor force, for example, represents a commitment for some minimum period of time.

If there are seasonal and trend components in the demand, these risks are increased for decisions regarding the pattern of production. The two extreme possibilities, level production or variable production rates to match requirements, both involve risks either for inventories or capacity requirements.

Decisions based on the forecasts cannot be regarded as either right or wrong in themselves, since we face a sequence of decisions where over-estimates in period 1 can be adjusted for in period 2 and so on. Just as with driving a car, which is also a continuous adjustment process, there is a significant reaction time before changes in direction can be effected if a sudden sharp curve comes into view. As with driving, if events take place wholly within the reaction time we can be placed in a very unfortunate position. In production-inventory systems reaction times may be fairly long because of information feedback time lags, and directions set by decisions remain in effect for a period of time before adjustments are made. The reasons for these time lags for making adjustments in schedules are that sales feedback information is periodic rather than continuous so we do not have a clear answer at all times telling us how good the last period decision was. Also, to change production rates ordinarily involves money for hiring or layoff, possible overtime costs, or costs of reorganization for the changed conditions. Before taking action, we wish to project into the future to estimate whether the current downturn is simply a random variation in demand which may be compensated by future higher than normal actual demands.

System 3, Closed Job Shop. In many ways the closed job shop presents problems similar to those of system 2 just discussed since the closed job shop may also produce inventoriable items. But the intermittent nature of production in a job shop makes a difference in the duration of the effects of a decision based on a forecast. Suppose we are dealing with a closed job shop that produces transmissions for an automobile company, perhaps 25 different inventoriable items. Each transmission is scheduled for a production run periodically so that the number produced must satisfy demand over a period of time. To set the number to produce at any one time intelligently (lot size), we would try to balance or minimize the incremental costs associated with producing the item in discrete lots rather continuously. In general, these costs are machine setup costs and planning costs which occur for each lot produced, plus inventory costs which depend on the lot size produced at one time. The order quantity which minimizes the sum of these costs is called the economic order quantity (EOQ). The EOQ for a transmission might be equivalent to three months' supply so the opportunity to redress the effects of a bad forecast occurs less often than for continuous systems.

Systems 4 and 5, Open Job Shop and One-Time Project. Forecasting to guide current operations for systems 4 and 5 does not depend on demand forecasting since all work is on the basis of firm orders or contracts. Current operations are more closely tied to the scheduling function which takes orders or contracts and translates them into demand for labor skills and equipment by a certain time schedule. Both systems 4 and 5 carry no finished goods inventories but instead hold an inventory of labor skills and equipment in readiness to produce. These systems have certain capabilities for sale which are more general in character. Thus, depending on the nature of the enterprise, they may offer a printing capability, a machining capability, a research and development capability in a field, or a construction capability. Thus forecasting future business is more closely allied to forecasting general economic and political events or forecasting the trends in technology in the particular industry in which the enterprise operates.

Forecasting Methodology

The forecasting methodology which we will discuss is applicable to the needs for guiding current operations for inventoriable items, that is, for systems 1, 2, and 3. As we just commented, the guidance of current operations for systems 4 and 5 is closely tied to the scheduling function which we will discuss later.

Components of Demand. Patterns of demand for specific products or services might vary widely but in general can be reduced to five components: average demand, trends in the average, seasonal effects, cyclic effects, and random variations. Figure 5 shows the general situation where four of the components are seen to be operating simultaneously (cyclic variations involving an analysis of the business cycle are beyond our scope). We need to be able to state a forecast for the upcoming period which takes account of all four components.

Looking at Figure 5 the average demand for the entire two-year period is meaningless since the trend is an important effect. Therefore, some kind of moving average is needed which emphasizes the recent experience and estimates the trend effect. Furthermore, the estimate of demand for the upcoming period must take account of the expected seasonal variation. Finally, we wish not to be influenced by the random variations in demand when making an estimate for the upcoming period, or preferably we might wish to state the expected demand with probable limits of variation from the expected value due to random causes.

Weighted Averages. A way of placing greater emphasis on the more recent demand data is simply to weight recent experience more heavily in

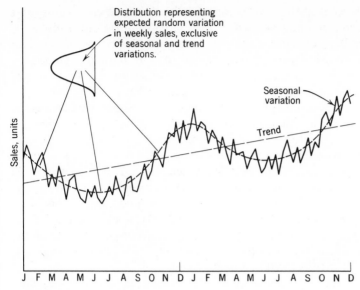

FIGURE 5. *Kinds of variation in demand which must be accounted for by forecasting.*

computing the moving average. The effect of a moving average is also to minimize random variations by averaging. One of the most convenient and easy-to-use methods of accomplishing differential weighting and smoothing is by *exponentially weighted moving averages*. The simplest exponential smoothing model estimates forecast average demand for the upcoming period $\bar{F}_t$ by adding or subtracting a fraction (α) of the difference between actual current demand D_t and the last forecast average $\bar{F}_{t-1}$. The new forecast average $\bar{F}_t$ is then:

$$\bar{F}_t = \bar{F}_{t-1} + \alpha(D_t - \bar{F}_{t-1}) \qquad (1)$$

The smoothing constant α is between 0 and 1 with commonly used values of 0.01 to 0.30. Equation (1) can be rearranged in a more convenient and possibly more understandable form as follows:

$$\bar{F}_t = \alpha D_t + (1 - \alpha)\bar{F}_{t-1} \qquad (2)$$

If $\alpha = 0.10$, then equation (2) says, forecast average in the upcoming period $\bar{F}_t$ will be determined by adding 10 percent of the new actual demand information D_t and 90 percent of the last forecast average $\bar{F}_{t-1}$. Since the new demand figure D_t includes possible random variation, we are discounting 90 percent of those variations. Obviously, then, small values of α will have a stronger smoothing effect than large values. Conversely, large values of α will react more quickly to real changes (as well as random variations in actual demand). The choice of α is normally guided by judgment, though studies could produce economically best or near-best values. Note that an extrapolation is not made.

The time periods represented by $\overline{F_t}$, and $\overline{F}_{t-1}$ are sometimes confusing. First, let us recognize that $\overline{F_t}$ does not represent an extension beyond known demand data. Rather, it is the most current smoothed average used to help guide current operations. In the true sense it is not a forecast at all but a statement of current demand. How then is $\overline{F_t}$ different from D_t? The latter figure is raw data containing components of random variations. The forecast average figure is smoothed to discount the random variation effect. Since no trend or seasonality is reflected in the model, extrapolation from $\overline{F_t}$, to infer a forecast is justified. Therefore, the forecast for the upcoming period $\overline{F}_{t+1}^*$ is taken directly as the computed value of $\overline{F_t}$. (Starred symbols, *, will represent extrapolated or forecasted values.)

Equation (2) actually gives weight to all past actual demand data, though this is not obvious. This occurs through the chain of periodic calculations to produce forecast averages each period. In equation (2), for example, the term $\overline{F}_{t-1}$ was previously computed from

$$\overline{F}_{t-1} = \alpha D_{t-1} + (1 - \alpha)\overline{F}_{t-2}$$

which includes the previous actual demand D_{t-1}. The $\overline{F}_{t-2}$ term was calculated in a similar way which included D_{t-2} and so on back to the beginning of the series. Therefore, the forecasts are based on a sequential process representing all of the previous actual demands.

Trend effects. If there were a trend present in the data, equation (2) would respond to it but with a lag. But the apparent trend each period is simply the difference between the last two forecast averages $\overline{F_t} - \overline{F}_{t-1}$. This difference represents another series which can be estimated and smoothed by exponentially weighted averages just as with average demand. Therefore, the new average trend adjustment $\overline{T_t}$ is:

$$\overline{T_t} = \alpha(\overline{F_t} - \overline{F}_{t-1}) + (1 - \alpha)\overline{T}_{t-1} \tag{3}$$

The expected demand $E(D_t)$ for the upcoming period including trend adjustment is the forecast average $\overline{F_t}$ computed in equation (2), plus a fraction of the new average trend adjustment $\overline{T_t}$ computed in equation (3):

$$E(D_t) = \overline{F_t} + \frac{(1 - \alpha)\overline{T_t}}{\alpha} \tag{4}$$

The term $(1 - \alpha)/\alpha$ is a correction for lag in $\overline{T}_t$, in response to a ramp increase or decrease. Note that the only facts and figures required to update a forecast are α, D_t, $\overline{F}_{t-1}$, and $\overline{T}_{t-1}$, yet all past actual demand data is weighted in the model but with rapidly decreasing weights as we proceed backward in time. If a large number of items were to be forecast, as is commonly true, the entire process could be computerized requiring minimum computer storage for each item, and the only new data to be supplied the computing program each period would be the current actual demand D_t.

Extrapolation and Forecast. As with the no trend model, equation (4) involves no extrapolation beyond known demand data. To extrapolate from equation (4) to forecast D^*_{t+1} requires that we add $\overline{T}_t$, the most recent average trend adjustment,

$$D^*_{t+1} = E(D_t) + \overline{T}_t \qquad (5)$$

Then, to extrapolate or forecast for n periods in the future,

$$D^*_{t+1} = E(D_t) + n\overline{T}_t \qquad (6)$$

Seasonal Adjustments. The basis for including a seasonal adjustment to an exponentially smoothed forecast model is to develop a *base series* which represents the seasonal cycle. A demand ratio of actual to base series demand is then computed for each period. This ratio is then smoothed, correcting for trend effects, resulting in an expected demand ratio. The expected demand $E(D_t)$ is computed through a period by period multiplication of actual period demand D_t by the smoothed ratio. The extrapolated forecast D^*_{t+1} is then computed as the product of the period expected ratio plus trend, and the base series figure for $t + 1$.

See references 2 and 5 for computed examples involving the simplest exponential model represented by equation (2) and the inclusion of trend effects represented by equation (4), as well as examples including seasonal effects.

The exponential smoothing methodology is a competent and efficient way of forecasting demand for current operations. Figure 6 is a record of actual sales and forecast sales for one item of paint at the Pittsburgh Plate Glass Company. Note that the exponentially smoothed forecast tracks the average, trend, and seasonal effects but discounts the most extreme demand variations as being simply random effects.

Of course, there is an entirely equivalent statistical methodology involving ordinary moving averages, trend estimation by regression analysis, and so on, but the numerical work required is greater, and it is not as well

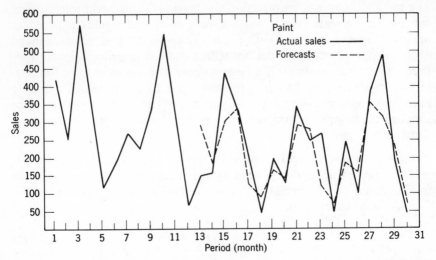

FIGURE 6. Bimonthly sales of one can size of one color of paint. Pittsburgh Plate Glass Co., from one central warehouse to dealers (5 years of data). From P. R. Winters, "Forecasting Sales by Exponentially Weighted Moving Averages," [16].

adapted to automatic computation since considerably more computer memory is required for each item to be forecast.

The use of forecast data is particularly important in the problems of inventories, aggregate planning and scheduling, and production control, which we shall now discuss in that order.

Exponential Forecasting with Adaptive Response

We noted previously that it is common to use fairly small values of α in exponential smoothing systems in order to filter out random variations in demand. When actual demand rates are changing gradually, the forecasting system can track the changes quite well. However, if demand changes suddenly a forecasting system using a small value of α will lag behind the actual change somewhat. Recent research efforts have focused attention on forecasting systems where the parameters involved are responsive to sudden changes in demand [8, 9, 10, 11, 12]. Trigg and Leach [12] propose to detect sudden changes automatically in computing systems by means of a tracking signal. A subroutine then increases the value of α in order to give more weight to recent data. When the system has stabilized, the value of α is reduced in order to be more effective in filtering out random variations in demand.

The tracking signal proposed by Trigg and Leach is:

$$\text{tracking signal} = \frac{\text{smoothed error}}{\text{smoothed absolute error}}$$

The two error figures are smoothed by the usual simple exponential methods. If the system is in control the tracking signal will fluctuate around zero. However, if biased errors occur the value of the tracking signal will move toward either plus or minus one. The tracking signal cannot go outside of the range ± 1.

In order to adapt the response rate of the forecasting system to changes in the tracking signal, the smoothing constant α is set equal to the tracking signal. Figure 7 is a graph of the comparative results of an exponential smoothing model with $\alpha = 0.1$ and a system with an adaptive response rate. Note that when a step change is introduced into the demand series the adaptive system follows the demand change quite well while the conventional exponential forecasting system lags behind the step change in demand substantially. After demand has stabilized at the new level, the adaptive system has reduced the value of α and both systems perform

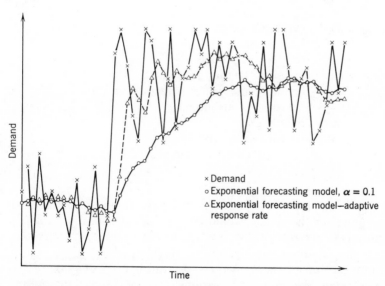

FIGURE 7. *Comparison of performance of conventional and adaptive exponential forecasting models in response to a step increase in demand. From D. W. Trigg and A. G. Leach, "Exponential Smoothing with an Adaptive Response Rate," Operational Research Quarterly, Vol. 18, No. 1, 1967, pp. 53–57.*

similarly. Trigg and Leach [12] also discuss more sophisticated models which take account of trend and seasonal variations.

INVENTORIES /

To see the extent of the inventory problem it is of value to examine the structure of a supply-production-distribution system for an inventoried product where the inventory problem is most pervasive. In Figure 8 we see diagrammed such a system showing physical flow with assumed handling and transit times at each of the stages. For example, the supplier's average two-day time is measured from the receipt of an order and does not include the information time lag from the factory purchasing office and other information time lags at the factory necessary to decide to place an order for raw materials. Similarly the other time values are those related to just physical activities for transit, production, handling at warehouses and delays between handlings, and so on. The point is that these times do not include delays due to lack of authorization to produce or ship. If we add all of the handling and transit times, they total:

> 2 days—supplier's handling
> 10 days—transit to factory
> 30 days—production process
> 1 day —transit to factory warehouse
> 2 days—handling and delays at factory warehouse
> 10 days—transit to distributors
> 4 days—handling and delays at distributor
> 5 days—transit to retailers
> 1 day —handling and delays at retailer
> _____
> 65 days   total

If the system volume were 1000 units per day, the in-process and in-transit inventory for the system would be the equivalent of 65 × 1000 = 65,000 units. Thus the rate of flow and the physical processing, handling, and transit time requirements demand a minimum of 65,000 equivalent units in inventory at all times. We say equivalent because prior to the finished goods stage the units are in various stages of completion, and the value of inventory would increase as we progress through the system. But these are minimum inventories just to carry on the entire process and are similar in concept to liquid in a pipeline. Thus we may call them "pipeline" inventories. The only way we can maintain a system flow rate of 1000 units

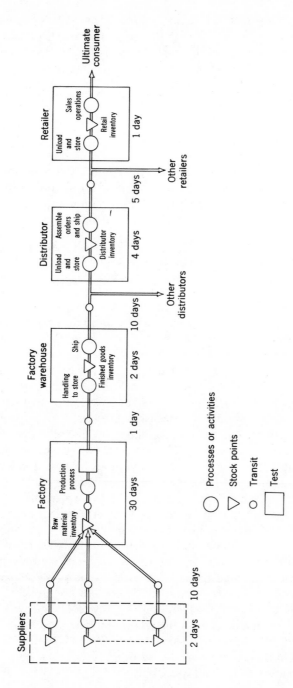

FIGURE 8. Supply-production-distribution system for an inventoried product showing physical flow, assumed handling and transit times, and major stock points (10 distributors 1000 retailers).

per day is to keep this pipeline full. As we shall see, the 65,000-unit inventory level for the pipeline is nowhere near the total inventory necessary for the system, but rather just the minimum necessary to sustain the supply-production-distribution process. If the flow rate increases or decreases, these pipeline inventory requirements will increase or decrease in direct proportion.

Inventories For Other Functions

There are two major factors which will require that system inventories be somewhat larger than those we have computed for Figure 8. These are related to the information lag times in the decision processes and the variability of demand.

Cycle Inventories. First, we must recognize that the system shown in Figure 8 does not have all of the time lags represented in it nor does it recognize how the inventory replenishment process will go on at each stage. In Figure 9 we have superimposed an information system on the physical flow system of Figure 8, showing some typical time lags for preparation of reports, decisions on order quantities, information transmission, and so on. For example, the typical retailer shown requires 10 days to review usage rates and inventory levels and prepare orders to replenish his inventories, and these orders require 2 days to be transmitted to the distributor. The retailer's replenishment cycle is then $10 + 2 + 2 + 5 + 1 = 20$ days (counting only 2 days at the distributor to prepare and ship orders). Since the retailer's replenishment cycle is 20 days, he must order 20 days in advance of the time he thinks he will really need the units, and he must order no less than 20 days' supply. The typical retailer's inventory will fluctuate then from a maximum at the time a new order is received to a minimum just before another order is received. If we assume that the retailer shown in the diagram is the average retailer, his sales average one unit per day, so he orders 20 units at one time each 20 days. His inventory levels fluctuate in a manner similar to Figure 10, with an average inventory level of ten units. Aggregating for the 1000 retailers then, there are 10,000 units in inventory due to the nature of the ordering cycle and the time cycle for replenishment. This cycle inventory is exclusive of the pipeline inventories which are not available for use because they are the average amount of inventory in motion. The cycle inventory, however, represents the amount available to the retailer for sale.

The distributor, of course, has a similar cycle stock. He requires 20 days to review needs and prepare orders requiring $20 + 2 + 1 + 10 = 33$ days for replenishment, ordering 33-days' supply each time or $33 \times 100 = 3300$

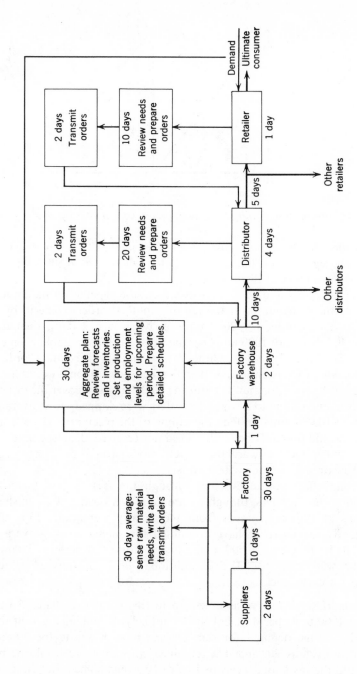

FIGURE 9. Supply-production-distribution system with some information and decision time lags added (10 distributors, 1000 retailers).

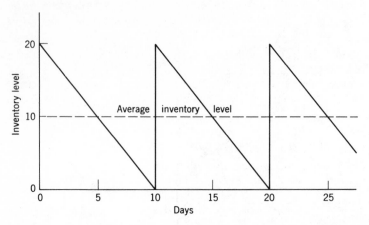

FIGURE 10.   Idealized diagram of the average retailer's inventory level.

units per order for the average distributor. His average cycle inventory is 1650, and aggregating for the ten distributors there are 16,500 units of average cycle inventory at distributors.

The cycle stock required at the factory warehouse depends on the timing of orders for the distributors. If the ten distributors' orders come in by a schedule, with one order for 2000 units arriving each 2 days, then the continuous supply rate of 1000 units per day from the factory could keep up without the need for cycle stock. On the other hand, if distributors' orders all arrive together each twenty days, then the factory warehouse would have widely fluctuating inventory levels requiring 20,000 units to cover the orders when received and falling to 0 when the orders were shipped, or an average cycle stock of 10,000 units. In fact, the timing of the receipt of orders from distributors would probably be neither ideal nor received all at one time, so that the average factory warehouse cycle stock would be some place between the extremes, perhaps 5000 units.

The cycling effect continues back through the factory raw material storage and at the suppliers, though we are no longer dealing with finished goods items at stages upstream from the factory warehouse. For just finished goods, however, we have accounted for 10,000 units in average inventory at the retailers, 16,500 at the distributors, and perhaps 5000 at the factory warehouse, or 31,500 additional units of finished goods inventories for cycle stocks.

Buffer Inventories.   We have assumed up to this point that demand was constant at 1000 units per day, but this is unlikely. Beginning again at the retail level, average demand for our average retailer during the 20-day replenishment cycle is 20, and if it remained constant there would be no difficulty and the inventory levels of Figure 10 would suffice. But suppose the 20-day demand followed a Poisson distribution so that 5 percent of the time 20-day demand would be 28 units or greater. If the retailer were satisfied in offering sales service at this level, that is, not running out of stock more than 5 percent of the time, he would keep an extra 8 units in inventory as a buffer or reserve, and the sawtooth inventory pattern of Figure 10 would be superimposed on an 8 unit minimum stock. If all 1000 retailers did this, there would be an extra 8000 units held as buffer inventories in the retail system.

Similarly, the average demand for the average distributor is 100 per day or 3300 during his 33-day replenishment cycle. His maximum expected demand might be 3500 assuming an even distribution of orders from retailers, requiring a buffer of 200 units, or 2000 for the ten distributors.

Finally, the factory warehouse must be prepared for larger than average demands from distributors, and its replenishment cycle is the longest of all. Production rates are reset only once each 30 days, and once changed it will take 32 days for additional output to become available to ship to distributors. If we take one-half of the 30-day review period and add it to the factory processing time plus transit and warehouse handling time of 32 days, we have an average lag time of 47 days. Average demand in 47 days we assume to be 47,000 units, and perhaps maximum expected demand is 55,000 units if distributors' orders were reasonably well spread out in time over the delay.

System buffer stocks for finished goods inventories then might total as much as 8000 units at retailers, 2000 units at distributors, and 8000 units at the factory warehouse, or an additional 18,000 units for the system. Buffer stocks of raw materials would also be required on some similar basis. At any rate, we can total the finished goods inventory requirements for the system as follows:

23,000—pipeline finished goods units (23 days × 1000 units/day)
31,500—cycle stock
18,000—buffer stock
―――――
72,500—total finished goods inventory

Thus, the pipeline inventories are less than a third of the total finished goods inventory requirement for the system. Carrying the fluid analogy stated previously for pipeline inventories a step further, we may envision a stream connecting a series of reservoirs discharging into the ocean. The pipeline inventories are the stream, and the stock points along the way are the reservoirs comprised of cycle and buffer stocks. The reservoirs can be opened or closed to maintain a flow rate in the stream or to temporarily increase or decrease the rate of flow. The 72,500 units are the minimum required for the system under the stated conditions.

We have already focused attention on the important basic parameters with which we must work if we propose to reduce the system inventories. The pipeline inventories are directly related to the various flow times stated. Reduce these times by whatever means, and pipeline inventories can be reduced in direct proportion. Thus emphasis on transport times in the distribution phase can have an important bearing on system finished goods inventories. Factory flow time is directly related to the design of production lines and other facilities. In the job shop we shall see that flow time is closely related to the scheduling function when we discuss job shop sequencing in Chapter 17.

The cycle stock is related to the replenishment cycle time and to the particular ordering policies used, that is, when to order and how much to order at one time. These ideas will be discussed in more detail in the next two chapters which deal exclusively with inventory models.

The buffer stocks are directly related to the variability of demand and the level of service which we wish to maintain and/or the back order or shortage costs we are willing to tolerate. These concepts of designing inventory systems which take into account the uncertainty of demand will be discussed in Chapter 9 on inventory control systems.

Decoupling Function. One of the major functions performed by inventories is the decoupling function. This function requires no additional inventories over and above those we have discussed but uses the existing inventories. To illustrate the decoupling function let us look at the simple factory system shown in Figure 11. This factory produces several products on only two machines, which perform the operations required on all of the products. Some products use only one of the machines, some have two operations as does the example shown, and some have three operations, doubling back to the first machine for the final operation. The point is that the machinery is time shared. Figure 11 shows the flow from raw material storage through the two machines to finished goods storage for one of the products. The flow diagram indicates that there are six storage delays in the process. Material is stored before and after each of the two machine operations in addition to raw material and finished goods storage. These storage delays cause an increase in the in-process inventory requirements of the system. How can we eliminate them?

The two storage delays that occur after operation 1 and before operation 2 could be eliminated or drastically reduced, by a change in layout that would physically connect machine 1 to machine 2 so that the output of the first operation was directly the input of the second operation. But recall that the example product shares the available time of the equipment. The equipment is used for other products, and the sequence is not always from machine 1 to machine 2. Flexibility in flow is demanded by the particular

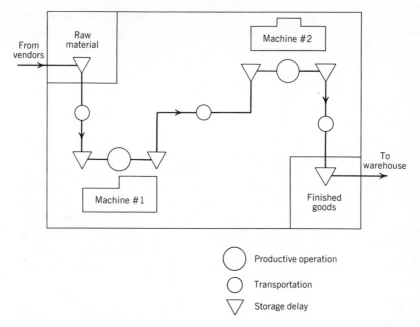

FIGURE 11. Schematic layout of operations and general flow of material.

production situation. If the demand for our example product were to increase to the point where it could more fully utilize the two machines, it might then be worthwhile to allocate the two machines solely for the use of the example product. To attempt to do this in the situation described, however, would result in very poor equipment utilization and somewhat higher equipment costs. The use of in-process inventories makes it possible to carry on the operations at machine 1 and machine 2 somewhat independently of each other. The coordination between operation 1 and operation 2 can be fairly loose. The decoupling effect of inventories in a production-distribution system is an extremely important function in many situations if low cost operations are to be achieved.

Looking back at Figure 9 we now see that inventories have made it possible to carry on all of the various activities, such as retailing, distributing, warehousing, and manufacturing, relatively independently and economically. If we had tried to "cut inventories to the bone" and get along with only pipeline inventories, we would be working on a "hand-to-mouth" basis at every stage in the system. Transport costs would be very high because we could not move goods in quantity. Machine setup costs would also go up drastically if equipment were time shared. Finally, service to customers would be very poor, requiring back orders for all demand in excess of the average rate of flow.

Seasonal Stocks. Seasonal inventories are of considerable importance also but are better discussed in relation to aggregate planning, discussed in Chapters 12 and 13.

Inventories and the Five Systems

Systems 1 and 2. Our previous discussion has centered on systems 1 and 2 so we shall not need to elaborate in detail. Obviously the range of problems regarding inventories depends on where the boundaries of the managerial system are drawn. If the system under managerial control is only retailing, then the inventory problem is one of replenishment by certain policies and rules with the greatest emphasis on choosing what to stock. If the system under managerial control is the distribution system, then the pipeline inventories become a larger fraction of total inventories. When the system under managerial control is a production-distribution system (system 2), the inventory management problem is much larger and more diverse, including raw materials, semifinished and finished goods.

Systems 3, Closed Job Shop. Inventory management for system 3 may include the previously stated problems of the production-distribution system, but in addition another important question is raised that is inventory related, the size of production runs. As we commented previously, small runs or lot sizes will lead to relatively high machine setup and other order preparation costs, while large runs will lead to high inventory costs. Mathematical models discussed in Chapter 8 seek a balance between these costs.

Systems 4 and 5, Open Job Shop and Large-scale Projects. Inventory management in custom shops is focused on raw material ordering and its timing and on allowances for scrap or spoiled work. In large projects, the timing of the receipt of raw materials can be important in minimizing inventory cost. Also the occurrence of scrap in the production process can result in reordering of raw material and the resetup of processes to rerun in order to obtain the required number of good items. Thus, we have a problem of achieving a balance between the cost or reruns and extra inventory costs due to scrap allowances in the original production run.

REVIEW QUESTIONS

1. Select some productive enterprise and develop a block diagram similar to Figure 1, but specific to the organization in question. For the same organization

identify the control points and determine whether the control points are controls over levels or over flow.

2. For the organization used as a basis for the answer to Question 1 isolate three classes of decisions made which are by their nature suboptimizations.

3. For the decisions involved in the answer to Question 2 develop block diagrams which show the interfunctional and environmental factors which enter into each decision.

4. What are the demand forecasting problems for each of the five kinds of productive systems?

5. Show that exponentially weighted averages do represent an average of all past demand data.

6. What is the effect of using small values of α in exponentially weighted forecasts? Of using large values of α?

7. How are seasonal effects accounted for in exponential forecasting models?

8. What are the pipeline inventories of a production-distribution system? Develop a specific model and compute the pipeline inventories for the system.

9. Why are cycle inventories necessary? Buffer inventories?

10. What are the variables under managerial control which make it possible to modify the levels of cycle stock? Buffer stock?

11. What is meant by the decoupling function of inventories?

PROBLEMS

1. Given the following five-year record of monthly demand for a product:

(a) Compute a three-month moving average forecast for the series.

(b) Compute an exponentially weighted forecast for the series using only equation (2) and $\alpha = 0.1$.

(c) Compute an exponentially weighted forecast which takes account of trend effects. $\alpha = 0.1$.

(d) Plot the demand data and the three forecasts and compare results.

Monthly Demand Data

	1965	1966	1967	1968	1969		1965	1966	1967	1968	1969
J	47	22	41	68	82	J	45	56	39	41	71
F	42	44	28	52	62	A	50	50	50	62	45
M	16	42	53	77	63	S	47	39	39	59	81
A	47	29	48	55	64	O	54	44	48	37	77
M	38	46	64	52	44	N	40	24	54	73	86
J	34	45	54	58	71	D	43	46	28	65	69

2. Current values for $\bar{F}_t$ and $\bar{T}_t$ are 62.45 and 0.063 units respectively, and $\alpha = 0.1$.

(a) Compute the forecast for the upcoming period, D^*_{t+1}.

(b) Compute the forecast for three periods hence, D^*_{t+3}.

3. A production-distribution system for a small appliance is made up of a factory, a factory warehouse, ten distributors, and a hundred retail outlets. The average handling, delay, and transit times at the various stages are as follows:

45 days—production process

2 days—transit to factory warehouse

2 days—handling and delays at factory warehouse

15 days—transit to distributors

5 days—handling and delays at distributors

8 days—transit to retailers

2 days—handling and delays at retailers

The average retailer's volume is two units per day, and all other stages are geared to this rate of flow.

(a) Compute the system equivalent pipeline inventory.

(b) Compute the system finished goods pipeline inventory.

4. The inventory replenishment process for the production-distribution system of Problem 3 involves the following delays and decision time lags when reordering inventory for replenishment:

Retailer. 5 days to review needs and prepare orders; 2 days to transmit orders to distributors.

Distributors. 30 days to review needs and prepare orders; 3 days to transmit orders to factory warehouse.

Factory Warehouse. 30 days to prepare aggregate plan, set new production levels, and prepare shedules for upcoming period.

Compute the required finished goods cycle stock.

5. Suppose that the enterprise described in Problems 3 and 4 wished to maintain a service level of 95 percent throughout the system. After making a statistical analysis, it has been found that the retail demand followed a Poisson distribution with mean of twenty units during the ten-day supply lead time; the distributor demand followed a negative exponential distribution with mean of 4,400 units during the twenty-two-day supply lead time; and the factory warehouse demand followed a normal distribution with mean of 124,000 units during the supply lead time of sixty-two days, with a standard deviation of 10,000 units. Compute the system finished goods buffer stock required.

6. Compute the required decoupling finished goods inventory between each pair of production and distribution phases in the system described in Problems 3, 4, and 5.

7. (a) Compute the total system finished goods inventory required for the enterprise described by Problems 3, 4, 5, and 6.

(b) What portion of the total finished goods inventory may be used to satisfy seasonal demand requirements?

REFERENCES

1. Brown, R. G., *Decision Rules for Inventory Management*, Holt, Rinehart, and Winston, Inc., New York, 1967.
2. Brown, R. G., *Statistical Forecasting for Inventory Control*, McGraw-Hill Book Co., New York, 1959.
3. Buchan, J., and E. Koenigsberg, *Scientific Inventory Management*, Prentice-Hall, Inc., Englewood Cliffs, N.J., 1963.
4. Buffa, E. S., *Modern Production Management*, John Wiley & Sons, Inc., 3rd ed., New York, 1969.
5. Buffa, E. S., and W. H. Taubert, *Production-Inventory Systems: Planning and Control*, Richard D. Irwin, Inc., Homewood, Ill., Revised Edition, 1972.
6. Holt, C. C., F. Modigliani, J. F. Muth, and H. A. Simon, *Planning Production, Inventories, and Work Force*, Prentice-Hall, Inc., Englewood Cliffs, N. J., 1960.
7. Magee, J. F., and D. M. Boodman, *Production Planning and Inventory Control*, McGraw-Hill Book Co., 2nd ed., New York, 1967.
8. Nerlove, M., and S. Wage, "On the Optimality of Adaptive Forecasting," *Management Science*, Vol. 10, No. 2, January, 1964, pp. 198–206.
9. Packer, A. H., "Simulation and Adaptive Forecasting as Applied to Inventory Control," *Operations Research*, Vol. 15, No. 4, July–August, 1967, pp. 600–679.
10. Pegels, C. C., "A Note on Exponential Forecasting," *Management Science*, Vol. 15, No. 5, January, 1969, pp. 311–314.
11. Rao, A. G., and A. Shapiro, "Adaptive Smoothing Using Evolutionary Spectra," *Management Science*, Vol. 17, No. 3, November, 1970, pp. 208–218.
12. Trigg, D. W., and A. G. Leach, "Exponential Smoothing with An Adaptive Response Rate," *Operational Research Quarterly*, Vol. 18, No. 1, 1967, pp. 53–59.
13. Schoderbek, P. P., *Management Systems*, John Wiley & Sons, Inc., New York, 2nd ed., 1971.
14. Starr, M. K., *Production Management*, Prentice-Hall, Inc., Englewood Cliffs, N.J., 1964.
15. Starr, M. K., *Systems Management of Operations*, Prentice-Hall, Inc., Englewood Cliffs, N.J., 1971.
16. Winters, P. R., "Forecasting Sales by Exponentially Weighted Moving Averages," *Management Science*, Vol. 6, No. 3, April, 1960.

chapter 8

ELEMENTARY
INVENTORY MODELS

It is understandable that businessmen are concerned about the problem of inventories. It is not uncommon for a manufacturing company to have 25 percent or more of its total invested capital tied up in inventories. On December 31, 1969, the TRW Company had 26 percent of its assets in inventories and the Lockheed Aircraft Corporation had over $500,000,000, or about 39 percent of its assets represented by inventories. The General Electric Company had nearly $1,482,000,000 and the General Motors Corporation more than $3,700,000,000 in inventories in December, 1969. Naturally, if good inventory management could change any of these totals by as much as even a few percent, we are talking about really big money.

The current emphasis in management science began with the analysis of inventory systems. In 1915, F. W. Harris [9] developed the first economic lot size equation, and this was probably the beginning of the use of mathematical models to represent management problems. In 1931, F. E. Raymond published his *Quantity and Economy in Manufacture* [14] in which he developed this idea much further, attempting to account for a wide variety of conditions. In the postwar period, the management science literature has been filled with analyses of inventory and production control systems, partly because of the great interest shown by the government and the military, as well as the interest shown by such progressive companies as the Eastman Kodak Company, the Procter and Gamble Company, Johnson and Johnson, and many others.

Management Objectives and Costs

It is important that models of inventory systems reflect true incremental costs associated with alternate plans or policies. These costs represent "out-of-pocket" expenditures or foregone opportunities of profit. Cost figures derived from the normal accounting records usually do not fit the requirements. The following types of cost items are often incremental costs in inventory models: Costs depending on the number of lots, production costs, handling and storing costs, cost of shortages, and capital investment costs.

Costs Depending on Number of Lots. In deciding on purchased lot quantities, there are certain clerical costs of preparing purchase orders that are the same regardless of the quantity ordered. These costs are important in deriving economic purchase quantities as we shall see; however, the cost figure used must be the true incremental cost of order preparation. It is not correct to derive such a figure simply by dividing the total cost of the purchasing operation by the average number of purchase orders processed. A large segment of the total costs of the purchasing operation are fixed, regardless of the number of orders issued. There is, however, a variable component, and this is the pertinent figure. Quantity discounts and shipping costs are other factors which influence the quantity of materials purchased at one time and, therefore, influence the levels of material inventories. A question parallel to the purchase quantity occurs within a production system in deciding the size of production orders, that is, the number of units to process at one time. Here, the preparation costs are the incremental costs of preparing production orders, setting up machines, and controlling the flow of orders through the shop. Intraplant material handling costs affect purchase lot quantities.

Production Costs. Some of the components of production costs which have a bearing on inventory models such as set-up, change-over, and material handling costs, have been discussed in the preceding paragraph. Certain other incremental costs, however, also have a direct bearing on inventory models. For example, overtime premium and the incremental costs of production fluctuation, such as hiring, training, and separation costs need to be balanced against the cost of carrying additional inventory. In this latter context, system inventories become an important part of the development of production-inventory programs which we cover in Chapter 13.

Costs of Handling and Storing Inventory. There are certain incremental costs associated with the level of inventories. They are represented by the costs of handling material in and out of inventory and storage costs, such as insurance, taxes, rent, obsolescence, spoilage, and capital costs. These incremental costs are commonly in proportion to inventory levels.

Cost of Shortages. An extremely important cost which never appears on accounting records is the cost of running out of stock. Such costs may appear in several ways. For example, within a production system a part shortage can cause idle labor on a production line or subsequent incremental labor cost to perform operations out of sequence, usually at higher than normal cost. There may be costs of avoiding shortages, such as expediting split lots. Shortage costs can be represented by profit foregone as when impatient customers take their business elsewhere. The realization of the importance of shortage costs raises the question, "What level of service is appropriate?"

Capital Costs. The opportunity cost of capital invested in inventory is an incremental cost of significance in designing inventory models. The cost figure itself is the product of inventory value per unit, the time that the unit is in inventory, and the appropriate interest rate. In general, the appropriate interest rate should reflect the opportunities for the investment of comparable funds within the organization, and, of course, it should not be lower than the cost of borrowed money. Since the funds are tied up in inventories, they cannot be used for the purchase of equipment, buildings, or other profit-producing investments. There is, therefore, an opportunity cost of having funds invested in inventory, and inventory models reflect this cost.

Management Objectives. The overall objective of management is to design policies and decision rules which view inventories in a "systems" context so that the broadly construed set of costs we have discussed generally are minimized. In a production-distribution system, the functions of inventories and their effects on costs are distributed throughout the system from raw material intake through all intermediate stages to the final point of sale. The result is that there are interactions between basic inventory policy and production planning, labor policy, production scheduling, facilities planning, customer service, etc. Although there are some operations which may be regarded as almost purely inventory situations, the most usual structure involves an interaction between what we think of as the limited inventory problem and many of the broad policies for operating the enterprise as a whole. We shall begin our analysis of inventory systems with the more limited and simple concepts and attempt to build a structure of concept and technique which tries to account for many of the interactions with the environment in which inventories exist.

The Classical Inventory Model

The classical inventory model assumes the highly idealized situation shown in Figure 1. Q units are ordered or manufactured at one time. The order is placed when the inventory level falls to a point where the normal usage would just use up the inventory within the fixed procurement lead time. The receipt of the order of lot size Q is perfectly timed so that at just the point in time when the inventory balance falls to zero, the order of size Q is received, the inventory balance is increased by Q units, and the cycle repeats. We will find this model useful in establishing the overall concepts with which we will be dealing. Let us establish the following list of symbols:

TIC = total incremental cost
TIC_0 = total incremental cost of an optimal solution
Q = lot size
Q_0 = optimal lot size
R = annual requirements in units
c_H = inventory holding cost per unit per year
c_P = preparation costs per order
c_S = shortage costs per unit per year
N_0 = number of orders or manufacturing runs per year for an optimal solution

Q = lot size, number purchased or manufactured at one time.
t = the time between procurement orders or manufacturing runs.

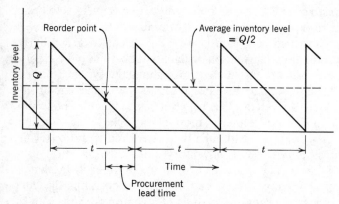

FIGURE 1. Graphic representation of inventory levels in the classical inventory model. Q = lot size, number purchased or manufactured at one time; t = the time between procurement orders or manufacturing runs. Lead time is less than order cycle time.

t = time between orders or manufacturing runs

t_0 = time between orders or manufacturing runs for an optimal solution

Objective. Our objective is to establish a mathematical model which expresses the relationship between Q, the variable under managerial control, and the incremental costs associated with the system. The incremental costs for the simple system we have defined are the costs associated with holding inventory and the costs associated with the procurement of an order of size Q. Therefore, the cost function we wish to minimize is:

$$TIC = \text{inventory holding costs} + \text{preparation costs}$$

We can see from Figure 1 that if Q is increased, the average inventory level, $Q/2$, will increase proportionately. If the inventory holding cost per unit per year is c_H, the annual incremental costs associated with inventory are

$$c_H \frac{Q}{2}$$

If the cost to hold a unit of inventory (interest costs, insurance, taxes, etc.) for a specific example was $c_H = \$0.10$, we could express the inventory holding cost function as $(0.10Q/2) = 0.05Q$. We could then plot this inventory holding cost function for different values of Q as we have done in Figure 2 curve (a).

Similarly, the annual preparation costs depend on the number of times that orders are placed per year and the cost to place an order. The number of orders required for an annual requirement of R will vary with the lot size Q of each order, or, R/Q. If it costs c_P to place an order, the annual preparation costs may be expressed as

$$c_P \frac{R}{Q}$$

If, for a specific example, $R = 1600$ units per year, and $c_P = \$5.00$, we could express the annual preparation costs as $(5.00 \times 1600/Q) = 8000/Q$. As with inventory holding costs, we can plot the preparation costs for this example for different values of Q, as we have done in Figure 2 curve (b).

Figure 2 curve (c) shows a graphic model of cost versus lot size, showing the total incremental cost curve, the calculations for which are shown in Table I. Looking at either Table I or Figure 2 curve (c), we note that the minimum total incremental cost, TIC_0, occurs when 400 units are ordered

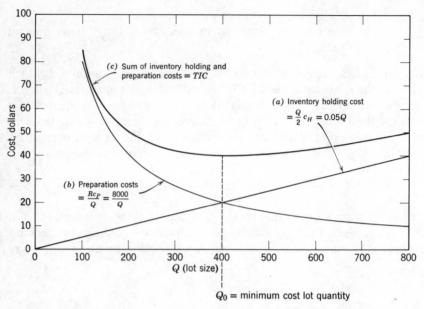

Q_0 = minimum cost lot quantity

FIGURE 2. Graphic representation of classical inventory model. $R = 1600$ units per year, $c_P = \$5.00$, and $c_H = \$0.10$.

TABLE I. Computation of points for cost versus lot size for curves of Figure 2. $R = 1600$ units per year, $c_P = \$5.00$, and $c_H = \$0.10$

(1)	(2)	(3)	(4)
	Inventory Holding Cost	Preparation Costs	
Lot Size, Q	$= \dfrac{Q}{2} \times c_H = 0.05Q$ (See Figure 2a)	$= \dfrac{Rc_P}{Q} = \dfrac{8000}{Q}$ (See Figure 2b)	TIC = Sum of Columns (2) + (3) (See Figure 2c)
100	5.0	80.0	85.0
200	10.0	40.0	50.0
300	15.0	26.7	41.7
$400 = Q_0$	20.0	20.0	40.0
500	25.0	16.0	41.0
600	30.0	13.3	43.3
700	35.0	11.4	46.4

at one time. This is a solution for the specific data given, and we can see that the general form of the total incremental cost curve has a single minimum point. Note that though the intersection of the preparation and holding cost functions does correspond to the minimum point of the *TIC* function for this model, this is not generally true.

A General Solution. Regardless of the data used for specific examples, the general form of the curves are similar to those shown in Figure 2, and we can express the relationships in a completely general way,

$$TIC = \frac{c_H Q}{2} + \frac{c_P R}{Q} \tag{1}$$

This is an equation for the total incremental cost curve, and we wish to find a general expression for Q_0, the lot size associated with the minimum point of the total incremental cost curve. Mathematically, this may be done by finding the value of Q for which the slope of the total incremental cost curve is zero. Using the calculus, the first differential of (1) with respect to Q is:

$$\frac{d(TIC)}{dQ} = \frac{c_H}{2} - \frac{c_P R}{Q^2} \tag{2}$$

recalling that the rule for differentiation of a simple variable $x = ay^n$ is $dx/dy = nay^{n-1}$. For the first term of (1) the equivalent form which must be differentiated is $c_H Q^1/2$, where $c_H/2$ is equivalent to the constant, a. Therefore $d(TIC)/dQ = (1)(c_H/2)Q^{1-1}$, since $Q^{1-1} = Q^0 = 1$, $d(TIC)/dQ = c_H/2$.

Similarly, the equivalent form of the second term of (1) is

$$c_P R Q^{-1}$$

where $c_P R$ is equivalent to the constant, a. Therefore,

$$\frac{d(TIC)}{dQ} = (-1)(c_P R)Q^{-1-1} = -c_P R Q^{-2} = -\frac{c_P R}{Q^2}$$

The value of equation (2) is, in fact, the slope of the line tangent to the total incremental cost curve. We wish to know the value of Q when this slope is zero; therefore, we set (2) equal to zero, and solve for Q_0:

$$\frac{c_H}{2} - \frac{c_P R}{Q_0^2} = 0$$

$$Q_0^2 = \frac{2c_P R}{c_H}$$

and

$$Q_0 = \sqrt{2c_P R/c_H} \tag{3}$$

The cost of an optimal solution may be derived by substituting the value Q_0, in equation (1).

$$TIC_0 = \frac{c_H Q_0}{2} + c_P \frac{R}{Q_0}$$

$$= \frac{c_H}{2} \sqrt{2c_P R/c_H} + \frac{c_P R}{\sqrt{2c_P R/c_H}}$$

Combining the two terms with the common denominator

$$2\sqrt{2c_P R/c_H}$$

we have

$$TIC_0 = \frac{\cancel{c_H} \times \dfrac{\cancel{2}c_P R}{\cancel{c_H}} + \cancel{2}c_P R}{\cancel{2}\sqrt{2c_P R/c_H}} = \frac{2c_P R}{\sqrt{2c_P R/c_H}}$$

and

$$\frac{\sqrt{(2c_P R)^2}}{\sqrt{2c_P R}} \cdot \sqrt{c_H} = \sqrt{2c_P c_H R} \tag{4}$$

The number of orders or manufacturing runs per year N_0 and the time between orders or manufacturing runs t_0, for an optimal solution are:

$$N_0 = \frac{R}{Q_0} \tag{5}$$

$$t_0 = \frac{Q_0}{R} = \frac{1}{N_0} \tag{6}$$

If we substitute the values for R, c_P, and c_H used in our example, we obtain,

$$Q_0 = \sqrt{2 \times 1600 \times \frac{5.00}{0.10}} = \sqrt{160,000} = 400 \text{ units}$$

$$TIC_0 = \sqrt{2 \times 5.00 \times 0.10 \times 1600} = \sqrt{1600} = \$40$$

$$N_0 = \tfrac{1600}{400} = 4 \text{ orders or manufacturing runs per year}$$

$$t_0 = \tfrac{1}{4} = 0.25 \text{ years between orders or runs}$$

An Inventory Model with Shortage Costs

If the assumption that back orders are zero in the classical model is relaxed, we have the graphical structure of Figure 3. Our problem now is to determine the minimum cost order quantity when shortages are allowed at cost c_S. The inventory level rises to only I_{max} on the receipt of Q because the difference $Q - I_{max}$ is assumed to meet back orders instantaneously.

When shortage costs are accounted for, the classical model becomes slightly more general—the model represented by equation (3) being a special case. The rationale for derivation parallels that given for the simple

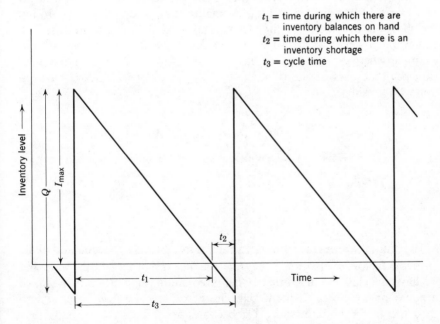

FIGURE 3.   Idealized structure of inventory levels with back orders of $Q - I_{max}$ allowed.

case, but it is somewhat more complex mathematically. Derivations may be found in references [3, 7], and the resulting formulas are

$$Q_0 = \sqrt{2c_P R / c_H} \cdot \sqrt{(c_H + c_S)/c_S} \tag{7}$$

$$TIC_0 = \sqrt{2c_P c_H R} \cdot \sqrt{c_S/(c_H + c_S)} \tag{8}$$

$$I_{\max_0} = \sqrt{2c_P R / c_H} \cdot \sqrt{c_S/(c_H + c_S)} \tag{9}$$

Note that when comparing equations (7) and (8) with the comparable formulas (3) and (4), with shortages, Q_0 is increased by the factor $\sqrt{(c_H + c_S)/c_S}$, and TIC_0 is decreased by the factor $\sqrt{c_S/(c_H + c_S)}$. The influence of shortages, then, is dependent on the relative size of c_H and c_S. If c_H is large relative to c_S, the effect of shortages on Q_0 and TIC_0 is considerable; that is, Q_0 will be increased and TIC_0 decreased compared to equations (3) and (4). If, on the other hand, c_H is small relative to c_S, minor changes in Q_0 and TIC_0 will result. The net effect of shortages costs on Q_0 and TIC_0 may at first seem to be strange. Recognize, however, that when the model permits shortages, average holding costs are reduced because of smaller average inventory balances. This will result in a larger Q_0. For the shortage case, TIC_0 is smaller than when shortages are not included because both holding costs and annual preparation costs are somewhat lower. For example, if we consider shortages in the previous example where $R = 1600$ per year, $c_P = \$5.00$ per order, $c_H = \$0.10$ per unit per year, and in addition, $c_S = \$0.50$ per unit per year, we have the following results:

$$Q_0 = \sqrt{(2 \times 5.00 \times 1600)/0.10} \sqrt{(0.10 + 0.50)/0.50}$$

$$= 400 \sqrt{1.2} = 400 \times 1.095 = 438 \text{ units}$$

$$TIC_0 = \sqrt{2 \times 5.00 \times 0.10 \times 1600} \sqrt{0.50/(0.10 + 0.50)}$$

$$= 40 \sqrt{0.833} = 40 \times 0.912 = \$36.50.$$

The limiting values of c_S provide valuable insight. As c_S becomes infinitely large the factor in equation (7), $\sqrt{(c_H + c_S)/c_S}$, becomes 1 in the limit and we have the classical inventory model of equation (3). This corresponds to a policy of no shortages permitted. On the other hand if c_S is set at zero then the factor and therefore Q_0 becomes zero. This corresponds to a policy of infinite backordering, hand-to-mouth supply, or supply only on the basis of special order.

The Effect of Quantity Discounts

The basic economic lot size formula assumes a fixed price. When quantity discounts enter the picture, additional simple calculations will determine if there is a net advantage. As an illustration, assume the basic data of our previous example, that is, $R = 1600$ units per year, $c_P = \$5.00$ per order, and $c_H = 10$ percent per year. Recall that the economic order quantity was computed as 400 units. In addition, however, assume that the purchase prices are quoted as \$1.00 per unit in quantities below 800 and \$0.98 per unit in quantities above 800. If we buy in lots of 800 we save \$32 per year on the purchase price plus \$10 on order costs, since only two orders need to to be placed per year to satisfy annual needs. This saving of \$42 per year must be greater than the additional inventory costs that would be incurred if the price discount is to be attractive. Under the 400 unit order size, average inventory is 200 units and inventory costs are $200 \times 1.0 \times 0.10 = \$20$. If orders of 800 units were placed, the inventory costs would be $400 \times 0.98 \times 0.10 = \$39$. There is a net gain of $42 - (39 - 20) = \$23$ by ordering in lots of 800 instead of in lots of 400. If the vendor had a second price break of \$0.97 per unit for lots of 1600 or more, a similar analysis shows that the incremental inventory costs outweigh the incremental price and order savings, so that there is no net advantage in purchasing in lots of 1600. Table II summarizes the calculation for all three cases.

TABLE II. Incremental cost analysis to determine net advantage or disadvantage when price discounts are offered

$R = 1600$ Units per Year, $c_P = \$5.00$ per Order, $c_H = 10$ percent per Year			
	Lots of 400 Units, Price = \$1.00 per Unit	Lots of 800 Units, Price = \$0.98 per Unit	Lots of 1600 Units, Price = \$0.97 per Unit
Purchase cost of a year's supply (1600 units)	\$1600	\$1568	\$1552
Ordering cost ($c_P = \$5.00$ per order)	20	10	5
Inventory holding cost (avg. inv. × unit price adjustment × c_H)	20	39	74
	\$1640	\$1617	\$1631

Formal Models with Price Breaks. We may generalize our ideas about the effect of quantity discounts by examining a formal model which takes price breaks into account. Recall that the lot size equation (3) did not need to consider price or value of the item because for every value of Q considered, the price was the same, that is, price was not an incremental cost. Let us now consider a lot size model which includes the value of the item as a factor. To reflect this idea, the total incremental cost associated with such a system may be expressed as follows:

$$TIC = \text{(annual cost of placing orders)}$$
$$+ \text{(annual purchase cost of } R \text{ items)}$$
$$+ \text{(annual holding cost for inventory)}$$

$$= c_P \frac{R}{Q} + kR + k \frac{Q}{2} F_H \tag{10}$$

where k = cost or price per unit, and F_H = *fraction* of inventory value, representing inventory holding cost on an annual basis $(kF_H = c_H)$.

Following the rationale developed previously, we seek the value of Q, Q_0, which minimizes this total incremental cost equation. This leads to

$$Q_0 = \sqrt{2c_P R / kF_H} \tag{11}$$

$$TIC_0 = \sqrt{2c_P kF_H R} + kR \tag{12}$$

The derivations of equations (11) and (12) parallel the derivations of equations (3) and (4).

We may now use formulas (11) and (12) in the analysis of inventory systems which involve a price break. For comparison, let us assume the data of Table II for the first price break at $b = 800$ units. Recall that in this example, the price per unit below the break point was $k_1 = \$1.00$ and that above 800 units, the price was $k_2 = \$0.98$ per unit. To fit in with the present model, we will now express the inventory holding cost factor as $F_H = 10$ percent of inventory value. The other data remain the same, that is, $R = 1600$ units per year, and $c_P = \$5.00$ per order.

In the logic of our analysis, let us first note that the total incremental cost curve TIC_2 will fall below the curve TIC_1. This is shown in Figure 4. The logical thing to do, then, is to calculate q_{2_0} to see if it falls within the range P_2 where the price $k_2 = \$0.98$ applies. Doing this we find that $q_{2_0} = 404$ units, using equation (11), which is less than the break point, $b = 800$ units. Since 404 corresponds to the minimum point on the TIC_2

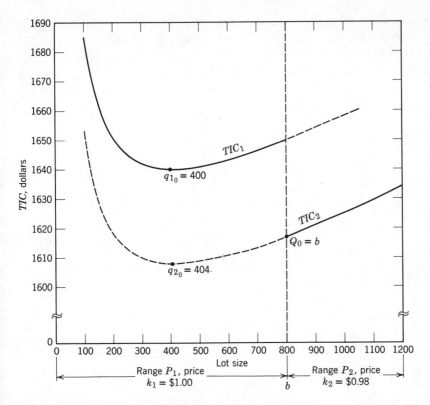

FIGURE 4. Total incremental cost curves for inventory model with one price break at b = 800 units. R = 1600 units per year, $c_p = \$5.00$, $F_H = 10$ percent of inventory value.

curve, we know that the lowest possible cost of TIC_2 within the range where the price k_2 applies is at the lot size $b = 800$ units. If it had happened that q_{2_0} was in the range P_2, this would have determined immediately that the economic lot size for the system, Q_0, was the value calculated q_{2_0}. Since this is not the case, however, we must continue our analysis to see if the minimum point on the curve TIC_1 is below TIC_2 at lot size $b = 800$ units. We may calculate TIC_{1_0} easily from equation (12), and its value is $1640. Also, we may calculate TIC_b using equation (10), and this we find to be $1617. The decision is now clear; $Q_0 = b = 800$, since TIC_2 at lot size b is less than TIC_{1_0}.

Compare these results with those obtained by the incremental cost analysis in Table II. This of course can be seen easily from the graphs of Figure 4. Constructing the curves for each case would be laborious, however, compared to the simple computations required to come to a decision. Figure 5 shows a decision flow chart for an inventory model with one price break, indicating the flow of calculations and resulting decisions. In some instances, the final result is obtained with one calculation, as when q_{2_0} falls in the lot size range P_2 where the price k_2 is valid. Where this is not

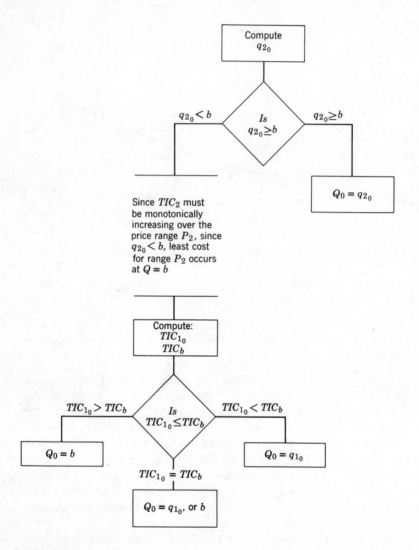

FIGURE 5. Decision flow chart for inventory model with one price break at the lot size b. Price k_1 applies in the lot size range P_1, price k_2 applies in the lot size range P_2.

the case, simple calculations for comparative total incremental cost yield a final result.

Using the same general rationale we can develop decision processes for inventory models with two or more price breaks. Also, models could be constructed for quantity discount situations that also took account of other factors, such as shortage costs and the value added into inventory through the accumulation of preparation costs [4, 8].

Determining the Length of Production Runs

Production order quantities and runs are based on the same general concepts as purchase order quantities, as we have noted previously, but the assumption that the order is received and placed into inventory all at one time is often not true in manufacturing runs. For many manufacturing situations the production of the total order quantity Q takes place over a period of time, and the parts go into inventory, not in one large batch, but in smaller quantities as production continues. This results in an inventory pattern similar to Figure 6 when the run extends over a considerable period of time. When the run time is perhaps 30–60 percent of the total cycle time t shown in Figure 6, the effect on the average inventory of the system should be accounted for. Let r = daily usage rate and p = daily production rate—assuming, of course, that $p > r$. Other symbols remain as previously defined. During the production period t_p, inventory is accumulating at the rate of the difference between production rate and usage rate, $p - r$. This rate of increase continues for the production period t_p, so that the peak inventory is $t_p(p - r)$, and the average inventory is

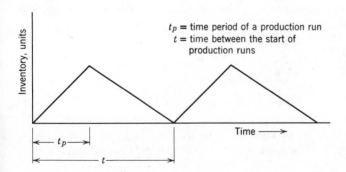

FIGURE 6. Diagram of inventory balance in relation to time when the lot Q is received in inventory over a period of time.

one-half this amount, or

$$\frac{t_p(p - r)}{2} \tag{13}$$

Also, since Q units are produced at the rate of p per day for t_p days, $Q = pt_p$, and $t_p = Q/p$. Substituting for t_p in (13), the average inventory of the system is

$$\frac{(p - r)Q}{2p} = \left(1 - \frac{r}{p}\right)\frac{Q}{2} \tag{14}$$

Proceeding as we have previously, let us now set up an equation for the total incremental costs of the system TIC. These costs are

$$TIC = \text{annual cost of setups} + \text{annual costs of holding inventory} \tag{15}$$

The annual setup cost is as before, the product of the cost of a setup, c_P, and the number of setups per year, R/Q. The annual cost of holding inventory is the product of the cost of holding a unit of inventory per year, c_H, and the average inventory, $(1 - r/p)Q/2$. Substituting these expressions in word equation (15), we have

$$TIC = \frac{c_P R}{Q} + \frac{c_H Q(1 - r/p)}{2} \tag{16}$$

This total incremental cost function has a minimum as with the previous cases, and we may derive the lot size Q_0, associated with that minimum cost in a way entirely parallel to the derivation of the previous lot size formulas. The results are

$$Q_0 = \sqrt{\frac{2c_P R}{c_H(1 - r/p)}} \tag{17}$$

$$TIC_0 = \sqrt{2c_P c_H R(1 - r/p)} \tag{18}$$

The optimal number of production runs of size Q_0 is, of course, $N_0 = R/Q_0$, and the optimal time between the start of production runs is $t_0 = Q_0/R = 1/N_0$.

Production Runs for Several Products. When a number of products share the use of the same equipment on a cyclical basis, the overall cycle length can be established in a way similar to the single product case just described. The more general problem, however, is not to determine the economical length of a production run for each product individually, but to determine jointly the runs for the entire group of products which share the use of the same facilities. If each part or product run is set independently, it is highly likely that some conflict of equipment needs would result unless the operating level is somewhat below capacity, where considerable idle equipment time is available. Examples of this situation are a steel rolling mill that must be set up to roll different sizes and types of steel, batch chemical processes using the same mixing vats, paper-making machines that produce several grades of paper, etc.

Conceptually, the problem of determining an economical cycle is the same as for the one-product case, that is, to determine the cycle length which will minimize the total of machine setup costs plus inventory holding costs, but jointly for the entire set of products.

The maximum inventory for a given product is $(p_i - r_i)t_p$, and the average inventory is $(p_i - r_i)t_p/2$. However, $Q_i = p_i t_p = R_i/n$. Therefore, average inventory can be expressed as

$$\frac{(p_i - r_i)t_p}{2} = (p_i - r_i)\frac{R_i}{2p_i n} = \left(1 - \frac{r_i}{p_i}\right)\frac{R_i}{2n} \tag{19}$$

The annual inventory cost for a given product is then the product of the average inventory, given by (19), and the cost to hold a unit in inventory per year, c_H, or

$$\frac{c_{H_i}R_i}{2n}\left(1 - \frac{r_i}{p_i}\right) \tag{20}$$

The annual inventory cost for the entire set of m products is, then, the sum of m expressions of the form of (20), or

$$\frac{1}{2n}\sum_{i=1}^{m} c_{H_i}R_i\left(1 - \frac{r_i}{p_i}\right) \tag{21}$$

The setup costs for a given product are given by c_{P_i}, in dollars per run. Therefore, the total setup cost per year for that product is nc_{P_i}, where n is the number of production runs per year. Finally, the total annual setup cost is the sum of nc_P for the entire set of m products, or

$$\sum_{i=1}^{m} nc_{P_i}$$

and since n is the same for all products, the total annual setup cost is

$$n \sum_{i=1}^{m} c_{P_i} \tag{22}$$

The total incremental cost associated with the entire set of m products is then

$$TIC = \text{annual setup cost} + \text{annual inventory holding cost}$$

$$= n \sum_{i=1}^{m} c_{P_i} + \frac{1}{2n} \sum_{i=1}^{m} c_{H_i} R_i \left(1 - \frac{r_i}{p_i} \right) \tag{23}$$

Our objective is to determine the minimum of the TIC curve with respect to n, the number of production runs. The first derivative of TIC with respect to n which we set equal to zero is

$$\frac{d(TIC)}{dn} = \sum_{i=1}^{m} c_{P_i} - \frac{1}{2n^2} \sum_{i=1}^{m} c_{H_i} R_i \left(1 - \frac{r_i}{p_i} \right) = 0$$

and the optimal number of runs, N_0 is

$$N_0 = \sqrt{\frac{\displaystyle\sum_{i=1}^{m} c_{H_i} R_i (1 - r_i/p_i)}{2 \displaystyle\sum_{i=1}^{m} c_{P_i}}} \tag{24}$$

The total cost of an optimal solution is found by substituting N_0 for n in (23), or

$$TIC_0 = N_0 \sum_{i=1}^{m} c_{P_i} + \frac{1}{2N_0} \sum_{i=1}^{m} c_{H_i} R_i \left(1 - \frac{r_i}{p_i} \right)$$

Substituting the expression for N_0 shown in (24) and simplifying leads to

$$TIC_0 = \sqrt{2 \sum_{i=1}^{m} c_{P_i} \sum_{i=1}^{m} c_{H_i} R_i \left(1 - \frac{r_i}{p_i} \right)} \tag{25}$$

Where R_i = annual requirements for the individual products, r_i = equivalent requirements per production day for the individual products, p_i = daily production rates for the individual products, c_{H_i} = holding cost per unit, per year for the individual products, c_{P_i} = setup costs per run for the individual products, and m = the number of products.

Let us work out an example for the determination of the cycle length for the group of ten products shown in Table III, which shows the annual sales requirements, sales per production day, daily production rate, production days required, annual inventory holding costs, and setup costs.

TABLE III. Sales, production, and cost data for ten products to be run on the same equipment

(1) Product Number	(2) Annual Sales, Units R_i	(3) Sales per Production Day (250 days per year) r_i	(4) Daily Production Rate p_i	(5) Production Days Required	(6) Annual Inventory Holding Cost c_{H_i}	(7) Setup Cost per Run c_{P_i}
1	10,000	40	250	40	$0.05	$ 20
2	20,000	80	500	40	0.10	15
3	5,000	20	200	25	0.15	35
4	13,000	52	600	21.7	0.02	40
5	7,000	28	1000	7	0.30	25
6	8,000	32	800	10	0.40	37
7	15,000	60	500	30	0.02	42
8	17,000	68	500	34	0.05	50
9	3,000	12	200	15	0.35	16
10	1,000	4	125	8	0.10	12
				230.7		$292

Table IV then shows the calculation of the number of runs per year calculated by equation (24). The minimum cost number of cycles which results in four per year, each cycle lasting approximately 59 days and producing one-fourth of the sales requirements during each run. The total incremental cost from equation (25) is TIC_0 = $2420.

It is interesting to compare now the jointly determined number of runs per year with the number that would have resulted had runs been determined independently for each of the ten products. Table V summarizes these calculations. Note that products 4, 7, and 10 would have two or fewer runs per year, and products 2, 5, and 6 would have more than six runs per year. Magee [10] states a rule of thumb that if "the minimum-cost number of runs for the product alone, for any one or more products is less than half the value for all products, the product is a possible candidate

TABLE IV. Determination of the number of runs, jointly, for ten products from equation (24)

(1) Product Number	(2) Ratio r_i/p_i Col. 3/Col. 4 from Table III	(3) $(1 - r_i/p_i)$	(4) $c_{H_i} R_i =$ Col. 2 × Col. 6 from Table III	(5) $c_{H_i} R_i$ $(1 - r_i/p_i)$ = Col. 3 × Col. 4	(6) c_{p_i}, Col. 7 from Table III
1	0.160	0.840	$ 500	$ 420	$ 20
2	0.160	0.840	2000	1,680	15
3	0.100	0.900	750	675	35
4	0.087	0.913	260	237	40
5	0.028	0.972	2100	2,041	25
6	0.040	0.960	3200	3,072	37
7	0.120	0.880	300	264	42
8	0.136	0.864	850	734	50
9	0.060	0.940	1050	987	16
10	0.032	0.968	100	97	12
				$10,207	$292

$$N_0 = \sqrt{\frac{10,207}{2 \times 292}} \approx 4 \text{ cycles per year}$$

for only occasional runs." Table V also summarizes the total incremental cost which would result if the number of runs for each product were determined independently. The figure of $1932 is $488 less than the total incremental cost figure of $2420 given by equation (25) when runs are determined jointly. The apparent cost saving through individual determination of production runs is, of course, illusory because it does not take account of congestion costs or possible shortage costs that might result from independent scheduling. On the other hand, at low shop loads the interferences and schedule conflicts should not appear with independent scheduling.

SUMMARY

The models developed in this chapter are meant to build a general conceptual framework for the analysis of inventory systems. Although they

TABLE V. Calculation of runs, independently for each product, from equation (17)

(1) Product Number	(2) $c_{H_i} R_i$ $(1 - r_i/p_i)$ from Col. 5, Table IV	(3) c_{P_i}, from Col. 7, Table III	(4) $\dfrac{Col.\ 2}{2 \times Col.\ 3}$	(5) $N_i = \sqrt{Col.\ 4}$	(6) TIC_{0_i}
1	420	$20	10.5	3.2	$ 130
2	1680	15	56.0	7.5	224
3	675	35	9.7	3.1	217
4	237	40	3.0	1.7	137
5	2041	25	40.8	6.4	101
6	3072	37	42.7	6.5	477
7	264	42	3.1	1.8	149
8	734	50	7.3	2.7	271
9	987	16	30.8	5.6	178
10	97	12	4.0	2.0	48
					$1932

may certainly be useful in some situations, they are not meant to be transplanted without modification into practical situations. Rather, they are meant to show some of the kinds of situations and factors that have been accounted for in simple inventory models. Actually, many more situations have been covered in the literature [2, 4, 6, 7, 8, 13, 15, 17, 19, 20]. With a knowledge of the general functions of inventories, management objectives, and the nature of costs which enter inventory models, we are in a position to consider the influence of variability of demand and basic systems of control which take account of these risks, as well as the effects on inventory planning of production planning and seasonal sales patterns.

REVIEW QUESTIONS

1. What is the nature of costs affected by inventories? Outline them and discuss each.

2. What are the kinds of costs related to inventories but dependent on lot quantities? In a practical situation, how do we derive these costs?

3. What are management's objectives in designing inventory systems? In the classical inventory model, which of the variables are controllable and which are outside the control of management?

4. What is the general effect of shortage costs on lot sizes?

5. Why must the classical lot size formula be modified if we are attempting to take quantity discounts into account?

6. Outline the rationale for determining the minimum cost purchase quantity Q_0 when a price discount is involved.

7. How is the determination of a production run different from the determination of a purchase lot size?

8. How does the production run problem change when a number of products share the use of the same equipment on a cyclical basis? Is the problem the same when the operating level is somewhat below capacity?

PROBLEMS

1. Compute the optimal lot size, Q_0, when $R = 10,000$ units per year, $c_P = \$5$, and $c_H = \$10$ per unit per year.

2. What is the total incremental cost for the conditions of Problem 1?

3. How much would Q_0 change if our estimate of c_P was in error and was actually only \$4 in Problem 1? What would be the difference in actual total incremental costs between the two solutions?

4. How much would Q_0 change if our estimate of c_H was in error, being only \$8, in Problem 1? What would be the difference in actual total incremental costs between the two solutions?

5. What is the effect on Q_0 for Problem 1 if shortages cost $c_S = \$1$ per unit per year? What is the total incremental cost of this solution?

6. Suppose that shortages are very expensive, perhaps \$100 per unit per year. What is the answer to Problem 5?

7. Suppose that for Problem 1 a price discount is offered so that orders placed in quantities below 125 cost \$100 each but for orders of 125 or above this quantity the price is \$95 each. Inventory holding cost is now expressed as 10 percent of the value of the item. In what quantities should the items be purchased? Use the rationale of Figure 5.

8. Determine the number of production runs for an item if $R = 15,000$ units per year, $c_P = \$25$, $c_H = \$5$ per unit per year, and $p = 100$ units per working day. There are 250 working days per year.

9. Determine the best production cycle for the following group of products, assuming 250 working days per year.

Product Number	Annual Sales, Units	Daily Production Rate	Annual Holding Cost per Unit	Setup Cost per Run
1	5,000	100	$1.00	$40
2	10,000	75	0.90	25
3	7,000	50	0.30	30
4	15,000	80	0.75	27
5	4,000	40	1.05	80
Total				$202

10. Carson Manufacturing Co. finds ordering costs for its materials and supplies fall into three major categories depending on urgency and the ordinary amount of follow up required. It therefore wishes to simplify its use of equation (3) for use by ordering clerks. For class 1, 2, and 3 items ordering costs are respectively $5, $15, and $40.

(*a*) Derive formulas for the three classes of items.

(*b*) Further examination shows that inventory carrying cost is virtually constant at 18 percent of cost value for all items. Derive further simplified formulas for the three classes of items.

11. Carson Manufacturing Co. converted its entire ordering procedure to the EOQ basis described by problem 10*b*. On examining one of the Class 3 items ($c_p = 40), however, they noted very high annual freight costs under the new policy. Freight costs have been $200 per order under the EOQ policy and would cost only $400 for a carload lot of 500 units. $R = 5000$ units per year, and the average value of the item is $222.22. Should Carson order in carload lots?

REFERENCES

1. Brown, R. G., *Decision Rules for Inventory Management*, Holt, Rinehart and Winston, 1967.
2. Buchan, J., and E. Koenigsberg, *Scientific Inventory Management*, Prentice-Hall, Englewood Cliffs, N.J., 1963.
3. Buffa, E. S., and W. H. Taubert, *Production-Inventory Systems: Planning and Control*, Richard D. Irwin, Inc., Homewood, Ill., Rev. ed., 1972.
4. Churchman, C. W., R. L. Ackoff, and E. L. Arnoff, *Introduction to Operations Research*, John Wiley & Sons, New York, 1957.
5. Eilon, S., *Elements of Production Planning and Control*, Macmillan Company, New York, 1962.
6. Fetter, R. B., and W. C. Dalleck, *Decision Models for Inventory Management*, Richard D. Irwin, Homewood, Ill., 1961.

7. Hadley, G., and T. M. Whitin, *Analysis of Inventory Systems*, Prentice-Hall, Englewood Cliffs, N. J., 1963.
8. Hannssman, F., *Operations Research in Production and Inventory Control*, John Wiley & Sons, New York, 1962.
9. Harris, F., *Operations and Cost* (Factory Management series), A. W. Shaw Company, Chicago, Ill., 1915, pp. 48–52.
10. Magee, J. F., and D. M. Boodman, *Production Planning and Inventory Control*, McGraw-Hill Book Company, New York, 2nd ed., 1967.
11. McMillan, C., and R. F. Gonzalez, *Systems Analysis—A Computer Approach To Decision Models*, Richard D. Irwin, Inc., Homewood, Ill., Rev. ed., 1968, Chap. 6.
12. Moore, F. G., and R. Jablonski, *Production Control*, McGraw-Hill Company, New York, 3rd ed., 1969.
13. Naddor, E., *Inventory Systems*, John Wiley & Sons, New York, 1966.
14. Raymond, F. E., *Quantity and Economy in Manufacture*, D. Van Nostrand Company, Princeton, N.J., 1931.
15. Starr, M. K., and D. W. Miller, *Inventory Control: Theory and Practice*, Prentice-Hall, Englewood Cliffs, N.J., 1962.
16. Thierauf, R. J., and R. A. Grosse, *Decision Making Through Operations Research*, John Wiley & Sons, Inc., New York, 1970, Chap. 7.
17. Veinott, A. F., "The Status of Mathematical Inventory Theory," *Management Science*, Vol. 12, No. 11, July 1966 (includes an exhaustive bibliography at end of paper).
18. Voris, W., *Production Control*, Richard D. Irwin, Homewood, Ill., 3rd ed., 1966.
19. Wagner, H. N., *Statistical Management of Inventory Systems*, John Wiley & Sons, New York, 1962.
20. Whitin, T. M., *The Theory of Inventory Management*, Princeton University Press, Princeton, N.J., 1953.

chapter 9

INVENTORY CONTROL SYSTEMS

Some of the major defects in the models developed in the previous chapter, so far as practical inventory policy is concerned, are the assumptions that requirements were known exactly and that the delivery of replenishment orders was perfectly timed. Also, those models did not place the inventory system in the context of the operating environment of the broader production-distribution system. In this chapter we shall attempt to introduce the idea of variability of demand and its influence on inventory policy, consider comparative systems for inventory control which take account of demand variability, and consider the impact of inventories on the problem of controlling production levels. In part V we shall develop models which focus on the impact of inventories in making aggregate production plans or programs, particularly in Chapter 13.

Variability of Demand

The source of our problem in dealing with variability of demands or requirements is focused on the lags inherent in the system for replenishment. If we could fill requirements immediately, there would be no problem. The elements of the problems caused by lags in the system were introduced in Chapter 7.

As we know, the demand for an item may vary considerably owing to random causes, upward or downward trends in demand, seasonal and cyclic variations. Figure 1 shows a sales curve which demonstrates three of these factors (cyclic variations dealing with the concept of the business cycle are beyond our scope). Let us begin with a consideration of expected random variation and how realistic inventory policy might take it into account. Figure 2 abstracts from Figure 1 just the random variations in sales from average expected levels. Such a distribution could be abstracted from sales records from which the trend and seasonal factors have been removed, through commonly known statistical procedures. The residual variation is then simply the variation due to chance causes, comparable in every way to expected random variation in any process.

Buffer Stocks. The variations in demand are absorbed through the provision of buffer stocks which must be maintained because of our inability to forecast random variations in demand of the type shown by Figure 2. The size of these planned extra inventories depends on the stability of demand in relation to our willingness to run out of stock. If we are determined almost never to run out of stock, these planned minimum balances must be very high. If service requirements permit stock runouts and back ordering, the safety stocks can be moderate. Figure 3 shows the general structure of inventory balance with a fixed-order quantity system.

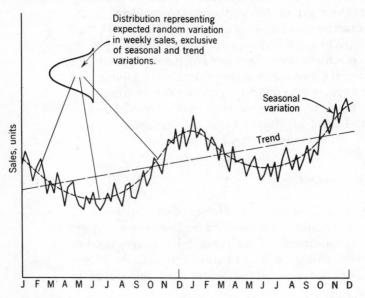

FIGURE 1. Three kinds of variation in demand which introduce risks into inventory policy.

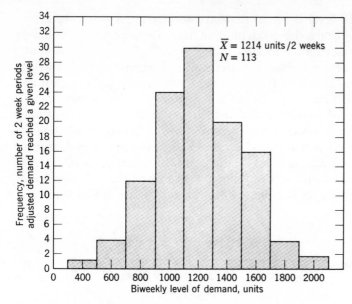

FIGURE 2. Distribution representing expected random variation in weekly sales, exclusive of seasonal and trend variations.

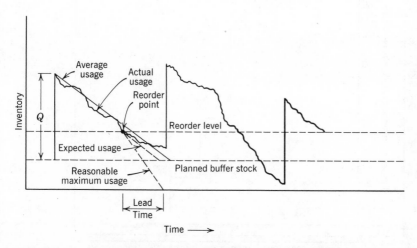

FIGURE 3. Structure of inventory balance for a fixed order quantity system, with safety stocks to absorb fluctuations in demand and in supply time. The buffer stock level is set so that a reasonable figure for maximum usage would draw down the inventory to zero during the lead time. Q is a fixed quantity ordered each cycle.

The buffer stock level is set so that inventory balances would be drawn down to zero during the constant lead time for supply, if we should experience near-maximum demand.

The rational determination of buffer stocks, then, turns on a knowledge of the probability distribution of demand together with a decision regarding the risk of stock runout that we are willing to accept. To be most useful, the probability distribution of demand can be expressed in a form shown by Figure 4. Figure 4 was constructed from Figure 2, first, by plotting the number of periods that adjusted demand exceeded a given level, second, by establishing a percentage scale to represent a derived probability scale, and third, by idealizing the distribution as shown by the dashed curve of Figure 4. Since the approximate average two-week usage is 1214 units, and

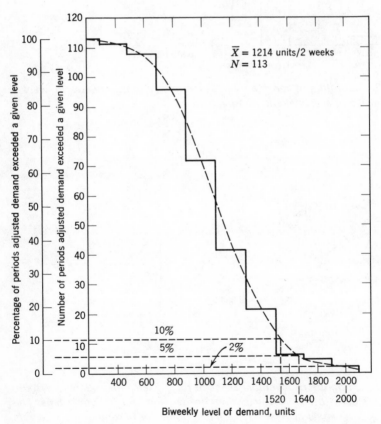

FIGURE 4. Distribution of percent of periods that demand exceeded a given level, developed from Figure 2.

assuming a normal lead time of 2 weeks, we could be 90 percent sure of not running out of stock by having the 1520 units on hand when the replenishment order is placed. The buffer stock is then $1520 - 1214 = 306$ units. If we wish to be 95 percent sure of not running out of stock, the buffer stock must be $1640 - 1214 = 426$ units. Similarly, to be sure that we have only a 2 percent risk of running out of stock, the buffer stock level must be increased to 768 units.

It is easy to see from the shape of the demand curve that, for high levels of protection, the buffer stock required goes up rapidly, and, therefore, the cost of providing this assurance goes up. This is shown by the calculations in Table I where we have assumed the demand curve of Figure 4, assigning a value of $50 to the item and inventory holding costs of 20 percent of value. The average inventory required to cover expected maximum usage rates during the lead time of 2 weeks is calculated for the three service levels shown. To offer service at the 95 percent level instead of the 90 percent level requires an incremental $1200 per year, but to move to the 98 percent level of service from the 95 percent level requires an additional $3600 in inventory cost.

The demand curve, then, provides a rational basis for the determination of buffer stock levels by helping to establish a reasonable maximum usage rate during the lead time. To establish this rate, however, management must decide what risk of stock runout is acceptable. In some instances this must be a judgment, but where a cost of shortages can be realistically assigned, a simple incremental cost analysis can determine whether additional protection is worthwhile. For example, for the data shown in Table I, there would be an incremental saving of $1578 in moving from the 90

TABLE I.   Cost of providing the three levels of service shown in figure 4, when the item is valued at $50 each and inventory holding costs are 20 percent

	Service Level		
	90%	95%	98%
Expected maximum usage for 2-week replenishment time	1520	1640	2000
Buffer stock required	306	426	786
Average inventory required for service level during replenishment period = $(I_{max} - Buffer)/2 + Buffer$	913	1033	1393
Value of average inventory at $50 per unit	$45,650	$51,650	$69,650
Inventory cost at 20%	$ 9,130	$10,330	$13,930

percent to the 95 percent level of service if the cost of a shortage was $1 each (1214 × 26 × 0.05 × 1.00). This incremental gain exceeds the incremental cost of $1200 shown in Table I. On the other hand, to move from the 95 percent to the 98 percent level the incremental gain is only $950 whereas the incremental cost is $3600 as shown in Table I. The 98 percent level of service is obviously too expensive in this instance.

In summary, we have a fairly general procedure. To determine buffer stocks, we must determine reasonable maximum usage rates during the lead time, and this requires the derivation of a demand distribution which reflects only the variation due to random fluctuations. Here, however, management must decide on a risk level for running out of stock, or if realistic shortage costs can be assigned, an incremental cost study can be made to determine the best risk level. If demand for the item is subject to seasonal variation or an upward or downward trend, the average of the distribution shifts, and it is necessary to reassess buffer stock level periodically. In such an instance, it would be better to express the demand distribution curve shown in Figure 4 in terms of deviations from expected mean values.

Practical Methods for Determining Buffer Stocks

The generalized methodology for setting buffer stocks when lead times are constant (just discussed) is too cumbersome for use in practical systems where large numbers of items may be involved. Computations are simplified considerably if we can justify the assumption that the demand distribution follows some particular mathematical function, such as the normal, Poisson, or negative exponential distributions. The general procedure is the same for all distributions: (a) determine the applicability of the normal, Poisson, or negative exponential distribution of demand *during lead time*, (b) establish a service level based on managerial policy or an assessment of the balance of costs, (c) define D_{max} during lead time based on the appropriate distribution and the service level, for example, if we have selected a service level of 10 percent then D_{max} is 1520 units in Figure 4, and (d) compute the required buffer stock from $B = D_{max} - \bar{D}$ where $\bar{D}$ is average demand and both D_{max} and $\bar{D}$ are based on the demand distribution over the constant lead time.

The three distributions have been found to be applicable in a number of situations at different stages in the supply-production-distribution system. For example, the normal distribution has been found to describe adequately many demand functions at the factory level, the Poisson distribution at the retail level, and the negative exponential distribution at the wholesale and retail levels [4]. When both demand and lead time are variable the determination of buffer stocks is more complex. In this situation, we are faced with an interaction between fluctuating demand and fluctuating lead times, and there is no simple mathematical analysis. Nevertheless, buffer stocks can be determined through a process of Monte Carlo simulation as long as we have a knowledge of the demand and lead time distributions. Since the simulation methodology is being used in such a situation, the distributions need not be described by any of the standard mathematical ones. Detailed examples of inventory models with variable demand and lead time are developed in reference [11].

Basic Inventory Control Systems

In attempting to develop automatic control systems for inventories, it is necessary to take account of random fluctuations in demand as just discussed and actual shifts in average demand of either a seasonal or long-term nature. The variables of the system which can be manipulated by management to develop a control system are the size of the replenishment order, the frequency of replenishment orders, the frequency of review and forecast of usage levels, and the method of information feedback on which the reviews are based. Alternate inventory control systems blend these factors in somewhat different ways.

The Fixed-Order Quantity System. This system is diagrammed in Figure 3. The system has a reorder level set which allows the inventory level to be drawn down to the buffer stock level within the lead time if average usage rates are experienced. Replenishment orders are placed in a fixed predetermined amount (not necessarily the minimum cost quantity, Q_0) timed to be received at the end of the lead time. The maximum inventory level becomes the order quantity Q plus the buffer stock I_{min}. The average inventory expected is, then $I_{min} + Q/2$. Usage rates are reviewed periodically in an attempt to react to seasonal or long-term trends of the type shown in Figure 1. At the time of the periodic reviews, the order quantity and buffer stock levels may be changed to reflect the new conditions. Demand for an item is ordinarily taken from the subsequent operation. Assume that we are considering the can of the capacitor shown in Figure 4 of Chapter 3. The capacitor is made in three sizes of electrical capacity. The can which houses the capacitor, however, is identical for all three sizes.

Figure 5 shows the chain of demand for the can as reflected back through the series of stock points and manufacturing operations. Customer orders are placed at the warehouse which maintains an inventory with controls

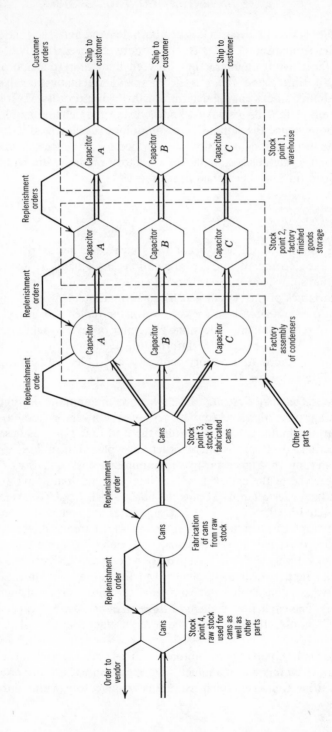

FIGURE 5. Chain of demand for the capacitor can, shown in Figure 4 of Chapter 3.

as described by Figure 3. When the warehouse inventory level falls to the reorder point, a replenishment order is sent to the factory, and the factory ships from its finished goods stock. When the finished goods inventory falls to a reorder point, however, a requisition is sent to the manufacturing department, and more condensers are assembled. To assemble the condensers, however, cans and other parts are requisitioned from stock point 3, a stock of fabricated cans. When the stock of fabricated cans falls to a reorder level, a shop order is written for a run of cans to be fabricated. The shop order requires raw stock which is drawn from stock point 4, raw material storage. When the inventory for the raw material falls to the reorder level, a purchase requisition is issued to vendors for replacement. Thus the demand for the capacitor can is reflected back in a chain involving 4 stock points and 2 factory operations. Figure 5 represents the structure of the information feedback system.

Fixed-reorder quantity systems are common where a perpetual inventory record is kept and with low-valued items such as nuts and bolts, where the inventory level is under rather continuous surveillance so that notice can be given when the reorder level is reached. One of the simplest methods for maintaining this close watch on inventory level is the use of the "two bin" system. In this system, the inventory is physically separated into two bins, one of which contains an amount equal to the reorder level. The balance of the stock is placed in the other bin, and day-to-day needs are drawn from it until it is empty. At that point it is obvious that the reorder level has been reached, and a stock requisition is issued. From that point on, stock is drawn from the second bin, which contains an amount equal to average usage over the lead time plus a buffer stock. When the stock is replenished by the receipt of the order, the physical segregation into two bins is made again and the cycle is repeated.

Fixed-reorder Cycle Systems. These systems focus control on a periodic basis, so that orders are placed weekly, monthly, or by some other cycle. The size of the order, however, is varied for each cycle to absorb the fluctuations in usage from period to period, as shown by Figure 6. The amount ordered covers normal usage during the procurement lead time plus the quantity necessary to replenish inventories to the level required for one cycle's usage plus buffer stock. This is, of course, the I_{max} level shown on Figure 6. Just as with lot size models, optimal relationships for the reorder cycle and I_{max} can be derived. See references [9, 13]. As with the fixed-quantity system, periodic reviews of usage rates are required to react to changes in the average usage rates of the type shown in Figure 1. Fixed-reorder cycle systems are prominent with higher valued items and where a large number of items are regularly ordered from the same vendor. With fixed-cycle ordering, freight cost advantages can often be gained by grouping these orders together for shipment. The common information feedback system for fixed-cycle systems is diagrammed in Figure 5, based on a chain of demand.

The main operating difficulties with the fixed cycle system described lie in the time lags in the information chain, and the apparently irresistible temptation to outguess shifts in requirement rates. The shifts in usage rates are most often simply random shifts, and the buffer stock has been designed to absorb these variations. If we respond to these random shifts in requirements we will surely drive ourselves insane. Suppose we are ordering on a monthly cycle the fabrication of cans for stock point 3 of Figure 5. Average requirements have been 500 cans monthly, but last month's requirements jumped to 600 units. If we assume that this will be a continuing requirement, we might decide to place an order for the current month which not only replenishes the 600 units drawn, but adds another 100 units to build up inventory to meet the expected continuation of 600 units per month. This makes a total order of 700 units. Suppose, however, that last months increase was simply a random fluctuation, and in a true expression of the capriciousness of random processes, requirements for this period turn out to be only 300 units. We now have a 400-unit excess inventory, and we need place an order for only 100 units for the coming period to meet average requirements. The result is that the random variations in demand from 600 units to 300 units have been translated into variations in shop orders for cans ranging from 700 units to 100 units. Demand variability has been amplified, leading to severe problems on the production floor in attempting to accommodate these wide variations.

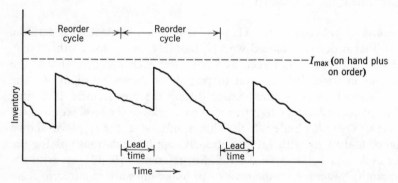

FIGURE 6. Fixed reorder cycle system of control. An order is placed at regular intervals which replenishes stock, based on the inventory balance on hand and on order plus the amount needed for one cycle.

The question of amplification of demand variability is of extreme importance in designing stable production-inventory control systems, and we shall consider it more carefully at a later point. The immediate question is, however, "How can we tell if a change in demand is merely a random fluctuation or a true shift in average requirements?" We have an obvious application of the principles of statistical control. Appropriate control limits could be established and requirements plotted in relation to the control limits. Variations in requirements that fall within the control limits may be ignored, since buffer stocks were designed to absorb them. When points fall outside the control limits the question may be raised whether planning figures for average requirements should be revised. Even then, adjustments in planning figures for requirements should be relatively modest, taking a wait and see attitude, in order to avoid the costly results of fluctuations as in the situation described in the previous paragraph.

Control Theory Applied to Inventory Systems. Engineers have been interested in the design of automatic control systems, and the result has been the development of concepts and systems of control which have been

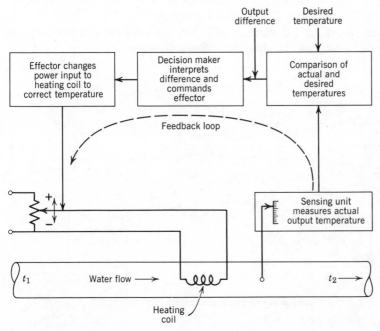

FIGURE 7. Diagram of elements of an automatic system for maintaining a given output temperature of water flow. The basic components of the feedback loop are common to automatic control systems.

applied largely in automation and other physical systems. These self-correcting systems establish automatic control over some variable (a dimension, temperature, pressure, etc.) through a feedback loop. Conceptually, the feedback loop is comprised of some *sensing unit* which measures the output of the variable being controlled, a *comparator* which compares the actual output with the desired level, and a *decision maker* which interprets the error information and finally commands the *effector* to make a correction in the proper magnitude and direction so that output will meet standards. Figure 7 shows a schematic representation of the maintenance of the temperature of flowing water under automatic control.

Many management control problems can be viewed in the same conceptual framework. For example, Figure 8 shows a diagram for information feedback, for the control of inventories and production levels. The parallels between the physical system and the inventory system are direct. From the principles of process control, we can learn some basic control concepts of considerable value in controlling inventories. These concepts are related to time lags and their effect on the stability of the system. Let us see what actual dynamic effects we might expect from an inventory system which was originally stable and now is stimulated by a 10 percent step increase in retail sales, the new sales level remaining stable.

Forrester [8], using a dynamic simulation model of the system shown in Figure 9 demonstrates the dynamic effects dramatically. There are three

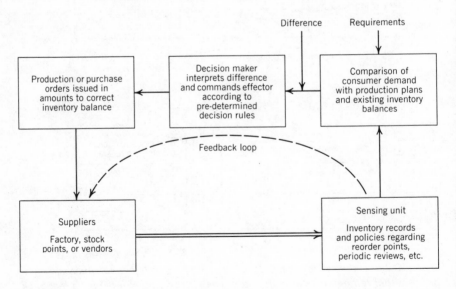

FIGURE 8. Information feedback loop for an inventory control system.

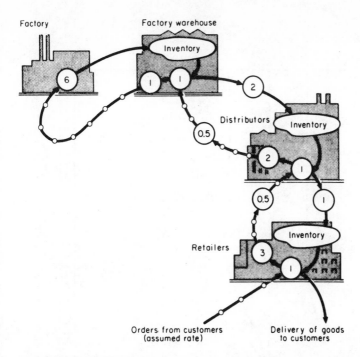

Factory

Factory warehouse

Inventory

6

1 1

2

Distributors

Inventory

0.5

2

1

0.5

1

Inventory

Retailers

3

1

Orders from customers
(assumed rate)

Delivery of goods
to customers

FIGURE 9.   Structure of a production-distribution system. Solid lines represent physical flow, lines with dots represent information flow, and circled numbers represent time delays in weeks. From J. Forrester, Industrial Dynamics,, [8].

levels of inventories in the system: factory warehouses, distributor, and retailer. The circled lines show the flow of orders for goods from customers to retailers, retailers to distributors, distributors to factory warehouse, and finally from the warehouse as orders for the factory to produce. The solid lines show the flow of the physical goods between each of the levels of the structure in response to the orders. The circled numbers represent the time delays in weeks for each of the activities to take place. Figure 10 shows the effect of the 10 percent step increase in retail sales on inventories at the three levels, as well as on factory production output. Whereas the sales increase was simple and orderly, the response of the inventory and production system shows wild oscillations which increase in magnitude as we go up stream in the system from the retail level to the distributor, factory warehouse, and to the actual factory output. As we will demonstrate in Chapter 21, reducing the time lags in the system, for example, by eliminating the distributor level, or reducing the time for clerical delays will reduce considerably the magnitude of the fluctuations.

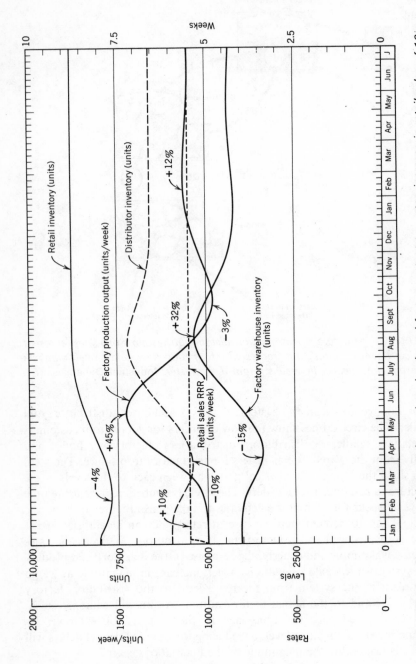

FIGURE 10. *Response of inventories at three levels and factory output to a step increase in retail sales of 10 percent. Adapted from J. Forrester, Industrial Dynamics, [8].*

More direct information feedback to the various stock points instead of through the chain of demand shown in Figure 5 will have important effects in stabilizing the entire system. We consider these dynamic effects more carefully and in greater detail in our Chapter 21 discussion of large-scale system simulation. At this point, however, a conclusion we might draw is that a more direct information feedback system similar to that shown in Figure 11 for the capacitor can production-inventory system will have a stabilizing effect so that no amplification of demand *variability* will take place at stock points up stream from the consumer inventory level. At each stock point in the system, then, we are working against actual consumer demand rather than against the secondary and tertiary effects of demand as reflected back through the chain. Reducing the lag in information flow has a stabilizing effect, regardless of the inventory system used and would be appropriate for both the fixed quantity and fixed cycle systems.

Base Stock System. The base stock system [10] is a blend of the fixed quantity and fixed cycle systems which uses an information feedback system similar to that diagrammed in Figure 11. In this system, stock levels are reviewed on a periodic basis, but orders are placed only when inventories have fallen to a predetermined "reorder level." At this point an order is placed to replenish inventories to the "base stock" level, which is sufficient for buffer stock plus a fixed quantity calculated to cover current usage needs. Periodic reviews of current usage rates can result in upward or downward revisions in the base stock levels. The base stock system has the advantages of close control associated with the fixed cycle system which makes it possible to carry minimum buffer stocks. On the other hand, since replenishment orders are placed only when the reorder point has been reached, fewer orders, on the average, are placed so that order costs are comparable to those associated with the fixed quantity systems. Since all stock points are working against consumer demand, we do not have the amplification of demand variability at points up stream. Therefore, buffer stocks can be reduced even further, since the extreme levels of maximum demand are not experienced. Another result is a reduction in the cost of production fluctuations (hiring, separation, and training), since smaller production fluctuations are also associated with the type of information feedback system used.

In the sections just completed we tried to show the influence of variability of demand on inventory models, and the importance of time lags in the system as a whole. The important concept to carry over into this section is that inventory models must take account of the environment in which they are operated and cannot be considered as an isolated problem.

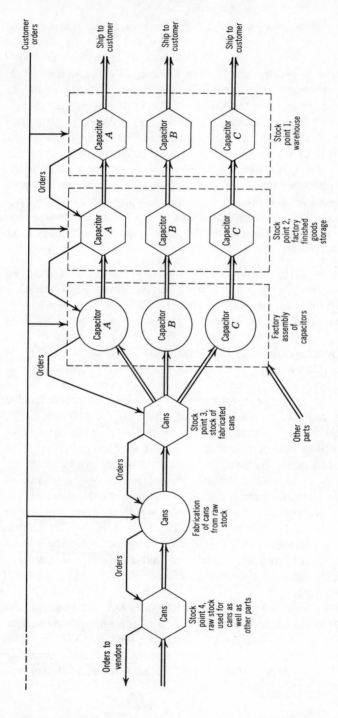

FIGURE 11. Current demand from customers fed back directly to stock points and operations so that all links in the production-inventory chain work against current demand.

We shall focus on the problem of operating a production-inventory system through the controlling of production levels. As we shall see, inventories play a major role.

Controlling Production Levels

When a basic production-inventory program has been developed, the result is a schedule of planned production levels and inventory balances based on forecasts of requirements. As sales proceed, however, we must have some system for compensating for the differences between planned and actual requirements in order to maintain inventories at proper levels. If actual requirements exceed plans, we run the risk of running out of stock, with resulting poor customer service and possible additional costs related to shortages. If actual requirements are below expectations, inventories will build up with resulting high carrying costs. Therefore, a control plan is needed which adjusts production and inventory levels in keeping with sales experience. Such a control plan might be accomplished by constructing periodically a new production program that takes into account existing inventories by adjustments in the short-run levels of production.

Our objective in this control plan is *to increase or decrease production levels in the period ahead, proportional to differences between actual and forecast sales, by an amount that minimizes the incremental costs of inventories and fluctuations of production levels.* If the planning period is fairly short, this adjustment of levels would continuously correct inventory levels to be in keeping with present demand, thus preventing stock-outs or the buildup of excessive inventories because of changes in demand. The basic elements of this control plan are comparable to those described earlier in this chapter and illustrated by Figure 8. We wish to construct a feedback control system where information on desired levels of inventories (indicated by current requirements) is compared with actual inventories to determine an error function which is fed back and compared with information on planned production levels for the coming period. By some predetermined rule, the production level is then adjusted to compensate for the demand fluctuation and bring inventories into line.

Decision Rules for Controlling Production Levels. Let us first state an obvious kind of rule for controlling production levels as actual requirements vary from forecasted requirements. The rule we will use for introductory purposes is that when actual requirements deviate from forecasts, we will add or subtract the difference as soon as possible to the amount produced in order to compensate for the variation from planned inventory levels. Let us illustrate with the forecast of requirements for 10 weeks shown in

TABLE II. Calculation of production levels and inventories when the difference between forecasted and actual requirements is absorbed entirely by changes in production level, 2 weeks hence. Beginning inventory is 500 units.

(1) Week	(2) Forecasted Requirements	(3) Planned Production	(4) Planned Inventories = Beginning Inventories + Col. 3 − Col. 2	(5) Actual Requirements	(6) Difference Between Actual and Forecasted Requirements, Col. 5 − Col. 2	(7) Actual Production Level = Planned Production + Difference Between Actual and Forecasted Requirements, 2 Weeks Ago; Col. 3 + Col. 6 for 2 Weeks Ago	(8) Actual Inventory Level = Beginning Inventory + Actual Production − Actual Requirements = Beginning Inventory + Col. 7 − Col. 5
0			500				500
1	590	600	510	595	5	600	505
2	590	600	520	430	−160	600	675
3	590	600	530	590	0	605	690
4	590	600	540	1000	410	440	130
5	600	600	540	50	−550	600	680
6	600	600	540	625	25	1010	1065
7	600	600	540	570	−30	50	545
8	600	600	540	575	−25	625	595
9	610	600	530	680	70	570	485
10	610	600	530	705	95	575	355
	5980	6000		5820		5675	

Actual average production rate = 567.5 units per week.
Actual average inventory level = 573 units.

column 2 of Table II. Column 3 shows the planned production program for the product, and the planned inventories are easily calculated in column 4. As we would expect, however, actual requirements vary from forecast as shown in column 5 and the difference between actual and forecast requirements in column 6. The production lead time is 2 weeks, so that when a deviation from forecasted requirements occurs we can change production rate for the production period two weeks hence. Therefore, no change occurs from production plans in the first 2 weeks shown in column 7, but the third week's production reflects the shortage in planned requirements of five units. Similarly, the fourth week reflects the overage of 160 units which occurred in the second week, and so on. Actual inventory levels shown in column 8 are simply beginning inventory plus the amount produced during the week (column 7) less the actual requirements (column 5).

We see that this rule does indeed compensate for the variations, with a 2-week time lag, but at what cost? Actual production levels vary from 50 units to 1000 units per week in the short space of 10 weeks. But, notice that over the 10 weeks, actual total requirements were quite close to forecasted total requirements. Variation from forecast was largely week-to-week variation. As a matter of fact, the week-to-week variation reflects the random variations described in the demand distribution of Figure 4. In other words, it was variation that we should have expected to occur. Perhaps there is a better way to absorb this variation than by direct changes in the production level.

Let us test the idea just stated. Why not damp the effects of variation in actual requirements from forecast by changing production level by only 50 percent of the difference instead of 100 percent as we did previously. This is shown in Table III, under "50% Reaction." The original forecast of requirements and production and inventory plans are identical to those of Table II, but notice that violent swings in both production and inventory levels have been damped out considerably. Why not carry this idea farther? What happens with a 10 or 5 percent reaction rate? This is also shown in Table III with additional stabilizing factors in the form of simple heuristic rules. With the 10 percent reaction we have included the additional restriction that we will not respond to the variation from forecast at all unless 10 percent of the difference exceeds 10 units. In addition, with the 5 percent reaction we have included the 10-unit minimum and the restriction that larger changes in production level are made only in increments of 10 units. Therefore, if 5 percent of the difference is 27.5 units as it is in the fifth week, a change in production level of 30 units is made in the seventh week. Notice the results of progressively decreasing reaction rates in Table III. The results are more stable production and inventory levels. Also note, however, that average inventory levels have increased as reaction rate was decreased.

The effect of reducing reaction rate could have been forecast. By using a

TABLE III. *Actual production and inventory levels when only 50 percent, 10 percent, or 5 percent of the difference between forecasted and actual requirements is absorbed by changes in production level from plan, 2 weeks hence. Buffer stocks absorb the balance of the variation. Data for forecasted and actual requirements and planned production and inventory levels are shown in Table II*

Week	50% Reaction		10% Reaction 10-Unit Minimum		5% Reaction 10-Unit Minimum, Increments 10 Units	
	Actual Production Level	Actual Inventory Level	Actual Production Level	Actual Inventory Level	Actual Production Level	Actual Inventory Level
0	—	500	—	500	—	500
1	600	505	600	505	600	505
2	600	675	600	675	600	675
3	603	688	600	685	600	685
4	520	208	584	269	590	275
5	600	758	600	819	600	825
6	805	938	641	835	620	820
7	375	743	545	810	570	820
8	613	781	600	835	600	845
9	585	686	600	755	600	765
10	587	568	600	650	600	660
Average for 10 Weeks	589	655	597	684	598	688

relatively low reaction rate we are assuming that most deviations in actual requirements from forecasts are simply random deviations, so why become excited about them? If the deviation looks large, perhaps we should increase or decrease production rate *a little*, just in case it really marks the beginning of a trend. The question is, then, what should be the reaction rate for optimal cost performance? It is a good question, but it is slightly premature. Let us first discuss the general aspects of the decision rule and develop the ideas of reaction rates, review periods, and their interrelations.

Our decision rule really operates in the following context:

1. A longer-term forecast of requirements on which is based a broad production program.

2. A shorter-term forecast or "review" to refine the forecast of requirements for the immediate periods ahead.

3. Based on this short-term review and forecast of requirements we can:

    a. Determine a production plan for these periods.

    b. Set planned inventory levels for these periods.

4. In the shortest-term planning period which is equal to the production lead time (the shortest notice used to change production levels in the period ahead), we can make a final adjustment in production level which takes account of the latest information we have regarding the comparison of actual and forecasted requirements.

5. The decision rule used is that production level in the immediate period ahead will be adjusted by some fraction k of the difference between actual and forecasted requirements for the current period.

In this context, we see that there are really two parameters we can manipulate to develop a model for the control of production levels. They are the value of k—the reaction rate—and the length of the review period mentioned in number 2 and 3 in the preceding outline. The importance of the reaction rate has already been discussed and demonstrated in the text material related to Tables II and III. In summary, k may take on values between the number 0 and 1.00, representing no reaction to deviations from forecasted requirements when $k = 0$, to 100 percent reaction and compensation when $k = 1.00$. In general terms, low values of k lead to stable production levels and relatively high buffer stock requirements, since variations from the plan must be absorbed by inventories. Conversely, high values of k lead to large production fluctuations and relatively low buffer stocks because variations from plan are absorbed by changing production levels. The significance of reaction rates in smoothing production rates is comparable to the smoothing constant α used in the exponentially smoothed forecasting methods discussed in Chapter 7.

The frequency of review also has a direct effect on both the magnitude of production fluctuations and the size of needed buffer stocks. The reason is easy to see in relation to the general principle of process control which we discussed in connection with Figures 7 and 8. The longer the period between reviews, P, the greater the chance that forecasts of requirements may not reflect the most current trends. Therefore, it is more likely that relatively large differences between actual and forecasted requirements would accumulate. For a given value of k, longer review periods lead to both relatively large production fluctuations and buffer stocks in order to provide the needed compensation. Short periods between reviews, then lead to closer control and relatively small production fluctuations and buffer stocks, whereas longer periods between reviews lead to looser control and larger production fluctuations and buffer stock requirements.

Determining k and P. Magee [10] derives two approximate formulas useful in solving the problem of determining the reaction rate k and the review period P for specific situations. He shows that the expected magnitude of production fluctuations is approximately proportional to

$$\sqrt{kP/(2 - k)} \tag{1}$$

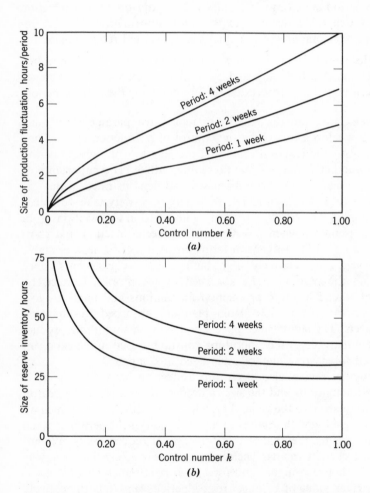

FIGURE 12. (a) *Magnitude of production fluctuations versus control number and length of review period.* (b) *Reserve inventory required versus control number and length of review period. By permission from* Production Planning and Inventory Control, *by J. F. Magee and D. M. Boodman, McGraw-Hill Book Company, 2nd ed., New York, copyright, 1967.*

and that the required factory buffer stock will be approximately proportional to

$$\sqrt{[T(2k - k^2) + P]/(2k - k^2)} \qquad (2)$$

where T = production lead time, P = length of review period, and k = reaction rate in decimals.

The cost of production fluctuation, then, is proportional to (1) and the cost of buffer stocks are proportional to (2). Figure 12 shows the relationship of reaction rates and review period to the size of production fluctuations and reserve inventory requirements, expressed in equivalent hours. For a specific case, then, suppose that at $k = 1.00$ we experience a production fluctuation cost of \$5000 and a buffer stock cost of \$500, when the review period and production lead times are each 1 week. Using formulas (1) and (2), we can compute points for the curves shown in Figure 13 to find a value of k approximating 0.075 for minimum total incremental cost. Further similar calculations with different review periods would yield a combination of k and P which would minimize incremental costs for the entire system. Obviously, the right combination for a specific case like that shown in Figure 13 depends on the relative magnitudes of inventory carrying cost and the cost of production changes.

Let us summarize at this point some of the aspects of the control of inventories under uncertainty in a production-inventory system. Previously in this chapter we discussed systems for controlling inventories that

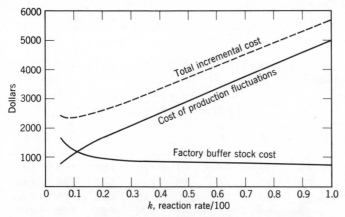

FIGURE 13. Relationship between incremental costs and k, when the cost of production fluctuations and factory buffer stocks are \$5000 and \$500, respectively, at k = 1. Review period and lead time are 1 week.

involved fixing the quantity ordered at one time, letting the frequency of ordering vary, fixing the frequency of ordering, letting the quantity ordered vary, and the base stock system which was a combination of the elements of the two different systems. Also, differences in the information feedback pattern and their effects were noted. In the operation of a production-inventory system we have noted that the cost of production fluctuations is also an important factor to take into account. By way of summary, let us now consider the overall comparison of systems of control.

A Comparative Example

Magee [10] relates a hypothetical case called the Hibernian Co. which compares operation and costs for different basic systems of production and inventory control. The example considers a company that manufactures and sells about 5000 small machines per year for $100 each. The factory supplies four warehouses located in strategic areas around the country, which in turn supply the customer. We shall show the calculated results for four alternate systems of control: an economical order quantity system, a two-week fixed reorder cycle system, a base stock system with a review period of 1 week and reaction rate of 100 per cent, and a base stock system with a 1-week review period but involving a production reaction rate of 5 percent.

Each of the four branches sold an average of 25 units per week, or 1300 units per year. This average rate was, of course, subject to considerable variation, and Table IV shows distributions of demand at each of the four branches for 1-week periods, 2-week periods, etc. For example, at any given branch, sales would be expected to exceed 37 units per week only 1 percent of the time, 67 units per 2-week period 1 percent of the time, and so on. Requirements aggregated at the factory warehouse, reflecting demand from all four of the branches, are shown in Table V for eight different time groupings. Figure 14 shows the structure of the production-distribution system.

1. *Economical fixed reorder quantity system (EOQ).* Using an economical fixed

TABLE IV. Distribution of demand at each of four branches by eight different time-period groupings

Percent of Periods Exceeding Levels Given	Units of Sales Period, Weeks							
	1	2	3	4	5	6	7	8
90	19	41	64	87	111	134	158	182
60	24	46	71	95	124	144	168	193
50	25	50	75	100	125	150	175	200
20	29	56	82	108	134	160	186	212
10	31.4	60	86	113	139	166	192	218
1	37	67	95	123	151	179	206	233

TABLE V. Distribution of demand on factory warehouse from branches by eight different time-period groupings

Percent of Periods Exceeding Levels Given	Units of Requirements in Period, Weeks							
	1	2	3	4	5	6	7	8
90	87	182	278	374	471	569	666	764
60	95	193	291	389	488	587	686	785
50	100	200	300	400	500	600	700	800
20	108	212	314	417	519	621	722	824
10	113	218	322	426	529	631	734	836
1	123	233	341	447	553	658	762	866

reorder quantity system, we must analyze the requirements for buffer stocks, cycle stocks, transit stocks, and reordering costs for the branches, as well as, buffer stocks, cycle stocks, in-process inventory ordering costs, and the cost of production fluctuations at the factory and warehouse.

Branches. At each branch, the economical quantity to be ordered at one time may be calculated if we know that $c_P = \$19$ ($6 clerical cost, $13 cost of packing, shipping, receiving, and stocking), $R = 1300$, and $c_H = \$5$. Q_0 is then,

$$\sqrt{(2 \times 19 \times 1300)/5} = 100 \text{ units}$$

Therefore, each branch would place an order for 100 units each, 4 weeks on the average, and the average *cycle stock* in each branch would be $100/2 = 50$ units. The branch *buffer stock* is based on a 1 percent risk of running out of stock. Since the total

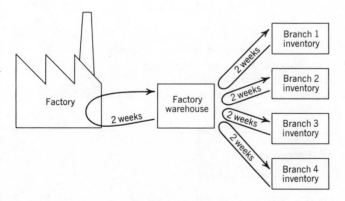

FIGURE 14. Structure of production-distribution system for Hibernian Bay Co.

lead time was 2 weeks, we can determine the reasonable maximum demand during that period from Table IV as 67 units. Since normal demand during the 2-week lead time would be 50 units, the buffer stock is then the difference, or 17 units. Finally, the average *transit stock* is equal to the delivery time multiplied by the average demand rate, or 50 units. Average branch inventory is then as follows:

$$
\begin{array}{lll}
\text{Buffer stock,} & 4 \times 17 = & 68 \text{ units} \\
\text{Cycle stock,} & 4 \times 50 = & 200 \\
\text{Transit stock,} & 4 \times 50 = & \underline{200} \\
& & 468 \text{ units}
\end{array}
$$

Since $c_H = \$5$ per unit per year, this average inventory of 468 units has an annual cost of \$2340. Since each branch places an order once every 4 weeks, on the average, there are 52 orders per year from the four branches which cost \$19 each or a total annual reordering cost of \$988.

Factory Warehouse and Factory. The factory warehouse is, of course, reflecting the aggregate demand from the four branches so that its economical order quantity reflects annual requirements, $R = 5200$ units, and its own inventory holding and preparation costs of $c_H = \$3.50$, and $c_P = \$13.50$. Calculating Q_0, as before, we obtain $Q_0 = 200$ units. Maximum 2-week demand from the branches (using a 1 percent run-out risk criterion) under the economical reorder quantity system is 233 units, so that *factory warehouse buffer stocks* are set at $233 - 200 = 33$ units. *Cycle stocks are* $200/2 = 100$ units, and *in-process inventories* in the factory average one-half the order quantity or 100 units. Total average inventory at the factory warehouse is therefore 233 units. On the average, 26 factory production orders per year must be issued at a cost of \$13.50 or \$351 per year. Table VI summarizes the inventory and ordering costs for the economical order quantity system. To this total we must add the *cost of production* fluctuations which occur with the economical order quantity system. Figure 15a shows a typical pattern of orders on the factory and the resulting factory production levels set. Note that very large fluctuations in production levels result and these fluctuations cost \$8500 per year.

TABLE VI.   Summary of incremental costs of economical order quantity system for Hibernian Co. from Magee [10]

Inventory costs	
Four branches	$ 2,340
Factory	816
Reorder costs	
Four branches	988
Factory	351
Production fluctuations	8,500
	$12,995

2. Fixed Reorder Cycle Systems.

Branches. Under the fixed reorder cycle system, each branch warehouse maintains its inventory sufficient to fill reasonable maximum demands during the review period

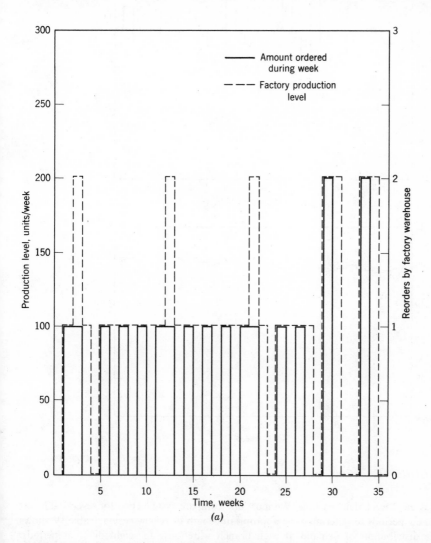

(a)

FIGURE 15. (a) *Factory orders and production level, economic reorder quantity system.* (b) *Production level, fixed reorder cycle system.* (c) *Production level, basestock system; reaction rate = 5 percent. Adapted by permission from* Production Planning and Inventory Control, *by J. F. Magee and D. M. Boodman, McGraw-Hill Book Company, 2nd ed., New York, copyright, 1967.*

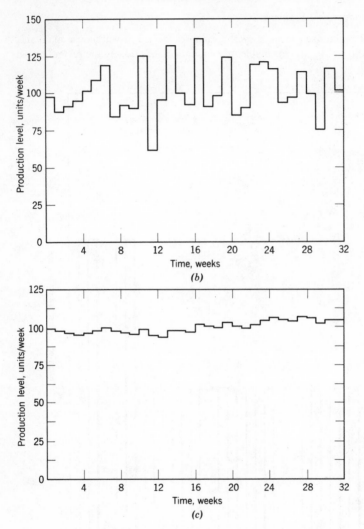

FIGURE 15. (Continued)

plus the 2-week delivery time. We must first compare system costs for several different review periods to determine the appropriate length of review period. Table IV shows the distribution of demand at each branch warehouse for eight different periods. Therefore, we can determine *buffer stock* requirements for each review period considered, at the 1 percent risk level, by looking at the numbers on the row for the percent of period sales exceeding the 1 percent level. The buffer stock requirements for a 1-week review period plus the 2-week lead time are $95 - 75 = 20$. Buffer stock requirements computed in the same way are shown for the various review periods in

Table VII. *Cycle stock* would average one-half of the normal shipment. A shipment is made once each period so that the average amount shipped would be 25 × (the number of weeks in the period). Table VII shows the appropriate cycle stocks for each review period. *Transit stock* remains at 50 units for each review period. The number of orders placed varies inversely with the length of the review period, therefore, 1-week period results in 52 orders per year at $19 per order or $988 per year. The branch ordering costs for the other periods are summarized in Table VII.

TABLE VII. Comparison of system costs for different lengths of review periods for the fixed reorder cycle system*

	Length of Review Period, Weeks					
	1	2	3	4	5	6
Branch warehouses, each branch						
Inventory						
Buffer stock	20	23	26	29	31	33
Cycle stock	12.5	25	37.5	50	62.5	75
Transit stock	50	50	50	50	50	50
Total	82.5	98	113.5	129	143.5	158
Annual inventory cost at $5	$ 412.5	$ 490	$ 567.5	$ 645	$ 717.5	$ 790
Ordering cost	990	495	330	250	195	165
Total	$1402.5	$ 985	$ 897.5	$ 895	$ 912.5	$ 955
Total, four branches	$5610	$3940	$3590	$3580	$3650	$ 3,820
Factory warehouse						
Buffer stock	41	47	53	58	62	67
Cycle stock	50	100	150	200	250	300
In-process stock	50	100	150	200	250	300
Total	141	247	353	458	562	667
Annual inventory cost at $3.50	$ 493	$ 865	$1235	$1630	$1967	$ 2,335
Ordering cost	700	350	235	175	140	120
Total factory warehouse cost	$1193	$1195	$1470	$1805	$2107	$ 2,455
Cost of changing production levels	$1600	$2250	$2760	$3180	$3560	$ 3,900
Total system costs	$8403	$7385	$7820	$8565	$9317	$10,175

*Modified from J. F. Magee and D. M. Boodman, Production Planning and Inventory Control, McGraw-Hill Book Company, New York, 2nd ed., 1967.

Factory Warehouse and Factory. Factory warehouse *buffer stocks* are set at the 1 percent risk level, and Table V shows the distribution of demand on the factory warehouse from branches by eight different time-period groupings. Since the factory lead time is 2 weeks, reasonable maximum demand must be calculated over the lead time plus one review period. For example, for a 1-week review period, maximum demand is 341 units and average usage is 300 units. The resulting buffer stock is the difference or 41 units. The factory buffer stocks shown in Table VII are computed from Table V in a parallel way. Factory warehouse *cycle stocks* and factory *in-process inventories* are equal to one-half the average requirements per period and are computed as shown in Table VII. The factory warehouse *ordering costs* are inversely proportional to the length of the review period and are calculated at $13.50 each. The cost of production changes is computed at $1600 annually for the close control resulting from a 1-week review period, and Magee [10] shows that the cost of production changes for the other review periods is proportional to $\sqrt{n}$, where n is the length of the review period. Figure 15*b* shows production levels for a 2-week period reorder system, which we see is the least cost plan of the six review periods analyzed in Table VII.

3. *Base Stock System, $k = 100$ Percent.* A third system for comparison is the general base stock system which we discussed in this chapter. Here the four branches report sales periodically and the factory consolidates demand from these sources and puts an equivalent amount into production. The branch stocks are then replenished when sales have exceeded a minimum shipment quantity. The two main questions to be tied down then, are, "How often should the branches report sales?", and "How big should the minimum replenishment shipment be?" The possible advantage of the base stock system compared to the fixed cycle system just discussed are:

1. If the branches can justify weekly sales reporting, production fluctuations and buffer stocks might be reduced even more.

2. It might be possible to make less frequent shipments from the factory to branches, thereby making further cost reductions.

Looking at Table VII, we see that if we go to weekly reporting periods instead of the 2-week period decided on, branch safety stocks can be reduced from 23 to 20 per branch resulting in an inventory cost reduction of $60. Similarly, factory warehouse buffer stocks would be reduced from 47 to 41, resulting in a modest reduction of $21. From the closer control of the 1-week review period, the cost of production changes goes down from $2250 to $1600 resulting in a net reduction of $650.

Recall that the value of $c_P = \$19$ was made up of $6 for clerical costs and $13 for shipping and related costs. Therefore, we can compute an economical shipping quantity as follows:

$$\sqrt{(2 \times 13 \times 1300)/5} = 82 \text{ units}$$

This means an average of 16 shipments annually to each branch, or a total cost of $16 \times 4 \times 13 = \$832$. This compares with 26 shipments required for the two week reorder period which totaled $1352, resulting in a net shipping cost reduction of $520.

These cost reductions are partially offset by increases in the cost of branch reports and cycle stock costs. A branch report costs $6 each, and there would be 52 of them required for each branch per year instead of 26, which results in a net increase in cost of $624. Finally, the cycle stock at the branches is increased from 25 units per branch to one-half the new average shipping quantity, or 41 units. This results in a net increase in cycle stock cost of $20. The net result is that the base stock system with $k = 100$ percent decreases net system costs by a modest $311.

4. *Base Stock System, k = 5 Percent.* If we now decrease the reaction rate at the factory to 5 percent, the cost of production changes is reduced and Figure 15c shows the startling stabilizing effect of the 5 percent reaction rate on production levels. From Table VII, for a review period of 1 week, we see that the cost of production changes is $1600. Recall that we stated earlier that the cost of production changes was proportional to equation (1). Thus we may compute the cost of production changes when the reaction rate is 5 percent by $1600 \times \sqrt{0.05/1.95} = \$256$. Similarly, using equation (2) and noting from Table VII that the factory buffer of 41 units costs $144 per year, when $k = 100$ percent, we can calculate the cost of buffer stock when $k = 5$ percent as $299.

Table VIII shows the final summary of incremental costs for the four systems. The base stock system with 1-week review and a reaction rate of 5 percent has the lowest total of $6673. This compares with $12,995 for the "so-called" economical order quantity system, more than twice the cost of the lowest cost system. Thus we see demonstrated what is perhaps the most important factor in the design of a production-inventory system. The lesson is that it must reflect the "systems" point of view, that is, consider not only inventory models in isolation, but take account of the interaction of inventory costs with other costs in the overall production system. The result is that the economical order quantity model represents a local optimum and other policies can contribute to a broader system optimum policy.

TABLE VIII.   *Comparative incremental costs for four systems*

	Economical Order Quantity System	2-Week Fixed Cycle Reorder System	Base Stock, 1-Week Reporting, k = 100%	Base Stock, 1-Week Reporting, k = 5%
Inventory costs				
Four branches	$ 2,340	$1960	$2220	$2220
Factory warehouse	816	865	844	1143
Reorder costs				
Four branches	988	1980	1456	1456
Factory warehouse	351	350	350	350
Branch reports	—	624	1248	1248
Cost of production fluctuations	8,500	2250	1600	256
Total incremental costs	$12,995	$8029	$7718	$6673

SUMMARY

In this chapter we have tried to develop the importance of the factor of demand variability and its impact on inventory planning. In doing this, we have developed the rational determination of buffer stocks and discussed systems inventory control which take account of the resulting risks. In connection with these systems of inventory control, the concepts of process control and information feedback were introduced and the important effects of time lags shown.

In considering the problems posed by inventories, we are forced to consider several levels of planning covering different time spans. These are as follows:

1. *Long-range plans for plant capacity.* Plant capacity may be affected by seasonal peaks, and there are capital costs associated with this capacity. What combination of in-plant capacity, use of seasonal inventories, overtime, and subcontracting will minimize the combined capital costs, seasonal inventory costs, labor costs, production fluctuation costs, and extra costs of subcontracting? Is new capacity justified?

2. *Intermediate-range plans for a few months to a year* in advance, which attempt to determine for the expectations of sales what will be the best allocation of the resources of existing capacity. We are asking what combination of production within periods, size of work force, and seasonal inventories will minimize the combined costs of production fluctuation, seasonal inventory cost, labor costs, and extra subcontracting costs. We shall pay particular attention to this subject in Chapter 13.

3. *Short-range plans for the immediate period ahead.* Since actual requirements will change from forecasts, we must take a last look within the lead time to change production level, but neither can we change production levels capriciously because large costs can be involved, nor can we ignore what might develop into a huge inventory buildup. The result is that we need a control system that minimizes in the short range the cost of inventories and production fluctuations.

4. *In the shortest range of planning*, we need automatic decision rules that dispatch work to each and every workplace and machine. There is no time to ponder the question at this point. We must develop an automatic rule which operates quickly and accurately, indicating the best sequence in which to process orders at a given machine or machine center. Here we are looking for models of

flow, such as those covered in Chapter 17, which will minimize inventory and idle labor costs while providing a high level of service to customers by completing their work on time.

Inventories have an important impact at all stages of planning and execution. The result is that we must view inventories in their multifunction role in the broad system from raw material input, flow through the production-distribution system, and to the consumer. They cannot be examined in isolation with realism.

REVIEW QUESTIONS

1. What are the three kinds of variations which we might expect in sales curves, which result in variability of demand?

2. Why is it that we wish to abstract just the random variations due solely to chance causes from the total variation in demand curves from all causes, for use in determining buffer stocks?

3. How can we determine what stock runout level to use for a specific situation?

4. Describe each of the three inventory control systems which take account of variability of demand which are described in this chapter.

5. What are the variables in inventory control systems that are subject to managerial control?

6. Which system has closer control over inventory levels, the fixed reorder quantity system or the fixed reorder cycle system?

7. What techniques may be applied to determine if an apparent change in demand is merely a random fluctuation or a true shift in average requirements?

8. Relate the general principles of process control to inventory control systems.

9. Describe the effects on retail inventories, distributor inventories, factory warehouse inventories, and on factory production levels when consumer demand changes, assuming the structure of a production distribution system as shown in Figure 9.

10. What is the nature of our objective in controlling production levels?

11. Compare the expected results when a production control rule is used with reaction rates of 100, 50, 10, and 5 percent.

12. In controlling production levels, what are the two main variables that are under our control?

13. What is the general relationship between reaction rates and the frequency of adjustment of production levels? Which combinations produce high costs of production fluctuation? High costs of reserve inventories?

14. How can equations (1) and (2) help to determine the best reaction rate to use in a specific situation?

15. Make a complete analysis of the four systems of control used in the Hibernian Co. case, checking all calculations, to show exactly where the different systems have relative advantages and disadvantages.

PROBLEMS

1. Weekly demand for a product exclusive of seasonal and trend variations is represented by the empirical distribution given below. What buffer stock would be required for the item to insure that one would not run out of stock more than 15 percent of the time? Five percent of the time? One percent of the time? Normal lead time is one week.

Weekly Demand, Units	Frequency, Number of Weeks Demand Reached a Given Level
0	0
20	2
30	5
40	10
50	9
60	20
70	30
80	25
90	18
100	17
110	10
120	8
130	6
140	3
150	2
Total	165

2. If the item for which data is given in Problem 1 has a unit value of $100, shortages costs of $10 each, and an annual inventory carrying cost of 25 percent of the average inventory value, which of the three levels of service would be most appropriate?

3. An organization is attempting to assess the cost of increasing its service level which is currently set at only 80 percent. Average demand during lead time is 18 units, and demand is reasonably well described by the Poisson distribution. Inventory holding costs are approximated by $c_H = \$10$ per unit per year. Calculate the buffer inventory costs required for service levels of 80, 90, 95, and 99 percent. What are the comparative costs if the distribution of demand during lead time follows

the negative exponential distribution? The normal distribution with $\sigma_D = 2, 4$, and 6 units?

4. Given a control number of 0.6, a decreased demand fluctuation of 600 units in the first period, and a forecasted production level of 15,000 units in the third period, what would be the revised production quantity set for period three? (Owing to lead times, it is not possible to adjust the production level for the second period.)

5. A company manufactures a single product for which the following table represents a schedule of forecasted and actual demand in units for one year.

Month	Forecasted Demand	Actual Demand
Jan.	23,000	23,000
Feb.	24,000	25,000
Mar.	21,000	20,000
Apr.	23,000	22,000
May	20,000	22,000
June	19,000	24,000
July	17,000	22,000
Aug.	14,000	15,000
Sept.	8,000	6,000
Oct.	10,000	13,000
Nov.	9,000	10,000
Dec.	10,000	14,000
Total	198,000	216,000
Average	16,500	18,000

The initial inventory is 15,000 units. The desired ending inventory is 20,000 units. The cost of storage is $1 per unit per month. It costs $1000 to change production from zero to 3000 units and $3000 to change production from 3000 to 6000 units. No change larger than 6000 units is possible in one period. Back orders are permitted at a cost of $5 per unit per period.

(a) What is the best production plan for the forecasted demand if one wishes to minimize pertinent costs?

(b) Assuming that the year is over, what is the best production plan for the actual demand utilizing the benefit of hindsight?

(c) To correct for deviations in actual demand as compared to forecasted demand, evaluate the choice of a control number of 0.25 versus one of 0.75. Assume that at the end of a month sufficient time exists to alter the planned production for the next month.

(d) What would be the cost impact of these two control numbers if the following additional rules were formulated.

(1) Determine the planned production change.

(2) Add or subtract the additional change due to the forecast error modified by the appropriate control number factor.

(3) If the total change is less than or equal to 1500, do not change production levels.

(4) If the total change is greater than 1500 but less than or equal to 4500, change production levels by 3000 units.

(5) If the total change is greater than 4500, change production levels by 6000 units.

(6) Subtract the production change as per rules (3), (4), and (5) from the total change indicated by rule (2) and add or subtract the result to the planned production change for two months hence.

REFERENCES

1. Biegel, J. E., *Production Control*, Prentice-Hall, Englewood Cliffs, N.J., 1971.
2. Bowman, E. H., "Production Scheduling by the Transportation Method of Linear Programming," *Journal of the Operations Research Society of America*, Vol. 4, No. 1, 1956, pp. 100–103.
3. Brown, R. G., *Decision Rules for Inventory Management*, Holt, Rinehart and Winston, New York, 1967.
4. Buchan, J., and E. Koenigsberg, *Scientific Inventory Management*, Prentice-Hall, Englewood Cliffs, N.J., 1963.
5. Buffa, E. S., and W. H. Taubert, *Production-Inventory Systems: Planning and Control*, Richard D. Irwin, Inc., Homewood, Ill., Rev. ed., 1972.
6. Eilon, S., *Elements of Production Planning and Control*, The Macmillan Company, New York, 1962.
7. Fetter, R. B., and W. C. Dalleck, *Decision Models for Inventory Management*, Richard D. Irwin, Homewood, Ill., 1961.
8. Forrester, J. W., *Industrial Dynamics*, MIT Press, Cambridge, Mass., 1961.
9. Hadley, G., and T. M. Whitin, *Analysis of Inventory Systems*, Prentice-Hall, Englewood Cliffs, N.J., 1963.
10. Magee, J. F., and D. M. Boodman, *Production Planning and Inventory Control*, McGraw-Hill Book Company, New York, 2nd ed., 1967.
11. McMillan, C., and R. F. Gonzalez, *Systems Analysis*, Richard D. Irwin, Inc., Homewood, Ill., Rev. ed., 1968, Chap. 4.
12. Moore, F. G., and R. Jablonski, *Production Control*, McGraw-Hill Book Company, New York, 3rd ed., 1969.
13. Naddor, E., *Inventory Systems*, John Wiley & Sons, New York, 1966.
14. Starr, M. K., and D. W. Miller, *Inventory Control: Theory and Practice*, Prentice-Hall, Englewood Cliffs, N.J., 1962.
15. Vassian, H. J., "Application of Discrete Variable Servo Theory to Inventory Control" *Journal of the Operations Research Society of America*, Vol. 3, No. 3, August 1955, pp. 272–282.
16. Voris, W., *Production Control*, Richard D. Irwin, Inc., Homewood, Illinois, 1961.
17. Wagner, H. M., *Statistical Inventory Management*, John Wiley & Sons, New York, 1962.

PART IV

LINEAR PROGRAMMING MODELS

chapter 10

LINEAR PROGRAMMING— SIMPLEX METHODS

Linear programming is one of the most important, far reaching developments in management science methodology. Many of the other model types have had their beginnings some time ago, and current efforts represent evolution and development based on relatively old fundamental ideas. This is true of inventory models, waiting line models, statistical models, and others. Linear programming, however, is a creation of the present era, dealing with some of the problems of allocating the resources of an enterprise. Perhaps the most general statement of the objective of programming is that *we wish to allocate some kind of limited resource to competing demands in the most effective way.* These kinds of problems are some of the most fundamental to the effective operation of an enterprise.

Typical Allocation Problems

Following is a description of a number of typical problems in operations management which have been approached by linear programming methods. They are diverse in their settings and in the methods required for their solution, and should spark our imagination to think of related or different problems that might be approached in the same general way. Some are stated generally, and others represent specific studies.

1. *Distribution of products from a set of origin points to a number of destinations* in a way which satisfies the demand at each destination and the supplies available at the origins and minimizes total transportation cost.

2. *Distribution of products from factories to warehouses*, similar to 1, but minimizing combined production and distribution costs; or if the products have different revenues in the various marketing areas, maximizing a function of revenue minus production-distribution costs.

3. *Multiple plant location studies*, where common products are produced with a decentralized complex of plants. Here we wish to evaluate various alternate locations for the construction of a new plant. Each different location considered produces a different allocation matrix of product from the factories to the distribution points because of differing production-distribution costs. The best new location is the one that minimizes total production-distribution costs for the entire system, and this, of course, is not necessarily the location which seems to have the lowest production cost. [3, page 379]

4. *Locational dynamics for multiple plants.* Here, the problem is somewhat similar to 3, but the question is, which plants to operate at what levels for a given total demand. Since additional capacity at each location can normally be obtained through overtime, and since certain overhead costs can be saved by shutting down a plant, there are conditions when total costs are minimized by shutting down a plant and supplying the total demand from the other plants, even though overtime costs are incurred. The plant to be shut down is not necessarily the high production cost plant— this depends on the relative importance of production and distribution costs. [3, page 385]

5. *Redistribution of empty freight cars* from their existing locations to the points where they are needed in a way that minimizes transportation costs.

6. *Allocation of limited raw materials used in a variety of products* so that total profit is maximized, meeting market demands insofar as is possible. [26, page 65]

7. *Allocation of production facilities when alternate routings are available.* Given the unit machine time for the alternate machine routes, total hours available on the different machine classes, requirements for the number of each product, and unit revenue for each product, linear programming can give a solution that

maximizes some profit function, minimizes cost, or meets some other management objective. [26, page 53]

8. *Blending Problems.* As an example, a paint manufacturer may need to prepare paint vehicles that are a blend of several constituents. The constituents, such as oil, thinner, etc., are available in limited quantity and in commercial blends of fixed proportions. Costs per gallon of the various possible raw materials are known. The problem is to determine the amount of each raw material such that the required amounts for the new blends are obtained at minimum cost. Another similar problem is the blending of animal feed to provide certain minimum nutrient values at minimum cost. [20, page 156]

9. *Maximizing material utilization.* Many times different stock sizes must be stamped or cut from standard raw material sizes. The problem is to determine the combination of cuts that will meet requirements for the amounts of the different sizes with a minimum trim loss. [20, Chapter 8]

10. *Development of a program for production, when demand is seasonal.* Here we are attempting to allocate available capacity to various production periods for the products to be produced in such a way that requirements for all products are met and combined incremental inventory and production costs are minimized. The incremental production costs may include overtime premium, turnover costs, and extra subcontracting costs. [5, 20, 26]

11. *Product mix problems.* Here we have a general class of problems of considerable interest. If we have production facilities that can be used to produce several different items which may have different costs, revenues, and market demands, we wish to know how best to allocate the available capacity to various products within the limitations of market demand. [5, 12, 26]

12. *Long-range planning.* The general capacity planning problem has been treated as being met by ownership, leases, or short-term contracts. A model cast in a linear programming framework may help in answering questions such as, (*a*) the effect of a given demand forecast on capacity plans, (*b*) the effects of changes in ownership costs, (*c*) the effect of changes in the costs of leased capacity, and (*d*) the sensitivity to forecast error of various decisions and costs [13].

Simplex methods of linear programming are more general in scope and application than the distribution-transportation methods which we shall discuss in Chapter 11. Distribution problems may be solved by the simplex method but usually with some additional time and effort. The simplex method, however, can be used where distribution methods cannot; hence, the field of application for simplex is considerably broader. In developing the conceptual framework for the simplex method, we will first use a graphical example to introduce the nature of the problem restrictions and objectives, show an algebraic solution, and finally present a detailed procedure for solution of more complex problems. The problems set up for illustrative purposes are necessarily simple; however, this is not a limitation of simplex methods or of linear programming. Actually, one of the great advantages of linear programming is the complexity and scale of problems that can be handled.

GRAPHIC
INTERPRETATION /

For simple problems we can show graphically how the restrictions of the linear programming problem limit the possible solution and how the objective function determines the optimum solution for a problem. This will help in the interpretation of the algebraic and procedural aspects of the simplex method.

As an example let us consider the facilities of a company which manufactures a line of refrigerators and air conditioners. The major manufacturing departments are the machine shop, the stamping department, the "unit" department, which makes the refrigeration units for both products, and separate final assembly lines for the refrigerators and air conditioners. The monthly capacities of the five departments are as follows:

Department	Capacity for Refrigerators		Capacity for Air Conditioners
Machine shop	7500	or	6000
Stamping	5000	or	9000
Unit	6000	or	7000
Refrigerator assembly	4000		—
Air conditioner assembly	—		5000

The first three departments produce both refrigerator and air conditioner parts in the proportions scheduled within the capacity restrictions indicated. For example, the machine shop could devote all of its capacity to the production of refrigerator parts—7500 refrigerator parts per month.

Alternately, it could produce parts for 6000 air conditioners, or proportionate combinations of the two products. The final assembly facilities for the two products are specialized and separate, as indicated by the capacity figures.

The contribution (sales value less variable cost) is $50 per refrigerator and $60 per air conditioner. (Recall from our discussion in Chapter 2 that contribution is a linear profit function.) We wish to know how many of each product to produce to maximize contribution, assuming we can sell what we make. We will remove this assumption of a sellers' market at a later point.

Let us set up the restrictions of the problem. We shall denote the number of air conditioners by x and the number of refrigerators by y. The simplest restrictions are those imposed by the two final assembly lines. They indicate that the number of air conditioners produced per month must be less than or equal to 5000 and that the number of refrigerators must be less than or equal to 4000. These restrictions are plotted in Figure 1. The shaded areas

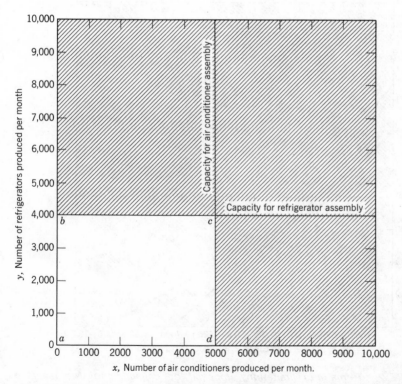

FIGURE 1. *Graphic illustration of the limitations imposed by the final assembly capacity of air conditioners and refrigerators.*

of Figure 1 indicate the parts of the graph that are eliminated as feasible solutions to the problem by the limitations of assembly line capacity. Any feasible solution to the problem must be a combination of air conditioners and refrigerators which falls within the area *abcd*.

The other restrictions are only slightly different. The machine shop capacity limits production to either 6000 air conditioners, 7500 refrigerators, or comparable combinations of both. This restriction is shown in Figure 2 as a straight line which goes through the points ($x = 0$, $y = 7500$) and ($x = 6000$, $y = 0$). This line further restricts the area of feasible solutions. The only combinations of air conditioner and refrigerator production which would not exceed the capacity of the machine shop are those that fall on or below the line.

Figure 2 also shows the limitations imposed by the capacities of the stamping and unit departments. The stamping department restriction is represented by a straight line that goes through the two points ($x = 0$,

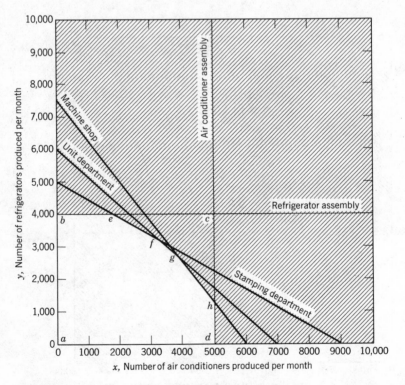

FIGURE 2. *Remaining limitations imposed by capacities of the machine shop, unit department, and stamping department. The area enclosed by* abefghd *includes all feasible solutions to the problem.*

$y = 5000$) and ($x = 9000$, $y = 0$). Combinations of air conditioner and refrigerator production which are equivalent fall on this straight line, for example, 900 air conditioners and 4500 refrigerators, or 4500 air conditioners and 2500 refrigerators. Finally, the unit department restriction is represented by a straight line that goes through the two points ($x = 0$, $y = 6000$) and ($x = 7000$, $y = 0$), which is shown also in Figure 2. The only combinations of air conditioner and refrigeration production that do not exceed the capacity of the unit department are those that fall on or below its line. Note that all the restrictions have been expressed as straight lines, that is, linear relationships. The term, "linear programming," is derived from the fact that all relationships within the model are linear.

Figure 2 shows clearly that the feasible solutions to our problem fall within the white area in *abefghd*. All combinations that fall in the shaded area exceed the capacity of one or more departments. The remaining question is then: Which of the feasible combinations will maximize contribution?

Maximizing Contribution

Recall that contribution was earned at the rate of $50 per refrigerator and $60 per air conditioner. Our objective function is then:

$$60x + 50y = \text{maximum}$$

Our objective is to produce the combination of air conditioners and refrigerators that is feasible and at the same time maximizes contribution. Let us select arbitrarily some contribution figure to see how the objective function looks graphically. At a total contribution of $180,000, for example, the objective function becomes:

$$60x + 50y = 180,000$$

when $x = 0$, $y = 3600$, and when $y = 0$, $x = 3000$

The line passing through these two points is shown as the $180,000 line in Figure 3. This line defines all combinations of air conditioner and refrigerator production that yield a total contribution of $180,000.

Now let us choose a larger value of contribution, perhaps $240,000. The objective function becomes:

$$60x + 50y = 240,000$$

when $x = 0$, $y = 4800$, and when $y = 0$, $x = 4000$

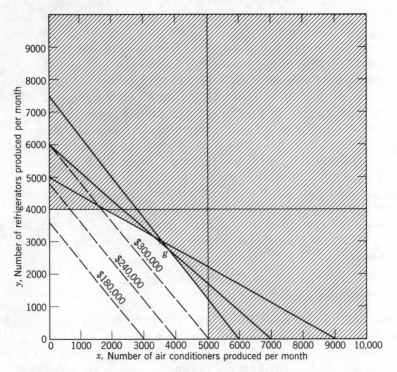

FIGURE 3. Contribution lines plotted to show the effect of larger and larger contributions. The maximum possible contribution within the polygon is defined by a contribution line through the point g.

The line passing through these two points is also shown in Figure 3 as the $240,000 line. It defines all combinations of air conditioner and refrigerator production that yield a total contribution of $240,000. Note that it is *parallel* to the $180,000 line. If we increase the contribution to $300,000, we have the $300,000 line shown in Figure 3. We can see now that we will be limited in the size of the total contribution by the point g. It defines the combination of air conditioner and refrigerator production that produces the largest possible contribution within the space of feasible solutions. Reading from the graph, the point g is approximately at the coordinate $x = 3800$, $y = 2700$. Since the point g is the intersection of the two lines which define the machine shop capacity and the unit department capacity, we can determine the point g exactly by solving the equations of these two lines simultaneously. These two equations are of the form $y = mx + b$, where m is the slope of the line and b is the y intercept. The two equations are:

Machine shop capacity,

$\frac{7500}{6000} = \frac{5}{4}$

$$y = -\tfrac{5}{4}x + 7500$$

Unit department capacity,

$$y = -\tfrac{6}{7}x + 6000$$

solving simultaneously, we have

$$7500 - \tfrac{5}{4}x = 6000 - \tfrac{6}{7}x$$

$$\tfrac{11}{28}x = 1500$$

$$x = 3818 \text{ air conditioners } (\text{MAX})$$

using $x = 3818$ in the first equation, we have

$$y = -\tfrac{5}{4}(3818) + 7500$$

$$= 2728 \text{ refrigerators } (\text{MAX})$$

the contribution of this solution is:

MAX # X $/unit = Contribtn

Contribution $= 60(3818) + 50(2728) = \$365{,}480$

Of course, this agrees with the values of the production program read approximately from the graph.

The graphical interpretation of linear programming can also be extended to three-dimensional space. For example, we could have shown three products, perhaps air conditioners, refrigerators, and stoves. The lines which represent restrictions on the problem would become planes. Feasible solutions would appear in a volume instead of an area, and optimal solutions would occur at the intersections of planes instead of lines. Beyond three-dimensional problems, there is no direct geometric representation.

The Effect of Changes in Objective Function

Let us assume for a moment that the objective function is slightly different, perhaps reflecting an increase in the profitability of air conditioners. Assume that the contribution from air conditioners has increased to \$62.50 per air conditioner and that the contribution for refrigerators has remained at

$50. The new objective function is $62.5x + 50y = $ maximum. We have shown plotted in Figure 4 iso-revenue lines for total contributions of $250,000, $300,000, and $350,000. We can see that the slope of the revenue lines is identical to the slope of the machine shop restriction line. We shall now have an entire family of alternate optimum solutions described by the line segment *gh*. All combinations of air conditioner and refrigerator production which fall on this line segment have the maximum possible total contribution.

Market Restrictions

Let us now examine what happens if we remove the assumption stated earlier that we were operating in an unlimited market. Suppose that market studies have indicated that we cannot expect to sell more than 4500 air

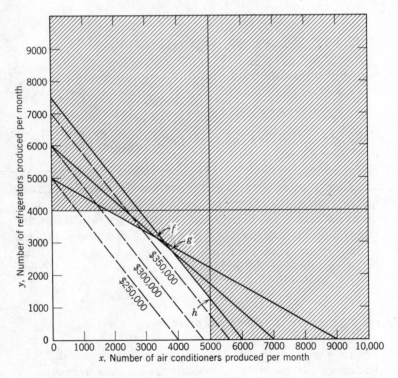

FIGURE 4. *Effect of change of relative profitability of the objective function produces a family of optimum solutions along the line segment* gh.

conditioners and 3000 refrigerators per month. These may be plotted as additional restrictions to feasible solutions, as indicated in Figure 5. Note that if we are considering our first objective function to be valid, the market restrictions have not changed the optimal solution, which is still indicated by the point *g*. That is, the controlling limitation is still determined by the capacities in the machine shop and in the unit department. If we are considering the second objective function, the family of alternate optimum solutions has been reduced to the line segment *gi* because of the limitations of the market for air conditioners. More severe market limitations would of course change this. If, for example, the market studies indicated a maximum sale of 4000 air conditioners and only 2000 refrigerators, all the plant capacities become irrelevant and the maximum total contribution is achieved by producing to meet market requirements, as may be verified by an examination of the graphical relationships.

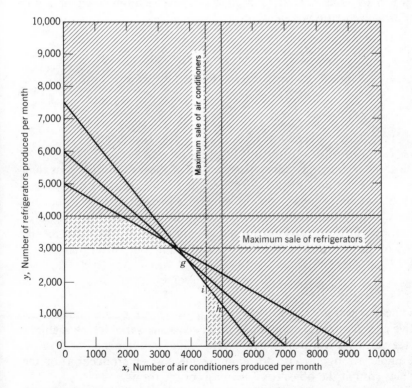

FIGURE 5. *Effect of market restrictions on the enclosed area of feasible solutions.*

A GENERAL STATEMENT OF THE
LINEAR PROGRAMMING PROBLEM /

Before proceeding to the algebraic interpretation of the simplex method let us now state a broad general mathematical statement of the linear programming problem. There are a number of common threads running through the 12 short statements of allocation problems at the beginning of the chapter which were not necessarily explicit, yet they are very important. Hadley [16] describes the general linear programming problem as follows: "*Given a set of m linear inequalities or equations in r variables, we are to find non-negative values of these variables which will satisfy the constraints and maximize or minimize some linear function of the variables.*" For example the m linear inequalities or equations in r variables might describe the capacity in m departments of a shop which can manufacture r products. The constraining set of linear inequalities or equations might be:

$$a_{11}x_1 + a_{12}x_2 + \cdots + a_{1r}x_r \leqslant b_1 \text{ (Dept. 1)}$$
$$a_{21}x_1 + a_{22}x_2 + \cdots + a_{2r}x_r \leqslant b_2 \text{ (Dept. 2)}$$
$$\cdot$$
$$\cdot$$
$$\cdot$$
$$a_{m1}x_1 + a_{m2}x_2 + \cdots + a_{mr}x_r \leqslant b_m \text{ (Dept. m)}$$

Each of these inequalities states that the sum of the ax's must be less than or equal to the limiting quantity b, where the b's are capacities to produce in each department, the x's are the quantities of each of the r products, and the a's are coefficients which indicate the amount of the resource required by each x (product). Another constraint in addition to the linearity of the variables is that they must all be non-negative, that is,

$$x_j \geqslant 0, \qquad j = 1, \ldots, r$$

Given these constraints, we are seeking to maximize or minimize some objective or criterion function made up of the same variables, though not all of the variables will have positive values, that is, some may be zero. In our example, we might wish to minimize the cost of production for the r products so that the objective function is of the form

$$C_1x_1 + C_2x_2 + \cdots + C_rx_r = Z$$

where Z is the total cost to be minimized, and the C's are the costs associated with each variable. The number of equations or inequalities m can be greater, less than, or equal to the number of variables r, and we seek the values of the x's subject to the constraints and to meeting the objective stated by the criterion function. The functions must be linear both in the constraints and in the objective function which implies that powers and products of the variables, such as x_1^2 or x_1x_2, are not allowed. Specific problem statements might call for either maximizing or minimizing the objective function, and the constraints may take the form of equations or inequalities of either the less than or equal to or greater than or equal to type.

We shall now proceed to illustrate specific cases of linear programming by first an algebraic interpretation and finally develop an efficient equivalent procedure for solving problems.

ALGEBRAIC
INTERPRETATION /

Let us take a slightly different problem and develop an algebraic solution consistent with the general statement, attempting to relate our methods to the graphic interpretation.

Assume the conditions of a plant which manufactures two products, which we designate by x and y. Each product is manufactured by a two-step process which involves machines A and B. The process time for the two products on the two machines is as follows:

Product	Machine A	Machine B	CONTRIB
x	2 hours	3 hours	$ 60
y	4 hours	2 hours	$ 50
Total	80 hrs	60 hrs	

For the period ahead, machine A has available 80 hours and machine B has available 60 hours.

The contribution (sales value minus variable cost) for product x is $60 per unit, and for y it is $50 per unit. The company faces a situation where it can sell as much as it can produce for the immediate planning period ahead and therefore wishes to know how many units of each of the two products it should produce to maximize its contribution.

Formulation of the Problem

Since we are limited only by the available hours on the two machines, we wish to make symbolically the common-sense statement that, for each of the two machines, the total time spent in the manufacture of product x and of product y cannot exceed the total time available. For machine A then, since product x requires two hours per unit and y four hours per unit, 2 (units of product x) + 4 (units of product y), must be less than or equal to 80 hours. Symbolically, this is:

$$2x + 4y \leqslant 80 \qquad (A\text{-}1)$$

And for machine B,

$$3x + 2y \leqslant 60 \qquad (B\text{-}1)$$

In addition, since the total contribution depends only on the amounts of the two products produced, the objective function is:

$$\text{Contribution} = 60x + 50y = \text{maximum} \qquad (C\text{-}1)$$

Let us pause for a moment to see how the problem looks graphically. Figure 6 shows the restrictions for the capacity of the two machines plotted for the limiting cases when the productive hours allocated to products x and y total 80 hours and 60 hours for machines A and B respectively. The objective function is also plotted for the two levels of total contribution, \$900 and \$1200, and it is easy to see that point c defines the combination of products x and y for which we will obtain maximum contribution.

Slack Variables

Formulations A-1 and B-1 are inequalities, that is, they state that the total time on machine A, for example, allocated to product x and y might not be as much as 80 hours. There could be some idle time. If we let W_A represent this idle time, we convert (A-1) to an equation with W_A taking up the slack:

$$2x + 4y + W_A = 80 \qquad (A\text{-}2)$$

And for machine B,

$$3x + 2y + W_B = 60 \qquad (B\text{-}2)$$

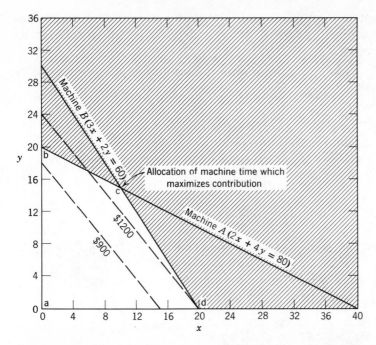

FIGURE 6. Graphical solution of example used for algebraic interpretation of the simplex method.

The only permissible values for the unknowns are zero, or some positive value, that is, we cannot produce negative amounts of the products or have negative idle time on the machines.

We now have two equations with four unknowns for which we wish to determine the values, x, y, W_A, and W_B. It can be shown that there is a solution to such a system, such that at least two of the unknowns are zero. The practical effect of this statement is that our problem becomes one of determining which two of the variables should be zero in order that contribution is maximum.

Initial Solution

To start, we first develop a trivial solution, which is nonetheless feasible and which we may then improve by a procedure that will take us, step by step, toward the optimum solution. Let us start with the worst possible solution, from the point of view of our objective function, in which W_A and W_B are assumed to be the variables with positive values, and x and y

are zero. In other words, all the available machine time is idle, since there is no production. First, we solve for W_A and W_B by transposing (*A*-2) and (*B*-2) as follows:

$$W_A = 80 - 2x - 4y \qquad (A\text{-}3)$$

$$W_B = 60 - 3x - 2y \qquad (B\text{-}3)$$

If x and y are zero, the values of W_A and W_B are

$$W_A = 80 - 2(0) - 4(0) = 80$$

$$W_B = 60 - 3(0) - 2(0) = 60$$

The value of the objective function is

$$\text{Contribution} = 60x + 50y = 60(0) + 50(0) = 0 \qquad (C\text{-}3)$$

which is the contribution expected when nothing is produced. Note that this initial solution is point a in Figure 6.

Improving the Initial Trivial Solution

Obviously, we can improve this initial solution by decreasing either W_A or W_B to zero and selecting either x or y as a variable with a positive value. The question is, however, which variable, x or y, should we choose first? The answer is that we wish to introduce the variable that will improve the contribution by the greatest amount.

Selecting the Key Variable. Which variable, x or y, would improve the total contribution most? We can tell by looking at the objective function. Each unit of x earns $60 as compared to only $50 for each unit of y. Therefore, it is x that we wish to increase from zero to some positive value.

Increasing x to the Maximum Possible. We know that allocating productive time to x will increase contribution. For each unit of x produced, we obtain a contribution of $60. How many x's should we produce, 1, 2, 10, 20, . . . ? Since we have found an advantageous shift in the allocation of available machine time, why not produce as many as possible? We will increase the value of x to the maximum possible without violating the restrictions of the problem. Equation *A*-2 shows us that if y and W_A were zero, the maximum value of x is

$$x = \frac{80 - 4 \times 0 - 0}{2} = 40 \qquad (A\text{-}4)$$

Equation B-2 tells us that if y and W_B are zero, the maximum value of x is

$$x = \frac{60 - 2 \times 0 - 0}{3} = 20 \qquad (B\text{-}4)$$

Key Equation. Equation B-2 is controlling, since in it a value of x greater than 20 is not permitted. This means then that we will increase x to the maximum and reduce W_B to zero. The two variables to have positive values are now x and W_A, y and W_B being zero. Equation B-2 is then the key equation, so we solve it for x:

$$x = \frac{60 - 2y - W_B}{3}$$

$$= 20 - \frac{2y}{3} - \frac{W_B}{3} \qquad (B\text{-}5)$$

Since the expression of x limits it to the maximum possible, we will substitute this expression for x in (A-3) and in the objective function.

$$W_A = 80 - 2\left(20 - \frac{2y}{3} - \frac{W_B}{3}\right) - 4y$$

which simplifies to

$$W_A = 40 - \tfrac{8}{3}y + \tfrac{2}{3}W_B \qquad (A\text{-}5)$$

The objective function then becomes

$$\text{Contribution} = 60(20 - \tfrac{2}{3}y - \tfrac{1}{3}W_B) + 50y$$

$$= 1200 + 10y - 20W_B \qquad (C\text{-}5)$$

Letting y and W_B become zero results in the following values of the four variables:

$$x = 20, \quad \text{from } (B\text{-}5)$$

$$W_A = 40, \quad \text{from } (A\text{-}5)$$

$$y = 0$$

$$W_B = 0$$

$$\text{Contribution} = 1200, \quad \text{from } (C\text{-}5)$$

This is an obvious improvement over the first solution, since the value of the objective function has now increased from zero to $1200. We can see from Figure 6 that the second stage of our solution is represented by point *d*.

Repeating the Procedure. Is it possible to improve on the solution just presented? Our test is a simple one. We look at the last statement of the objective function, (*C*-5). Here we see that the total value of the objective function would increase if we could increase the value of *y* above zero (*y* is positive in *C*-5). For every unit of *y* produced, we would add $10 to the total contribution. Also, we can see from (*C*-5) that total contribution would increase if we could decrease W_B (W_B is negative in *C*-5); however, we know that W_B is already zero so that it is impossible to reduce it any more. Therefore we select *y* as the variable to increase.

How Much Can **y** *Be Increased?* As before, we look to the equations that represent the current stage of solution, (*A*-5) and (*B*-5). From (*A*-5), the maximum value of *y* occurs when W_A and W_B are zero, or $y = 15$. (W_B was already zero at this stage of solution.) From (*B*-5) the maximum value of *y* occurs when *x* and W_B are zero, or $y = 30$.

Equation *A*-5 is the more restrictive and is, therefore, selected as the *key equation.* We solve (*A*-5) for *y*:

$$y = 15 + \tfrac{1}{4}W_B - \tfrac{3}{8}W_A \qquad (A\text{-}6)$$

Substituting this value of *y* in (*B*-5) and the last statement of the objective function, (*C*-5), we obtain

$$x = 10 + \tfrac{1}{4}W_A - \tfrac{1}{2}W_B \qquad (B\text{-}6)$$

$$\text{Contribution} = 1350 - \tfrac{15}{4}W_A - \tfrac{35}{2}W_B \qquad (C\text{-}6)$$

When W_A and W_B are zero, the values of the variables and of the objective function are as follows:

$$x = 10$$

$$y = 15$$

$$W_A = 0$$

$$W_B = 0$$

$$\text{Contribution} = 1350$$

We see that this is point *c* in Figure 6, and we have noted before that this was the optimal solution by inspection of Figure 6. How can we tell that this is true from the algebraic interpretation? We look at the last statement of the objective function (*C*-6) to see if it can be increased without violating any of the restrictions of the problem. We note that the only possible way that contribution could increase is by decreasing either W_A, W_B, or both. Since the solution at this stage already specifies that W_A and W_B are at their minimum values of zero, and since none of the variables can take on negative values, there is no way to increase contribution. We have the optimal solution.

Shadow Prices.   Now that we have identified an optimal solution, we wish to provide the manager with the maximum decision making information. He knows now the optimal combination of products x and y to produce, that is, 10 and 15 units, respectively. He also knows that the total contribution to profit and overhead of this solution is $1350. But what are the marginal gains and losses that he would experience by altering the solution? The answers are contained in the last statement of the objective function (*C*-6) which was

$$\text{Contribution} = 1350 - \tfrac{15}{4}W_A - \tfrac{35}{2}W_B$$

Recall that since W_A and W_B were zero in the optimal solution, the net contribution was $1350. But what is the significance of the coefficients $-15/4$ and $-35/2$ of W_A and W_B? They indicate the net contribution of W_A and W_B in the objective function and are called shadow prices. Specifically, the net contribution of W_A is $-15/4 = -\$3.75$. In other words, for every unit of W_A added in the solution at this point (idle time on machine *A*), contribution declines by $3.75. But conversely, if the original capacity of machine *A* had been 81 hours instead of 80, net contribution could have been increased by $3.75. The meaning of the shadow prices then is that they represent *the value of a marginal unit of capacity* in the final solution. Indeed the shadow prices had this equivalent meaning at every stage of the solution. In the initial statement of the objective function (*C*-3) x and y had marginal contribution rates of 50 and 60, respectively, and W_A and W_B had zero rates. In the second stage of solution (*C*-5), y had a contribution rate of 10 and W_B a rate of -20.

The shadow prices define the opportunities available and focus managerial attention on them. The optimal solution states what to do now, given the constraints on capacity. The shadow prices raise questions about what should be done, that is, in this case, should capacity be increased? The optimal solution is a satisfying result which can possibly promote complacency. The shadow prices are disturbing and provoke thought.

One final observation about the shadow prices is of value. The total contribution of the machine capacities are also indicated by the shadow prices. For machine A, we noted the shadow price of $-\$3.75$ per hour of idle time. There is possible a total of 80 idle hours on $3.75 \times 80 = \$300$. For machine B the shadow price was $-35/2 = -\$17.50$ and a maximum idle time of 60 hours, or $17.50 \times 60 = \$1050$. The sum of the two values of machine capacity is $300 + 1050 = \$1350$, the total contribution of the optimum solution. In other words, in the optimum solution the total value of producing x and y in the quantities of 10 and 15 units, respectively, is equal to the total value of the capacities defined by the potential idle times W_A and W_B which are not in the final solution.

Value of the Simplex Method

It seems as though we have performed a great deal of computation and manipulation to solve so simple a problem, one which was obvious by graphical methods. The value of the simplex method, however, is for large-scale problems where there is no graphic equivalent. In these complex cases, the simplex method saves time and effort by taking us to the optimal solution in a finite number of steps, each step bringing us closer to the optimum. Note that the initial solution was at point a of Figure 6, the second solution at d, and the third at c, all corners of the polygon a, b, c, d. There were many combinations of the four variables that we did not even consider as we converged on the optimal solution.

For example, in proceeding from a to d, we considered none of the many feasible solutions along the line ad, which would have yielded progressively larger values of contribution, as the value of x increased. Instead, we jumped from a to d. Similarly, we did not consider any of the feasible solutions along the line dc, although each one would have progressively yielded a larger contribution as we converged on the optimum. For example, the point ($x = 16$, $y = 6$) results in $W_A = 24$, $W_B = 0$, and contribution $= \$1200$.

Also, we did not consider any of the feasible solutions that fell inside the polygon. We should note that all these other solutions which we did not consider are feasible solutions that involve more than two of the four variables as positive values. By requiring that we deal only with solutions where two, and only two, variables could be positive, we can jump from corner to corner, rather than move more slowly in more steps along the lines of the polygon. The solutions that involve only two of the four variables are called *basic solutions*. There are only four such basic solutions in our example, at points a, b, c, and d.

In the larger scale problems, we are doing the same sort of thing, that is, moving from one basic solution to a better one, leaping over an entire set of other feasible solutions that are in-between. These basic solutions are always at the corners of two- and three-dimensional problems and conceptually at the equivalent of the corners of multidimensional problems in hyperspace.

✓ *Alternate Optimum Solutions.* Now let us consider the effect of a slightly different objective function in the example. Suppose that the contribution of y is only \$40 instead of \$50. The objective function becomes:

$$60x + 40y = \text{maximum}$$

The objective function line is now parallel to the line segment cd in Figure 6 so that we have an entire family of optimum solutions. Two of these optima would be basic solutions (points c and d) with a total contribution of \$1200 (the new maximum contribution). All the combinations of x and y that fall along the line segment cd also give the maximum contribution of \$1200, but they are not basic solutions because they will involve some idle machine time—that is, more than two of the variables x, y, W_A, and W_B have positive values. If we take the point ($x = 16$, $y = 6$), $W_A = 24$ and $W_B = 0$, as noted before. We call the optimum solutions of this type "derived optima."

This procedure is the simplex method. The basic procedure can be used with problems of great complexity. To apply the procedure to complex problems, it will be useful to reduce it to a set of rigorous rules which can be applied rather mechanically to save time and to reduce the computation required to a minimum. In such a procedure, it is important to retain contact with the meaning of each step so that we have more than just a mechanical procedure. We shall attempt to do this by using the same example as was used for the algebraic interpretation, and by relating our manipulations to what we did in the algebraic procedure.

THE SIMPLEX PROCEDURE /

Recall that after the addition of the slack variables to account for idle time, our two restricting equations for machines A and B were respectively:

$$2x + 4y + W_A = 80$$
$$3x + 2y + W_B = 60$$

and the objective function was

$$60x + 50y = \text{maximum}$$

Since idle time contributes nothing to contribution, we could also write the objective function as follows, without changing its value:

$$60x + 50y + (0)W_A + (0)W_B = \text{maximum}$$

To minimize the recopying of x, y, W_A and W_B, let us arrange the two restricting equations with the variables at the heads of columns and the coefficients of these variables in rows to represent the equations.

	x	y	W_A	W_B
80	2	4	1	0
60	3	2	0	1

The usual form is to reverse the right- and left-hand sides of the equations so that the constants 80 and 60 now appear on the left, with the equal sign dropped. For machine A, we have entered the coefficient 0 under column W_B, since W_B does not apply to machine A, and similarly for W_A in the equation for machine B. Next we place the coefficients from the objective function above the variables, and to the left we place beside the constants 80 and 60 two columns which identify the variables in the solution and their contribution rates in the objective function. This is shown in Table I. Table I also shows the condition of the matrix for the initial solution. Recall that in the algebraic interpretation we started with an initial trivial solution where all the available machine time was idle. The stub of the matrix identifies the variables in the solution which are nonzero and shows their values, as well as showing in the far left column the contribution to the objective function that each of these variables makes.

TABLE I. Initial simplex matrix

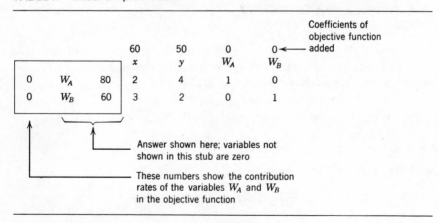

Before proceeding, let us name the various parts of the matrix. Figure 7 shows the nomenclature of the various parts of the matrix. The objective row contains the coefficients which show the contribution rates of each of the variables in the objective function. For example, the contribution of each unit of x is \$60 per unit, y is \$50, etc. The variable row simply identifies the variable associated with each of the coefficients in the various columns. The solution stub will always contain three columns. The variable column shows the variables that have positive values at a given stage of solution, and variables not shown in the stub have a value of zero. The constant column shows the value of each of the variables in the solution. The objective column shows the contribution rates of the solution variables, and these coefficients come from the objective row. For example, in the initial solution shown, the coefficients above W_A and W_B are zeros. The body and identity will vary in size, depending on the particular problem. The identity will be that portion of the matrix showing the coefficients for slack variables.

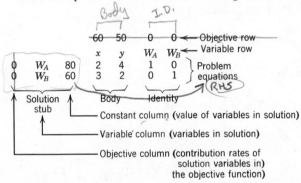

FIGURE 7.   Nomenclature of the simplex matrix.

Improving the Initial Solution

To improve the initial solution, we must have a measure of the potential improvement that we would make in the objective function by bringing some of the variables which are now zero into the solution, instead of the variables that are now in the solution. To determine measures of potential improvement for the simplex method, we will develop an *index row* (shadow prices) which will be placed just below the present initial matrix. These index numbers will appear under the constant column, the body, and the identity. They are calculated from the formula:

Index number = Σ (numbers in column) × (corresponding number in objective column) − (number in objective row at head of column)

Recall that the numbers in the objective column represent the contribution rates of the variables which are in the solution represented by the matrix. The numbers in the column are the coefficients of the variable for which the index number is being computed. What we have then, essentially, is a measure of the contribution of the present variables in the solution weighted by the coefficients of a variable we propose to introduce. We then subtract from this the contribution rate for that variable at the head of the column. If the algebraic sum is negative, the practical meaning is that the variable in question would contribute more to the objective than one or more of the variables now in the solution, that is, they are marginal contribution rates, or what we have called shadow prices. We can see, then, that negative numbers in the index row will indicate variables which are good candidates for changes in allocation.

For our problem, the index row numbers are as follows:

1. Index number for constant column,

$$= (80 \times 0 + 60 \times 0) - 0 = 0$$

2. Index number for first column of body,

$$= (2 \times 0 + 3 \times 0) - 60 = -60$$

3. Index number for second column of body,

$$= (4 \times 0 + 2 \times 0) - 50 = -50$$

4. Index number for first column of identity,

$$= (1 \times 0 + 0 \times 0) - 0 = 0$$

5. Index number for second column of identity,

$$= (0 \times 0 + 1 \times 0) - 0 = 0$$

We now place the index numbers in the initial simplex matrix, as indicated in Table II. We see in this instance that the index row is merely the objective row preceded by minus signs. *This occurs when the objective column contains all zeros.*

The larger the negative number, the greater the potential improvement. If all the numbers under the body and identity of the index row were zero or positive, no further improvement could be obtained, which would indicate that the solution presented in the stub was an optimal solution.

TABLE II.   Initial simplex matrix with index row included

			60	50	0	0	
		0	x	y	W_A	W_B	
0	W_A	80	2	4	1	0	
0	W_B	60	3	2	0	1	
		0	−60	−50	0	0	← Index row

Selecting the Key Column and Key Row.   We see from Table II that the column headed by the variable x has the greatest improvement potential, so we select it as the *key column*. This selection means that the variable x will be introduced into the solution in favor of W_A or W_B. To determine whether x will replace W_A or W_B, we must select a key row. To do this, we *divide each number in the constant column by the corresponding positive nonzero number in the key column*. The resulting quotients are compared, and the *key row* is selected as the row yielding the smallest nonnegative quotient. For our problem, the quotients are:

$$\text{First row,} \quad \tfrac{80}{2} = 40$$

$$\text{Second row,} \tfrac{60}{3} = 20 \text{ (key row)}$$

Through the selection of the key row, we are determining which of the two problem equations will limit the value of x. See equations A-4 and B-4 to verify that we have performed exactly the same computation as we did at that point.

Since the second row limits the value of x, it is designated the key row, and the number at the intersection of the key row and key column is designated the *key number*. Table III shows the initial matrix with the key column, key row, and key number identified.

TABLE III.   Initial simplex matrix with key column, row, and number identified

Matrix I			60	50	0	0	
			x	y	W_A	W_B	
0	W_A	80	2	4	1	0	
0	W_B	60	3	2	0	1	←———Key row
			−60	−50	0	0	

Key column ⟶   ⟵ Key number

Developing an Improved Solution

With the key column and key row selected, we can now prepare a new table representing an improved solution. The first step in developing the new table is to calculate the coefficients for the *main row*. This main row appears in the relative position in the new table as the key row in the preceding table. It is computed by dividing the coefficients of the key row by the key number. Table IV shows this development. The variable and its objective number from the head of the key column, that is, x and 60, are placed in the stub of the main row replacing W_B and 0 from the previous table. The balance of the objective and variable columns in the stub is copied from the previous table, and the new table developed to this point now appears as Table V.

TABLE IV. *Simplex matrix with main row of new table*

Matrix I			60	50	0	0
			x	y	W_A	W_B
0	W_A	80	2	4	1	0
0	W_B	60	3	2	0	1
			-60	-50	0	0
Matrix II						
		20	1	$\frac{2}{3}$	0	$\frac{1}{3}$ ← Main row

TABLE V. *Simplex matrix with variable and objective columns completed*

Matrix I			60	50	0	0
			x	y	W_A	W_B
0	W_A	80	2	4	1	0
0	W_B	60	3	2	0	1
			-60	-50	0	0
Matrix II						
0	W_A					
60	x	20	1	$\frac{2}{3}$	0	$\frac{1}{3}$

Now all of the remaining coefficients in the new table, including the constant column, the body, identity, and index row can be calculated by the following formula:

$$\text{New number} = \text{old number} - \frac{\begin{pmatrix} \text{corresponding} \\ \text{number of} \\ \text{key row} \end{pmatrix} \times \begin{pmatrix} \text{corresponding} \\ \text{number of} \\ \text{key column} \end{pmatrix}}{\text{key number}}$$

1. First row, constant column,

$$\text{new number} = 80 - \frac{60 \times 2}{3} = 40$$

2. First row, first column of body,

$$\text{new number} = 2 - \frac{3 \times 2}{3} = 0$$

3. Index row, first column of body,

$$\text{new number} = -60 - \frac{3 \times (-60)}{3} = 0$$

The remaining coefficients can be calculated in the same way and the completed improved solution is shown in Table VI.

TABLE VI.   Simplex matrix with first iteration completed

			60	50	0	0
Matrix I			x	y	W_A	W_B
0	W_A	80	2	4	1	0
0	W_B	60	3	2	0	1
			-60	-50	0	0
Matrix II						
0	W_A	40	0	$2\frac{2}{3}$	1	$-\frac{2}{3}$
60	x	20	1	$\frac{2}{3}$	0	$\frac{1}{3}$
		1200	0	-10	0	20

Let us pause for a moment to determine what we have accomplished by this manipulation and to relate it to the previous algebraic solution. First, in generating the main row for the second table, we have done the equivalent of solving the equation for machine B for the variable x as was done by equation B-5. Note that the coefficients for each of the variables in the main row are the same as those in equation B-5, ignoring sign. In generating the balance of the numbers to complete the table by the formula for "new numbers," we are doing the equivalent of substituting the value of x determined by equation B-5 in the equation for machine B and in the objective function. To check this, note that the coefficients, ignoring sign, for the row above the main row are the same as those in equation A-5, and those in the row below the main row are the same as those in equation C-3.

The solution at this stage is:

$$W_A = 40$$
$$x = 20$$
$$y = 0$$
$$W_B = 0$$

The values in the constant columns of the stub indicate this, y and W_B being zero since they are not in the stub at all. The value of the objective function (contribution) for this solution is $1200, given in the constant column, index row. Table VI, however, shows that the solution can still be improved since a -10 appears in the index row under the variable y.

Since the index row has only one negative number, which is under the variable y, it is selected as the key column for the next iteration. The key row is selected in the same way as before. The two quotients are:

$$\text{First row,} \quad 40/\tfrac{8}{3} = 15 \quad \text{(key row)}$$
$$\text{Second row,} \quad 20/\tfrac{2}{3} = 30$$

The first row has the smallest nonnegative quotient, so it is selected as the key row. A new main row is calculated as before, by dividing the coefficients in the main row by the key number. The new variable y and its objective number are entered in the stub, and the new numbers in the body, identity, and index row are computed as before. The remaining variable and its objective number are copied from the preceding interation table; Table VII shows the new solution.

The new solution in Table VII is optimal since no further improvement is

TABLE VII. *Simplex matrix, second and final iteration completed*

Matrix I

			60	50	0	0
			x	y	W_A	W_B
0	W_A	80	2	4	1	0
0	W_B	60	3	2	0	1
			−60	−50	0	0

Matrix II

0	W_A	40	0	$2\frac{2}{3}$	1	$-\frac{2}{3}$
60	x	20	1	$\frac{2}{3}$	0	$\frac{1}{3}$
		1200	0	−10	0	20

Matrix III

50	y	15	0	1	$\frac{3}{8}$	$-\frac{1}{4}$
60	x	10	1	0	$-\frac{1}{4}$	$\frac{1}{2}$
		1350	0	0	$3\frac{3}{4}$	$17\frac{1}{2}$

indicated in the index row. The values of the variables for the optimal solution are:

$$x = 10$$
$$y = 15$$
$$W_A = 0$$
$$W_B = 0$$

The value of the objective function for the optimal solution is shown as $1350. Of course, all these values check with our previous algebraic solution and with the graphical solution. Note also that the final index row yields the shadow prices obtained previously for W_A and W_B.

Procedure Summary

1. *Formulate the problem and the objective function.*
2. *Develop the initial simplex matrix*, including the initial trivial

solution and the index row numbers. The index row numbers in the initial matrix are calculated by the formula:

$$\text{Index number} = \Sigma \left[\begin{pmatrix} \text{numbers} \\ \text{in} \\ \text{column} \end{pmatrix} \times \begin{pmatrix} \text{corresponding} \\ \text{number in} \\ \text{objective} \\ \text{column} \end{pmatrix} \right] - \begin{pmatrix} \text{number in} \\ \text{objective} \\ \text{row at head} \\ \text{of column} \end{pmatrix}$$

3. *Select the key column*, the column with the most negative index number in the body or the identity.

4. *Select the key row*, the row with the smallest nonnegative quotient obtained by dividing each number of the constant column by the corresponding positive, nonzero number in the key column.

5. *The key number* is at the intersection of the key row and key column.

6. *Develop the main row of the new table*.

$$\text{Main row} = \frac{\text{numbers in key row of preceding table}}{\text{key number}}$$

The main row appears in the new table in the same relative position as the key row of the preceding table.

7. *Develop the balance of the new table*.
   a. The variable and its objective number at the head of the key column are entered in the stub of the new table to the left of the main row, replacing the variable and objective number from the key row of the preceding table.
   b. The remainder of the variable and objective columns are reproduced in the new table exactly as they were in the preceding table.
   c. The balance of the coefficients for the new table are calculated by the formula:

$$\text{New number} = \text{old number} - \frac{\begin{pmatrix} \text{corresponding} \\ \text{number of} \\ \text{key row} \end{pmatrix} \times \begin{pmatrix} \text{corresponding} \\ \text{number of} \\ \text{key column} \end{pmatrix}}{\text{key number}}$$

8. Repeat (iterate) steps 3 through 7c until all the index numbers (not including the constant column) are positive. An optimal solution then results.

9. The interpretation of the resulting optimum solution is as follows: The solution appears in the stub. The variables shown in the variable column have values shown in the corresponding rows of the constant column. The value of the objective function is shown in the constant column, index row. All variables not shown in the stub are equal to zero. The shadow prices which indicate the value of a marginal unit of capacity are shown in the index row of the final solution.

Checking the Work. The simplest and most effective check of the work in progress is to establish a check column to the right of the simplex matrix. The numbers in the check column are simply the algebraic sum of all the numbers in a given row, beginning with the constant column and adding all the coefficients to the right. This check column can be established for each row, including the index row. All transformations of the numbers in the check column are the same as for any of the other numbers in the table. After transformation, the algebraic sum of the row coefficients should equal the transformed number in the check column. If it does not, an error has been made, and it should be traced and corrected before proceeding. Table VIII shows the three iterations of our illustrative problem with the check column included.

TABLE VIII. *Completed solution from Table VII with check column*

Matrix I							
			60	50	0	0	
			x	y	W_A	W_B	Check
0	W_A	80	2	4	1	0	87
0	W_B	60	3	2	0	1	66
			-60	-50	0	0	-110
Matrix II							
0	W_A	40	0	$2\frac{2}{3}$	1	$-\frac{2}{3}$	43
60	x	20	1	$\frac{2}{3}$	0	$\frac{1}{3}$	22
		1200	0	-10	0	20	1210
Matrix III							
50	y	15	0	1	$\frac{3}{8}$	$-\frac{1}{4}$	$16\frac{1}{8}$
60	x	10	1	0	$-\frac{1}{4}$	$\frac{1}{2}$	$11\frac{1}{4}$
		1350	0	0	$3\frac{3}{4}$	$17\frac{1}{2}$	$1371\frac{1}{4}$

Degeneracy in the Simplex Solution. Degeneracy in the simplex solution can be recognized at the time that the key row is being selected. If a tie exists between two or more rows for the smallest nonnegative quotient at that time, the problem is degenerate. Table IX shows this situation. Dividing the constant column by the corresponding number in the key column, we have:

$$\text{Row 1}: \frac{40}{4} = 10$$

$$\text{Row 2}: \frac{30}{3} = 10$$

TABLE IX.   Degeneracy in the simplex matrix. Rows 1 and 2 are tied for key row

			12	10	0	0	0
			A	B	W_1	W_2	W_3
0	W_1	40	4	2	1	0	0
0	W_2	30	3	1	0	1	0
0	W_3	20	1	3	0	0	1
		0	−12	−10	0	0	0

A tie exists, and there is the possibility that if the wrong row is selected as the key row, the variable in the stub of the other row may disappear. The problem may begin to cycle at this point, and an optimum solution could not be obtained. The degeneracy is resolved by the following procedure:

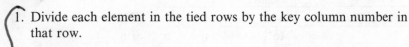

1. Divide each element in the tied rows by the key column number in that row.
2. Compare the resulting ratios, column by column, from left to right, first in the identity and then in the body.
3. The first comparison that yields unequal ratios breaks the tie.
4) The key row is the row that has the algebraically smaller ratio.

Applying this procedure to the degenerate problem of Table IX we begin our paired comparison in the left-hand column of the identity. The ratios in column W_1 are:

$$\text{Row 1}: \frac{1}{4}$$

$$\text{Row 2}: 0$$

The second row yields the algebraically smaller ratio and therefore is selected as the key row. The regular simplex procedure may then be resumed. This procedure for resolving degeneracy is general and can be applied at any stage of the solution to any size matrix.

The problem of Table IX may be taken as an exercise, including a check column. (Answer: $A = 8$, $B = 4$, $W_2 = 2$)

Exercises Involving Variations and Other Objective Functions

Cost of Idle Equipment. In our illustrative example we assumed that there was no cost attached to idle equipment. This, of course, is not necessarily true. There may be standby heating or lighting costs, routine maintenance or machine rental. Any incremental costs incurred by a machine, department, or other productive unit, while it is idle should be included. This, of course, does not include fixed costs but only those costs which can be avoided by choosing some reasonable alternative plan of action.

Idle equipment costs appear in the objective function. They are represented by negative coefficients of the slack variables. For example, let us assume that the idle costs for our previous illustrative problem were $30 per hour for machine A and $25 per hour for machine B. The new objective function would be:

$$60x + 50y - 30W_A - 25W_B = \text{maximum}$$

Exercise

Determine the optimum allocation of machine time when idle equipment costs stated above are included. Use a check column to insure accuracy.

Maximizing the Number of Units Produced. Our previous illustrative problems have been concerned with maximizing a profit function. We may, however, reconstruct our objective to maximize the total number of units of x and y produced. The objective of maximum number of units of output might be appropriate where a delivery date must be met which involves a large penalty for default. Also, wartime conditions often produce maximum production goals, cost being only a secondary objective.

In our illustrative example, if we had wished to maximize the total number of units of x and y produced, the objective function would be

$$x + y = \text{maximum}$$

The basic relationships restricting capacity for machines A and B would of course remain the same.

Exercise

Develop an optimum solution to the problem of maximizing the number of units produced, using the restricting equations for our previous illustrative example.

Minimizing an Objective Function.   The procedure with which we have been dealing is a maximizing one. Suppose that we had wished to maximize the time that the equipment was in use. Using the same illustrative example as a background, the objective function would have been

$$W_A + W_B = \text{minimum}$$

This of course has the effect of maximizing the time that the equipment was being used. Since the procedure we have developed is for maximizing an objective function, we simply multiply the foregoing statement by -1 and obtain

$$-W_A - W_B = \text{maximum}$$

This does not alter the objective function, but makes it possible for us to use the maximizing procedure that we have developed.

We may also achieve the objective of minimizing a given objective function by changing one simple rule in the simplex procedure. When selecting the *key column*, the largest *positive* number in the index row is selected, rather than the largest negative number. All other steps remain exactly the same.

Requirements

To this point, we have dealt only with restrictions to a problem. In our illustrative example, both machines A and B have maximum amounts of time available. There may be situations, however, where we are given a requirement that some combination of the variables must be greater than or equal to a given number. For example, the inequality

$$3x + 2y \geqslant 12$$

has a requirement of at least 12. To convert this statement to an equation, we must *subtract* a slack variable, and the result is

$$3x + 2y - W_1 = 12$$

As it stands, however, this equation cannot be used in the simplex matrix, because the coefficient for W_1 is -1. The *simplex method requires that each equation have one (and only one) nonzero entry in the identity and that this* *entry must have a coefficient of + 1.* We can accomplish this by adding an artificial variable U, which will appear in the identity. Our equation becomes

$$3x + 2y - W_1 + U_1 = 12$$

The slack variable W_1 will now appear in the body of the simplex matrix and the artificial variable U_1 appears in the identity, satisfying the requirement of only one nonzero entry in the identity with a coefficient of $+1$. The artificial variable is included simply as a computational device that permits us to stay within the rules of the simplex method. Consequently, the artificial variable is not wanted in an optimum solution. To be sure that the artificial variable will always be zero in the optimum solution, we may assign an arbitrarily large negative contribution to it in the objective function which we shall call $-M$. The $-M$ is in reality an overwhelming cost in relation to the positive contributions in the objective function, so that as the objective function is maximized through the usual procedure, the artificial variable is driven to zero.

Equations

A problem may state that a certain combination of variables must total some exact quantity. To fit this into the requirements of the simplex matrix we must have a variable for the identity, which can be accomplished through the use of an artificial variable. For example, the equation

$$2x + 3y = 90$$

can be modified to fit into the simplex format by adding an artificial variable U, and the equation becomes

$$2x + 3y + U = 90$$

As with the handling for requirements, a $-M$ contribution is assigned to the artificial variable U in the objective function so that the artificial variable is always zero in the optimum solution.

Approximations

It may be that a particular problem requires only that some combination of the variables involved should be approximately equal to some number, so that some flexibility is allowed. For example, we may state this as

$$2x + 4y \approx 40$$

(The symbol $\approx$ means "approximately equal to.") This statement may be prepared for the simplex matrix by both adding and subtracting slack variables:

Approximation

$$2x + 4y - W_1 + W_2 = 40$$

The two slack variables permit $2x + 4y$ to be either slightly larger or slightly smaller than 40. The slack variable W_1 represents the amount by which $2x + 4y$ exceeds 40, and the slack variable W_2 represents the amount by which $2x + 4y$ is less than 40. The approximation, modified by the two slack variables, is now prepared for inclusion in the simplex matrix. The slack variable W_1 will appear in the body, and the slack variable W_2 will appear in the identity. We wish to minimize the value of the slack variables so that $2x + 4y$ will be as close as possible to 40, and this may be accomplished in the objective function by assigning the coefficient -1 to both slack variables in the objective function. In this example, the objective function might be

$$60x + 50y - W_1 - W_2 = \text{maximum}$$

Example

To summarize the way in which different types of relationships are prepared for inclusion in the simplex matrix, let us take an example that involves the four types of relationships which we have discussed—restrictions, requirements, equations, and approximations. Assume that our objective function is

$$30x + 25y = \text{maximum}$$

subject to

$$4x + 2y \leqslant 60$$
$$2x + 3y \geqslant 50$$
$$3x + 9y = 65$$
$$5x + 2y \approx 40$$

Adding and subtracting the appropriate slack and artificial variables, we have the following four equations for inclusion in the simplex matrix:

$$4x + 2y + W_1 = 60$$

$$2x + 3y - W_2 + U_1 = 50$$

$$3x + 9y + U_2 = 65$$

$$5x + 2y - W_3 + W_4 = 40$$

We now modify the objective function to include the slack and artificial variables:

$$30x + 25y + 0W_1 + 0W_2 - W_3 - W_4 - MU_1 - MU_2 = \text{maximum}$$

Rearranging the objective function so that the sequence of the variables is divided between the body and the identity, we can develop the initial simplex matrix for this problem as shown in Table X.

TABLE X. Initial simplex matrix for a problem involving restrictions, requirements, equations, and approximations

			30	25	0	−1	0	−M	−M	−1
			x	y	W_2	W_3	W_1	U_1	U_2	W_4
0	W_1	60	4	2	0	0	1	0	0	0
−M	U_1	50	2	3	−1	0	0	1	0	0
−M	U_2	65	3	9	0	0	0	0	1	0
−1	W_4	40	5	2	0	−1	0	0	0	1

The Dual Problem

Simplex problems formulated in the way that we have illustrated in the previous examples are called *primal* problems. It is interesting to note that the same basic problem may be solved in a different way, essentially by reversing the rows and columns. Turning the problem around in this way results in what is called the *dual* problem. A solution to the dual problem can easily be converted into a solution of the original problem, that is, the primal. This is useful when we have a problem with a large number of rows and a small number of columns. In such a case, if we solved the dual problem, instead of the primal, there would be less total work and effort involved. The rules of thumb are as follows:

1. Select the way of formulating the simplex matrix that presents the smaller number of rows.
2. If both the primal and the dual have the same number of rows, select the simplex matrix that presents the smaller number of columns.

Let us illustrate the formulation of the dual problem, using as an example our previous illustrative problem, augmented by two additional restrictions. The problem may be stated as:

$$\text{Maximize: } 60x + 50y, \text{ subject to,}$$

$$2x + 4y \leqslant 80$$

$$3x + 2y \leqslant 60$$

$$x \leqslant 15$$

$$2y \leqslant 36$$

If we were going to solve the problem as before, that is, the primal problem, we might begin by arranging the coefficients in rows and columns as follows:

		60	50
		x	y
	$80 \geqslant$	2	4
	$60 \geqslant$	3	2
	$15 \geqslant$	1	0
	$36 \geqslant$	0	2

We have not, as yet, added in the necessary slack variables. We can now convert the problem to a dual problem by the following five steps:

1. *Assign a new variable to each row*

		60	50
		x	y
V_1	$80 \geqslant$	2	4
V_2	$60 \geqslant$	3	2
V_3	$15 \geqslant$	1	0
V_4	$36 \geqslant$	0	2

2. *Write the constant column of the primal as the objective row of the dual, reversing the algebraic signs.* The objective row for the dual of our problem is then:

$$-80 \quad -60 \quad -15 \quad -36$$

3. *Write the objective row of the primal as the constant column of the dual, reversing the inequality signs.* The constant column of the dual of our problem is then:

$$-80 \quad -60 \quad -15 \quad -36$$

$$60$$

$$50$$

4. *Write the remainder of the rows of the primal problem as the columns of the dual.* This results in:

	-80	-60	-15	-36
	V_1	V_2	V_3	V_4
60	2	3	1	0
50	4	2	0	2

5. *Add slack and artificial variables as required by the restrictions or requirements of the dual problem.* Since the conversion of the problem from primal to dual changed our original restrictions to requirements, the resulting initial dual matrix is as follows:

	-80	-60	-15	-36	0	0	$-M$	$-M$
	V_1	V_2	V_3	V_4	W_A	W_B	A_1	A_2
60	2	3	1	0	-1	0	1	0
50	4	2	0	2	0	-1	0	1

This is a simplex matrix and may be solved in the usual way. Table XI shows the final optimal solution of the dual problem. For comparison Table XII shows the optimal solution for the primal.

Let us now compare the two tables so that we may see where to find in either table the answers to either the primal or dual problems.

1. *Values for the basic variables of the primal are found in the dual solution under the slack variables columns, index row.* The basic variables of the primal are x and y; in Table XI we find their optimal values in the index row under the slack variables. Their

TABLE XI. Optimum solution for dual simplex problem

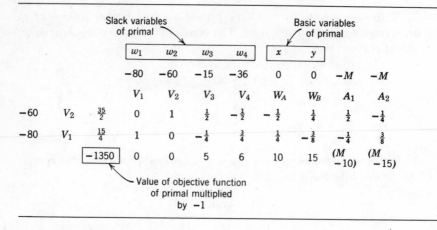

			Slack variables of primal				Basic variables of primal			
			w_1	w_2	w_3	w_4	x	y		
			-80	-60	-15	-36	0	0	$-M$	$-M$
			V_1	V_2	V_3	V_4	W_A	W_B	A_1	A_2
-60	V_2	$\frac{35}{2}$	0	1	$\frac{1}{2}$	$-\frac{1}{2}$	$-\frac{1}{2}$	$\frac{1}{4}$	$\frac{1}{2}$	$-\frac{1}{4}$
-80	V_1	$\frac{15}{4}$	1	0	$-\frac{1}{4}$	$\frac{3}{4}$	$\frac{1}{4}$	$-\frac{3}{8}$	$-\frac{1}{4}$	$\frac{3}{8}$
		$\boxed{-1350}$	0	0	5	6	10	15	$(M-10)$	$(M-15)$

Value of objective function of primal multiplied by -1

TABLE XII. Optimum solution for primal of dual problem shown in Table XI

			60	50	0	0	0	0
			x	y	W_1	W_2	W_3	W_4
0	W_3	5	0	0	$\frac{1}{4}$	$-\frac{1}{2}$	1	0
50	y	15	0	1	$\frac{3}{8}$	$-\frac{1}{4}$	0	0
60	x	10	1	0	$-\frac{1}{4}$	$\frac{1}{2}$	0	0
0	W_4	6	0	0	$-\frac{3}{4}$	$\frac{1}{2}$	0	1
		1350	0	0	$\frac{15}{4}$	$\frac{35}{2}$	0	0

values are 10 and 15, respectively. This may be verified by looking in Table XII, constant column.

2. *The values for the slack variables of the primal are found in the dual solution under the columns for basic variables, index row.* The dual solution of Table XI shows the values in the index row for the four basic variables to be 0, 0, 5, and 6. Therefore, we know that the optimal values in the primal problem are, $W_1 = 0$, $W_2 = 0$, $W_3 = 5$, and $W_4 = 6$. Checking with the primal solution of Table XII, we see that this is true.

3. *The value of the objective function is in the same location in both the primal and dual matrices, but of opposite sign.* Therefore, in the dual solution we find the value of the objective function to be -1350, whereas in the primal it is $+1350$.

To summarize, let us repeat the steps required to convert a primal problem to its equivalent dual. The steps are:

1. Assign a new variable to each row.

2. Write the constant column of the primal as the objective row of the dual, reversing algebraic signs.

3. Write the objective row of the primal as the constant column of the dual, reversing the inequality signs.

4. Write the remainder of the rows of the primal problem as columns of the dual.

5. Add slack and artificial variables as required by the restrictions or requirements of the dual and solve by the usual simplex methods.

SUMMARY

The range of application of the linear programming technique is, of course, limited by the requirement that all the mathematical functions involved be linear in form. Quite often, however, the functions may not actually be linear but can be reasonably approximated by a straight line. Also, although a function may be nonlinear over its entire range, it may be approximated by a straight line in the operating portion of the curve, that is, the portion of the curve that is of practical significance in the problem at hand. There are other programming techniques which can be used in the nonlinear cases, however, and these are dealt with in some of the references listed.

The examples we have used to illustrate the basic steps of the simplex method have been trivial ones. Linear programming, however, is not restricted to these trivial problems, and as mentioned earlier, part of the great power of the technique is that very complex large-scale situations can be handled. In larger scale problems the real difficulty is a computational one; that is, the number of man-hours required to develop a solution. The digital computer is, of course, the final answer to this problem, and library programs for linear programming models are commonly available.

REVIEW QUESTIONS

1. Relate the adjective, "linear," to the nature of the restrictions and the objective function as shown in the graphical solution of linear programming.

2. Figure 2 shows the effect of the restrictions on stamping department, unit

department, machine shop, and assembly department capacity in limiting the feasible solutions to the problem. What other restrictions are implicit in Figure 2?

3. What is the practical result of having an objective function that is parallel to the critical line segment of the polygon of feasible solutions in the graphical representation of linear programming?

4. Are market restrictions fundamentally different from capacity restrictions in determining the polygon of feasible solutions?

5. Outline the steps required in the algebraic solution of linear programming problems. Express the procedure in the form of a flow chart.

6. What is the significance of shadow prices? How can they be used by managers in decision making?

7. Outline the procedure for simplex solution of linear programming problems. Express the procedure in the form of a flow chart and show that the steps are equivalent to those in the algebraic procedure.

8. Contrast the effect of "requirements," "restrictions," and "equations" in the simplex procedure.

9. What is the function of slack and artificial variables in the simplex procedure?

10. What are the *primal* and the *dual* forms of the linear programming model? What are the circumstances under which we would select one format over the other?

11. Can we obtain answers to the primal problem from the solution to the dual, and vice versa? If so, how?

PROBLEMS

1. A company manufacturing television sets and radios has four major departments: chassis, cabinet, assembly, and final testing. Monthly capacities are as follows:

	Television Capacity		Radio Capacity
Chassis	1500	or	4500
Cabinet	1000	or	8000
Assembly	2000	or	4000
Testing	3000	or	9000

The contribution of television is $30 each and the contribution of radio is $5 each. Assuming that the company can sell any quantity of either product, determine the optimal combination of output.

2. An oil company has two additives, x and y, which they mix into their premium grade gasoline. After careful analysis the following restrictions have been determined:

   a. If more than one-half pound of total additives are used per tank car, the additives form harmful deposits on carburetors.

b. $2x + y$ cannot be less than one-half pound, or the gasoline will not have its normal distinctive color (a major selling point).

c. One pound of additive x will add 100 equivalent octane units per tank car, and one pound of additive y will add 200 equivalent octane units per tank car. The total number of equivalent units per tank car cannot be less than 60 to insure performance standards.

d. Additive x costs \$150 per pound and additive y costs \$400 per pound. Graphically determine the optimum additive mixture. Algebraically check the results and compute the total cost per tank car.

3. A company makes three products, x, y, and z, out of three materials p_1, p_2, and p_3. The three products use units of the three materials according to the following table.

	p_1	p_2	p_3
x	2	0	3
y	3	2	2
z	0	5	4

The unit contributions of the three products are:

Product	Contribution
x	\$3
y	\$5
z	\$4

and the availabilities of the three materials are:

Material	Amount Available, Units
p_1	8
p_2	10
p_3	15

Determine the optimal product mix.

4. Once upon a time Lucretia Borgia invited 50 enemies to dinner. The *piece de resistance* was to be poison. In those crude days only two poisons were on the market, poison X and poison Y. Before preparing the menu, however, the remarkably talented young lady considered some of the restrictions placed on her scheme:

(a) If she used more than one-half pound of poison, the guests would detect it and refuse to eat.

(b) Lucretia's own private witch, a medieval version of the modern planning staff, once propounded some magic numbers for her in the following doggerel:

One Y and X two,
If less than half,
Then woe to you.

(c) Poison X will kill 75 and poison Y will kill 200 people per pound.

(d) Poison X costs 100 solid gold pieces per pound, and poison Y 400 solid gold pieces per pound.

After devising a menu to cover up the taste of the poison, Lucretia found she was very short of solid gold pieces. In fact, unless she were very careful she would not be able to have another scheduled poisoning orgy that month. So she called in her alchemist, a very learned man, and told him about her problem. The alchemist had little experience in solving problems of this type, but he was able to translate the four restrictions into mathematical statements.

$$(1) \quad X + Y \leqslant \tfrac{1}{2}$$

$$(2) \quad 2X + Y \geqslant \tfrac{1}{2}$$

$$(3) \quad 75X + 200Y \geqslant 50$$

$$(4) \quad 100X + 400Y = \text{cost}$$

Assist the alchemist in solving this problem. The penalty for failure will be an invitation to next month's dinner.

5. A mining company owns two different mines that produce a given kind of ore. After the ore is crushed, it is graded into three classes: high-grade, medium-grade, and low-grade ores. There is some demand for each grade of ore. The mining company has contracted to provide a smelting plant with 12 tons of high-grade, 8 tons of medium-grade, and 24 tons of low-grade ore per week. It costs the company $200 per day to run the first mine and $160 per day to run the second. These mines have different capacities, however. In a day's operation the first mine produces 6 tons of high-grade, 2 tons of medium-grade, and 4 tons of low-grade ore, whereas the second mine produces daily 2 tons of high-grade, 2 tons of medium-grade, and 12 tons of low-grade ore. How many days a week should each mine be operated to fulfill the company's orders most economically? (*Hint:* Let x be the number of days per week that mine 1 operates, and y the number of days per week that mine 2 operates. Solve by the graphical method.)

6. A company sells two different products, A and B. The selling price and incremental cost information are as follows:

	Product A	Product B
Selling price	60	40
Incremental cost	30	10
Contribution	30	30

The two products are produced in a common production process and are sold in two different markets. The production process has a capacity of 30,000 man-hours. It takes three hours to produce a unit of A and one hour to produce a unit of B. The market has been surveyed, and the company officials feel that the maximum number of units of A that can be sold is 8000; the maximum for B is 12,000 units. Subject to these limitations, the products can be sold in any combination.

(a) Formulate the above problem as a linear programming simplex problem; that is, write the appropriate equations.

(b) Solve this problem by graphical methods.

7. A company makes four products, v, x, y, and z, which flow through four departments, drill, mill, lathe, and assembly. The hours of department time required by each of the products per unit are:

	Drill	Mill	Lathe	Assembly
v	3	0	3	4
x	7	2	4	6
y	4	4	0	5
z	0	6	5	3

The unit contributions of the four products and hours of availability in the four departments are:

Product	Contribution
v	$9
x	$18
y	$14
z	$11

Department	Hours Available
Drill	70
Mill	80
Lathe	90
Assembly	100

Determine the optimal product mix.

8. A company makes five products u, v, x, y, and z, which flow through five departments, blanking, forming, straightening, brazing, and assembly, requiring the following processing times.

Time Required

Product	Blanking	Forming	Straightening	Brazing	Assembly
u	1 hr	1 hr	2 hr	0	1 hr
v	1 hr	0	½ hr	1 hr	2 hr
x	2 hr	3 hr	0	½ hr	1 hr
y	0	2 hr	2 hr	1 hr	2 hr
z	½ hr	1 hr	½ hr	2 hr	1 hr

The contribution of each product is as follows:

Product	Contribution
u	$8 per unit
v	$9 per unit
x	$13 per unit
y	$15 per unit
z	$7 per unit

Time available in the various departments and the estimated incremental cost of idle time are:

Department	Time Available	Estimated Incremental Cost of Idle Time per Hour
Blanking	115 hrs	$12
Forming	100 hrs	$8
Straightening	140 hrs	$3.50
Brazing	90 hrs	$30
Assembly	110 hrs	$12

Formulate the problem in the simplex matrix.

9. A refinery operating in Nebraska uses four crude oils: Oklahoma, West Texas, Wyoming, and Pennsylvania. These crudes have different delivered prices as indicated below. The refinery makes four basic end products: regular gasoline, high-test gasoline, diesel fuel, and fuel oil. The catalytic cracking and reforming characteristics of the refinery dictate a limited and different product mix for the different crudes. Data is as follows:

Crude	Delivered Price per Gallon, cents	Optimal Throughput for Each Crude			
		Regular Gas	High-Test Gas	Diesel Fuel	Fuel Oil
Oklahoma	7	30%	10%	40%	20%
West Texas	6	20%	10%	60%	10%
Wyoming	5	10%		30%	60%
Pennsylvania	9	30%	50%	20%	
Present market requirement, gallons	—	2000	1500	2800	3300

Formulate the problem in a simplex matrix with the objective of minimizing crude costs.

10. A company makes three products, x, y, and z, out of seven materials. The material requirements and contributions for each of the three products are as follows:

Unit Material Requirements

Product	P_1	P_2	P_3	P_4	P_5	P_6	P_7
x	3		2	1			
Alternate x		3		4			1
y		2	1			2	
Alternate y	1			2	3		
z				4		2	1
Alternate z			2		6		

Product	Unit Contribution
x	$6
y	$5
z	$9

The amounts of each material that are available are:

P_1	100 units
P_2	115 units
P_3	135 units
P_4	90 units
P_5	85 units
P_6	140 units
P_7	170 units

Formulate the problem in the primal simplex matrix with the objective of maximizing contribution. Convert the problem to the dual formulation.

INTERPRETATION

11. Mesa plastics, Inc. is a bulk producer of sheet plastic material which they sell in three sizes (thicknesses). They have two plants located on the same site. Plant B is of later design and was specifically built to produce sizes 1 and 2 economically since these two sizes had the largest demand. However, Plant B is less economical than A for size 3. Time requirements for the three products in the two plants, and the variable hourly costs and time availability for Plants A and B are:

Hours per 100 Pounds

Size	Plant A	Plant B	
1	0.25	0.20	*CONSTRAINTS*
2	0.40	0.25	
3	0.35	0.40	
Variable costs/hour	$250	$300	
Maximum available hours per week	100	100	

Sales revenue and maximum demand for the three products are:

Size	Sales Revenue/100 Pounds	Maximum Demand per Week, 100 Pounds
1	$100	310
2	$120	300
3	$150	125

Management is considering how production should be allocated for the upcoming period to the two plants in order to maximize contribution, and the following optimal simplex solution has been obtained:

ANSWERS →

			37.5	40	20	45	62.5	30	0	0	0	0	0
			x_{1A}	x_{1B}	x_{2A}	x_{2B}	x_{3A}	x_{3B}	W_A	W_B	W_1	W_2	W_3
0	W_A	10	0	0	0.0875	0	0	0.15	1	1.25	−0.25	−0.3125	−0.35
40	x_{1B}	125	0	1	−1.25	0	0	2	0	5	0	−1.25	0
37.5	x_{1A}	185	1	0	1.25	0	0	−2	0	−5	1	1.25	0
45	x_{2B}	300	0	0	1	1	0	0	0	0	0	1	0
62.5	x_{3A}	125	0	0	0	0	1	1	0	0	0	0	1
		33,250	0	0	21.875	0	0	37.5	0	12.5	37.5	41.875	62.5

What interpretation of the solution would you give management, particularly regarding possible future profits and how they could be obtained?

REFERENCES

1. Bertoletti, M. E., J. Chapiro, and H. R. Rieznik, "Optimization of Investment— A Solution by Linear Programming," *Management Technology, No. 1*, January 1960, pp. 64–75.

2. Bowman, E. H., and R. B. Fetter, *Analysis for Production and Operations Management*, Richard D. Irwin, Inc., Homewood, Ill., 3rd ed., 1967.

3. Buffa, E. S., *Modern Production Management*, John Wiley & Sons, New York, 3rd ed., 1969.

4. Charnes, A., and W. W. Cooper, *Management Models and Industrial Applications of Linear Programming*, 2 Volumes, John Wiley & Sons, New York, 1961

5. Charnes, A., W. W. Cooper, and R. Ferguson, "Optimal Estimation of Executive Compensation by Linear Programming," *Management Science*, Vol. 1, No. 2, January 1955, pp. 138–151.

6. Charnes, A., W. W. Cooper, and R. Ferguson, "Blending Aviation Gasolines— A Study in Programming Interdependent Activities," *Econometrica*, Vol. 20, No. 2, April 1952, pp. 135–159.

7. Dantzig, G. B., *Linear Programming and Extensions*, Princeton University Press, Princeton, N.J., 1963.

8. Eisemann, K., and W. N. Young, "Study of a Textile Mill with the Aid of Linear Programming," *Management Technology, No. 1*, January 1960, pp. 52–63.

9. Enrick, N. L., *Management Operations Research*, Holt, Rinehart and Winston, New York, 1965.

10. Fabian, T., "A Linear Programming Model of Integrated Iron and Steel Production," *Management Science*, Vol. 4, No. 4, July 1958, pp. 415–449.

11. Fabian, T., "Blast Furnace Production—A Linear Programming Example," *Management Science*, Vol. 14, No. 2, October, 1967.

12. Ferguson, R. O., and L. F. Sargent, *Linear Programming*, McGraw-Hill Book Company, New York, 1958.

13. Fetter, R. B., "A Linear Programming Model for Long-Range Capacity Planning," *Management Science*, Vol. 7, No. 4, July 1961, pp. 372–378.

14. Goetz, B. E., *Quantitative Methods—A Survey and Guide for Managers*, McGraw-Hill Book Co., New York, 1965.

15. Greene, J. H., K. Chatto, C. R. Hicks, and C. B. Cox, "Linear Programming in the Packing Industry," *Journal of Industrial Engineering*, Vol. X, No. 5, 1959, pp. 364–372.

16. Hadley, G., *Linear Programming*, Addison-Wesley Publishing Co., Reading, Mass., 1962.

17. Hanssmann, F., and S. W. Hess, "A Linear Programming Approach to Production and Employment Scheduling," *Management Technology, No. 1*, January 1960, pp. 46–52.

18. Henderson, A., and R. Schlaifer, "Mathematical Programming," *Harvard Business Review*, May–June 1954.

19. McMillan, C., *Mathematical Programming*, John Wiley & Sons, Inc., New York, 1970.

20. Metzger, R. W., *Elemental Mathematical Programming*, John Wiley & Sons, New York, 1958.

21. Metzger, R. W., and R. Schwarzbek, "A Linear Programming Application to Cupola Charging," *Journal of Industrial Engineering*, Vol. XII, No. 2 March–April 1961, pp. 87–93.

22. Naylor, T. H., and E. T. Byrne, *Linear Programming*, Wadsworth Publishing Co., Belmont, Calif., 1963.

23. Thierauf, R. J., and R. A. Grosse, *Decision Making Through Operations Research*, John Wiley & Sons, Inc., New York, 1970.

24. Vajda, S., *Readings in Linear Programming*, John Wiley & Sons, New York, 1958.

25. Vajda, S., *The Theory of Games and Linear Programming*, John Wiley & Sons, New York, 1956.

26. Vazsonyi, A., *Scientific Programming in Business and Industry*, John Wiley & Sons, New York, 1958.

chapter 11

LINEAR PROGRAMMING— DISTRIBUTION METHODS

Distribution methods of linear programming developed around the classic problem of distributing goods from a set of origin points (perhaps factories) to multiple destinations (perhaps warehouses) at a minimum cost. The basic problem can be formulated and solved in the simplex format, but the special methodology developed in this chapter is simpler and easier to understand and is computationally faster. Since insights into the model are somewhat easier than for the simplex format, we can also gain a deeper understanding of allocation problems in general by studying distribution methods.

STEPPING-STONE METHOD
FOR DISTRIBUTION PROBLEMS /

We begin our survey of distribution (transportation) type problems using methods for solution commonly termed, "stepping-stone methods." The stepping-stone method is discussed particularly because the nature of the problems and solution makes close contact with all phases of the solution possible and one obtains a "feel" for what he is doing and why.

As a setting for an illustrative problem, let us assume the distribution situation indicated by Figure 1. Here we see that we have three factories located in Chicago, Detroit, and Atlanta,

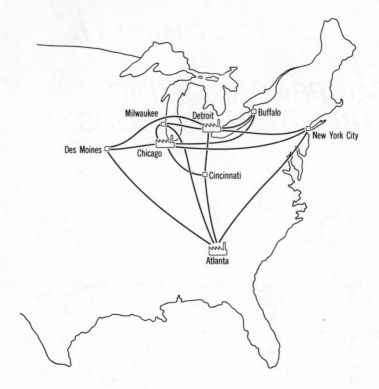

FIGURE 1. Geographical locations of factories and distribution points.

which produce some identical products. The distribution system of the organization has established five major distribution points that serve various market areas in Milwaukee, Cincinnati, Des Moines, Buffalo, and New York City. The three factories have capacities which determine the availability of product, and the market demand in the five major areas determine the requirements to be met. The problem in general, then, is one of determining an allocation of the available product at the three factory locations to the five distribution points in a way that meets the demands and minimizes the cost of distribution for the entire system. Data for our illustrative problem are shown in Table I. We see that there are 19,000 units available at the Detroit plant, 28,000 at Chicago, and 25,000 at Atlanta, or a total of 72,000. Similarly, demands in the five market areas are indicated in the bottom row of the table and also total 72,000 units, although, as we shall see later, this is not a necessary requirement for solution.

These figures of units available and required are commonly termed the "rim conditions." We have also shown in Table I the distribution costs per

TABLE I. Summary of quantities of product available and required, and distribution costs per thousand. *costs*
(Distribution or Transportation Matrix)

To Dist. Points From Factories	Milwaukee (V)	Cincinnati (W)	Des Moines (X)	Buffalo (Y)	New York City (Z)	Available, at Factories 1000's
Detroit (A)	42	42	44	40	44	19
Chicago (B)	34	42	40	46	48	28
Atlanta (C)	46	44	42	48	46	25
Required, at Dist. Points 1000's	11	13	7	17	24	72

thousand units for all combinations of factories and distribution points.
These figures are shown in the small boxes, for example, the distribution
cost between the Chicago plant and the Milwaukee distribution point is
$34 per thousand units. For convenience in notation, we have labeled the
plants A, B, and C and the distribution points V, W, X, Y, and Z. Table I
is commonly termed the "distribution or transportation matrix." Our
measure of effectiveness is distribution cost, and we wish to distribute the
72,000 units available from the factories A, B, and C to the distribution
points V, W, X, Y, and Z in such a way that the total distribution cost is
at a minimum, within the restrictions imposed by units available and
required.

An Initial Solution

We shall make a beginning by assigning the various units available in an
arbitrary way, ignoring the distribution costs. We begin in the upper left-
hand corner of the matrix (the so-called northwest corner) and we note that
A has 19 (thousand) units available and V needs 11 (thousand). We assign
the 11 from A to V. (See Table II; circled numbers represent assigned
product, for example, 11 in box AV means 11,000 units to go from A to V.)
We have not yet used up A's supply, so we move to the right under column
W and assign the balance of A's supply, 8, to W. Looking at the requirements for W, we note that it has a total requirement of 13, so we drop
down to row B and assign the balance of W's requirements, 5, from B's

TABLE II. Northwest initial solution

To From	V	W	X	Y	Z	Available 1000's
A	42 (11)	42 (8)	44 ✕	40 ✕	44 ✕	19
B	34 ✕	42 (5)	40 (7)	46 (16)	48 ✕	28
C	46 ✕	44 ✕	42 ✕	48 (1)	46 (24)	25
Required, 1000's	11	13	7	17	24	72

Total distribution cost:

$$
\begin{aligned}
AV, \quad 11 \times 42 &= 462 \\
AW, \quad 8 \times 42 &= 336 \\
BW, \quad 5 \times 42 &= 210 \\
BX, \quad 7 \times 40 &= 280 \\
BY, \quad 16 \times 46 &= 736 \\
CY, \quad 1 \times 48 &= 48 \\
CZ, \quad 24 \times 46 &= \underline{1104} \\
& \$3176
\end{aligned}
$$

supply of 28. We then move to the right again and assign a portion of the balance of B's supply of 7 to X. We continue in this way, stair-stepping down the matrix until all the arbitrary assignments have been made, as in Table II. The total distribution cost, \$3176, is calculated in Table II below the matrix. Note that we have 7 squares with assignments (n rows $+ m$ columns $- 1$) and 8 open squares, that is, squares without assignments.

Improving the Initial Solution

Is the initial northwest corner solution shown in Table II the best possible? We can answer this by successively examining the open squares to see if total distribution cost is reduced by shifting assignments to them. When all possible shifts in assignments of this nature have been made, we can be certain that we have an optimum solution. Let us examine such a procedure. First, we want to be sure that any shift made conforms to the restrictions of available and required units as shown in the rim conditions of the distribution matrix. Let us select the first open square in the first column, square BV. If we were to add 1 (thousand) unit each to BV and AW and subtract the same amount from AV and BW, we would still satisfy the restrictions of availability and requirements. Table III shows us that such a shift would be advantageous because we would be shifting from higher cost routes to lower cost routes. We would be adding 1000 units each to routes BV and AW at a cost of $34 + 42 = \$76$ and subtracting 1000 units each from AV and BW at a saving of $42 + 42 = \$84$, or a net decrease of $84 - 76 = \$8$ per 1000 units.

TABLE III. Evaluation of square BV *for possible improvement*

From \ To	V		W		X		Y		Z		Available 1000's
A	(−) ⑪	42	⑧ (+)	42		44		40		44	19
B	(+)	34	⑤ (−)	42	⑦	40	⑯	46		48	28
C		46		44		42	①	48	㉔	46	25
Required, 1000's	11		13		7		17		24		72

Evaluation of square BV: for shifting one unit to BV, change in cost is:

$$+34 - 42 + 42 - 42 = -8.$$

Since this is a net improvement in cost, increase the assignment for BV to the maximum possible. This is limited by the assignment for BW which can be reduced by only 5. Maximum improvement at BV is, therefore, $5(-8) = -40$. New total distribution cost $= 3176 - 40 = \$3136$.

Since we have found an advantageous shift, we want to take advantage of it by increasing the assignment at BV to the maximum. The shift in assignments is limited to 5 units, however, because that is the existing assignment at BW, and we cannot reduce it below zero. Therefore, the maximum improvement in the solution that we can effect at BV is 5000 units at a distribution cost saving of $8 per thousand, or $40. The new total distribution cost is now $3136. We make the changes in assignment indicated, and the resulting assignments to the four squares affected are indicated in Figure 2.

We now proceed systematically through the table, column by column, evaluating each open square, making shifts in assignments when they are

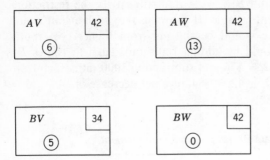

FIGURE 2. Resulting assignments to the four squares affected by the evaluation of square BV.

advantageous. The pattern required to evaluate a given open square is not necessarily a rectangular one as in Tables III and IV, however. We must have a closed path starting at the square to be evaluated, with right angle turns only at squares that already have assignments, proceeding either clockwise or counterclockwise. Squares may be skipped to get to the corners as illustrated in Table IV. No diagonal movement is permitted. Beginning at the square being evaluated, we assign a plus sign, since we propose to add a load, and alternate with minus and plus signs as we go

TABLE IV.   Evaluation of square CV for possible improvement

To From	V	W	X	Y	Z	Available 1000's
A	⑥ ⎸42	⑬ ⎸42	⎸44	⎸40	⎸44	19
B	(−) ⑤ ⎸34	⎸42	⑦ ⎸40	⑯(+) ⎸46	⎸48	28
C	(+)◄ ⎸46	⎸44	⎸42	①(−) ⎸48	㉔ ⎸46	25
Required, 1000's	11	13	7	17	24	72

Evaluation of square CV: for shifting one unit to CV, change in cost is:

$$+46 - 34 + 46 - 48 = +10.$$

This would result in a net increase in total cost and therefore the changes are not made.

around the closed path. There is only one closed path to evaluate for a given open square if the initial arbitrary solution has been properly established. By adhering to the closed path idea which we have expressed, we insure that proposed shifts in assignments do not violate the restrictions of the rim conditions of availability and requirements, since in each row and column we add and subtract the same amount so that the totals are unaffected by the shifts in assignments that we make.

We proceed systematically through the table evaluating each open square, column by column or row by row, making shifts in assignments when they are advantageous. The next open square for evaluation in column V is CV. Square CV is evaluated in Table IV, and we see that if we were to make the shift in allocations indicated, there would be a net increase in total distribution cost. Therefore, the changes are not made. Proceeding to column W we pass over square BW, since the evaluation of square BV by Table III indicates immediately that BW will only increase total cost.

The next square is CW which is evaluated in Table V. Here we see an illustration of a more complex closed path for the evaluation of an open square. Note that in each row and column affected there is a plus sign and a minus sign so that the rim restrictions are not violated by the proposed change in assignments. Table V indicates that CW would also result in a net increase in total costs; therefore, the changes are not made. As we proceed systematically through the table, evaluating each open square,

TABLE V.   Evaluation of square CW *for possible improvement*

To ⟍ From	V	W	X	Y	Z	Available 1000's
A	(+) ⑥ 42	(−) ⑬ 42	44	40	44	19
B	(−) ⑤ 34	42	⑦ 40	⑯ (+) 46	48	28
C	46	(+) 44	42	① (−) 42	㉔ 48 46	25
Required, 1000's	11	13	7	17	24	72

Evaluation of square CW: for shifting one unit to CW, change in cost is:

$$+44 - 48 + 46 - 34 + 42 - 42 = +8.$$

This would result in a net increase in total cost and therefore the changes are not made.

we may find that squares which previously indicated no improvement may later yield improvement because of subsequent changes made. This process is continued until all open squares show no further improvement.

An Optimal Solution. At this point, an optimal solution has been obtained and is shown in Table VI. The total distribution cost required by the optimal solution is $2986, which is $190 less than the original northwest corner solution. This reduction in total distribution cost can be accomplished by the column-by-column evaluation of thirteen open squares, five of which yield improvement. The first time through the table, no improvement is obtained from *CV*, *BW*, *CW*, *CX*, *AZ*, and *BZ*, but squares *BV*, *AX* and *AY* yield improvement. The second time through the table, *BW* and *CW* yield improvement. At this point the solution is optimal, because reevaluation of all open squares shows no further improvement possible. Table VI shows the resulting optimal solution and indicates the evaluations of the open squares by the small figures in the lower left-hand corners of the squares. Note that all open squares show that distribution costs would either increase or not change at all by further shifts in assignments.

Alternate Optimal Solutions. The fact that open squares *CX* and *AZ* in Table VI have zero evaluations is important and gives us flexibility in determining the final plan of action. These zero evaluations allow us to generate other solutions which have the same total distribution cost as the optimal solution generated in Table VI, just as we were able to develop derived optimal solutions in the simplex method. To take an example,

TABLE VI. *An optimal solution. Evaluation of all squares without assignments in this table results in no further improvement*

To \ From	Milwaukee (V)	Cincinnati (W)	Des Moines (X)	Buffalo (Y)	New York City (Z)	Available, 1000's
Detroit (A)	42 +8	42 (2)	44 +4	40 (17)	44 0	19
Chicago (B)	34 (11)	42 (10)	40 (7)	46 +6	48 +4	28
Atlanta (C)	46 +10	44 (1)	42 0	48 +6	46 (24)	25
Required, 1000's	11	13	7	17	24	72

Total distribution cost = $2986.

TABLE VII.   Alternative basic optimum solution

To / From	V	W	X	Y	Z	Available 1000's
A	42 +8	42 (2)	44 +4	40 (17)	44 0	19
B	34 (11)	42 (11)	40 (6)	46 +6	48 +4	28
C	46 +10	44 0	42 (1)	48 +6	46 (24)	25
Required, 1000's	11	13	7	17	24	27

since open square CX has a zero evaluation we may make the shifts in allocations indicated by its closed path and generate the alternate basic optimal solution shown in Table VII. Similarly, we could generate another basic optimal solution by shifting assignments to open square AZ as shown in Table VIII. Also note that we could derive a different basic optimal solution from Table VII by taking advantage of the fact that open square AZ has a zero evaluation; or following a similar procedure, we could derive a fourth alternate basic optimum solution from Table VIII by taking advantage of the fact that open square CX has a zero evaluation. We have discovered for this example an entire family of solutions that are all equally good, and optimal.

TABLE VIII.   Second alternate basic optimum solution

To / From	V	W	X	Y	Z	Available, 1000's
A	42 +8	42 0	44 +4	40 (17)	44 (2)	19
B	34 (11)	42 (10)	40 (7)	46 +6	48 +4	28
C	46 +10	44 (3)	42 0	48 +6	46 (22)	25
Required, 1000's	11	13	7	17	24	72

TABLE IX.   Alternate optimum solution derived from Table VI

To \ From	V	W	X	Y	Z	Available, 1000's
A	42 +8	42 (2)	44 +4	40 (17)	44 0	19
B	34 (11)	42 (10½)	40 (6½)	46 +6	48 +4	28
C	46 +10	44 (½)	42 (½)	48 +6	46 (24)	25
Required, 1000's	11	13	7	17	24	72

But we are not yet finished, for we can generate literally dozens of other optimal solutions from each of the five basic optimal solutions we have just discussed. Let us go back to our original optimal solution shown in Table VI. Recall that we derived a second optimal solution shown in Table VII by shifting 1000 units to open square CX which had a zero evaluation. But it was not necessary for us to shift the entire 1000 units to CX. We could have shifted only 500 units, or 400, or 300, or any fractional amount of the 1000 units. Table IX shows one of these solutions where 500 units have been shifted to CX. This solution as well as any of the others which would involve shifting fractional amounts of 1000 units to CX has the same total distribution cost as the original optimal solution. We see that where we have optimal solutions containing open squares with zero evaluations we have great flexibility in distribution at minimum cost. Where fractional shifts are permitted, we have in fact an infinite number of alternate optimal solutions. This may often make it possible to satisfy nonquantitative factors in the problem and still retain a minimum distribution cost solution.

Degeneracy in Distribution Problems.   Another aspect of the mechanics of developing a solution is the condition known as degeneracy. Degeneracy occurs in distribution problems when, in shifting assignments to take advantage of a potential improvement, more than one of the existing assignments go to zero. Degeneracy can also occur in an initial solution which does not meet the requirements stated below. Examination of the problem in Table X shows that degeneracy is about to happen. Note that the problem in Table X is only slightly different from the example we have been using, that is, the requirements for V and X have been changed.

TABLE X. *Evaluation of square AX produces degeneracy*

To From	V	W	X	Y	Z	Available, 1000's
A	(−) ⑥————⑬————→ (+) 42	42	44	40	44	19
B	(+) ⑥←————————— ⑥ (−) 34	42	40	⑯ 46	48	28
C	46	44	42	① 48	㉔ 46	25
Required, 1000's	12	13	6	17	24	72

This problem was set up in the usual way, and an initial northwest corner solution was established. The open squares were evaluated column by column as before, and changes in assignments were made when they indicated potential improvement.

In Table X we are evaluating square AX by the closed path pattern shown. Potential improvement is indicated, since a unit of allocation reduces transportion costs by \$4 per thousand. We wish to press this advantage to the maximum by shifting as much as possible to AX. We are limited, however, by both squares AV and BX, each of which has an allocation of 6000 units assigned to them. When the shift in assignment is made, both AV and BX go to zero. This is shown in the resulting matrix of Table XI.

TABLE XI. *Problem now degenerate, squares AV, BW, CW, BX, CX, AY, and AZ cannot be evaluated*

To From	V	W	X	Y	Z	Available, 1000's
A	42	⑬ 42	⑥ 44	40	44	19
B	⑫ 34	42	40	⑯ 46	48	28
C	46	44	42	① 48	㉔ 46	25
Required, 1000's	12	13	6	17	24	72

We now have only six allocations instead of seven as before, and we do not meet the restriction on the stepping-stone method of solution which we stated earlier, that is that the number of allocations must be $m + n - 1$. The practical effect of this is that several of the open squares, namely, AV, BW, CW, BX, CX, AY, and AZ, cannot be evaluated in the usual way because a closed path cannot be established for them.

The degeneracy can be resolved, however, by regarding one of the two squares where allocations have disappeared as an allocated square with an extremely small allocation, which we shall call an ϵ allocation. This is illustrated in Table XII. Conceptually, we shall regard the ϵ allocation as being infinitesimally small so that it does not affect the totals indicated in the rim. The ϵ allocation, however, does make it possible to meet the $m + n - 1$ restriction on the number of allocations so that evaluation paths may be established for all open squares. The ϵ allocation is then simply manipulated as though it were no different from the other allocations.

TABLE XII.   Degeneracy resolved by use of the ϵ allocation

To \ From	V	W	X	Y	Z	Available, 1000's
A	42 ϵ	42 (13)	44 (6)	40	44	19
B	34 (12)	42	40	46 (16)	48	28
C	46	44	42 (1)	48 (24)	46	25
Required, 1000's	12	13	6	17	24	72

If in subsequent manipulations the ϵ allocation square is the one that limits shifts in assignments, it is simply shifted to the square being evaluated, and the usual procedure is then continued. This is illustrated in Table XIII where we are attempting to evaluate square AZ by the closed path shown. A potential improvement of $8 per 1000 units is indicated, but the limiting allocation at a negative square is the ϵ allocation. The net effect of adding and subtracting the ϵ allocation around the closed path is to move the ϵ allocation from square AV to AZ. The procedure is then continued as before until an optimal solution is obtained.

TABLE XIII.   Shift of ϵ allocation when it is limiting

To \ From	V	W	X	Y	Z	Available, 1000's
A	(−)(ϵ) 42	(13) 42	(6) 44	40	(ϵ)(+) 44	19
B	(+)(12) 34	42	40	(−)(16) 46	48	28
C	46	44	42	(+)(1) 48	(24)(−) 46	25
Required, 1000's	12	13	6	17	24	72

As the procedure continues it may happen that the ϵ allocation disappears. This is illustrated in Table XIV where we are evaluating the open square *CX*. Potential improvement of $4 per 1000 units is indicated, and here we are limited not by the ϵ allocation but by the allocation of 6000 units at *AX*. In making the adjustments we add and subtract 6000 units around the closed path according to the signs indicated, and the result is that the ϵ allocation at *AZ* becomes 6000 units. We now have seven squares with positive allocations, and the ϵ allocation is no longer needed. In carrying through the solution of larger scale problems, degeneracy could appear and disappear in the routine solution of a problem, or we might sometimes have more than one ϵ allocation. Also, optimal solutions may be degenerate.

TABLE XIV.   Disappearance of the ϵ allocation when it falls at a positive corner of an evaluation path

To \ From	V	W	X	Y	Z	Available, 1000's
A	42	(13) 42	(−) (6) 44	40	(+) (ϵ) 44	19
B	(12) 34	42	40	(16) 46	48	28
C	46	44	(+) 42	(1) 48	(24)(−) 46	25
Required, 1000's	12	13	6	17	24	72

Unequal Supply and Demand

We may now bring up the question of the handling of a problem where supply and demand are not equal. Suppose, for example, that supply exceeded demand. This situation is shown in Table XV where there is available a total of 50 units from the three points of origin at *A*, *B*, and *C*. Demand at the five distribution points *V*, *W*, *X*, *Y*, and *Z*, however, totals only 47 units. This situation can be handled in the problem by creating a dummy distribution point to receive the extra three units. The nonexistent distribution point is assigned zero distribution costs, since the product will never be shipped. The optimal solution then assigns 47 of the 50 available units in the most economical way to the five real distribution points and assigns the balance to the dummy department.

TABLE XV.   *Distribution matrix with supply exceeding demand*

To\From	V	W	X	Y	Z	Dummy	Available
A	10	3	2	5	7	0	10
B	9	8	5	6	6	0	15
C	4	8	7	8	7	0	25
Required	4	10	7	14	12	3	50

When demand exceeds supply, we can resort to a modification of the same technique. In this instance, we create a dummy factory to take up the slack. Again zero distribution costs are assigned for the dummy factory, since product will never be shipped. The solution then assigns the available product to the distribution points in the most economical way. The solution shows which distribution points should receive "short" shipments in order that total distribution costs are minimized.

TECHNIQUES FOR
SIMPLIFYING PROBLEM SOLUTION /

First, we can simplify the arithmetic complexity considerably by two methods. A little thought about the illustrative example we used will convince us that it is the cost differences that are important in determining the optimal allocation rather than their absolute values. Therefore, we can reduce all costs by a fixed amount, and the resulting allocation will be unchanged. In our illustrative example, we may subtract 34 from all distribution cost values so that the numbers with which we must work are of such magnitude that many evaluations can be accomplished by inspection. Another simplification in the arithmetic may be accomplished by expressing the rim conditions in the simplest terms. For example, in our illustrative problem we expressed the rim conditions in thousands of units so that we were able to work with two digit numbers only.

Getting an Advantageous Initial Solution. The northwest corner initial solution is actually not used a great deal in practice, since it is ordinarily a rather poor solution which will involve a number of steps to develop an optimal solution. Placing the lowest cost cell in the northwest corner gives us an advantageous start. The usual procedure is to start with some solution by inspecting the most promising routes, entering allocations which are consistent with the rim conditions. In establishing such an initial solution, the only rules to be observed are that there must be exactly $m + n - 1$ allocations, and it must be possible to evaluate all open squares by the closed path methods previously discussed. If the initial solution turns out to be degenerate, it is a simple matter to increase the allocations to the exact number required by resorting to the ϵ allocation. There are a number of short-cut methods which are commonly used such as row minimum, column minimum, matrix minimum, and VAM. They all have merits; but we shall discuss VAM in some detail because it seems particularly valuable for hand computation of problems of fairly large scale. Of course, computer solutions should be used for large scale problems, if at all possible.

Vogel's Approximation Method (VAM) [10]

VAM makes possible a very good initial solution which in fact is usually the optimal solution. The technique is a simple one and reduces considerably the amount of work required to develop a solution. We shall use as an example the same problem used to illustrate the stepping-stone method. Table XVI shows the distribution matrix with the distribution costs all reduced by the constant amount, $34. The steps in determining an initial VAM solution are as follows:

1. *Determine the difference between the two lowest distribution costs for each row and each column.* This has been done in Table XVI, and the figures at the heads of columns and to the right of the rows represent these differences. For example, in column V the three distribution costs are 8, 0, and 12. The two lowest costs are 8 and 0, and their difference is 8. In row A the two lowest distribution costs are 6 and 8, or a difference of 2. The other figures at the heads of the columns and to the right of the rows have been determined in a similar way.

2. *Select the row or column with the greatest difference.* For the example we are using, the row or column with the greatest difference is column V which has a difference of 8.

3. *Assign the largest possible allocation within the restrictions of the rim conditions to the lowest cost square in the row or column selected.*

TABLE XVI. *Distribution matrix with initial VAM row and column differences shown*

From \ To	8 ↓ V	0 W	2 X	6 Y	2 Z	Available	
A	8	8	10	6	10	19	2
B	0	8	6	12	14	28	6
C	12	10	8	14	12	25	2
Required	11	13	7	17	24	72	

TABLE XVII.   First VAM assignment satisfies V's requirement. Row and column VAM differences are recalculated

	↓ 8̶	0	2	6	2		
To \ From	V	W	X	Y	Z	Available	
A	8 X	8	10	6	10	19	2
B	0 (11)	8	6	12	14	28	6̶2 (8-6)
C	12 X	10	8	14	12	25	2
Required	11	13	7	17	24	72	

This has been done in Table XVII. Under column V the lowest cost square is BV with a cost of 0, and we have assigned 11 units to that square. The 11-unit assignment is the largest possible because of the restriction imposed by the number required at distribution point V.

4. *Cross out any row or column completely satisfied by the assignment just made.* For the assignment just made at BV, the requirements for V are entirely satisfied, so we may cross out the other squares in that column, since we can make no future assignments to them. This is shown in Table XVII.

5. *Recalculate the differences as in Step 1, except for rows or columns that have been crossed out.* This has been done in Table XVII where row B is the only one affected by the assignment just made.

6. *Repeat Steps 2 to 5 until all assignments have been made.*
   a. Column Y now exhibits the greatest difference; therefore, we allocate 17 units to AY, since it has the smallest distribution cost in column Y. Since Y's requirements are completely satisfied, the other squares in that column are crossed out. Differences are recalculated. This entire step is shown in Table XVIII.

TABLE XVIII. Second VAM assignment satisfies Y's requirement. Row and column VAM differences are recalculated

	8̸	0	2	6̸ ↓	2		
To \ From	V	W	X	Y	Z	Available	
A	8 X	8	10	6 (17)	10	19	2
B	0 (11)	8	6	12 X	14	28	6̸2
C	12 X	10	8	14 X	12	25	2
Required	11	13	7	17	24	72	

TABLE XIX. Third VAM assignment

	8̸	0	2̸ ↓	6̸	2		
To \ From	V	W	X	Y	Z	Available	
A	8 X	8	10 X	6 (17)	10	19	2
B	0 (11)	8	6 (7)	12 X	14	28	6̸2̸6
C	12 X	10	8 X	14 X	12	25	2
Required	11	13	7	17	24	72	

b. The recalculated differences now show five of the columns and rows with a difference of 2. The lowest cost square in any column or row is BX which has a cost of 6. We assign 7 units to BX which completely satisfies the requirements at X. Table XIX shows the allocation of 7 units at BX, the crossing out of the other squares in column X, and the recalculation of cost differences for the remaining rows and columns.

c. Row B now shows a cost difference of 6 and we allocate 10 units to the low cost square BW as shown in Table XX. This completes row B. Recalculated cost differences now show all remaining cost differences in rows and columns to be 2. The lowest cost square available is AW so we allocate 2 units there to complete row A. This step is also shown as a part of Table XX.

TABLE XX.   Fourth and fifth VAM assignments

To \ From	V	W	X	Y	Z	Available	
	~~8~~ 0 ~~2~~ ~~6~~ 2						
A	8 X	8 (2)	10 X	6 (17)	10 X	19	~~2~~ ←
B	0 (11)	8 (10)	6 (7)	12 X	14 X	28	~~6 2 8~~ ←
C	12 X	10 1	8 X	14 X	12 2|4	25	2
Required	11	13	7	17	24	72	

d. The last two allocations at CW and CZ are made by inspection of the rim conditions. This is shown in Table XXI. An evaluation of the open squares in Table XXI shows that this solution is optimal, being identical to the optimal solution shown in Table VI.

TABLE XXI.   Final assignments at CW and CZ balance with rim restrictions and yield VAM initial solution which is optimal

From \ To	V	W	X	Y	Z	Available
A	8 X	8 ②	10 X	6 ⑰	10 X	19
B	0 ⑪	8 ⑩	6 ⑦	12 X	14 X	28
C	12 X	10 ①	8 X	14 X	12 ㉔	25
Required	11	13	7	17	24	72

Modified Distribution Method (MODI)

The MODI method for improving an initial solution is an alternate to the stepping-stone method. The main difference is that the MODI method selects the particular open square that will yield the most improvement by a set of index numbers calculated for the rows and columns. The shifts in allocation are then made for that square, according to the usual rules of a closed path. Revised index numbers then indicate the next best open square, and the procedure is repeated until an optimal solution is obtained. The index numbers are referred to as R for row index numbers and K for column index numbers. In the MODI method, the beginning solution may be the northwest corner solution, or some other feasible solution, as before. The VAM initial solution is preferable since it will probably involve fewer steps to an optimal solution.

Calculating R and K Values.   Given some initial solution, an index number is calculated for each row and column. These numbers, together with the "costs" associated with each square, are used to evaluate open squares. We will let R and K represent the row and column numbers and use subscripts to identify the rows and columns, that is, R_A is the row number for row A, etc. The costs associated with each square will be denoted by C, therefore C_{AX} is the cost for square in AX. Then for a *square with an assignment*, and only for squares with assignments, we establish the following formula:

$$R + K + C = 0$$

We begin with the northwest corner initial solution for the illustrative example used in the stepping-stone method to illustrate the procedure. Table XXII shows the initial northwest corner solution. We assume that $R_A = 0$ to get started; therefore based on square AV, we can calculate K_V as follows:

$$K_V = -R_A - C_{AV} = 0 - 8 = -8$$

TABLE XXII. *Northwest corner initial solution with* R *and* K *values entered to evaluate open squares by MODI*

To / From	$K_V = -8$	$K_W = -8$	$K_X = -6$	$K_Y = -12$	$K_Z = -10$	Available
$R_A = 0$	8 (11)	8 (8)	10	6	10	19
$R_B = 0$	0	8 (5)	6 (7)	12 (16)	14	28
$R_C = -2$	12	10	8	14 (1)	12 (24)	25
Required	11	13	7	17	24	72

Square	Calculation	Improvement
BV	$0 + (-8) + 0 = -8$	Yes
CV	$(-2) + (-8) + 12 = 2$	No
CW	$(-2) + (-8) + 10 = 0$	No
AX	$0 + (-6) + 10 = 4$	No
CX	$(-2) + (-6) + 8 = 0$	No
AY	$0 + (-12) + 6 = -6$	Yes
AZ	$0 + (-10) + 10 = 0$	No
BZ	$0 + (-10) + 14 = 4$	No

Also, knowing that $R_A = 0$, we can calculate K_W:

$$K_W = -R_A - C_{AW} = 0 - 8 = -8$$

Now that we have K_W we can calculate R_B at the square BW as follows:

$$R_B = -K_W - C_{BW} = 8 - 8 = 0$$

Stepping down the squares with assignments in this fashion, we can calculate the balance of R and K values as follows:

$$K_X = -R_B - C_{BX} = 0 - 6 = -6$$

$$K_Y = -R_B - C_{BY} = 0 - 12 = -12$$

$$R_C = -K_Y - C_{CY} = 12 - 14 = -2$$

$$K_Z = -R_C - C_{CZ} = 2 - 12 = -10$$

These values are entered in the headings of rows and columns in Table XXII.

Evaluating Open Squares by MODI

The open squares are evaluated by adding algebraically the R, K, and C values associated with them. This is done for all the open squares of our example in Table XXII, below the matrix. Squares that yield negative numbers are squares that would result in improvement if the assignments were shifted to them, according to the closed path patterns which we have used before. The square that yields the largest negative number would result in the greatest improvement, and we should select that square to make shifts in assignments. (Comparable to selecting the key variable in the simplex method.) In Table XXII the largest negative number is -8 for square BV. We therefore make the changes in assignment to the maximum possible, according to its closed path as we did in our previous procedure. These changes are shown in the matrix of Table XXIII.

Since the assignments are now changed, some of the R and K values will change. Table XXIII also shows the new R and K values based on the set of squares with assignments in the new matrix. Open squares are then evaluated by the new R, K, and C values as before. In this instance, however, we have simply shown the evaluations as small numbers in the lower left-hand corners of the open squares. The largest negative number again identifies

TABLE XXIII. Assignment changes indicated by Table XXII are made. New MODI R and K values and the evaluation of open squares are shown

To \ From	$K_V = -8$	$K_W = -8$	$K_X = -14$	$K_Y = -20$	$K_Z = -18$	Available
$R_A = 0$	8 ⑥	8 ⑬	10 / −4	6 / −14	10 / −8	19
$R_B = 8$	0 ⑤	8 / 8	6 ⑦	12 ⑯	14 / 4	28
$R_C = 6$	12 / 10	10 / 8	8 / 0	14 ①	12 ㉔	25
Required	11	13	7	17	24	72

the open square which would result in the greatest improvement. In this instance, it is square AY.

The Optimal Solution by MODI

This procedure is continued until assignments are obtained where the R, K, and C values yield non-negative evaluations for all open squares. Table XXIV shows the optimal solution which is identical with that obtained by the stepping-stone method in Table VI. The MODI evaluations in lower left-hand corners of the open squares are now all non-negative, indicating no further improvement can be obtained.

Mathematical Formulation of Distribution-Type Models

A mathematical formulation of our distribution problem is now in order. The following are three word statements which we wish to express with mathematical symbolism, using our distribution example for illustrative purposes:

1. The sum of units sent to distribution points V, W, X, Y, and Z equals the amount available at each of the supplying factories.

TABLE XXIV. Optimal solution with MODI R *and* K *values and open square evaluations*

To \ From	$K_V=0$	$K_W=-8$	$K_X=-6$	$K_Y=-6$	$K_Z=-10$	Available
$R_A=0$	8 0	8 (2)	10 4	6 (17)	10 0	19
$R_B=0$	0 (11)	8 (10)	6 (7)	12 6	14 4	28
$R_C=-2$	12 10	10 (1)	8 0	14 6	12 (24)	25
Required	11	13	7	17	24	72

For example, for factory A, we say that the sum of units sent to V, W, X, Y, and Z equals 19. We will have three equations like this, one each for A, B, and C.

2. The sum of units received from factories A, B, and C equals the amount required for each of the receiving distribution points. For example, for distribution point V, the sum of units received from A, B, and C equals 11. We will have five equations like this, one each for V, W, X, Y, and Z.

3. Our objective is to minimize the sum of the products of units allocated times distribution costs for all routes. There will be one such equation.

To state these ideas mathematically, let us call the assigned loads x. The subscripts will identify which x we mean. Therefore, the first three equations that identify the distribution of product available are for A, B, and C, respectively:

$$x_{AV} + x_{AW} + x_{AX} + x_{AY} + x_{AZ} = 19 \tag{1}$$

$$x_{BV} + x_{BW} + x_{BX} + x_{BY} + x_{BZ} = 28 \tag{2}$$

$$x_{CV} + x_{CW} + x_{CX} + x_{CY} + x_{CZ} = 25 \tag{3}$$

Also, the five equations that identify the units of product received by V, W, X, Y, and Z respectively are:

$$x_{AV} + x_{BV} + x_{CV} = 11 \tag{4}$$

$$x_{AW} + x_{BW} + x_{CW} = 13 \tag{5}$$

$$x_{AX} + x_{BX} + x_{CX} = 7 \tag{6}$$

$$x_{AY} + x_{BY} + x_{CY} = 17 \tag{7}$$

$$x_{AZ} + x_{BZ} + x_{CZ} = 24 \tag{8}$$

Finally, the *objective function* is:

$$42x_{AV} + 42x_{AW} + 44x_{AX} + 40x_{AY} + 44x_{AZ}$$
$$+ 34x_{BV} + 42x_{BW} + 40x_{BX} + 46x_{BY} + 48x_{BZ}$$
$$+ 46x_{CV} + 44x_{CW} + 42x_{CX} + 48x_{CY} + 46x_{CZ} = \text{minimum} \tag{9}$$

The first eight equations represent the model. The ninth formulates our objective. The method of solution is linear programming, and a specific solution is represented by the optimum assignment matrix in Table VI.

Zeros in the Matrix

We note that in the optimal solution, represented by Table VI, there are only seven routes that end up with assignments. Therefore, there are eight others where the x's are zero. This is not an accident. As we pointed out previously, it is true that if we have m sources and n destinations in the problem, then *no more than $m + n - 1$* of the routes will have a positive value of x. In our case, there will be at least $15 - (3 + 5 - 1) = 8$ zeros. This is fundamental to linear programming. (Note that alternate solutions derived from basic optimum solutions can have split loads.)

Now let us see if the knowledge of the number of zeros in the matrix can help us to understand something about linear programming. Recall that basic algebra taught us that two unknowns and two independent equations can be solved simultaneously. In our case we have fifteen unknowns and only eight problem equations plus an objective function, but we know that at least eight of the unknowns are zero, so in reality we have one more equation than we need. As a matter of fact, what we did to solve our problem was start with an arbitrary solution in which we assumed that 8 x's were zero, and the other 7 x's were assigned values that were consistent with the rim conditions. We then proceeded systematically to improve the solution, which involved changing our minds several times as to which of the x's should be zero. We could have taken a trial-and-error approach to solving the problem, each time calculating the total cost for the solution. To do so, we would have to take all combinations of zero assignments, solve for the remaining x's to determine their values, and finally compute the total distribution cost by means of the objective function. By tabulating the total distribution cost associated with each combination of assignments, we could finally select the optimum solution by finding the one with the lowest total distribution cost; however, we would have to have computed for all possible combinations to be sure that the combination we had selected was the best possible. Linear programming takes us to the optimum solution much more directly and gives us a test for knowing when we have it, so that we need not put in additional effort.

Linear programming determines which of the variables are zero and gives the value of those that are not zero for the optimum solution. If someone had told us which of the x's were zero to begin with, our problem would have been very simple. Let us see that this is true. From Table VI, the optimum solution, we can see where these zeros should be. They are:

$$x_{AV},\ x_{AX},\ x_{AZ},\ x_{BY},\ x_{BZ},\ x_{CV},\ x_{CX},\ \text{and}\ x_{CY}$$

If we substitute the value of zero for each of these eight variables in our first eight equations, we have:

$$\overset{0}{\cancel{x_{AV}}} + x_{AW} + \overset{0}{\cancel{x_{AX}}} + x_{AY} + \overset{0}{\cancel{x_{AZ}}} = 19 \tag{1a}$$

$$x_{BV} + x_{BW} + x_{BX} + \overset{0}{\cancel{x_{BY}}} + \overset{0}{\cancel{x_{BZ}}} = 28 \tag{2a}$$

$$\overset{0}{\cancel{x_{CV}}} + x_{CW} + \overset{0}{\cancel{x_{CX}}} + \overset{0}{\cancel{x_{CY}}} + x_{CZ} = 25 \tag{3a}$$

$$\overset{0}{\cancel{x_{AV}}} + x_{BV} + \overset{0}{\cancel{x_{CV}}} = 11 \tag{4a}$$

$$x_{AW} + x_{BW} + x_{CW} = 13 \tag{5a}$$

$$\overset{0}{\cancel{x_{AX}}} + x_{BX} + \overset{0}{\cancel{x_{CX}}} = 7 \tag{6a}$$

$$x_{AY} + \overset{0}{\cancel{x_{BY}}} + \overset{0}{\cancel{x_{CY}}} = 17 \tag{7a}$$

$$\overset{0}{\cancel{x_{AZ}}} + \overset{0}{\cancel{x_{BZ}}} + x_{CZ} = 24 \tag{8a}$$

From this we obtain directly the fact that $x_{BV} = 11$ (from $4a$), $x_{BX} = 7$ (from $6a$), $x_{AY} = 17$ (from $7a$), and $x_{CZ} = 24$ (from $8a$). Then from ($1a$) we know that $x_{AW} = 2$ since $x_{AY} = 17$. From ($2a$) we know that $x_{BW} = 10$, since $x_{BV} = 11$ and $x_{BX} = 7$. Finally, from ($3a$) we know that $x_{CW} = 1$ since $x_{CZ} = 24$. We still have equation ($5a$) which we have not used, although we now have all the values of our unknowns. We can check some of our values with it, and we find that $x_{AW} + x_{BW} + x_{CW} = 13$. Of course, these values also check with the values obtained previously and displayed in our optimal distribution matrix.

We can see that the distribution methods of linear programming make a great contribution to the *practical* solution of these types of problems. If linear programming did not exist, we could only guess at solutions, perhaps finding an improved solution from time to time based on some individual's insight. To consider the trial-and-error approach, however, would be impractical or even impossible for problems of the magnitude encountered in business and industrial practice.

Production programming

A production program is, of course, an allocation of available capacity to demand, and it can be placed in the framework of a formal linear programming model. In general terms, we are attempting to allocate available production capacity to various periods in a way which meets requirements while minimizing some function of incremental inventory and production costs. The incremental production costs may include overtime premium, turnover costs, extra subcontracting costs, etc.

An Example—The Camtor Company

Ferguson and Sargent [4] describe the Camtor Company case (fictitious name), a manufacturer of a quality line of cameras and projectors, as an application of distribution methods of linear programming to determine a least cost production program which satisfies fluctuating sales demand from a given plant capacity, maintaining a relatively fixed level of employment. The program was constructed to minimize inventory and outside purchase costs. The requirements for cameras and projectors follow a seasonal pattern with maximum sales in October, November, and early December, reflecting the Christmas trade. Relatively low sales occur during January and February, with gradual increases beginning in late March, continuing through April and May to meet the vacation demand. Within the manufacturing division of the company, production releases are issued quarterly, each release authorizing approximately 3 months supply.

Table XXV summarizes the basic data for thirty parts, for which a linear programming solution was developed (the problem has been scaled down for presentation). In Table XXV we are given machine hour requirements by quarters for each of the thirty parts, as well as cost data on the comparative advantage of purchasing and inventory holding cost. We see from the total requirements by quarters that the seasonal swing is in the ratio 10,190/5504 = 1.85. Also, the planned capacity figures in hours indicate an increasing overload as the year progresses, totaling 7994 hours. The inventory carrying cost has been expressed in dollars per quarter for one hour's production.

To construct a distribution matrix, we note that we have requirements in each of four quarters for each of thirty different parts. These requirements form the 120 rows of the distribution matrix, and total 31,794 hours. Similarly, we have capacity available in four quarters totaling 23,800 hours and we have presumably unlimited

TABLE XXV. *Camptor Company basic data for linear programming model to smooth production for seasonal requirements*

		Requirements, Machine Hours Quarter					Incremental Cost to Purchase instead of Manufacture. M Signifies Always Manufactured	Inventory Carrying Cost per Quarter per Hour of Production, dollars
		1	2	3	4	Total		
Part	1	500	700	900	1,000	3,100	20.00	1.25
	2	300	375	400	500	1,575	15.00	1.46
	3	100	140	180	200	620	10.00	0.833
	4	480	600	640	800	2,520	7.75	3.12
	5	120	150	160	200	630	6.50	0.417
	6	400	560	720	800	2,480	6.50	0.104
	7	75	105	135	150	465	6.00	0.417
	8	{250	350	450	500}	2,495	6.00	0.146
		{180	225	240	300}			
	9	60	75	80	100	315	5.75	0.104
	10	75	105	135	150	465	5.00	0.125
	11	150	210	270	300	930	4.50	0.083
	12	60	75	80	100	315	4.25	0.833
	13	{100	140	180	200}	1,250	3.75	0.017
		{120	150	160	200}			
	14	120	150	160	200	630	3.50	0.073
	15	100	140	180	200	620	2.00	0.625
	16	50	70	90	100	310	1.75	0.417
	17	60	75	80	100	315	0.75	0.250
	18	120	150	160	200	630	0.00	0.042
	19	60	75	80	100	315	−0.75	0.104
	20	{100	140	180	200}	935	−1.00	0.012
		{60	75	80	100}			

capacity to purchase outside. Purchasing then takes up the slack between requirements and manufacturing capacity and becomes a fifth source of capacity. We have then a distribution matrix of 120 rows and 5 columns, the cost elements of which are inventory carrying cost for the 4 columns representing manufacture, and incremental cost to purchase (over and above in-plant manufacturing cost) representing the cost element in the purchase column. Figure 3 shows the elements of the matrix for three typical parts. Part 23 is typical of the parts that are never purchased outside. Part 1 is typical of parts that can be either manufactured or purchased, but which represent those parts where there is a marked cost disadvantage in purchasing. Part 19 is representative of the parts that could be either manufactured or purchased, but which represent those parts having a cost advantage in purchasing.

Each of the cost elements under the 4 columns for manufacturing are computed as follows. If the item is to be manufactured in the first quarter, for example, we assume

TABLE XXV. (Continued)

	Requirements, Machine Hours Quarter					Incremental Cost to Purchase instead of Manufacture. M Signifies Always Manufactured	Inventory Carrying Cost per Quarter per Hour of Production, dollars
	1	2	3	4	Total		
21	60	75	80	100	315	−3.00	0.059
22	200	280	360	400	1,240	−3.25	0.417
23	100	140	180	200	620	M	0.625
24	350	490	630	700	2,170	M	6.25
25	240	300	320	400	1,260	M	0.625
26	350	490	630	700	2,170	M	0.833
27	300	375	400	500	1,575	M	2.08
28	{ 50 / 30	70 / 38	90 / 40	100 } / 50 }	468	M	0.208
29	84	105	112	140	441	M	0.083
30	100	140	180	200	620	M	0.083
Total requirements	5,504	7,338	8,762	10,190	31,794		
Capacity†	5,600	5,800	6,000	6,400	23,800		
Overload	−96	1,538	2,762	3,790	7,994		

*Adapted from R. O. Ferguson and L. F. Sargent, Linear Programming, McGraw-Hill Book Company, New York, 1958.

†Capacity is the effective available capacity allowing for downtime, setup, and expected production efficiency. Braces indicate parts used in both cameras and projectors.

Part number	Quarter	Allocated hours					Requirements (hours)	
		Manufacture				Purchase (Slack)	By quarters	Total
		First quarter	Second quarter	Third quarter	Fourth quarter			
23	1	0	+M	+M	+M	+M	100	620
	2	+0.63	0	+M	+M	+M	140	
	3	+1.25	+0.63	0	+M	+M	180	
	4	+1.88	+1.25	+0.63	0	+M	200	

Cost of carrying inventory. (Zero if produced in quarter needed.) (If produced before needed, cost is value from Table XXV, x number of quarters in advance of need.)

Incremental cost if part purchased instead of being manufactured. M means overwhelming cost and therefore, not admissible in solution. Values from Table XXV.

Part number	Quarter	First quarter	Second quarter	Third quarter	Fourth quarter	Purchase (Slack)	By quarters	Total
1	1	0	+M	+M	+M	+20	500	3100
	2	+1.25	0	+M	+M	+20	700	
	3	+2.50	+1.25	0	+M	+20	900	
	4	+3.75	+2.50	+1.25	0	+20	1000	

Part number	Quarter	First quarter	Second quarter	Third quarter	Fourth quarter	Purchase (Slack)	By quarters	Total
19	1	0	+M	+M	+M	−0.75	60	315
	2	+0.10	0	+M	+M	−0.75	75	
	3	+0.21	+0.10	0	+M	−0.75	80	
	4	+0.31	+0.21	+0.10	0	−0.75	100	

Machine hours available	5600	5800	6000	6400	7994 (Slack)	31,794

FIGURE 3. Basic form of distribution matrix for allocating requirements for various parts to four manufacturing quarters and parts to be purchased so that incremental costs of carrying inventories and purchasing are minimized. Employment levels are held relatively steady. Adapted from R. O. Ferguson and L. F. Sargent [4].

that there is no incremental cost to carry inventory, since it cannot be manufactured later and still meet requirements. In the first quarter, however, we can manufacture parts in advance which may be required for the second, third, or fourth quarters. Therefore, an incremental carrying cost is justified. If the part is made one quarter in advance, one quarter's incremental carrying cost would be justified. If the part is to be made two quarters in advance of requirements, two quarters' incremental carrying cost is justified, etc. For example, for part 23 under the column, "First quarter," the costs are zero if the part is made in the first quarter, 0.625 (from Table XXV) if made for second-quarter requirements, 1.25 if made for third-quarter requirements = 0.625 × 2, etc. Looking across the row for part 23, quarter one, we find a cost of 0 under the first quarter, but the letter M (indicating an overwhelming cost so that the allocation is not admissible in a solution) under each of the other three columns. This merely indicates that a requirement in the first quarter cannot be manufactured in a subsequent quarter and still meet the requirements of solution.

Results. Table XXVI shows the final results of the allocation made by the distribution model. For each quarter it shows the hours allocated for each part to be made for that quarter and for future quarters, as well as the parts to be purchased outside to meet requirements in the quarter. The solution represents a minimum inventory carrying cost-incremental purchase cost solution. Ferguson and Sargent discuss a number of alternate programs which represent variations of the basic program just presented. Specifically they are as follows:

1. Scheduling an exactly constant load of 5800 machine hours per quarter.

2. Increasing the forecast by 10 percent as a hedge.

3. Revising the program for the last quarter to correct for earlier unplanned variations.

4. Determining the profitability of including additional machine capacity.

5. Correcting for decreases in the forecast.

6. Determining the economy of overtime operation during the peak requirements period.

SUMMARY

Now that we have covered the basic methodology for distribution problems of linear programming, there are some important variations and conditions which follow easily and extend the range of application of distribution methods. The first is the inclusion in our objective of minimizing combined

TABLE XXVI. Four quarter program showing allocation of 31,794 require linear programming. Adapted from R. O. Ferguson and L. F. Sargent [4].

Part Number	First Quarter Program Make Hours for Quarter				Buy Hours for Quarter				Second Quarter Program Make Hours for Quarter				Buy Hou for Quar		
	1	2	3	4	1	2	3	4	1	2	3	4	1	2	3
1	500									700					
2	300									375					
3	100									140					
4	480									600					
5	120									150					
6	400	560			19						720	172			
7	75									105					
8	430									575					
9	60									75	80	100			
10	75									105					
11					150									210	
12					60									75	
13					220									290	
14					120									150	
15					100									140	
16					50									70	
17					60									75	
18					120									150	
19					60									75	
20					160									215	
21					60									75	
22					200									280	
23	100									140					
24	350									490					
25	240									300					
26	350									490					
27	300									375					
28	80									108					
29	84	105	112	140											
30	100	140	180	200											
Total Hours	5600				1360				5800				1805		

production plus distribution costs. In the illustrative example that we used, it is probable that the production costs at the three factory locations were not identical. The addition of these different production costs in the matrix would undoubtedly result in a different allocation of capacity to demand.

to "make" or "buy" for thirty parts. Solution by distribution methods of

	Third Quarter Program							Fourth Quarter Program						
Make Hours for Quarter			Buy Hours for Quarter				Make Hours for Quarter				Buy Hours for Quarter			
2	3	4	1	2	3	4	1	2	3	4	1	2	3	4
	900									1000				
	400									500				
	180									200				
	640									800				
	160									200				
	509									100				
	135									150				
	690									800				
		96			39									150
					270									300
					80									100
					340									400
					160									200
					180									200
					90									100
					80									100
					160									200
					80									100
					260									300
					80									100
					360									400
	180									200				
	630									700				
	320									400				
	630									700				
	400									500				
	130									150				
6000					2179					6400				2650

In problems where we wish to determine which plants to operate and at what levels, we may wish to determine whether or not it would be more economical to use overtime capacity with attendant higher costs in one location, and produce less at other factory locations. This can be handled easily by regarding the overtime production at each location as a separate source of supply. The production cost at these overtime sources is of course somewhat higher than it would be for regular time production; however, the expanded production-distribution matrix will handle this with no difficulty.

It would be realistic to consider problems where the revenue obtained for products distributed in different marketing areas varies. In this instance, we wish to deal not with a cost matrix, but with a contribution matrix, that is, revenue—production costs—distribution costs. Our objective now will be to maximize a measure of profit rather than to minimize costs. This requires only a minor change in our usual procedure. Since the figures in the matrix now represent a measure of profit rather than costs, we would make changes in allocation when using the stepping-stone method where such a change would result in an increase in contribution. In making shifts in allocations, however, we are still limited by the smallest allocation at a negative square in the closed path. In establishing an initial solution by the VAM method for a contribution matrix, we would compute differences for the two highest contribution figures in a given row or column, instead of the smallest cost figures as we had indicated when dealing with a cost matrix. In the MODI method for improving a solution, maximizing a profit function means simply that squares that yield positive numbers are squares that would result in improvement if the assignments were shifted to them, according to the closed path patterns. The square that yields the largest positive number would yield the greatest improvement. Otherwise the procedure is identical.

REVIEW QUESTIONS

1. What is the general nature of problems for which linear programming provides a general model?

2. What is the structure of the northwest corner initial solution to distribution-type problems?

3. How do we know whether or not a shift in assignments is advantageous in the stepping-stone method? How do we know when an optimal solution has been obtained?

4. Is it possible to have more than one optimal allocation in a distribution problem? What is the practical significance of this?

5. If fractional assignments are allowed and alternate optima exist, how many alternate optimal solutions could be generated?

6. What conditions produce degeneracy in distribution problems? In initial solutions?

7. How can the condition of degeneracy be resolved in a distribution problem?

8. How can unequal supply and demand be handled in the distribution matrix?

9. Outline Vogel's Approximation Method (VAM). Does it result in an optimal solution?

10. Why does the Modified Distribution Method (MODI) provide a more efficient means of improving an initial solution? How many variables will result from a 4 × 5 distribution matrix? How many of the variables will have a zero allocation?

11. How would an objective function proportional to profits rather than to costs affect the practical procedures of solving distribution-type problems?

PROBLEMS

1. A company has factories at *A*, *B*, and *C* which supply warehouses at *D*, *E*, *F*, and *G*. Monthly factory capacities are 70, 90, and 115 respectively. Monthly warehouse requirements are 50, 60, 70, and 95 respectively. Unit shipping costs are as follows:

	To			
From	D	E	F	G
A	$17	$20	$13	$12
B	$15	$21	$26	$25
C	$15	$14	$15	$17

Determine the optimum distribution for this company to minimize shipping costs.

2. A company with factories at *A*, *B*, and *C* supplies warehouses at *D*, *E*, *F*, and *G*. Monthly factory capacities are 20, 30, and 45 respectively. Monthly warehouse requirements are 10, 15, 40, and 30 respectively. Unit shipping costs are as follows:

	To			
From	D	E	F	G
A	$6	$10	$6	$8
B	$7	$9	$6	$11
C	$8	$10	$14	$6

Determine the optimum distribution for this company to minimize shipping costs.

3. A company has factories at *A*, *B*, and *C* which supply warehouses *D*, *E*, *F*, and *G*. Monthly factory capacities are 300, 400, and 500 respectively. Monthly

warehouse requirements are 200, 240, 280, and 340 respectively. Unit shipping costs are as follows:

	To			
From	D	E	F	G
A	$7	$9	$9	$6
B	$6	$10	$12	$8
C	$9	$8	$10	$14

Determine the optimum distribution for this company to minimize shipping costs.

4. A company has factories at *A*, *B*, and *C* which supply warehouses at *D*, *E*, *F*, and *G*. Monthly factory capacities are 160, 150, and 190 respectively. Monthly warehouse requirements are 80, 90, 110, and 160 respectively. Unit shipping costs are as follows:

	To			
From	D	E	F	G
A	$42	$48	$38	$37
B	$40	$49	$52	$51
C	$39	$38	$40	$43

Determine the optimum distribution for this company to minimize shipping costs.

ANS:
1) 8935

5. A company has factories at *A*, *B*, *C*, and *D* which supply warehouses at *E*, *F*, *G*, *H*, and *I*. Monthly factory capacities are 200, 225, 175, and 350 respectively. Monthly warehouse requirements are 130, 110, 140, 260, and 180 respectively. Unit shipping costs are as follows:

	To					Avail
From	E	F	G	H	I	
A	$14	$19	$32	$9	$21	200
B	$15	$10	$18	$7	$11	225
C	$26	$12	$13	$18	$16	175
D	$11	$22	$14	$14	$18	350
Reqd	130	110	140	260	180	

Determine the optimum distribution for this company to minimize shipping costs. (*Hint.* Use VAM for initial solution and MODI to evaluate.)

Ans: $5040

6. A company has factories at A, B, and C which supply warehouses at D, E, F, and G. Monthly factory capacities are 250, 300, and 200 respectively for regular production. If overtime production is utilized, the capacities can be increased to 320, 380, and 210 respectively. Incremental unit overtime costs are $5, $6, and $8 per unit respectively. The current warehouse requirements are 170, 190, 230, and 180 respectively. Unit shipping costs between the factories and warehouses are:

	To			
From	D	E	F	G
A	$8	$9	$10	$11
B	$6	$12	$9	$7
C	$4	$13	$3	$12

Determine the optimum distribution for this company to minimize costs.

7. A company with factories at A, B, C, and D supplies warehouses at E, F, G, and H. Monthly factory capacities are 100, 80, 120, and 90 respectively for regular production. If overtime production is utilized, the capacities can be increased to 120, 110, 160, and 140 respectively. Incremental unit overtime costs are $5, $2, $3, and $4 respectively. Present incremental profits per unit excluding shipping costs are $14, $9, $16, and $27 respectively for regular production. The current monthly warehouse requirements are 110, 70, 160, and 130 respectively. Unit shipping costs are as follows:

	To			
From	E	F	G	H
A	$3	$4	$5	$7
B	$2	$9	$6	$8
C	$4	$3	$8	$5
D	$6	$5	$4	$6

Determine the optimum distribution for this company.

8. A manufacturer wishes to develop a production program in aggregate terms for the coming year. Cost and inventory data are as follows:

$$
\begin{aligned}
&\text{Cost of production per unit, regular time,} && C_R = \$\ 40 \\
&\text{Cost of production per unit, overtime} && C_o = \$\ 60 \\
&\text{Cost of storage per unit per period,} && C_I = \$\ 20 \\
&\text{Beginning inventory, units,} && I_0 = 1000 \\
&\text{Ending inventory, units,} && I_n = \ \ 700
\end{aligned}
$$

Data on production requirements and capacities are as follows:

Production Periods	Production Require-ments, Units	Maximum Production per Period on Regular Time	Maximum Production per Period on Overtime
1.	700	630	126
2.	1,000	630	126
3.	1,000	630	126
4.	900	630	126
5.	600	600	120
6.	600	600	120
7.	500	600	120
8.	600	600	120
9.	300	600	120
10.	300	600	120
11.	300	600	120
12.	400	600	120
	7,200	7,320	1,464

Determine an optimum production program by the distribution method of linear programming. Evaluate the optimum program in terms of the logic of the results.

9. What is the typical format for a simplex matrix of a distribution type problem? As an example, set up the initial simplex matrix for the problem represented by the distribution matrix of Table I.

REFERENCES

1. Bertoletti, M., "Planning Continuous Production by Linear Programming," *Management Technology, No. 1*, January 1960, pp. 75–81.
2. Bowman, E. H., "Production Scheduling by the Transportation Method of Linear Programming," *Operations Research*, Vol. 4, No. 1, 1956, pp. 100–103.
3. Charnes, A., and W. W. Cooper, *Management Models and Industrial Applications of Linear Programming*, 2 Volumes, John Wiley & Sons, New York, 1961.
4. Ferguson, R. O., and L. F. Sargent, *Linear Programming*, McGraw-Hill Book Company, New York, 1958.
5. Fetter, R. B., "A Linear Programming Model for Long Range Capacity Planning," *Management Science*, Vol. 7, No. 4, 1961. pp. 372–378.
6. Henderson, A., and R. Schlaifer, "Mathematical Programming," *Harvard Business Review*, May–June 1954.

7. McMillan, C., *Mathematical Programming*, John Wiley & Sons, Inc., New York, 1970.
8. Metzger, R. W., *Elementary Mathematical Programming*, John Wiley & Sons, New York, 1958.
9. Naylor, T. H., and E. T. Byrne, *Linear Programming*, Wadsworth Publishing Co., Belmont, Calif., 1963.
10. Reinfeld, N. V., and W. R. Vogel, *Mathematical Programming*, Prentice-Hall, Englewood Cliffs, N.J., 1958.
11. Thierauf, R. J., and R. A. Grosse, *Decision Making Through Operations Research*, John Wiley & Sons, Inc., New York, 1970.
12. Vazsonyi, A., *Scientific Programming in Business and Industry*, John Wiley & Sons, New York, 1958.

PART V

OPERATIONS PLANNING AND CONTROL— PLANNING, SCHEDULING, AND CONTROLS

chapter 12

AGGREGATE PLANNING, SCHEDULING, AND PRODUCTION CONTROLS

AGGREGATE PLANNING /

Aggregate planning and scheduling is a process of developing firm plans for the upcoming period and tentative plans for possibly up to a year in advance, all in aggregate terms. The fact that the plans are aggregate in nature merely means that they are designed to deal with productive effort as a whole, not in terms of detailed plans and schedules for individual products. It means that some common unit must be found to represent all products, such as gallons, pounds, barrels, or possibly equivalent machine hours. In our meaning of the term, aggregate planning actually includes a schedule and usually specifies the production rate to be set and employment levels for at least the upcoming period. Other key factors follow from this, such as a specification of the amount of overtime to be worked, the amount of subcontracting, and ending finished goods inventories. Aggregate planning makes it possible for high level management to make the broad important decisions allocating the productive resources of the organization. More detailed plans by individual products can be made subsequently within the constraints set by the aggregate plan.

As a basis for discussion and defining the nature of the aggregate planning problem, let us return to the production-distribution system of Figures 8 and 9 of Chapter 7. At first we assumed a constant demand rate of 1000 units per day for the system as a whole. Later, when we talked about buffer stocks, we relaxed that assumption and stated that we would expect random variations in demand around the average and used this fact as a basis for the concepts of buffer stocks to perform the function of absorbing random variations. Now, however, we wish to introduce the possibility of trends in average demand and seasonal demands, while raising the important questions, "How will the system react to trends and seasonals?" and, "What kinds of policies, decision rules, and decision models can guide us in selecting optimum strategies in the face of changing demands including trends and seasonals?" These questions are of great importance because they involve the possibility of changing production rates and employment levels.

Recall Figure 6 of Chapter 7, showing the record of bimonthly sales of a paint item and the exponentially smoothed forecast plotted on the same diagram. Actual sales, even the smoothed forecast, vary tremendously during the year because of seasonality, but in addition note the declining trend in average sales in the early record. The forecast of sales raises the question of how we will allocate our own capacity resources to meet expected sales requirements. Presumably we can increase effective production rate by greater use of overtime, by hiring additional personnel, by putting on additional shifts, and in some cases by subcontracting; or accomplish reductions in production rate by reversing these actions.

Thus by resorting to these various possibilities where appropriate, we could increase and decrease production rates to follow the forecast demand curve. But changing production rates by any of these means has costs associated with them. Overtime normally costs 1.5 times the hourly rates and may be less productive; to hire personnel costs money for recruiting, selection, placement, and training; to lay off or fire personnel may involve unemployment compensation and/or severance costs as well as the costs to process the changes; as we noted in Chapter 2, there are semifixed costs required to put on additional shifts as well as shift premium payroll costs; subcontracting if it is possible is presumably more expensive than in-plant production.

The alternative to changing production rates through a combination of the means just stated is to absorb all or part of the large fluctuation in demand by additional *seasonal inventory*. These inventories are similar in function to buffer stocks in that they absorb demand fluctuations, but the fluctuations they absorb are the seasonal fluctuations rather than random fluctuations in demand. Figure 1 shows a simple plan for partially absorbing seasonal sales requirements by seasonal inventory accumulations and by changing production rates. *The problem, then, is to determine a plan or*

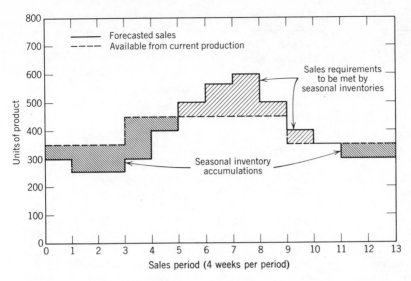

FIGURE 1. Sales forecasts and production plan showing peak seasonal sales met by accumulated seasonal inventories.

course of action which uses the combination of available capacities from the regular work force, hiring and layoff, overtime, additional shifts, subcontracting, and inventories, and minimizes the affected costs. Thus higher management can make the key decisions on production rate and employment levels on a broad general basis. These decisions in turn set the allowable amounts of overtime, inventory buildup or drain, and so on. The broad general plan in "aggregate" terms then becomes a basis for developing detailed schedules of individual products and the use of facilities. The following example shows how widely the costs of alternate plans might vary.

An Example

Table I shows a forecast of production requirements and buffer stocks for a year hence. The expected production requirements for each month take account of the fact that production must lead the time of expected sale. We see that there is a pronounced seasonal swing in the requirements, apparently equal to 11,000/3000 = 3.67 (peak in July, 11,000; low point in February and March, 3000). Actually, however, the magnitude of the seasonal swing is much greater from the point of view of the production plan because of the variation of working days available in each month, emphasized by the fact that the plant shuts down for two weeks in August for vacations. The resulting seasonal swing in requirements per production day is from 136 units per day in March to 682 units per day in August, or a ratio 682/136 = 5.02.

TABLE I. Forecast of production requirements and buffer stocks

Month	Expected Production Requirements	Cumulative Production Requirements	Required Buffer Stocks	Production Days	Cumulative Production Days
January	4,000	4,000	2,500	22	22
February	3,000	7,000	2,200	18	40
March	3,000	10,000	2,200	22	62
April	4,000	14,000	2,500	21	83
May	7,000	21,000	3,200	22	105
June	9,000	30,000	3,500	21	126
July	11,000	41,000	4,000	21	147
August	9,000	50,000	3,500	13	160
September	6,500	56,500	3,200	20	180
October	6,000	62,500	2,800	23	203
November	5,500	68,000	2,700	21	224
December	4,000	72,000	2,500	20	244
			34,800		

$$\text{Average buffer stock} = \frac{34,800}{12} = 2900 \text{ units}$$

Table I also shows the required buffer stocks for each month which average 2900 units.

Figure 2 shows a graph of the cumulative production requirements calculated in Table I. By adding, for each month, the buffer stock requirements to the cumulative requirements curve, we can obtain a curve of cumulative maximum requirements. The importance of this cumulative requirements curve in preparing alternate production plans is that *any line representing the way requirements are to be produced must fall entirely above the cumulative maximum requirements line to provide the stock needed for sale and still provide the desired protection against stock runout.* Three such plans are shown in Figure 2, and we shall discuss them in greater detail. For any plan, the seasonal inventory (inventory over and above buffer stock) for a given point in time is represented by the distance between the curve for the production plan in question and the cumulative maximum requirements curve. An example of the seasonal inventory at the sixtieth day for plan 3 is shown in Figure 2. Although a chart similar to Figure 2 is of the greatest value for comparing alternate feasible plans, a chart similar to Figure 3 may be more meaningful in visualizing the differences between the alternate plans in relation to the projected requirements. Figure 3 shows the production rates in units per day for the three plans.

Plan 1 calls for level production which will result in high seasonal inventory costs, but will minimize labor, turnover, and subcontracting costs. Plan 2 follows the requirements curve quite closely, and this, of course, results in very low inventory

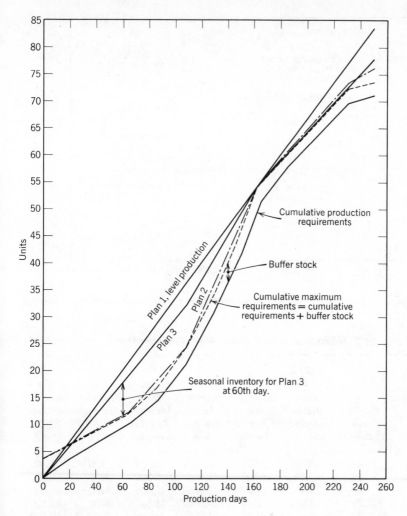

FIGURE 2. Cumulative requirements with three alternate programs which meet maximum requirements.

costs. The costs associated with changing production levels, however, are bound to be high. Plan 3 is a compromise between the extremes of plans 1 and 2. To come to a decision on which of the three plans might be best, we must have additional data about the plant and its costs.

Normal production capacity is 400 units per day, and we can obtain up to 480 units per day by using overtime capacity. The use of overtime capacity, however, adds $10 per unit to the cost of the product. Also, we may exceed the 480 unit per day

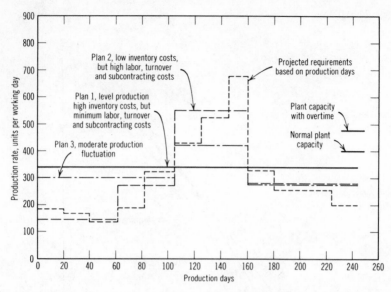

FIGURE 3. Comparison of three production programs that meet requirements.

TABLE II. Calculation of seasonal stock for production plan 3

(1)	(2)	(3)	(4)	(5)	(6)	(7)	(8)
		Produc-tion	Produc-tion	Cumu-lative	Cumu-lative Maximum	Seasonal Stock =	Seasonal Stock × Prod. Days =
	Produc-tion	Rate, units	in	Produc-tion	Require-ments	Col. 5 −	Col. 2 ×
Month	Days	per day	Month			Col. 6	Col. 7
January	22	300	6600	6,600	6,500	100	2,200
February	18	300	5400	12,000	9,200	2800	50,400
March	22	300	6600	18,600	12,200	6400	140,800
April	21	300	6300	24,900	16,500	8400	176,300
May	22	300	6600	31,500	24,200	7300	160,500
June	21	420	8820	40,320	33,500	6820	143,300
July	21	420	8820	49,140	45,000	4140	87,000
August	13	420	5460	54,600	53,500	1100	14,300
September	20	280	5600	60,200	59,700	500	10,000
October	23	280	6440	66,640	63,300	3340	76,800
November	21	280	5880	72,520	70,700	1820	38,250
December	20	280	5600	78,120	74,500	3620	72,300
	244						972,150

Average seasonal stock = 972,150/244 = 3985 units.

limit through the use of subcontracting, but at an extra cost of $15 per unit, compared to in-plant normal time production. Inventory carrying cost is $60 per year per unit, and to change production rate by 20 units per day requires the employment or separation of 40 men at a cost of hiring and training of $200 per employee. With this basic data, we may now compute the incremental costs of seasonal stock, labor turnover, overtime premium, and subcontracting for each of the three alternate plans. Table II shows the calculation of seasonal stock for production plan 3. The seasonal stocks for plans 1 and 2 may be computed in a comparable way.

Table III summarizes the comparative incremental costs for the three production programs. Note that plan 2 has the lowest total incremental cost of $253,210. Recall that plan 2 resulted in relatively low inventory costs achieved by varying production rate, using overtime and subcontracting to absorb the peak requirements. Plan 2 is not necessarily the plan with minimum possible costs; however, other plans could be analyzed in a comparable way. Plan 2 has some important disadvantages which are not easy to measure in a quantitative way. It involves a large labor force fluctuation which could have an effect on employee morale and on community relationships. Also, if these employees are of relatively high skills and scarce, it would be important to minimize turnover. The quantitative difference in monetary values resulting from the analysis may be balanced by the manager against the intangible values.

TABLE III. Comparative incremental costs for three production programs

	Plan 1 Level Production	Plan 2	Plan 3
Average seasonal stock, units	5100	791	3985
Average buffer stock, units	2900	2900	2900
Total average inventory, units	8000	3691	6885
Peak capacity required:			
(Plan 1 = 100)	100	165	126
Incremental costs:			
Seasonal stock cost[1]	$308,000	$ 47,460	$239,100
Labor turnover cost[2]	0	104,000	48,000
Overtime premium[3]	0	44,000	11,000
Subcontracting cost[4]	0	57,750	0
	$308,000	$253,210	$298,100

[1] Inventory carrying cost computed at $60 per unit per year.
[2] A change in production rate of 20 units per day requires the employment or separation of forty men, at a cost of hiring and training an employee of $200.
[3] Units produced at overtime labor rates cost $10 per unit extra.
[4] Units produced by subcontractors cost $15 per unit extra.

This graphical example shows how widely alternate production programs could vary in cost but still leaves open the question of how to generate optimum decisions. Also, the graphic model is static, thereby assuming that the forecast remains fixed and all we need to do is develop a plan to meet requirements. Actually conditions and forecasts keep changing, and we need a dynamic decision process which makes possible a sequence of decisions each of which takes account of ending conditions and the then existing forecasts. The aggregate planning problem has been approached in many different ways. First, it has been put into the framework of a linear programming model, and we will examine the simplex format and the distribution model format. The aggregate planning problem has also been approached by quadratic programming in a form called the Linear Decision Rule. Finally, the aggregate planning problem has also been approached by heuristic programming methods and by computer search methods. We shall examine and compare these specific methods in the next chapter.

Aggregate Planning and the Five Systems

Aggregate planning is directly applicable to all manufacturing situations where inventoried items are involved. Thus systems 2 and 3, production-distribution and closed job shop systems, involve the general situation we have discussed. System 1, the distribution system, has an equivalent of aggregate planning which stems directly from the demand forecast so that required inventories to service expected demand can be provided for. System 4, the open job shop, and system 5, the one-time project, have no finished goods inventories to use as trade-offs for other resources. On the other hand, since the total demand for a large project is known because a contract exists, we may regard the PERT project schedule, which we will discuss at a later point in this chapter, as an aggregate plan in a sense. By smoothing the project schedule's need for manpower or other resources, we are in effect attempting to minimize the equivalent of production fluctuations. We will consider PERT and CPM methods for scheduling and smoothing in Chapter 18.

PRODUCTION
SCHEDULING AND CONTROL /

The production scheduling and control function varies widely with the five systems. With system 1 it is simple since the "operations" phase is uncomplicated, dealing with handling and storing activities and shipping. In general, the shipping schedule is comparable to production schedules in other systems and the related activities, such as handling, assembling and packing orders, will be geared to the shipping schedule.

Scheduling and Control for High Volume Production Systems

Scheduling for the production phases of system 2, production-distribution systems for high volume standardized products, is nearly done when the aggregate schedule has been developed. The aggregate schedule incorporates the basic decisions setting production rates and employment levels. But there remains an interaction between production rate and employment level and the question of deciding how the aggregate production rate will be divided among the individual products.

The production rate-employment level interaction has some important implications. A given output rate (number of equivalent units per period in the aggregate schedule) can possibly be achieved in different ways by overtime or undertime with the same work force or by changing the size of the work force. But the aggregate plan has specified the combinations of these alternatives to be used. Now to implement the aggregate decisions we must get down to details.

Suppose the aggregate plan calls for an increase in production rate from 1000 to 1200 gallons in the upcoming period to be achieved by an expansion of the work force from 500 to 520 men and the use of 2000 hours of overtime. In order to deal with the reshuffled work assignments, we must first break down the aggregate production rate to rates for individual products. Sales patterns and percentages may guide in this effort, but since the aggregate plan has placed limitations on total output the individual products are competing for limited capacity. What is the relative profitability of the items and are there minimum quantities which must be produced for sales service reasons? These data can enter an allocation model to develop answers for optimum product mix. The product mix problem may be approached by a linear programming model by the general methods covered in Chapter 10. If the constraints on capacity are not severe, a simple percentage breakdown of the aggregate production rate by individual products is often used. With the product mix established, raw material requirements become known.

Given a product mix, the next question is how to absorb the 20 additional men into the production system. Recall in Chapter 6, on the design of systems, we discussed the line balance problem. If the basic production rate is to be changed, this means a rebalancing of facilities to the new rate.

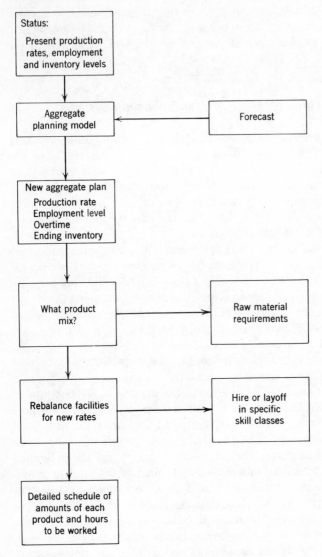

FIGURE 4. Development of schedules for high volume standardized product systems.

If the aggregate plan had called for a change in rate without a change in employment level, the scheduling function could achieve this by working the lines either longer or shorter hours. With a change in labor force, however, the basic balance of the system must be changed. This means restructuring jobs on the line to match the requirements of the new rate or simply rebalancing the lines to absorb 20 more men in our particular example. Now we are in a position to specify to the personnel function the types of men and their labor skills that are necessary. We are also now in a position to develop a detailed schedule for the upcoming period of the amounts of each product to be produced and the hours to be worked by facilities and personnel. Figure 4 summarizes the overall process.

The control over the schedule is achieved by a reporting of actual output and hours worked compared to schedule. Corrective action can be taken mainly through altering the hours worked when the facilities balance has been set.

Scheduling and Control for Job Shops

The basic schedule and control problems for systems 3 and 4 are the same, though the closed job shop, since it is producing a forecastable line of products, can engage in some form of aggregate planning. Recall the basic situation in intermittent manufacturing systems where equipment is grouped by functions performed, and the routings or operation sequences of individual orders vary widely. In thinking of the scheduling problem, it must also be kept in mind that the performance times for operations are predictable but only with fairly wide variance. These performance times will best be described by an estimated mean and standard deviation. Finally, the equipment breakdown and maintenance problem is also interposed as a factor affecting the stochastic nature of order flow through a job shop.

The flow through a job shop might best be described as a network of waiting lines, as we show in Figure 5. Each machine center is receiving orders for processing from many other machine centers as dictated by the routings of individual orders. Because of variability in waiting and performance time at previous machine centers, it is difficult to predict exactly when a given order will be received at machine center X, for example. When the order does arrive, other orders may already be waiting for processing so our order takes its place in line (queue) and waits until a machine and man in combination are available. It is then processed in a time appropriate for the job (which is in general different from the time required for other orders). When the material handling system is ready and available, the completed order will move to the next machine center in its routing to repeat the same kind of sequence of events. Thus the flow process is probabilistic.

Perhaps then we can describe the flow of orders through a job shop as being represented by a network of queues or waiting lines and the con-

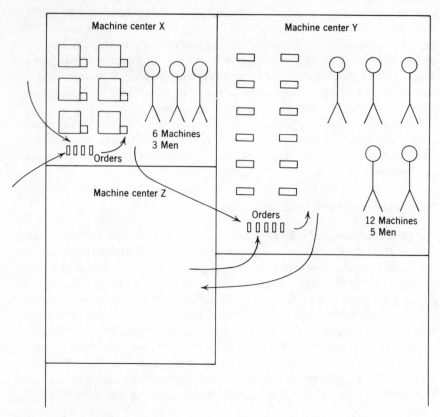

FIGURE 5. Structure of order flow to machine centers, waiting in line for processing, and proceeding to the next waiting line.

ceptual framework for analyzing the problem as consisting of waiting line models which we discuss separately in Chapter 14. Waiting line models make it possible to predict in limited cases the average time an order must wait to be processed, the processing time, and the total time in the machine center, as well as the number of orders in line and in the system for known conditions of order arrival rates. One of the major variables which can be experimented with in such systems is the priority system used for orders, that is, first come first served, last come first served, remaining processing time, etc. A great deal of research effort has been expended in comparing different priority systems (methods of sequencing orders) by simulation methodology and Chapter 17 discusses some of this work.

The essence of job shop scheduling systems, therefore, is to establish required processes and routings for orders and release them to the shop.

The scheduling of individual operations then takes place locally at the machine center by the order sequencing rules and labor assignment rules used. Such scheduling procedures are referred to as "loading systems." In some instances there is central control in terms of established priority rules to be used for sequencing but currently in most situations it is left to the judgment of the foreman to sequence orders and assign men as he thinks best by an assessment of purely local conditions.

Control is accomplished through an information system which reports the progress of individual orders through the shop. Depending on the degree of central control, when orders are running late compared to due dates, the priority system used may automatically increase the priority of late orders and/or special expediting personnel may be assigned to follow the progress of "hot orders" and work with individual foremen in completing the required processing. Modern data processing methods have improved the reporting and control process by placing remote information pickup points in the shop to obtain the latest status of orders and their locations. The data processing system, using priority updating routines, may give daily reports to all departments, showing the orders located there, their due dates and latest priorities. Department foremen can then use these reports to plan daily work loads and schedules.

As we imply in Figure 5, the limiting resource in job shop systems is usually labor rather than machine capacity. With more machinery than labor available, the system is very flexible in its ability to meet peaks of demand in departments especially if part of the labor pool in one machine center which is underloaded can be moved to the area where the heavy demand exists.

Schedule and Control of Large Projects

The key thing which distinguishes scheduling and control of large projects is the complexity resulting from the very large number of activities required on possibly a very large number of components and parts. Since the project by its nature is a one-time affair, the cost of all of the planning and scheduling required must be absorbed by the project. Because of the interlaced network of activities and the technological precedence requirements of the activities, it is not obvious to see how best to schedule projects of any size.

A relatively simple example serves best to show the nature of the problem and to indicate the general modes of analysis which have proved effective. Table IV shows a list of the activities required to rebuild a tool cutter grinder, together with the required times and the precedence relationships of the activities. From the precedence relationships, we can develop a

TABLE IV. Rebuilding a tool cutter grinder. Activities required, times, immediate predecessors, and earliest start and finish times of activities*

Activ-ity Code	Activity Name	Days Re-quired	Imme-diate Pre-decessors	ES, Earliest Start Time	EF, Earliest Finish Time
A	Disconnect and move	0.2	—	0	0.2
B	Connect power and pretest	0.2	A	0.2	0.4
C	Remove electrical units	0.2	B	0.4	0.6
D	Clean machine	0.3	C	0.6	0.9
E	Remove and disassemble mechanical units	0.2	C	0.6	0.8
F	Clean machine parts	0.4	D	0.9	1.3
G	List mechanical parts	0.5	F	1.3	1.8
H	Order machine parts	0.5	G	1.8	2.3
I	Receive machine parts	1.0	H	2.3	3.3
J	Paint cross slides	25.0	I	3.3	28.3
K	Machine parts	1.5	G	1.8	3.3
L	Inspect and list electrical parts	1.0	K	3.3	4.3
M	Paint motor	1.0	L	4.3	5.3
N	Assemble motor	0.8	P, Q, R	7.3	8.1
O	Machine saddle	2.5	H	2.3	4.8
P	Machine slides	2.0	V	5.3	7.3
Q	Machine table	2.0	L	4.3	6.3
R	Paint machine	2.0	M	5.3	7.3
S	Scrape slides	1.0	N	8.1	9.1
T	Scrape table	1.0	G	1.8	2.8
U	Scrape saddles	0.5	E	0.8	1.3
V	Machine gibs	2.0	K	3.3	5.3
W	Install spindle	1.0	J, O, T	28.3	29.3
X	Assemble parts	1.0	J, O, S, T	28.3	29.3
Y	Scrape gibs	0.5	U	1.3	1.8
Z	Assemble head	1.0	J, O, T	28.3	29.3
AA	Install motor and electrical parts	0.3	Y	1.8	2.1
BB	Assemble cross slides	0.4	J, O, T	28.3	28.7
CC	Connect power and test	0.5	AA, BB, Z, W, X	29.3	29.8
DD	Touch-up, move, reinstall	0.3	CC	29.8	30.1

*Data from R. D. Archibald and R. L. Villoria, Network-Based Management Systems, John Wiley & Sons, New York, 1967.

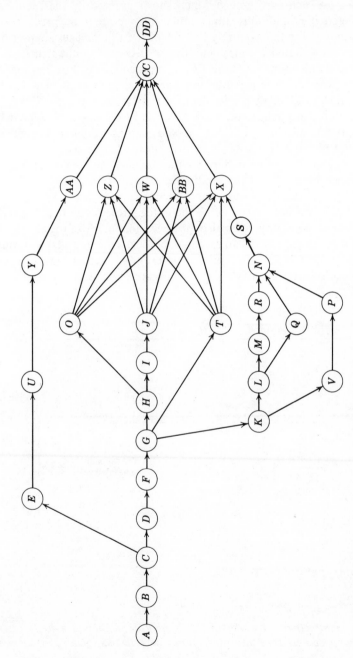

FIGURE 6. Network of precedence relationships for the activities required to rebuild a tool cutter grinder.

network diagram such as Figure 6 which shows graphically the required sequences of activities. This diagram is similar in structure to the precedence diagram developed for the assembly line balancing problem in Chapter 6. Working from the activity times and the precedence requirements, the earliest start and finish times (ES and EF) for each activity can be developed as shown in Table IV. For example, the earliest start time for activity B is the early finish time for its predecessor, activity A, and so on.

Given the precedence relations and the ES's and EF's, a feasible schedule of the activities could be developed, as shown graphically in Figure 7. Figure 7 is not necessarily a good schedule, but it is a feasible one.

Notice in Figure 7 the line defined as the "critical path schedule line." This line connects the EF's of the limiting set of activities. The schedule of these activities is particularly important, because if you delay the start of any one of them you necessarily delay the entire project due to the inter-locking precedence relations. Note also, however, that many of the activities have slack, that is, their start times could be delayed somewhat without affecting the project completion time. For example, activity AA has as necessary successors only activity CC (see Figure 6) so that AA could be

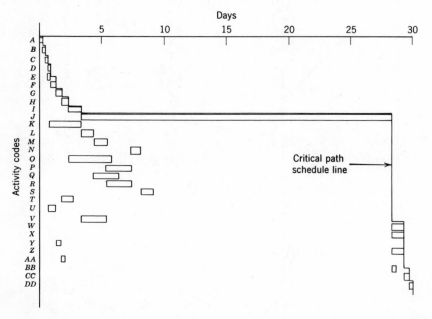

FIGURE 7. Gantt chart schedule for the project of rebuilding a tool cutter grinder showing earliest start and finish times of activities, given precedence relationships.

delayed as much as 27.2 days without affecting any other activity. Some of the activities can be delayed only if other activities are also delayed. For example, *Y* can be delayed only if *AA* is also delayed but *AA* has 27.2 days slack so the actual schedules of both activities could be shifted considerably.

Thus, we see that the flexibility we have available for generating other possibly better feasible schedules comes from the slack in the original *ES* schedule. For example, the schedule of Figure 7 appears to require a burst of effort at the beginning and at the end of the schedule with a long wait in between. The schedule's demand for resources (labor in this instance) could be smoothed considerably. In some instances, there may be resource constraints so that we must either smooth the need for the resource or delay the project completion time to accommodate the constraint on the resource.

Network scheduling techniques are currently very important and are popularly known as PERT (Performance Evaluation and Review Technique) and CPM (Critical Path Methods). They are similar, but not identical, in detail. These methods have been computerized so that given the precedence relationships and the time requirements it is a simple matter for a computer program to develop a set of limiting start and finish times for the activities. Also, heuristic and simulation programs have been developed which smooth the need for resources and in some instances accommodate resource constraints. The controls on such schedules are also commonly computerized with reports of the status of all activities and the generation of new revised schedules when activities become delayed. We shall cover the details of these network planning scheduling and control techniques in Chapter 18 on network programs.

MAINTENANCE /

Productive systems which create goods in the physical sense almost invariable involve a substantial inventory of plant and equipment, and in some instances the equipment is quite sophisticated. The plant and equipment require maintenance to remain effective as a producing unit. Also, the present-day information systems reflect varying degrees of sophistication with electronic computer and even partial on-line real time systems already in use. These assets, that is, plant, producing, and information system equipment, normally account for the dominant share of the value of the physical assets of an enterprise. Organizations whose product is a service also may depend on systems involving sophisticated equipment:

computers in banks; complex reservation systems, together with the ground facilities and airplanes for airlines; complex X-ray machines, laboratory equipment, and so on, in hospitals.

The effectiveness and the reliability of the system as a whole will depend on how well these complicated systems and components work. If a lathe bearing is defective, dimensions on parts produced may not meet standards, and costs of inspection and rework go up, or defective products will go out to customers. If equipment on a production line regularly breaks down, the interdependent nature of the operations may require the stoppage of the entire line with the attendant very large idle labor costs. If the data processing system of a bank is not reliable, customer service will decline as well as the number of customers. If the laboratory equipment of a hospital gives erroneous data, then diagnoses and treatments may be wrong. If the reservation system for an airline is regularly out of order, customer service will decline, and if aircraft maintenance is poor, the results can be catastrophic.

The importance of the maintenance function varies, but in general it is charged with the responsibility of maintaining the reliability of operational systems. Our interest is not in the nuts and bolts, grease, and mechanics but in the operations management policies and procedures which can contribute to optimum system performance. These policies and procedures are centered specifically on *preventive maintenance*, the *size of maintenance crews*, and an assessment of the degree of needed *slack in the system* to provide flexibility in case of serious breakdown.

Preventive Maintenance

Carefully designed preventive maintenance programs are based on a knowledge of the breakdown frequencies of components within the system being maintained. Knowing the breakdown-time distribution and other relevant cost data, we can determine whether or not it is economical to anticipate a breakdown and replace critical components before they fail or simply to wait and let it happen, replacing the component at that time. It is not a simple and clear-cut picture to deal with.

First, if the breakdown-time distribution is widely variable, then it will be difficult or impossible to anticipate breakdowns, that is, if the probability of failure is fairly equally likely over a broad range from perhaps 100 hours to 2000 hours of operation. On the other hand, if the breakdown-time distribution exhibits low variability, then we can forecast with fair accuracy when to expect a breakdown, and it *may* be economical to use a preventive breakdown policy. But even under these circumstances whether or not it will actually be worthwhile depends on the balance of costs (preventive maintenance versus repair cost, downtime costs, and repair component costs) in the particular situation.

If it takes just as long (costs just as much) to perform preventive maintenance as it does to repair the equipment after it breaks down, there may be no advantage to preventive maintenance. But if the downtime costs are heavy (e.g., when an entire production line is held up), the balance of costs swing in favor of preventive maintenance. Opportunity costs of lost sales can also enter such models when the system is operating at full capacity to meet demand, since output which can be sold may be reduced due to breakdown. Machine breakdown-time distributions in fact represent the arrival rate distribution of a waiting line model and we shall cover basic waiting line models in Chapter 14 and their particular application to the maintenance problem in Chapter 15.

Maintenance Crew Sizes

The size of the maintenance crew is a critical factor with respect to the level of maintenance service which can be expected. In general maintenance crew sizes need to be large enough so that they are *idle* a fair fraction of the time in order to give economical service. The reason why this seeming anomaly is true is that downtime costs continue while the machine waits for service. Thus, an assessment of the balance of idle time costs of mechanics and the downtime costs makes it economical to have a crew size somewhat bigger than would be required just to meet the average maintenance demand. Again, waiting line models provide a conceptual framework for the analysis of these kinds of problems, and the general simulation methodology which we shall discuss in Chapter 16 is applicable in the determination of optimum crew sizes. A specific example of repair crew size determination methods at the Eastman Kodak Company is discussed in Chapter 16.

System Slack for Maintenance

The design of the production system does of course interact with the maintenance problem. If the production system has routing flexibility, as in intermittent system designs, then a breakdown will ordinarily have only local effects because other processes do not depend on the broken down machine, and the order can probably be rerouted to another equivalent machine. The broken down machine can then be repaired when a mechanic is available. The slack in machine capacity has provided parallel paths so that if one path breaks down another takes over. The use of parallel systems is a common way of increasing reliability and has been used effectively in missile systems where a failure is extremely costly.

In continuous production systems, we are more likely to resort to preventive maintenance than parallel paths unless downtime experience with a particular machine is very severe. With continuous systems some of the flexibility of the intermittent system can be achieved by the use of in-process inventories at strategic points. If a certain machine is a common offender, then its effect on the production line as a whole can be reduced by building up a bank of in-process inventory between it and the operation which follows. Then a breakdown in the machine can occur and not stop the line as a whole as long as the in-process inventory bank holds out. The material bank is, of course, performing the inventory decoupling function which we discussed earlier in Chapter 7, making it possible to carry on activities relatively independently.

The management of maintenance operations is more difficult than may be commonly thought because of the complex interaction of probabilistic breakdown, probabilistic service time, the relative costs of components, and the complex scheduling problem which results with so much uncertainty. While there is some management science methodology which is applicable, as we have indicated, there is also a great deal of art and judgment involved in actual managerial operations of maintenance systems.

QUALITY CONTROL /

The question of product quality has been raised several times previously; in the section on product design and production design of products in Chapter 3, in process selection and layout where the production system design is developed to conform to quality standards in Chapter 6, and in the just completed section on maintenance where policies and procedures are designed to keep the production system operating according to the quality standards originally set.

To understand the quality function in an enterprise is to understand how it threads through the various stages of policy and conception of quality, relative to markets, product design, production system design, the actual production process, and the distribution, installation, and use of the product. Quality may be thought of in four general phases as shown in Figure 8.

Guiding Policies. As used in quality control the term "quality" is a relative one implying a specification of quality level. An organization may

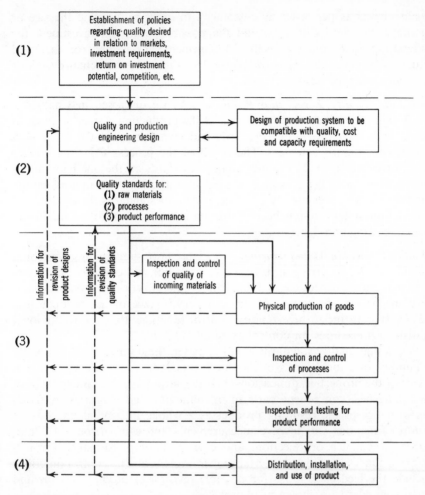

FIGURE 8. Schematic representation of the role of quality control throughout the planning, production, and distribution of a product.

plan to offer products and services at high, medium, or low levels, or across the board, since substantial markets may exist at all levels. At any rate, the conception of the meaning of quality for an organization is a managerial function which when expressed gives direction and focus for the enterprise. Management in deciding on the quality levels to shoot for must be concerned with how the ultimate consumer measures quality and what factors are of importance to him. Management needs to concern itself with the sensitivity of required investment and production cost to differences in quality levels as perceived by customers, in order to estimate the size of markets, competitive factors, and the possible return on investment for different product quality levels. Management's assessment of the total situation becomes the basis for phase 2 in Figure 8, the actual design of products and production systems.

Designing Quality Levels into Products. As we discussed in Chapter 3 the design of products and the design of the production system go hand in hand, with each providing standards and constraints for the other in a cooperative iterative process. The result of the process from the quality point of view is a set of product quality standards on the one hand and a production system design which is capable of meeting the standards on the other hand. The presumably matched system of standards for quality and production system design become the basis for the control of quality in manufacturing and distribution.

Quality Control in Manufacturing. In Figure 8 we show quality control in manufacturing occurring in three ways: inspection and control of incoming raw materials, inspection and control of manufacturing processes, and final inspection and testing of the end performance of the product as a whole. It is in these three quality control functions that the well-known statistical procedures for control are used.

Given that quality standards are already set, these standards may specify a number of critical kinds of measurements. These measurements are in terms of the properties, dimensions, and the surface finish characteristics of raw materials, component parts in manufacture, and measures of actual performance of the resulting product as a whole. In general, the quality control functions will involve measurements and comparison with standards, acceptance or rejection, and correction of performance through information feedback loops. On a broader level the quality control functions include the feed-back loops for possible revision of product designs and quality standards as shown in Figure 8.

In attempting to implement the quality standards, the quality control function is faced with another problem of balancing incremental gains and incremental losses. By increasing the effort to control the quality of incoming raw materials, processes, and final product performance, we can reduce costs due to scrap, rework, and customer dissatisfaction as shown in Figure 9. On the other hand, increasing the quality control effort in itself is expensive and increasingly so, because of more inspection, machine maintenance and setup costs, and labor idle time due to control interference. Thus there is some optimal effort which balances the two opposing cost pressures as shown in Figure 9. Part of the problem in designing quality

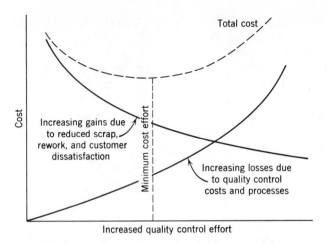

FIGURE 9. *Incremental gains and losses due to increased quality control effort.*

control procedures is in developing cost models which have the objective of achieving this balance.

Process control is a statistical technique which tracks the output of individual production processes with the objective of determining (with reasonably small time lag) when the process which generates the measurements is probably out of control. Corrective action can then be taken before scrap losses become large. Process control techniques utilize probability control limits on the measurements taken which are commonly plotted on *control charts* that show graphically when a process has a high probability of being out of control. When a sample shows an out-of-control condition the process is stopped and corrective measures taken. The bases for the design of process controls are covered separately in Chapter 19 on models of statistical control.

A different statistical technique known as *acceptance sampling* provides control for incoming materials by filtering out lots containing items which probably do not meet standards. Sample sizes can vary from very small to 100 percent inspection (variations in control effort) and in general, the probability of finding lots which do not meet standards increases with sample size. Lots which are rejected on the basis of the sample are either returned to the supplier or are screened by 100 percent inspection. Acceptance sampling is commonly used for incoming raw materials or sometimes at intermediate stages of the overall production process. The bases for designing acceptance sampling plans are covered separately in Chapter 20.

Quality Control in Distribution, Installation, and Use. Product defects can occur in the packing, handling, and distribution phases, so that to implement the quality standards originally set, attention must be given to the events which follow the production process. This has been recognized through the design of packaging and distribution systems for product protection. The performance of many products is also affected by the way the system is installed and used. Since some kind of guarantee of performance is either expressly made or implied, a total concept of quality control must often give attention to the installation and use phases.

Obviously, organizing for quality control involves more than the mere establishment of an inspection department in manufacturing. The schematic diagram of Figure 8 indicates that organizing for quality involves coordination at many different levels and at many different points in a product life cycle.

The emphasis of the quality control function is different for the five different production systems which we have discussed. Systems 2 and 3, the production-distribution system for high volume standardized products and the closed job shop have in general the full range of functions indicated by Figure 8. The possible difference between the two systems is that for system 2 some of the quality check points can be built into production lines as a part of the production system design. Control for system 1 is of course limited to the distribution, installation, and use phases. Quality control for systems 4 and 5, the open job shop and project systems, has its emphasis more on inspection with a much less likely possibility of using statistical methodology.

LABOR AND COST CONTROL /

Cost control is concerned with the operating decisions which remain after the basic decisions have been made which set the design of products and of the production system, and after the other operating plans and control systems have been set. These other plans and control systems are of course the inventory controls, the aggregate production plans and detailed schedules of production, the maintenance policies and procedures, and the quality controls. Obviously, many if not most of these other plans and controls have been concerned with costs too, including labor as well as other costs. But there still remains a degree of freedom or two which represents operating decisions in the final deploying of men, machines, and materials on the production floor. Decisions must be made regarding the actual assignment of men and machines for a given task or production order, and how best to utilize materials, gain the cooperation of the work force, and so on. Most of these decisions are the responsibility of first-line supervisors and foremen. Cost control (through a system of budgets and reports) attempts to set up current cost standards that hold the supervisor responsible for cost performance, in order to encourage him to make the decisions in the interest of the organization within his sphere of control.

Most of the decisions are at a level of detail missed by the broader control systems, yet when they are made in the interest of the organization they contribute strongly to cost effectiveness. Many of these kinds of alternate decisions are so close to the actual work performance that they can only be seen by the individuals who are very close to the actual situation, such as foremen or workers. Thus, cost improvement programs involve foremen and sometimes workers in training programs designed to teach the basics of production economics and work methods improvement, coupled with incentive and reward systems which make it worthwhile to contribute ideas.

Although the methods of cost control are largely those of budgets, cost standards, and reports, the concepts of statistical control (which we cover in Chapter 19) are finding a widening field of application and have been used as an aid to controls over cost, labor turnover, accident rates, and so on.

The emphasis in labor and cost control varies considerably with the five systems. The degree of prior planning and other controls is greatest with continuous systems eliminating many of the possible local options. Part of the reason for this is simply the fact that the production system has been designed to operate in a much more rigid fashion. The greatest responsibility falls on first-line supervisors and foremen in the intermittent systems by the very nature of the tremendous flexibility in the production system. In the job-shop systems, for example, even after the scheduling function has done its work, the final decisions for the deployment of men and machines are usually left to the foremen. Particularly in the custom manufacturing situations typified by systems 4 and 5, even the basic production methods have not been determined in detail as a manufacturing plan, leaving the foreman and workers the option of defining methods to be used.

SUMMARY

As a summary of the seven major problems of operations planning and control, we have developed Table V with brief comments about the problems in relation to the five types of productive systems.

TABLE V.   Summary comments for the five productive systems in relation

Problems Systems	Forecasting	Inventories	Aggregate Planning and Scheduling
System 1, distribution systems	Forecasts a direct basis for inventory and activity levels.	Control of cycle and buffer stocks represents the heart of the operations function. (See Chapters 8 and 9.)	Largely in the form of forecasts of demand.
System 2, production-distribution systems for high volume standardized products	Forecasts for current operations important but errors can be compensated for by subsequent decisions. Need for relatively broad planning horizon places emphasis on forecasts up to a year in advance and on long range forecasts.	Cycle, buffer, and pipeline inventories define minimum aggregate inventory levels for given levels of operations. Decoupling function of inventories makes crucial contribution to low cost operation. (See Chapters 8 and 9.)	Represents crucial decisions allocating major resources and committing them for some minimum period of time. (See Chapter 13.)
System 3, closed job shop	Same as for system 2.	Same as for system 2, but in addition the size of production runs is a problem unique to the closed job shop. (See Chapter 8.)	Same as for system 2.
System 4, open job shop	Contracts and orders fix demand for current operations but forecasts need to assess the likelihood of future demand beyond current operation levels.	Inventory problems are related to in-process flow time and estimating run size to obtain balance between scrap and rework costs versus in-process inventory cost. (See Chapter 8.)	Contracts and orders fix loads for current operations. Aggregate planning focused on master load plan.
System 5, large-scale one-time projects	Project contracts fix demand for current operations but forecasts need to assess the likelihood of future projects.	Same as for system 4 but in addition long project times make timing of receipt of raw materials a problem in balancing delay costs versus in-process inventory costs. (See Chapters 8 and 18.)	Network planning and scheduling establishes basis for resource leveling and feasible aggregate schedules. (See Chapter 18.)

major problems of operation and control

Detailed Scheduling and Control	Maintenance	Quality Control	Labor and Cost Control
Shipping schedule directly controlled by orders.	Maintenance and reliability of information and control hardware. (See Chapters 14–16 on waiting lines, and simulation.)	Focused largely on product protection and guarantees in use.	Costs centered on inventory and transportation costs.
Adjust production rates of individual products to aggregate plan. Rebalance lines and adjust size of work force to conform to aggregate plan.	Maintenance is of great importance due to possible heavy downtime costs of production lines, placing an emphasis on preventive maintenance. (See Chapters 15 and 16.)	Quality function extends throughout organization. Statistical techniques as in acceptance sampling and process control, applicable in manufacturing. (See Chapters 19 and 20.)	Degree of prior planning in the design of the production system and controls minimizes options left to foreman and workers. Automation minimizes importance of labor cost control.
Sequencing of orders and labor assignment procedures at machine centers form policies and procedures for scheduling. (See Chapter 17.)	Alternate paths makes preventive maintenance less important. (See Chapters 15 and 16.)	Same as for system 2.	Large options left to foremen for work and machine assignments and in some instances for work methods.
Same as for system 3.	Same as for system 3.	Quality standards set by customer. Emphasis is on inspection with less possible use of statistical techniques.	Same as for system 3.
Network planning and scheduling provides basis for detailed schedules and controls. (See Chapter 18 on Network Programs.)	Same as for systems 3 and 4.	Same as for system 4.	Large options left to foremen and workers including work methods used.

Most, although certainly not all, of the applications of mathematical and simulation models to operations management have been in the operation and control phases. We see throughout this chapter extensive references to other specific chapters and sections of the book that deal with statistical models, simulation models, waiting line models, and programming models of various kinds, including linear programming, quadratic, heuristic, and computer search programs of aggregate planning, and network programs.

REVIEW QUESTIONS

1. Define the aggregate planning problem in terms of its structural characteristics, objectives, managerial decision variables, and uncontrollable variables.

2. How is the aggregate planning problem different for each of the five productive systems?

3. Describe the production scheduling and control problem for system 2.

4. Describe the flow of orders through a job shop as a network of queues.

5. What is meant by the term "loading system" to describe job shop scheduling?

6. What would happen to the flexibility available in processing orders through a job shop if all available machines were fully manned? What would happen to labor utilization under these circumstances?

7. What is the meaning of the term "critical path schedule"?

8. How can slack be used to generate improved schedules in large project scheduling?

9. What are the characteristics of the breakdown-time distribution which favor the use of preventive maintenance?

10. What is the nature of the balance of pertinent costs which favors the use of preventive maintenance?

11. Describe the role of quality in at least four levels of a production-distribution system.

12. Describe the general cost model associated with controlling quality.

13. Contrast the concepts of acceptance sampling with those of process control. What is the nature of statistical technique applicable to each?

14. What discretion is left to first line supervision for labor and cost control in each of the five productive systems?

15. Using Table V summarize the seven major problems of significance in the operation and control of the five productive systems. Indicate the kinds of analysis found useful in each category.

PROBLEMS

1. The data in Table VI show expected production requirements for an item together with buffer stock requirements and available production days in each month. Develop a chart for cumulative requirements and cumulative maximum requirements similar to Figure 2 in the text. Beginning inventory is 4200 units.

TABLE VI

Month	Production requirements	Required buffer stocks	Production days
January	10,000	2,000	22
February	8,000	1,600	18
March	4,000	800	22
April	3,000	600	21
May	3,000	600	22
June	2,500	500	21
July	4,000	800	21
August	6,000	1,200	13
September	8,000	1,600	20
October	12,000	2,400	23
November	15,000	3,000	21
December	12,000	2,400	20
	87,500	17,500	244

2. Using the data of problem 1, compare the total incremental costs involved in level production, a plan that follows maximum requirements quite closely, and some intermediate plan. Normal plant capacity is 400 units per working day. An additional 20 percent can be obtained through overtime but at an additional cost of $15 per unit. Inventory carrying cost is $40 per unit per year. Changes in production level cost $6000 per 10 units in production rate. Extra capacity may be obtained from subcontracting at an extra cost of $20 per unit.

3. In Table VII there is list of activities required to install a gas forced air furnace, together with estimates of activity times, and the required sequencing of activities by their codes. Develop a network diagram that shows the established precedence relationships.

4. (a) Develop a Gantt chart schedule of the activities for the furnace installation project, similar to Figure 7 of the text.
   (b) Which of the activities have slack in their schedules and how much?
   (c) Which activities have no slack and therefore define the critical path?

TABLE VII.   Installation of a gas forced air furnace. Codes, activity list, estimated times, and immediate predecessors

Activity code	Activity	Time, days	Immediate predecessors
A	Start	0	—
B	Obtain delivery of furnace unit	10	A
C	Obtain delivery of piping	5	A
D	Obtain delivery of dampers and grilles	14	F
E	Obtain delivery of duct work	10	F
F	Design duct work layout	2	A
G	Install duct work and dampers	12	D,E
H	Install grilles	1	G
I	Install furnace unit	1	B
J	Install gas piping	5	C
K	Connect gas pipes to furnace	0.5	I,J
L	Install electric wiring	2	B
M	Install furnace controls and connect to electrical system	1	I,L
N	Test final installation	0.5	H,K,M
O	Clean up	0.5	N

REFERENCES

1. Buffa, E. S., *Modern Production Management*, John Wiley & Sons, Inc., 3rd ed., New York, 1969.
2. Buffa, E. S., and W. H. Taubert, *Production-Inventory Systems: Planning and Control*, Richard D. Irwin, Inc., Homewood, Ill., Rev. ed., 1972.
3. Duncan, A. J., *Quality Control and Industrial Statistics*, Richard D. Irwin, Inc., Homewood, Ill., 1955.
4. Goldman, A. S., and T. B. Slattery, *Maintainability: A Major Element of System Effectiveness*, John Wiley & Sons, Inc., New York, 1964
5. Holt, C. C., F. Modigliani, J. F. Muth, and H. A. Simon, *Planning Production, Inventories, and Work Force*, Prentice-Hall, Inc., Englewood Cliffs, N.J., 1960.
6. Kirkpatrick, E. G., *Quality Control for Managers and Engineers*, John Wiley & Sons, Inc., New York, 1970.
7. Schoderbek, P. P., *Management Systems*, John Wiley & Sons, New York, 2nd ed., 1971.
8. Starr, M. K., *Production Management*, Prentice-Hall, Inc., Englewood Cliffs, N.J., 1964.
9. Vance, L. L., and J. Neter, *Statistical Sampling for Auditors and Accountants*, John Wiley & Sons, Inc., New York, 1956.

chapter 13

PRODUCTION-
INVENTORY
PROGRAMS

One of the most significant programming problems in operations management is the development of production-inventory plans used as a basis for managerial decisions on aggregate production rates and the size of the work force. The process involving these decisions is generally known as aggregate planning or aggregate planning and scheduling. Recall that we discussed the general nature of the problems involved in some detail in Chapter 12. The results of aggregate planning usually specify the production rate to be set and employment levels for at least the upcoming period and perhaps forecasts or estimates for several periods in advance. Other key factors follow from these decisions, such as a specification of the amount of overtime to be worked, the amount of subcontracting to be engaged in, and ending finished goods inventories.

There are a number of different approaches to the aggregate planning problem which have been developed. The earliest of these methods were graphic in nature and were discussed in Chapter 12. There are several difficulties with the graphic methods, however. First, graphic methods are not optimizing in any sense and do not generate alternate proposals. They make it possible to visualize some of the effects of alternate programs, but the analyst must supply the alternate programs to be evaluated. In addition, graphic methods are static in character and do not take into account the need for flexibility in adjusting the production program as new actual demand data becomes available. Some of the more sophisticated methods and models tend to meet these objections. These models fall into the general classifications of linear programming methods, the Linear Decision Rule (LDR), heuristic methods, and computer search methods in the form of the Search Decision Rule (SDR).

Linear Programming Methods

The aggregate planning problem has been represented in the format of both simplex and distribution models of linear programming.

Bowman [6] proposed the distribution model of linear programming as a mode for aggregate planning in 1956. The model focused on the objective of assigning units of productive capacity such that combined production plus storage costs were minimized and sales demand met, all within the constraints of available capacity. The rim conditions in the distribution matrix form the constraints that sales requirements must be met on the one hand, and that capacity limitations in the form of initial inventory, regular time production capacity, and overtime production capacity be met on the other hand. Both beginning and ending inventory must be specified for the program developed over the N periods in the planning horizon. The matrix elements are costs. The criterion function to be minimized is combined regular production, overtime production, and inventory cost. The output of the process is a program which specifies the amount of regular and overtime production in each of the periods of the planning horizon. The basic matrix can be extended to more than one product by establishing a separate column in each period for each product. Problem 8 at the end of Chapter 11 required this solution format, and the Camptor Company, presented as an example in that chapter, was a variation of the basic model proposed by Bowman.

Distribution methods of linear programming have *serious limitations* for the aggregate planning problem. The most serious disadvantages are that the distribution model does not account for production change costs, and there is no cost penalty for back ordering or lost sales. Thus, resulting programs may call for changes in production levels in one period (requiring an expanded work force) only to call for the discharging of these workers one or two periods hence. Since the distribution model assigns no cost to hiring and laying off workers, it calls for such decisions with abandon. In addition, the linearity requirement is often too severe.

The *simplex method* of linear programming makes it possible to include production level change costs and inventory shortage costs in the model.

McGarrah [36, pp. 124–127] proposes a simplex model for aggregate planning in which the production change cost function is segmented into four linear functions, thus covering a broad range of change costs but still meeting the requirement for linearity in the model. His inventory penalty cost functions reflect linear inventory holding costs which result from carrying too much inventory, as well as stock-out and backordering costs resulting from not carrying enough stock. Perhaps the biggest disadvantage of the model is that it has a planning horizon of only one period.

Simplex models which have larger horizon times have also been developed by Hanssmann and Hess [26] and by McGarrah [36, pp. 127–129]. The Hanssmann-Hess model establishes work force and production rate as independent variables with regular payroll, hiring, layoff, overtime, inventory, and shortage costs as dependent variables and allows a preset planning horizon time. We shall delay specific comment on the Hanssmann-Hess model since it is stated in exactly the same general format as the following discussion of the Linear Decision Rule. Industrial applications of the simplex model are reported by Eisemann and Young [14] in a study of a textile mill and by Greene, Chatto, Hicks, and Cox [24] in the packing industry.

The Linear Decision Rule

The Linear Decision Rule (LDR) is a quadratic programming approach for making aggregate employment and production rate decisions. It was developed by Holt, Modigliani, Muth, and Simon [28, 29, 30] and was tested in a paint factory. The LDR is based on the development of a quadratic cost function for the company in question, the components of the cost function being regular payroll, hiring, layoff, overtime, inventory holding, back ordering, and machine setup costs. The quadratic cost function is then used to derive two linear decision rules for computing work force levels and production rate for the upcoming period based on forecasts of aggregate sales for a planning horizon. The two linear decision rules are optimum for the model.

Cost Functions. Figure 1 shows the form of the four components of the cost function. The size of the work force is adjusted in the model once per month with the implied commitment to pay employees at least their regular time wages for the month. This is indicated in Figure 1a. The costs of labor turnover are indicated in Figure 1b. These costs result from hiring or laying off workers, and the LDR model approximates these costs with a quadratic function.

If the size of the work force is held constant for the month, then changes

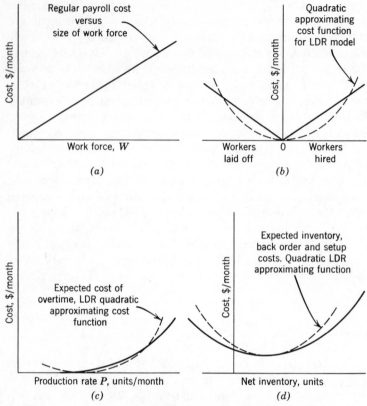

FIGURE 1. *Approximating linear and quadratic cost functions used by the Linear Decision Rule (LDR) model.*

in production rate can be absorbed by overtime and undertime. Undertime is the cost of idle labor at regular payroll rates. The overtime cost depends on the size of the work force, W_t, and on the aggregate production rate P_t. The form of the overtime-undertime cost function in relation to production rate is shown in Figure 1c, being approximated by a quadratic function. Whether overtime or undertime costs will occur for a given decision depends on the balance of costs defined by the horizon time. For example, in responding to the need for increased output the costs of hiring and training must be balanced against the overtime costs, or conversely the response to a decreased production rate would require the balancing of layoff costs against the costs of undertime.

Figure 1d shows the general shape of the net inventory cost curve. When inventories deviate from ideal levels, either extra inventory costs must be absorbed if inventory levels are too high or costs of back ordering or lost sales will occur if inventory levels are too low. In the LDR, the optimal aggregate inventory level for each paint is defined by the sum of the optimal average safety stock and one-half the optimal batch size. The optimal batch size for each paint is determined by economic order quantity formulas. Therefore, one of the costs which will vary with changes in aggregate inventory is machine setup cost. Thus, as aggregate inventory is reduced, the average production batch size will be decreased in order to maintain a balanced inventory resulting in incremental machine setups. The meaning of "net inventory" is simply inventory minus back orders.

The total incremental cost function developed for the paint factory application of the LDR is simply the sum of the four component cost functions. The problem is to minimize the sum of the monthly incremental cost function over the planning horizon time of N months:

$$C_N = \sum_{t=1}^{N} C_t \tag{1}$$

Where C_N is the total cost for N periods and C_t is the monthly cost made up of the four cost components as follows:

$$
\begin{aligned}
C_t = [(c_1 W_t) & \qquad \text{Regular payroll costs} \\
+ c_2(W_t - W_{t-1})^2 & \qquad \text{Hiring and layoff costs} \\
+ c_3(P_t - c_4 W_t)^2 + c_5 P_t - c_6 W_t & \qquad \text{Overtime costs} \\
+ c_7(I_t - c_8 - c_9 O_t)^2], & \qquad \text{Inventory-connected costs}
\end{aligned}
\tag{2}
$$

subject to the restraints,

$$I_{t-1} + P_t - O_t = I_t \qquad t = 1, 2, \ldots, N \tag{3}$$

Equations (1), (2), and (3) are general in form and applicable to a broad range of situations. By estimating the values of the c's, a specific factory cost structure can be specified such as the one for the paint factory:

$$C_N = \sum_{t=1}^{N} \{[340W_t] + [64.3(W_t - W_{t-1})^2] + [0.20(P_t - 5.67W_t)^2 \\ + 51.2P_t - 281.0W_t] + [0.0825(I_t - 320)^2]\} \tag{4}$$

Optimal Decision Rules for the Paint Factory. Two specific decision rules for production rate P_t and work force size W_t were obtained by differentiating equation (4) with respect to each decision variable. The result of this process is contained in equations (5) and (6) for the paint company.

$$P_t = \begin{Bmatrix} +0.463O_t \\ +0.234O_{t+1} \\ +0.111O_{t+2} \\ +0.046O_{t+3} \\ +0.013O_{t+4} \\ -0.002O_{t+5} \\ -0.008O_{t+6} \\ -0.010O_{t+7} \\ -0.009O_{t+8} \\ -0.008O_{t+9} \\ -0.007O_{t+10} \\ -0.005O_{t+11} \end{Bmatrix} + 0.993W_{t-1} + 153.0 - 0.464I_{t-1} \quad (5)$$

$$W_t = 0.743W_{t-1} + 2.09 - 0.010I_{t-1} + \begin{Bmatrix} +0.0101O_t \\ +0.0088O_{t+1} \\ +0.0071O_{t+2} \\ +0.0054O_{t+3} \\ +0.0042O_{t+4} \\ +0.0031O_{t+5} \\ +0.0023O_{t+6} \\ +0.0016O_{t+7} \\ +0.0012O_{t+8} \\ +0.0009O_{t+9} \\ +0.0006O_{t+10} \\ +0.0005O_{t+11} \end{Bmatrix} \quad (6)$$

Equations (5) and (6) may then be used to compute decisions for each upcoming month. Equation (5) determines the aggregate production rate and equation (6) the aggregate size of the work force. The equations are easy to use, requiring only data on last month's work force size and ending inventories plus forecasts of aggregate sales for each of twelve months in advance (the forecast horizon can be shorter or longer).

Results for the Paint Company. The two decision rules represented by equations (5) and (6) were applied to a past six-year record of known decisions in the paint company. Two kinds of forecasts were used as inputs, a perfect forecast and a moving average forecast. The actual order pattern was extremely variable involving both the 1949 recession and the Korean War. The graphical record of actual factory performance compared with the simulated performance of the LDR is shown in Figures 2 and 3 for production rates and work force levels. Additional graphical results of overtime hours, inventories, and back orders are contained in references

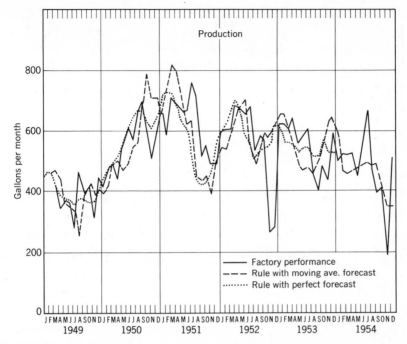

FIGURE 2. Comparative performance of the Linear Decision Rule with actual factory performance for production rates. (Figures 2 and 3 are from C. C. Holt, F. Modigliani, and H. H. Simon, "A Linear Decision Rule for Production and Employment Scheduling," Management Science, Vol. II, No. 2, October, 1955, pp. 1–30.)

[10, 30]. Cost comparisons are shown in Table 1. Costs were reconstructed for the six-year period of actual operation and projected for the decision rules based on the cost structure originally estimated from paint company data. The LDR with a perfect forecast yields the lowest cost. The difference between the costs for the perfect and moving average forecasts may be regarded as a measure of the value of improved forecasting. The cost difference between actual company performance and the LDR performance with the moving average forecast was $173,000 per year.

Modifications and Extensions of LDR.   Since the original development of LDR, several investigators have modified and extended the basic conceptual framework. Sypkens [46] expanded the basic model to include plant capacity as an independent decision variable in addition to W_t and P_t. Of course, short range capacity for these kinds of productive systems is set in the conventional LDR model through the determination of the work force

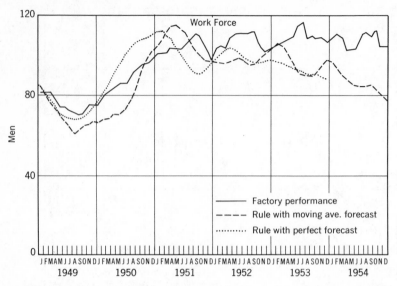

FIGURE 3. *Comparative performance of the Linear Decision Rule with actual factory performance for work force size.*

size, W_t; however, there are some instances where fundamental physical capacity adjustments can also be made to advantage. Sypkens cites two types of production systems where physical capacity adjustments can be made as a part of the aggregate planning model. The first is a system where the capacity can be divided physically into a large number of identical production units, each able to perform the essential operations. Examples would be a trucking firm or a steel components plant consisting of a large number of identical machines, such as turret lathes. A second type of production system where a variable capacity model has some validity is the typical job shop, where a large number of production units each have a different function in the total productive process. Sypkens notes that theoretically it seems impossible to increase the capacity of such a production facility by a small fraction because of the apparent need to increase the capacity of each individual unit by some fraction. On the surface, it seems that a capacity increase in such a system could be achieved only by replacing the entire system, thus making a small capacity expansion impractical. This is true, however, only if the capacity of all production units is exactly the same. In reality, however, the plant capacity is commonly determined by the machine or machine group with the limiting or bottleneck capacity. Therefore, it is often possible to increase the capacity of a plant in small steps by increasing the capacity of the bottleneck machine group.

TABLE I.   Cost comparisons for 1949 to 1953

| | | Decision Rule | |
Costs (Thousands of Dollars)	Company Performance	Moving Average Forecast	Perfect Forecast
Regular payroll	$1940	$1834	$1888
Overtime	196	296	167
Inventory	361	451	454
Back orders	1566	616	400
Hiring and layoffs	22	25	20
Total Cost $\begin{cases} \$ \\ \% \end{cases}$	4085 139%	3222 110%	2929 100%

From C. C. Holt, F. Modigliani, and H. A. Simon, ibid.

Another modification of the basic LDR model involves the extension to the multiproduct situation. Chang and Jones [11] generalized the LDR methodology to yield aggregate and disaggregate planning and scheduling information, extending the conceptual framework to take account of longer product cycles. An assumption implicit in most aggregate planning models is that all of the effort required to produce the product occurs during the same period that the product was completed. This is realistic for bulk processing, such as paint, and for many small products, but not for products involving long fabrication and assembly cycles. Chang and Jones extended their multiproduct model by incorporating a labor distribution matrix giving the fraction of total labor hours for product i required in month r for the product cycle time.

Bergstrom and Smith [3] extended the basic LDR model involving both multiproducts and the inclusion of a revenue term. The objective function of their model, therefore, becomes one of maximizing contribution to fixed costs and overhead. Beyond the general multiproduct extension incorporated in [11], Bergstrom and Smith have included a crucially different concept with respect to the demand function. In the original LDR formulation and all of the other modifications, the demand forecast has been fixed and specified. Instead Bergstrom and Smith have estimated revenue versus sales curves for each product. The amount to be sold then is dependent on price and other possible parameters, for example, differential promotional budgets. The total revenue for any volume of output is the product of that volume and the price as determined from the demand curve.

Comparison of the Hanssmann–Hess and LDR Models. Since the Hanssmann–Hess [26] linear programming simplex model for aggregate planning is equivalent to the LDR model in terms of components and general structure, we are in a position now to compare them. Decisions are in terms of aggregate work force and production rates in both models, and the cost criterion function involves the same components. The basic difference between the two models, then, is in the contrast between linear and quadratic functions and in the optimizing procedure. It is difficult to choose which type of cost functions would be better, since both impose severe limitations in the structure of the cost model: linear functions for one, quadratic functions for the other. A recent comparative study by Kolenda, see references [10, 35], of the results obtained by the models indicates that they are comparable. In actual situations, the various cost components are probably neither all linear nor all quadratic, so that both models are subject to similar defects.

Preliminary Evaluation of LDR. The Linear Decision Rule has many important advantages. First, the model is optimizing, and the two decision rules, once derived, are simple to apply. On the other hand, the quadratic cost structure may have severe limitations and probably does not adequately represent the cost structure of any organization. In addition, there are no constraints on the size of work force, overtime, inventory, and capital. Heuristic and computer search methods are free of mathematical forms in constructing cost models for specific company situations and seem to offer considerable promise. We shall discuss briefly two alternate heuristic approaches and then present computer search methods.

Heuristic Programs

There are two rather different proposals for handling the aggregate planning problem by heuristic programming models. The first developed by Bowman uses the past average managerial performance to derive coefficients for decision rules. We shall call his proposal the "Management Coefficients Model." The second heuristic model is called Parametric Production Planning and was developed by Jones.

Bowman's *Management Coefficients Model* [5] determines the coefficients for the production rate and size of work force decision rules through statistical analysis of management's own past decisions. Recall that in the Linear Decision Rule the coefficients were determined through mathematical analysis. Bowman's theory is that management is sensitive to the same criteria used in analytical models but that managerial behavior tends to be highly variable rather than off-center. Thus he states that management's performance can be improved considerably simply by applying the decision rules more consistently, since in terms of the usual U-shaped criterion function variability is more costly than being slightly off-center from optimum decisions, but consistent in those decisions. Applications are discussed in references [5, 10].

Parametric Production Planning is a heuristic programming model developed by Jones [34]. Parametric Production Planning is dependent on two linear feedback decision rules, one for size of work force and one for production rate, as with LDR and the Management Coefficients Model. Each decision rule is defined by two parameters resulting in a four-dimensional space in which we wish to find, for a specific application, the combination of parameters which is associated with minimum cost operation. Two of the parameters determine the fraction of desired work force and production rate to be achieved, and the other two determine the relative weights to be placed on the forecasts for each period for each of the two rules. A search procedure is used to determine the best combination of the four parameters by evaluating alternate sets through the cost structure of the firm being analyzed. There are no limitations in mathematical form to the cost functions as there are with LDR and linear programming. Instead the cost functions should be the best estimates which can be constructed. The parameters chosen are then incorporated into the two decision rules to make the rules specific for the firm being analyzed. The result is that while the decision rules are not optimal in the sense of a mathematically provable optimum, Parametric Production Planning produces production plans involving costs which are not easily reduced.

Applications of Parametric Production Planning are reported by Jones in four different situations. The first was the paint factory analyzed by means of the LDR; the second was a hypothetical firm, Company X, which involved a perfect forecast and comparison with a comparable linear programming model; the third also involved Company X and comparison with the comparable linear programming model, but the perfect forecast was replaced with an imperfect one; and, the fourth involved a comparative application between Parametric Production Planning, LDR, and a linear programming model in making decisions in a complex management simulation game. The results for the paint company showed that Parametric Production Planning yielded decisions which were almost the same as those given by the optimum LDR. The results in terms of comparative costs for the two models are given in Table II. The cost differences are minor, and we must conclude that for practical purposes the results are the same.

When Jones compared Parametric Production Planning with linear programming in the setting of the hypothetical Company X he found that Parametric Production Planning yielded discretionary costs about 8 percent

TABLE II. Comparative costs for the paint company resulting from the use of the Linear Decision Rule and Parametric Production Planning

	Linear Decision Rule*	Parametric Production Planning
Hiring and layoff costs	$ 20,778	$ 19,039
Overtime costs	150,478	157,591
Payroll costs	1,857,052	1,852,892
Storage costs	26,221	25,940
Total costs	$2,054,529	$2,055,462

From C. H. Jones, "Parametric Production Planning," Management Science, Vol. 13, No. 11, July 1967, pp. 843–866.
*These results were achieved by using the coefficients on page 61 of Holt, Modigliani, Muth, and Simon. Planning Production, Inventories, and Work Force, Englewood Cliffs, N.J., 1960. If the slightly different coefficients on page 17 of Holt, Modigliani, and Simon, "A Linear Decision Rule for Production and Employment Scheduling," Management Science, October 1955, are used, the costs become $20,284, $127,684, $1,881,622, and $25,168 to a total of $2,054,759. Although the total costs are very similar, the slight difference in rounding moves $23,000 of costs from regular payroll to overtime.

higher than for linear programming when the perfect forecast was used, but when erroneous forecasts were used the cost performance of Parametric Production Planning was about 8.5 percent lower than for linear programming.

In the management simulation game setting, three alternate models were constructed in order to make decisions: linear programming, the LDR, and Parametric Production Planning. At the end of eight comparable periods of play, "the Parametric Production Planning firm had achieved a profit about $70,000 higher than the linear programming firm and $170,000 higher than the LDR firm. In order to put these relative costs into perspective, the total profit for each firm was over $4 million and the sum of money expended by each firm for hiring and firing, overtime, extra inventory costs, and other discretionary costs was about $1 million." Jones states further that:

> The poor showing of the Linear Decision Rule firm can be attributed to the poor fit of the quadratic curve to some costs that were essentially linear. This was most damaging when the linear overtime costs were approximated by a shallow parabola.
> This firm (the linear programming firm) turned out to be particularly suitable for linear programming because our sales forecasting procedures were fairly good and did not deteriorate badly with an increasing time span. The average absolute percentage of error for forecasts one, two, three, and four periods in

advance was respectively 5.4, 5.1, 6.0, and 8.2 percent. Most of the differences in profit between the Parametric Production Planning firm and the linear programming firm were due to lost sales which occurred when the linear programming firm suddenly found itself faced with peak sales forecasts higher than it had expected and chose to lose sales rather than pay the costs of immediate large production and employment expansions. By contrast the production smoothing through the previous trough had left the Parametric Production Planning firm with a larger inventory to help in achieving the large sales.

It appears as though the Parametric Production Planning model has significant advantages over both linear programming and the LDR in that mathematical form does not constrain the cost structure used by Parametric Production Planning and smoothing effects built into the model give it a more stable response than linear programming.

Optimization Techniques

There are numerous optimization techniques that can be used to solve mathematical models of the aggregate planning problem. Some are strictly analytical in nature—differential calculus, Lagrangian multipliers, linear programming, dynamic programming, etc.; others are quasi-analytical, such as the many gradient following techniques; and still others are strictly heuristic in nature. Both the quasi-analytical and heuristic techniques offer the user only the hope of finding a global optimum but not a guarantee. At the present time, no single optimization technique can be used to solve all mathematical models. This means that optimization is, in reality, still an art involving a careful match between technique and model. This match must be skillfully made with constant concern for the fundamental fact that a solution to a model can be no better than the model itself. Consequently, the model builder faces the dilemma that the more complicated and realistic he makes the model, the lower his probability of finding the global optimum.

In the past, this complexity problem was so serious that the model builder had to restrict his attention to simple models that could be solved by analytic techniques. Today the computer has made possible many new quasi-analytical and heuristic search techniques. These techniques have significantly increased the probability of finding the global optimum of a complex model and have placed before the model builder a very powerful set of mathematical tools. One such set of tools is known as direct computer search procedures or, more succinctly, "direct search."

"Direct Search" consists of the sequential examination of a finite set of feasible trial solutions of the criterion function. A single trial evaluation is produced by specifing values for each independent variable, evaluating the criterion function, and recording the result. Each trial value is compared to the best previous value. If an improvement is observed, the trial value is accepted; if not, it is rejected. The direct search procedure is normally terminated when a predetermined number of trial valuations has been made, or the computer time limit is exceeded.

"Pattern Search" is a particular type of direct search developed by Hooke and Jeeves [31], and later modified by Weisman, Wood, and Rivlin [53] and by Taubert [50]. Their heuristic establishes a base point, or particular setting of the independent variables, and then looks for a pattern by means of an exploratory search in which each independent variable is sequentially perturbed, first in the forward coordinate direction and then in the reverse, until an improvement in the criterion function is found. The amount of the perturbation, or step size, for each independent variable is modified as the search progresses. The step size heuristic is complex but in general depends on whether a success or failure was experienced during the previous exploratory search phase. Successes produce larger step sizes (the search becomes bolder), while failures produce smaller step sizes (the search becomes more cautious).

Once a successful pattern has been established the search routine moves through N-dimensional space to a new point based on a set of heuristics. See [10]. This movement is called a pattern move. A local exploration is then conducted in an attempt to find another successful pattern. Each pattern move is followed by a sequence of exploratory moves until the function cannot be reduced, or the computer time limit is exceeded.

The pattern search technique has been successfully used to solve complicated nonlinear optimization problems and appears to require significantly less computer time than other methods. The success of this type of heuristic stems from its ability to remain on the crest of a sharp ridge while searching N-dimensional space for an optimum. By following a one-dimensional ridge the heuristic reduces the effective dimensionality of the problem and hence reduces the computer time required for its solution. The interested reader will find a complete documented FORTRAN listing of this method in [10, 50].

SEARCH DECISION RULE
FOR AGGREGATE PLANNING */*

Taubert [50] modified the Hooke-Jeeves Pattern Search Program [31, 50, 53] as a vehicle for experimenting with the aggregate planning problem, which we shall now refer to as the

Search Decision Rule (SDR). To test the feasibility of using such a program, the paint company example (originally used to test the Linear Decision Rule) was selected because of the availability of published data and comparative results.

In general terms, the criterion function which represents the costs to be minimized over the planning horizon time can be expressed as a function of production rates and work force levels:

$$C_N = f[P_1, W_1, P_2, W_2 \ldots P_N, W_N] \qquad (7)$$

where the notation $C_N = f[\ ]$ is read C_N is a function of the variables listed in the brackets. Therefore, each period that is included in the planning horizon requires the addition of two dimensions to the criterion function, one each for production rate and work force level. The criterion function developed for the paint company was given as equation (4). The original program used was written to handle a maximum of twenty independent variables, and, therefore, the planning horizon time was limited in the analysis of the paint company to 10 months. (The modified adaptive pattern search program has been expanded to handle many more independent variables.) Beginning inventory, work force levels, and monthly sales were taken from the data given in [30]. The search routine was set to end whenever the decrease in the objective cost function found by SDR's exploration of the response surface was less than 0.5×10^{-6}. After computing a set of decisions for the first month, the program automatically updated the sales forecasts (using a perfect forecast) over the planning horizon of 10 months and reset the initial starting vector so that an entire 24-month sample (or more) could be computed in one continuous run. In order to restrict the search, two constraints were added restricting production rate to 1000 gallons per month and work force to 150 men as maximum values.

Table III shows a sample of the SDR output for the first month of factory operation. The computer output gives the first month's decision as well as an entire program for the planning horizon of 10 months. In the lower half of the table the program prints out the component cost of payroll, hiring and firing, overtime, inventory, and totals for the entire planning horizon. Thus a production manager is not only provided with the immediate decisions for the upcoming month, but also the projected decisions based on monthly forecasts for the planning horizon time and the economic consequences of each month's decision.

Table IV gives a month-by-month comparison for the first 24 months between the results obtained by SDR as compared to the use of the two optimum decision rules for the LDR. The month-by-month decisions are

TABLE III.   SDR output for the first month of paint factory operation (perfect forecast)

A. SDR Decisions and Projections

Month	Sales (Gallons)	Production (Gallons)	Inventory (Gallons)	Work Force (Men)
0			263.00	81.00
1	430	471.89	304.89	77.60
2	447	444.85	302.74	74.10
3	440	416.79	279.54	70.60
4	316	380.90	344.44	67.32
5	397	374.64	322.08	64.51
6	375	363.67	310.75	62.07
7	292	348.79	367.54	60.22
8	458	358.63	268.17	58.68
9	400	329.83	198.00	57.05
10	350	270.60	118.60	55.75

B. Cost Analysis of Decisions and Projections (Dollars)

Month	Payroll	Hiring and Firing	Overtime	Inventory	Total
1	26,384.04	743.25	2,558.82	18.33	29,704.94
2	25,195.60	785.62	2,074.76	24.57	28,080.54
3	24,004.00	789.79	1,555.68	135.06	26,484.53
4	22,888.86	691.69	585.21	49.27	24,215.03
5	21,932.79	508.43	1,070.48	0.36	23,512.06
6	21,102.86	383.13	1,206.90	7.06	22,699.93
7	20,473.22	220.51	948.13	186.43	21,828.29
8	19,950.99	151.70	2,007.33	221.64	22,331.66
9	19,395.30	171.76	865.74	1,227.99	21,660.79
10	18,954.76	107.95	−1,396.80	3,346.46	21,012.37
					241,530.14

From W. H. Taubert, "Search Decision Rule for the Aggregate Scheduling Problem," Management Science, Vol. 14, No. 6, February, 1968.

not identical but are very close to each other and the 24-month production totals differ by only 2 gallons. The total cost of the SDR plans and schedules exceeds the LDR costs by only $806, or 0.11 percent. This difference may be accounted for by the fact that the SDR used a planning horizon of only 10 months as compared to the 12-month horizon used by the LDR.

Other interesting results developed from the computer runs. For example, the SDR program in certain instances was minimizing total costs over the planning horizon by selecting certain combinations of work force and production rate which resulted in a negative overtime cost contribution to the criterion function. Note for example in Table III, the overtime cost of −$1396.80 for the tenth month. Since it is illogical for either overtime or undertime to make a negative contribution to total costs, the overtime cost function developed by Holt et al. was examined more carefully, and it was found indeed possible for negative overtime cost contributions to

TABLE IV. A comparison of LDR and SDR decisions for the first 24 months of operation with paint company data (perfect forecast)

Month	Monthly Sales (Gallons)	Production (Gallons)		Work Force (Men)*		Inventory (Gallons)		Monthly Cost (Dollars)	
		LDR	SDR	LDR	SDR	LDR	SDR	LDR	SDR
0				81	81	263	263		
1	430	468	472	78	78	301	305	29,348	29,705
2	447	442	443	75	74	296	301	27,797	79,930
3	440	416	418	72	71	272	279	26,294	26,460
4	316	382	385	69	68	337	348	24,094	24,415
5	397	377	376	67	66	317	327	23,504	23,436
6	375	368	366	66	64	311	318	22,879	22,672
7	292	360	360	65	63	379	386	22,614	22,539
8	458	382	382	65	63	303	309	23,485	23,322
9	400	377	379	66	64	280	288	23,367	23,331
10	350	366	366	67	64	296	304	22,846	22,569
11	284	365	359	69	67	377	379	23,408	23,004
12	400	404	401	72	70	381	380	25,750	25,654
13	483	447	447	75	74	345	344	28,266	28,367
14	509	477	479	79	78	313	314	30,180	30,408
15	500	495	498	83	81	307	312	31,310	31,479
16	475	511	510	87	86	343	348	32,422	32,481
17	500	543	547	91	90	386	394	34,858	35,074
18	600	595	592	96	94	380	387	38,119	38,216
19	700	641	642	100	98	321	328	40,849	41,110
20	700	661	659	103	101	282	287	41,848	41,898
21	725	659	658	105	103	216	220	41,945	41,981
22	600	627	624	106	105	244	245	39,074	38,940
23	432	605	601	107	106	417	413	38,134	37,928
24	615	653	655	109	108	455	454	41,785	42,003
Totals		11,621	11,619	1,972	1,936	7,859	7,970	734,176	734,982

From W. H. Taubert, ibid.
*Rounded to the next largest number of men.

occur. When the overtime cost is plotted as a function of production rate, as it was by Holt et al. (see Figure 1c) a quadratic cost function is shown. Actually, however, overtime cost is given as a function of both production rate and size of work force, as shown by equations (2) and (4), and when iso-cost contours were developed as a function of P_t and W_t, it was found that negative overtime cost contributions as high as $3000 were possible for low production rates, and contributions as high as $2000 were possible over almost the entire range of productive capacity. Consequently, the computer search program was behaving in a very logical way when it used these negative overtime costs to help minimize the criterion function. Holt et al. had added two constants to the basic overtime cost function, "to improve the overall approximation" [30, p. 11]. Nevertheless, the magnitude of the error is small. The important point is simply the observation that the LDR model can produce negative overtime costs and that this is illogical.

Horizon Time Effects

It is interesting to examine the usefulness of an extended horizon time. With SDR, it was an easy matter to vary the forecast horizon time and measure the results in terms of percentage increases in the 24-month total cost and in computer time requirements. Figures 4 and 5 show the results for the paint company. In Figure 4 we see that reducing the forecast horizon time from 10 to 5 months increases total cost by only 1.28 percent; however, in Figure 5 we see that computer time is reduced by almost a factor of 3. While computer time per decision is very small for the paint company example (19 seconds on an IBM 7094, 3 seconds on an IBM 360/75), in more complex problems one might wish to make a trade off between horizon time and computing cost. Also, in more complex problems it might be advantageous to reduce horizon time and use the released independent variables in building a more effective and realistic model.

With the incentives of the horizon time-computing cost tradeoff and the possible released independent variables in mind, Sikes [45] investigated methods by which the necessary horizon might be reduced. In addition he noted that the smaller the horizon the less forecast data is required to drive the model. Since the reliability of forecasts decreases as they become more distant, a smaller horizon becomes even more attractive from a practical point of view.

Furthermore, the behavior of the SDR projections over the planning horizon as indicated in Table IIIA exhibits strange characteristics near the end of the horizon. The projected decisions show that for the last three months production rates are substantially below sales and continuing to

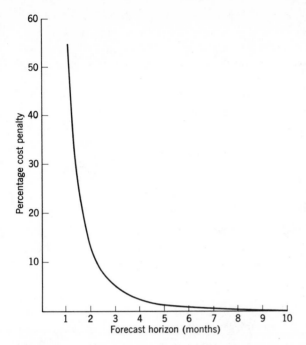

FIGURE 4. Percentage cost increase versus the length of the forecast horizon. From W. H. Taubert, "A Computer Search Solution of the Aggregate Scheduling Problem," Management Science, Vol. 16, No. 6, February, 1968, pp. 343–359.

decline, the difference being made up by draining inventories. (Note that these are projected decisions which are finalized in subsequent iterations.) That these projected decisions are in error is shown clearly by the finalized optimum values for the same months shown in Table IV. SDR was in fact performing very logically by sloughing off inventory in the final months of the projections because it saw a finite horizon and assumed a "going out of business" stance, minimizing costs by producing less and dumping inventories near the end of the planning horizon. While the magnitude of the finite horizon effect on final solutions yielded by SDR is obviously miniscule for planning horizons of approximately six months or more, the observation of the behavior of the projections provided Sikes with insight for eliminating the effect and reducing the required size of the horizon in SDR solutions.

PROPX. After experimenting with several techniques Sikes [45] found a simple method for establishing boundary conditions on inventories to be

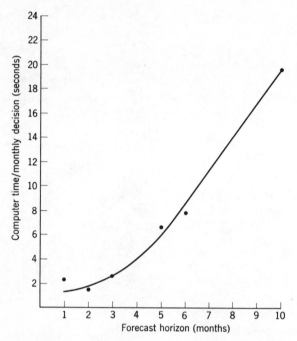

FIGURE 5. Computer time versus forecast horizon. From W. H. Taubert, "A Computer Search Solution of the Aggregate Scheduling Problem," Management Science, Vol. 14, No. 6, February, 1968, pp. 343–359.

most effective and termed it PROPX. He imposed an artificial penalty on the low-ending inventories during the periods near the end of the planning horizon. These penalties were progressively greater as the planning horizon approached its limit, since the tendency toward inventory drain increased by this general pattern. Thus he "propped up" the ending inventories.

Recall that for the paint company the inventory-related cost function from equation (4) was $c_7(I_t - c_8)^2$, where c_7 and c_8 were computed as 0.0825 and 320 gallons, respectively. c_8 is the optimum ending inventory. Therefore, there are N terms in the SDR objective function of the form,

$$CINV(J) = c_7[I(J) - 320]^2, \quad J = 1, 2, \ldots, N$$

where J is the index on periods with $J = 1$ corresponding to month t. When PROPX is applied the program computes values of $CINV(J)$ by multiplying c_7 by the respective values of an n-dimensional vector whose Jth value is PROP(J).

Sikes finally settled on a PROP function which grew geometrically over the horizon range $1 \leqslant J \leqslant N$. In the construction used, $\text{PROP}(1) = 1$ and $\text{PROP}(N) = \text{PROPX}$. The result is that during the decision-making phase of SDR, higher penalties for inventory deviations from the minimum cost level of 320 are imposed for the last $N - 1$ periods. In the assessment phase, however, there results no unnatural distortion of the cost of the decisions actually finalized since c_7 remains unchanged for the first month of the planning horizon.

Sikes carried out computational experiments involving values of PROPX ranging from 1 to 60. For the paint company he found that $\text{PROPX} = 15$ minimized total costs for 24 months of operation using a horizon of $N = 10$ months.

The significance of the PROPX technique for the paint company is shown in Figure 6 which relates planning horizon to percentage cost penalty for two different values of PROPX. The curve for $\text{PROPX} = 1$ involves no adjustment for ending inventories and is similar to Figure 4. When

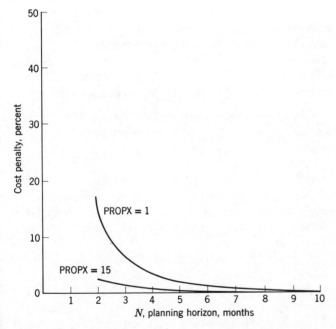

FIGURE 6.   *Cost penalties versus planning horizon for PROPX = 1 and 15. From T. W. Sikes, "The Search Decision Rule Applied to Aggregate Planning: Improved Efficiency and Stochastic Extension," unpublished Ph.D. Dissertation, UCLA, 1970.*

PROPX = 15, however, the penalties for using horizons shorter than 10 months are 2.4 percent for $N = 2$, 1.25 percent for $N = 3$, 0.68 percent for $N = 4$, and 0.41 percent for $N = 5$. Obviously the PROPX technique provides an effective means of reducing the planning horizon with very small cost penalty in a simple environment such as the paint company. Tests of the PROPX technique in the more complex environment of the search company (to be discussed on pp. 434–439) indicate that the technique may have more general application.

The Effect of Forecast Errors

Sikes also experimented with the effects of forecast errors in the paint company environment. To accomplish this he developed a stochastic extension of the SDR paint company model in which the actual sales S_t were assumed to be those given as sales data, and forecasts F_t were, $F_t = S_t - \delta_t$, where δ_t is a random forecasting error independent of S_t. The forecasting error was normally distributed with mean 0. Variances of δ_t, Var(δ_t), were assumed equal from month to month. In the stochastic model, SDR based its decisions on the inaccurate forecasts F_t but computed inventories, and the costs of decisions, based on the actual sales S_t. Sikes ran a series of experiments, three of which are reported here: those dealing with unrevised forecasts, the value of perfect information, and those dealing with revised forecasts. Sample sizes were $k = 30$, and a horizon of $N = 3$ months was used with a value of PROPX = 13 for all of the experiments.

Unrevised Forecasts. Sikes made runs using the paint company cost model and sales data, observing total costs for a 24-month period for Var(δ_t) = 0, 400, 900, 1600, 3600, 6400, 10,000, and 20,000. In general there is a linear increase of mean costs with Var(δ_t). To gain perspective, note that for Var(δ_t) = 10,000 (standard deviation 100) the average cost penalty was $777,053 − $741,848 = $35,205 or only 4.8 percent more than the costs obtained with perfect forecasts. Yet the forecast error is relatively large since the average actual sales for the 24 months was 468 gallons, yielding a coefficient of variation of 21.4 percent.

The composition of the $35,205 cost penalty is shown in Table V which indicates that the majority of the increased costs are in the inventory and overtime categories, with a relatively small increase in hiring-layoff costs resulting in a smaller regular payroll cost. Apparently, for the paint company excellent decisions in the face of forecast uncertainty are to absorb fluctuations through overtime and inventories.

The Value of Perfect Information. In a second set of experiments, Sikes determined the amount of the cost penalty attributable to each of the three months of the planning horizon. He did this by making three runs for

TABLE V. Composition of cost increases when Var(δ) = 10,000 compared to perfect forecasts*

	Regular Payroll Costs	Hiring- Layoff Costs	Overtime Costs	Inventory Related Costs	Total Costs
Var(δ) = 0					
(Perfect forecasts)	$629,405	$13,247	$95,004	$ 4,192	$741,848
Var(δ) = 10,000	628,394	19,263	108,311	21,085	777,053
Cost difference	− $ 1,011	$ 6,016	$13,307	$16,893	$ 35,205

*From T. W. Sikes, "The Search Decision Rule Applied to Aggregate Planning: Improved Efficiency and Stochastic Extension," Unpublished Ph.D. Dissertation, UCLA, 1970.

comparison: (a) with forecast errors in all three months of the forecast horizon, (b) with a perfect forecast for the first month, and (c) with a perfect forecast for the first two months of the three month horizon. Runs were made for Var(δ_t) ranging from 0 to 10,000 and total costs for 24 months were computed. For Var(δ_t) = 10,000 the cost difference between (a) and (b) was $22,782 or 65 percent of the total cost penalty due to forecast errors for all three months of the horizon. This effect suggests further support for the shorter planning horizons since forecast errors beyond three months would have little effect.

Revised Forecasts—The Value of Improved Forecasting. In this set of experiments Sikes made it possible for the forecasts to be revised each month, incorporating a progressively lower variance of forecast error as that month grows closer to the current period. The presumption was made that the variance of forecast errors could be progressively reduced by 50 percent as the month draws closer to the current period. In one set of runs this was compared with a forecasting system in which the variance of the first month's forecast could be further cut in half. For example, if the basic variance Var (δ_t) = 10,000, the 24-month cost difference was only $5,200 or $2,600 per year. This suggests that there is a relatively small value to be placed on improved forecasting for the paint company situation.

APPLICATIONS OF SDR IN MORE COMPLEX ENVIRONMENTS /

It is clear that the SDR can duplicate the performance of the LDR in the simple environment of the paint company. Having available the known optimum solution for the paint company has provided an excellent vehicle for experimentation with a flexible technique such as SDR. In order to test the SDR methodology in more complex environments, a hypothetical organization called the search company was created, followed by more extensive applications in an applied research laboratory and in an integrated steel mill. We shall discuss the results of these applications in sequence.

The Search Company—A Complex Multi-Shift Manufacturing Enterprise

The Search Company cost model was developed in 1967 by Buffa and Taubert [9, 10] to represent the operation of a manufacturing facility with second shift capability. As a general enterprise situation the search company is not unlike the paint company, though it is not the paint company, since the kind of additional data needed was not available for the paint company. Nevertheless, many of the cost values come from the paint company example, and the model is driven with paint company sales data.

 As a point of departure for the cost structure of the Search Company, let us refer to Figure 1 in Chapter 2 which represents something close to the actual cost volume relationships as we pass through a wide range of production rates. The total cost function shown in Figure I of Chapter 2 is characterized by semi-fixed costs associated with the start up of first, second, and third shifts. Also, increased congestion and delay costs, and the relative ineffectiveness of newly hired labor, caused a decline in labor productivity as volume approaches the limits of shift capacity. As the limits of shift capacity are approached there is an increased use of overtime capacity with the attendant higher costs. For these reasons, and possibly others, the total cost function is not linear, especially near the critical volumes associated with shift additions or deletions. Neither is it quadratic or any other simply stated mathematical function. It is unique to itself, and, though we have tried to represent something "typical", each enterprise has its own unique function. Profit occurs in a "pocket" within the shift capacity range, declining and possibly disappearing in the zone near shift capacity and the start up of an additional shift because of the diseconomies just noted. The Search Company model is guided in the cost components included by the general structure of Figure 1 of Chapter 2.

 The Search Company has three independent variables under managerial control and all decisions produced by the model are in the terms of direct work force size (WD_t) and indirect work force size (WI_t) in men, and production rate (P_t) in gallons. All of the nine cost components shown in Figure 7 are functions of one or more of the independent variables. Note

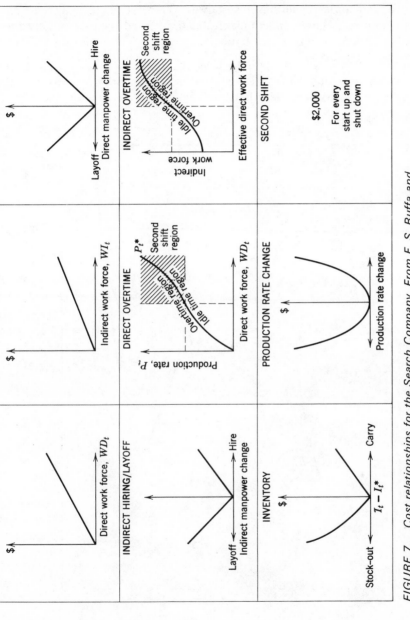

FIGURE 7. Cost relationships for the Search Company. From E. S. Buffa and W. H. Taubert, "Evaluation of Direct Computer Search Methods for the Aggregate Planning Problem." Industrial Management Review, MIT Press, Fall 1967, pp. 19–36.

that both linear and nonlinear cost functions are involved. The productivity functions which describe the use of direct and indirect overtime involve 7th and 6th order equations respectively. The inventory stock out and production rate change functions are quadratic, and the cost penalty for invoking a second shift is a step function.

Results. The SDR formulation views the cost model as an eighteen dimensional response surface, (three decisions per month over a six month planning horizon). The Search Company model was run on the SDR

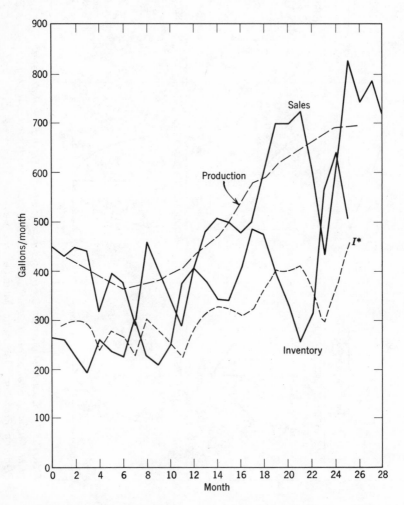

FIGURE 8. Sales, production rate decisions, and inventory levels for the Search Company. From E. S. Buffa and W. H. Taubert [9].

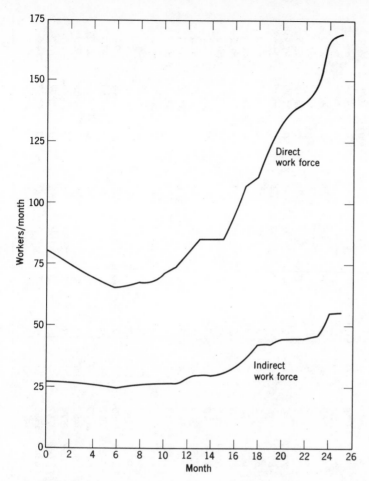

FIGURE 9. Direct and indirect work force decisions made by SDR for the Search Company. See Figure 8 for production decisions and inventory data. From E. S. Buffa and W. H. Taubert [9].

program driven with the first thirty months of the paint company sales data to produce a 24-month record of decisions. Figures 8 and 9 display graphically the results of decisions made by SDR, and Table VI summarizes the cost results of the decisions. Note the stable and smooth response of the three SDR decisions in the face of widely varying sales. SDR invokes the second shift in the seventeenth month. Beginning with the eleventh month unit costs rise substantially reflecting the lower productivity of labor, higher overtime costs, and heavy hiring costs. Although there is no guar- antee that the decisions are optimal, the results appear to be quite reason-

TABLE VI. Cost results of SDR decisions for the Search Company

Month	Direct Work Force Pay-roll	Over-time	Hire Cost	Lay-off Cost	Indirect Work Force Pay-roll	Over-time	Hire Cost	Lay-off Cost	Inventory Carry Cost	Stock-out Cost	Pro-duction Change Cost	Shift Change Cost	Total Costs	Unit Cost
1	26,490	0	0	371	7424	69	0	0	0	76	183	0	34,613	81.0
2	25,442	0	0	370	7301	0	0	0	0	428	66	0	33,607	81.3
3	24,655	0	0	278	7176	0	0	45	0	952	40	0	33,146	82.5
4	23,659	0	0	351	7030	0	0	0	97	0	66	0	31,203	81.3
5	22,855	0	0	284	6919	0	0	40	0	130	44	0	30,273	81.3
6	22,186	0	0	236	6833	0	0	0	0	135	31	0	29,421	81.0
7	22,507	2	66	0	6859	19	0	0	377	0	8	0	29,838	81.0
8	23,078	0	117	0	6942	9	0	0	0	517	23	0	30,686	81.2
9	23,077	250	0	0	6944	35	0	0	0	439	2	0	30,748	80.6
10	24,309	0	254	0	7124	0	33	0	0	1	77	0	31,798	80.1
11	25,058	0	189	0	7239	0	0	0	754	0	35	0	33,275	81.8
12	27,096	0	419	0	7589	1	64	0	660	0	261	0	36,089	83.0
13	28,884	0	360	0	7925	19	61	0	345	0	165	0	37,720	82.7
14	28,876	1013	0	0	7972	157	0	0	81	0	46	0	38,145	81.6
15	28,877	4266	0	0	8462	209	89	0	106	0	472	0	42,482	84.2
16	32,196	4786	683	0	9019	849	101	0	483	0	637	0	48,753	89.7
17	36,593	5489	905	0	10,294	1369	232	0	828	0	738	2000	58,447	100.6
18	37,831	5675	255	0	11,436	577	208	0	567	0	41	0	56,590	95.9
19	41,959	6268	850	0	11,436	2719	0	0	0	7	388	0	63,627	103.0
20	44,823	0	590	0	11,965	3492	96	0	0	437	193	0	61,596	96.8
21	47,050	7056	458	0	11,967	4514	0	0	0	1983	135	0	73,164	112.0
22	48,360	7254	270	0	12,198	4787	0	0	0	152	56	0	73,077	110.2
23	50,471	7344	435	0	12,344	5395	27	0	1371	0	143	0	77,529	114.0
24	56,665	1884	1275	0	15,073	2847	496	0	1381	0	111	0	79,732	114.8

From E. S. Buffa and W. H. Taubert [9].

able. Unfortunately the complexity of the Search Company cost model precludes solution by any of the analytic model–optimal solution techniques so that it is not possible to make the kind of direct comparison made for the paint company.

The computer runs were made on a direct coupled IBM 7040-7090 and required an average of forty seconds per set of monthly decisions. Later runs were made on an IBM 360/75 which required an execution time averaging five seconds to search and determine a set of decisions for each month.

SDR Applied to Search Laboratory I

In 1968 Taubert [50] developed an aggregate planning cost model to represent the operations planning problems of an applied research laboratory. While the name "Search Laboratory" is fictitious, the laboratory is in fact a division of a large aerospace firm housed in a 100,000 square feet facility employing a staff of 400. Approximately 300 of the staff are classified as direct technical employees, the balance being indirect administrative support for the operations of the laboratory. The fact that this application of SDR occurs in a nonmanufacturing environment helps to show the pervasiveness of aggregate planning concepts as well as the SDR methodology.

Both the government and the corporation fund the specific research programs, and the output of the laboratory is a direct function of the quality of the scientific staff. The laboratory offers a capability through its scientific staff and facilities, and this capability could be severely impaired by widely fluctuating employment even though the operating environment is characterized by wide fluctuations in government sales and rapid shifts in technology. The operations planning problem is centered in a monthly decision by the director to determine the size of the scientific and administrative staff as well as the allocation of the scientific staff to government contracts, corporate research programs, and overhead. Overhead charges arise when there are no contracts or corporate research programs available for scientists. This charge is in addition to the charges normally made to overhead for the usual indirect costs. Thus, overhead is used as a buffer to absorb fluctuations in the demand for scientific manpower. The independent decision variables incorporated in the aggregate planning model are four in number as follows:

1. The size of the scientific staff
   (a) WS_t, manpower allocated to government contracts
   (b) WR_t, manpower allocated to corporate research programs
   (c) WO_t, manpower allocated to overhead
2. WI_t, the size of the administrative support staff

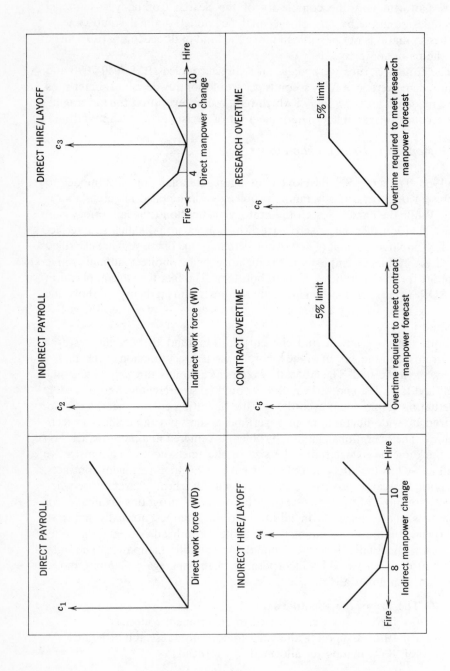

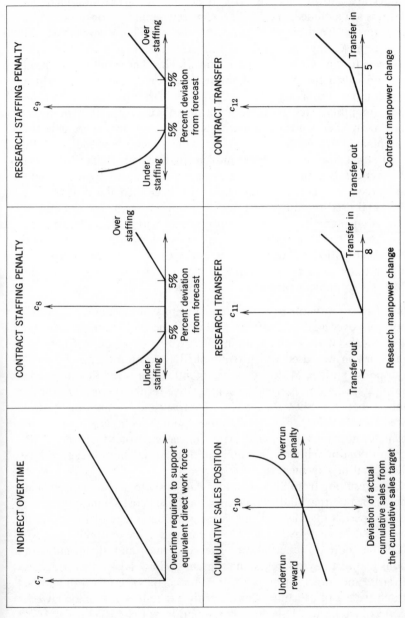

FIGURE 10. The twelve cost relationships entering the Search Laboratory cost model. From W. H. Taubert, "The Search Decision Rule Approach to Operations Planning," unpublished Ph.D. Dissertation, UCLA, 1968. Figure 55, p. 222.

441

Cost Model. The twelve cost relationships entering the search laboratory cost model are shown in Figure 10. Note that a variety of functional relationships are included, such as linear, piecewise linear, constraints, and nonlinear forms. Taubert also built into the model a complete set of equations representing the overhead rate structure used to compute the overhead rate for any given set of decision variables. The resulting overhead rate is then used to compute the monthly government sales volume which in turn is compared to a cumulative sales target. The inputs to the decision system are monthly forecasts of contract manpower, research manpower, overhead manpower, and a cumulative sales target which represents the financial plan of the laboratory. An important factor not indicated by Figure 10 is a two-month forecast implementation lag which also has a smoothing effect. If a manpower forecast is not met exactly by the straight time manpower decision plus allowable overtime, then the difference is computed and used to adjust the forecast for the subsequent two months. Thus, the total manpower forecast must be met within these constraints, and it is part of the director's operations planning problem to determine the best combination of decision variables which will accomplish the objective. Failure to meet the manpower requirements increases costs and this effect is also implemented in the cost model.

Results. Taubert validated the cost model against the financial record of the laboratory over a 5.5 year period. Following the validation, the decision system was operated for each month in the 5.5 year test period. A 6 months' planning horizon was used which required SDR to optimize a 24 dimensional response surface (4 decisions per month for a 6 months' planning horizon). Figure 11 summarizes the comparative results. Figure 11a shows the contrast between SDR decisions on contract and research manpower compared with forecasts. Figure 11b shows a similar comparison of actual management decisions compared with forecasts. Note that the SDR decisions respond much more smoothly to fluctuating manpower forecasts than did actual management decisions.

The costs resulting from SDR decisions compared to actual management decisions indicated that SDR would have produced cost savings. Over the 5.5 year test period the SDR advantage ranged from a high of 19.7 percent to a low of 5.2 percent, averaging 11.9 percent over the entire test period. The SDR decisions produced lower overhead rates and significant cost reductions in direct payroll, research program staffing, sales target penalties and rewards, and direct hiring costs. It achieved these results through the more extensive use of overtime. Computer time requirements on the UCLA IBM 360/91 averaged 10 seconds per monthly search. References [47] and [50] contain a complete description of the model as well as the results of the Search Laboratory I application.

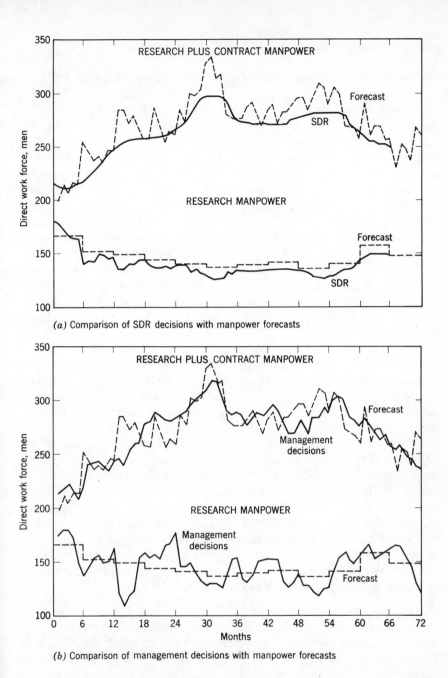

(a) Comparison of SDR decisions with manpower forecasts

(b) Comparison of management decisions with manpower forecasts

FIGURE 11.   Results of SDR decisions for Search Laboratory I compared to forecasts and actual management decisions. From W. H. Taubert, "The Search Decision Rule Approach to Operations Planning," unpublished Ph.D. Dissertation, UCLA, 1968, Figures 60 and 61, p. 243.

SDR and Search Laboratory II (Three Departments)

Following the successful application of SDR to the aggregate planning problem of Search Laboratory I, Taubert increased the complexity by disaggregating the decision variables for the size of the scientific staff in three different departments. In effect, each department was considered as a minature laboratory with its own contract and research manpower forecast as well as cumulative sales targets. Thus, the allocation of scientific staff to government contracts, corporate research programs, and overhead had to be made in each of the three departments. This resulted in nine independent decision variables related to the size and allocation of scientific staff. With the addition of the decision variable concerning the size of the administrative support staff there resulted ten decision variables over a six-month planning horizon, or a 60 dimensional response surface.

The departmental forecasts were designed with a diverse mix of increasing, decreasing, and sinusoidal manpower demands. The monthly department forecasts were structured so that their sum equalled the aggregate forecasts used in the Search Lab I model in order that direct comparisons of aggregate results could be made between the two models. While some transferring of personnel between departments was allowed, this practice was limited to represent the fact that in general scientists are not interchangeable and cannot be readily shifted from one department or technical expertise to another simply to meet fluctuating manpower requirements. Thus, transfers were limited to a total of two men in any one month with the further limitation that a maximum of one could be transferred between any two departments. Residual departmental manpower adjustments then had to be handled by hiring and layoff decisions.

The cost components of the model follow the structure of Figure 10. However, the Search Laboratory II model required that those cost elements relating to direct scientific manpower had to be computed on a departmental level. In addition a departmental transfer cost was added to charge both departments involved in a transfer up to one week's pay for the transfer of a man, reflecting learning curve effects.

Results. Figure 12 shows the results over a 42 month period. Figure 12 shows clearly that research manpower assignments have been used as a buffer to smooth the total departmental manpower level, particularly in Department 2. Also note how overhead manpower charges (shown by the shaded areas) are also used as buffers to absorb fluctuations. A total of 31.6 man-months of overhead were used for this buffering purpose during the 42 months of operation. This compares to two man-months used by the Search Laboratory I model. The greater use of overhead is a logical result of the limitation of transfers between departments.

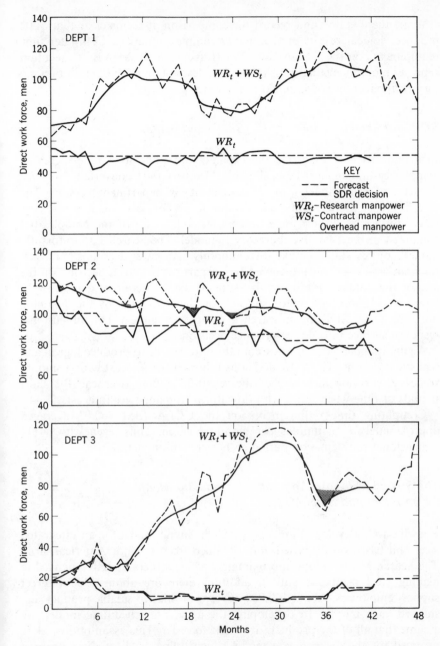

FIGURE 12.   Result of SDR application to Search Laboratory II. From W. H. Taubert, "The Search Decision Rule Approach to Operations Planning," unpublished Ph.D. Dissertation, UCLA, 1968, Figure 64, p. 262.

While there is no valid record for comparison, it seems clear that SDR produces logical results in this highly complex situation. Computer time requirements on the UCLA IBM 360/91 averaged 36 seconds of execution time per monthly evaluation. A complete description of the Search Laboratory II application is contained in reference [50].

SDR and Search Laboratory III (Six Departments)

In a final attempt to probe the capability of SDR to handle increased complexity and higher dimensionality, Taubert [49] converted the three department cost model into an equivalent six department version. The resulting cost model contained 12 manpower forecasts, a monthly sales target for each of the 6 departments, as well as all of the complexities contained in the Search Laboratory II model. The Search Laboratory III model requires SDR to make three monthly manpower decisions (contract, research, and overhead) in each of six departments, plus a decision on the size of the indirect administrative support staff. Therefore, a total of 19 monthly decisions are made in each of the 6 months of the planning horizon. Thus, SDR must search a complex nonlinear 114 dimensional response surface in order to produce decisions.

Again, it appeared that SDR continued to be able to produce logical and realistic decisions. The SDR decisions followed the forecast with a smooth response, carrying members of the scientific staff in overhead for short periods of time when faced with downturns in manpower forecasts.

Computing time requirements on the UCLA IBM 360/91 averaged approximately two minutes per monthly search. Thus, even with a 114 dimensional problem, computing costs were still moderate.

The Search Mill—An Aggregate Scheduling Model for an Integrated Steel Mill

Redwine [43] developed an aggregate scheduling model for an integrated steel mill based on disguised data obtained from a major American firm. The Search Mill employs approximately 5500 workers directly involved in making steel products, and in addition there are about 1800 indirect support employees. About 120,000 net tons of finished salable products are shipped each month. In developing the aggregate scheduling model, we assume that all of the products are made to order. This assumption will be dropped for the disaggregate model which follows. All of the data used were collected during the calendar years 1968 and 1969.

Figure 13 is a flow diagram for the ten major processes of the Search Mill.

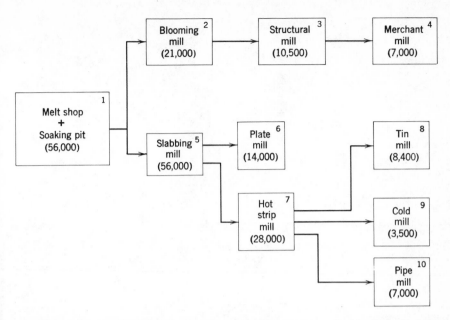

FIGURE 13. Flow diagram for the major processes of the Search Mill. Numbers in the upper right hand corners of boxes are the facility numbers, numbers in parentheses are weekly capacities in tons.
Figures 13 and 14 are from C. N. Redwine, "A Mathematical Programming Approach to Production Scheduling in a Steel Mill," unpublished Ph.D. Dissertation, UCLA, 1971.

For the aggregate scheduling model there are three independent variables under managerial control, direct work force size (WD_t) and indirect work force size (WI_t) in men, and production rate (P_t) in tons of salable steel products produced during the month. The planning horizon was 12 months, resulting in a 36 dimensional cost surface for which we wish to determine the cost minimum. Figure 14 shows the general shape of functions which control affected costs.

Results. Table VII shows the comparison between actual management decisions and the decisions produced by the SDR aggregate planning model. SDR decisions yield a cost reduction of $4.53 million for the year which would result in a 6.56 percent saving.

Table VIII shows that the biggest single difference between the costs of the actual decisions and the SDR decisions is in the payment of direct overtime. This difference actually comes about during the months of January, February, and March of 1969. The SDR foresees the amount of

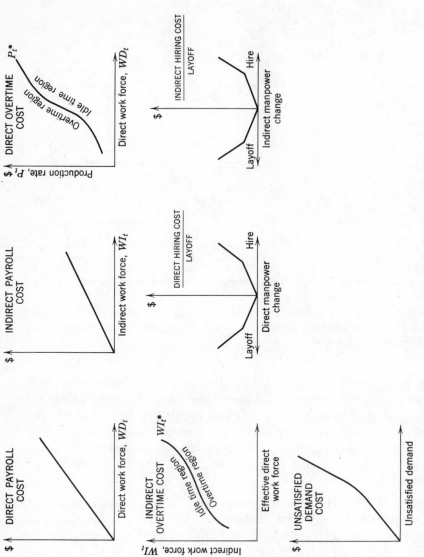

FIGURE 14. Cost relationships for the Search Mill. Adapted from C. N. Redwine [43]. A Mathematical Programming Approach to Production Scheduling in a Steel Mill, unpublished Ph.D. Dissertation, UCLA, 1971.

TABLE VII.   Comparison between actual and SDR decisions for aggregate scheduling model for the Search Mill

Year	Month	Actual Production (Tons × 10⁻³)	SDR Production (Tons × 10⁻³)	Actual Direct Employees	SDR Direct Employees	Actual Indirect Employees	SDR Indirect Employees
1968	Jul.	132.823	132.822	5827	5662	1801	1760
	Aug.	116.109	116.171	5778	5513	1805	1713
	Sep.	115.435	115.435	5700	5501	1789	1708
	Oct.	111.553	111.553	5491	5407	1798	1679
	Nov.	104.770	104.773	5352	5081	1805	1578
	Dec.	98.763	99.149	5083	5000	1810	1557
1969	Jan.	120.218	120.473	5048	5546	1815	1697
	Feb.	113.551	113.856	5275	5471	1811	1692
	Mar.	133.442	134.853	5450	5681	1808	1708
	Apr.	118.188	119.089	5468	5530	1815	1717
	May	123.636	124.633	5513	5577	1808	1731
	Jun.	125.996	126.003	5706	5589	1829	1738

Tables VII–XI are from C. N. Redwine, A Mathematical Programming Approach to Production Scheduling in a Steel Mill, Unpublished Ph.D. Dissertation, UCLA, 1971.

TABLE VIII.   Costs of actual and SDR decisions for the aggregate scheduling model for the Search Mill

Type of Cost	Actual Decisions	SDR Decisions
	(Dollars × 10⁻⁶)	
Direct Payroll	50.648	50.545
Indirect Payroll	14.144	13.221
Direct Overtime	2.726	.017
Indirect Overtime	.188	.085
Direct Hire/Fire	.399	.538
Indirect Hire/Fire	.014	.081
Unsatisfied Demand	.891	.000
Totals	69.012	64.488

work coming and hires over 500 direct employees between December 1968 and January 1969, whereas actually direct employees were laid off between those months and the rate of growth was only about 200 per month during February and March.

Another difference between the SDR and the actual decisions is in the handling of indirect employees. The SDR exhibits a greater willingness to hire and layoff indirect employees than the Search Mill management. Possibly the indirect hire/layoff costs are thought by the management to be higher than those shown in Figure 14. The unsatisfied demand penalties of Table VIII are somewhat different, but it must be remembered that the SDR was working with perfect sales forecasts while the actual decisions were made under conditions of some (but not great) uncertainty.

Search Mill—Disaggregate Scheduling Model

The ideas behind the disaggregate scheduling model are fundamentally the same as those of the aggregate scheduling model. However, instead of considering the production and employment levels of the Search Mill as a whole we now consider the operations planning problem for each cost center. The Search Mill is made up of ten cost centers as follows:

(1) iron and steel making division

(2) slabbing mill

(3) blooming mill

(4) structural mill

(5) merchant mill

(6) plate mill

(7) hot strip mill

(8) tin mill

(9) cold mill

(10) pipe mill

These cost centers correspond to the ten facilities shown in Figure 13. Because the data available for each cost center is not as complete as for the Search Mill as a whole, the disaggregate scheduling model will be somewhat more hypothetical than was the aggregate scheduling model. However, the production and employment levels given will be quite realistic.

For each cost center the shape of the curve P_t^*, the maximum possible production without using overtime, is the same as that of Figure 14. These productivity curves were appropriately scaled down to reflect the actual levels of production and employment in each cost center. For each month in the scheduling horizon the SDR must now determine the optimal number of direct employees and the level of production for each of the 10 cost centers. Since indirect employees support all cost centers, they are not broken down by cost center. Thus the number of indirect employees required will depend solely on the total direct equivalent work force, just as it did in the aggregate scheduling model.

The assumption that all steel products are made to order is dropped, and we assume that all products of the structural mill and the merchant mill are stocked and a linear inventory cost function is defined. Each of the remaining eight cost centers deal only with made-to-order products.

Each of the ten cost centers now does its own hiring and laying off of direct employees. However, transfers between cost centers are permitted. In fact, a company policy will be enforced which requires that transfers will take precedence, whenever possible, over hiring or laying off. A cost of one week's pay was assessed for each direct employee transferred between cost centers. This rule guarantees that there will be no new hires during a month if any cost center is laying off.

The nonlinear programming model has 21 variables for each month in the planning horizon: ten P_t, ten WD_t, and WI_t. A 6-month planning horizon was used resulting in a 126 dimensional cost surface to be minimized.

Results. A comparison of results is shown in Tables IX, X, and XI. The SDR decisions result in a savings of more than $2.5 million over the six month period, which represents a savings of 7.3 percent. As in the case of the aggregate scheduling problem, the savings are due primarily to hiring more direct personnel early in 1969 to take care of the larger production requirements. The SDR was more willing than the management to transfer direct employees between cost centers. In practice, the goal of keeping cost centers somewhat autonomous is probably pursued vigorously.

SUMMARY

The SDR methodology at the present stage of development seems to offer the broadest capability available for handling the aggregate planning problem. The applications to date indicate that there is a substantial advantage in being able to represent the enterprise cost or profit model realistically. The Search Laboratory models II and III seemed to indicate

TABLE IX. Comparison of actual versus SDR levels of production in net tons for disaggregate scheduling. Model of the Search Mill

| | Actual Production | | | | | | SDR Decisions | | | | | |
| | 1968 | | | 1969 | | | 1968 | | | 1969 | | |
Cost Center	Oct.	Nov.	Dec.	Jan.	Feb.	Mar.	Oct.	Nov.	Dec.	Jan.	Feb.	Mar.
Iron and Steel Making	111,553	104,770	98,763	120,218	113,551	133,442	111,599	104,770	99,260	120,218	113,751	133,442
Slabbing Mill	104,618	97,946	87,107	98,387	89,293	106,068	104,664	97,946	87,604	98,387	89,493	106,070
Blooming Mill	6,935	6,824	11,656	21,831	24,258	27,374	6,935	6,824	11,656	21,831	24,258	27,374
Structural Mill	6,935	6,824	11,656	21,831	24,258	27,374	6,935	6,824	11,656	21,831	24,258	27,374
Merchant Mill	2,856	2,827	2,385	2,152	2,936	4,009	2,856	2,827	2,385	2,152	2,936	4,009
Plate Mill	39,839	42,803	38,084	41,914	38,595	42,222	39,885	42,803	38,084	41,914	38,595	42,222
Hot Strip Mill	74,779	55,143	49,023	56,473	50,698	63,846	74,779	55,143	49,520	56,473	50,898	63,848
Tin Mill	28,100	21,617	20,779	22,484	21,496	28,543	28,100	21,617	20,779	22,484	21,496	28,543
Cold Mill	1,000	2,299	2,560	2,402	2,624	3,492	1,000	2,299	2,560	2,402	2,624	3,492
Pipe Mill	12,152	14,075	8,630	7,796	7,051	11,778	12,152	14,075	8,630	7,796	7,051	11,778

TABLE X.   Comparison of actual versus SDR number of direct employees for disaggregate scheduling. Model of the Search Mill

Cost Center	Actual Direct Employees						SDR Decisions					
	1968			1969			1968			1969		
	Oct.	Nov.	Dec.	Jan.	Feb.	Mar.	Oct.	Nov.	Dec.	Jan.	Feb.	Mar.
Iron and Steel Making	2,213	2,159	2,042	2,049	2,120	2,195	2,181	1,903	1,900	1,900	2,203	2,283
Slabbing Mill	87	85	80	79	84	86	88	85	75	75	75	88
Blooming Mill	109	106	111	107	113	114	100	100	100	120	120	119
Structural Mill	131	127	134	127	134	135	120	120	120	146	146	143
Merchant Mill	148	144	137	132	143	147	145	143	120	120	147	160
Plate Mill	357	351	330	328	343	354	345	359	327	356	333	357
Hot Strip Mill	423	400	379	377	394	408	440	386	360	395	360	416
Tin Mill	1,308	1,275	1,209	1,200	1,256	1,300	1,350	1,247	1,188	1,289	1,239	1,350
Cold Mill	161	157	149	144	155	161	140	140	154	140	158	170
Pipe Mill	554	548	512	505	532	550	560	560	500	500	500	560

TABLE XI. Comparison of actual versus SDR
number of indirect employees for disaggregate
scheduling. Model of the Search Mill

		Number of Employees	
Year	Month	Actual	SDR
1968	Oct.	1,798	1,716
	Nov.	1,805	1,656
	Dec.	1,810	1,600
1969	Jan.	1,815	1,677
	Feb.	1,811	1,676
	Mar.	1,808	1,847

that there are no great difficulties for SDR to handle multiple products or departments and that dimensionality limits have not yet been reached.

The results of the PROPX experiments in the paint and Search Company environments suggest that a shorter planning horizon may be adequate when the concepts of PROPX are used. However, this technique has not yet been tested in the more highly complex environments characterized by the Search Laboratories models II and III. If the technique has broad application, there will be considerable practical significance for SDR since variables would be released for more effective use in the decision system and less forecast data would be needed. The stochastic extensions suggest that aggregate planning systems may not be highly sensitive to forecast errors.

On the other hand, SDR does not produce a guaranteed global optimum, and managers must make the trade-off between the advantages cited and the desire or need for a guaranteed optimum solution. We must always remember, however, that it is the model which is optimized in analytical methods. Whether or not the real world counterpart of the model is also optimized by the decisions depends on how closely the model represents reality.

REVIEW QUESTIONS

1. Discuss the nature of the aggregate planning and scheduling problem. What are the general costs which are affected? What is the form of these costs?

2. What is the general mathematical form of the cost components included in the Linear Decision Rule model?

3. Describe the process by which the generalized statement of costs given by equation (2) is made specific for a firm like the paint company as given in equation (4).

4. What is the general process by which the two specific decision rules represented by equations (5) and (6) for the paint company are derived from the cost equation (4)?

5. Describe the modifications and extensions of LDR. What are the conditions under which it may be of value to include plant capacity as an independent variable? What, if any, are the limitations of LDR in a multi-product format? How have Bergstrom and Smith coupled the production and marketing functions in their extension of LDR?

6. How are the coefficients in the decision rules determined for the Management Coefficients Model?

7. Why might we term the Parametric Production Planning Model as optimum seeking?

8. Compare the performance of the Parametric Production Planning Model with the Linear Decision Rule and linear programming models.

9. What is the basis of operation for the Search Decision Rule?

10. Compare the results obtained by the Search Decision Rule with the Linear Decision Rule for the paint company.

11. What is the meaning of a negative overtime cost contribution to a criterion function? Why is it possible for this to happen in the Linear Decision Rule?

12. What is the nature of the trade-off between forecast horizon and computer time for SDR?

13. Why does SDR make projected decisions which dump inventories near the end of the planning horizon?

14. What is the rationale behind the PROPX technique? What is the practical effect of PROPX for the paint company?

15. What is the effect of forecast errors for the paint company? What is the value of perfect forecast information in aggregate planning models based on Sikes' experiments?

16. Compare the complexity and realism of the paint company, Search Company, Search Laboratories I, II, III models. What alternatives to SDR could have been used for solution in the more complex model cases?

17. Account for the substantial increases in product unit costs near the capacity limits for one shift operation and after the second shift was invoked in the Search Company example.

18. Make a comparative evaluation of the following aggregate planning models: linear programming, LDR, Management Coefficients, Parametric Production Planning, and SDR.

PRODUCTION CONTROL GAME /

The game which follows is illustrative of a relatively simple situation where the players are pitted against a simulated environment. Its simplicity makes it possible to play them without the use of a computer. The game deals with the decision of setting production levels for 26 two-week periods in a year in such a way that the total incremental costs are minimized. The game is played for two basic conditions of the environment: (a) when orders average 100,000 cases per period, but vary randomly from this mean rate, and (b) when the average order pattern follows a seasonal curve, with random variation from the average seasonal curve.

Condition 1. You are the production control manager of a company making a single product. Your plant has unlimited capacity within the potential sales range. Orders for your product vary from period to period, and it is your job to devise a production plan that will fill shipping orders each period from available inventory. The goal of the plan should be to minimize the total annual costs for holding inventories, failing to meet orders on time, and changing the current production rate.

Since it takes time to change the production rate, there is a one period interval between the time that you make a decision and the time that the change goes into effect. Thus a decision made at the end of the first period goes into effect during the second period. Any change in the output level must be in thousand-case lots and may not be less than five-thousand cases nor more than ten-thousand cases. Excess production is stored in plant warehouses up to a total capacity of 240,000 cases. Inventory above this amount may be stored in outside facilities at extra cost.

At the beginning of the year, the following rules and conditions apply:

1. Opening inventory—to be furnished by game referee.

2. Current shipments average 100,000 cases per period with the following approximate distribution:
   a. 76 percent of the time shipments will be between 70,000 and 130,000 cases per period.
   b. 96 percent of the time shipments will be between 50,000 and 150,000 cases per period.

3. To change the production rate costs $5000 per change, regardless of the magnitude of the change.

4. There is an inventory holding charge of $200 per year for each 1000 cases of average inventory. In addition, each 1000 cases stored in outside facilities costs $500 per year.

5. There is a charge of $750 per period for each 1000 cases ordered which cannot be shipped because of insufficient inventory. (100 per cent back-order rate.)

6. The plant shuts down for vacation during the thirteenth period. Orders continue to be shipped, although production is zero.

Procedure. Figure 15 shows the work sheet to be used. Beginning inventory at the time play starts in period one will be furnished by the game referee.

(1)	(2)	(3)	(4)	(5)	(6)	(7)
Two–Week Period Number	Beginning Inventory, 1000's	Production Level Set, 1000's	Available = Beginning Inventory in Period + Previous Period's Production, 1000's	Orders in Period, Sampled from Order Distribution, 1000's	Ending Inventory = Available − Orders, 1000's	Excess Inventory Over 240, 1000's
0		90				
1	300	90	390	70	320	80
2						
3						
4						
5						
6						
7						
8						
9						
10						
11						
12						
13		Vacation				
14						
15						
16						
17						
18						
19						
20						
21						
22						
23						
24						
25						
26						

FIGURE 15.   Work sheet-production and inventory control game.

1. Enter the figure for beginning inventory furnished by the game referee on line 1 under column 2.

2. Set the initial production level for period zero and period one and enter in column 3.

3. Calculate "available" (column 4), the sum of beginning inventory (column 2) for the period plus "production" (column 3) for the previous period.

4. Decide on production levels for the next period by entering the amount in column 3 for period two.

5. Record "orders" for period one in column 5. This figure will be read by the game referee and represents a Monte Carlo sampling from the order distribution. As an example, the orders for period one are shown as 70 in Figure 15.

6. Calculate "ending inventory" (column 6) by subtracting orders for the period from the total available for the period.

7. Calculate "excess inventory" (column 7) by subtracting 240 from the ending inventory for the period. For the example shown in Figure 15, the excess inventory which must be stored at extra cost in outside facilities is 80.

8. Transfer the figure for ending inventory to column 2, beginning inventory for the next period.

9. Repeat for 26 periods making sure to account for the vacation in the 13th period during which time no production will occur, but during which orders will be delivered. If during any period orders exceed the amounts available, simply record negative ending inventory and beginning inventory for the next period. This takes account of the 100 percent back-order rule.

Cost Calculations	Condition 1	Condition 2
1. Production changes. Multiply the number of changes made in the year by $5000 per change.	_____	_____
2. Inventory holding cost. Total ending inventories for each 2-week period, divide by 26 and multiply the number of 1000 cases resulting by $200. (Do not deduct shortages.)	_____	_____
3. Outside storage facilities. Total excess inventory (over 240,000 for each 2-week period), divide by 26 and multiply by $500.	_____	_____
4. Stock shortage cost. Determine the number of 1000 case shortages and multiply by $750.	_____	_____
5. Total yearly cost.	$_____	$_____

FIGURE 16. Form for calculating costs.

10. Compute incremental costs. Using the form shown in Figure 16, calculate costs for production changes, inventory costs, excess inventory costs, and stock shortage costs. The total of these four costs represents a measure of the effectiveness of the sequence of decisions made.

Condition 2. In the second condition of the game, all rules for play remain the same. The only thing which has changed is that the order pattern exhibits a seasonality, as shown by Figure 17. Shipments are seasonal, but still average 100,000 cases per period over the entire year. The variability of the order distribution is still expressed by the relative deviation from mean values as indicated previously. Thus, while the average order level for the fifth period is 60,000 cases, as indicated by Figure 17, in any given fifth period, random variation could result in a minimum of no orders, or a maximum of orders for 120,000 cases.

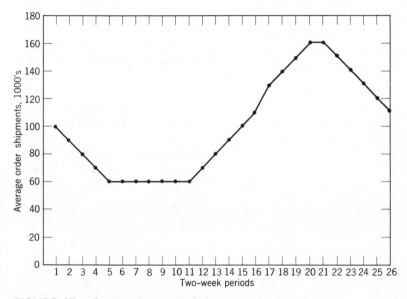

FIGURE 17.   Seasonal pattern of shipments.

REFERENCES*

1. Babb, E. M., and T. H. Yu, "Analysis of Factors Affecting Least-Cost Size of Plant." *Management Science*, Vol. 16, No. 10, June, 1970, pp. 607–613.
2. Bellman, R., "Dynamic Programming and the Smoothing Problem," *Management Science*, Vol. 3, No. 1, October, 1956, pp. 111–113.
3. Bergstrom, G. L., and B. E. Smith, "Multi-Item Production Planning—An

---

*References with asterisk are also reprinted in their entirety in E. S. Buffa, Editor, *Readings in Production and Operations Management*, John Wiley & Sons, Inc., New York, 1966.

Extension of the HMMS Rules," *Management Science*, Vol. 16, No. 10, June, 1970, pp. 614–629.

4. Bishop, A. B., and T. H. Rockwell, "A Dynamic Programming Computational Procedure for Optimal Manpower Loading in a Large Aircraft Company," *Operations Research*, Vol. 6, 1958, pp. 835–848.

5. *Bowman, E. H., "Consistency and Optimality in Managerial Decision Making," *Management Science*, January, 1963.

6. *Bowman, E. H., "Production Scheduling by the Transportation Method of Linear Programming," *Operations Research*, Vol. 4, No. 1, February, 1956, pp. 100–103.

7. Bowman, E. H. and R. B. Fetter, *Analysis for Production and Operations Management*, 3rd ed., Richard D. Irwin, Inc., Homewood, Ill., 1967.

8. Buffa, E. S., "Aggregate Planning for Production," *Business Horizons*, Fall 1967.

9. Buffa, E. S., and W. H. Taubert, "Evaluation of Direct Computer Search Methods for the Aggregate Planning Problem," *Industrial Management Review*, MIT Press, Fall 1967, pp. 19–36.

10. Buffa, E. S., and W. H. Taubert, *Production-Inventory Systems: Planning and Control*, Richard D. Irwin, Inc., Homewood, Ill., Rev. ed., 1972, Chaps. 5, 6, and 7.

11. Chang, R. H., and C. M. Jones, "Production and Workforce Scheduling Extensions," *AIIE Transactions*, Vol. 2, No. 4, December, 1970, pp. 326–333.

12. Davidon, W. C., "Variable Metric Method for Minimization," AEC Research and Development Report, AN–5990 (Rev) 1959.

13. Dianich, D., "An Application of Nonlinear Programming to Approximate Optimal Management Control Decisions with Time-Dependent Resource Availability," Unpublished Ph.D. Dissertation, George Washington University, 1971.

14. *Eisemann, K., and W. M. Young, "Study of a Textile Mill with the Aid of Linear Programming," *Management Technology*, No. 1, January, 1960.

15. Fabian, T., "Blast Furnace Production—A Linear Programming Example," *Management Science*, Vol. 14, No. 2, October, 1967, pp. 1–27.

16. Fan, L. T., *The Continuous Maximum Principle*, John Wiley & Sons, Inc., New York, 1966.

17. Fan, L. T., C. L. Hwang, and F. A. Tillman, "A Sequential Simplex Pattern Search Solution to Production Planning Problems," *AIIE Transactions*, Vol. 1, No. 3, Sept., 1969, pp. 267–273.

18. Fan, L. T., and C. Wang, *The Discrete Maximum Principle*, John Wiley & Sons, Inc., New York, 1964.

19. Feltham, G. A., "Some Quantitative Approaches to Planning for Multiproduct Production Systems," *The Accounting Review*, Vol. XLV, No. 1, January, 1970, pp. 11–26.

20. Ferguson, R. O., and L. F. Sargent, *Linear Programming*, McGraw-Hill Book Co., New York, 1958.

21. Fletcher, R., and M. Powell, "A Rapidly Convergent Descent Method for Minimization," *The Computer Journal*, Vol. 6, 1963, pp. 163–168.

22. Fletcher, R., and C. Reeves, "Function Minimization by Conjugate Gradients, "*The Computer Journal*, Vol. 7, 1964, pp. 149–154.
23. Gordon, J. R. M., "A Multi-Model Analysis of an Aggregate Scheduling Decision," Unpublished Ph.D. dissertation, Sloan School of Management, M.I.T., 1966.
24. *Greene, J. H., K. Chatto, C. R. Hicks, and C. B. Cox, "Linear Programming in the Packing Industry," *Journal of Industrial Engineering*, Vol. 10, No. 5, 1959.
25. Hadley, G., *Nonlinear and Dynamic Programming*, Addison-Wesley, Reading, Mass., 1964.
26. *Hanssmann, F., and S. W. Hess, "A Linear Programming Approach to Production and Employment Scheduling," *Management Technology*, No. 1, January, 1960.
27. Holloway, C. A., "A Mathematical Programming Approach to Identification and Optimization of Complex Operational Systems, with the Aggregate Planning Problem as an Example," Unpublished Ph.D. dissertation, UCLA, 1969.
28. Holt, C. C., F. Modigliani, J. F. Muth, and H. A. Simon, *Planning Production, Inventories and Work Force*, Prentice-Hall, Inc., Englewood Cliffs, N.J., 1960.
29. Holt, C. C., F. Modigliani, and J. F. Muth, "Derivation of a Linear Decision Rule for Production and Employment," *Management Science*, Vol. 2, No. 2, January, 1956, pp. 159–177.
30. *Holt, C. C., F. Modigliani, and H. A. Simon, "A Linear Decision Rule for Production and Employment Scheduling," *Management Science*, Vol. 2, No. 1, October, 1955, pp. 1–30.
31. Hooke, R., and T. A. Jeeves, "A Direct Search Solution of Numerical and Statistical Problems," *Journal of the Association for Computing Machinery*, April, 1961.
32. Hwang, C. L., L. T. Fan, and L. E. Erickson, "Optimum Production Planning by the Maximum Principle," *Management Science*, Vol. 13, No. 9, May, 1967, pp. 751–755.
33. Hwang, C. L., and L. T. Fan, "The Application of the Maximum Principle to Industrial and Management Systems," *Journal of Industrial Engineering*, Vol. 17, No. 11, November, 1968, pp. 589–593.
34. Jones, C. H., "Parametric Production Planning," *Management Science*, Vol. 13, No. 11, July, 1967, pp. 843–866.
35. Kolenda, J. F., "A Comparison of Two Aggregate Planning Models," Unpublished Master's Thesis, Wharton School, 1970.
36. McGarrah, R. E., *Production and Logistics Management: Text and Cases*, Chap. V., John Wiley & Sons, Inc., New York, 1963.
37. McGhee, R. B., "Some Parameter Optimization Techniques," *Digital Computers User's Handbook*, M. Klerer and G. A. Korn, Editors, McGraw-Hill Book Co., New York, 1967.
38. Metzger, R. W., *Elementary Mathematical Programming*, John Wiley & Sons, Inc., New York, 1958.
39. Mugele, R. A., "A Program for Optimal Control of Nonlinear Processes," *IBM Systems Journal*, September, 1962, pp. 2–17.

40. Nelder, J. A., and R. Mead, "A Simplex Method for Function Minimization," *Computer Journal*, Vol. 7, 1964, pp. 308–313.

41. Nemhauser, G. L., and H. L. Nuttle, "A Quantitative Approach to Employment Planning," *Management Science*, Vol. 11, No. 8, June, 1965, pp. 155–165.

42. Pontryagin, L. S., V. G. Boltyanskii, R. V. Gamkrelidze, and E. F. Mischenko, *The Mathematical Theory of Optimal Processes*, New York: Interscience, 1962. (English translation by K. N. Trirogoff.)

43. Redwine, C. N., *A Mathematical Programming Approach to Production Scheduling in a Steel Mill*, Unpublished Ph.D. dissertation, UCLA, 1971.

44. Silver, E. A., "A Tutorial on Production Smoothing and Work Force Balancing," *Operations Research*, Vol. 15, No. 6, Nov.–Dec., 1967, pp. 985–1,010.

45. Sikes, T. W., "The Search Decision Rule Applied to Aggregate Planning; Improved Efficiency and Stochastic Extension," Unpublished Ph.D. dissertation, UCLA, August, 1970.

46. Sypkens, H. A., "Planning for Optimal Plant Capacity," Unpublished Master's Thesis, Sloan School of Management, M.I.T., 1967.

47. Taubert, W. H., "A Case Study Problem in Aggregate Manpower Planning," in M. J. C. Martin and R. A. Denison, *Case Exercises in Operations Research*, John Wiley & Sons, Inc., London, 1971.

48. Taubert, W. H., "A Search Decision Rule for the Aggregate Scheduling Problem," *Management Science*, Vol. 14, No. 6, February, 1968, pp. 343–359.

49. Taubert, W. H., The Search Decision Rule: A New Approach to Operations Planning," paper presented at the 36th National Meeting, ORSA, Miami, Florida, Nov. 10, 1969.

50. Taubert, W. H., "The Search Decision Rule Approach to Operations Planning." Unpublished Ph.D. dissertation, UCLA, 1968.

51. Tuite, M. F., "Merging Marketing Strategy Selection and Production Scheduling: A Higher Order Optimum," *Journal of Industrial Engineering*, Vol. 19, No. 2, February, 1968, pp. 76–84.

52. Van De Panne, C., and P. Bosje, "Sensitivity Analysis of Cost Coefficient Estimates: The Case of Linear Decision Rules for Employment and Production," *Management Science*, Vol. 9, No. 1, October, 1962, pp. 82–107.

53. Weisman, J., C. F. Wood, and L. Rivlin, "Optimal Design of Chemical Process Systems," *Chemical Engineering Progress Symposium Series, Process Control and Applied Mathematics*, Vol. 61, No. 55, 1965.

54. Welam, U. P., "Constrained Nonlinear Programming Applied to Aggregate Planning and Scheduling," Mimeographed Paper, Göteborg, Sweden, 1969.

55. Wilde, D. C., and C. S. Beightler, *Foundations of Optimization*, Prentice-Hall, Inc., Englewood Cliffs, N.J., 1967.

56. Zoller, K., "Optimal Disaggregation of Aggregate Production Plans," *Management Science*, Vol. 17, No. 8, April 1971, pp. 533–549.

chapter 14

BASIC WAITING
LINE MODELS

Many types of production problems are described by the buildup of waiting lines (queues) of some input to the production system, or subsystem. Other more complex systems are well characterized by a network of queues, such as the job shop. Processing takes place within the system and the interplay of the timing of the *arrivals* and the required time for processing determines such important characteristics of the situation as the probable length of the waiting line, the average number in the line including the one being serviced, the average time that an input waits, and the average time that an input spends both waiting and being processed. If this information can be determined, we are often in a position to construct special models of the balance of costs which will serve as guides to decision making.

The original work in waiting line, or queuing theory was done by A. K. Erlang, a Danish telephone engineer. Erlang started his work in 1905 in an attempt to determine the effect of fluctuating service demand (arrivals) on the utilization of automatic dial equipment. It has been only since the end of World War II that work on waiting line models has been extended to other kinds of problems. There are a wide variety of seemingly diverse problem situations which are now recognized as being described by the general waiting line model. In all instances, we have an input that arrives at some facility for service or processing. The time between the arrival of individual inputs at the service facility is commonly random. Similarly, the time for service or

TABLE I. Waiting line model elements for some commonly known situations

Unit Arriving	Service or Processing Facility	Service or Process Being Performed
Ships entering a port	Ships	Docks	Unloading and loading
Maintenance and repair of machines	Machine breaks down	Repair crew	Repair machine
Assembly line, not mechanically paced	Parts to be assembled	Individual assembly operations or entire line	Assembly
Doctor's office	Patients	Doctor, his staff and facilities	Medical care
Purchase of groceries at a supermarket	Customers with loaded grocery carts	Checkout counter	Tabulation of bill, receipt of payment and bagging of groceries
Auto traffic at an intersection or bridge	Automobiles	Intersection or bridge with control points such as traffic lights or toll booths	Passage through intersection or bridge
Inventory of items in a warehouse	Order for withdrawal	Warehouse	Replenishment of inventory
Job shop	Job order	Work center	Processing

processing is commonly a random variable. Table I shows the waiting line model elements for a number of commonly known situations.

There are four basic structures of waiting line situations which describe the general conditions at the servicing facility. The simplest situation is where arriving units form a single line to be serviced by a single processing facility, for example, a one-man barber shop. This is called the single-channel, single-phase case. If the number of processing stations is increased (two or more barbers), but still draws on the one waiting line, we have a multiple-channel, single-phase case, since a customer can be serviced by any one of the barbers. A simple assembly line has a number of service facilities in series or tandem and is the single-channel, multiple-phase case. The multiple-channel, multiple-phase case might be illustrated by two or more parallel production lines. Figure 1 shows the four cases diagrammed and labeled. Variations in the four basic structures may be in the queue discipline, that is, the order in which inputs are taken out of the waiting

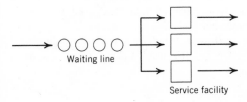

(a) Single channel, single phase case.

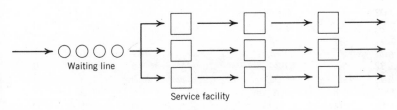

(b) Multiple channel, single phase case.

(c) Single channel, multiple phase case.

(d) Multiple channel, multiple phase case.

FIGURE 1. *Four basic structures of waiting line situations.*

line. We have implied a first come–first served queue discipline in the diagrams, but obviously other priority systems could be used. Also, combinations of the basic structures could exist as with the job shop network of queues.

An Example

A simple example will serve to help us gain some insight into the nature of the waiting line problem. Assume that we are observing and recording the activities of a mechanic who is maintaining a large bank of automatic machines. When a machine breaks down or needs service, the mechanic is called. He services the machines in the order of breakdown (first come–first served). The mechanic is the equivalent of the service facility, and machine breakdowns represent arrivals. We have the structure of the single-channel, single-phase case as diagrammed in Figure 1. We begin our record at 8:00 AM, Monday, recording the time when machines break down, when service begins and ends and thereby produce the history for twenty breakdowns shown in Table II. The time at which machines break down is of course random, and therefore the time between arrivals is random. In Table II the average time between arrivals is approximately 2 hours. The mechanic begins service immediately, or as soon as possible if he is already servicing another machine. The time per service varies considerably, depending on the nature of the trouble. It may be that a minor adjustment is needed requiring only 1 or 2 minutes. On the other hand, a part failure may require 2 or 3 hours for repair.

TABLE II.   Record of twenty machine breakdowns with service history. Average time between breakdowns is approximately 2 hours, average service time is approximately 1 hour

Time of Machine Breakdown	Time Required for Service, minutes	Service Begins at	Service Ends at	Idle Time of Mechanic, minutes	Down Time of Machine, minutes	Number of Machines Waiting for Service
Mon., 8:16 am	20	Mon., 8:16 am	Mon., 8:36 am	16	20	0
11:28	9	11:28	11:37	172	9	0
3:03 pm	64	3:03 pm	4:07	206	64	1
3:53	1	4:07	4:08	0	15	0
6:03	21	6:03	6:24	115	21	0
9:28	56	9:28	10:24	184	56	1
9:32	30	10:24	10:54	0	82	0
11:02	198	11:02	Tues., 2:20 am	8	198	2
Tues., 1:07 am	30	Tues., 2:20 am	2:50	0	103	1
1:15	10	2:50	3:00	0	105	0
5:31	58	5:31	6:29	151	58	1
5:46	41	6:29	7:10	0	84	0
10:26	120	10:26	12:26 pm	196	120	1
11:53	40	12:26 pm	1:06	0	73	0
3:28 pm	75	3:28	4:43	142	75	0
6:25	120	6:25	8:25	102	120	0
9:22	68	9:22	10:30	57	68	1
10:14	180	10:30	Wed., 1:30 am	0	196	2
11:13	78	Wed., 1:30 am	2:48	0	215	1
11:25	2	2:48	2:50	0	205	0
Totals	1221			1349	1887	

Time machines wait for service to begin
$$= \text{(total machine down time)} -- \text{(total machine service time)}$$
$$= 1887 - 1221 = 666 \text{ minutes}$$

The record of Table II shows the typical pattern of such a situation. Sometimes the mechanic has nothing at all to do. In three instances these periods of idleness exceed three hours. But sometimes, owing to the pattern of machine breakdowns in relation to required service times, the mechanic has a backlog of work, that is, a waiting line of machines needing service.

Let us now change one of the important conditions to see the effect on the idle time of the mechanic, the machine waiting time, and the waiting line of machines to be repaired. Table III shows a typical record for the new condition where the average time between arrivals has been reduced from 2 hours to 1.5 hours, with the average service time remaining at about 1 hour. The increased arrival rate has had a dramatic effect. The mechanic's idle time is less than half of the previous figure. In addition, the time that machines waited for service to begin, and the average waiting line length

TABLE III. Record of twenty machine breakdowns and service history with average time between breakdowns reduced to approximately 1.5 hours. Average service time remains unchanged at approximately 1 hour

Time of Machine Breakdown	Time Required for Service, minutes	Service Begins at	Service Ends at	Idle Time of Mechanic, minutes	Down Time of Machine, minutes	Number of Machines Waiting for Service
Mon., 9:31 am	24	Mon., 9:31 am	Mon., 9:55 am	91	24	0
10:41	194	10:41	1:55 pm	46	194	2
11:16	11	1:55 pm	2:06	0	170	2
11:24	60	2:06	3:06	0	222	1
2:04 pm	136	3:06	5:22	0	198	1
4:59	81	5:22	6:43	0	104	0
9:19	22	9:19	9:41	156	22	0
10:16	35	10:16	10:51	35	35	1
10:33	60	10:51	11:51	0	78	1
11:28	58	11:51	Tues., 12:49 am	0	81	0
Tues., 3:44 am	38	Tues., 3:44 am	4:22	175	38	1
3:48	17	4:22	4:39	0	51	0
6:23	15	6:23	6:38	104	15	1
6:27	110	6:38	8:28	0	121	2
7:38	22	8:28	8:50	0	72	2
8:06	87	8:50	10:17	0	131	1
8:39	126	10:17	12:23 pm	0	224	2
10:23	12	12:23 pm	12:35	0	132	1
11:18	20	12:35	12:55	0	97	0
1:48 pm	74	1:48	3:02	53	74	0
Totals	1202			660	2083	

Time machines wait for service to begin
$$= \text{(total machine down time)} - \text{(total machine service time)}$$
$$= 2083 - 1202 = 881 \text{ minutes}$$

have both increased. The relative changes in these measures of effectiveness are somewhat greater than the increase in arrival rate.

Tables II and III both reflect the nature of the typical waiting line situation. Because of the random nature of arrivals, we may at times have long periods between breakdowns, but sometimes two or three breakdowns may occur almost simultaneously. Similarly, since the time required for service varies considerably and is a random process, long service times may occur at the time that several machines are down, causing long waiting times, or, the reverse pattern may be true. The resulting length of waiting line and waiting time, and the idle time of the service facility depend on the distribution of arrivals and of service times.

DISTRIBUTION OF
ARRIVALS AND SERVICE TIMES /

The common basic waiting line models have been developed on the assumption that *arrival rates* follow the Poisson distribution and that *service times* follow the negative exponential distribution. This situation is commonly referred to as the Poisson arrival–exponential holding time case. These assumptions are often quite valid in operating situations.

Poisson Arrival Rates

The Poisson distribution of arrival rates occurs frequently in the real world. Figures 2, 3, and 4 are examples of cases that have been validated by statistical analysis. Figure 2 is based on a broad study by Nelson [8] of the distributions of arrival rates and processing times in a Los Angeles jobbing machine shop. The frequency of arrivals of job orders at fifteen machine centers for a period of three months was tabulated. Table IV summarizes the data on the distribution of arrival rates, and Figure 2 shows the graphs for two of the machine groups compared to the theoretical distribution of the Poisson. The distributions for the entire set of fifteen machine centers were subjected to careful statistical tests in comparison to the Poisson, using the chi square goodness of fit test. It was concluded that the distributions of arrival rates for all fifteen machine centers were not significantly different from the Poisson distribution.

Figure 3 shows the comparison between the actual distribution of order rates and the Poisson distribution. This study took place at the Kodak Park Works of the Eastman Kodak Company, and the distribution represented the rate at which orders for mixed chemicals needed by several production departments in the company were received at a storeroom.

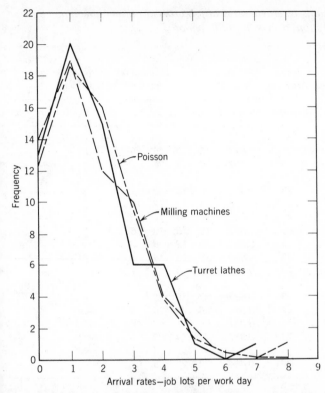

FIGURE 2. Comparison of the distribution of arrival rates at two machine centers in a jobbing machine shop with the Poisson distribution. Adapted from Rosser T. Nelson [8].

Statistical tests again indicate that the actual distribution was described adequately by the Poisson. Figure 4 shows comparisons of actual distributions of arrival rates with the Poisson and normal distribution in traffic studies.

Although we cannot say with finality that distributions of arrival rates are always described adequately by the Poisson, there is much evidence to indicate that this is often the case. We might have reasoned that this should be true, because the Poisson distribution corresponds to completely random arrivals, since it is assumed that an arrival is completely independent of other arrivals as well as of any condition of the waiting line. We should note, however, that completely random arrivals are probably as unusual as completely ordered ones. The practical question is whether or not the Poisson distribution is a reasonable approximation.

TABLE IV. *Distributions of arrival rates of job orders to fifteen machine centers in a jobbing machine shop, over a 3-month period**

Machine Group	Number of Machines in Group	Total Arrivals in 3 Months	Mean Arrival Rate, Arrivals per Work Day	Distribution of Arrivals— Job Lots per Work Day								
				0	1	2	3	4	5	6	7	8
Engine lathes	7	120	1.935	11	14	21	4	9	2	1	—	—
Turret lathes	6	104	1.677	13	20	15	6	6	1	—	1	—
Automatic lathes	3	6	0.097	57	4	1	—	—	—	—	—	—
Hollow spindle lathes	1	27	0.435	40	18	3	1	—	—	—	—	—
Milling machines	6	107	1.726	14	19	12	10	4	2	—	—	1
Saws	2	77	1.242	25	14	11	9	1	2	—	—	—
Drill presses	3	95	1.532	15	18	18	6	3	1	1	—	—
Punch presses	2	37	0.597	39	12	8	3	—	—	—	—	—
Boring machines	2	33	0.532	39	16	4	3	—	—	—	—	—
Slotters	1	14	0.226	51	9	1	1	—	—	—	—	—
Hydrostatic pipe tester	1	33	0.532	37	19	5	—	1	—	—	—	—
Upsetters	2	57	0.919	25	22	10	5	—	—	—	—	—
Shapers	2	5	0.081	59	1	2	—	—	—	—	—	—
Wheelabrator	1	24	0.387	44	14	3	—	1	—	—	—	—
Pipe threading machine	1	30	0.484	37	20	5	—	—	—	—	—	—

*Adapted from Rosser T. Nelson [8].

The commonly used symbol for average arrival rate in waiting line models is the Greek letter lambda (λ), arrivals per time unit. It can be shown that when the arrival rates follow a Poisson process with mean arrival rate λ, the time between arrivals follows a negative exponential distribution with mean time between arrivals of $1/\lambda$. This relationship between mean arrival rate and mean time between arrivals does not necessarily hold for other distributions. The negative exponential distribution, then, is also representative of a Poisson process, but describes the time between arrivals, and specifies that these time intervals are completely random. Negative exponential distributions are shown in Figures 5 and 6. Both the Poisson and negative exponential distributions are tabulated in the Appendix as Tables V and VI respectively.

Exponential Service Times

The commonly used symbol for average service rate in waiting line models is the Greek letter mu (μ), the number of services completed per time unit. As with arrivals, it can be shown that when service rates follow a Poisson

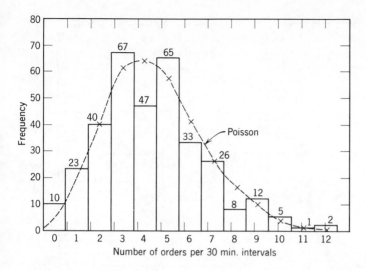

FIGURE 3. Distribution of order rates for mixed chemicals compared to the Poisson distribution. From O. J. Feorene [5].

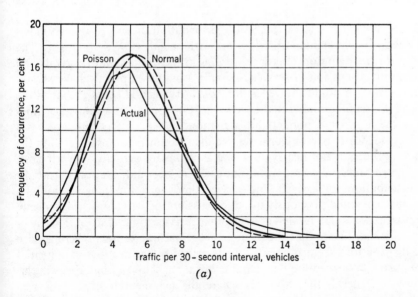

FIGURE 4. Arrival rates in traffic studies. From C. W. Churchman, R. L. Ackoff, and E. L. Arnoff [3].

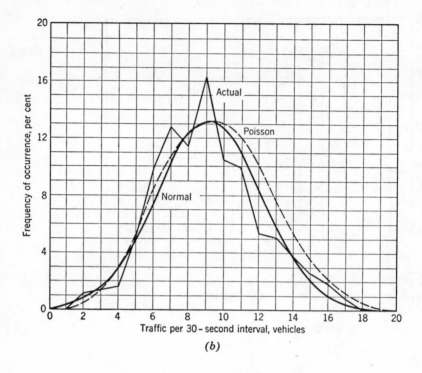

(b)

process with mean service rate μ, the distribution of service times follows the negative exponential distribution with mean service time $1/\mu$. The reason for the common reference to *rates* in the discussion of arrivals and *times* in the discussion of service is simply a matter of practice. We should hold it clearly in mind, however, for both arrivals and service, that in the general Poisson model, rates follow the Poisson distribution and times follow the negative exponential distribution.

The evidence that real world service distributions commonly follow the Poisson process is not nearly as strong as it was for arrivals. Nevertheless, in some instances the assumption appears to be valid. Nelson's study of the distributions of arrivals and service times in a Los Angeles jobbing machine shop cited previously in our discussions of arrivals did *not* indicate that the exponential model fit the actual service time distributions adequately for all of the machine centers. The machine centers where service time distributions seemed adequately described by the negative exponential were turret lathes, milling machines, boring machines, and the wheelabrator. In general, the instances where the exponential hypothesis was reasonable occurred in the machine centers with the largest mean processing time.

Nelson's study indicated that other mathematical distributions such as the hyperexponential and the hyper-Erlang were better descriptions of the actual distributions. Figure 5 shows the distributions and fitted curves for the drill presses and the upsetters. A visual comparison indicates that the negative exponential distribution does not yield the best fit, and this was also indicated by statistical analysis.

Other evidence indicates that in some cases the negative exponential distribution fits. Figure 6, for example, shows that service time at a tool

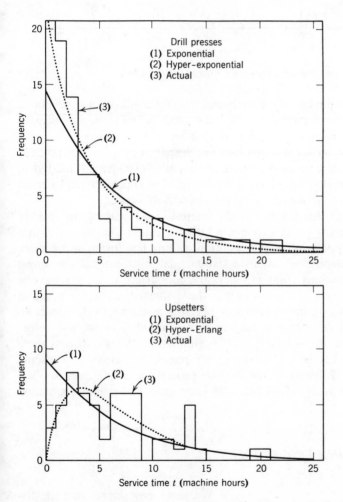

FIGURE 5. *Comparison of actual and theoretical distributions for two machine groups. From Rosser T. Nelson [8].*

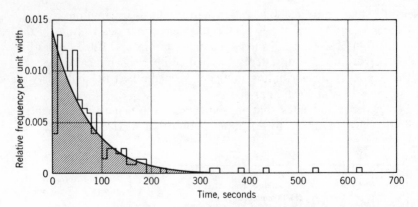

FIGURE 6. Service time at a tool crib. From G. Brigham [1].

crib was nearly exponentially distributed. The duration of local telephone calls not made from a pay station has also been shown to be exponential.

The net result of our discussion is that we cannot assume without a careful check that service distributions are described by a Poisson process. We may expect some instances where the negative exponential fits, but in many instances service times have been shown to be approximated by some unimodal distribution, usually somewhat positively skewed.

We might ask at this point, why the interest in establishing the validity of the Poisson and negative exponential distributions? The answer is that where the assumptions hold, the resulting waiting line formulas are quite simple. The Poisson and negative exponential distributions are single parameter distributions, that is, they are completely described by one parameter, the mean. The result is that the mathematical derivations and resulting formulas are not complex. Where the assumptions do not hold, the mathematical development may be rather complex, or we may resort to other techniques for solution, such as simulation. We will discuss these techniques at a later point; however, our present objective is to discuss waiting line models based on the Poisson process for arrivals and service, the situation commonly referred to as Poisson arrival rates and exponential holding times.

INFINITE WAITING LINE MODELS /

We must now make another distinction in the classifications of waiting line models, between situations where the waiting line may theoretically become infinite and where the maximum length of the waiting line is finite. In practice we would apply infinite waiting line models where the number in line could grow very large. From Figure 4 we see that the high average rate of arrivals of 1100 autos per hour does indeed imply the potential of the very large waiting line. In contrast, consider the case of maintaining a bank of ten automatic machines. The breakdown of a machine is considered to be an arrival. Obviously, the maximum possible waiting line of machines to be serviced is ten. It is finite and requires a different analysis resulting in a model different from that of the infinite waiting line problem.

Single-Channel, Single-Phase Case

We assume that the following conditions are valid: (a) Poisson arrival rates; (b) negative exponential service times; (c) first come–first served queue discipline; (d) the mean service rate μ is greater than the mean arrival rate λ.

The probability of an arrival occurring in the short interval Δt is simply $\lambda(\Delta t)$. Also since the average service rate is μ the probability of a unit leaving the system during Δt is $\mu(\Delta t)$. Since Δt is a very short interval, we assume that the probability of more than one arrival or departure during Δt is zero, because the factor $(\Delta t)^n$ will be extremely small or zero for any number of arrivals n greater than one. Thus, we have only the three possible events during Δt, a net addition of one unit in the system by an arrival but no departure, a net reduction of one unit by a departure but no arrival, and the maintenance of the status quo by both an arrival and a departure. This situation is shown in Figure 7 for four different starting conditions at time t of units in the system of $l = 0, 1, 2$, and n. When the number of units in the system is $l = 0$ only two possible end conditions at $t + \Delta t$ are possible since no departure is possible. The general situation when $l > 0$ is shown for $l = n$. When we begin with n units in the system at time t then the ending conditions at time $t + \Delta t$ are one of the three possibilities, $l = n - 1$, $l = n$, or $l = n + 1$.

As stated previously, the probability of an arrival is $\lambda(\Delta t)$ and of a departure $\mu(\Delta t)$. Therefore, the probability of each of the ending conditions can be stated as shown in Figure 7. For example, if $l = 0$ at time t, the probability that $l = 1$ at $t + \Delta t$ is $P_1 = \lambda(\Delta t)$, and since there are only two possibilities the probability that $l = 0$ at $t + \Delta t$ is $P_0 = 1 - \lambda(\Delta t)$. For the general case when $l = n$ at time t (where $n > 0$), the probability that $l = n - 1$ at $t + \Delta t$ is $P_{n-1} = \mu(\Delta t)$, the probability of a departure with no arrival. Similarly, the probability that $l = n + 1$ at $t + \Delta t$ is $P_{n+1} = \lambda(\Delta t)$, the probability of an arrival with no departure occurring. Finally,

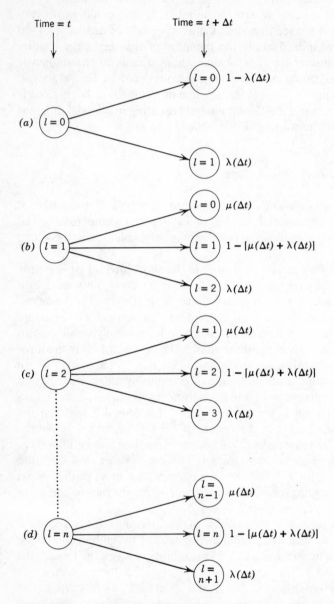

FIGURE 7. Probabilities of the occurrence of each ending condition for the number of units in the system, l.

the third possibility that the number of units in the system will remain the same at time $t + \Delta t$ is simply $P_n = 1 - [\mu(\Delta t) + \lambda(\Delta t)]$, since the sum of the probabilities must total 1.

We are now in a position to develop a set of equations for the probability of various ending conditions of the number of units in the system l. Referring to Figure 7 there are two ways we can have $l = 0$ at $t + \Delta t$: when $l = 0$ at t and no arrival occurs so that $l = 0$ at $t + \Delta t$, and when $l = 1$ at t and a departure but no arrival occurs so that $l = 0$ at $t + \Delta t$. The probability of $l = 0$ is then the product of the probabilities that $l = 0$ at t and at $t + \Delta t$ for the first, plus the product of the probabilities that $l = 1$ at t and $l = 0$ at $t + \Delta t$, or

$$P_0 = [1 - \lambda(\Delta t)]P_0 + \mu(\Delta t)P_1 \tag{1}$$

Similarly P_1 can occur in three ways (see Figure 7), and

$$P_1 = \lambda(\Delta t)P_0 + [1 - \mu(\Delta t) - \lambda(\Delta t)]P_1 + \mu(\Delta t)P_2 \tag{2}$$

Finally P_n takes the following general form:

$$P_n = \lambda(\Delta t)P_{n-1} + [1 - \mu(\Delta t) - \lambda(\Delta t)]P_n + \mu(\Delta t)P_{n+1} \tag{3}$$

Equation 1 may be solved for P_1 in terms of P_0

$$P_1 = \frac{\lambda}{\mu} P_0 \tag{4}$$

Also equation (3) may be solved for P_{n+1} in terms of P_n and P_{n-1} as follows:

$$P_{n+1} = \frac{\mu + \lambda}{\mu} P_n - \frac{\lambda}{\mu} P_{n-1} \tag{5}$$

By substituting $n = 1$, and equation (4) for P_1, we can obtain an expression for P_2 as follows:

$$P_{1+1} = \frac{\mu + \lambda}{\mu} P_1 - \frac{\lambda}{\mu} P_{1-1}$$

$$P_2 = \frac{\mu + \lambda}{\mu} P_1 - \frac{\lambda}{\mu} P_0$$

but,

$$P_1 = \frac{\lambda}{\mu} P_0$$

from (4), therefore,

$$P_2 = \frac{\mu + \lambda}{\mu} \left(\frac{\lambda}{\mu} P_0 \right) - \frac{\lambda}{\mu} P_0$$

$$= \frac{\lambda}{\mu} \left(\frac{\mu + \lambda}{\mu} - 1 \right) P_0$$

$$= \left(\frac{\lambda}{\mu} \right)^2 P_0$$

Following the same general procedure the probabilities of various values of l can be shown to be in the same form so that

$$P_n = \left(\frac{\lambda}{\mu} \right)^n P_0 \tag{6}$$

The sum of the probabilities must total 1, or

$$\sum_{n=0}^{\infty} P_n = 1$$

Substituting equation (6) for P_n, we have

$$\sum_{n=0}^{\infty} \left(\frac{\lambda}{\mu} \right)^n P_0 = 1 = P_0 \sum_{n=0}^{\infty} \left(\frac{\lambda}{\mu} \right)^n$$

and

$$P_0 = \frac{1}{\sum_{n=0}^{\infty} \left(\frac{\lambda}{\mu} \right)^n}$$

but

$$\sum_{n=0}^{\infty} \left(\frac{\lambda}{\mu} \right)^n$$

is an infinite geometric progression whose sum is

$$\frac{1}{1 - \lambda/\mu}$$

therefore

$$P_0 = \frac{1}{1/(1 - \lambda/\mu)} = 1 - \frac{\lambda}{\mu} \tag{7}$$

Substituting equation (7) for P_0 in equation (6)

$$P_n = \left(\frac{\lambda}{\mu}\right)^n \left(1 - \frac{\lambda}{\mu}\right) \tag{8}$$

Equation (8) can then be used to compute the probability of any number of units in the system, given the four conditions stated at the beginning of this section.

Average Line Lengths and Waiting Times. Average values for waiting line lengths and waiting times are often useful in cost models. The average number of units in the system L (including the one being processed) is simply the sum of the products of n and P_n for all n

$$L = \sum_{n=0}^{\infty} nP_n \tag{9}$$

Substituting the value of P_n from equation (8) we have

$$L = \sum_{n=0}^{\infty} n \left(\frac{\lambda}{\mu}\right)^n \left(1 - \frac{\lambda}{\mu}\right)$$

$$= \left(1 - \frac{\lambda}{\mu}\right) \sum_{n=0}^{\infty} n \left(\frac{\lambda}{\mu}\right)^n$$

but the term $\sum_{n=0}^{\infty} n \left(\frac{\lambda}{\mu}\right)^n$ may be expanded into a geometric series whose sum is

$$\frac{(\lambda/\mu)}{(1 - \lambda/\mu)^2}$$

therefore

$$L = \frac{(1 - \lambda/\mu)(\lambda/\mu)}{(1 - \lambda/\mu)^2}$$

which reduces to

$$L = \frac{\lambda}{\mu - \lambda} \tag{10}$$

L is the mean number of units in the system, including the one being served. Other useful related formulas are as follows:

Mean number in waiting line

$$L_q = \frac{\lambda^2}{\mu(\mu - \lambda)} = L - \left(\frac{\lambda}{\mu}\right) \tag{11}$$

Mean waiting time

$$W_q = \frac{\lambda}{\mu(\mu - \lambda)} = \frac{L_q}{\lambda} \tag{12}$$

Mean time in system including service

$$W = \frac{1}{\mu - \lambda} = W_q + \frac{1}{\mu} = \frac{L}{\lambda} \tag{13}$$

At first glance, it might seem that the difference between the mean number in the system and the mean number in the waiting line $(L - L_q)$ should be 1, the unit being served. A check of the formulas, however, indicates that this is not true; the difference is less than 1. A moment's reflection indicates the intuitive reason. Sometimes, because of the random nature of arrivals and service times, the service facility is idle so that the average number being served per unit of time must be less than 1. Also, note that the difference between the mean time in the system and the mean waiting time $(W - W_q)$ is simply the average time for service $1/\mu$, as we would expect.

If we take the ratio between the mean arrival rate and the mean service rate, we have an index of the utilization of the service facility. The ratio is commonly called the utilization factor and is denoted by the Greek letter rho (ρ). If the two rates are equal, $\rho = 1$, theoretically the service facility could be used 100 percent of the time. But let us see what actually happens to the queue as ρ varies from zero to one. Figure 8 summarizes the result of computing L_q for different values of ρ. As ρ approaches unity, the number waiting in line increases rapidly and approaches infinity. We can also see that this is true by examining equations (10), (11), (12), and (13). In all cases, $\mu - \lambda$ appears in the denominator. When λ and μ are equal, $\mu - \lambda$ is zero and the value of L, L_q, W, or W_q becomes infinitely large. In practical situations, this never really happens because arrivals may not choose to wait if the line is already very long, or someone takes action either to reduce the arrival rate or increase the processing rate in order to remedy the situation. We see now one of the requirements of any practical system: μ must always exceed λ, otherwise we cannot have a stable system. If units are arriving faster on the average than they can be processed, the waiting line will be continuously increasing and no steady state will be achieved.

When conditions of arrival and service rate are such that the average length of the waiting line increases as noted in Figure 8, we can reason that the probability that the service facility will be idle must become rather small. Equation (8) allows us to calculate this probability rather easily.

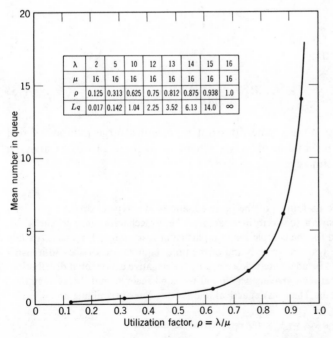

λ	2	5	10	12	13	14	15	16
μ	16	16	16	16	16	16	16	16
ρ	0.125	0.313	0.625	0.75	0.812	0.875	0.938	1.0
L_q	0.017	0.142	1.04	2.25	3.52	6.13	14.0	∞

FIGURE 8. *Relationship of queue length to the utilization factor ρ.*

The probability of 0 units in the system (service facility idle), P_0, is

$$P_0 = \left(1 - \frac{\lambda}{\mu}\right)\left(\frac{\lambda}{\mu}\right)^0$$

and, since $\left(\dfrac{\lambda}{\mu}\right)^0 = 1$,

$$P_0 = \left(1 - \frac{\lambda}{\mu}\right) = (1 - \rho)$$

This is the probability that the service facility will be idle, and checks our intuition that utilization of the facility plus idleness should total 100 percent.

Constant service times modify the formulas for the mean number in the waiting line and mean waiting time only slightly. The formulas are:

Mean number in waiting line

$$L_q = \frac{\lambda^2}{2\mu(\mu - \lambda)} \tag{14}$$

Mean waiting time

$$W_q = \frac{\lambda}{2\mu(\mu - \lambda)} \tag{15}$$

Whereas constant service time does not represent a large number of real situations, it is reasonable in cases where a machine processes arriving items by a fixed time cycle.

An Example

Let us illustrate the usefulness of the basic equations in a typical decision problem. Suppose that we have a tool crib in a factory where mechanics come to check out special tools needed for the completion of a particular task assigned to them. A study is made of the time between arrivals and of the time required for service. Both distributions are found to be adequately described by the negative exponential distribution. The average time between arrivals was found to be 60 seconds and the average time for service 50 seconds. The Poisson arrival and service rates per minute are:

$$\lambda = \tfrac{1}{60} \times 60 = 1 \text{ arrival per minute}$$

$$\mu = \tfrac{1}{50} \times 60 = 1.2 \text{ services per minute}$$

Let us determine the magnitude of waiting line lengths, waiting time and the percent of idle time of the attendant, using equations (10), (11), (12), and (13).

$$L_q = \frac{\lambda^2}{\mu(\mu - \lambda)} = \frac{1^2}{1.2(1.2 - 1.0)} = \frac{1}{1.2 \times 0.2} = 4.17 \text{ mechanics in line}$$

$$L = \frac{\lambda}{\mu - \lambda} = \frac{1}{1.2 - 1.0}$$

$$= 5 \text{ mechanics in line, including the mechanic being served}$$

$$W_q = \frac{\lambda}{\mu(\mu - \lambda)} = \frac{1}{1.2(1.2 - 1.0)} = \frac{1}{1.2 \times 0.2}$$

$$= 4.17 \text{ minutes per mechanic}$$

$$W = \frac{1}{\mu - \lambda} = \frac{1}{1.2 - 1.0} = 5 \text{ minutes waiting time, including service}$$

Idle time $= 1 - \rho = 1 - \dfrac{1}{1.2} = 0.1667$, or 16.67 percent idle time of the attendant

If the attendant is paid \$2 per hour and the mechanics are paid \$4 per hour, what service level should be established? What cost function do we wish to minimize? If we add more attendants, the waiting line and mechanics' waiting time will be reduced, but the idle time of the attendants will be increased. Therefore, what we wish to do is to determine the number of attendants that will minimize the combined cost of attendants' idle time, plus the cost of mechanics' waiting time. For one attendant, the cost of idle time is:

$$8 \times 0.1667 \times 2.00 = \$2.67 \text{ per day}$$

If mechanics arrive at the rate of 1 per minute, then 480 are served in an 8-hour day, and the daily cost of waiting time is

480 (waiting time per mechanic in hours)(hourly pay rate)

$$= 480 \times \frac{W_q}{60} \times 4.00 = 480 \times \frac{4.17}{60} \times 4.00 = \$133.44 \text{ per day}$$

Obviously, with one attendant, we are incurring a very large waiting time cost ($33\frac{1}{3}$ hours per day) in relation to the cost of the attendants' idle time, and more attendants to step up the effective service rate will be justified. But before we can proceed with our analysis we must have information about the next most complex situation, because if we add a second, third, or fourth attendant, we are dealing with the multiple-channel, single-phase situation.

Multiple-Channel, Single-Phase Case

In the multiple-channel case we assume the same conditions of Poisson arrivals, exponential service times, and first come–first served queue discipline. The effective service rate $M\mu$ must be greater than the arrival rate λ, where M is the number of channels. First, it is necessary to calculate P_0, the probability that there are zero units in the system (service facility idle), since the basic formulas all involve P_0 in their simplest forms.

$$P_0 = \frac{1}{\left[\sum_{n=0}^{M-1} \frac{(\lambda/\mu)^n}{n!}\right] + \left[\frac{(\lambda/\mu)^M}{M!\left(1 - \frac{\lambda}{\mu M}\right)}\right]}$$

and substituting $r = \lambda/\mu$,

$$P_0 = \frac{1}{\left[\sum_{n=0}^{M-1} \frac{r^n}{n!}\right] + \left[\frac{r^M}{M!\left(1 - \frac{r}{M}\right)}\right]} \tag{16}$$

where n is an index for the number of channels, the calculation of the term $\sum_{n=0}^{M-1} \frac{r^n}{n!}$ being the sum of $\frac{r^n}{n!}$ for all of the numbers of channels ranging from $n = 0$ to $n = M - 1$. The notation $n!$ means n factorial, that is, to multiply the declining series of numbers beginning with the value of n, declining to 1. For example, $6! = 6 \cdot 5 \cdot 4 \cdot 3 \cdot 2 \cdot 1 = 720$.

Then the formulas parallel to the single channel case are:

Mean number in waiting line

$$L_q = \frac{(r)^{M+1}}{(M-1)!(M-r)^2} \cdot P_0 \tag{17}$$

Mean number in system, including those being serviced

$$L = L_q + r \tag{18}$$

Mean waiting time

$$W_q = \frac{r^{M+1}}{\lambda(M-1)!(M-r)^2} \cdot P_0$$

$$= \frac{L_q}{\lambda} \tag{19}$$

Mean time in system, including service

$$W = W_q + \frac{1}{\mu}$$

$$= \frac{L}{\lambda} \tag{20}$$

Although the relationships are somewhat more complex, especially for a large number of channels, we can see that we need calculate only one of the conditions, L_q, L, W_q, or W, and all of the others may be calculated quite simply through the interrelationships that exist.

The Effect of Increasing the Number of Channels. To compare the effects of increasing the number of channels, it is useful to plot curves for line lengths and waiting times versus the utilization factor which may now be generalized as $\rho = \lambda/M\mu$, where M is the number of channels. Figures 9 and 10 show line lengths and waiting times for $M = 1, 2, 3, 4, 5$, and 10. If, for example, we were faced with a situation where $\rho = 0.9$ for the single-channel case, then L_q is approximately 8 from Figure 9. Adding a second channel reduces the utilization factor to $\rho = 0.9/2 = 0.45$, which results in $L_q = 0.23$ from Figure 9. The effects are surprisingly large, that is, we can obtain disproportionate gains in waiting time by increasing the number of channels. We can see intuitively that this might be true from Figure 8 since queue length (and waiting time) begins to increase very rapidly at about $\rho = 0.8$. A rather small increase in the capacity of the system (decrease in ρ) at these high loads can produce a large decrease in line length and waiting time.

Let us return now to the tool crib example. If a second tool crib attendant were added, the utilization factor becomes $\rho = 1/(2 \times 1.2) = 0.417$, whereas previously it was 0.833. Reading approximate values from the curves of Figure 9, $L_q = 0.175$ and $W_q = 0.175/\lambda = 0.175/1 = 0.175$ minute per mechanic. The cost of mechanics' waiting time is now reduced to:

$$480 \times \frac{0.175}{60} \times 4 = \$5.60 \text{ per day}$$

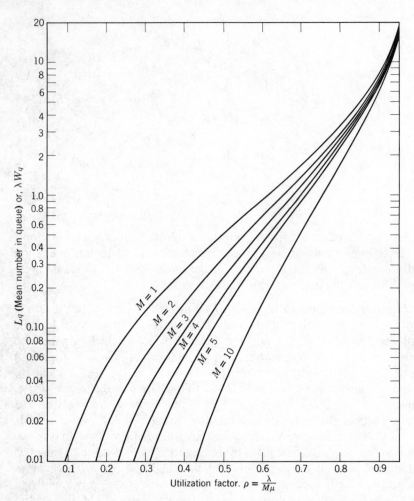

FIGURE 9. L_q *(Mean number in queue) or* λW_q *for different values of* M, *versus the utilization factor* ρ. $L_q = \lambda W_q$.

The idle time of the attendants has increased by 8 hours, however, since there is no more work to be done than before—it is simply distributed between two attendants. The new idle time cost is then,

$$\$2.67 + \$2 \times 8 = \$18.67 \text{ per day}$$

The combined cost of waiting plus idle time is much less ($24.27) when two

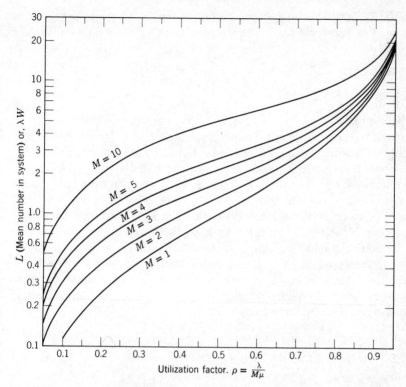

FIGURE 10. L *(Mean number in system) or* λW *for different values of* M, *versus the utilization factor* ρ. L $= \lambda W$.

attendants are available than when only one was available ($136.11). We can also see without further detailed analysis that it would not be economical to add a third attendant, since the incremental cost of doing so would be $16.00 per day and the waiting time cost with two attendants is only $5.60 per day.

The Effect of Pooling Facilities. This effect can also be seen from Figure 9. Suppose, for example, that since we find a second attendant is warranted following our previous analysis, the proposal is made to decentralize and have two separate tool cribs. What effect will this have on waiting time costs? With two separate tool cribs we will assume that half the mechanics go to each, so that the average arrival rate at each crib is now 0.5 arrivals per minute. The utilization factor is then $\rho = 0.417$ and waiting time per mechanic is $L_q/\lambda = 0.3/0.5 = 0.6$ minute from Figure 9. This translates into a waiting time cost for the two tool cribs of

$$\frac{0.6}{60} \times 480 \times 4 = \$19.20 \text{ per day}$$

This compares to $5.60 per day waiting time cost for the single facility with two attendants previously calculated. We can see intuitively why there is greater total waiting time in the decentralized system if we visualize the two tool cribs functioning side by side. If the attendant for crib 1 were busy servicing a mechanic with a second mechanic waiting, the second mechanic could obtain immediate service if the attendant for crib 2 were idle. With the two cribs physically decentralized, however, both the second mechanic's waiting time and the crib 2 attendant's idle time would continue at that point. The result is clear. One large facility can give better service than an equivalent number of small facilities. The above calculation, of course, accounts only for the waiting time costs. In the case of the tool crib a centralized facility would have other economic advantages and disadvantages such as reduced total investment in tools and increased transportation time by mechanics.

FINITE WAITING LINE MODELS /

Many practical waiting line problems which occur in production systems have the characteristics of finite waiting line models. This is true whenever the population of machines, men, or items which may arrive for service is limited to a relatively small finite number. The result is that we must express arrivals in terms of a unit of the population rather than as an average rate. In the infinite waiting line case the average length of the waiting line is effectively independent of the number in the arriving population, but in the finite case the number in the queue may represent a significant proportion of the arriving population, and therefore the probabilities associated with arrivals are affected. The resulting mathematical formulations are somewhat more difficult computationally than for the infinite queue case. Fortunately, however, *Finite Queuing Tables* [10] are available which make problem solution very simple. Although there is no definite number that we can point to as a dividing line between finite and infinite applications, the finite queuing tables have data for populations from 4 up to 250, and this may be taken as a general guide. We have reproduced these tables for populations of

5, 10, 20, and 30 in the Appendix, Table III, to illustrate their use in the solution of finite queuing problems. The tables are based on a finite model for exponential times between arrivals and service times, and a first come–first served queue discipline.

Use of the Finite Queuing Tables

The tables are indexed first by N, the size of the population. For each population size, data are classified by X, the service factor (comparable to the utilization factor in infinite queues), and by M, the number of parallel channels. For a given N, X, and M, two factors are listed in the tables, D (the probability of a delay; that is, if a unit calls for service, the probability that it will have to wait) and F (an efficiency factor, used to calculate other important data). To summarize, we define the factors just expressed plus those which may be calculated as follows:

N = population (number of machines, customers, etc.)

T = mean service time (repair time, length of telephone conversation, process time, etc.)

U = mean run time, or mean time between calls for service, *per population unit*

X = service factor = $\dfrac{T}{T + U}$

M = number of service channels

D = probability of delay (probability that if a unit calls for service, it will have to wait)

F = efficiency factor

L_q = mean number in waiting line = $N(1 - F)$

W_q = mean waiting time = $L_q(T + U)/(N - L_q) = \dfrac{T}{X}\left(\dfrac{1 - F}{F}\right)$

H = mean number of units being serviced = $FNX = L - L_q$

J = mean number of units running = $NF(1 - X)$

$M - H$ = average number of servers idle

The procedure for a given case is as follows:

1. Determine the mean service time T, and the mean running time U, based on data or measurements of the system being analyzed.

2. Compute the service factor $X = T/(T + U)$.

3. Locate the section of the tables listing data for the population size N.

4. Locate the service factor calculated in 2 for the given population.

5. Read the values of D and F for the number of channels M, interpolating between values of X when necessary.

6. Compute values for L_q, W_q, H, and J as required by the nature of the problem.

An Example

Let us take as an illustrative example the case of tire curing. After tires have been assembled, they go to curing presses where the various layers of rubber and fiber are vulcanized into one homogeneous piece and the final shape including the tread is molded. Different tires require somewhat different curing times which may range up to 90 minutes or more. The press operator can unload and reload a press in 3 minutes, so that one operator would normally service a bank of curing presses, and each press may be molding tires of a different design, so that presses are "arriving" for service at nearly random times. The presses automatically open when the preset cure time is complete.

In servicing a bank of thirty presses, the operator is ranging over a wide area of approximately 90 feet by 200 feet. Indicator lights flash on, signifying that the press is ready for service, and the operator walks to the open press, unloading and reloading it. Sometimes, of course, the position of the open press may be quite close to the operator so that his walk is fairly short. In rare instances the operator is at one extreme end of the area and the press requiring service is at the other extreme end, requiring a fairly long walk. Thus the operator's tasks in rendering service are made up of walking plus unloading and reloading the presses. The average time for the operator's activity is 3 minutes and is approximated by the negative exponential distribution.

When a press is idle, waiting to be serviced, the only costs which continue are the services to the press, mainly heat supply. The cost of supplying this heat is $4.00 per hour per press. Operators are paid $3.50 per hour, and contribution per tire is $5.00.

Let us determine the number of operators (number of channels) to be used when the average cure time of tires being produced is 80 minutes for conditions when market demand is less than plant capacity and when it is above plant capacity.

The Solution

To state our objective we wish to determine the number of servicing operators which will minimize the combined costs of downtime due solely to waiting for service and the cost of heat supplied to the presses while waiting and the loss of contribution when demand is above capacity and any additional output can be sold. When demand is below capacity, we assume that management is adjusting the number of presses in operation, hours worked, or even the number of shifts worked to match output to demand. We will calculate costs for 24 hours of operation.

1. *Value of wasted heat due to presses waiting for service.* Since $T = 3$ minutes and $U = 80$ minutes,

$$X = \frac{T}{T + U} = \frac{3}{3 + 80} = 0.036$$

for $N = 30$, and $X = 0.036$ we have the following values from the tables:

M	F
3	*0.998*
2	*0.988*
1	*0.853*

and, we compute L_q and W_q,

M	$L_q = N(1 - F)$	$W_q = \dfrac{L_q(T + U)}{N - L_q}$
3	*0.06 presses*	*0.166 min./press/cycle*
2	*0.36 presses*	*1.008 min./press/cycle*
1	*4.41 presses*	*14.30 min./press/cycle*

Since the presses are running, being serviced, or waiting to be serviced, the percent of time that they are waiting is

$$\frac{W_q}{U + T + W_q} \times 100$$

and we may calculate the cost of waiting time for thirty presses and 24 hours of operation:

M	*Percent Waiting Time* $= \dfrac{W_q}{U + T + W_q} \times 100$	*Cost for Thirty Presses and 24 Hours of Operation at \$4/hr.* $= 24 \times 4 \times L_q$
3	*0.2*	*\$ 5.76*
2	*1.2*	*34.56*
1	*14.7*	*423.36*

2. *Value of operator's idle time.* Recall that $H = FNX$ is the average number of units being serviced at any one time. If there are M channels, there are $M - H$ channels idle at any one time, so we may calculate easily the opportunity value of operator idle time for 24 hours of operation:

M	H = FNX	Average Number of Operators Idle = M − H	Cost of Idle Time for 24 Hours at Pat Rate, $3.50/hr.
3	1.078	1.922	$161.45
2	1.067	0.933	78.37
1	0.921	0.079	6.64

When demand is less than capacity, our decision is based on the balance of costs of wasted heat due to presses waiting and of operators' idle time:

M	Cost of Wasted Heat Due to Presses Waiting	Cost of Operator's Idle Time	Total
3	$ 5.76	$161.45	$167.21
2	34.56	78.37	112.93
1	423.36	6.64	430.00

The use of two operators to service the thirty presses is indicated, since this situation produces the lowest combined cost of wasted heat and operator idle time. Now let us see if conditions change sufficiently when demand exceeds capacity to warrant a change of operating policy.

3. *Value of lost marginal profit due to presses waiting for service, when demand exceeds capacity and additional tires can therefore be sold.* If there were no waiting time the average output from the thirty presses would be $30(60/83) = 21.7$ tires per hour. Also, we may calculate the average number of presses running at any point in time by $J = NF(1 - X)$. Every 83 minutes of run time produces a tire on the average, therefore:

M	Average Number of Presses Running = J = NF(1 − X)	Average Output per Hour = J $\frac{60}{83}$	Output Lost per Hour Due to Waiting = 21.7 − Average Output	Cost of Output Lost = (output lost) ($5)(24)
3	28.86	20.86 tires	0.84 tires	$100.80
2	28.57	20.65	1.05	126.00
1	24.67	17.83	3.87	464.40

Finally, the total of downtime costs due to waiting plus the cost of operator idle time is:

M	Value of Wasted Heat Due to Presses Waiting	Cost of Output Lost	Cost of Operator's Idle Time	Total
3	$ 5.76	$100.80	$161.45	$268.01
2	34.56	126.00	78.37	238.93
1	423.36	464.40	6.64	894.40

Therefore, two operators is also the best number to service the bank of thirty machines when demand exceeds capacity.

There are a number of other important phases of the preceding problem which we are not attempting to deal with here, but which could be analyzed from the data in the *Finite Queuing Tables* and the relationships which were developed earlier. For example, is the decision to use two operators sensitive to the number of presses in operation? How sensitive is it to changes in average cure time (a different product mix)? Curves could easily be developed for average output versus average cure time for different numbers of presses operating, indicating the zones for using 1, 2, 3, etc. operators to serve the presses. Other elements of the operation of the press room, which in themselves are finite queuing problems, are the changeover of presses to different tire sizes, and the mechanical maintenance of the presses. We can see that these problems interact with the overall problem of production programming the output of the press room.

SUMMARY

Waiting line models and concepts are among the most used of quantitative methods today. The common assumptions of Poisson arrivals and negative exponential holding times are reasonable in quite a number of instances. In many cases where they are not appropriate we have a nonhomogeneous situation, where two or more basic conditions are mixed—for example, the service times of a punch press department that handled both repair work (very small orders) and production work (large orders). In such a case the resulting distribution of service times really reflects two basic distributions. We should note also that the first come–first served queue discipline assumed by the formulas is most commonly valid for what we might call external lines (i.e., those involving customers) and that other queue disciplines involving priorities are common internally, such as in job-shop scheduling.

Note that we did not cover any of the multiple-phase cases, situations involving arrival and/or service distributions other than the Poisson, and queue disciplines other than first come–first served. It is felt that these more complex structures are best handled through the technique of computer simulation, which will be covered later. Also, because of work done by P. M. Morse [7] and others, there is considerable knowledge about the machine maintenance problem which will be covered separately in Chapter 15.

REVIEW QUESTIONS

1. Outline and compare the four alternate structures of waiting line situations discussed. Suggest a physical example of each.

2. If arrival rates follow the Poisson distribution, what would the distribution of the times between arrivals be?

3. What evidence is there that arrival rates in actual situations do in fact follow the Poisson distribution?

4. What evidence is there that service times follow the negative exponential distribution in actual processing situations?

5. Contrast infinite and finite waiting line models. What is the characteristic of the situation which makes the distinction between the two kinds of waiting line models?

6. Why is it not true that the difference between the mean number in the system L and the mean number in the waiting line L_q is simply the number of items being served?

7. Explain in physical terms why the waiting line may become infinitely long when the utilization factor is 1.

8. What are the effects on waiting time costs of pooling facilities?

PROBLEMS

1. Trucks arrive at a dock in a Poisson manner at the rate of 8 per hour. Service time distribution is closely approximated by the negative exponential. The average service time is 5 minutes.

a. Calculate the mean number in the waiting line.

b. Calculate the mean number in the system.

c. Calculate the mean waiting time.

d. Calculate the mean time in the system.

e. Calculate the probability of six units being in the system.

f. Calculate the utilization factor.

2. People arrive at a theater ticket booth in a Poisson distributed arrival rate of 25 per hour. Service time is a constant at 2 minutes.

a. Calculate the mean number in the waiting line.

b. Calculate the mean waiting time.

c. Calculate the utilization factor.

3. A taxi cab company has 4 taxi cabs at a particular location. Customer arrival rates and service rates are Poisson distributed. The average arrival rate is 10 per hour. The average service time is 20 minutes.

a. Calculate the utilization factor.

b. From Figure 9 determine the mean number in the waiting line.

c. From Figure 10 determine the mean number in the system.

d. Test the answers to *b* and *c* by the formula $L = L_q + r$.

e. Determine the mean waiting time.

f. Determine the mean time in the system.

4. Using the data in Problem 3:

a. What would the utilization factor be if the number of taxi cabs were increased from 4 to 5?

b. What would be the effect of this change on the mean number in the waiting line as determined by Figure 9?

c. What would be the effect of this change on the mean number in the system as determined by Figure 10?

d. What would be the effect of reducing the number of taxi cabs from 4 to 3?

5. A stenographer has five persons for whom she performs stenographic services. Arrival rates are Poisson distributed, and service times follow the negative exponential distribution. The average arrival rate is 5 jobs per hour. The average service time is 10 minutes.

a. Calculate the mean number in the waiting line.

b. Calculate the mean waiting time.

c. Calculate the mean number of units being serviced.

d. Calculate the mean number of units running.

6. A trucking company has docking facilities with Poisson distributed arrival and service rates. Trucks arrive at the rate of 10 per hour and the unloading rate is 2 trucks per man hour. The time to unload a truck is inversely proportional to the number of workers unloading. The docking facility permits either one or two trucks to be unloaded at the same time. Under the present system, the entire crew works on the same truck until unloading is completed. Each man on the dock crew is paid $2.00 per hour. The cost of an idle truck and driver is estimated to be $15.00 per hour.

a. Determine the optimal number of workers for this docking facility and the average hourly cost.

b. What would be the effect of a 10 percent increase in arrival rate on the optimal number of men? On the utilization factor?

c. What change in average hourly cost would result if the men were split into two crews?

d. What advantages would be gained by such a split?

e. Is such a split analogous to the facilities pooling as exemplified in the chapter?

7. A hospital has thirty beds in one particular section. Calls from patients follow a Poisson process and the distribution of the times required is approximated by the negative exponential. The mean call rate is 20 calls per hour and the mean service time is 8 minutes. The hospital believes that patients should have immediate service at least 80 percent of the time because of possible emergencies. Qualified nurses of this type are paid $3.00 per hour.

a. Determine the required number of nurses for this section and the hourly cost.

b. Determine the average idle time and the cost of this idle time.

c. Assuming a nonprofit organization, how much extra must a patient pay for the 80 percent criterion than if the immediate service level were placed at 50 percent?

8. A hotel beauty shop has Poisson process arrival and service rates of 3 per hour and 1.25 per hour respectively. Beauty operators are paid $1.75 her hour plus tips, time and one half for over 40 hours per week. Incremental profit averages $1.00 per customer; fixed expenses are $100.00 per week, and the shop operates on a 6 day 48 hour week. Because of competitive factors, the management does not want customers to wait more than 15 minutes on the average.

a. Determine the optimal number of beauty operators.

b. Determine the weekly profit.

c. Evaluate the possibility of remaining open an extra hour each night if the average demand would be 10 percent less than normal.

d. How much can the shop afford to pay per week for advertising that will increase business 5 percent?

REFERENCES

1. Brigham, F., "On a Congestion Problem in an Aircraft Factory," *Operations Research*, Vol. 3, No. 4, 1955, pp. 412–428.

2. Bierman, H., C. P. Bonini, and W. H. Hausman, *Quantitative Analysis for Business Decisions*, Richard D. Irwin, Homewood, Ill., Rev. ed., 1969.

3. Churchman, C. W. R., R. L. Ackoff, and E. L. Arnoff, *Introduction to Operations Research*, John Wiley & Sons, New York, 1957.

4. Cox, D. R., and W. L. Smith, *Queues*, Methuen and Co., London, and John Wiley & Sons, New York, 1961.

5. Feorene, O. J., "The Gentle Art of Simulation," *Proceedings, Twelfth Annual Industrial Engineering Institute*, Berkeley-Los Angeles, 1960, pp. 15–22.

6. Malcolm, D. G., "Queuing Theory in Organization Design," *Journal of Industrial Engineering*, November–December 1955, pp. 19–27.

7. Morse, P. M., *Queues, Inventories, and Maintenance*, John Wiley & Sons, New York, 1958.
8. Nelson, R. T., "An Empirical Study of Arrival, Service Time, and Waiting Time Distributions of a Job Shop Production Process," Research Report No. 60, *Management Sciences Research Project*, UCLA, 1959.
9. Panico, J. A., *Queuing Theory*, Prentice-Hall, Inc., Englewood Cliffs, N. J., 1969.
10. Peck, L. G., and R. N. Hazelwood, *Finite Queuing Tables*, John Wiley & Sons, New York, 1958.
11. Prabhu, N. U., *Queues and Inventories*, John Wiley & Sons, Inc., New York, 1965.
12. Saaty, T. L., *Elements of Queuing Theory*, McGraw-Hill Book Company, New York, 1961.
13. Saaty, T. L., "Resume of Useful Formulas in Queuing Theory," *Operations Research*, Vol. 5, No. 2, 1957.
14. Sasieni, M., A. Yaspan, and L. Friedman, *Operations Research*, John Wiley & Sons, New York, 1959.
15. Takács, L., *Introduction to the Theory of Queues*, Oxford University Press, New York, 1962.
16. Thierauf, R. J., and R. A. Grosse, *Decision Making Through Operations Research*, John Wiley & Sons, Inc., New York, 1970.

chapter 15

WAITING LINES
AND MAINTENANCE

With the rapid and continuous development of mechanization and automation, the problem of machine maintenance has become one of particular interest to production and operations management. We can view the problem as one of maintaining the reliability of the entire production system. In general, this reliability can be maintained and improved by the following:

1. *Increasing the size of repair facilities and crews* so that average machine downtime is reduced because maintenance crews are less likely to be busy when a breakdown occurs, or in some cases because a larger crew may be able to repair a machine more quickly.

2. *Utilizing preventive maintenance* where practical so as to replace critical parts before they fail. It is often possible to do this on second and third shifts and thereby not interfere with normal production schedules. Whether preventive maintenance is worthwhile or not depends on the distribution of breakdowns, the relation of preventive maintenance time to repair time, as we shall see, and the relative importance of downtime costs.

3. *Providing for slack in the system* at critical stages so that we have parallel paths available. This means excess capacity so that some machines can be down without affecting the delay costs to any great degree.

4. *Making individual components within a machine or the machines within the system more reliable* through improvements in engineering design. For example, special lubrication systems that may extend the life of working parts.

5. *Decoupling successive stages of the production system by inventories* between operations. The resulting independence of operations localizes the effect of a breakdown so that operations preceding and following the machine that is down are less likely to be affected.

To accomplish increased reliability by any of these means is costly, and therefore we can justify it only insofar as the costs of attaining it are offset by cost reductions in idle labor, scrap, lost business, etc. Number 4 in the preceding list may be regarded as an engineering design problem coupled with economic analysis. Number 5 interacts with problems of facility layout and inventory control, which are in themselves separate subjects which we cover elsewhere. Numbers 1, 2, and 3, however, represent ideas which may be approached through the general methodology of waiting line models, and hence they will be the focus of our interest in this chapter.

Breakdown-Time Distributions

Breakdown-time distribution data are basic if we hope to be able to formulate any general policies concerning maintenance through the mechanism of waiting line models. The basic data might be gathered in the form of the number of hours or days that machines operate free of breakdowns. This data then could be formed into distributions which show the frequency with which a machine has a given free run time. These distributions take different shapes, depending on the nature of the equipment with which we are dealing. For example, a simple machine with few moving parts would tend to break down at nearly constant intervals following the last repair. That is, they exhibit minimum variability in their distribution of free run times. Curve *a* of Figure 1 would be fairly typical of such a situation. A large percent of the breakdowns occur near the average breakdown time U, and only a few occur at the extremes. Obviously, we are in a rather good position to deal with such a situation, because the relatively small variability in the distribution makes it possible for us to predict with reasonable accuracy when the bulk of breakdowns will occur and, therefore, we can anticipate the breakdown with some preventive maintenance policy.

If a machine is more complex, having many parts, each part has a failure distribution. When all these are grouped together in a single distribution

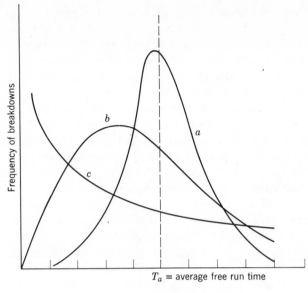

T_a = average free run time

Run time free of breakdowns ──────➤

FIGURE 1. Frequency distributions of run time free of breakdowns representing three degrees of variability in free run time.

of the free run time between breakdowns for any cause, we expect to find greater variability because the machine can break down for any one of a number of reasons. Some breakdowns could occur shortly after the last repair, or any time. Therefore, for the same average breakdown time U, we would find much wider variability of breakdown time as in curve b Figure 1. Curve b has the same average free run time U as does curve a, but the probability of breakdown is more evenly distributed throughout the range.

To complete the picture of representative distributions of free run time, curve c is representative of a distribution with the same average breakdown time U, but with very wide variability. A large proportion of the breakdowns with a distribution such as curve c occur just after repair, and on the other hand, a large proportion have a long free running time. Curve c may be typical of machines that require "ticklish" adjustments. If the adjustments are made just right, the machinery may run for a long time, but if not, readjustment and repair may be necessary almost immediately.

In waiting line models for maintenance, we normally deal with distributions of the percentage of breakdowns that exceed a given run time, such as Figure 2. They are merely transformations of the distributions of free run time typified by those in Figure 1. Taking curve *a* of Figure 1 as an example, we may convert it to the breakdown-time distribution of curve *a* in Figure 2 in the following way. If the vertical scale of Figure 1 is converted to the percentage of breakdowns that occur instead of the frequency of breakdowns, we can then easily plot the percentage of breakdowns that exceed a given run time. First, we know that all the breakdowns, or 100 percent, exceed an average run time of zero. To obtain curve *a* in Figure 2, we simply subtract successively the percentages that occur at different free run times. We can see by examination of Figure 2 that almost 60 percent of the breakdowns exceeded the average breakdown time *U*, and that very few of the breakdowns occurred after $2U$.

In practice, actual breakdown-time distributions can often be approximated by standard distributions, three of which are shown in Figure 2. Curve *b* is actually the negative exponential distribution which we discussed in connection with waiting line theory, corresponding to completely random breakdowns. From this point on, our reference will be to the breakdown-time distributions plotted in Figure 2, recognizing that the basic data for breakdown-time distributions would be accumulated as a distribution of the frequency of free run time as in Figure 1.

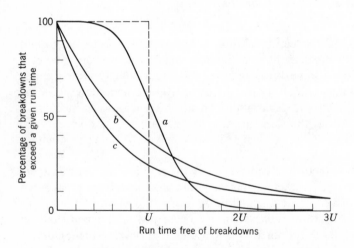

FIGURE 2. *Breakdown time distributions. Curve* a *exhibits low variability from the average breakdown time* U. *Curve* b *is the negative exponential distribution and exhibits medium variability. Curve* c *exhibits high variability, and the dashed line represents a constant breakdown-time. Adapted from P. M. Morse [4].*

Preventive Maintenance versus Repair (Single Machine)

Let us assume a preventive maintenance policy that provides for an inspection and perhaps replacement of certain critical parts after the machine has been running for a fixed time, called the preventive maintenance period. The maintenance crew takes an average time T_m to accomplish the preventive maintenance. This is the preventive maintenance cycle. A certain proportion of the breakdowns will occur before the fixed cycle has been completed, and for these cases the maintenance crew will repair the machine, taking an average time T for the repair. This is the repair cycle. These two patterns of maintenance are diagrammed in Figure 3.

The probability of occurrence of the two different cycles depends on the specific breakdown-time distribution of the machine and the length of the standard preventive maintenance period. If the distribution has low variability and the standard preventive maintenance period is perhaps only 80 percent of the average free run time U, actual breakdown would occur rather infrequently, and most of the cycles would be preventive maintenance cycles. If the distribution were more variable for the same standard preventive maintenance period, more actual breakdowns would occur before the end of the standard period. Shortening the standard preventive maintenance period would obviously result in fewer actual breakdowns, and lengthening it would have the opposite effect for any distribution.

Assuming that either a preventive maintenance or a repair puts the machine in shape for a running time of equal probable length, the percentage of time that the machine is working can be plotted as the ratio of the standard preventive maintenance period and the average run time U for the breakdown-time distribution. Figure 4 shows the relation of the percentage of time that the machine is working and the ratio of the standard period

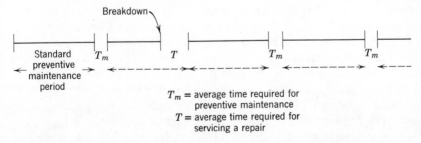

T_m = average time required for preventive maintenance
T = average time required for servicing a repair

FIGURE 3.   Illustrative record of machine run time, preventive maintenance time T$_m$, *and service time for actual repairs* T.

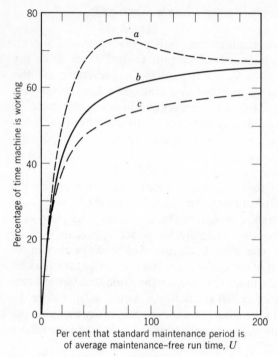

FIGURE 4. *Percentage of time a machine is working for the three distributions of breakdown time shown in Figure 2. Preventive maintenance time* T_m *is 20 percent of* U, *and repair time is 50 percent of* U. *Adapted from P. M. Morse* [4].

to the average run time U for the three distributions of breakdown-times shown in Figure 2.

Note that, in general, when the standard period is short, say less than 50 percent of U, the machine is working only a small fraction of the time. This is because the machine is down so often owing to preventive maintenance. As the standard period is lengthened, more actual breakdowns occur which require repair. For curves b and c this improves the fraction of time the machine is running because the combination of preventive maintenance time and repair time produces a smaller total of downtime.

Curve a, however, has a peak in it, or an optimum preventive maintenance period which maximizes the percentage of machine working time. What is different about curve a? It is based on the low variability breakdown-time distribution from Figure 2. For curve a, lengthening the maintenance period beyond about 70 percent of U reduces the fraction of machine working time because actual machine breakdowns are more likely. For the more variable distributions of curves *b* and *c* this is not true, because breakdowns are more likely throughout their distributions than they are in curve *a*.

Guides to a Preventive Maintenance Policy

Some generalizations about preventive maintenance policy can be made through the concepts which we have developed. First, preventive maintenance is generally applicable to machines with breakdown-time distributions that have low variability, exemplified by curve *a* of Figure 2. In general, distributions with less variability than the negative exponential, curve *b*, are in this category. The reasons are that low variability means that we can predict with fair precision when the majority of breakdowns will occur. A standard preventive maintenance period can then be set which anticipates breakdowns fairly well.

Equally important, however, is the relation of preventive maintenance time to repair time. If it takes just as long to perform a preventive maintenance as it does to repair the machine, there is no advantage in preventive maintenance, which has the effect of reducing the amount of time that the machine can work. Thus if we are attempting to maximize machine running time, the machine spends a minimum amount of time being down for maintenance if we simply wait until it breaks down. This is shown by Figure 5, where we compare the percentage of the time a machine is working when repair time is greater than preventive maintenance time and when the two times are equal. Both curves are based on the low variability distribution of curve *a*, Figure 2. Note that curve *d* exhibits an optimum, but curve *e* does not. For curve *e*, the percentage of time that the machine works continues to increase as the standard maintenance period is lengthened, which results in more repairs and fewer maintenance cycles. Clearly, there is no advantage in preventive maintenance when $T_m = T$ from the point of view of maximum machine working time. To sum up, preventive maintenance can be useful when breakdown-time distributions exhibit low variability and when the average time for preventive maintenance is less than the average time for repair after breakdown.

The effect of downtime costs can modify the conclusions just stated, however, Suppose that we are dealing with a machine in a production line. If the machine breaks down, the entire line may be shut down, with very high idle labor costs resulting. In this situation, preventive maintenance is more desirable than repair *if* the preventive maintenance can take place during second or third shifts, vacations, or lunch hours, when the line is normally down, anyway. This is true even when $T_m \geqslant T$. The determination

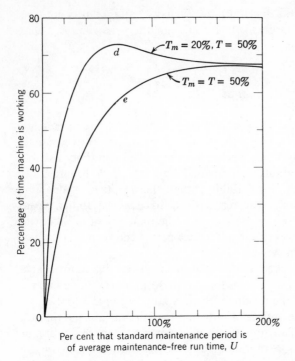

FIGURE 5. *Comparison of percentages of machine working time when preventive maintenance time is less than repair time, curve* d, *and when they are equal, curve* e. *Curve* d *is identical with curve* a, *Figure 4.* T$_m$ *and* T *are expressed as percentages of the average breakdown time* U.

of the standard preventive maintenance period would require a different, but similar, analysis in which the percentage of machine working time was expressed as a function of repair time only, since preventive maintenance takes place outside of normal work time. An optimal solution would be one that minimized the total of downtime costs, preventive maintenance costs plus repair costs. The effect of the downtime costs would be to justify shorter standard preventive maintenance periods and to justify making repairs more quickly (at higher cost) when they do occur. There are many situations, however, where extra manpower on a repair job would not speed it up. In such cases, total repair time might be shortened by overtime on multiple shifts and weekends, with attendant higher costs. Optimal solutions would specify the standard preventive maintenance period, the machine idle time, and the repair crew idle time, which strike a balance between downtime costs and maintenance costs.

A special case exists when sales are such that the plant must operate at full capacity to meet demand. Under these circumstances, reduced machine working time due to repair and preventive maintenance reduces the number of units which can be sold and, therefore, affects income. Optimal maintenance policy is then even more heavily weighted in favor of shortening standard preventive maintenance periods and pouring in more effort to repair machines quickly when breakdowns occur. Morse [(4), pp. 165–166] has developed basic models that fit this special case in which an income-less-maintenance cost function is maximized.

Maintaining Several Machines (Single Repair Crew)

The single machine situation that we have been discussing contains basic elements of general policy which can be carried over into the multimachine case. When several machines must be serviced, however, our problem more closely resembles the usual finite waiting line model. If we assume that all the machines have the same breakdown-time distribution, breakdowns are comparable to arrivals in the finite waiting line model, and the repair crew is the service station. As machines break down, the crew services them in the average time T as before. If the crew is already working on a machine, successive machines that break down must wait for service, and the costs associated with downtime will grow with the delay. We can reduce the chance that this will happen by increasing the size of the crew in some instances, but this solution also costs money and will increase the cost of crew idle time, waiting for breakdowns to occur. The problem, then, is one of striking a balance between the downtime costs of the machines and the idle time costs of the maintenance crew as before.

When the breakdown times and the repair times follow the exponential distribution, we may use the *Finite Queuing Tables* [5] to obtain solutions to a wide variety of specific problems. Figures 6, 7, and 8 show data computed from the *Finite Queuing Tables* for 4, 6, 8, 10, and 15 machines.

The curves for Figures 6, 7, and 8 give the percent of machines running, the percent of time that the repair crew is busy, and a factor related to the waiting time, all plotted in relation to the service factor X, as defined for use in the *Finite Queuing Tables*. Recall that the service factor is $X = T/(T + U)$, where T is the average time for service and U is the average free run time. We could compute from Figure 6, for example, the average output expected from a given bank of machines and a given service factor. Figure 7 gives directly the percent of time that the repair crew is busy for a given service factor. For example, if $X = 0.1$, then from Figure 8, $W_q(X/T) = 0.125$ for eight machines. If $T = 1$ hour, then $W_q = 0.125 \times$

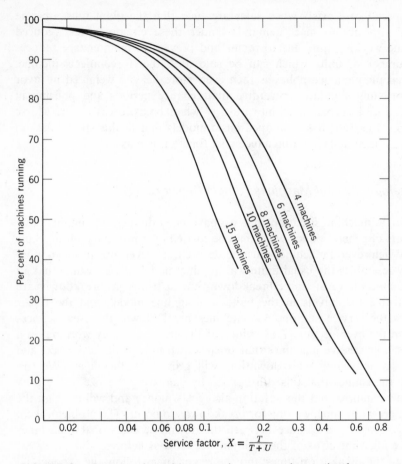

FIGURE 6. *Percent of machines running versus the service factor.*

$1/0.1 = 1.25$ hours. If T were expressed in working days, then W_q is waiting time in working days.

Multiple Machines—Multiple Repair Crews

The multiple machine–multiple repair crew case is, of course, simply an extension of the single repair crew case. Figures 9, 10, and 11 present data on the average number of machines in running order, the percent of time that the repair crew is busy, and a factor related to the waiting time, plotted in relation to the service factor for different numbers of machines

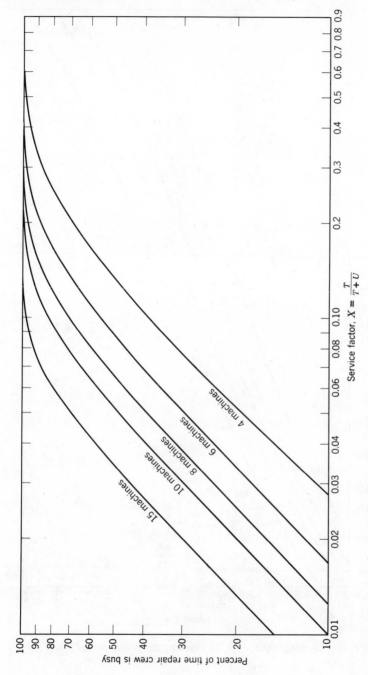

FIGURE 7. Percent of time repair crew is busy versus the service factor.

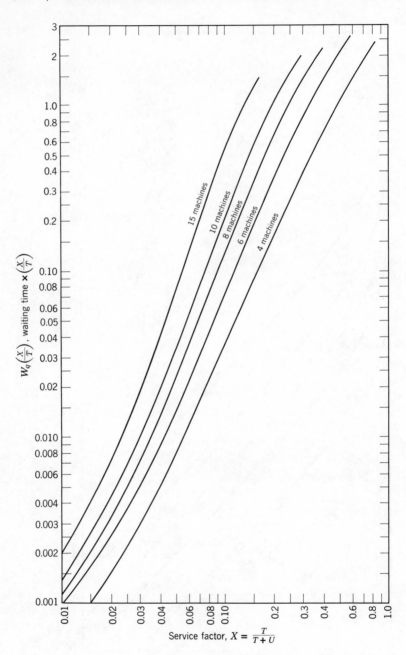

FIGURE 8. Waiting time × (X/T) versus the service factor.

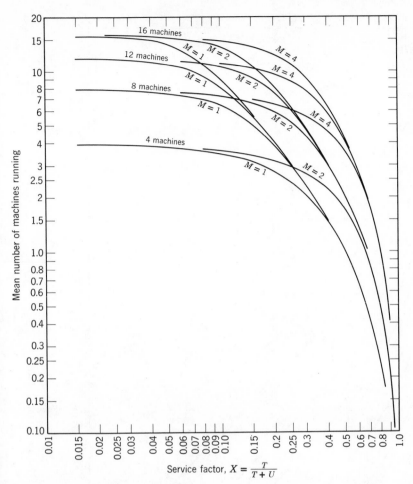

FIGURE 9. *Mean number of machines running versus the service factor for different numbers of machines and repair crews,* M.

and repair crews. Again, these charts will allow us to make calculations for specific cases.

Interpretation of the charts requires some care. For example, what would be the effect on the mean number of machines in running order, and on the combined waiting plus maintenance time, if one large repair crew could service a machine in half the time of two separate but smaller repair crews working independently? If we assume sixteen machines to be maintained, with an average negative exponential breakdown time of

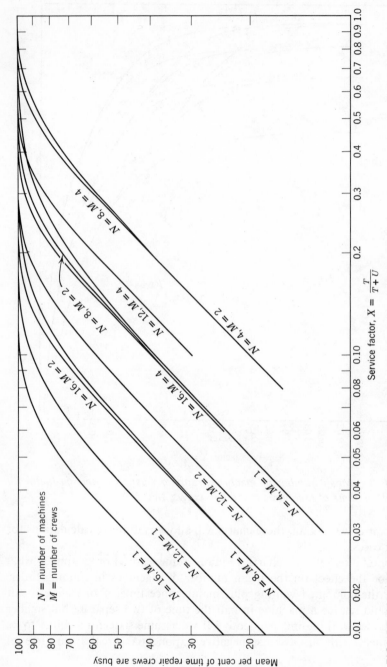

FIGURE 10. *Mean percent of time repair crews are busy versus the service factor for different numbers of machines and repair crews.*

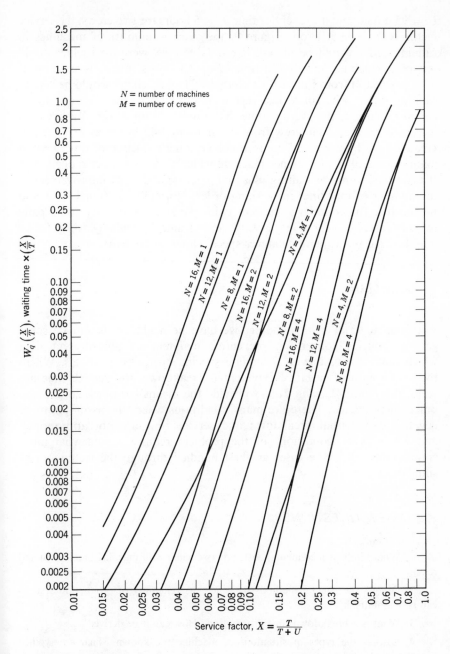

FIGURE 11. Waiting time × (X/T) versus the service factor for different numbers of machines and repair crews.

$U = 95$ hours, and if the service time $T = 5$ hours for two crews, the service factor is $X = 0.05$. From Figure 9, the average number of machines in running order would be fifteen. If one large crew were used which could service a machine in half the time, $T = 2.5$ hours, the service factor is $X = 0.026$, and from Figure 9 an average of 15.4 machines would be kept in running order. The single fast repair crew is better than the two slower crews. Of course, the average time that a machine must wait for service is increased by the single crew from 0.7 hour to 1.42 hours as may be calculated from Figure 11. There is, however, a net reduction of time spent in maintenance of 2.5 hours per machine which results in a net reduction in the combined time of waiting plus maintenance and a net improvement in the number of machines in working order. Normally, of course, it would not be true that one large crew of twice the size could carry out repairs twice as fast; however, Figures 9, 10, and 11 and the *Finite Queuing Tables* may be used to evaluate whatever specific alternatives exist.

SUMMARY

With the material in this chapter we have been able to formulate some general policies concerning preventive maintenance and present data which make it possible to formulate specific operational models. Where the assumption of negative exponential breakdown and service time are valid, the *Finite Queuing Tables* provide the means for quick solution to practical problems. There are many conditions where the assumptions of negative exponential breakdown and service time are not appropriate, and where other conditions of the problem require a somewhat more complex model. These cases are best handled through the techniques of simulation.

REVIEW QUESTIONS

1. What kinds of incremental costs are associated with machine breakdown and repair?

2. Discuss the general methods by which the reliability of production systems can be maintained.

3. What is a breakdown-time distribution? How can it be derived?

4. Discuss the types of situations of machine breakdown which are typified by curves *a*, *b*, and *c*, respectively, in Figure 2.

5. What are the general conditions for which preventive maintenance is appropriate for a *single* machine?

6. If it takes just as long to perform a preventive maintenance as it does a repair, is there any advantage to preventive maintenance? How can high downtime costs modify this? What is the effect if preventive maintenance can be achieved during off hours when the machine is normally not working?

7. Compare the problem of maintaining a bank of machines to the general waiting line model.

8. What would be the effect on the mean number of machines in running order, and on the combined waiting plus maintenance time, if one large repair crew could service a machine in half the time of two separate but smaller repair crews working independently, assuming the multiple machine case?

PROBLEMS

1. A group of twenty machines is serviced by 6 repairmen. Breakdown and service rates follow the Poisson distribution. The average breakdown rate is 3 per 8-hour shift for each machine, and the mean repair time is 1½ hours.
   a. Determine the average number of machines running.
   b. Determine the average waiting time of a machine.
   c. What is the probability that a repairman will be immediately available when a machine breaks down?
   d. What is the cost per shift of repairman idle time? (Repairman average earnings = $3.50 per hour.)

2. A lathe department with 8 machines has mean Poisson process breakdown for each machine and repair rates of 2.4 and 8.7 per 8-hour shift respectively.
   a. From Figure 6, determine the percent of machines running.
   b. From Figure 7, determine the percent of time the repair crew is busy.
   c. From Figure 8, determine the average waiting time.
   d. What is the average number of machines waiting for service?

3. An automatic screw machine department has 16 machines. Service is required on these machines at random as approximated by the Poisson distribution. The distribution of service times follows the negative exponential. The mean number of calls for service is 3 per hour for each machine. The mean service time is 2.8 minutes per call.
   a. From Figure 9, determine the average number of machines running for 1, 2, and 4 operators.
   b. From Figure 10, determine the percent of time the operators are busy for 1, 2, and 4 operators.
   c. From Figure 11, determine the average amount of waiting time for 1, 2, and 4 operators.

4. A milling machine department has 10 machines. Breakdowns follow a Poisson process and average 0.4 per 8-hour shift for each machine. The service rate is 2.1 per 8-hour shift and also follows the Poisson process. Repairmen are paid $4.50 per hour and work individually. Machine downtime is estimated to cost $7.00 per hour. What is the optimal number of repairmen for this department?

5. A steel rolling mill is operated 24 hours a day by a crew of 30 men with the following cost structure:

Average hourly wage	$4.00 per hour
Fringe benefits	10 percent of labor cost
Fuel expense (not stopped for short periods)	$50.00 per hour
Power expense	$15.00 her hour
Heat and lights expense	$5.00 per hour
Water expense	$0.50 per hour
Expendable tools expense	$1.50 per hour
Depreciation expense	$8.00 per hour
Factory burden	$200.00 per hour

The breakdown rate follows the Poisson process and is 2 per hour. The distribution of repair times is approximated by the negative exponential; the mean service rate is 5 minutes if done by one repairman and varies inversely with the number of repairmen. Repairmen are paid $10 per hour (including fringe benefits).

a. Determine the optimal number of repairmen for this rolling mill.

b. What proportion of the time will repairman be idle?

c. What would be the effect of assigning some value to fill-in work done by repairmen in their idle time?

6. A group of thirty machines has Poisson process breakdown rates of 2 per hour for each machine and a Poisson process service rate of 10 per hour. If preventive maintenance is done on these machines at night while they are idle, the daytime breakdown rates can be reduced by 40 percent. The cost of downtime is estimated to be $8 per hour, and capable repairmen are paid $5 per hour. The cost of second-shift preventive maintenance is estimated to be $500 per week. What cost advantage or disadvantage would be realized by adopting this plan? (5-day, 40-hour week.)

7. A group of twenty machines has Poisson process breakdown rates of three per hour for each machine and a Poisson service rate of 20 per hour. Management is considering the installation of a system of preventive maintenance. It is believed that by instituting various levels of preventive maintenance, breakdown rates can be decreased. To do this, however, repair time and the cost of repair parts will necessarily increase because of parts being replaced before they are completely worn out. After a study of maintenance records and machine design, the following estimates of various preventive maintenance levels have been prepared:

Level	Breakdown Rate	Service Time	Repair Parts
L_1	−30%	+20%	+50%
L_2	−40%	+35%	+80%
L_3	−50%	+75%	+120%

Downtime is estimated to cost $9 per hour. Capable repairmen are paid $6 per hour.

Present repair part cost averages $1 per breakdown. Determine the optimal number of repairmen and preventive maintenance level.

8. At a building materials yard trucks are loaded with a payloader-type tractor. Because of the varying travel distances, the distribution of truck loading time follows the negative exponential distribution. The truck arrival rate follows a Poisson process. The mean service time is 6 minutes, and the arrival rate is 8 per hour. The waiting time per hour for a truck and driver is estimated to be $10. How much could the company afford to pay per day for an overhead hopper system that could fill any truck in 2 minutes? (Assume that the present tractor could adequately service the conveyors loading the hoppers.)

REFERENCES

1. Barlow, R., and L. Hunter, "Optimum Preventive Maintenance Policies, *Operations Research*, Vol. 8, pp. 90–100, 1960.
2. Bovaird, R. L., "Characteristics of Optimal Maintenance Policies," *Management Science*, Vol. 7, No. 3, pp. 238–254, April 1961.
3. Fetter, R. B., "The Assignment of Operators to Service Automatic Machines," *Journal of Industrial Engineering*, September–October 1955, pp. 22–29.
4. Morse, P. M., *Queues, Inventories, and Maintenance*, John Wiley & Sons, New York, 1958.
5. Peck, L. G., and R. N. Hazelwood, *Finite Queuing Tables*, John Wiley & Sons, New York, 1958.
6. Weiss, G. H., "A Problem in Equipment Maintenance," *Management Science*, Vol. 8, No. 3, pp. 266–278, April 1962.

chapter 16

SIMULATION MODELS

Simulation models of operations systems have been growing
rapidly and promise to become a dominant technique for
assisting management in the decision-making process for day-to-
day problems, as well as for comparing basic alternatives of
operating policy. With simulation models, we can determine
the effects of dozens of alternate policies without tampering
with the actual physical system. The result is that we do not
risk upsetting the existing system without prior assurance that
the changes contemplated will be beneficial. In a very real sense
then, the common reference to simulation as management's
laboratory is true.

Business and industry have already made important applications of the simulation technique, ranging from models of
relatively simple waiting line situations, to models of integrated
systems of production. For example, Warren Alberts of United
Air Lines reports a model of an airline maintenance facility in
which 100 days of operation are simulated [23]. Brown discusses
a general purpose inventory controls simulator [23]. The
simulator makes it possible to evaluate customer service, the
number of orders placed, the production workload, and the
total investment for the comparison of alternate systems of
control. Feorene of Eastman Kodak Company has published
reports of a machine maintenance simulation which makes it
possible to determine the optimum number of maintenance
mechanics for various conditions [10]. When Rowe was with
the General Electric Company, he developed a job shop

simulator and used it for evaluating alternate dispatch decision rules [25]. Forrester has developed dynamic simulation models of the Sprague Electric Company production-distribution system which show time-varying effects of changing market conditions and various alternate policies [11]. Another important branch of applications of simulation has been in the development of management games. In management simulation games, the characteristics of a business, or some subsystem of a business are simulated. Individuals or teams then give the model inputs in the form of key decisions, and they determine the effects of these decisions through the simulation model. Through this gaming technique, years of decision-making experience can be collapsed into a few hours.

In general, simulation is useful in situations where mathematical analysis is either too complex or too costly. If a particular type of problem can be shown to be well represented by a mathematical model, the analytical approach will ordinarily be somewhat cheaper to follow. Quite often, however, we find situations where the problem faced is incredibly complex, because of a maze of interacting variables, or where the problem itself may be relatively simple in structure, but involves a projection of mathematical analysis into unknown areas. An example of the latter would be a simple waiting line model where the nature of the distributions of arrivals for service times does not fit the standard ones for which analytical solutions have been worked out. In such situations, we might spend a great deal of time attempting to work out a mathematical analysis for the specific empirical distribution, or may fail in this attempt. To simulate the unique problem, however, would be relatively simple.

A simulation model may be constructed which represents the essential features of the system under study. Then, by "driving" the simulation model with input data, we may observe the reactions of the system components and of the system output. As with any model, the ultimate value of the simulation model is determined by how well it predicts behavior of the system under study. One of the advantages of simulation models, however, is their relative flexibility in adaptation to the requirements of the real system. Simulation, then, often provides a bypass for difficult or impossible mathematical analysis. For the complex problems to which we have referred, simulation is by no means a cheap mode of analysis. It does, however, provide an approach to many problems which could not be attacked by other known techniques.

In our discussion we first introduce Monte Carlo methods that make it possible to introduce statistical variation into simulation models. This also serves to introduce the general concepts of simulation modeling. A number of applications are discussed in this chapter to illustrate Monte Carlo methods as well as the general simulation technique. In Chapter 21 we consider large-scale system simulation for both static and dynamic situations. These larger-scale models may or may not require Monte Carlo techniques. They are simply larger in scale, more complex, and in the case of dynamic models, have some special features of considerable interest for operations management. In Chapter 17, we discuss job shop scheduling research which has been very largely based on simulation. These sequencing models have been useful in providing a testing ground for priority dispatch rules and for developing and testing practical means for sequencing operations on production lines. The great complexity of these kinds of problems makes simulation the logical mode of analysis. Furthermore, the job shop planning and control systems discussed in Chapter 17 involve simulation of the shop as an operating part of the system.

SIMULATED SAMPLING /

Simulated sampling, known generally as Monte Carlo, makes it possible to introduce data into a system which have the statistical properties of some empirical or other distribution. If the model involves the flow of orders according to the actual demand distribution experienced, we can simulate the "arrival" of an order by Monte Carlo sampling from the actual distribution, so that the timing and flow of orders in the simulated system parallels the actual experience. If we are studying the breakdown of a certain machine due to bearing failure, we can simulate typical breakdown times through simulated sampling from the distribution of bearing lives. Let us take an example to illustrate how simulated sampling is achieved.

Suppose we are dealing with the maintenance of a bank of thirty machines, and, initially, we wish to estimate what level of service can be maintained by one mechanic. We can see that we have the elements of a waiting-line situation, with machine breakdowns representing arrivals, the mechanic being the service facility, and repair time representing service or processing time. Of course, if the distributions of breakdown and service times followed the negative exponential, the simplest procedure would be to use the formulas and calculate the average time that a machine waits, the mechanic's idle time, etc. We can see by inspection of Figures 1 and 2 that the distributions are not similar to the negative exponential, so that we decide to simulate. Our procedure is as follows:

1. *Determine the distributions of time between breakdowns and service time.* If they were not available directly, we would have to make a study to determine these distributions, or, hopefully, records of the breakdown

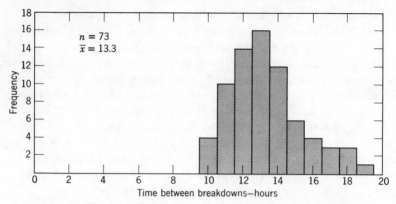

FIGURE 1. Frequency distribution of the time between breakdowns for 30 machines.

and repair of machines may be available from which the distributions may be constructed. Figures 1 and 2 show the distributions of breakdowns and repair times for 73 breakdowns, and will be the basis for our simulation.

2. *Convert the frequency distributions to cumulative probability distributions* (*see Figures 3 and 4*). This conversion is accomplished by summing the frequencies that are less than or equal to each breakdown or repair time and plotting them. The cumulative frequencies are then converted to percents by assigning the number 100 to the maximum value. As an example, let us take Figure 1 and convert it to the cumulative distribution of Figure 3. Beginning at the lowest value for breakdown time, 10 hours, there are four occurrences. Four is plotted on the cumulative chart for the break-

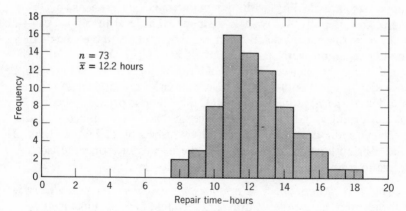

FIGURE 2. Frequency distribution of the repair time for 73 breakdowns.

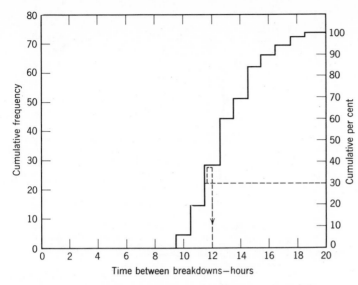

FIGURE 3. *Cumulative distribution of breakdown times.*

down time, 10 hours. For the breakdown time, 11 hours, there were 10 occurrences, but there were 14 occurrences of 11 hours or less, so the value 14 is plotted for 11 hours. For the breakdown time, 12 hours, there were 14 occurrences recorded, but there were 28 occurrences of breakdowns for 12 hours or less.

Figure 3 was constructed from Figure 1 by proceeding in this way. When the cumulative frequency distribution was completed, a cumulative percent scale was constructed on the right of Figure 3 by assigning the number 100 to the maximum value, 73, and dividing the resulting scale into 10 equal parts. This results in a cumulative empirical probability distribution. From Figure 3 we can say that 100 percent of the breakdown time values were 19 hours or less; 99 percent were 18 hours or less, etc. Figure 4 was constructed from Figure 2 in a comparable way.

3. *Sample at random from the cumulative distributions to determine specific breakdown times and repair times to use in simulating the repair operation.* We do this by selecting numbers between 0 and 100 at random (representing probabilities in percent). The random numbers could be selected by any random process, such as drawing numbered chips from a box. The easiest way is to use a table of random numbers, such as those included in Table IV of the Appendix. (Pick a starting point in the table at random and take two-digit numbers in sequence in that column, for example.)

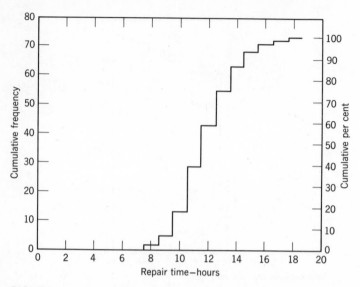

FIGURE 4. Cumulative distribution of repair times.

The random numbers were used to enter the cumulative distributions to obtain time values. An example is shown in Figure 3. The random number 30 is shown to select for us a breakdown time of 12 hours. We can now see the purpose behind the conversion of the original distribution to a cumulative distribution. Only one breakdown time can now be associated with a given random number. In the original distribution, two values would result because of the bell shape of the curve. By using random numbers to obtain breakdown time values in this fashion from Figure 3, we will obtain breakdown time values in proportion to the probability of occurrence indicated by the original frequency distribution. As a matter of fact, at this point we can construct a table of random numbers that select certain breakdown times. For example, reading from Figure 3, the random numbers 6 through 19 give us a breakdown time of 11 hours, etc. This is the same as saying that 5 percent of the time we would obtain a value of 10 hours, 14 percent of the time we would obtain a breakdown time of 11 hours, etc. Table I shows the random number equivalents for Figures 3 and 4.

Sampling from either the cumulative distributions of Figures 3 and 4 or from Table I will now give breakdown times and repair times in proportion to the original distributions, just as if actual breakdowns and repairs were happening. Table II gives a sample of 20 breakdown and repair times determined in this way.

TABLE I.   Random numbers used to draw breakdown times and repair times in proportion to the occurrence probabilities of the original distributions

Breakdown Times		Repair Times	
These Random Numbers ⟶	Select These Breakdown Times	These Random Numbers ⟶	Select These Repair Times
1–5	10 hours	1–3	8 hours
6–19	11	4–7	9
20–38	12	8–18	10
39–60	13	19–40	11
61–77	14	41–59	12
78–85	15	60–75	13
86–90	16	76–86	14
91–95	17	87–93	15
96–99	18	94–97	16
100	19	98–99	17
		100	18

4. *Simulate the actual operation of breakdowns and repairs.* The structure of what we wish to do in simulating the repair operation is shown by the flow chart of Figure 5. This operation involves the selection of a breakdown time and determining whether or not the mechanic is available. If the mechanic is not available, the machine must wait until he is, and we may compute that wait time easily. If the mechanic is available, the question is, did the mechanic have to wait? If he did, we compute the mechanic's idle time. If the mechanic did not have to wait, we select a repair time and proceed according to the flow chart, repeating the overall process as many times as desired, providing a mechanism for stopping the procedure when the desired number of cycles has been completed.

The simulation of the repair operations is shown in Table III. Here we have used the breakdown times and repair times selected by random numbers in Table II. We assume that time begins when the first machine breaks down and cumulate breakdown time from that point. The repair time required for the first breakdown was 15 hours, and since this is the first occurrence in our record, neither the machine nor the mechanic had to wait. The second breakdown occurred at 18 hours, but the mechanic was available at the end of 15 hours, so he waited 3 hours for the next breakdown to occur.

We proceed in this fashion, adding and subtracting, according to the requirements of the simulation model to obtain the record of Table III.

TABLE II. Simulated sample of twenty breakdown and repair times

Breakdown Times		Repair Times	
Random Number	Breakdown Time from Figure 3	Random Number	Repair Time from Figure 4
83	15	91	15
97	18	4	9
88	16	72	13
12	11	12	10
22	12	30	11
16	11	32	11
24	12	91	15
64	14	29	11
37	12	33	11
62	14	8	10
52	13	25	11
9	11	74	13
64	14	97	16
74	14	70	13
15	11	15	10
47	13	43	12
86	16	42	12
79	15	25	11
43	13	71	13
35	12	14	10

The summary at the bottom of Table III shows that for the sample of twenty breakdowns, total machine waiting time was 11 hours, and total mechanic's idle time was 26 hours. To obtain a realistic picture we would have to use a much larger sample. Using the same data on breakdown time and repair time distributions, 1000 runs using a computer yielded 15.9 percent machine wait time and 7.6 percent mechanic's idle time. Of course the mechanic is presumably paid for an 8 hour day regardless of the division between idle and service time; however, knowing idle time available may be a guide to the assignment of "fill-in" work.

If a computer were programmed to simulate the repair operation, we would place the two cumulative distributions in the memory unit of the computer. Through the program, the computer would generate a random number and thereby select a breakdown time. By comparing cumulative breakdown time with cumulative mechanic's time, the computer could

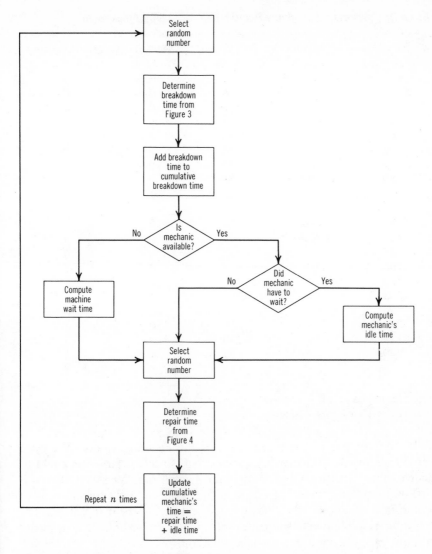

FIGURE 5. Flow chart showing structure of repair simulation.

determine whether or not the mechanic was available, and if he was available, whether or not he had to wait. The computations of machine wait time, or mechanic's idle time, would be routinely made, and the computer would be directed to select another random number, thereby determining a repair time. The other necessary computations could then be

TABLE III.   Simulated breakdown and repair for twenty breakdowns

Time of Breakdown	Time Repair Begins	Time Repair Ends	Machine Wait Time	Repair Mechanics Idle Time
0	0	15	0	0
18	18	27	0	3
34	34	47	0	7
45	47	57	2	0
57	57	68	0	0
68	68	79	0	0
80	80	95	0	1
94	95	106	1	0
106	106	117	0	0
120	120	130	0	3
133	133	144	0	3
144	144	157	0	0
158	158	174	0	1
172	174	187	2	0
183	187	197	4	0
196	197	209	1	0
212	212	224	0	3
227	227	238	0	3
240	240	253	0	2
252	253	263	1	0

Total machine wait time = 11 hours
Total mechanic's idle time = 26 hours

made, the computer holding in memory the resulting values. The cycle would then repeat as many times as directed, so that a large run could be made easily and with no more effort than a small run. When a computer is used the simulation model can become very realistic, reflecting all sorts of contingency situations which may be representative of the real problem. The following example of the simulation of optimal repair crew sizes is meant to show an application in a realistic situation.

EXAMPLES OF SIMULATION /

Simulation of Optimal Repair Crew Size

Feorene [10] reports a study made at the Eastman Kodak Company of the size of repair crews. A group of twenty automatic machines were being maintained by a crew of six mechanics. Production forecasts indicated the need for two more machines to meet capacity needs, and this raised the question of whether or not the size of the repair crew should be enlarged. The basic structure of the simulation is parallel to the simple one presented previously; however, a new variable has been added, the number of mechanics. We will note that the specific conditions in effect are reflected in the data used and in the structure of the simulation model.

After careful study, the following data were gathered from the maintenance and down-time records available in the production department:

1. A breakdown-time distribution which showed the length of time that the machines would run before requiring service. Of course, this distribution determines the "arrivals" to the maintenance system. Figure 6 shows the breakdown-time distribution, and in this instance, the distribution happens to follow the negative exponential quite closely.

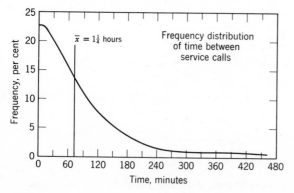

FIGURE 6. Breakdown time distribution for a bank of automatic machines. Figures 6–16 are adapted from O. J. Feorene [10].

2. An analysis of records showed that two-thirds of the time, the machines could be serviced while they were operating and continuing to produce. The other third of the time, the machine had to be shut down while the repairs and adjustments were made. In this latter instance, the mechanic remained at the machine after it was functioning again in order to make final adjustments.

3. A distribution of the service time required when the machine was down, being serviced by the mechanic. This distribution is shown in Figure 7.

4. A distribution of the time spent by the mechanic with the machine after it had been started again, in order to make final adjustments

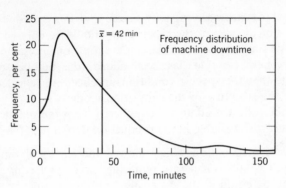

FIGURE 7.   Service-time distribution for downtime calls.

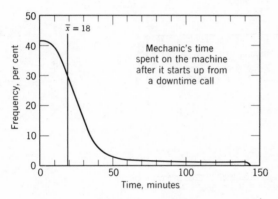

FIGURE 8.   Run-in time distribution, the time spent by the mechanic after the machine starts up from a downtime call.

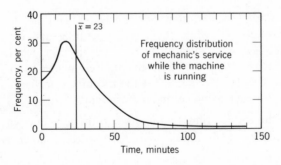

FIGURE 9.   Service-time distribution for run calls.

and insure that it was ready for service. This is the mechanic's "run-in" time and is shown in Figure 8.

5. A distribution of the mechanic's service time in those instances in which the machine could be serviced while it was still operating (Figure 9). This is the mechanic's service time for the run-calls which represent 67 percent of the cases.

The Simulation. Figure 10 shows the structure of the simulation model used. Note the five places in the model where Monte Carlo methods of sampling from the empirical distributions were involved.

The simulation model was programmed for a computer and simulation runs were made for different levels of production (that is, number of machines in operation), each time computing costs for different numbers of mechanics servicing the system. The incremental costs were those associated with machine down-time and maintenance labor cost. One of the curves for twenty-two machines available is shown in Figure 11, and we note that even with the two additional machines, the minimum cost is achieved with only four mechanics instead of the six used prior to the study. Note, however, that if five mechanics are employed and one is absent the cost goes down *slightly*, but if four are employed and one is absent the cost goes up *sharply*. The recommendations indicated by simulation were installed, and the results vindicated the model. Obviously, the study represented an immediate net gain for the company, and in addition provided a model which could be used again to evaluate future projected loads.

Simulation of a Mixed Chemicals Distribution System

Another application carried out at Eastman Kodak Company [10] involved a department that mixed chemicals for use in two general locations in nearby buildings. The general pattern was that orders were placed with the mixed chemicals department by the using departments, ordinarily to be delivered within 1 hour because of close scheduling of a series of operations in the using departments. A marshaling area was set aside in the mixed chemicals department for hand trucks loaded with filled orders waiting for call from the using departments. Although the using department had placed an order for a specific time, there was considerable variation from the order time in the actual call time, as we shall see. After being called for, the order was delivered to the using department by means of the hand truck, so that the truck was unavailable for an additional period of time before it was returned to the mixed chemicals department for reuse. This trucking time also had considerable variation and was different for

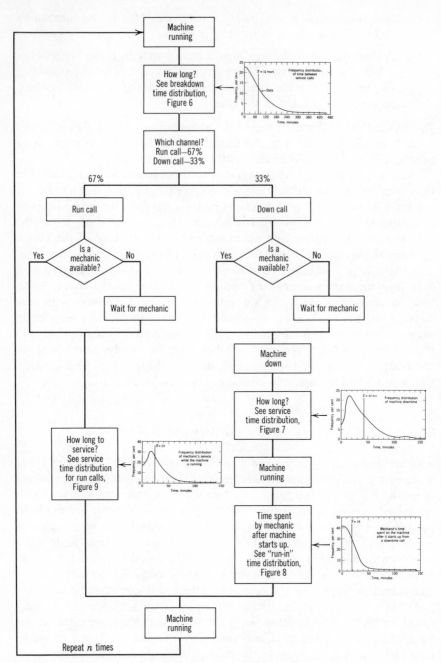

FIGURE 10. Structure of simulation model for the determination of optimal repair crew size.

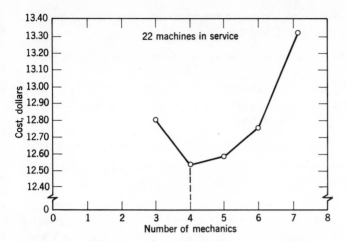

FIGURE 11.   *Curve of cost versus number of mechanics in repair crew for 22 machines in service.*

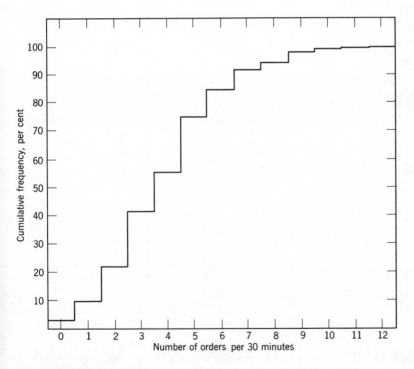

FIGURE 12.   *Cumulative order distribution for mixed chemicals.*

the two using departments. At any given moment, there were as many as thirty-three hand trucks in the system.

The Problem. A projected increase in production requirements seemed to indicate the need for additional trucks as well as an increase in the size of the marshaling area. Considerable congestion had already developed with the existing system. The real question which evolved was, how many trucks are necessary to operate the system?

The Simulation. To simulate the system, the following data were gathered:

1. A distribution of the order rates. Figure 12 shows a cumulative distribution of the number of orders placed per 30-minute interval.
2. The distribution of order-call time. Figure 13 shows a cumulative distribution of call times, indicating that orders might be called for as much as 1½ hours before the order time, or as much as 3 hours after the order time.

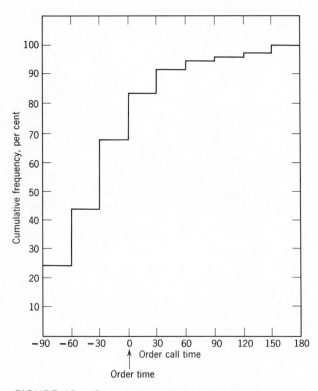

FIGURE 13. Cumulative call-time distribution.

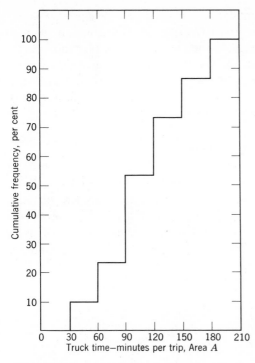

FIGURE 14. Cumulative truck-time distribution for Area A.

3. The truck destinations. An analysis of truck destinations revealed that 58 percent of the orders were for area A and 42 percent for area B.

4. A distribution of the time spent for a round trip by trucks with orders going to each of the two using departments. Figures 14 and 15 show cumulative distributions of truck time for areas A and B respectively.

The system was then simulated for various numbers of trucks available. Figure 16 shows the simple structure of the simulation. Simulated sampling takes place at five points in the system: the determination of orders from Figure 12, the determination of the destination of orders, the determination of call time from Figure 13, and the determination of truck times from either Figure 14 or 15, depending on destination. In simulating the operation of the system, it is necessary to work trucks through the system, depending on order rates, destinations, call times, and truck times, so that we may keep track of the number of trucks being used and the number of trucks available for use. The simulation indicated that the existing production level could be met with twenty-four trucks in the system, nine less than the original figure. This reduction in the number of trucks eliminated the congestion in the aisles and marshaling area, and eliminated the need for an expansion of the marshaling area which was originally thought to be necessary. Also, the model could be used to estimate needs for other production levels if conditions were to change.

Simulation of Steel-Making Operations

A somewhat more complex model is illustrated by the simulation of six open-hearth furnaces and related operations by the steel company of Wales Limited, as reported by Neate and Dacey [22]. The simulation study was initiated following a trial carried out on one open-hearth furnace using the new technique of enriching preheated combustion air with oxygen during the charging period. The analysis for the trial period had shown that the

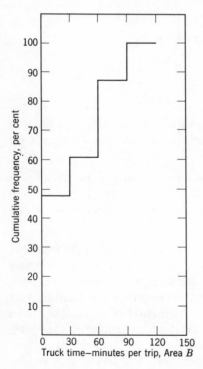

FIGURE 15. Cumulative truck-time distribution for Area B.

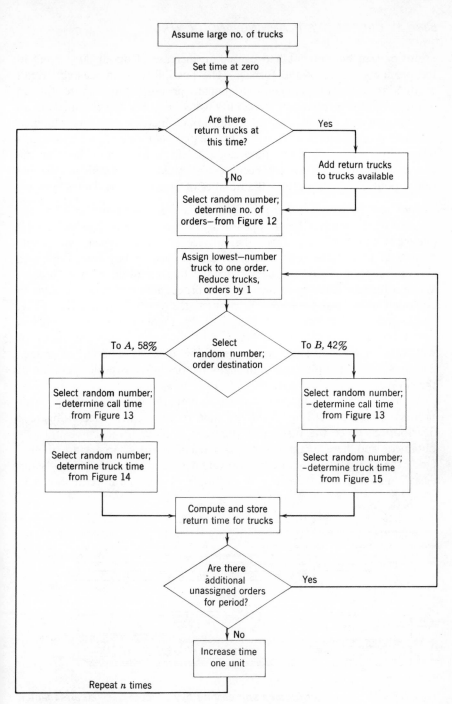

FIGURE 16.   Structure of mixed chemicals simulation.

use of oxygen enrichment had caused an increase of about 20 percent in the production rate of the furnace. The possibility of increasing overall production by using oxygen enrichment prompted the desire for an estimate of the production capability when using the technique on all furnaces. It was unlikely that a proportionate increase could be obtained because of the limitations imposed by ancillary equipment and by congestion delays. As we shall see, there is considerable interaction between the operation of the six furnaces because of limited crane facilities, teeming (ingot pouring) facilities, and the number of unpredictable delays.

Layout and Process. Figure 17 shows the general layout of the area covered by the study. The six open-hearth furnaces are charged with solid materials and hot metal from the furnace bay, are tapped, and ingots poured at one of the four platforms on the casting bay side. Figure 18 shows a simplified flow process chart for the operation of one furnace. When a furnace is ready to tap, the first procedure is to obtain a crane to position the ladle and remove the molten steel when tapping is complete. At this point, there may be a delay if the available cranes are already in use in connection with other furnaces, with the pouring of ingot molds, or with other activities. The occurrence of this delay is random, of course, and depends on the interaction of many factors in the overall operation of the shop.

After the furnace is tapped, it must be prepared for a new charge. This process is called "fettling," and the time required varies according to a distribution. Once the furnace is prepared, a charging machine must be obtained, and here again a delay can occur if the chargers are in use. Once the charger is obtained, however, a second delay called a "scrap delay" may occur if there is not an ample supply of full-scrap boxes in

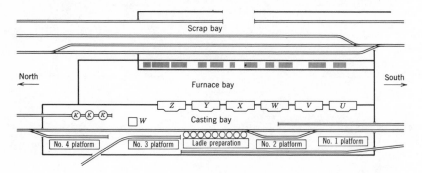

FIGURE 17.   Layout of furnace and casting bays. Figures 17–20 are adapted from R. Neate and W. J. Dacey [22].

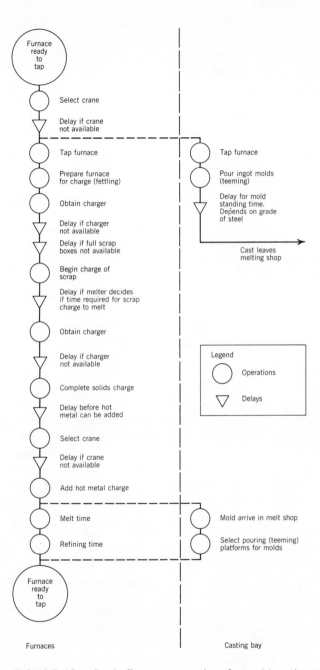

FIGURE 18. Basic flow process chart for melting shop operations.

position. If scrap material is available, however, the charging process begins. If after a period of charging and before the solids charge is complete, the melter considers it undesirable to add any more scrap to the furnace, there is an "assimilation delay" during which the furnace digests the scrap already charged into it. Following the assimilation delay, it may be that a charger is again unavailable, in which case a second charger delay may occur. The charge of solid material is then completed. A delay dictated by the process now occurs before hot metal can be added. When the time arrives for the addition of hot metal, a crane must be obtained, and a second crane delay may occur. The hot metal is then added to the furnace, and the steel-making process continues through a melt time and a refining time, both of which are variable. At the end of the refining time, the furnace is again ready to tap.

During the operations of the furnace just described, the casting bay and its associated equipment are used at two different times. First, the furnace is tapped into a large ladle, and this ladle is moved to one of the teeming platforms to pour ingot molds. These molds stand on the platform for a period of time, depending on the grade of steel, and finally the entire cast is moved out of the melting shop. Second, prior to the time of tapping, empty molds are brought into the shop and placed in one of the four platform positions.

Simulation. To simulate the operation of the melting shop, it is necessary to take account of all of the furnace times which are variable through the Monte Carlo sampling process. Looking at the simulation flow chart of Figure 19, these Monte Carlo samplings occur when determining fettle times, melt times, and refine times. The delays in the system are computed internally within the simulation model. A 5-minute time unit was adopted for the model, and the basic simulation flow chart revolves around two questions which are asked in sequence at each 5-minute interval. The first question is, "Is there a furnace ready to tap?" If there is, the sequence of simulated operations of crane selection, furnace tapping, and fettling must be accounted for. If there is no furnace ready to tap, the second question is, "Is there a furnace ready to charge?" If there is a furnace ready to charge, the entire sequence of simulated operations following must be accounted for, computing the delays if they are appropriate, adding in the fixed and simulated sampled times as required to update furnace time for the particular furnace which is being charged. If the answer to the second question is no, the system updates all six furnace times by the next 5-minute interval and asks the two questions again. The procedure is repeated the desired number of times through the computer program and stopped automatically when completed.

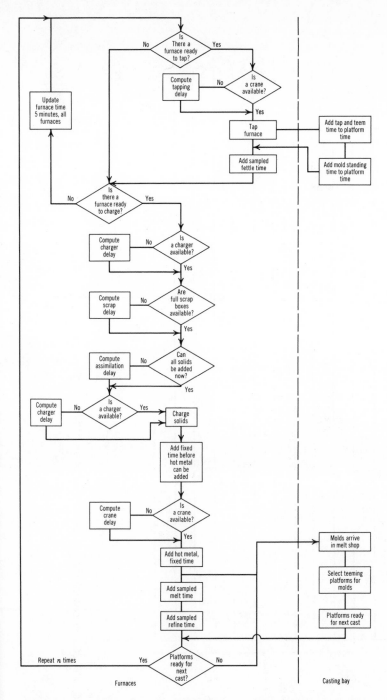

FIGURE 19. Structure of simulation for melting shop operations.

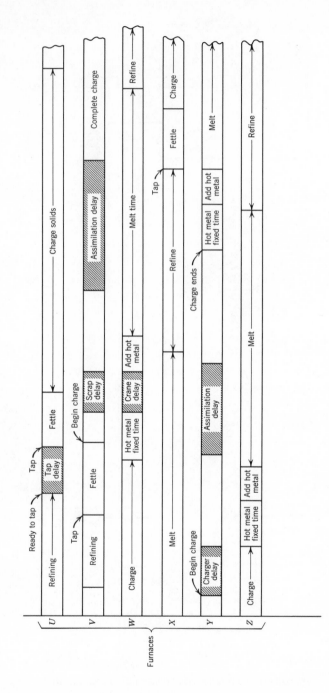

FIGURE 20. Simulation chart for 7 hours of operation.

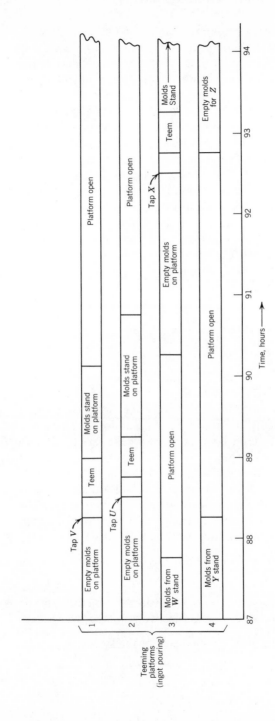

FIGURE 20. (Continued)

Figure 20 shows a graphical simulation chart for 7 hours of simulated operation. In essence, a time record is being kept for each of the six furnaces and the four teeming platforms. When the model detects that a furnace is ready to tap or ready to be charged, appropriate times are added to the time record for that furnace. Some of these times are based on Monte Carlo sampling, such as the melt time; some are fixed times for each occurrence, such as the time for addition of hot metal; and some of the times are computed, such as the delays waiting for equipment. The output of the simulation system yields information indicating the simulated output of the shop for the period of simulation—found by adding the number of casts— and the values of the various delays in the system. With the model, proposed changes in operating procedures can be evaluated prior to installation. For example, what would be the effect on output of increasing the number of cranes, chargers, or other limiting ancillary equipment? The effects of such changes are not immediately obvious because of the complex inter- action of so many factors in the operating system. The simulation model, however, could be used to evaluate their effect.

General Purpose System Simulator [12]

Geoffrey Gordon of the Advanced Systems Development Division, IBM, has developed a computer processor that makes possible the simulation of many kinds of systems when they can be described adequately by a block diagram developed in a manner consistent with the computer processor. Whereas this seems at first to be a limitation, a study of the simulator indicates that the clever conception of a wide variety of blocks of different characteristics, taken in various combinations, makes possible the repre- sentation of a multitude of actual systems.

The simulation allows the user to follow the flow through the system and observe the effects of blocking caused either by the need to timeshare facilities or caused by limited capacity of parts of the system. Outputs of the program give information on:

1. The amount of traffic flowing through the system, or parts of the system.

2. The average time and the time distribution for traffic to pass through the system, or between selective points in the system.

3. The extent to which elements of the system are loaded.

4. Queues in the system.

Simscript [*16, 29*]

Markowitz, Hausner, and Karr of the RAND Corp. have developed a simulation programming language called SIMSCRIPT. This computer language is similar in general concept to FORTRAN, but is specifically designed to accommodate simulation programs.

The implications of the existence of the General Purpose System Simulator and SIMSCRIPT are tremendous, for once they are learned, programming time is considerably reduced.

SUMMARY

The examples were chosen to illustrate applications of different kinds of activities and various levels of complexity. For example the Eastman Kodak studies of mechanics and of mixed chemicals are largely illustrative of the Monte Carlo technique in practical situations. The simulation of steel making was meant to show how a more complex system with many interdependent variables can be handled.

REVIEW QUESTIONS

1. Discuss the general situation in which simulation is preferable to mathematical analysis.

2. What are Monte Carlo methods, and what is their place in simulation?

3. In simulated sampling, why do we normally convert frequency distributions to cumulative probability distributions?

4. In the example of simulated sampling (machine breakdown and repair) used in this chapter, how can we be sure that the occurrence of machine breakdowns and the repair times are representative of the true situation?

5. Discuss the example of the determination of repair crew size at the Eastman Kodak Company. Given the existence of the simulation model, how could it be of continuing usefulness to the company in evaluating current practices and policies?

6. Discuss the simulation of the mixed chemicals distribution system at Eastman Kodak Company. How could this simulation model be of continuing usefulness to the organization?

7. The objective of the simulation of steel making operations given as an example in this chapter was to determine the capacity of operations. How else might such a model be used?

PROBLEMS

1. A sample of 100 arrivals of customers at a checkout station of a small store are according to the following distribution:

Time between Arrivals, minutes	Frequency
0.5	2
1.0	6
1.5	10
2.0	25
2.5	20
3.0	14
3.5	10
4.0	7
4.5	4
5.0	2
	100

A study of the time required to service the customers by adding up the bill, receiving payment, making change, placing packages in bags, etc., yields the following distribution:

Service Time, minutes	Frequency
0.5	12
1.0	21
1.5	36
2.0	19
2.5	7
3.0	5
	100

a. Convert the distributions to cumulative probability distributions.
b. Using a simulated sample of 20, estimate the average percent customer waiting time and the average percent idle time of the server.

2. The manager of a drive-in restaurant is attempting to determine how many "car hops" he needs during his peak load period. As a policy he wishes to offer service such that average customer waiting time does not exceed 2 minutes. How many car hops does he need if the arrival and service distributions are as follows, and any car hop can service any customer? Simulate for various alternate numbers of car hops with a sample of twenty arrivals in each case.

Time Between Successive Arrivals, minutes	Frequency	Service Time, minutes	Frequency
0	10	0	0
1.0	35	1.0	5
2.0	25	2.0	20
3.0	15	3.0	40
4.0	10	4.0	35
5.0	5		100
	100		

3. A company maintains a bank of machines which are exposed to severe service, causing bearing failure to be a common maintenance problem. There were three bearings in the machine that caused trouble. The general practice had been to replace bearings when they failed. However, excessive down-time costs raised the question whether or not a preventive policy was worthwhile. The company wished to evaluate three alternate policies:

a. The current practice of replacing bearings that fail.
b. When a bearing fails, replace all three.
c. When a bearing fails, replace that bearing plus other bearings that have been in use 1700 hours or more.

Time and cost data are as follows:

Maintenance mechanics time:
Replace 1 bearing   5 hours
Replace 2 bearings   6 hours
Replace 3 bearings   7 hours
Maintenance mechanic's wage rate $3 per hour
Bearing cost $5 each
Down-time costs $2 per hour

A record of the actual working lives of 200 bearings results in the following distribution:

Bearing Life, hours	Frequency
1100	3
1200	10
1300	12
1400	20
1500	27
1600	35
1700	30
1800	25
1900	18
2000	15
2100	4
2200	1
	200

Simulate approximately 20,000 hours of service for each of the three alternate policies.

4. Following the structure of the flow chart of Figure 16, and the cumulative distributions of Figures 12, 13, 14, and 15, simulate the mixed chemicals operation for 20 cycles.

REFERENCES

1. Armour, G. C., and E. S. Buffa, "A Heuristic Algorithm and Simulation Approach to the Relative Location of Facilities," *Management Science*, Vol. 9, No. 2, January, 1963.

2. Banbury, J., and R. J. Taylor, "A Study of Congestion in the Melting Shop of a Steelworks," *Operations Research Quarterly*, Vol. IX, No. 2.

3. Basil, D. C., P. R. Cone, and J. A. Fleming, *Executive Decision Making Through Simulation*, Charles E. Merrill, Columbus, Ohio, 1965.

4. Bonini, C. P., *Simulation of Information and Decision Systems in the Firm*, Prentice-Hall, Inc., Englewood Cliffs, N.J., 1963.

5. Bowman, E. H., and R. B. Fetter, *Analysis for Production and Operations Management*, Richard D. Irwin, Homewood, Ill., 3rd ed., 1967.

6. Buffa, E. S., G. C. Armour, and T. E. Vollmann, "Allocating Facilities with Craft," *Harvard Business Review*, March–April, 1964.

7. Colman, H., and C. P. Smallwood, *Computer Language: An Autoinstructional Introduction to Fortran*, McGraw-Hill Book Company, New York, 1962.

8. Emshoff, J. R., and R. L. Sisson, *Design and Use of Computer Simulation Models*, The Macmillan Company, New York, 1970.

9. Evans, G. W., G. F. Wallace, and G. L. Sutherland, *Simulation Using Digital Computers*, Prentice-Hall, Inc., Englewood Cliffs, N.J., 1967.

10. Feorene, O. J., "The Gentle Art of Simulation," *Proceedings, Twelfth Annual Industrial Engineering Institute*, University of California, Berkeley–Los Angeles, 1960.
11. Forrester, J., *Industrial Dynamics*, MIT Press, Cambridge, Mass., 1961.
12. Gordon, G., *A General Purpose System Simulator*, IBM Advanced Systems Development Division, October, 1961.
13. Greenlaw, P. S., L. W. Herron, and R. H. Rawden, *Business Simulation: In Industrial and University Education*, Prentice-Hall, Inc., Englewood Cliffs, N.J., 1962.
14. Jones, H. G., and A. M. Lee, "Monte Carlo Methods in Heavy Industry," *Operations Research Quarterly*, Vol. VI, No. 3.
15. Malcolm, D. G., "System Simulation-A Fundamental Tool for Industrial Engineering," *Journal of Industrial Engineering*, Vol. IX, No. 3, May–June 1958.
16. Markowitz, H. M., B. Hausner, and H. W. Karr, *SIMSCRIPT: A Simulation Programming Language*, Memorandum RM-3310-PR, The Rand Corp., Santa Monica, Calif., November, 1962.
17. McMillan, C., and R. F. Gonzales, *Systems Analysis*, Richard D. Irwin, Inc., Homewood, Ill., Rev. ed., 1968.
18. Meier, R., W. T. Newell, and H. L. Pazer, *Simulation in Business and Economics*, Prentice-Hall, Inc., Englewood Cliffs, N.J., 1969.
19. Mitchner, M., and R. P. Peterson, "An Operations Research Study of the Collection of Defaulted Loans," *Operations Research*, Vol. V, No. 4, August, 1957.
20. Mize, J. H., and J. G. Cox, *Essentials of Simulation*, Prentice-Hall, Inc., Englewood Cliffs, N.J., 1968.
21. Naylor, T. H., J. L. Balintfy, D. S. Burdick, and K. Chu, *Computer Simulation Techniques*, John Wiley & Sons, New York, 1966.
22. Neate, R., and W. J. Dacey, "A Simulation of Melting Shop Operation by Means of a Computer," *Process Control and Automation*, Vol. V, No. 7, July, 1958.
23. Report of System Simulation Symposium, Cosponsored by AIIE, ORSA, and TIMS, New York, May, 1957.
24. *Report of System Simulation Symposium No. 2*, Cosponsored by AIIE, ORSA, and TIMS, New York, February, 1959.
25. Rowe, A. J., "Application of Computer Simulation to Sequential Decision Rules in Production Scheduling," *Proceedings, Eleventh Industrial Engineering Institute*, University of California, Berkeley–Los Angeles, 1959, pp. 33–43.
26. Sasieni, M., A. Yaspan, and L. Friedman, *Operations Research*, John Wiley & Sons, New York, 1959.
27. Schiller, D. H., and M. M. Lavin, "Determining Required Warehouse Dock Facilities," *Operations Research*, Vol. IV, No. 2, April, 1956.
28. Thierauf, R. J., and R. A. Grosse, *Decision Making Through Operations Research*, John Wiley & Sons, Inc., 1970.
29. Wyman, F. P., *Simulation Modeling: A Guide to Using Simscript*, John Wiley & Sons, Inc., New York, 1970.

chapter 17

JOB SHOP SCHEDULING

The job shop scheduling problem is commonly recognized as the most complex scheduling problem in existence. The complexity stems from the fact that the nature of the system requires that virtually everything is left flexible: part or product designs, routes through the system, processes to be used, processing times, etc. Progress in understanding the nature of the system was made when it was characterized as a network of queues with arrivals and departures at each work center described by probability distributions. The usual system, however, was so complex that analytical approaches of waiting line theory were useless. Thus, while the general concepts of waiting line analysis as described in Chapter 14 are useful in understanding the nature of the flow process in a job shop, the formulas themselves make no contribution toward problem solving. With the availability of large scale computers, however, a complex network of queues can be simulated. The general concepts of Monte Carlo simulation discussed in Chapter 16 apply, and simulation has been the dominant technique used in studying job shop scheduling. Early research in job shop scheduling pointed to the queue discipline as being an important variable which could be manipulated and a great deal of the research has been focused on queue discipline (priority dispatch decision rules) through the mechanism of computer simulation.

SEQUENCING MODELS
FOR JOB SHOP SCHEDULING *I*

Interest in job shop scheduling has centered on the sequencing problem for a number of years. We discussed the general problem of job shop scheduling in Chapter 12. The sequencing problem, stated in general terms, is to determine the sequence in which jobs or orders are to be processed at each of the series of machine centers. We recognize, of course, that the sequencing problem is only a part of the overall problem of controlling the flow of orders in a job shop. The production planning of the required processing and routing requirements, material procurement, and other planning precedes the sequencing problem, and follow-up or control to insure on-time completion of orders follows the sequencing problem.

The first simulation studies of alternate queue disciplines were by Rowe [29, 30] in 1958 using a job shop simulation of a General Electric Company plant as the focus for study. Though the Rowe study recognized both labor and machines as possible limiting resources and involved no assumptions concerning arrival rates, most of the work which followed, by Baker and Dzielinski [2] in 1960, Conway and Maxwell [7] in 1962, Nanot [24] in 1963, and Carroll [6] in 1965, has been in the context of a machine-limited shop involving the assumptions of Poisson arrival rates and exponential service times. Studies involving the dual resources of machines and labor appeared again in 1962 with a study by Allen [1] and Nelson's more recent studies [25, 26]. Studies based in actual operating data for machine- and labor-limited systems have been carried out at General Electric by Rowe [29] and Allen [1], and at the Hughes Aircraft Company by LeGrande [22]. Harris [13, 14] carried out an investigation in a Los Angeles job shop to examine the assumptions involved in using the conceptual framework of queuing networks as a basis for job shop scheduling research.

We shall divide our discussion of sequencing models for job shop scheduling into an analysis of studies made on machine-limited systems, studies on labor-limited systems, and comments on studies involving actual shop data. Finally, we shall consider briefly the characteristics of integrated systems of job shop scheduling which incorporate some of the results of sequencing models.

Machine-Limited Systems

A machine-limited system is one in which it is assumed that the only critical resource is machines and that labor is always immediately available when an order has been assigned to a machine center. The result is that order waiting time occurs only when machines are not available. Early theoretical work by Smith [31] in 1956 had pointed to the shortest operation time (SOT) rule as having minimum possible order flow and waiting time for single stage systems. The SOT rule sequences orders with the shortest operation time first. Since Smith's mathematical analysis showed that the SOT rule was optimal for single stage systems, it seemed that the remaining question was how the SOT rule and others would perform in more realistic situations represented by a complex network of queues. It was at this point, of course, that mathematical analysis failed and continuing research turned to the simulation methodology.

The early simulation studies were largely exploratory, being designed to screen a large number of possible priority dispatching rules (queue disciplines). The simulation studies of Rowe in 1958 and Baker and Dzielinski in 1960 had both pointed to the attractiveness of the SOT rule for complex systems on the basis of certain criteria. Two massive studies to screen a wide range of possible priority dispatch decision rules followed the preliminary findings of Rowe, and Baker and Dzielinski. The Conway [7] study at RAND Corporation tested 92 different rules (some with changes in parameters only), and the Nanot [24] study involved sample sizes as high as 145,000 for ten different decision rules in six different shop structures using 125 hours of IBM 7094 computer time. We shall summarize the results of the Nanot study after considering a basis for classifying priority dispatch decision rules.

One common classification of priority rules is on the basis of horizon. A *local rule* establishes priorities entirely on the basis of the characteristics of the job order, for example, its processing time or due date. A broader horizon rule might take into account overall work load, projected delay time downstream, or other characteristics. Another basis of classification separates decision rules into those that are static versus those that are dynamic. A static rule is one in which the relative priorities remain the same once assigned. A dynamic priority rule, however, assigns a priority which changes with time. For example, with a due date priority, orders waiting in the queue gain in relative priority with time, since the longer they wait the less likely it is that a new arrival will have an earlier due date.

The Nanot Study

The Nanot Study involved six different job shop structures, testing ten different priority dispatching rules with over 2.44×10^6 orders processed through these systems. The six shop structures were as follows:

Job Shop 1—four centers, medium load, pure job shop routing.

Job Shop 2—four centers, high load, pure job shop routing.
Job Shop 3—eight centers, low load, quasi flow shop routing.
Job Shop 4—eight centers, medium load, quasi flow shop routing.
Job Shop 5—two centers, medium load, pure job shop routing.
Job Shop 6—eight centers, low load, pure job shop routing.

Pure job shop routings are those in which an order leaving one machine is equally likely to go to any other machine in the shop. Pure flow shop routings are those in which there is only one routing that orders can follow.

The ten static and dynamic local rules tested by Nanot were as follows:

Rule 1 (FCFS)   —first come, first served.
Rule 2 (SOT)   —shortest operation time.
Rule 3 (SS)   —static slack, that is, due date minus time of arrival at machine center.
Rule 4 (SS/PT)   —static slack/remaining processing time.
Rule 5 (SS/RO)   —static slack/remaining number of operations.
Rule 6 (FISFS)   —first in system, first served, commonly known as the due date system.
Rule 7 (LCFS)   —last come, first served.
Rule 8 (DS)   —dynamic slack (time remaining to due date, less remaining expected flow time).
Rule 9 (DS/PT)   —dynamic slack/remaining processing time.
Rule 10 (DS/RO)—dynamic slack/remaining number of operations.

Nanot included a number of explicit assumptions. The arrival rates of orders in the system followed a Poisson process, and the service times followed the negative exponential distribution. There was only one queue for each machine center and labor was assumed to be available. Lot splitting was not permitted and transportation time between machine centers was zero. Neither subcontracting nor overtime was allowed, and machine breakdowns, scrap, and other interruptions were not allowed to occur. Setup time was considered to be a part of the processing times for each operation.

Results. The SOT rule consistently had the lowest mean flow time, but the standard deviations of the FCFS and FISFS rules were in general lower. The significance of the standard deviation measure of performance is shown in Figures 1 and 2 where typical flow time curves are plotted versus fractiles of orders processed. The flow time curves were similar for all shop conditions. Figure 1 shows the flow time curves up to the 0.90 fractile. The shaded area includes Rules 1, 3, 5, 6, and 8, (FCFS, SS, SS/RO, FISFS, and DS). The SOT rule consistently performed the best in the zero to 0.90 range and was almost linear. Rule 4 (SS/PT) was consistently the worst performer.

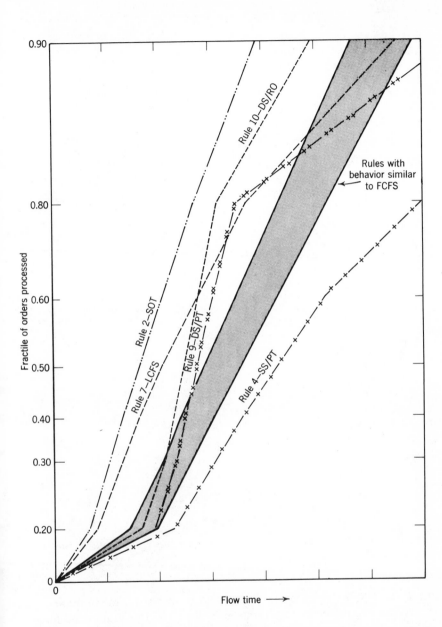

FIGURE 1. *Typical flow time curves for alternate priority dispatching decision rules. (Figures 1 and 2 are from Y. R. Nanot,* An Experimental Investigation and Comparative Evaluation of Priority Disciplines in Job Shop-Like Queueing Networks, *Unpublished Ph.D. Dissertation, UCLA, 1963.)*

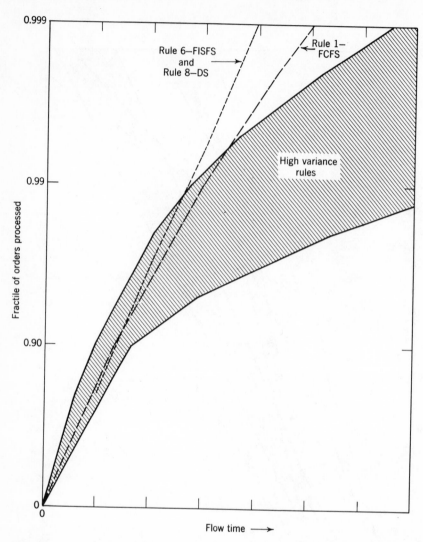

FIGURE 2. Typical flow time curves for alternate priority dispatching rules at higher fractiles.

Rule 7 (LCFS) exhibits some interesting properties. For the single server Poisson-exponential system this rule leads to the same expected flow time as the first come–first served rule but can be shown to have greater variance in flow time [31]. This appears to be true also for the network systems studied by Nanot. For the lower fractiles in Figure 1, the

LCFS rule flow times are consistently smaller than those obtained by FCFS for at least 80 percent of all orders. From a practical point of view, the LCFS rule is widely used. For example, in machine shops, orders waiting to be served at a machine center are often located in stacked boxes. When the machine is ready for the next order, it is much easier to remove the top box than attempt to get at the one on the bottom.

Figure 2 shows flow time performance beyond the 0.90 fractile. Rules 1, 6, and 8 (FCFS, FISFS, and DS) are plotted individually, and the other rules fall into the shaded area, the upper limit of which is the SOT rule. The high variance rules caused about 1 percent of the orders to have flow times averaging from 4 to 15 times the mean flow time under the FCFS rule.

The effect of system configuration was investigated through the mechanism of an analysis of variance. The results showed that the differences due to the use of different priority dispatching rules was highly significant but that the differences due to system configuration (effect of shop size and differences in routing) were very much less significant.

The Shortest Operation Time Rule (SOT)

Since the SOT rule exhibits excellent flow time characteristics, and because the rule is simple to use, considerable further research has been done. Smith's [31] mathematical analysis showed that for single stage systems using the SOT rule the following statements were true:

1. The total completion time is minimized.

2. The average completion time is minimized.

3. The average number of jobs in process is minimized.

4. The average waiting time is minimized.

5. If lateness is defined for a given job as the difference between completion time and due date, the average lateness is minimized.

Any rule that accomplishes these objectives is of considerable practical as well as theoretical interest. The one big disadvantage of the SOT rule is that there may be very long waiting times for individual orders or jobs even though average waiting time has been minimized. The theoretical analysis also leaves several other questions open. Among them are: Do conclusions with regard to the optimality of the rule extend to the more realistic multimachine case, comparable to real job shops? How accurately must processing times be known, that is, is the performance of the rule sensitive to errors in the estimated processing times? Is the rule sensitive to shop size, that is, does it work well with a one-machine or small shop but break down in the more complex situation representative of medium to large shops? A number of studies, including the Nanot study just discussed, tend to confirm the extension of the rule from the single-machine case to the more complex network of queues. A study by Conway and Maxwell [7] addresses itself to the first as well as to the other questions.

To consider more complex systems, Conway and Maxwell used a computer simulation of waiting line networks in which comparisons were made between the SOT rule and others. In some of the simulated experiments, shop size was varied, and other runs were made to determine if the effectiveness of the rule would break down if the estimates of processing time were progressively poorer. The results showed that the mean flow time superiority of the SOT rule does transfer to the more complex multi-machine case and that the rule is not sensitive to shop size, shop loading, or errors in estimating the process times.

Finally, the question of the disadvantage of the rule which results in a very long waiting time for a few jobs was dealt with by considering modified SOT rules. For example, a truncated SOT rule places an upper limit on the amount of waiting time for any order. If the order remains in the waiting line as long as this time limit, it then moves to the head of the line and is processed. Of course, some of the advantage of the SOT rule is lost by the modified rule. For example, when the waiting time limit was set as 2.5 times the mean waiting time for a first come–first served rule, about two-thirds of the advantage in idle time of the SOT rule over the first come–first served rule was lost.

The advantages of the SOT rule are its simplicity in application and its relative effectiveness for average flow time. Its disadvantages are in its characteristic high flow time variance.

C over T Rules

Carroll [6] performed an extensive set of simulation experiments to investigate a family of priority dispatch decision rules characterized in general by the ratio of delay cost to processing time, that is, c/t, or COVERT. Carroll's objective was to find a rule which retained the basic performance values of the SOT rule but which reduced the extreme lateness of a few of the orders. The basic COVERT rule and its variants establishes a trade-off between potential delay costs and the processing time for tasks. Carroll established the cost of delay as simply the incremental change in order tardiness and assumes that all orders incur the delay cost penalties at the same rate. Thus the COVERT rules involve dynamic priority concepts as well as aspects of the SOT rule. In general, then, the COVERT rule gives the highest priority to orders with the largest ratio of expected tardiness to operation time, that is, c/t.

The priority numbers range between zero and 1. If the slack time for an order exceeds its expected waiting time in the system, its priority index is zero since there should be no difficulty in meeting its due date. The computations of the priority index numbers are slightly complex though not difficult.

Experimental Results. Carroll tested the COVERT rule against six other rules in a set of simulation experiments that involved both single- and multiple-component orders (multiple-component orders are assembled units). Results are shown in Table I and Figure 3 for a sample run with single-component orders and a pure job shop configuration comprised of eight machines. The mean tardiness of the COVERT rule is shown to be superior even to the truncated SOT rule. Table I also shows the COVERT rule to be superior in mean wait time to the first three bench-mark rules but not as good as the SOT and truncated SOT rules. Figure 3 shows dramatically the effectiveness of the COVERT rule in minimizing order lateness.

TABLE I. Mean tardiness and wait times for six priority dispatch decision rules. Pure job shop, eight machines, single component orders, utilization = 0.80, 3072 orders

Rule	Mean Tardiness per Order	Mean Wait Time
FCFS (first come—first served)	36.6	14.4
FISFS (first in system—first served)	24.7	14.2
SS/RO (static slack per remaining operation)	16.2	13.9
SOT (shortest operation time)	11.3	7.0
TSOT (truncated SOT)	4.6	8.0
COVERT	2.5	10.3

From D. C. Carroll, Heuristic Sequencing of Single and Multiple Component Jobs, *Unpublished Ph.D. Dissertation, MIT, 1965.*

Sensitivity tests at other utilization levels indicated no significant difference in performance of the COVERT rule except that at the low utilization levels differences between rules were less significant, though the COVERT rule maintained its superiority. Carroll suggests that this indicates that the sequencing function is less important with a light shop load. Other sensi-

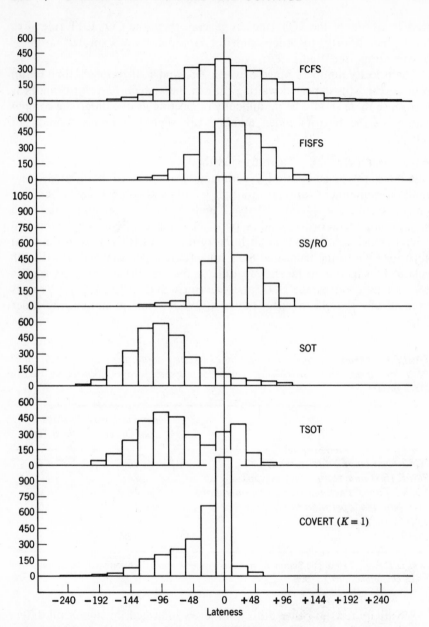

FIGURE 3. Lateness frequency distributions for six rules, pure job shop single-component order, 3072 orders, utilization = 0.80. From D. C. Carroll, Heuristic Sequencing of Single and Multiple Component Jobs, *Unpublished Ph.D. Dissertation, Sloan School of Management, Massachusetts Institute of Technology, 1965.*

tivity experiments with different flow allowances (time allowed between start and due dates) showed that the COVERT rule performed well at both extremes. Carroll tested the COVERT rule in other situations involving shops with multiple machines in each work center and with multiple-component orders in both kinds of shops and obtained similar general results. The COVERT rule seems to offer considerable promise in dealing with the disadvantages of the SOT rule while maintaining its benefits.

Labor-Limited Systems

A more realistic assumption about job shops is that they are labor limited rather than machine limited, or possibly in some circumstances jointly labor and machine limited. The usual situation is that not all machines are manned simultaneously so that labor can be used as a flexible but limiting resource to operate different machines at different times depending on the needs of the work load. Previously, we have considered priority dispatch decision rules for sequencing orders on machines. In a labor-limited system other basic questions are raised, for example: What are effective labor assignment procedures and how do these procedures interact with sequencing rules? What are the effects of various degrees of centralized control for labor assignment?

Nelson [26] was motivated in part by the conclusions of an empirical study by Harris [14] and developed a general model for studying labor- and machine-limited systems. The Nelson model is small in size but efficient in terms of the number of variables we can manipulate in assessing the effects and interactions of a wide variety of alternate policies and procedures. Figure 4 shows the schematic diagram of Nelson's general model. The design and control parameters of the model are as follows:

Design Parameters:
m the number of machine centers in the system.
c_i the number of identical machines in machine center i, ($i = 1$, $2, \ldots, m$).
n the number of machine operators in the labor force.
e_{ji} the efficiency of laborer j on any machine in machine center i, ($i = 1, 2, \ldots, m; j = 1, 2, \ldots, n$).
Control Parameters:
l the machine center selection procedure used in central control.
q_i the queue discipline used at machine center i, ($i = 1, 2, \ldots, m$).
d_i the degree of centralized labor assignment control exercised at machine center i, ($i = 1, 2, \ldots, m$).

The work load parameters of the model are the arrival and service

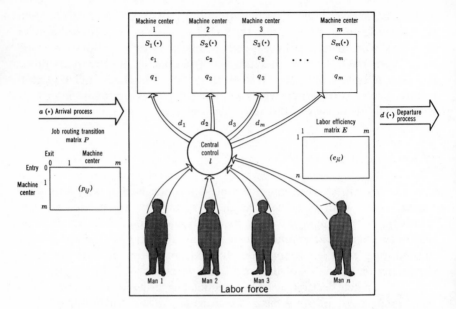

FIGURE 4. General model—schematic diagram. (Figures 4 and 5 are from R. T. Nelson, "Labor and Machine Limited Production Systems," Management Science, Vol. 13, No. 9, May 1967, pp. 648–671.)

probability density functions and their parameters and the job routing transition matrix which can be specified as pure job shop, pure flow shop, and all intermediate degrees. Labor assignment to the processing of jobs or orders is dependent on the degree of centralized control over each of the machine centers. A value $d_i = 1$ represents completely centralized control wherein each operator on completing a service operation at machine center i is given his next work assignment by central control. On the other hand, when $d_i = 0$ the operator remains in his work center as long as there is any job in its queue, returning to central control for assignment only when there is no work remaining. Intermediate values of the degree of centralized control may also be specified. The assignment of operators to machine centers in central control is governed by a machine center selection procedure l which operates in conjunction with the queue discipline q_i at the machine centers to form the complete labor assignment procedure.

Experimental Design. In a series of initial experiments, Nelson established a simple version of his general model involving a system consisting of just two machine centers, each with two identical machines and a variable number of operators. The job or order arrival process was Poisson with unit mean arrival rate. A pure job shop mode was adopted and service rates followed identical exponential distributions for all machines. The mean service rate was adjusted to the number of operators in order to establish comparable work loads for all experiments, and average labor utilization was set at $^8/_9$. Nelson then systematically varied the number of operators in the system, the central control machine center selection procedure, and the machine center queue disciplines. The number of operators was varied from one through four and when $n = 4$ there was an operator for each machine in the system resulting in machine limitation. Three different queue disciplines were used:

$q = 1$, first come–first served (FCFS).
$q = 2$, first in system–first served (FISFS).
$q = 3$, shortest operation time (SOT).

Five different machine selection procedures were used for centralized labor assignment:

$l = 0$, random assignment of idle labor among machine centers with work in queue.
$l = 1$, assignment of labor according to the labor- and machine-limited systems counterpart of the FCFS queue discipline for machine-limited systems.
$l = 2$, assignment of labor according to the labor- and machine-limited systems counterpart of the FISFS queue discipline for machine-limited systems.
$l = 3$, assignment of labor according to the labor- and machine-limited systems counterpart of the SOT queue discipline for machine-limited systems.
$l = 4$, assignment of labor to the machine center with the most jobs in queue, LNGQ.

The degree of centralized labor assignment control over each of the machine centers was fixed at its maximum level ($d_1 = d_2 = 1$) corresponding to completely centralized control. The labor efficiency matrix set all operators at full efficiency.

Experimental Results. The most effective combination of machine center selection procedure and queue discipline in terms of minimum mean flow time was LNGQ-SOT, that is, the machine center selection procedure of the longest queue in combination with the queue discipline of the shortest operation time. On the other hand, when the procedures were ranked in terms of minimum variance of flow time and the smallest maximum flow time, the combination LNGQ-FISFS was the most effective.

When the results were plotted in the form of Figure 5, the independent effects of changes in size of labor force, machine center selection procedure, and queue discipline for order sequencing stood out. Figure 5 does not contain a plot for all of the data but for just the selected values involving three and four operators. Note that there is no machine center selection procedure required when $n = 4$ since all machines are fully manned. Changes in machine center selection procedure seem to have relatively small effect in both mean and variance of flow time. However, changes in queue discipline for order sequencing showed large effects. Nelson notes that the results for the variance of flow time give increasing values for the queue disciplines FISFS, FCFS, and SOT respectively.

Certainly the most interesting effect indicated in Figure 5 is that attributed to changes in the size of the labor force. Large increases in mean and variance resulted from increases in the labor force from three to four

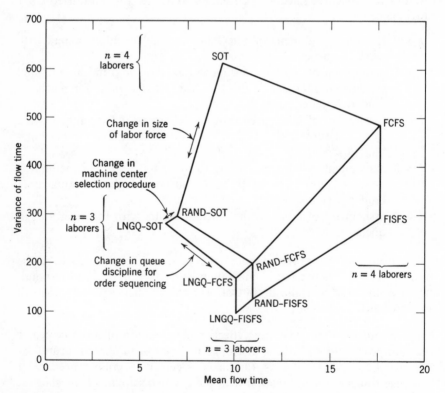

FIGURE 5. *Mapping of mean flow time versus variance to show independent effects of changes in size of labor force, machine center selection procedure, and queue discipline.*

operators, for all three queue disciplines. Table II shows the mean flow time and flow time for selected fractiles of orders processed in relation to size of work force. In each case the values given are those obtained by the use of the most effective labor assignment procedure (combination of l and q) for the fractile and work force size. The average utilization of the labor force was maintained at the same level for each value of n, so that we have a measure of physical flexibility.

TABLE II. Time in system statistics versus size of labor force

Size of Labor Force n	Mean f '	Job Flow Time Distribution-Fractile,							
		.20	.40	.60	.80	.90	.95	.99	.999
4	9.4	1.63	3.48	6.09	11.70	18.97	28.74	76.42	101.20
3	6.4	1.08	2.26	3.99	7.79	12.85	20.25	51.45	68.94
2	5.0	0.80	1.60	2.86	5.38	9.24	15.84	51.49	67.32
1	4.2	0.62	1.24	1.85	3.76	7.20	13.90	53.65	122.40

From R. T. Nelson, "Labor and Machine Limited Production Systems," Management Science, Vol. 13, No. 9, May 1967, pp. 648–671.

The results show that the mean value of flow time decreases as the size of the work force decreases. The same behavior is exhibited up to the 0.98 fractile. It seems that the labor-limited system offers a degree of flexibility not found in the machine-limited system. In addition, as the ratio of machines to work force increases flexibility increases, with the exception of the extreme upper tail for a work force of size one. Apparently a machine-limited system loses its flexibility since labor cannot be reassigned to machine centers where the load is heavy. The queues at some work centers will be empty at times and thus the average utilization of labor will decrease and flow time will increase. Nelson gives the following example of how the advantage of the flexibility of labor-limited systems might be used.

We can consider the models used in the experiments with a single machine in each machine center and a work force consisting of two laborers. For the sake of this example we shall assume a FCFS queue discipline. The mean time in system (flow time) for this machine-limited system as computed from queueing theory is $f' = 16$. Suppose now that a decision is made to add one more machine in each machine center identical to the machine previously there. The experimental results of the $n = 2$ experiments with FCFS indicate that f' for the new system is 8.7. The nearly 50% improvement in the average time in system can be expected to result in an increased work load due to improved service to the customer with respect to competitors. The increased work load will increase f' until a new equilibrium is attained. The end result will be a more flexible system offering better service at a higher volume with the original labor force. The only costs incurred in the transition are investment in equipment and training.

The degree of centralized control of labor assignment was studied by Nelson with the system involving three laborers. The machine center selection procedure used by central control was LNGQ in combination with the three queue disciplines. With the combination LNGQ-FCFS the use of full central control as opposed to no central control led to a 7 percent decrease in system flow time and a 14 percent decrease in the variance of flow time. With the combination LNGQ-FISFS the corresponding decreases were 7 and 28 percent respectively. With the combination LNGQ-SOT the use of full central control decreased mean flow time by 12 percent but the variance increased by 30 percent. The detailed flow time data by fractiles indicated that the effects of the degree of central control were quite different for the three labor assignment procedures used. Nelson concludes that in terms of flow time statistics the LNGQ-SOT labor assignment procedure would be relatively better for systems characterized by less centralized labor assignment control and that the other two procedures might perform better in systems characterized by central control.

Studies with Actual Shop Data

It is interesting that the three well-known studies which have been carried out in an actual shop environment have all reflected the realistic conditions of the labor-limited system. The original Rowe [29] study used a General Electric Company plant as a basis for the model. The LeGrande [22] study carried out under Rowe's direction at the Hughes Aircraft Company. Finally, an interesting study by Allen [1] carried out at a General Electric Company plant examines the performance of alternate decision rules under declining load. This latter study is of particular interest since it raises new questions.

In studying the effects of declining load, Allen was particularly interested in the SOT rule because it had been shown to perform well, in terms of mean flow time, under "steady state" conditions. Allen wished to reexamine the SOT rule for the short run situation when shop load was rapidly declining. The General Electric Company shop used as a basis for the study consisted of 78 machines classified into 18 machine groups. It was assumed in the simulation studies that any machine in a machine group could perform the required operations with the same setup and processing time. The work force of 40 men were classified in 13 labor classes.

All men in a given labor class were interchangeable. As a whole, the system was labor limited except for certain machine groups, such as the boring mills, where machine capacity was limited.

Experiments and Results. Allen was interested in the situation where no additional work was released to the shop after the initial load so that actual run out of the orders takes place. His objective was to examine alternate priority dispatch decision rules in order to determine which would maintain labor utilization at as high a level as possible until additional orders were received. One of the factors thought to be important in improving labor utilization was the possible use of alternate routing. Approximately one-third of the required operations could be performed at more than one machine group for the order mix studied. The eight decision rules tested are listed at the bottom of Table III. Alternate routing decisions were deferred until the order became available for the operation in question and was therefore regarded as a part of dispatching. The

TABLE III. Average labor utilization figures for eight priority dispatching rules under conditions where no additional work was released to the shop after the initial load, so that run-out takes place

	Average Labor Utilization—Percent							
	Rule 1	*Rule 2*	*Rule 3*	*Rule 4*	*Rule 5*	*Rule 6*	*Rule 7*	*Rule 8*
Weeks 1–10	*85.1*	*81.8*	*83.4*	*79.5*	*86.7*	*86.5*	*87.9*	*88.3*
Weeks 7–10	*62.8*	*54.5*	*58.5*	*49.5*	*66.8*	*66.3*	*69.8*	*70.8*

Rule 1	*(SOT-AR),*	*Shortest operation time with alternate routing.*
Rule 2	*(LOT-AR),*	*Longest operation time with alternate routing.*
Rule 3	*(RAND-AR),*	*Random rule with alternate routing.*
Rule 4	*(RAND),*	*Random rule without alternate routing.*
Rule 5	*(LOT-SOT),*	*LOT until week 6, then SOT.*
Rule 6	*(SOT B-LOT),*	*SOT on bottleneck machines, LOT elsewhere.*
Rule 7	*(TC-SOT),*	*Two class SOT rule. Jobs divided into two classes, those requiring additional processing beyond the operation in question and those not. Higher priority always given to the first class and jobs ordered within classes by SOT.*
Rule 8	*(TC-SW),*	*Two class switching rule. Jobs divided into two classes as in rule 7, but within classes jobs were ordered by LOT until week 6 and by SOT thereafter.*

Data for Tables III and IV from M. Allen, A Detailed Simulation of a Non-Stock Production Leveling Problem, *Unpublished S.M. Thesis, MIT, 1962, or from (1).*

specific method of alternate routing used by Allen in the simulation was to reexamine each queue once each shift. If the backlog of orders was such that some of those in a queue could not possibly be processed in the forthcoming shift, an attempt was made to reroute the order into some other queue which did not have a backlog of work equal to one shift.

Average labor utilization figures for the eight decision rules are shown in Table III. The effect of alternate routing can be seen by examining the contrast between the utilization figures for rules 3 and 4. Of the first four simple rules, the SOT-AR rule has the highest utilization. This led Allen to test four additional more complex rules, all of which involved the SOT rule in some way. Rule 8, the two-class switching rule, yielded the highest utilization figures.

Flexibility Experiments. Allen also performed simulation experiments to determine the degree of additional labor flexibility which might result if it were assumed that the entire 40-man work force were pooled into one extremely versatile labor class which could operate all machines in the shop. Table IV shows the comparative results for four different decision rules. The results show a strong preference for the more flexible labor force for all rules tested, both in terms of average labor utilization and weeks to empty the shop.

TABLE IV.   Average labor utilization in percent and weeks to empty the shop with 13 and 1 labor classes

	13 Labor Classes				1 Labor Class			
	Rule 1 SOT-AR	Rule 2 LOT-AR	Rule 3 RAND-AR	Rule 4 RAND	Rule 1 SOT-AR	Rule 2 LOT-AR	Rule 3 RAND-AR	Rule 4 RAND
Average utilization, 10 weeks	85.1	81.8	83.4	79.5	91.9	93.8	93.6	89.5
Weeks to empty shop	27	27	27	27	20	19	19	19

Allen then made a second simulation run where it was assumed that five of the 40-man work force could operate all machines in the shop, the other 35 remaining in the 13 labor class structure. He reports that much of the advantage of the one-class shop was retained since the number of weeks to empty the shop remained at only 19, however, no average labor utilization figures were given.

We may also compare the relative merits of labor and machine flexibility by examining Table IV. Comparing the performances for rules 3 and 4, RAND-AR and RAND, for the thirteen- and one-class shops, we note that the average improvement in 10-week utilization due to alternate routing was only 4 percentage points compared to 10.1 percentage points attributable to labor flexibility. Allen notes that the alternate routing flexibility effect seems to be relatively independent of the labor flexibility effect though no statistical analysis was made to establish independence.

JOB SHOP PLANNING AND CONTROL SYSTEMS /

As we commented earlier, the job shop sequencing models are only a part of an overall system for planning and control, and we shall now attempt to embed the concepts derived from sequencing models in an overall system. We must recognize that we are in fact attempting to visualize the broad information requirements of such an organization. There are essentially two kinds of job shop scheduling and control systems: (*a*) loading systems where sequencing rules such as those we have discussed are used as a mechanism to maximize the flow of orders and labor utilization, and to minimize order tardiness, and (*b*) systems which attempt to schedule in detail starting and finishing times of each operation to be performed. Most actual systems are of the loading type.

The important characteristic which distinguishes loading systems is simply that no detailed schedule of the use of men and machines is generated centrally. Instead, the shop is loaded based on priority dispatch decision rules of one sort or another. If any kind of detailed schedules are made, they would be developed locally by foremen who can see the problems to be faced. This does not mean, however, that all control is local, for the priority dispatch decision rules are developed centrally and are meant to be followed.

In order to try to place job shop sequencing models in context, we shall discuss the loading system installed in the Hughes Aircraft Company and an interactive system at Western Electric which yields a detailed schedule.

The Hughes Loading System

The Hughes Aircraft Company is a large aerospace firm which bids on design, development, and manufacture of complex electronics systems. The particular shop described by the example has a diverse product mix of machined and sheet metal parts, machine assemblies, wave guides, and etched circuit boards flowing through functionally grouped work and machine centers. There are approximately 2000 to 3000 orders being processed at any one time with an average of seven operations per order. The average total processing time for an order is 2.5 hours. There are approximately 1000 machines and/or work centers in the shop which are grouped into 120 functional machine or work centers. The work centers are manned by 400 direct workers so that the entire system is labor limited and the average order cycle time is 3 to 4 weeks. We should note that the control system which we shall describe is a part of a broader system which involves bidding, product definition, operational planning, operations, and operational control. The Hughes loading system was reported at different stages of development by LeGrande [22], Steinhoff [32], and Bulkin, Colley, and Steinhoff [5], and a summary of the end operating system is described in the latter reference.

The vital components of the system are a weekly *Shop Load Forecast* for each machine group and a *Job Shop Simulation Scheduler* routine which produces a Daily *Order-Schedule Report* and a Daily *Hot-Order Visibility Report*. The entire system is computer based, and the two daily reports as well as the weekly load forecast are based on daily updated fabrication open-order master files.

System as a Whole. The broad outlines of the entire system are shown in Figure 6. Operational process planning is developed from engineering blueprints to yield the critical data of processes to be performed, standard process times, and standard flow allowances. These data are placed in the disc file. When a fabrication requirement notice is received from one of the assembly product-line departments, a fabrication order is transmitted to data processing which initiates the preparation of a fabrication shop order and establishes an open order in the fabrication open-order master file. A deck of master job cards is also produced which accompanies the order through the shop. These papers are then sent to a fabrication order control prerelease center from which orders are dispatched to the shop. After release to the shop, the master job cards are used in conjunction with plastic location cards at machine groups to actuate the remote data collection devices. At the end of the day, a paper tape containing all order moves transacted during the day is used to update current order locations and to code completed operations in the fabrication open-order file. The fabrication open-order master file contains, on a daily updated basis, the information on every open order and is the heart of the system which produces the three documents, the *Weekly Shop Load Forecast*, the *Daily Order-Schedule Report*, and the *Daily Hot-Order Visibility Report*.

The *Weekly Shop Load Forecast* is generated from information in the Fabrication Open-Order Master File for each machine group and projects

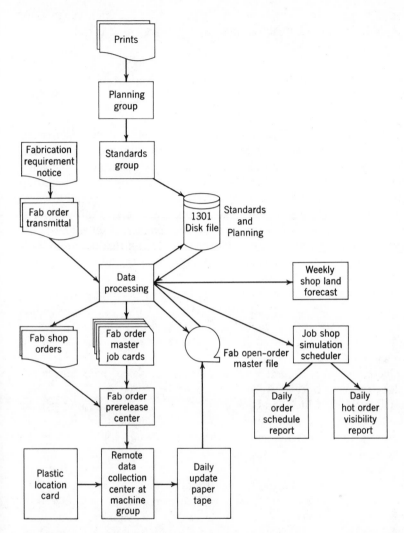

FIGURE 6. Hughes Aircraft Company's production, planning, and control system. Adapted from M. H. Bulkin, J. L. Colley, and H. W. Steinhoff, "Load Forecasting, Priority Sequencing, and Simulation in a Job Shop Control System," in Readings in Production and Operations Management, E. S. Buffa, ed., John Wiley & Sons, New York, 1966.

the anticipated load for each machine or work center for 10 weeks in advance. The projected work load for each machine center in standard hours is divided into total active load and preshop load (orders not yet released to the shop) and is further subdivided into orders which are on schedule, behind schedule, or held due to lack of production plans, material, tooling, etc. The shop load forecast can then be used to establish manpower and machine needs for the present and future weeks in each machine group.

Order Scheduling. The *Daily Order-Schedule Report* and the *Hot-Order Visibility Report* are developed by the Job Shop Simulation Scheduler. These documents are used by shop foremen and expediters in the daily sequencing of orders at the machine groups in the shop. The simulation scheduler was developed by Steinhoff [32] as a computing routine used to simulate one shift of shop activity and to generate the two daily reports. The priority dispatch decision rule used in the simulation scheduler is the dynamic slack time per operation rule (DS/RO). Recall that dynamic slack time is computed as the number of days remaining to the due date, less the remaining number of days of processing time. The resulting priority index is then dynamic slack divided by the number of remaining operations. Actually, the priority rule used at Hughes Aircraft Company is a two-class rule, since hot orders are segregated and processed first in the sequence of their priority numbers followed by the processing of all other orders in priority sequence.

The *Operation of the Simulation Scheduler* involves first the computation of the slack time per operation for every order in the open-order file. There are two labor classes which can be assigned to one or more machine groups. The simulation program then makes an initial assignment for each order in the open file to the machine group indicated in the current location of the file. When all orders in the file have been assigned to their respective "current location" machine groups, the orders in each machine group are ranked in priority sequence with hot orders first. These orders are then assigned sequentially until either all available machines or men have been exhausted. For those machine groups serviced by a common labor pool, and for which the availability of men is the capacity limitation, the machine group with the highest priority job will be serviced first.

When the initial assignment of orders has been completed, the simulation process begins. An event clock is used to record operation completions at the machine groups based on the estimated run times. On the completion of an operation in the simulation a new priority index is computed for the order and it is moved to its next location, where it is placed in the queue in the proper priority sequence or actually processed if men and machine resources are available. At the machine group where the operation completion occurred the job at the head of the queue is processed. This continues for one shift, and all activity taking place during the simulation is recorded and used to generate the daily operating reports.

The *Order-Schedule Report* shows the orders in the machine group at the beginning of the shift followed by the orders expected to arrive during the shift. Within these two categories the orders are further subdivided into hot orders and other orders. Finally within these two categories the orders are sequenced in terms of the established priority numbers. Orders which are already behind schedule have negative slack and are listed with negative priority numbers. The foreman uses the information in the *Order-Schedule Report* to plan the shift work load. From the report he knows which orders are in his machine groups, their priorities, and the work content, as well as the number of hot orders which will arrive that day. The *Hot-Order Visibility Report* segregates those orders which should be pushed, and this report is an aid to expediters in the performance of their jobs.

The Hughes loading system, by incorporating the daily simulation scheduler, has the effect of providing department foremen with a *feasible* daily schedule. The simulator makes it possible to anticipate bottlenecks and develop alternate routing where possible. Note that the DS/RO was one of the high variance decision rules according to the Nanot study reported earlier in this chapter. As noted previously, however, it was actually used as a two-class rule at Hughes and we have no comparative test results of the rule in this form. This decision rule was apparently used based on the results of the previous study by LeGrande [22] at the Hughes Aircraft Company where this rule performed well on the basis of weighted criteria designed to emphasize on-time completion of orders.

Western Electric Interactive System [11]

An interesting development which uses the capabilities of time-shared computing has promise for the job shop scheduling problem. Jones and coworkers [10, 11] developed interactive scheduling systems which use either typewriter or display terminals and thereby place the production supervisor, or a scheduler, in a loop with a computer program. By interacting with the computer program the scheduler develops and/or alters a schedule. Schedules are generated by making choices from among sets of decision rules, for example, rules for the acceptance or rejection of orders, rules for sequencing orders, and rules for allocating the use of overtime. The scheduler develops a schedule by testing the effects of various combinations of possibilities, simulating various alternate assignments and their effects.

Godin and Jones [11] developed a small scale application of the interactive scheduling concept in one of the coil winding shops of the Western Electric Company. Of the 200 types of coils manufactured, approximately 65 are active at any point in time and each type is usually being produced for three or four different orders. There are 20 of one type winding machine and 2 of a second type, and the work force consists of from 20 to 35 machine operators working on two or three shifts depending on shop load. Because of differences in skills not all operators can wind all types of coils, and performance against standard varies considerably for various combinations of operators and coil types. Similarly, some machines cannot be used to wind some types of coils. The production supervisor must assign workers and machines to each order in a way which balances pressures for on time deliveries against the other factors which make for production effectiveness.

The system allows for the production supervisor to consider seven variables in constructing schedules:

Skill levels of workers
Skill needs of products
Capability of machines
Availability of workers, machines, and materials
Quantities required
Completion dates
Existing machine setups

Conversational Language. The system functions through a main program and 23 sub-routines. To communicate with the program through the typewriter terminal a simple conversational language was developed. A single key stroke indicates a whole series of commands. The keys are identified by a plastic overlay on the keyboard, for example, the overlay shows "Load" over the exclamation point key. When this key is depressed, the computer understands it as a request to print the winding shop load on the printer.

Figure 7 is an illustration of how the supervisor can converse with the computer program through simple commands which evoke responses or questions from the program. The supervisor answers questions with the information requested. For example, in the seventh line of Figure 7 the program requests, "TYPE IN THE DECISION RULE YOU WISH TO USE." The supervisor responds with the code '6', which calls a preprogrammed decision rule.

The language used in the interactive process is designed to emphasize the computer's subordinate role. The computer speaks in the first person

```
JO  TYPE CURRENT DAY,WEEK,MONTH,END DAY,WEEK,MONTH
REPLY CO,'1,2,6,2,2,6'
OO  TYPE NUMBER OF WEEKS IN EACH MONTH
REPLY OO,'5'
OO  TYPE NUMBER OF DAYS IN EACH WEEK
REPLY OO,'5,5,5,5,5'
JO  TYPE IN THE DECISION RULE YOU WISH TO USE
REPLY CO,'6'
  START OF SHIFT  1        ON DAY  1      OF WEEK  2
  PHASE 1......INDICA         MACHINES
OO  READY.
```

FIGURE 7. How the supervisor and the computer converse. Each computer message begins with 00 and is followed by the supervisor's response beginning with REPLY 00. Some symbols represent function buttons such as the Q, which represents the command GO, and the + sign, which represents the command PRINT THE CURRENT SHOP STATUS. From V. Godin, and C. H. Jones, "The Interactive Shop Supervisors," Industrial Engineering, November, 1969.

in a helpful manner as follows: "SORRY, I CANNOT UNDERSTAND YOUR REQUEST. TRY AGAIN." Or, "I SUGGEST SMITH, M. ON CODE 2588AB ON MACHINE NO. 2." Or, "I NEED HELP ASSIGNING GREGG, F."

Simulation and Reports. The computer program can carry out simulations of shop schedules so that the supervisor can test various alternate assignments and try to anticipate future problems. Simulations can be run in a completely automatic mode with no human intervention, but it is more likely to simulate in interactive mode. When the interactive mode is used the supervisor enters two parameters which set the guidelines for the system. The first tells the computer how long it may keep an operator on the same coil type before manual reassignment is necessary, and the second tells what region the computer program may search when suggesting assignments for operators. In addition to these two parameters a normal daily run includes the open order file and the operator-machine job assignments already in existence. The latter input is generated through the use of a small prepunched card deck.

Given the current operator-machine job assignments, the computer program starts to simulate shop activity, automatically reassigning an operator to a new job on the same coil type whenever possible. If the range of the first guideline parameter would be exceeded by such reassignment, the program informs the supervisor that he must make the new assignment manually. At the same time, the program uses the second parameter to search the open order file and the history file for a high efficiency job for the operator in question. Based on this search, the supervisor is offered one or two suitable assignments for the operator.

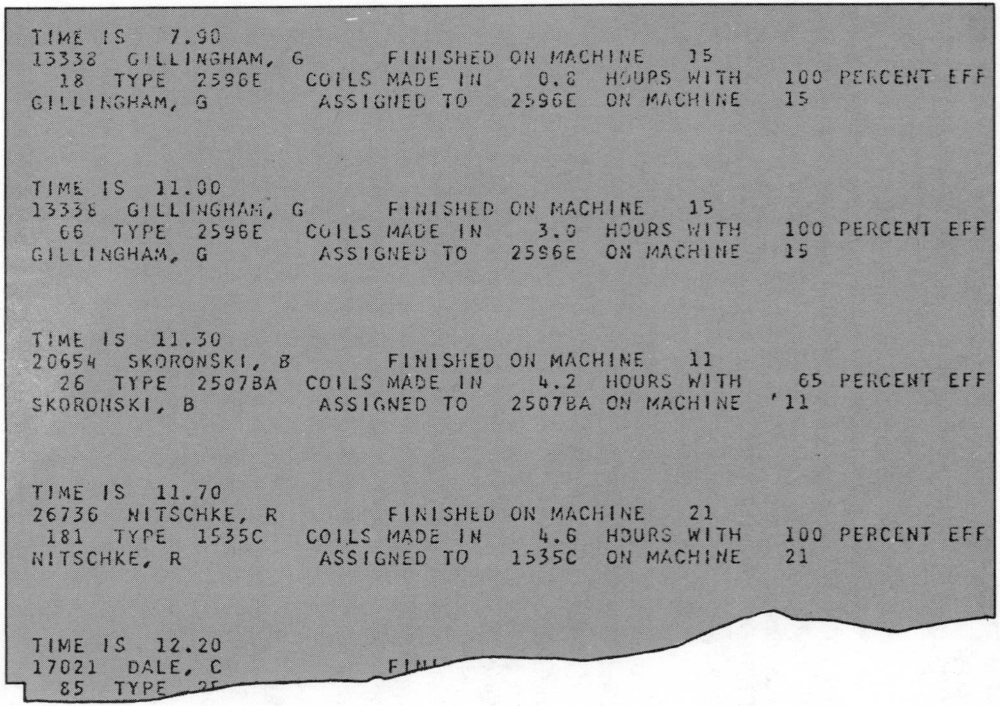

```
TIME IS   7.90
15338  GILLINGHAM, G   FINISHED ON MACHINE 15
   18  TYPE 2596E   COILS MADE IN   0.8  HOURS WITH  100 PERCENT EFF
GILLINGHAM, G   ASSIGNED TO   2596E ON MACHINE 15

TIME IS  11.00
15338  GILLINGHAM, G   FINISHED ON MACHINE 15
   66  TYPE 2596E   COILS MADE IN   3.0  HOURS WITH  100 PERCENT EFF
GILLINGHAM, G   ASSIGNED TO   2596E ON MACHINE 15

TIME IS  11.30
20654  SKORONSKI, B   FINISHED ON MACHINE 11
   26  TYPE 2507BA   COILS MADE IN   4.2  HOURS WITH   65 PERCENT EFF
SKORONSKI, B   ASSIGNED TO   2507BA ON MACHINE '11

TIME IS  11.70
26736  NITSCHKE, R   FINISHED ON MACHINE 21
  181  TYPE 1535C   COILS MADE IN   4.6  HOURS WITH  100 PERCENT EFF
NITSCHKE, R   ASSIGNED TO   1535C ON MACHINE 21

TIME IS  12.20
17021  DALE, C   FIN
   85  TYPE 2F
```

FIGURE 8. Simulation shows what happens as jobs begin and end. From
V. Godin, and C. H. Jones, "The Interactive Shop Supervisor," Industrial
Engineering, November, 1969.

The length of the simulation run is normally two to four days, however, the length of run is not restricted. When the simulation run is complete a summary of activity over the simulated period is typed out as shown in Figure 8.

Various reports can be called for at any time that the system is in operation such as shop status, a history of work by operator or by machine, load summarized by standard hours, etc. Figure 9 shows an example of a shop status report.

Concluding Comments

Sequencing models based largely on simulation studies have provided important new methodology and concepts for production line balancing and for job shop scheduling. The job shop scheduling research has by no

MACHINE	CODE	E.NO.	NAME
1	2588S	15982	DOWLER, B
2	2588L	20654	SKORONSKI, B
3	2588BM	13338	GILLINGHAM, G
4	2588AS		
5	2588C	34149	HYLAND, B
6	2588BY		
7	2588AN	30264	KRAMER, J
8	2588BT	13989	GREGG, F
9	2507AJ	10460	FLEMING, M
10	2588CM		
11	0		
12	2588CH	26499	STARR, B
13	2588BF	18884	MERCEIN, C
14	2596C	23979	ANDERSON, D
15	2596A		
16	2588AF	17021	DALE, C
17	1535G	88888	JETER, B
18	2507AK	11631	ALDRIDGE, L
19	2588BW	25448	JORDAN, H
20	2588AP		
21	1535F	26736	NITSCHKE, R

FIGURE 9. This display of shop status can be obtained from the computer any time the system is in operation. From V. Godin, and C. H. Jones, "The Interactive Shop Supervisor," Industrial Engineering, November, 1969.

means come to a final conclusion, and most job shop scheduling systems currently use very little of the generated knowledge. Part of the reason for this is that crystal-clear conclusions have not yet been forthcoming. One thing seems clear from the development of computer-based control systems like the one at Hughes—such systems can improve operations and probably increase the size of shop that can be managed effectively.

REVIEW QUESTIONS

1. Define the terms machine-limited and labor-limited job shop systems.

2. What is a local priority dispatch rule? A dynamic priority rule?

3. Based on the results of Nanot's experiments, which two priority rules would be best if on-time completion of orders were the dominant criterion?

4. Does it appear that the SOT Rule (shortest operation time) can be salvaged as an effective and practical rule by altering it through truncation?

5. Is the COVERT Rule simply a modification of the SOT Rule? By what rationale does it achieve excellent order tardiness characteristics?

6. Describe Nelson's concept of a complete labor assignment procedure in labor-limited production systems.

7. Based on Nelson's experimental results, what was the most effective machine center selection procedure for labor assignment?

8. Rationalize why labor-limited production systems are more flexible than machine-limited systems.

9. What was Nelson's conclusion on the effectiveness of centralized control of labor assignment?

10. Summarize the results of Allen's studies of decision rules under declining load.

11. Outline the Hughes' loading system. How does it provide a feasible schedule to shop foremen?

12. Outline the Western Electric interactive scheduling system. Would you classify it as a loading or detailed schedule system?

13. Compare the advantages and disadvantages of the Hughes and Western Electric systems.

REFERENCES

1. Allen, M., "The Efficient Utilization of Labor Under Conditions of Fluctuating Demand," Chapter 16 in *Industrial Scheduling*, J. F. Muth and G. L. Thompson, eds., Prentice-Hall, Inc., Englewood Cliffs, N.J., 1963.

2. Baker, C. T., and B. P. Dzielinski, "Simulation of a Simplified Job Shop," *Management Science*, Vol. VI, No. 3, April 1960, pp. 311–323.

3. Bowman, E. H., "The Schedule Sequence Problem," *Operations Research*, Vol. VII, September, 1959, pp. 621–624.

4. Buffa, E. S., and W. H. Taubert, *Production-Inventory Systems: Planning and Control*, Richard D. Irwin, Inc., Homewood, Ill., Rev. ed., 1972.

5. Bulkin, M. H., J. L. Colley, and H. W. Steinhoff, Jr., "Load Forecasting, Priority Sequencing, and Simulation in a Job-Shop Control System," Chapter 11 in, *Readings in Production and Operations Management*, E. S. Buffa, ed., John Wiley & Sons, Inc., New York, 1966. Also published in similar form in *Management Science*, Vol. 13, No. 2, October, 1966, pp. 29–51.

6. Carroll, D. C., *Heuristic Sequencing of Single and Multiple Component Jobs*, Unpublished Ph.D. Dissertation, Sloan School of Management, Massachusetts Institute of Technology, 1965.

7. Conway, R. W., and W. L. Maxwell, "Network Scheduling by the Shortest Operation Discipline," *Operations Research*, Vol. X, No. 1, 1962, pp. 51–73. Reprinted as Chapter 17 in *Industrial Scheduling*, J. F. Muth, and G. L. Thompsons, eds., Prentice-Hall, Inc., Englewood Cliffs, N.J., 1963.

8. Elmaghraby, S. E., and R. T. Cole, "On the Control of Production in Small Job-Shops," *Journal of Industrial Engineering*, Vol. XIV, No. 4, July–August, 1963, pp. 186–196.

9. Emery, J., "An Approach to Job Shop Scheduling Using a Large-Scale Computer," *Industrial Management Review*, Vol. III, Fall 1961, pp. 78–96.

10. Ferguson, R. L., and C. H. Jones, "A Computer Aided Decision System," *Management Science*, Vol. 15, No. 10, June, 1969, pp. 550–561.

11. Godin, V., and C. H. Jones, "The Interactive Shop Supervisor," *Industrial Engineering*, November, 1969, pp. 16–22.

12. Grindlay, A. A., *Tandem Queues with Dynamic Priorities*, Western Management Science Institute, Working Paper No. 14, UCLA, September, 1962.

13. Harris, R. D., *An Empirical Investigation of a Job Shop as a Network of Queueing Systems*, Unpublished Ph.D. Dissertation, UCLA, 1965.

14. Harris, R. D., *An Empirical Investigation and Model Proposal of a Job Shop-Like Queueing System*, Western Management Science Institute, Working Paper No. 84, UCLA, July, 1965.

15. Jackson, J. R., "Job Shop-Like Queueing Systems," *Management Science*, Vol. X, No. 1, October, 1963, pp. 131–142.

16. Jackson, J. R., "Networks of Waiting Lines," *Operations Research*, Vol. V, August, 1957, pp. 518–521.

17. Jackson, J. R., "Queues with Dynamic Priority Disciplines," *Management Science*, Vol. VIII, No. 1, 1961, pp. 18–34. Reprinted as Chapter 19 of *Industrial Scheduling*, J. F. Muth, and G. L. Thompson, eds., Prentice-Hall Inc., Englewood Cliffs, N.J., 1963.

18. Jackson, J. R., *Scheduling a Production Line to Minimize Maximum Tardiness*, Management Sciences Research Project, Research Report No. 43, UCLA, 1955.

19. Jackson, J. R., "Simulation Research on Job Shop Production," *Naval Research Logistics Quarterly*, Vol. IV, December, 1957.

20. Jackson, J. R., "Some Problems of Queueing with Dynamic Priorities, *Naval Research Logistics Quarterly*, Vol. VII, September, 1960, pp. 235–250.
21. Kusnick, A. A., "Management and Engineering Information Systems," *Industrial Management Review*, Spring, 1966, pp. 3–16.
22. LeGrande, "The Development of a Factory Simulation System Using Actual Operating Data," *Management Technology*, Vol. III, No. 1, May, 1963. Reprinted as Chapter 9 in *Readings in Production and Operations Management*, E. S. Buffa, ed., John Wiley & Sons, New York, 1966.
23. Mann, A. S., "On the Job Shop Scheduling Problem," *Operations Research*, Vol. VIII, October, 1960, pp. 219–223.
24. Nanot, Y. R., *An Experimental Investigation and Comparative Evaluation of Priority Disciplines in Job Shop-Like Queueing Networks*, Ph.D. Dissertation, UCLA, 1963. Also Management Sciences Research Project, Research Report No. 87, UCLA, 1963.
25. Nelson, R. T., *Dual Resource Constrained Series Service Systems*, *Operations Research*, Vol. 16, No. 2, March–April, 1968. Also published as, Western Management Science Institute, Working Paper No. 113, UCLA, February, 1967.
26. Nelson, R. T., "Labor and Machine Limited Production Systems," *Management Science*, Vol. 13, No. 9, May, 1967.
27. Nelson, R. T., "Waiting-Time Distributions for Application to a Series of Service Centers," *Operations Research*, Vol. VI, November–December, 1958, pp. 856–862.
28. Reiter, S., "A System for Managing Job-Shop Production," *Journal of Business*, Vol. XXXIV, No. 3, July, 1966, pp. 371–393.
29. Rowe, A. J., "Application of Computer Simulation to Sequential Decision Rules in Production Scheduling," *Proc.: Eleventh Annual Industrial Engineering Institute*, University of California, Berkeley-Los Angeles, February, 1959.
30. Rowe, A. J., "Towards a Theory of Scheduling," *Journal of Industrial Engineering*, Vol. XI, March, 1960, pp. 125–136.
31. Smith, W. E., "Various Optimizers for Single Stage Production," *Naval Research Logistics Quarterly*, Vol. III, March, 1956, pp. 59–66.
32. Steinhoff, H. W., Jr., "Daily System for Sequencing Orders in a Large-Scale Job Shop," Chapter 10 in *Readings in Production and Operations Management*, E. S. Buffa, ed., John Wiley & Sons, Inc., New York, 1966.

chapter 18

NETWORK PROGRAMS

Network programming as a fundamental methodology developed apparently simultaneously by the DuPont Company in concert with the Univac Division of Remington Rand Corporation (now Sperry Rand Corporation), and the Navy Office of Special Projects working with the Booz-Allen and Hamilton Company and the Missile Systems Division of Lockheed Aircraft Company. The initial development at the DuPont Company was directed toward achieving better control of the engineering function. For that purpose there was created an Integrated Engineering Control Group (IEC) under the direction of J. S. Sayer, and in 1956 M. R. Walker of DuPont and J. E. Kelley, Jr., of Remington Rand started a project directed toward the control of maintenance of chemical plants at DuPont. The critical path method (CPM) of scheduling and controlling large projects was the outgrowth of this effort. In 1957 the Navy was faced with the task of planning and controlling the Polaris Project, an enormous task involving approximately three thousand separate contracting organizations. To accomplish this the Navy set up a team under the Navy Office of Special Projects to develop a special control technique. The result of this effort was the well-known Program Evaluation and Review Technique (PERT) now known as Performance Evaluation and Review Technique. The Polaris Project was an outstanding success [20], and PERT is now required in some form for all government defense contractors. With the publicized success of PERT in 1959 the CPM technique was released publicly by

DuPont which had apparently maintained its secrecy until that point. The basic conceptual framework and methodology of the two techniques are very nearly the same.

The techniques of network programming are largely applicable to the scheduling and control of large-scale, one-time projects. Our discussion in Chapter 12 serves as a general introduction to the present material. Recall at that time we developed our discussion around the activities required to rebuild a Tool Cutter Grinder and developed a feasible Gantt chart schedule for accomplishing the activities. For illustrative purposes, we shall develop that same example in terms of PERT and CPM. Our initial discussion will be in terms of the planning, scheduling, and control problems in the context of the PERT methodology. We shall then discuss the differences between the PERT and CPM methods.

The complexity of large-scale one-time projects puts a premium on the network planning phase. Just the development of the production plan as a network of operations yields a tremendous improvement over traditional managerial methods, because to develop the network chart requires the determination of the individual operations or activities to be done: how they will be performed, the equipment needed, the required kinds of labor skills, the required sequence of operations, the possible simultaneity of operations or activities, and estimates of activity time requirements. Given all of this information, it is possible to schedule the effective use of available resources. The development of a rational schedule requires attention to careful timing and sequencing of required activities to complete the project in minimum time or (what we called previously) the *critical path schedule*.

One of the most important results of the generation of a feasible schedule is the development of permissible slack in the timing of certain activities. This slack in the schedule gives management a degree of flexibility in achieving the schedule. An extremely important aspect of this flexibility is that it may be used to level the labor requirements to some extent over the entire project or make it possible to use limited equipment for several operations without conflict and without extending the overall project time. Computer scheduling programs have been developed to help achieve answers to this limited resources problem. Finally, when a feasible schedule of activities of men and equipment has been developed, there still remains the reporting and control of activities involving the rescheduling of some activities where necessary. The reporting and control problem is a complex one because of the large number of activities going on simultaneously, and computer based reporting and control systems have been developed to meet this problem.

Network Planning Methods

In network planning models each activity must be assigned a definite beginning and end point, and these points in time are called "events." An event has no time duration in itself, but the activities occur between events in the PERT methodology. A project may then be defined as a collection of interrelated activities connected by events and leading to the accomplishment of the project activities. Network planning in the framework of PERT reduces to three phases: activity analysis, arrow diagramming, and node numbering.

In the *activity analysis* phase, planners are determining the list of activities required, methods to be used, tools and equipment required, and the technological precedence relationships of the activities. This process is normally carried on by professional planning personnel who work with everyone concerned to derive lists of activities and other pertinent data, such as Table I. Table I shows the activities required, activity time requirements in days, and the technological precedence requirements to rebuild a Tool Cutter Grinder.

The second phase, *arrow diagramming*, must be based on a complete, verified, and approved list of activities. The arrow diagram makes no attempt to relate the project to a time scale but instead attempts to show the interrelationships between activities. These interrelationships stem from the technological sequencing requirements rather than from scheduling considerations. Each activity is represented by an arrow; the tail of the arrow indicates the start of an activity and the arrow head the completion, the arrow length having no significance. Thus a sequence of arrows represents a sequence of activities, and the nodes, represented by small circles, define the events. Figure 1 represents the arrow diagram for the set of activities listed in Table I. (Note that Figure 1 is not identical to the precedence diagram shown in Figure 6 on page 395. We shall discuss the differences and similarities when we discuss CPM.) Our present interest is in the structure of the diagram and how it represents the technological precedence relationships. Note that activities A, B, C must proceed in that sequence. However, activities L and Q can proceed separately and independently of activities V and P so long as both are completed prior to the beginning of activity N. Note also that three of the activities are represented by dashed lines and have zero time requirements as shown. These activities are called dummy activities and are inserted to establish certain sequential requirements. For example activity X must be preceded by activities J, and S as shown in Table I. Note, however, from

TABLE I. Rebuilding a tool cutter grinder. Activities required, times, and immediate predecessors*

Activity Code	Activity Name	Days Required	Immediate Predecessors
A	Disconnect and move	0.2	—
B	Connect power and pretest	0.2	A
C	Remove electrical units	0.2	B
D	Clean machine	0.3	C
E	Remove and disassemble mechanical units	0.2	C
F	Clean machine parts	0.4	D
G	List mechanical parts	0.5	F
H	Order machine parts	0.5	G
I	Receive machine parts	1.0	H
J	Paint cross slides	25.0	I
K	Machine parts	1.5	G
L	Inspect and list electrical parts	1.0	K
M	Paint motor	1.0	L
N	Assemble motor	0.8	P, Q, R
O	Machine saddle	2.5	H
P	Machine slides	2.0	V
Q	Machine table	2.0	L
R	Paint machine	2.0	M
S	Scrape slides	1.0	N
T	Scrape table	1.0	G
U	Scrape saddles	0.5	E
V	Machine gibs	2.0	K
W	Install spindle	1.0	J, O, T
X	Assemble parts	1.0	J, O, S, T
Y	Scrape gibs	0.5	U
Z	Assemble head	1.0	J, O, T
AA	Install motor and electrical parts	0.3	Y
BB	Assemble cross slides	0.4	J, O, T
CC	Connect power and test	0.5	AA, BB, Z, W, X
DD	Touch-up, move, reinstall	0.3	CC

*Data from R. D. Archibald and R. L. Villoria, Network-Based Management Systems, John Wiley & Sons, New York, 1967.

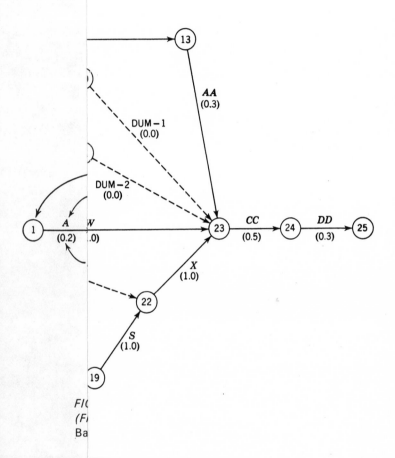

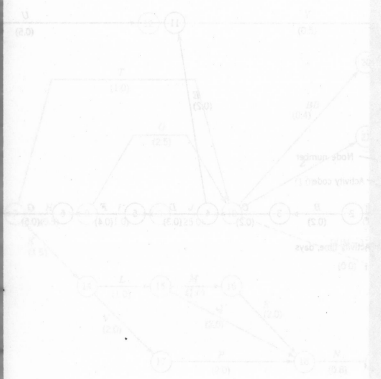

FIGURE 1. Arrow diagram for rebuilding Cincinnati No. 2 coke oven...
Figures 1 to 3 are adapted from R. D. Archibald and R. L. Villoria, Network-Based Management Systems, John Wiley & Sons, New York, 1967.

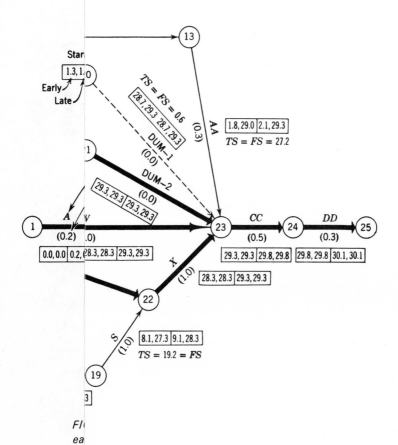

Start

Early

Late

Fl

ea

FIGURE 2. Arrow diagram for rebuilding Cincinnati No. 2 cutter panel. Early and late start and finish times, and critical path indicated.

Figure 1 that all activities ending in node 10 need to precede activity X. The relationship of activity J preceding X is established through DUM-3, a dummy activity requiring no performance time.

The node numbering shown in Figure 1 follows simple rules. An arrow is designated by the numbers of the nodes it connects, i, j, where i represents the tail and j the arrow head. The node numbers are then such that for each arrow i is always less than j, that is, $(i < j)$. The purpose of establishing this convention is so that efficient routines can construct all of the logical relationships of an arrow diagram and prevent the occurrence of closed loops.

A network diagram such as Figure 1 provides a clear basis for planning the entire project showing its scope in a form that can be easily interpreted and understood. The mere preparation of the diagram produces a great deal of the overall benefit since it requires that someone has thought carefully about the activities and their relationships. The diagram becomes a basis for the development and refining of the objectives of the project and for training project personnel. However, the next logical use of the diagram is in generating and evaluating alternate schedules.

Critical Path Scheduling

The arrow diagram of Figure 1 showing the required activities, the precedence relationships, and the estimated activity times, is now the critical input to the development of a first feasible schedule which we shall call the Critical Path Schedule. As we shall see, the critical path through the network is so termed because a delay in any of the activities which fall on the critical path will delay the project as a whole. We shall first discuss a deterministic critical path schedule based on the activity times given in Table I and shown in parentheses near the activity codes in Figure 1. Probabilistic network scheduling methods will be discussed in the next major section of this chapter. The time values shown in Table I and Figure 1 are expected times, and from these basic values we can compute "earliest" and "latest" start and finish times, as well as slack values representing the time performance flexibility in the network. All of these computations can be performed automatically with existing computer routines.

Earliest Start and Finish Times. If we start with zero as an arbitrary starting time for the project, then for each activity there is a relative earliest starting time (ES) which is the earliest possible time that the activity can begin, assuming that all of the preceding activities are also started at their ES. The earliest finish time for that activity (EF) is ES + activity time. The procedure for computing *ES* and *EF* manually from a network such as Figure 1 is as follows:

1. Place the value of the project start time to the left of the beginning activity in the position shown for the early start time in Figure 2. In Figure 2 we see a zero for the *ES* for activity *A*. The early finish time is then *ES* + activity time, or 0.2 days for activity *A*.

2. Now consider any new unmarked activities, all of whose predecessors have been marked with their *ES*'s and *EF*'s, and mark to the left of the new activity in the *ES* position the largest number in the *EF* position of its immediate predecessors. This number is the *ES* time for the new activity. For activity *B* the *ES* is 0.2 days since that is the *EF* time of the preceding activity.

3. Add to this number the activity time and mark the result in the *EF* position for activity *B*, 0.2 + 0.2 = 0.4 days.

4. Continue through the entire network until the "finish" activity has been reached.

To complete the computations accurately, we must take account of the effects at nodes where several arrowheads terminate. The following activity will take its *ES* from the largest *EF* of any of its immediate predecessors including dummy activities. For example, following node 22, activity *X* must take account of both activity *S* and DUM-3. The largest *EF* of the two turns out to be 28.3 for activity *S* which then becomes the *ES* for activity *X*. If we continue through the entire network in this way, the *ES* and *EF* for the final activity *DD* are respectively 29.8 and 30.1 days (see the computer output shown in Figure 3).

Latest Start and Finish Times. If we assume that the target for completing the project is the *EF* time of 30.1 days, then we have defined the latest finish time (*LF*) as 30.1 days, allowing no slack in the project as a whole. Therefore, the latest start time (*LS*) for the terminal activity is *LF*—activity time. The *LS* and *LF* times for each activity can now be determined by working backwards from activity *DD* as follows:

1. Mark the values of *LF* and *LS* in their proper positions for the finish activity *DD*. For the Tool Cutter Grinder project shown in Figure 2, *LF* = 30.1, and *LS* = 29.8 days.

2. Consider any new unmarked activity, *all of whose successors have been marked*, and mark in the *LF* position for the new activity the *smallest LS* time marked to the left of any of its immediate successors. In other words, *LF* for an activity equals the earliest

CRITICAL PATH SCHEDULE   JOB NO. 50787

DATE ISSUED 7–17–62   PAGE 1

OPERATION CODE	i	j	DAYS REQ'D	EARLIEST START	EARLIEST FINISH	LATEST START	LATEST FINISH	DAYS SLACK	FREE SLACK
A	1	2	.2	.0	.2	.0	.2	.0	**
B	2	3	.2	.2	.4	.2	.4	.0	**
C	3	4	.2	.4	.6	.4	.6	.0	**
D	4	5	.3	.6	.9	.6	.9	.0	**
E	4	11	.2	.6	.8	27.8	28.0	27.2	.0
F	5	6	.4	.9	1.3	.9	1.3	.0	**
G	6	7	.5	1.3	1.8	1.3	1.8	.0	**
H	7	8	.5	1.8	2.3	1.8	2.3	.0	**
I	8	9	1.0	2.3	3.3	2.3	3.3	.0	**
J	9	10	25.0	3.3	28.3	3.3	28.3	.0	**
K	7	14	1.5	1.8	3.3	21.0	22.5	19.2	.0
L	4	15	1.0	3.3	4.3	22.5	23.5	19.2	.0
M	15	16	1.0	4.3	5.3	23.5	24.5	19.2	.0
N	18	19	.8	7.3	8.1	26.5	27.3	19.2	.0
O	8	10	2.5	2.3	4.8	25.8	28.3	23.5	23.5
P	17	18	2.0	5.3	7.3	24.5	26.5	19.2	.0
Q	15	18	2.0	4.3	6.3	24.5	26.5	20.2	1.0
R	16	18	2.0	5.3	7.3	24.5	26.5	19.2	.0
S	19	22	1.0	8.1	9.1	27.3	28.3	19.2	19.2
T	7	10	1.0	1.8	2.8	27.3	28.3	25.5	25.5
U	11	12	.5	.8	1.3	28.0	28.5	27.2	.0
V	14	17	2.0	3.3	5.3	22.5	24.5	19.2	.0
W	10	23	1.0	28.3	29.3	28.3	29.3	.0	**
X	22	23	1.0	28.3	29.3	28.3	29.3	.0	**
Y	12	13	.5	1.3	1.8	28.5	29.0	27.2	.0
Z	10	21	1.0	28.3	29.3	28.3	29.3	.0	**
AA	13	23	.3	1.8	2.1	29.0	29.3	27.2	27.2
BB	10	20	.4	28.3	28.7	28.9	29.3	.6	.0
CC	23	24	.5	29.3	29.8	29.3	29.8	.0	**
DD	24	25	.3	29.8	30.1	29.8	30.1	.0	**
DUM-1	20	23	.0	28.7	28.7	29.3	29.3	.6	.6
DUM-2	21	23	.0	29.3	29.3	29.3	29.3	.0	**
DUM-3	10	22	.0	28.3	28.3	28.3	28.3	.0	**

** Critical Operations

FIGURE 3.   Sample output of network analysis program for the Tool Cutter Grinder.

LS of the successors for that activity. In Figure 2, then, activity CC takes its $LF = 29.8$ from the LS time of activity DD.

3. Subtract from this number the activity time which becomes the LS for the activity. For activity CC, $LS = 29.8 - 0.5 = 29.3$.

4. Continue backwards through the chart until all LS and LF times have been entered in their respective positions.

Slack and Critical Path. Total slack (TS) for an activity is the maximum time that the activity can be delayed beyond its ES without delaying the project completion time. The critical activities are those which are in the sequence of the longest time path through the network, and therefore the activities on this path all have minimum possible TS. Since for our example the target date and the EF for activity DD, the finish activity, are the same, all critical activities will have zero TS. The project target date may of course be later than the EF of the finish activity, in which case all activities on the critical path would have the same TS equal to the difference. Then, all noncritical activities will have greater TS than critical activities. Note that this is true in Figure 3, which shows the computer output for the network of Figures 1 and 2.

Free Slack (FS) is the amount of time that an activity can be delayed without delaying the ES of any other activity. Free Slack for an activity never exceeds its TS. Free slack for an activity is computed as the difference between the EF for that activity and the earliest of the ES times of all of its immediate successors. For example, activity T has $FS = 25.5$, since the earliest ES of its four successors is 28.3 and its own EF is 2.8.

Probabilistic Network Methods

Because time estimates of activities were highly uncertain, the original PERT methodology attempted to take uncertainty into account by assuming that the activity time estimates were probability distributions and the critical path a probabilistic critical path. Then the schedules for all of the activities reflected the uncertainty of the activity times.

To apply the probabilistic methods, *three time estimates* are developed for each activity as a basis for specifying the probability distributions of activity times. The three different time estimates are:

The *optimistic time*, "a," is the shortest possible time in which the activity may be accomplished if all goes well. The estimate is based on the assumption that the activity would have no more than one chance in 100 of being completed in less than this time.

The *pessimistic time*, "b," is the longest time that an activity should take under adverse conditions, but barring acts of nature. This time estimate is based on the assumption that the activity would have no more than one chance in 100 of being completed in time larger than b.

The *most likely time*, "m," is the modal value of the distribution.

The PERT computational algorithm reduces these three time estimates to a single average estimate, t_e, the mean of a Beta distribution. The estimates of the mean and variance of the distribution may be computed by the following:

$$\bar{x} = \tfrac{1}{6}(A + 4M + B)$$

$$s^2 = [\tfrac{1}{6}(B - A)]^2$$

where A, B, and M are estimates of the values of a, b, and m respectively, and $\bar{x}$ and s^2 are estimates of the mean and variance, t_e and σ^2.

Figure 4 shows the general relationship of the specified time values for two sample distributions.

Probabilistic Critical Path. In the standard PERT algorithm the computation of early and late start and finish times are similar to those already discussed for deterministic time values, since the three time values specifying the distribution are reduced to the expected time t_e. The basic assumption in PERT is that each activity has a probability distribution; the actual deviations from the expected time values for any one path are the sum of the many individual activity deviations; and the total accumulated deviation of a path will be a random variable with normal probability distribution.

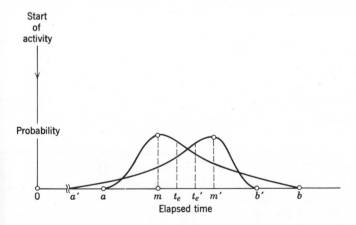

FIGURE 4. *PERT time estimates; a = optimistic time, b = pessimistic time, m = modal or most likely time, t_e = expected time for two distributions.*

The assumption is that since there are many activities, the individual differences from t_e in the distributions will cancel each other out.

Management can associate a particular date with any node in the diagram since any path has an associated probability distribution. This date is then compared to the probability distribution of the critical path up to that node and a probability of completion by that date is obtained. This assignment of probabilities to completion dates is a very powerful planning and control tool. Management can plan, reschedule, or even renegotiate contracts on the basis of expected outcomes and stated risk levels. Obviously, however, the output is no better than the input data, and there is a danger that the very existence of the precise probability statements made tends to give an aura of accuracy which may not necessarily be justified.

Criticism of the PERT methods and statistics have raised fundamental questions. Grubbs [12] shows that the mean and variance values used by PERT for the beta distribution are for individual values of time selected at random and not for some average of random variables. Fulkerson [11] shows that the expected critical path lengths in PERT networks are always optimistic and generates an improved estimate.

Monte Carlo methods have been used by Van Slyke [23] to simulate the time through networks plotting cumulative probability time distributions of the results. Thus he could assign an index of criticality to each and every activity which indicated the probability that the activity in question would be on the critical path.

Finally, MacCrimmon and Ryavec [19] made an extensive analytical study of PERT assumptions which should be read by all those who plan to use the technique.

Critical Path Methods

The differences between PERT and CPM are in the details of the preparation of the arrow diagram and in the fact that CPM normally uses only the single time estimate and so would follow the deterministic model of PERT described earlier.

The CPM procedure represents activities as occurring at the nodes, and the arrows represent the sequences of activities required to carry through the project. There is an advantage to the CPM mode of arrow diagramming in that it is not necessary to invoke the use of the dummy activity. Figure 6 in Chapter 12 is the CPM arrow diagram for the Tool Cutter Grinder project which may be compared with the comparable PERT diagram shown in Figures 1 and 2 of this chapter. The analysis in developing the early and late starting and finishing times as well as slack times is identical with the deterministic PERT procedure described previously. Though normally the CPM procedure uses only the deterministic model there is of course no reason why it could not be developed using the probabilistic methods as well.

PERT and CPM are entirely equivalent methodologies. Computer programs exist for both methods for either the deterministic or probabilistic models. The fact that the probabilistic model was developed in the aerospace setting is understandable when we consider the uncertainty of time performance in research and development work. Nevertheless, the Department of Defense has more recently dropped the use of the three time estimates in favor of the deterministic model because of arbitrary use of the time estimates and because in some instances projects such as the Minuteman Missile have exceeded computer size capabilities.

Project Scheduling and Control

When the critical path schedule, represented by Figures 1 and 2 for the Tool Cutter Grinder project, has been completed the scheduling process is not done but an important input to the scheduling process has been developed. With the data of the critical path schedule together with the available slack times for the noncritical activities, we can consider the various alternatives which might either shorten the schedule or reduce its cost. Some of the possibilities for attaining improved schedules involve cost-time trade-offs, where additional effort selectively allocated might possibly shorten the schedule and reduce costs, and the possibility of leveling the use of resources such as labor and equipment.

Least Costing. The concept of least costing is related to the allocation of overall resources (expenditures) to the various activities. The shape of the cost-time curve for an activity forms the basis for reallocation. Cost-time curves such as those represented in Figure 5 show that under some circumstances activity time can be reduced by resorting to a "crash program." In other instances, it might be possible to allocate fewer resources and accept a "slow" schedule at lower cost. These cost-time trade-off concepts are not equally applicable to all kinds of activities, and so care must be taken in applying them.

If the original critical path schedule is unsatisfactory in that the latest finish time (*LF*) does not meet the project deadline then management might wish to use the cost-time trade-off to shorten the schedule, particularly if there was a penalty for not meeting the project completion time. By drawing resources from noncritical activities and allocating them to

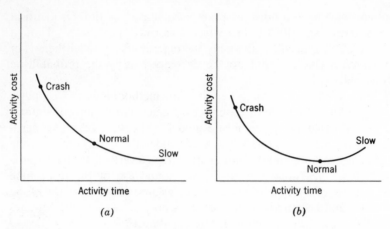

FIGURE 5.   Typical activity time-cost curves.

critical ones, the schedule may possibly be shortened. The technique is to add resources to activities whose cost time curves have the smallest slopes, that is, change in cost per unit change in time. By decreasing resource allocations to noncritical jobs (thus increasing their activity times) with the largest slopes, it is possible to take advantage of the differential slope characteristics to achieve either a shortened schedule, a lower total cost, or both.

Various formal methodologies have been proposed to achieve shortened schedules and/or lower project costs. Linear programming models have been proposed by Fulkerson [11] and Kelley [14]. Other approaches to the problem have been proposed by Berman [2] and Moder and Phillips [21], and a summary of various methodologies is provided by Davis [6].

Scheduling with Limited Resources.   The simplest approach to scheduling with limited resources is to level the demand for the particular resource, using the flexibility made available by slack in order to shift the timing of activities which use the limited resource. Simulation as a general methodology has been used to good effect in this process. In applying simulation, a first attempt at leveling might set a maximum of the scarce resource just below the highest peak level of the beginning critical path schedule. The execution of the simulation program would then follow the arrow diagram, setting the clock time at zero, beginning all activities leaving node 1 while keeping track of the amount of the resource used and available. As the simulation clock is advanced and activities are completed, resources are returned to the "available" pool. When new activities are started, resources are drawn from this pool. If at some point the resource pool is temporarily

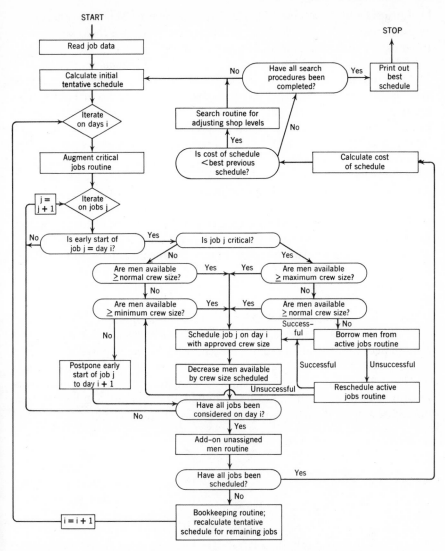

START

Read job data

Calculate initial tentative schedule

Have all search procedures been completed? — No → (loop back)

Yes → Print out best schedule → STOP

Search routine for adjusting shop levels

Yes ↓

Is cost of schedule < best previous schedule? — No → (back to search)

Yes ↑

Calculate cost of schedule

Iterate on days i

Augment critical jobs routine

j = j + 1

Iterate on jobs j

Is early start of job j = day i? — No →

Yes → Is job j critical?

No ↓ — Are men available ≥ normal crew size?

Yes → Is job j critical? Yes → Are men available ≥ maximum crew size?

No ↓ — Are men available ≥ minimum crew size?

No ↓ — Are men available ≥ normal crew size?

Successful → Schedule job j on day i with approved crew size

No → Borrow men from active jobs routine

Postpone early start of job j to day i + 1

Decrease men available by crew size scheduled

Successful / Unsuccessful — Reschedule active jobs routine

Unsuccessful →

Have all jobs been considered on day i? — No →

Yes ↓

Add-on unassigned men routine

Have all jobs been scheduled? — Yes →

No ↓

i = i + 1

Bookkeeping routine; recalculate tentative schedule for remaining jobs

FIGURE 6. *SPAR flow diagram. (Figures 6 and 7 are from J. D. Wiest, "A Heuristic Model for Scheduling Large Projects with Limited Resources,"* Management Science, *Vol. 13, No. 6, February 1967, pp. 359–377.)*

exhausted, the simulation program resorts to built in decision rules, for example, the activity may be delayed, or the program may "bump" noncritical activities and reassign resources to the critical ones.

Formal models for scheduling with limited resources have been proposed by Burgess and Killebrew [4], Dewitte [7], Wiest [24], and others. The Wiest model, called SPAR, is of particular interest since there seems to be the most published data available concerning it.

SPAR (*Scheduling Program for Allocation of Resources*) [24]. The SPAR program is written in FORTRAN to handle projects as large as 1200 single resource activities, network diagrams as large as 500 nodes in as many as 12 shops over a time span of 300 days. Wiest's model focuses on available resources which it allocates, period by period, to activities listed in the order of their earliest start times (*ES*). Beginning with the first period, activities are scheduled by selecting from the list of those currently available listed in the order of total slack. The most critical activities have the highest probability of being scheduled first. Activities are scheduled as long as there are available resources. When an activity fails to be scheduled in one period an attempt is made to schedule it in the following period. Eventually all postponed activities will become critical and move to the top of the priority list of available jobs. Figure 6 is the flow diagram for SPAR. Some of the detailed rules which guide the program are centered in a number of scheduling heuristics, which are designed to increase the utilization of the resources and/or to shorten the schedule.

Wiest has applied the SPAR program in a number of situations. The space vehicle project is of particular interest because of its size and requirement for several different resources. The project required engineering design and development, utilizing five different types of engineers and involving 300 activities. Figure 7 shows a comparative composite manpower loading chart for both a resource limited and unlimited schedule. The limited resources line shows the results after SPAR was applied. The total

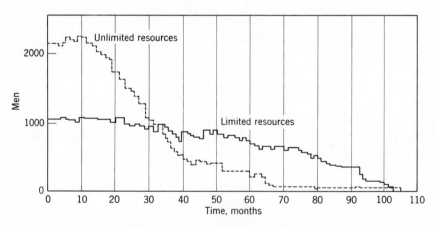

FIGURE 7. Space vehicle project, manpower loading schedule.

length of the project was shortened by 5 months with a much more even utilization of available resources.

Project Control by Network Methods

Control procedures occur throughout the network planning and scheduling processes which we have described. Controls are in effect during the preparation of the arrow diagram, during the scheduling phase, and during

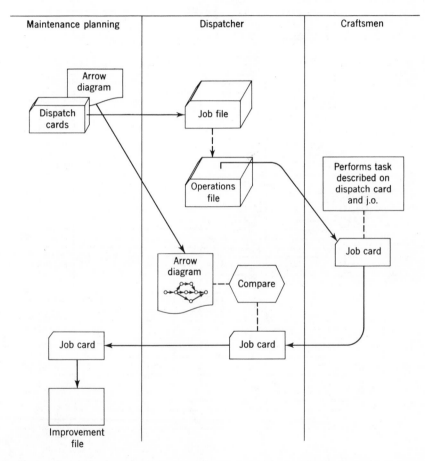

FIGURE 8. Flow diagram for dispatching phase of control of performance in machine tool rebuilding. Figures 8 and 9 are from R. D. Archibald and R. L. Villoria, Network-Based Management Systems, *John Wiley & Sons, New York, 1967.*

CRITICAL PATH SCHEDULE — START DATE July 9 — ORDER: 50787 — DATE: 7-17-62

Equip. Descrip: Grinder, Cinn #2 Tool & Cutter — SERIAL: 1D2T 1Z 442
Equip. No: — AREA CC B & J — PROD. CC

No	OPERATION	JOB	MEN	HRS.	ES	EF	LS	LF	CP	T	I	J
10	DISCONNECT	211										
		181										
11	UNLOAD OR MOVE	175	1	.5			7/9	7/9	*	0.2	1	2
		176	2	.5			7/9	7/9	*			
12	CONNECT POWER & PRE-TEST	181	1	1.0			7/9	7/9	*	0.2	2	3
		185	1	1.0			7/9	7/9	*			
		140	1	2.0			7/9	7/9	*			
13	REMOVE ELECTRICAL UNITS	181	1	1.0			7/9	7/9	*	0.2	3	4
		140	1	.5			7/9	7/9	*			
14	CLEAN MACHINE	179	1	4.0			7/9	7/9	*	0.3	4	5
15	INSPECT & LIST ELECT. PARTS	181	1	1.0			8/14	8/15	27	0.2	4	11
16	REMOVE & DISS MECH. UNITS	140	1	6.0			7/9	7/10	*	0.4	5	6
		147	1	6.0			7/9	7/10	*			
		211										
16+17	CLEAN MACHINE PARTS	150	1	8.0			7/9	7/10	*	0.5	6	7
18	LIST SPNDL.REPLACEMT PARTS	140										
19	LIST MECHANICAL PARTS	140	1	8.0			7/9	7/10	*	0.5	7	8
20	ORDER SPNDL.REPLACEMENT PARTS	MP										
21	ORDER MACH. MFR'S PARTS	MP	1				7/10	7/11	*	1.0	8	9
22	RECEIVE MFR'S NO-STOCK NOTICE	MP										
23	DRAFT TOOL ROOM PARTS	FE										
24	ORDER TOOL ROOM PARTS	MP										
25	RECEIVE MACH. MFR'S PARTS	MP	1				7/11	8/15	*	25.0	9	10
26	RECEIVE SPNDL.REPLACEMT PARTS	MP										
27	RECEIVE TOOL ROOM PARTS	MP										
28												
30	MACHINE BED	143										
31	MACHINE SADDLE	143	1	24.0			8/6	8/7	19	1.5	7	14
32	MACHINE SLIDES	143	1	16.0			8/7	8/8	19	1.0	14	15
33	MACHINE COLUMN	143										
34	MACHINE TABLE	143	1	16.0			8/8	8/9	19	1.0	15	16
35	MACHINE RAM	143										
36	MACHINE HEAD	143										
37	MACHINE GIBS	143	1	12.0			8/13	8/14	19	0.8	18	19
38	MACHINE PARTS	143	1	40.0			8/10	8/15	23	2.5	8	10
39	MACHINE TURRET OR CARRIER	143										
40	SCRAPE BED	140										
		147										
41	SCRAPE SADDLE(S)	140	1	16.0			8/9	8/13	19	2.0	17	18
		147										
42	SCRAPE SLIDE(S)	140	1	16.0			8/9	8/13	20	2.0	15	18
		147										
43	SCRAPE COLUMN	140										
		147										
44	SCRAPE TABLE	140	1	16.0			8/9	8/13	19	2.0	16	18
		147										
45	SCRAPE RAM	140										
		147										
46	SCRAPE HEAD	140										
		147										
47	SCRAPE GIBS	140	1	8.0			8/14	8/15	19	1.0	19	22
90	Dummy	147								0.0	20	23
91	Dummy									0.0	21	23
92	Dummy									0.0	10	22

FIGURE 9. Calendar schedule output for machine tool rebuilding.

(PAGE 2)

No.	Operation	Job	Men	Hrs.	ES	EF	LS	LF	CP	T	·I	J
48	SCRAPE TURRET OR CARRIER	140										
		147										
49												
50	PAINT HEAD	207										
51	PAINT GEAR BOX	207										
52	PAINT APRON(S)	207										
53	PAINT FEED UNITS	207										
54	PAINT CROSS SLIDES	207	1	6.0			8/14	8/15	25	1.0	7	10
55	PAINT MOTOR	207	1	2.0			8/15	8/15	27	.5	11	12
56	PAINT MACHINE	207	1	16.0			8/7	8/9	19	2.0	14	17
57	PAINT UNITS	207										
58												
59												
60	ASSEMBLE HEAD	140	1	14.0			8/15	8/16	*	1.0	10	23
		147										
61	ASSEMBLE GEAR BOX	140										
		147										
62	ASSEMBLE APRON	140										
		147										
63	ASSEMBLE FEED UNITS	140										
		147										
64	ASSEMBLE CROSS SLIDES	140	1	14.0			8/15	8/16	*	1.0	22	23
		147										
65	ASSEMBLE MOTOR9S) & UNITS	181	1	6.0			8/15	8/16	27	.5	12	13
66	ASSEMBLE TURRET OR CARRIER	140										
		147										
67	HANDLE PARTS	150	1	8.0			8/15	8/16	*	1.0	10	21
68	ASSEMBLE HYD. & LUB SYSTEM	211										
70	INSTALL HEAD	140										
		147										
		211										
71	INSTALL GEAR BOX	140										
		147										
72	INSTALL APRON	140										
		147										
73	INSTALL FEED UNITS	140										
		147										
74	INSTALL CROSS SLIDE	140										
		147										
75	INSTALL MOTORS & ELECT.PARTS	181	1	2.0			8/16	8/16	27	.3	13	23
76	INSTALL TURRET OR CARRIER	140										
		147										
77	INSTALL SPINDLE	140	1	6.0			8/15	8/16	1	.4	10	20
		147										
78												
80	MAKE AND INSTALL GUARDS	191										
81	BUILD SKID AND ATTACH	201										
82	WELD	200										
83	CONNECT POWER & POST TEST	181	1	1.0			8/16	8/16	*	.5	23	24
		185	1	1.0			8/16	8/16	*			
		140	1	6.0			8/16	8/16	*			
84	TOUCH-UP & LOAD OUT OR MOVE	207	1	2.0			8/16	8/16	*	.3	24	25
		175	1	1.0			8/16	8/17	*			
		176	2	1.0			8/16	8/17	*			
85	CONNECT MACHINE	181										
		185										
		211										

Total Hr. _____

FIGURE 9. (Continued)

the performance phase of a project. Perhaps the first point of control is in the project definition phase when lists of activities are being developed. The control point is in the approval of the activity list, and this step is commonly deferred until the arrow diagram has been developed, presuming that the preparation of the arrow diagram provides a check on the activity list.

Control of performance involves the generation of reports, commonly computer based. The most important factor in these reports is an up to date schedule. Based on an information feedback system concerning the progress and completion of activities, a new critical schedule can be produced daily or weekly to reflect the latest revisions in time estimates and the changing pattern of criticality of activities.

Figure 8 shows a flow diagram for some of the control phases for machine tool rebuilding at the Hughes Tool Company for which the tool cutter grinder example was a part. When the critical path schedule has been developed, a calendar schedule is prepared through a program which established earliest and latest starting dates and other data as shown in Figure 9. The maintenance planning group then prepares dispatch cards from the data in the calendar schedule. When an operation is "critical" this condition is flagged on the card. If an operation is not critical the total slack time is printed on the card. The entire process is computerized and among other things indicates the availability of men in various crafts, so that manpower limitations will be considered in the computations during the manpower scheduling phase. Rescheduling because of manpower limitations is automatic, and a computer output shows whether or not the critical path has changed and indicates which operations will be affected by the changes.

SUMMARY

Network planning and scheduling methods were born out of necessity as the size and complexity of one-time projects outran the capability of traditional managerial planning and control methods. It is interesting that two equivalent methodologies developed independently to meet the needs. Perhaps the most important future developments in network planning will be in the continuing advances and use of scheduling models which are designed to cope with the limited resources problem, such as Wiest's SPAR program. Such programs are not at all in common use at the present time. Coupled with a data processing system, the information available for control of performance through network methods is very much better than it was even 10 years ago. Jones and Taubert have applied the SDR methodology discussed in Chapter 13 to limited resource networks and this approach appears to have promise. [3].

REVIEW QUESTIONS

1. Try to account for the reasons why the deterministic methods of network planning developed in a situation like the maintenance operations of the Dupont Company while the probabilistic network planning methods developed in the Aerospace Industry.

2. Why is it necessary that an arrow diagram not be cyclic in nature?

3. What are the rules for node numbering?

4. Explain the purpose of a dummy activity.

5. What is the meaning of the term critical path?

6. Define the term total slack; free slack.

7. Define the terms optimistic time, pessimistic time, and most likely time.

8. What is the value to management of a probabilistic critical path?

9. Explain the concepts of crash, normal, and slow schedules in relation to cost-time curves.

10. Explain the concepts of least costing in obtaining lower project costs and/or shorter time schedules.

11. Discuss the concepts of resource leveling when resources are unlimited.

12. Contrast the concepts of resource leveling, when resources are unlimited, with those used by Wiest in his heuristic program for limited resources.

PROBLEMS

1. Listed in Table II is a set of activities, sequence requirements, and estimated activity times required for the renewal of a pipeline. Prepare both a PERT and CPM project diagram.

2. For the data of Problem 1 and the arrow diagram generated there:
(a) Compute ES, EF, LS, and LF for each of the activities.
(b) For the data generated in (a) compute slack for the system. Which activities can be delayed beyond their respective ES's without delaying the project completion time of 65 days? Which activities can be delayed, and by how many days, without delaying the ES of any other activity?
(c) Determine the critical path for the pipeline renewal project.

3. In Table III there is additional information in the form of optimistic, most likely, and pessimistic time estimates for the pipeline renewal project. Compute variances for the activities. Which activities have the greatest uncertainty in their completion schedules? Which have the least?

4. Suppose due to penalties in the contract that each day that the pipeline renewal project can be shortened is worth $100. Which of the following would you do and why?

(a) Shorten t_e of activity B by four days at a cost of $100.

(b) Shorten b of activity G by five days at a cost of $50.

(c) Shorten t_e of activity O by two days at a cost of $150.

(d) Shorten t_e of activity O by two days by drawing resources from activity N, which lengthens its t_e by two days.

5. Table II indicated the crew requirements per day for each activity in the pipeline renewal project.

(a) Prepare a crew size versus time chart representing the deployment of manpower for the *ES* schedule generated in Problem 2. Assume that men on all crews are completely interchangeable, that is, that any man can do any task.

TABLE II.

Activity	Letter Code	Code of Immediate Predecessor	Activity Time Requirement, (Days)	Crew Requirements per Day
Assemble crew for job	A	—	10	—
Use old line to build inventory	B	—	28	—
Measure and sketch old line	C	A	2	—
Develop materials list	D	C	1	—
Erect scaffold	E	D	2	10
Procure pipe	F	D	30	—
Procure valves	G	D	45	—
Deactivate old line	H	B,D	1	6
Remove old line	I	E,H	6	3
Prefabricate new pipe	J	F	5	20
Place valves	K	E,G,H	1	6
Place new pipe	L	I,J	6	25
Weld pipe	M	L	2	1
Connect valves	N	K,M	1	6
Insulate	O	K,M	4	5
Pressure test	P	N	1	3
Remove scaffold	Q	N,O	1	6
Clean up and turn over to operating crew	R	P,Q	1	6

TABLE III.

Activity Code	Optimistic Time Estimate of a	Most Likely Time Estimate of m	Pessimistic Time Estimate of b	Expected Time Estimate of t_e
A	8	10	12	10
B	26	26.5	36	28
C	1	2	3	2
D	0.5	1	1.5	1
E	1.5	1.63	4	2
F	28	28	40	30
G	40	42.5	60	45
H	1	1	1	1
I	4	6	8	6
J	4	4.5	8	5
K	0.5	0.9	1.9	1
L	5	5.25	10	6
M	1	2	3	2
N	0.5	1	1.5	1
O	3	3.75	6	4
P	1	1	1	1
Q	1	1	1	1
R	1	1	1	1

(b) Now assume that the man-days allocated for each activity can be deployed in any way. For example, activity L has a crew requirement of 25 men per day for 6 days from Table II or 150 man-days. These 150 man-days may be allocated over any chosen activity time; for example, 10 men per day for 15 days or vice versa. In order to try to achieve load leveling of the total crew, reallocate the man-days required for each activity so that no activity has a labor rate greater than a crew size of 10 men per day. This will require extending the activity times of some activities.

(c) (i) Compute the schedule statistics and new critical path.

   (ii) Prepare a new crew size versus time chart representing the deployment of manpower, but with the restriction that maximum total crew size per day is 10, using available slack as necessary. Also, use available slack to make this labor schedule as compact as possible; that is, the smallest number of fluctuations in overall crew size, and condensed in time span.

REFERENCES

1. Archibald, R. D., and R. L. Villoria, *Network-Based Management Systems*, John Wiley & Sons, New York, 1967.

2. Berman, E. B., "Resource Allocation in a PERT Network under Continuous-Time Cost Functions," *Management Science,* July, 1964.

3. Buffa, E. S., and W. H. Taubert, *Production-Inventory Systems: Planning and Control,* Richard D. Irwin, Inc., Homewood, Ill., Rev. ed., 1972, Chapters 13 and 14.

4. Burgess, A. R., and J. B. Killebrew, "Variation in Activity Level on a Cyclical Arrow Diagram," *Journal of Industrial Engineering,* Vol. XIII, No. 2, March–April, 1962, pp. 76–83.

5. Clark, C. E., "The Optimum Allocation of Resources among the Activities of a Network," *Journal of Industrial Engineering,* January–February, 1961.

6. Davis, E. W., "Resource Allocation in Project Network Models—A Survey," *Journal of Industrial Engineering,* Vol. XVII, No. 4, April, 1966, pp. 177–188.

7. Dewitte, L., "Manpower Leveling in PERT Networks," *Data Processing for Science/Engineering,* March–April, 1964.

8. Elmaghraby, S. E., "On Generalized Activity Networks," *Journal of Industrial Engineering,* Vol. XVII, No. 11, November, 1966, pp. 621–631.

9. Elmaghraby, S. E., "On the Expected Duration of PERT Type Networks," *Management Science,* Vol. 13, No. 5, January, 1957, pp. 299–306.

10. Elmaghraby, S. E., "The Theory of Networks and Management Science, II," *Management Science,* Vol. 17, No. 2, October, 1970, pp. 54–71.

11. Fulkerson, D. R., "Expected Critical Path Lengths in PERT Networks," *Operations Research,* Vol. 10, No. 6, November–December, 1962, pp. 808–817.

12. Grubbs, F. E., "Attempts to Validate Certain PERT Statistics or 'Picking on Pert,'" *Operations Research,* Vol. 10, No. 6, November–December, 1962, pp. 912–915.

13. Johnson, R. A., F. E. Kast, and J. E. Rosenzweig, *The Theory and Management of Systems,* McGraw-Hill Book Company, New York, 2nd ed., 1967.

14. Kelley, J. E., Jr., "Critical Path Planning and Scheduling Mathematical Basis," *Operations Research,* Vol. 9, No. 2, May–June, 1961, pp. 296–320.

15. Klingel, A. R., Jr., "Bias in PERT Project Completion Time Calculations for a Real Network," *Management Science,* Vol. 13, No. 4, December, 1966, pp. 194–201.

16. Levin, R. I., and C. A. Kirkpatrick, *Planning and Control with PERT/CPM,* McGraw-Hill Book Co., New York, 1966.

17. Levy, F. K., G. L. Thompson, and J. D. Wiest, "Multi-Shop Work Load Smoothing Program," *Naval Research Logistics Quarterly,* March, 1963.

18. Levy, F. K., G. L. Thompson, and J. D. Wiest, "The ABCs of the Critical Path Method," *Harvard Business Review,* September–October, 1963, pp. 98–108.

19. MacCrimmon, K. R., and C. A. Ryavec, "An Analytical Study of the PERT Assumptions," *Operations Research,* January–February, 1964; repr. as Chapter 30 in *Readings in Production and Operations Management,* E. S. Buffa, ed., John Wiley & Sons, Inc., New York, 1966.

20. Malcolm, D. G., J. H. Roseboom, C. E. Clark, and W. Fazar, "Application of a Technique for Research and Development Program Evaluation," *Operations Research,* Vol. 7, No. 5, September–October, 1959; repr. as Chapter 29 in

Readings in Production and Operations Management, E. S. Buffa, ed., John Wiley & Sons, New York, 1966.

21. Moder, J. J., and C. R. Phillips, *Product Management with CPM and PERT*, Reinhold Corporation, New York, 1964.

22. Shaffer, L. R., J. B. Ritter, and W. L. Meyer, *The Critical Path Method*, McGraw-Hill Book Co., New York, 1965.

23. Van Slyke, R. M., "Monte Carlo Methods and the PERT Problem," *Operations Research*, Vol. 11, No. 5, September–October, 1963, pp. 839–860.

24. Wiest, J. D., "A Heuristic Model for Scheduling Large Projects with Limited Resources," *Management Science*, Vol. 13, No. 6, February, 1967, pp. 359–377.

25. Wiest, J. D., "Heuristic Programs for Decision-Making," *Harvard Business Review*, September–October, 1966, pp. 129–143.

26. Wiest, J. D., "Some Properties of Schedules for Large Projects with Limited Resources," *Operations Research*, Vol. 12, No. 3, May–June, 1964; repr. as Chap. 31 in *Readings in Production and Operations Management*, E. S. Buffa, ed., John Wiley & Sons, New York, 1966.

27. Wiest, J. D., and F. K. Levy, *A Management Guide to PERT/CPM*, Prentice-Hall, Inc., Englewood Cliffs, N.J., 1969.

chapter 19

MODELS OF
STATISTICAL
CONTROL

Statistical analysis in operations management was introduced in 1924 by Walter Shewhart in a Bell Telephone Laboratories memorandum. In the years that followed, Shewhart, Dodge, and others also did early work in the concept of acceptance inspection. Much of Shewhart's thinking on these subjects was published in 1931 in his book, *Economic Control of Quality of Manufactured Product* [7]. In it, he introduced the basic concepts of statistical quality control, a field that has become an important and accepted part of production management. Industrial plants all over the country use the control chart methods which Shewhart introduced, and quality control has become a professional specialty. In the broader picture, the acceptance of statistical concepts of quality control represented a breakthrough in the way of thinking about many operations problems. Today there are many applications of statistical analysis in industry. *Work sampling*, which we discussed in Chapter 5, is becoming an accepted way of developing production standards. When an industrial engineer makes a time study, he is apt to consider how many readings are required in order to be confident of the result. The research worker in the operations field leans heavily on a branch of statistics called *experimental design*, in order to structure his experiments so that precise statements can be made about the results. *Correlation and regression analysis* is used to develop occupational tests, which may help to select workers who have a higher than average probability of success on the job. These and other applications in production make a knowledge of statistical analysis important for today's operations management personnel.

Universe and Sample. A sample is drawn from a *universe* or *population* and is, therefore, a subset of a universe or population. To draw the distinction, a *finite universe* might be a lot of 1000 parts produced on a lathe. Any of the dimensions produced might in themselves be considered a finite universe. If we measured the diameters of all 1000 parts, the result would be a distribution of the diameters of that universe. If we selected 100 parts from the 1000 and measured their diameters, we would have a sample distribution of diameters. If we let the selection of the sample of 100 parts be based strictly on chance, we have a *random sample*. An *infinite universe* might be represented by the time required for a worker to perform the lathe operation. If we timed a few cycles of the operation, we could form a *sequential sample* of the time required. If we timed these cycles at random intervals, we would have a random sample. If at each random interval we timed five cycles and averaged them, we would have a *sampling distribution* of averages of five. Taking samples at random intervals comes close to random sampling as possible in many instances, but, being ordered in time, the samples are not random in the same sense as random samples selected from a carload of grain, for example.

It is often true that the entire universe data are difficult or laborious and expensive to obtain or impossible as in the case of an infinite universe. Therefore, one of the important objectives of statistics is to infer from a sample distribution the characteristics of the universe distribution. Characteristics of the universe, such as the average, variance, and range (these terms will be defined later), are called *parameters*. These characteristics calculated from a sample are called *statistics*.

Notation. It is of some importance to retain the distinction just made between *parameters* and *statistics*, and we shall attempt to do this by using a system of notation. In general, when we are referring to the parameters of a universe, we shall use one set of symbols, and when we are referring to the statistics of a sample, we shall use another set. In most instances, we shall be dealing with statistics rather than parameters. The notation is as follows:

μ = the population mean (parameter)
$\bar{x}$ = the mean of a sample drawn from the population (statistic)
σ^2 = the population variance (parameter)
s^2 = the variance of a sample drawn from the population (statistic)

TABLE I.   Diameters of 200 shafts measured to the nearest 0.001 inch

1.0039	0.9956	1.0026	1.0004	1.0005
1.0014	0.9996	0.9994	0.9977	1.0023
0.9980	1.0025	1.0043	1.0004	0.9989
1.0000	1.0028	0.9954	0.9974	0.9992
0.9973	0.9994	1.0009	1.0033	1.0005
0.9996	0.9998	1.0026	1.0031	1.0034
1.0010	0.9995	0.9976	1.0009	0.9991
0.9999	0.9979	0.9983	0.9972	0.9998
1.0003	0.9968	1.0013	1.0007	1.0041
1.0037	1.0012	0.9985	1.0018	0.9987
1.0021	1.0008	1.0014	1.0000	1.0016
1.0006	1.0015	0.9971	1.0020	1.0046
0.9976	0.9988	1.0021	0.9990	1.0039
0.9978	0.9975	0.9988	1.0008	0.9986
1.0006	0.9984	1.0005	0.9948	1.0023
0.9943	1.0022	0.9985	0.9964	1.0005
0.9993	0.9967	1.0006	1.0008	0.9959
1.0016	0.9958	1.0056	0.9982	0.9999
0.9970	0.9996	0.9997	1.0009	0.9979
1.0005	0.9991	0.9989	1.0017	0.9993
1.0001	0.9997	0.9989	1.0020	0.9969
1.0049	1.0010	0.9981	1.0002	1.0001
0.9997	0.9963	0.9990	1.0031	0.9984
0.9992	0.9997	1.0000	1.0003	1.0027
1.0035	1.0002	0.9999	1.0016	1.0022
0.9998	0.9995	0.9997	0.9978	1.0007
0.9998	1.0009	1.0029	0.9996	1.0011
1.0012	0.9984	1.0033	0.9990	1.0013
1.0019	0.9992	1.0025	1.0002	0.9999
0.9981	0.9970	1.0011	1.0015	1.0013
1.0007	0.9985	0.9982	0.9980	1.0001
1.0000	0.9995	0.9984	1.0050	1.0003
1.0001	1.0010	0.9988	1.0008	0.9987
0.9983	1.0005	1.0028	0.9991	0.9993
1.0023	1.0004	1.0001	0.9989	0.9983
1.0015	0.9986	0.9993	1.0006	0.9982
0.9975	1.0010	1.0019	1.0000	0.9966
1.0030	0.9995	0.9987	0.9979	0.9999
0.9991	1.0019	0.9994	1.0017	1.0003
1.0018	1.0012	1.0015	0.9990	0.9996

Descriptive Statistics

One major area of the study of statistics has to do with precise and efficient ways of describing what otherwise would be a mass of data which would communicate very little worthwhile information. Table I illustrates this point. It lists measurements of the diameters of a sample of 200 shafts from a production lot of 10,000. By scanning the table we can pick out the maximum reading, 1.0056 inches, and the minimum reading, 0.9943 inches, but any generalization about the diameters of the 200 shafts is difficult. Similarly, inferences about the entire lot of 10,000 shafts are difficult.

Frequency Distributions. The situation is improved by grouping the data into a frequency distribution. To do this we tabulate the number of shaft measurements that fall into certain class intervals, as in Table II. Immediately we observe some characteristics of the data that were difficult to see before. For example, we see that the high and low readings represent a small minority of the cases, and that a large percent of the shafts measured somewhere between 0.9982 inch and 1.0018 inch, with the largest number, 22, occurring around 1.000 inch. When the data are plotted in what is called a histogram, as in Figure 1, the general relationships show up clearly. We see that we have a fairly symmetrical bell-shaped distribution of the measurements, centering on 1.000 inch.

TABLE II. Frequency distribution of the data in Table I

Class Limits, inches		Frequency, numbers of shafts	Class Limits, inches		Frequency, numbers of shafts
From	To		From	To	
1.0053–1.0057		1	0.9993–0.9997		21
1.0048–1.0052		2	0.9988–0.9992		18
1.0043–1.0047		2	0.9983–0.9987		15
1.0038–1.0042		3	0.9978–0.9982		12
1.0033–1.0037		5	0.9973–0.9977		7
1.0028–1.0032		6	0.9968–0.9972		6
1.0023–1.0027		8	0.9963–0.9967		4
1.0018–1.0022		11	0.9958–0.9962		2
1.0013–1.0017		14	0.9953–0.9957		2
1.0008–1.0012		17	0.9948–0.9952		1
1.0003–1.0007		20	0.9943–0.9947		1
0.9998–1.0002		22			

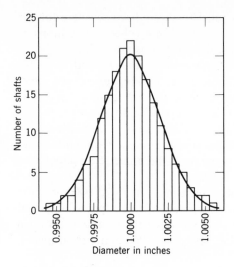

FIGURE 1. Histogram of the 200 shaft-diameter measurements.

The Normal Distribution. The smooth bell-shaped curve that has been superimposed on the histogram of Figure 1 is called the normal or Gaussian distribution. We see that the distribution of diameter measurements fairly well approximates the normal distribution. The name *normal distribution* does not imply that distributions which do not approximate it are abnormal. The curve for the normal distribution has a specific mathematical function, so that for a distribution to approximate normality, the occurrence frequencies must follow closely the general pattern indicated in Figure 1. There are statistical tests which can be used to determine how closely a distribution approximates normality. If there is anything "normal" about the normal distribution, it is, perhaps, the fact that a large number of actual distributions in industry, science, and nature can be closely approximated by it. Thus a large part of statistical method is based on the normal distribution. Table I in the Appendix gives areas under a standardized normal curve.

There are a number of other important distributions which are useful in operation's management. For example, the Poisson and the negative exponential distributions are greatly used in waiting-line theory and are useful in determining buffer inventory levels. Their distributions are tabulated as Tables V and VI in the Appendix. The statistics dealing with proportions or fractions are of great importance in quality control by attributes; that is, where parts are classified into two groups, good and not good. The distributions that are applicable here are the binomial and the

Poisson distributions. Techniques parallel to those discussed here for the normal distribution have been developed for these other distributions as well as for situations where no specific distribution is implied.

If we consider a normal distribution with mean, μ, and standard deviation, σ, it is true that 68.27 percent of the area under the curve (equivalent to the frequency of occurrence in the histogram) is included within the limits $\mu \pm \sigma$; 95.45 percent is included within the limits $\mu \pm 2\sigma$; and 99.73 percent is included within the limits $\mu \pm 3\sigma$ (see Figure 2). The significance of Figure 2 is that we can now make a probability statement about values that we presume come from the universe or population from which the sample distribution is drawn.

Using the shaft diameter example, which had an $\bar{x} = 1.000$ inch and $s = 0.0020$ inch, we can say that there is a 95.45 percent probability that shafts coming from the lot or universe from which the sample was drawn will have outside diameters measuring between 0.9960 and 1.0040 inches,

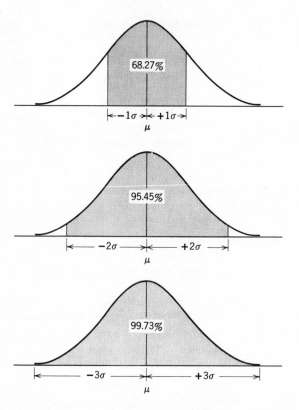

FIGURE 2.   Areas under the normal curve for different sigma limits.

and that there is only a 4.55 percent probability that shafts will measure outside these limits. Similarly, virtually all shafts will measure between 0.9940 and 1.0060 inches, and there is only a 0.27 percent chance that any shafts will measure outside these limits. (See Figure 3 for the relationships of the sample statistics to the histogram of the sample of 200 shafts.) The latter probability is very small; although we are aware that it could happen, we might be suspicious that shafts measuring beyond these limits do not really come from the manufacturing process that produced the dimensions of the sample of 200 from which we established the distribution. In other words, the machine may be out of adjustment, or the cutting tool may have worn, etc. At least the probability is high that there is some assignable cause for the measurement that is greater or less than expected. These are ideas on which

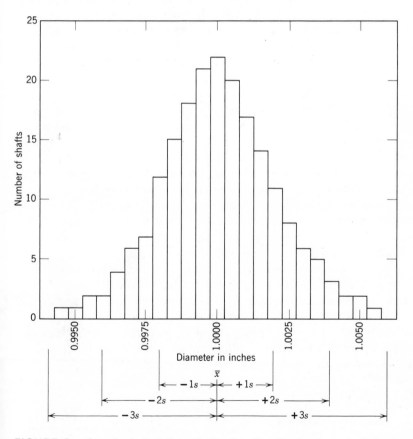

FIGURE 3. Standard deviation limits for the distribution of shaft-diameter measurements, based on Table II.

statistical quality control and control charts are based. See Table I in the Appendix for other values.

Variability in Processes

Any real process exhibits variation. In production processes, for example, variations occur in dimensions, in the percent of parts that meet specification, in chemical composition of materials, and in many other ways. In clerical operations we expect variation in the number of clerical errors produced. In shipping operations we would expect variation in transit time. In personnel we expect variation in absenteeism and in turnover. These and other situations are representative of what we expect. In most processes, a complex of causes of variation stemming from several sources contribute to what we would term the "normal" variation of the process.

For example, in a production process, this complex of causes of variation stems mainly from differences in the performance of machines and workers, minor differences in work methods between workers, variations in materials, differences in atmospheric conditions of temperature and humidity, and others. The machine is not capable of perfection; it may contribute to variation because of "play" in its mechanical system, and changes in atmospheric conditions may add to or subtract from this effect. Employees are subject to all sorts of pressures in their work and private life which may contribute to variations in work methods and performance. The materials used may vary in dimensions or composition and contribute to normal variation in the parameters of the output of the system.

These normal variations are referred to by statisticians as stemming from random or "chance" causes. In general, we cannot do anything about these random variations without altering the system; that is, we may be able to design a new machine that is capable of greater normal precision, or perhaps control the temperature and humidity of the environment surrounding the production system. These kinds of changes would produce a new normal variation resulting from a new system of chance causes.

Statistical control theory is designed to separate relatively large causes of variation, due to some change in the normal pattern, from the variations due to chance causes. These larger individual sources of change are called "assignable" causes. For example, the common assignable causes in a production process are:

1. Differences among workers.
2. Differences among machines.

3. Differences among materials.

4. Differences due to interaction between any two or all three of these factors.

A comparable set of possible assignable causes could be developed for any process. For example, assignable causes for variation in absenteeism might be disease epidemics, changes in interpersonal relations at home or in an employee's work situation, and others.

When a process is in a state of control, variations that occur in the number of defects, the size of a dimension, chemical composition, turnover, absentee rates, etc., are due only to chance variations. With statistical control methods, we set up standards of expected normal variation due to chance causes so that when variations due to one or more of the assignable causes are superimposed, it becomes obvious that something basic has changed. It is then possible to investigate immediately to find the assignable cause of variation and correct it, before the nonstandard condition has gone on too long. These mechanisms of statistical control are called control charts.

Conceptual Framework for Control Charts

If we begin with a set of measurements taken in sequence, we may form the data into a distribution and compute the mean and standard deviation of the distribution. If we may assume that the data come from a normally distributed parent distribution, recall from our previous discussion that we may make precise statements about the probability of occurrence associated with measurements that are a given number of standard deviation units from the mean value. Specifically:

68.26% of the values normally fall within $\mu \pm \sigma$
95.45% of the values normally fall within $\mu \pm 2\sigma$
99.73% of the values normally fall within $\mu \pm 3\sigma$

These percentage values represent the area under the normal curve between the given limits and, therefore, state the probability of occurrence for values that come from the current normal distribution. For example, the chances are 95.45 out of 100 that a measurement taken at random will fall within the 2σ limits and only 4.55 that it will fall outside these limits. These values, as well as decimal values of σ come from tables for the normal probability curve. Table I in the Appendix gives these values. The *natural tolerance* of a process is commonly taken as $\mu \pm 3\sigma$.

Control Chart for Individual Measurements (Samples of one)

If, for the mean and standard deviation of a normally distributed variable, we have established *standards* that are based on the typical distribution resulting from *normal conditions*, we can use these data to construct a control chart. By plotting sample measurements on the chart, we can observe readily if the points are maintained within control limits, or if there is a tendency for drift to one limit or the other. We know that if the successive samples are representative of the original standard universe, the probability is very small that any sample measurements would fall outside the 3*s* limits established. If sample measurements do fall outside these limits, we have reason to believe that something has changed which is producing nonstandard conditions, and the cause may be investigated and corrected. Thus a control chart signals when corrective action is required. Figure 4 shows a control chart for the shaft data based on our previous calculations of the mean and standard deviation.

Although other than the 3*s* limits can certainly be used for control charts, these limits have actually been adopted as standard. With these limits, the probability is extremely small of labeling a point as out of control, when in fact the normal condition exists. Therefore, when the chart calls for action, it is probably warranted.

What Control Limits? If we look at Figure 4 we note that the process generating the shaft diameter measurements appears to be in a state of statistical control by the criteria adopted there, that is, control limits of $\bar{x} \pm 3s$. We could very well have adopted other standards for the control limits, however. For example, if the limits $\pm 2s$ had been adopted, the next to the last point plotted would fall outside these limits. This would call for an investigation to determine if this "out of limits" observation did in fact signal that the process average measurement had shifted upward. If the investigation disclosed that the process had not changed, the investigation and the cost to make it would have been wasted. On the other hand, if the control limits had been $\pm 3s$, as originally shown, and the process had in fact shifted, the observation in question would have been ignored and more scrap product would have been produced in the interim between the time of that sample and the time when a subsequent sample would fall outside the broader limits.

Thus we have a problem in setting control limits of balancing these two kinds of costs—the cost of investigation and the inspection system against the cost of losses when no investigation is made, but when in fact the process is out of control. In general terms, if the cost of investigation is high relative to possible losses if the process continues out of control, the

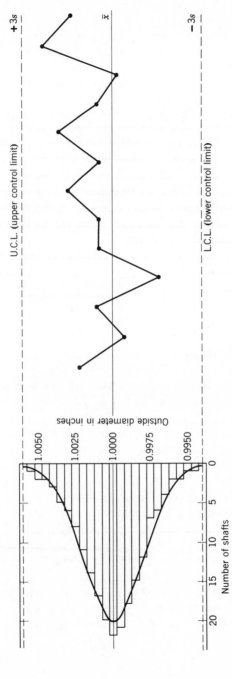

Figure 4. Control chart for the measurements of the diameters of the shafts.

limits should be relatively broad, perhaps $\pm 3s$. Conversely, when the potential loss is high relative to the cost of investigation, we need more sensitive control limits, perhaps closer to $\pm 2s$. All too commonly the balance of these costs is ignored in setting control limits, perhaps because the general practice in industrial quality control, where these techniques were originated, has been standardized at the limits of $\bar{x} \pm 3s$. This may well have had the effect on management personnel of their not considering statistical controls in situations where possible losses were relatively great.

Thus in specifying a control plan there are three interrelated decisions: the sample size, the sample frequency, and the control limits.

(a) $\bar{X} + \bar{R}$

(b) p-charts

(c) C-charts

Kinds of Control Charts. Three basic kinds of control charts are commonly used for statistical control methods. They are: (*a*) control charts for variables when the parameter under control is some measurement of a variable, such as a dimension of a part or the time required for work performance; (*b*) control charts for attributes when the parameter under control is a proportion or fraction, such as the fraction of defective parts in samples, the fraction of idle time for a machine, or the fraction of workers absent; and, (*c*) control charts for the number of defects per unit, such as the number of blemishes on the surface of a unit area of glass.

Control Charts for Variables

Recall that the control chart shown as Figure 4 was a "variables" chart since it was set up to control the outside diameter of the shaft, measured to the nearest 0.0001 inch. Note, however, that it was based on individual measurements (sample of one) and that the normality of the data had already been established. It is much more common, however, that control charts are constructed for averages of small samples rather than for individual measurements. One important reason for this is that *although a universe distribution may depart radically from normality, the sampling distribution of means of random samples will be approximately normal if the sample size is large enough*. This statement is of great importance, for it gives us some assurance that the probabilities associated with the control limits previously stated will apply. Figure 5 demonstrates that the deviation from normality can be fairly great, and yet the sampling distribution of the means of samples as small as $n = 5$ will follow the normal distribution quite closely.

If we take samples of $n = 4$ from the shaft data distribution (Figure 3) and determine an average for each sample, we have a new distribution. We regard each sample mean as an observation, and if we plot a frequency

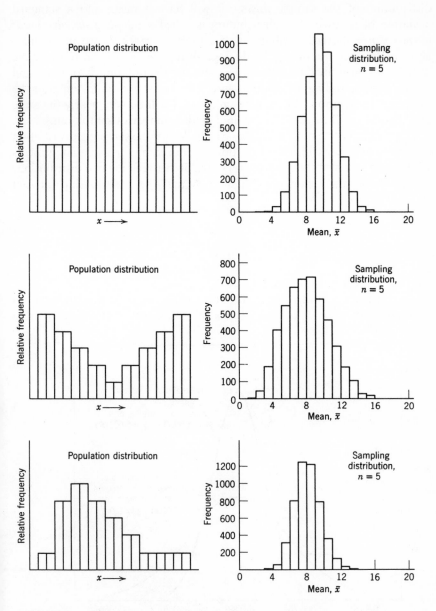

FIGURE 5. Normality of sampling distributions. The three distributions on the left are populations from which 5000 samples of n = 5 *were drawn at random. The resulting sampling distributions are shown on the right.*

distribution of the sample means, it will have a mean and a standard deviation of its own. This distribution is called *a sampling distribution of means of n* = 4 (the distributions of sample averages shown in Figure 5 are sampling distributions). To distinguish the *statistics* from those of the distribution of individual observations, we use the notation $\bar{\bar{x}}$ for the grand mean of the sampling distribution and $s_{\bar{x}}$ for the standard deviation of the sampling distribution. We expect that $\bar{x}$ and $\bar{\bar{x}}$ will be very nearly the same and that they will be equal in the limit as the number of samples increases.

The standard deviation will be much smaller for the sampling distribution of means, however, since the variation is reduced by the averaging process within each sample. The resulting relationship between the two distributions for the shaft data is shown in Figure 6. Actually the relationship between s and $s_{\bar{x}}$ is given by:

$$s_{\bar{x}} = \frac{s}{\sqrt{n}}$$

where n is the size of the sample.

To construct a control chart for the means, we need first to establish standard values for $\bar{x}$ and $s_{\bar{x}}$. Means of subsequent samples are plotted

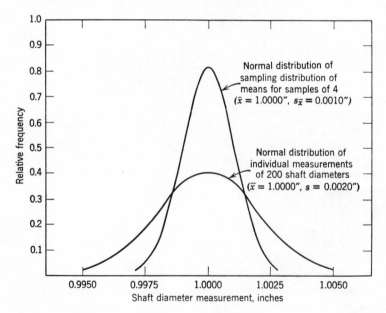

FIGURE 6. *Relation between the distribution for individual observations and the sampling distribution of samples of* n = *4 for the shaft-diameter data.*

again, and action would be called for if a sample mean should fall outside the control limits.

The reasons why sample means fall outside the control limits are, of course, related to the technology of the processes being controlled. For example, if parts were being produced on a lathe, they would tend to become oversized as the cutting tool became worn. Changes of this general nature tend to reflect themselves in the mean of the sampling distribution. If, however, the bearings of the lathe spindle had worn, it would be reflected by an increase in variability of the sampling distribution, and we would expect points to go outside of both control limits. The control chart can then show up changes in the mean of the distribution actually being generated as well as in the variability of the distribution, and combinations of changes in the mean and in the variability. Figure 7 summarizes these possible changes. Where changes in variability are particularly important, a special control chart on a measure of variability can be constructed, as we shall see.

$\bar{X}$ and R *Control Charts*

Setting Standards for Process Average and Control Limits. Suppose we have taken a set of measurements on a process for which we wish to set up standards for the process average and for control limits, so that future measurements may be plotted on the control chart to determine if the process is remaining in a state of statistical control. How do we determine if the data that we propose to use for the determination of process average and control limits are themselves in control? It could well have happened that during the period over which the data were gathered, nonstandard conditions occurred resulting in a shift in either the process average, the standard deviation, or both. If the process average does shift, the resulting calculated estimate of the standard deviation will reflect this. To guard against this possibility, we may compute a separate s for each of the small samples by the usual formula and average them. The means of the subgroup samples can then be plotted on a control chart based on $\bar{x} \pm 3s_{\bar{x}}$, to see whether or not changes in the process average have occurred during the period over which the preliminary data were gathered. The result is that the size of the subgroup should be relatively small and the period of time over which the preliminary data is gathered should be great enough so that changes in the process which occur between the sampling intervals may be recognized.

Practical Procedures for $\bar{X}$ Charts. As a practical matter, practitioners in the statistical control field use a short-cut method for calculating control

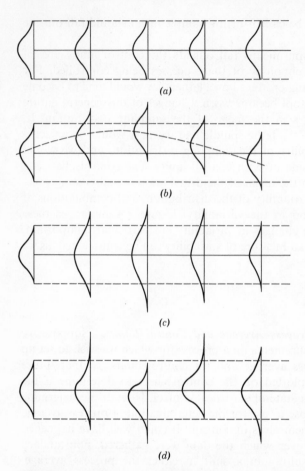

(a)

(b)

(c)

(d)

FIGURE 7. Changes in mean value, in variability, and in both measures in relation to specified process mean and control limits. (a) Process in control; (b) mean value out of control; (c) variability out of control; (d) both mean and variability out of control.

limits, using the range as a measure of variability instead of the standard deviation. A table of factors is then used to calculate directly the upper and lower control limits. Table II in the Appendix gives these factors for the computation of the $3s$ control limits commonly used. The procedure required is simply to determine the range for each of the samples and then to determine $\overline{R}$, the arithmetic mean of the ranges. The three standard deviation control limits are then calculated by:

$$\bar{\bar{x}} \pm A_2 \overline{R}$$

where A_2 is a factor from Table II in the Appendix, depending on the size of the subsample.

Control Charts on Measures of Variability. In developing the control chart for means, we use the sampling distribution of means and calculated control limits. We can as well take some measure of variability as the statistic, for example, the standard deviation or the range. For each subsample of size n, we can calculate a sample standard deviation. If we made a frequency distribution of these standard deviations, we would have a distribution which approximates the normal distribution. This distribution of sample standard deviations would itself have a mean and a standard deviation. We could, therefore, use this distribution of sample standard deviations to establish a control chart, which would tell us when the *variability* of the thing which is being controlled is greater or less than normal.

In statistical control work, the statistic chosen is usually the *range* instead of the standard deviation, because of the ease with which it can be computed for the successive samples and the fact that the range is fairly stable for small samples. For each sample the difference between the highest and lowest measurement is plotted on the control chart for ranges. The control chart for ranges represents the distribution of ranges for samples of size n. This distribution has an average $\bar{R}$ and a standard deviation s_R. The $3s_R$ limits have the same general significance as before. The probability that a sample range will fall outside the limits is only 0.27 percent if it comes from the original universe. Therefore, when sample ranges do fall outside the control limits, we can presume that something has happened to cause greater than expected variability.

Practical Procedures for Constructing R Charts. Just as with the $\bar{X}$ chart, a table of factors has been derived to simplify the calculation of the control limits for R charts. Using the data from Table II in the Appendix, for D_3 and D_4 listed for the appropriate sample size, the $3s$ control limits for the R chart are:

$$UCL_R = D_4\bar{R}$$
$$LCL_R = D_3\bar{R}$$

An Application of $\bar{X}$ and R Charts. Suppose that we are involved in a study to determine the time required for an employee to perform a certain task. The job methods for the task have been studied carefully and standardized, and among other data gathered for the work measurement study are the 100 stopwatch readings of the actual time required for 100 cycles of the repetitive part of the task. Table III shows these 100 readings in

TABLE III.   100 stopwatch readings for a repetitive task. Cycle times, minutes

				Sample Number					
1	2	3	4	5	6	7	8	9	10
1.98	2.24	1.95	1.83	1.94	2.12	1.79	2.16	2.21	2.26
1.75	2.09	1.72	1.91	1.42	2.38	1.86	2.12	1.72	1.84
2.01	1.84	2.04	1.68	2.08	2.19	2.06	2.01	2.01	1.87
2.09	2.25	2.13	1.94	2.26	1.98	1.70	1.96	2.05	1.82
2.04	2.09	2.08	2.02	1.88	2.30	2.12	2.24	2.04	2.29

				Sample Number					
11	12	13	14	15	16	17	18	19	20
1.81	1.76	2.17	2.03	2.43	2.55	2.10	1.78	1.63	2.18
2.10	1.79	1.99	1.92	1.84	2.17	2.26	1.88	2.23	1.92
2.19	2.06	2.25	2.03	1.87	2.00	1.87	1.57	1.71	1.98
2.06	1.82	2.05	2.07	2.20	2.31	1.89	1.84	2.08	1.99
1.84	2.44	2.08	2.08	2.14	2.14	1.90	1.62	2.02	1.99

minutes, divided into the subsamples of $n = 5$ by which they were gathered. Each sample of five readings was taken at random times in the order of the sample numbers as shown. Table IV shows the sample means for each of the twenty samples, the grand mean of which is $\bar{\bar{x}} = 2.01$ minutes. Table V shows the range in minutes for each of the twenty samples, and the average of the ranges is calculated as $\bar{R} = 0.43$ minute. The preliminary control limits for the $\bar{X}$ chart are then calculated as follows:

$$UCL = \bar{\bar{x}} + A_2\bar{R}$$

$$= 2.01 + 0.577 \times 0.43 = 2.26 \text{ minutes}$$

$$LCL = \bar{\bar{x}} - A_2\bar{R}$$

$$= 2.01 - 0.577 \times 0.43 = 1.76 \text{ minutes}$$

TABLE IV.   Sample means for twenty samples of stopwatch readings (n = 5, $\bar{\bar{x}}$ = 2.01) (sequence of samples is by rows)

1.97	2.10	1.98	1.88	1.92	2.19	1.91	2.10	2.01	2.02
2.00	1.97	2.11	2.02	2.10	2.24	2.00	1.74	1.93	2.01

TABLE V.   Ranges for twenty samples of stopwatch readings (n = 5). (Sequence of samples is by rows.) $\bar{R} = 0.43$ minutes

0.34	0.41	0.41	0.34	0.84	0.40	0.42	0.28	0.49	0.47
0.38	0.68	0.26	0.16	0.59	0.55	0.39	0.31	0.60	0.26

These preliminary control limits and the preliminary center line for the grand mean are plotted in Figure 8 together with the twenty sample means shown in Table IV. The chart seems to indicate that we have a stable data-generating system with the exception of sample No. 18 which falls below the lower control limit line. It is entirely possible, of course, that this sample mean represents one of the chance occurrences of a mean falling outside the three standard deviation limits. However, we also know that the chance that this will occur is only 0.27 percent, and, therefore, an investigation is made immediately to determine if a cause can be assigned. The investigation reveals the fact that the operator had been following a nonstandard method at that time because of a material shortage. One small part had been left off the assembly to be added at a later time when the material was available. This resulted in a mean time value somewhat lower than expected. Since an assignable cause was determined, sample

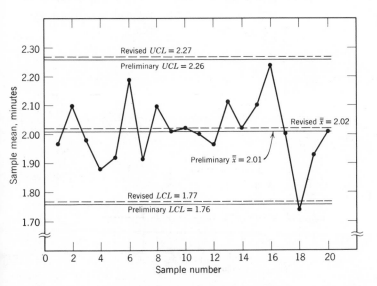

FIGURE 8.   X̄ Chart for the data of Table III showing preliminary control limits and revised limits after data for sample No. 18 have been eliminated. Values plotted from Table IV.

No. 18 was eliminated from the data and new revised grand mean and control limits computed as shown. The elimination of sample No. 18 also affects $\overline{R}$, which enters into the calculation of revised control limits.

The control limits for the R chart are determined in a similar way:

$$UCL_R = D_4\overline{R}$$

$$= 2.115 \times 0.43 = 0.91 \text{ minutes}$$

$$LCL_R = D_3\overline{R}$$

$$= 0 \times 0.43 = 0$$

Figure 9 shows the preliminary control limits for the R chart as calculated above. The center line for the R chart is the average of the sample ranges, $\overline{R} = 0.43$ minutes. The 20 sample ranges are shown in Figure 9, and we see that throughout the twenty samples variability within the samples remained stable within the control limits. Nevertheless, since sample No. 18 has been eliminated on the basis of the $\overline{X}$ chart, it must also be eliminated to calculate revised control limits for the R chart.

The revised center lines and control limits for the two charts of Figures 8 and 9 now represent reasonable standards for comparison of future samples. The basic calculations for determining the control limits and center lines for $\overline{X}$ and R charts remain the same, regardless of the variable being measured. In industrial product quality control, the measurement

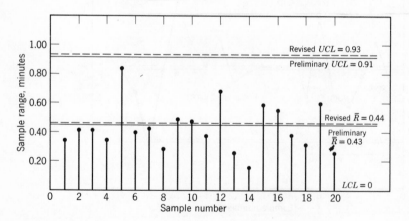

FIGURE 9. R *Chart for data of Table III showing preliminary control limits and revised limits after data for sample No. 18 have been eliminated because of out-of-control mean. Values plotted from Table V.*

is commonly a dimension, in work measurement it is time, and in many cost control problems it would, of course, be dollars.

Control Charts for Attributes (p-Charts)

In control charts for attributes, the population is divided into two classifications: defective parts versus good parts in a production process, the number of errors versus the number of error-free calculations in a clerical operation, the number absent versus the number present for an absenteeism control, the proportion of idle time versus the proportion of working time in a work sampling study, etc. In each instance we may calculate the proportion or fraction that represents the parameter we wish to control. The probability distribution that is applicable in a situation such as those mentioned is the binomial distribution. The mean $\bar{p}$ and the standard deviation s_p for the binomial distribution are given by:

$$\bar{p} = \frac{x}{n} = \frac{\text{number in classification}}{\text{total number observed}}$$

$$s_p = \sqrt{\frac{\bar{p}(1 - \bar{p})}{n}}$$

where n = the size of the subsample.

Following the general ideas for control charts which we have discussed, the control limits are normally set at the process average plus and minus three standard deviations; that is, they are set at $\bar{p} \pm 3s_p$.

Let us take as an example of the application of a p-chart the control of the number of clerical errors that occur in the posting of a journal. Table VI shows a record of the number of errors that occurred in each of twenty samples of $n = 200$. For each sample the error fraction has been calculated as p = number of errors/200. The average error fraction $\bar{p}$ is calculated by totaling the errors that occurred in the combined set of 20 samples divided by the total number of observations, and is shown below Table VI. Also, below Table VI are shown the calculation of s_p and the control limits adopted. Figure 10 shows the resulting control chart with the 20 sample points plotted. Note that samples 15 and 16 fall above the upper control limit. In this instance, investigation showed that at the time of those 2 samples construction work in the office was going on to remodel part of the area. Apparently the confusion and noise had affected the accuracy of the employee doing the posting, and this was regarded as an assignable cause of variation. In establishing the process average and the control limits, we would eliminate these 2 samples from our data to calculate

TABLE VI. Record of the number of clerical errors in posting a journal (n = 200). Calculation of $\bar{p}$ and control limits shown below

Sample Number	Number of Errors	Error Fraction	Sample Number	Number of Errors	Error Fraction
1	11	0.055	12	7	0.035
2	7	0.035	13	9	0.045
3	4	0.020	14	5	0.025
4	1	0.005	15	17	0.085
5	5	0.025	16	18	0.090
6	13	0.065	17	9	0.045
7	6	0.030	18	5	0.025
8	5	0.025	19	7	0.035
9	3	0.015	20	0	0.000
10	0	0.000	Total	131	
11	5	0.025			

$$\bar{p} = \frac{131}{20 \times 200} = 0.033$$

$$s_p = \sqrt{\frac{0.033 \times 0.967}{200}} = 0.0126$$

$$3s_p = 0.038$$

$$UCL = \bar{p} + 3s_p = 0.033 + 0.038 = 0.071$$

$$LCL = \bar{p} - 3s_p = 0.033 - 0.038 = 0$$

a revised process average and control limits, just as we did with the data for Figures 8 and 9.

p-Charts for Variable Sample Size. In the example of the control of clerical errors just shown, the sample size was constant. It often happens, however, that sample sizes vary from one sample to the next. This is particularly true when 100 percent inspection is being used and output volume varies from day to day. If the sample size varies only slightly, control limits may be computed, based on the average sample size. When there is wide variation in sample size, we may compute new control limits for each sample, or convert the deviations from process average into standard deviation units. Control charts based on the latter method are called stabilized *p*-charts.

Table VII shows a record of 20 samples of the number of defective parts in a production process. Note that the sample size varies. In the last 3 columns of Table VII we have calculated the data necessary for variable

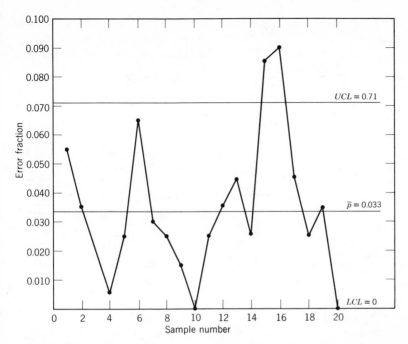

FIGURE 10. p-*Chart for clerical errors in posting a journal.* (p̄ *and control limits are preliminary; data and calculations from Table VI.)*

control limits. The value of $3s_p$ is calculated for each sample. This may be done most simply by computing the value of $3\sqrt{0.099 \times 0.901} = 0.894$, and dividing by $\sqrt{n}$ for each sample. Figure 11 shows the resulting control chart with the variable control limits and the sample points plotted.

A stabilized *p*-chart for the same data is shown in Figure 12, with supporting calculations shown in Table VIII. In Table VIII we have calculated s_p for each of the samples, and determined the variation of p from $\bar{p}$, $(p - \bar{p})$, for each sample. In the last column, then, we determine the number of standard deviation units of variation from $\bar{p}$ for each sample by dividing the deviation by s_p. The control chart plotted in Figure 12 shows the control limits at plus and minus three standard deviation units from $\bar{p}$.

Control Charts for Defects per Unit (c-Charts)

As we mentioned previously, sometimes the parameter to be controlled cannot be expressed as a simple proportion such as was true with *p*-charts.

TABLE VII. Record of the number of defective parts in a production process, variable sample size. Calculation of variable control limits is shown

Sample Number	Sample Size	Number of Defective Parts	Fraction Defective	$3s_p =$ $3\sqrt{\dfrac{0.099 \times 0.901}{n}}$	UCL = $\bar{p} + 3s_p$	LCL = $\bar{p} - 3s_p$
1	95	8	0.084	0.092	0.191	0.007
2	90	6	0.067	0.094	0.193	0.005
3	100	9	0.090	0.089	0.188	0.010
4	105	10	0.095	0.087	0.186	0.012
5	105	8	0.076	0.087	0.186	0.012
6	120	7	0.058	0.082	0.181	0.017
7	115	14	0.122	0.083	0.182	0.016
8	80	7	0.088	0.100	0.199	0
9	90	9	0.100	0.094	0.193	0.005
10	80	17	0.213	0.100	0.199	0
11	90	12	0.133	0.094	0.193	0.005
12	100	10	0.100	0.089	0.188	0.010
13	100	8	0.080	0.089	0.188	0.010
14	110	10	0.091	0.085	0.184	0.014
15	130	6	0.046	0.079	0.178	0.020
16	100	8	0.080	0.089	0.188	0.010
17	110	9	0.082	0.085	0.184	0.014
18	110	10	0.091	0.085	0.184	0.014
19	90	20	0.222	0.094	0.193	0.005
20	80	10	0.125	0.100	0.199	0
Totals	2000	198				

$$\bar{p} = \frac{198}{2000} = 0.0990$$

In weaving, for example, the number of defects per 10 square yards of material might be the parameter to be controlled. In such instances, each defect is in itself minor, but a large number of defects per unit might be objectionable. The probability distribution commonly applicable in this situation is the Poisson distribution. In the Poisson distribution the standard deviation s_c is equal to the square root of the mean value $\bar{c}$. The result is that the calculation of control limits is extremely simple.

Let us take as an example the data in Table IX which shows a record of the number of paint defects per unit for metal desk equipment painted by a dipping process. The defects are all types of paint defects, such as dimples and blemishes. The calculation of $\bar{c}$, s_c, and the control limits are shown below Table IX. The resulting c-chart is shown in Figure 13.

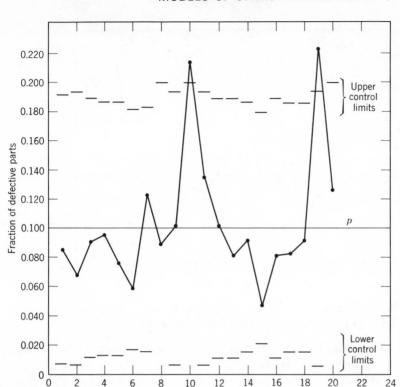

FIGURE 11. p-*Chart with variable control limits. Data and calculations from Table VII.*

If points were to have fallen outside the control limits, an investigation to determine if an assignable cause exists would proceed as before. Assignable causes in this example might be changes in paint viscosity, mixture, drying temperatures, etc. Preliminary and revised control limits and mean value would be determined as before. Also, c-charts with varying control limits due to varying sample size may be constructed as was true for p-charts.

SUMMARY

The concept of statistical control represents the epitome of management control by the exception principle. Probability controls are set so that random variations, owing entirely to uncontrollable chance causes, are ignored.

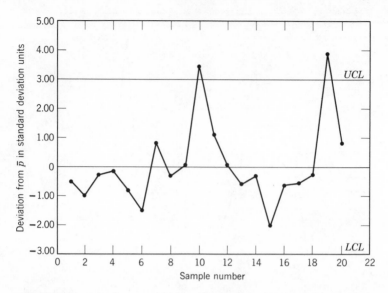

FIGURE 12.   Stabilized p-Chart. Sample points show deviation in standard deviation units from p̄. Data and calculations are in Table VIII.

When a deviation that is larger than expected occurs, however, probability controls signal this fact immediately and call into play a corrective procedure. The result is that managerial personnel do not waste their time on the random variations, but their attention is called immediately when the probability is high that a real change in the process being controlled has occurred.

As we have pointed out, the selection of a control plan should be set so that there is a balance between the cost of investigation and the cost of letting a process continue that is out of control. The three factors which influence these costs and which may be set by the designer of the control system are the control limits, the sample size, and the interval between samples. Although it is not common to set the levels of these three factors by a careful investigation, models have been developed which have this objective [1].

Finally, although the basic ideas and procedures for statistical control have been developed in a framework for industrial quality control, we should recognize that the principles are broadly applicable to the control of any parameter which can be measured and sampled. Thus, whereas initial applications were in the field of statistical quality control, it is becoming much more common to find the use of these methods in work measurement, cost control, control of labor turnover, absenteeism, and so on.

TABLE VIII.   Calculation of sample points for a stabilized p-chart. Data for sample sizes and defectives are from Table VII

Sample Number	Sample Size	Number of Defective Parts	Fraction Defective	$s_p = \dfrac{\sqrt{0.099 \times 0.901}}{\sqrt{n}}$	$p - \bar{p}$	$\dfrac{p - \bar{p}}{s_p}$
1	95	8	0.084	0.0306	−0.015	−0.49
2	90	6	0.067	0.0313	−0.032	−1.02
3	100	9	0.090	0.0296	−0.009	−0.30
4	105	10	0.095	0.0290	−0.004	−0.14
5	105	8	0.076	0.0290	−0.023	−0.79
6	120	7	0.058	0.0273	−0.041	−1.50
7	115	14	0.122	0.0276	+0.023	+0.83
8	80	7	0.088	0.0333	−0.011	−0.33
9	90	9	0.100	0.0313	+0.001	+0.03
10	80	17	0.213	0.0333	+0.114	+3.43
11	90	12	0.133	0.0313	+0.034	+1.09
12	100	10	0.100	0.0296	+0.001	+0.03
13	100	8	0.080	0.0296	−0.019	−0.64
14	110	10	0.091	0.0283	−0.008	−0.28
15	130	6	0.046	0.0263	−0.053	−2.02
16	100	8	0.080	0.0296	−0.019	−0.64
17	110	9	0.082	0.0283	−0.017	−0.60
18	110	10	0.091	0.0283	−0.008	−0.28
19	90	20	0.222	0.0313	+0.123	+3.93
20	80	10	0.125	0.0333	+0.026	+0.78
Totals	2000	198				

$$\bar{p} = \frac{198}{2000} = 0.099$$

REVIEW QUESTIONS

1. What are assignable causes and chance causes in a process?

2. What are the common assignable causes in production processes?

3. What is the probability that a measurement drawn from a normal distribution will fall within the $3s$ limits?

4. What is the probability that a measurement drawn from some distribution other than the normal will fall within the $3s$ limits?

TABLE IX. Record of the number of paint defects per unit for metal desk equipment painted by dipping

Item Number	Number of Defects per Unit	Item Number	Number of Defects per Unit
1	19	12	10
2	16	13	22
3	23	14	5
4	11	15	23
5	15	16	22
6	12	17	14
7	17	18	6
8	11	19	13
9	20	20	6
10	15	Total	293
11	13		

$$\bar{c} = \frac{293}{20} = 14.65 \text{ defects per unit}$$

$$s_c = \sqrt{\bar{c}} = \sqrt{14.65} = 3.83$$

$$UCL = \bar{c} + 3s_c = 14.65 + 3 \times 3.83 = 26.14$$

$$LCL = \bar{c} - 3s_c = 14.65 - 3 \times 3.83 = 3.16$$

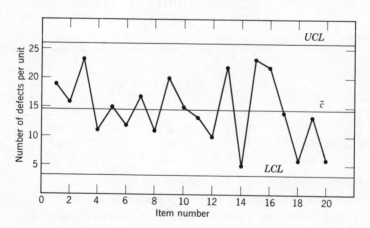

FIGURE 13. c-Chart for paint defects per unit. Data and calculations for control limits in Table IX.

5. When the potential loss is high relative to the cost of investigation, should control limits be relatively broad, perhaps $\pm 3s$?

6. Which would be the more sensitive control limit, $\pm 3s$ or $\pm 2s$?

7. Why are variables control charts normally constructed for small samples rather than for individual measurements?

8. What is the relationship between $s_{\bar{x}}$, the standard deviation of the sampling distribution, and s, the unbiased estimate of the standard deviation of the population distribution?

9. Outline the procedures required to construct $\bar{X}$ and R control charts.

10. Can $\bar{X}$ and R charts be constructed for measures of variability?

11. What statistical distribution is appropriate for control charts for attributes (p-charts)?

12. Could a control chart be constructed that allowed for continuous variation of control limits, as in the situation where a tool might wear as a process progressed?

13. What is the appropriate statistical distribution for control charts for defects per unit (c-charts)?

14. What is the area of application of c-charts?

15. Discuss the concept of statistical control in relation to the general principle of "management control by the exception principle."

PROBLEMS

1. Figure 14 shows a drawing of a 3-inch V-belt pulley which is made up of two identical flanges formed by presses, a hub which is produced on turret lathes, and a set screw which is purchased. The flanges are spot welded to the hub, and the two flanges are spot welded together, as specified. Finally, the entire pulley is cadmium plated. Trouble has been experienced in holding the tolerance specified for the length of the hub, $1.00'' \pm 0.040''$. Ten samples of four pulleys each yield the data as shown in Table X.

    a. Determine the natural tolerance of the process generating the hub length. Is the present turret lathe process capable of meeting the specified tolerance?

    b. Assuming that tool wear is the only predictable variable in the above process, at what average hub length should the process be centered whenever a tool change or adjustment is made? Sketch the distribution relationships and explain.

    (c) Determine preliminary control limits, based on data given, for $\bar{X}$ and R charts to control the cutoff operation of the turret lathe, assuming samples of $n = 4$.

    (d) Under normal conditions, the width of the cutoff tool wears at the rate of 0.001 inch per hour of use. Determine the appropriate control limits and

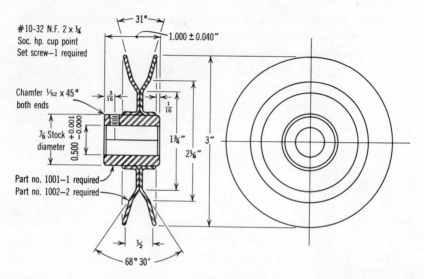

FIGURE 14. Drawing of a V-belt pulley. Tolerance on wobble ±0.010 from center. Tolerance on concentricity ±0.010 from center. Fractional tolerances ±$\frac{1}{64}$. Angular tolerances ±$\frac{1}{2}$°. Finish: Cadmium plated all over 0.0003 ± 0.0001. Notes: 1. Press fit flanges to hub. 2. Spotweld flanges to hub, two spots each side. 3. Spotweld flanges together—four spots. 4. Flange material: SAE #1010 deep-drawn steel. 5. Hub material: SAE #X1112 cold-finished screw stock.

TABLE X. Ten samples of n = 4, pully hub length, inches

Sample No.	Sample Average x̄	Sample Range R
1	1.007	0.013
2	1.008	0.022
3	0.991	0.018
4	0.993	0.014
5	0.998	0.019
6	1.008	0.026
7	0.996	0.024
8	0.995	0.011
9	0.999	0.021
10	0.995	0.024
Totals	9.990	0.192

$$\bar{\bar{X}} = .999 \qquad \bar{R} = .0192$$

trend of average hub length for the samples of $n = 4$ which reflect the known rate of tool wear. Plot the results. How often should the tool be sharpened and reset if the process is otherwise in control?

(e) How will the tool wear affect the control limits and process average for the *R* chart?

2. When assembling the pulleys by pressing the flanges on the hubs by an arbor press, the flanges tend to split excessively in instances when the hub is relatively large and the flange hole relatively small, and when the flange material is relatively hard, even though all these factors are within their stated tolerances. In addition, if the press fit between hub and flange is loose, the spot-welding operation tends to pull the flanges off the axis of rotation so that the pulley may be rejected because of excessive "wobble." Inspection of daily production results in rejection of pulleys for these reasons. Table XI is a record of 10 days'. production and rejections. Construct a *p*-chart with variable control limits. Is the process in control? Construct a stabilized *p*-chart for the same data. Which distribution is applicable in this case?

TABLE XI. Ten days production, and rejections due to flange splitting

Day	Amount Produced	No. of Defectives
1	5,205	85
2	6,100	120
3	5,725	105
4	5,345	150
5	4,250	75
6	3,975	50
7	4,345	95
8	5,270	120
9	6,075	155
10	7,005	110
Totals	53,295	1,065

3. The plating process for the pulleys can produce defective parts either because of too thick or too thin a plating, or because of defective appearance, which shows up in surface defects. We shall assume that the plating thickness is controlled by a *p*-chart. We wish to establish control over surface defects by means of a *c*-chart. Periodic samples of ten plated pulleys are drawn from the output of the process, are inspected, and the number of surface defects are counted. A record of ten samples is shown in Table XII; determine the preliminary control limits for a *c*-chart, construct the chart, and plot the ten samples. Is the process in control?

TABLE XII. Platting surface defects
in 10 samples of n = 100

Sample No.	No. of Defects per Sample
1	5
2	7
3	2
4	10
5	7
6	11
7	13
8	10
9	4
10	7
Total	76

REFERENCES

1. Bowman, E. H., and R. B. Fetter, *Analysis for Production and Operations Management*, Richard D. Irwin, Homewood, Ill., 3rd ed., 1967.
2. Duncan, A. J., *Quality Control and Industrial Statistics*, Richard D. Irwin, Homewood, Ill., 3rd ed., 1965.
3. Enrick, N. L., *Quality Control and Reliability*, Industrial Press, New York, 5th ed., 1966.
4. Grant, E. L., *Statistical Quality Control*, McGraw-Hill Book Company, New York, 3rd ed., 1964.
5. Hoel, P. G., and R. J. Jessen, *Basic Statistics for Business and Economics*, John Wiley & Sons, Inc., New York, 1971.
6. Kirkpatrick, E. G., *Quality Control for Managers and Engineers*, John Wiley & Sons, Inc., New York, 1970.
7. Shewhart, W. A., *Economic Control of Quality of Manufactured Product*, D. Van Nostrand Co., Princeton, N.J., 1931.
8. Tippett, L. H. C., *Technological Applications of Statistics*, John Wiley & Sons, New York, 1950.
9. Vance, L. L., and J. Neter, *Statistical Sampling for Auditors and Accountants*, John Wiley & Sons, New York, 1956.

chapter 20

ACCEPTANCE SAMPLING

Acceptance sampling is another statistical control technique which has proved to be of considerable value. The statistical control chart, which we discussed in Chapter 19, has the objective of controlling the process itself. The probability controls signal when adjustments and corrections to the process must be made, so that the condition does not continue for a considerable period of time. But suppose, however, that the parts already exist, or in a clerical operation, that the journals have already been posted. Is the lot of parts a good lot? Are the data in the journals accurate? We could reexamine each part, or recheck each entry and calculation to determine the answer; however, this inspection effort or audit may be expensive. On the other hand, if we accept the lot of parts without further inspection, or if we assume that the journal entries are correct, we may be faced with other kinds of costs. For example, if the parts were to be used in a subsequent production process, the occurrence of defective items could cause increased assembly costs and reworking. If the defective parts go out to customers, the costs of rehandling and replacement must be faced, to say nothing of a possible loss of customer good will. If the accounting data about which we spoke is assumed to be correct, but in fact contains errors, subsequent costly wrong decisions may be made on the basis of the information in the records. For example, an incorrect inventory balance record could lead to a decision not to reorder the material just yet, resulting in a material shortage. The material shortage in turn could cause a bottleneck in production, resulting in delays, idle labor, and possibly lost orders. In general then, we are faced with two kinds of costs which we wish to balance in proportion to the relative risks involved.

In the simplest case of acceptance sampling, we draw a random sample of size n from the total lot N, and decide whether or not to accept the entire lot based on the sample. If the sample signals a decision to reject the lot, it may then be subject to 100-percent inspection, sorting out bad parts, or finding errors in the entries of accounting records, as the case may be. Just as with the models of statistical control, acceptance sampling techniques were developed in the field of industrial quality control. Nevertheless, we should generalize on the concepts presented because they are applicable to the acceptance or rejection of any kind of data, whether it be physical measurements of parts (such as in industrial quality control) or data such as the occurrence of errors in an accounting system. In general, acceptance sampling is appropriate when:

1. Possible losses by passing defective items, or data, are not great, and the cost to inspect or audit is relatively high. In the limiting situation, this can mean no inspection at all.

2. Inspection requires the destruction of the product; for example, when it is necessary to determine the strength of parts by pulling them apart. Inferring the acceptability of an entire lot from a sample is necessary in these instances.

3. Further handling of any kind is likely to induce defects or errors; or when mental or physical fatigue is an important factor in the inspection or auditing process. In either instance, a sampling plan may actually pass fewer defective items than would 100 percent inspection, and it also costs less.

Just as with statistical control, parallel acceptance sampling procedures are available for both the situation where we simply classify items as good or bad (sampling by attributes) and where we make actual measurements of some kind that indicate how good or bad the item is (sampling by variables).

ACCEPTANCE SAMPLING BY ATTRIBUTES /

As with statistical control procedures, we shall consider here situations where the items being sampled may be classified into two groups, either acceptable or defective. In all instances, regardless of what we may be dealing with, some standard of acceptability has been established; and given those standards, the classification of acceptable and defective is made. If we are dealing with a manufactured part, a dimension may have a standard of acceptance of 1.00 ± 0.001 inches. If the part dimension falls within these tolerance limits, it is classified as acceptable. If it falls outside these tolerance limits, it is classified as defective. If we are dealing with accounting data, for example, the entries are either correct or in error. In any case, we wish to develop procedures whereby when we sample from the items of data available (the lot) the probability of acceptance by the sampling plan will be high, if in fact the entire lot is acceptable. On the contrary, if in fact the lot from which we sample is poor, we want the probability of acceptance to be relatively low. The curve of the actual quality of the lot plotted against the probability of acceptance by the sampling plan is called the operating characteristic curve.

Operating Characteristic (OC) Curves

The OC curve for a particular combination of sample size n and acceptance number c shows how well the plan discriminates between good and bad lots. The acceptance number c indicates the number of defectives in the sample if the entire lot from which the sample was drawn is to be accepted. Figure 1 is an OC curve for a sampling plan with a sample size $n = 100$ and acceptance number $c = 2$. In this plan, if 0, 1, or 2 defectives were found in the sample of $n = 100$, the lot would be considered acceptable. If

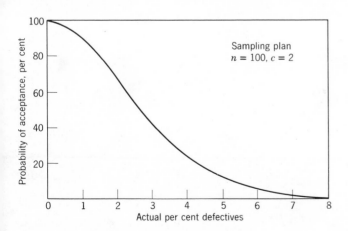

FIGURE 1. Operating characteristic (OC) curve for a sampling plan with n = 100 and c = 2. Plotted from data in Table I.

more than two defectives were found, the lot would be rejected. If for the plan, the *OC* curve of which is shown in Figure 1, the actual lot quality were 1 percent defectives, samples of $n = 100$ would accept the lot as satisfactory about 91.5 percent of the time and reject it about 8.5 percent of the time. In other words, the probability of finding 0, 1, or 2 defectives in random samples from such a lot is 91.5 percent, whereas the probability of finding more than 2 defectives is only 8.5 percent. Note, however, that if the actual quality of the lot were somewhat worse than 1 percent defective —5 percent—the probability of accepting these lots falls drastically to about 13 percent. This is the situation that we would like to have in a sampling plan. If the actual quality is good, we want there to be a high probability of acceptance, but if the actual quality is poor, we want the probability of acceptance to be low. The *OC* curve, then, shows how well a given plan discriminates between good and poor lots.

The discriminating power of a sampling plan depends heavily on the size of the sample, as we might expect. Figure 2 shows the *OC* curves for sample sizes of 100, 200, and 300, with the acceptance number remaining in proportion to sample size. Note that the *OC* curve becomes somewhat steeper as the sample size goes up. If we compare the discrimination power of the three plans represented in Figure 2, we see that all three would accept lots of about 1.4 percent defectives about 83 percent of the time (the approximate crossover points of the three curves). If actual quality falls to 5.0 percent defectives, however, the plan with $n = 100$ accepts lots about 13 percent of the time, $n = 200$ about 3.0 percent of the time, and

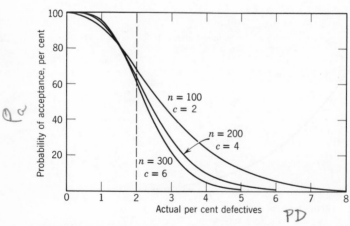

FIGURE 2.   OC curves for different sample sizes with acceptance numbers in proportion to sample size.

$n = 300$ less than 1 percent of the time. The plans with larger sample sizes are definitely more effective.

What happens to the *OC* curve if only the acceptance number changes? Figure 3 shows *OC* curves for a sample of $n = 100$ and acceptance numbers of $c = 0, 1, 2,$ and 3. Note that the four curves remain approximately parallel in their middle ranges so that the effect is mainly to change the level of the *OC* curve so that lower acceptance numbers make the plan "tighter," that is, they hold outgoing quality to lower percents defective. This is a generalization, of course, since there is some interaction between sample size and acceptance number in determining the discriminating power as well.

A plan that discriminates perfectly between good and bad lots would have an *OC* curve that was vertical, that is, it would follow the dashed line of Figure 2. For all lots having percent defectives to the left of the dashed line, the probability of acceptance is 100 percent. For all lots having percent defectives to the right of the line, the probability of acceptance is zero. Unfortunately, the only plan that could achieve this discrimination is one requiring 100 percent inspection. Therefore, the justification of acceptance sampling turns on a balance between inspection costs and the probable cost of passing defectives, as we have already noted. By making sampling plans more discriminating (increasing sample sizes) or tighter (decreasing acceptance numbers), we can approach any desired level of outgoing quality that we please, but at increasing inspection costs. This increased inspection effort would result in lower probable costs of passing defective parts, and at some point the combination of these costs is a minimum.

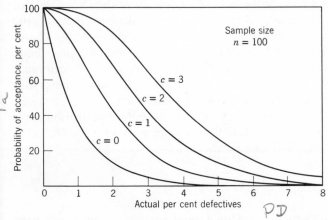

FIGURE 3. OC *curves with different acceptance numbers for a sample size of* n = *100.*

This minimum point defines the most economical sampling plan for a given situation.

Stated simply, then, to justify a 100 percent sample, the probable losses due to passing of defectives would have to be large in relation to inspection costs. On the other hand, to justify no inspection at all, inspection costs would have to be very large in relation to probable losses due to passing defective parts or data. Between these extremes, there exists a risk of not accepting lots which are actually good and a risk of accepting lots when actually they are bad. The first risk is called the producer's risk and the second, the consumer's risk. We shall discuss the definition of these risks more precisely in a moment. Perhaps the most usual situation in industry is no inspection at all since it often costs little to discard defective items if they do not fit at the assembly stage.

Determining OC Curves. The OC curve can be constructed easily from the normal or Poisson distributions. If lots are large, perhaps greater than ten times the size of the sample, probabilities for the OC curve are given by the binomial distribution. If samples are also large, however, the normal or Poisson distributions may be used. Specifically, the rules of thumb are as follows:

1. If $p'n > 5$, the probabilities can be determined from the normal distribution whose mean is p' and standard deviation $\sqrt{p'(1 - p')/n}$.

2. If $p'n \leqslant 5$, the Poisson distribution gives better results.

In the most usual situation, the lot percent defective is small, and the lots themselves relatively large, so that the Poisson distribution is used to calculate the values for the probability of acceptance of the OC curve. For each value of the lot percent defective, we may calculate $(PD \times n)/100$ and determine the probability of acceptance from the curves of the Thorndike chart shown in Figure 4. These curves are the cumulative probability curves of the Poisson distribution and give the probability of occurrence of c or less defectives in a sample of n selected from an infinite universe in which the percent defective is PD. Thus these curves serve as a generalized set of OC curves for single sampling plans, when the Poisson distribution is applicable. Table I shows the calculation of eight points for the OC curve of Figure 1, using the Thorndike chart.

Producer's and Consumer's Risks

Let us now return to the definition of producer's and consumer's risks by referring to a typical OC curve. Figure 5 shows graphically the following four definitions:

TABLE I. Calculation of values of P_a, probability of acceptance in percent, from the Thorndike Chart for the sampling plan n = 100, c = 2; OC curve shown in Figure 1

PD, Actual Percent Defectives	$\dfrac{PD \times n}{100}$	Probability of Two or Less Defectives, in Percent = 100 × Value from Figure 4 = P_a
0	0	100.0
1	1.0	91.5
2	2.0	68.0
3	3.0	42.0
4	4.0	24.0
5	5.0	12.0
6	6.0	6.0
7	7.0	3.0
8	8.0	1.5

AQL = Acceptable quality level. Good quality for which we wish to have a high probability of acceptance.

α = Producer's risk. The probability that lots of the quality level *AQL* will *not* be accepted. Usually α = 5 percent.

LTPD = Lot tolerance percent defective. The dividing line selected between good and bad lots. Lots at this level of quality are regarded as poor quality, and we wish to have a low probability for their acceptance.

β = Consumer's risk. The probability that lots of the quality level *LTPD* will be accepted. Usually β = 10 percent.

When we set levels for each of these four values we are determining two critical points on the *OC* curve which we desire, points *a* and *b* in Figure 5. Note that a rational choice of α and β depends on economic analysis as discussed previously.

Specification of Single Sampling Plans

Although the specification of the four values *AQL*, α, *LTPD*, and β do specify the characteristics of the *OC* curve which is desired, the question we must now answer is, "What sample size *n* and acceptance number *c* will produce an *OC* curve approximating the one specified?"

Use of the Thorndike Chart. Let us take as an example the following specifications: *AQL* = 2 percent, *LTPD* = 8 percent, α = 5 percent, and

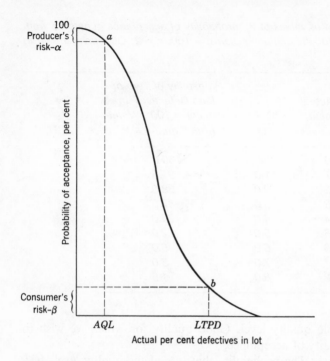

FIGURE 5. *Complete specifications of a sampling plan. An OC curve which goes through the points a and b meets the requirements stated by α and AQL, and β and LTPD, thus specifying a sampling plan with a given n and c.* (AQL = *acceptance quality level;* LTPD = *lot tolerance per cent defectives.*)

$\beta = 10$ percent. The values for the horizontal scale in the Thorndike chart are $PD \times n/100$, and we are interested in values at the points where the probability of acceptance P_a is 95 percent $(1 - \alpha)$, and for β, 10 percent. Therefore, let us tabulate the values of $PD \times n/100$ at these two points for each value of c. These values are listed in Table II. For example, If we locate the horizontal line $\beta = 10$ percent and find its intersection with $c = 0$, we may read $PD \times n/100 = 2.30$.

Similarly, we may check the values when $c = 1$, 2, etc., and for the 95 percent line as well. The last column of Table II is then simply the ratio of column 3 to column 2 for each value of c. Now, of course, the value of PD that we have in mind for the 95 percent level is our specification value of $AQL = 2$ percent, and similarly at the 10 percent level, our value of $LTPD = 8$ percent. Since column 4 is the ratio of these two values, it is in fact the ratio of $LTPD:AQL$ for the plan we seek. Our ratio is, $LTPD:AQL = {}^8/_2 = 4$. The value of 4 falls between 4.06 at

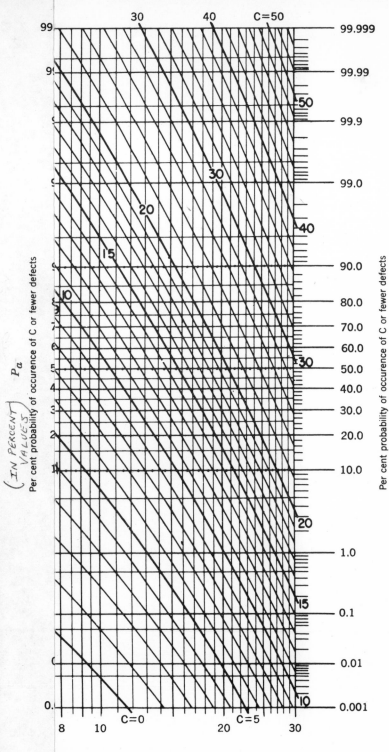

FIGURE 4. The Thorndike chart. Cumulative probability distribution curves of the Poisson Distribution. Adapted from H. F. Dodge and H. G. Romig, Sampling Inspection Tables, John Wiley & Sons, New York, 2nd ed., 1959.

TABLE II.   Table for determining sampling plans with specified AQL and LTPD and with α and β near 5 percent and 10 percent respectively*

(1)	(2)	(3)	(4)
Acceptance Number	Value of $\frac{PD \times n}{100}$ at $P_a = 95\%$, from Figure 4	Value of $\frac{PD \times n}{100}$ at $P_a = 10\%$, from Figure 4	Ratio, Col. 3 : Col. 2 = LTPD/AQL
0	0.051	2.30	45.10
1	0.355	3.89	10.96
2	0.818	5.32	6.50
3	1.366	6.68	4.89
4	1.970	7.99	4.06
5	2.613	9.28	3.55
6	3.285	10.53	3.21
7	3.981	11.77	2.96
8	4.695	12.99	2.77
9	5.425	14.21	2.62
10	6.169	15.41	2.50
11	6.924	16.60	2.40
12	7.690	17.78	2.31
13	8.464	18.96	2.24
14	9.246	20.13	2.18
15	10.040	21.29	2.12

*Adapted from F. E. Grubbs, "On Designing Single Sampling Inspection Plans," Annals of Mathematical Statistics, Vol. XX, p. 256.

$c = 4$ and 3.55 at $c = 5$. We must now decide whether to hold α and let β float, or vice versa. If, for example, we set $c = 4$ and hold α at 5 percent, then $PD \times n/100 = AQL \times n/100 = 1.970$. We can then solve for the sample size:

$$n = \frac{1.970 \times 100}{2} = 99$$

Our sampling plan is then $n = 99$, $c = 4$, based on the specifications $AQL = 2$ percent, α = 5 percent, and $LTPD = 8$ percent (see Table III). But what has happened to the value of β? We may check easily by reference to the Thorndike chart. Since we have now fixed $n = 99$ and $c = 4$, $LTPD \times n/100 = 8 \times 99/100 = 7.92$. At this value of $PD \times n/100$ for $c = 4$, we read the actual value of $β = 10.5$ percent. Table IV shows the

TABLE III. Sampling plans for c = 4 and c = 5 when α is fixed and β is allowed to float and when β is fixed, allowing α to float. AQL = 2 percent, LTPD = 8 percent

c Fixed at 4		c Fixed at 5	
α Fixed at 5%, β Floats	β Fixed at 10%, α Floats	α Fixed at 5%, β Floats	β Fixed at 10%, α Floats
$n = \dfrac{1.970 \times 100}{2}$	$n = \dfrac{7.99 \times 100}{8}$	$n = \dfrac{2.613 \times 100}{2}$	$n = \dfrac{9.28 \times 100}{8}$
$= 99$	$= 100$	$= 131$	$= 116$

values of n, c, $α$ and $β$ for each of the four plans that meet the basic requirements specified.

We see that plan 1 increases very slightly the probability of accepting lots of 8 percent quality, while holding the other specifications. Plan 2 increases slightly the probability of rejecting lots of good quality; that is, $AQL = 2$ percent while holding the specification for $β$. Plan 3 holds $α$ at 5 percent, but reduces the probability of accepting bad lots to the value of 5 percent. Plan 4 decreases the probability of rejecting good lots while holding $β = 10$ percent. In summary, plans 1 and 2 come the closest to meeting the original specifications, and the choice between them depends on which emphasis is desired.

Other Values of α and β.   Table II was constructed for the usual values of $α$ and $β$, but it is easy to see that a comparable table could be constructed from the Thorndike chart for any values of $α$ and $β$ that we may desire, so that the methods described are general.

TABLE IV. Actual α's and β's for the four plans derived. AQL = 2 percent, LTPD = 8 percent

Plan Number	Sample Size, n	Acceptance Number, c	α Percent	β Percent
1	99	4	5	10.5
2	100	4	5.4	10
3	131	5	5	5
4	116	5	3	10

Plans with Specified LTPD, β, and Minimum Total Inspection for a Given Average PD.   Tables have been developed that give sampling plans with minimum total inspection for specified values of $LTPD$, the process average of percent defectives, and β. These are known as the Dodge-Romig *Sampling Inspection Tables* [3]. The Dodge-Romig tables give the various plans that for selected values of incoming quality and various lot sizes have a minimum of total inspection, including the 100 percent inspection of rejected lots. The tables are organized according to the $LTPD$, with listings under 0.5, 1.0, 2.0, 3.0, 4.0, 5.0, 7.0, and 10.0 percent.

As an alternate to the tables, we present Figures 6, 7, and 8 which may be used to determine sampling plans with minimum total inspection for a given process average percent defectives, $LTPD$, and β. Let us construct an example with the following data: $LTPD = 8$ percent, $\overline{PD} = 4$ percent, $\beta = 10$ percent, and $N = 1000$. The procedure is as follows:

1. Calculate the tolerance number of defectives in the lot $= LTPD \times N/100 = 8 \times 1000/100 = 80$.

2. Calculate the ratio $\overline{PD}/LTPD = {}^4\!/_8 = 0.50$.

3. Enter Figure 6 with the values calculated in 1 and 2 to determine the acceptance number, c. The nearest value is $c = 11$.

4. Enter Figure 7 with the tolerance number of defectives in the lot $= 80$ and $c = 11$ to find on the vertical scale, $LTPD \times n/100 = 16$.

5. From the data determined in 4, calculate the sample size, $n = 16 \times 100/LTPD = 16 \times 100/8 = 200$.

6. Enter Figure 8 with the tolerance number of defectives in the lot $= 80$, and the ratio $\overline{PD}/LTPD = 0.50$ to find on the right-hand vertical scale, $LTPD \times I_{min}/100 = 23$.

7. With the data from 6, calculate the minimum average number inspected per lot, $I_{min} = 23 \times 100/LTPD = 23 \times 100/8 = 287.5$.

We have now determined a sampling plan with the following characteristics:

$$c = 11$$
$$n = 200$$
$$I_{min} = 287.5$$
$$\beta = 10 \text{ percent}$$

The average number inspected per lot includes, of course, a pro-rata amount for the 100 percent inspection of rejected lots. If AQL had been

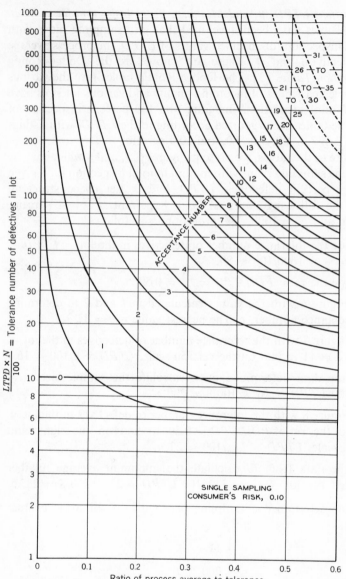

FIGURE 6. Chart for finding the acceptance number for minimum total inspection single sampling plans. LTPD and β specified $\overline{PD}$ given. Figures 6–8 are adapted from H. F. Dodge and H. G. Romig, Sampling Inspection Tables, John Wiley & Sons, New York, 2nd ed., 1959.

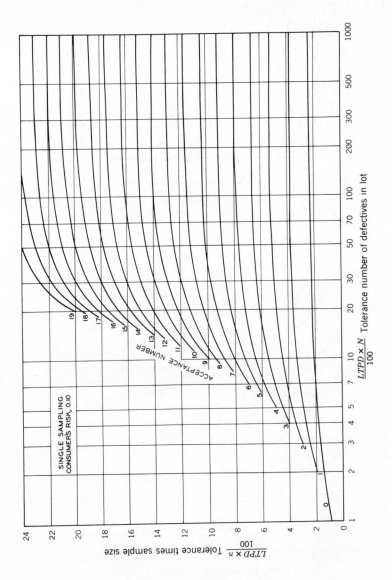

FIGURE 7. Chart for finding sample size for minimum total inspection single sampling plans. LTPD and β specified. P̄D given.

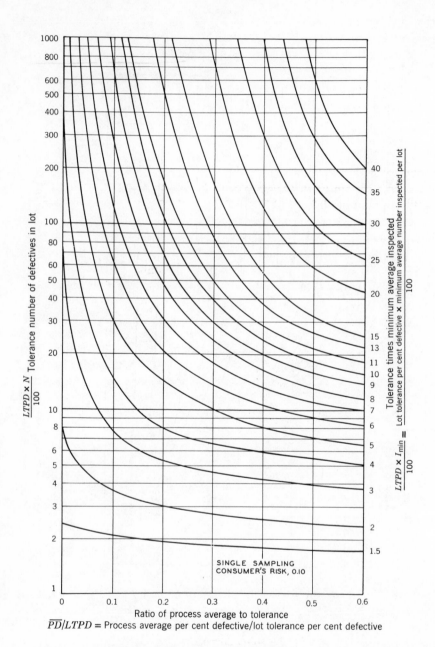

FIGURE 8. Chart for finding the minimum amount of inspection per lot for single sampling plans when LTPD and β are specified and $\overline{PD}$ given.

specified as 3 percent, we could now go to the Thorndike chart to determine the value of α as before. Here it would be $\alpha = 2.5$ percent. The Dodge-Romig charts furnish a convenient means of determining sampling plans with minimum total inspection over a wide range of conditions.

Average Outgoing Quality (AOQ) Curves

When a sampling plan rejects a lot, the most usual procedure is that the lot is subjected to 100 percent inspection. It can be shown, then, that the sampling plan gives definite assurance that the average outgoing quality will not exceed a certain limit. (Average outgoing quality refers to the average quantity, or percent, defective.) Figure 9 shows the flow of good and rejected parts in a typical sampling plan and the basis for calculating the average outgoing quality, AOQ. The random sample of size n is inspected, and any defectives found in the sample are replaced by good parts so that the sample ends up with only good parts. Based on the number of defectives, c', found in the sample, the entire lot is accepted if $c' \leq c$ and rejected if $c' > c$. If the lot is rejected it is subjected to 100 percent inspection, and all defectives found are replaced by good parts. In this instance, the entire lot of N parts is free of defectives. If, however, the lot is accepted by the sample, we run the risk that some defective parts have passed. The average number of defectives is easy to calculate. If the average incoming quality percentage is PD, acceptance occurs with the probability P_a (taken directly from the OC curve for the percent defective PD). The average number of defectives is then simply the product of the fraction defectives received, times the *number* remaining in the lot, weighted by the probability that acceptance occurs, or $(P_a/100)(PD/100)(N - n)$. The average outgoing quality AOQ in *percent* is then:

$$AOQ = \frac{\text{Average number of defectives}}{\text{Number of parts in lot}} \times 100 = \frac{P_a(PD)(N - n)}{100N}$$

From the foregoing relationship we can now develop a curve for any given sampling plan which shows the AOQ for any level of incoming quality. Such a curve can be plotted by assuming different values of actual incoming quality, determining from the OC curve the probability of acceptance for that incoming quality P_a. These figures can then be substituted in the formula to compute AOQ. Each calculation for different incoming quality levels determines a point on the AOQ curve, as indicated in Figure 10. The AOQ curve of Figure 10 is based on a sampling plan with $n = 100$, $c = 2$, and $N = 1000$, the OC curve of which is shown in Figure 1.

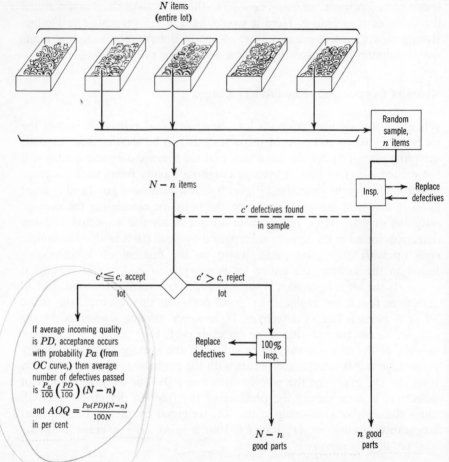

FIGURE 9. Flow of good and rejected parts in a typical acceptance sampling plan, showing the basis for calculating average outgoing quality.

Note the interesting characteristics of the AOQ curve. First, there is a maximum or limiting quality which can be passed, on the average. This peak of the curve is called the average outgoing quality limit ($AOQL$). There is an $AOQL$ for every sampling plan, which depends on the characteristics of the plan. We can reason why the AOQ curve takes the shape illustrated. When good quality is presented to the sampling plan, for example, 0 to 2 percent, the probability of acceptance is relatively high so that most of the defectives will be passed. As we go beyond 2 percent incoming quality, however, the probability of acceptance is declining and,

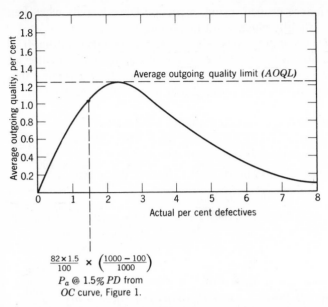

$$\frac{82 \times 1.5}{100} \times \left(\frac{1000 - 100}{1000}\right)$$

P_a @ $1.5\% \ PD$ from
OC curve, Figure 1.

FIGURE 10. Average outgoing quality (AOQ) *curve for a sampling plan with* n = 100, c = 2, *and lot size* N = 1000. OC *curve shown in Figure 1.*

therefore, the probability of 100 percent inspection is increasing so that a larger share of defectives is screened out. This accounts for the fact that the outgoing quality improves as incoming quality becomes worse.

The essence of the characteristics of the sampling plan shown in Figure 10 is simply that average outgoing quality never exceeds approximately 1.25 percent for the plan given, regardless of incoming quality. The amount of inspection required to maintain quality standards automatically adjusts to the situation. If incoming quality is very poor, perhaps 6 percent, the sampling plan reacts by rejecting lots much more frequently, calling for 100 percent inspection so that average outgoing quality is about 0.32 percent. On the other hand, if incoming quality is excellent, perhaps 1 percent, the sampling plan more frequently passes the lots, and the amount of inspection required is small. Inspectors will usually be spending their time screening bad lots and not wasting their time going over good lots.

The level of *AOQL* which should be selected for a given situation depends on the consequences of bad quality. If subsequent operations can catch further defectives without disrupting production, *AOQL* can be fairly loose. These probability controls over outgoing quality are ideal, especially since we can first specify the level of quality which is demanded by technical and economic considerations and then set up controls which guarantee the average performance needed, using inspection labor heavily when bad lots occur and only slightly when good lots occur.

AOQ without Replacement. We have shown the determination of the AOQ curve for the situation when defectives are replaced to maintain the lot size N; however, we could calculate in a parallel way AOQ assuming that all defectives are discarded, with rejected lots being 100 percent inspected as before.

In this situation, the average outgoing quality is calculated by:

$$AOQ = \frac{\text{Average number of defectives}}{\text{Number of parts in lot after defectives discarded}} \times 100$$

$$= \frac{(P_a/100)(PD/100)(N - n)}{N - (PD/100)n(PD/100)(1 - P_a/100)(N - n)} \times 100$$

which reduces to, oR

$$AOQ = \frac{P_a \times PD(N - n)}{N - [(PD/100)n + (1 - P_a/100)(PD/100)(N - n)]} \times 100$$

This analysis of AOQ curves assumes, of course, that the inspection process itself does not introduce defectives; where the inspection process does introduce errors, the level of the AOQ curve is raised.

Single Sampling Plans with Specified AOQL and Minimum Total Inspection for a Given PD

It is also possible to design single sampling plans that specify in advance $AOQL$ and, at the same time, minimize total inspection for a given process average $\overline{PD}$. Again, the Dodge-Romig *Sampling Inspection Tables* [3] provide us with a convenient means of selecting a sampling plan which fits requirements, just as was true with plans that specified $LTPD$, discussed previously. Tables are given by Dodge-Romig for values of $AOQL$ of 0.1, 0.25, 0.5, 0.75, 1.0, 1.5, 2.0, 2.5, 3.0, 4.0, 5.0, 7.0, and 10.0. They also show the OC curves for all the $AOQL$ curves shown in the tables.

Single Sampling Plans with Specified AOQL Protection. Just as with $LTPD$ protection, the Dodge-Romig tables for $AOQL$ protection can be reduced to a chart with some side calculations necessary. We will summarize this procedure with the use of Figure 11 and Table V. Let us assume that we have a lot of $N = 1800$ parts which come from a process where the average percent defectives is known to be $\overline{PD} = 1$ percent. We wish to

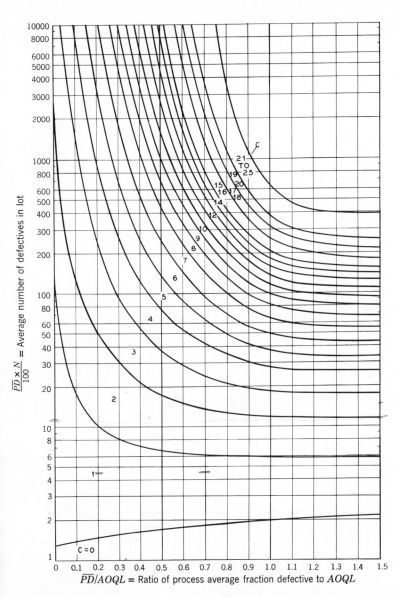

FIGURE 11. Chart for determining the acceptance number, c; AOQL protection Figures 11–12 are from H. F. Dodge and H. G. Romig, Sampling Inspection Tables, *John Wiley & Sons, New York, 2nd ed., 1959.*

TABLE V. Values of the factor y for given values of the acceptance number c. (AOQL protection)*

Given c	y	Given c	y	Given c	y	Given c	y
0	0.3679						
1	0.8400	11	7.233	21	14.66	31	22.50
2	1.371	12	7.948	22	15.43	32	23.30
3	1.942	13	8.670	23	16.20	33	24.10
4	2.544	14	9.398	24	16.98	34	24.90
5	3.168	15	10.13	25	17.76	35	25.71
6	3.812	16	10.88	26	18.54	36	26.52
7	4.472	17	11.62	27	19.33	37	27.33
8	5.146	18	12.37	28	20.12	38	28.14
9	5.831	19	13.13	29	20.91	39	28.96
10	6.528	20	13.89	30	21.70	40	29.77

*Adapted from H. F. Dodge and H. G. Romig, Sampling Inspection Tables, *John Wiley & Sons, New York, 2nd ed., 1959.*

determine a sampling plan which will give protection of $AOQL = 3$ percent. Our procedure is as follows:

1. Calculate $\overline{PD}/AOQL = \frac{1}{3} = 0.33$.
2. Calculate $(\overline{PD} \times N)/100 = (1 \times 1800)/100 = 18$.
3. From Figure 11, using the data from 1 and 2, the zone $c = 2$ is appropriate.
4. From Table V, $y = 1.371$ for $c = 2$.
5. Calculate the sample size n by the formula,

$$n = \frac{yN}{(AOQL/100)N + y}$$

$$= \frac{1.3710 \times 1800}{(0.03 \times 1800) + 1.371} = 45$$

From the foregoing procedure then, the sampling plan that will give the desired $AOQL$ protection is $n = 45$ and $c = 2$.

Double Sampling

Double sampling, which has the advantage of lower inspection costs for a given level of protection, is accomplished by taking a smaller sample initially. Based on this sample, the lot is either accepted or rejected, or no final decision is made. In the latter instance a second sample is drawn and a decision finally made to reject or accept the lot, based on the combined sample. This basic structure is shown in Figure 12, where we see that two acceptance numbers, c_1 and c_2, have been chosen. If the number of defectives in the first sample is less than c_1, the lot is accepted at that point. If the number of defectives found exceeds the larger acceptance number c_2, the lot is immediately rejected and subjected to 100 percent inspection. If, however, the number of defectives is between c_1 and c_2, a second sample is taken, and if the total number of defectives found in the *combined sample* exceeds c_2, the lot is rejected and subjected to 100 percent inspection. If the number of defectives found at this point is less than c_2, the lot is accepted.

The advantage of double sampling lies in the possible reductions in the total amount of inspections required. This occurs because the initial sample is smaller than that required by a comparable single sampling plan. If the

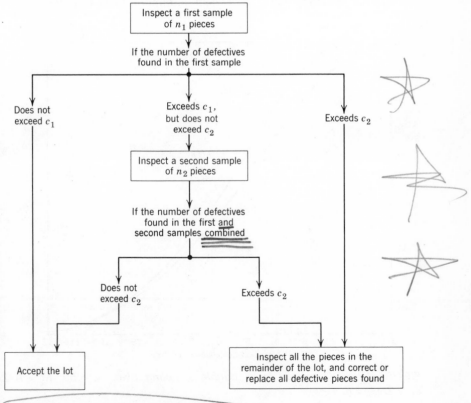

FIGURE 12.   Double sampling inspection.

lot can be accepted or rejected on the basis of the first sample, there will be a saving in total inspection. This saving in inspection is the greatest for large lot sizes and when incoming quality is normally quite good. There is a seeming advantage to the layman in the idea of "giving it a second chance." Actually this is illusory, because the probability of acceptance is determined by the *OC* curve for any plan, and a single sampling plan can be designed that yields greater discrimination between good and bad lots than a given double sampling plan. The disadvantage of double sampling is that the inspection load varies considerably. Figure 13 shows the *OC* curves for the first sample and for the combined sample of a double sampling plan with $n_1 = 50$, $n_2 = 100$, $c_1 = 2$, and $c_2 = 6$.

As with single sampling, double sampling plans have been constructed for minimum total inspection where we wish to specify *LTPD* and where we wish to specify *AOQL*, for a given process average percent defectives, $\overline{PD}$.

Double Sampling Plans with LTPD Specified. The Dodge Romig tables give double sampling plans that yield minimum total inspection for a

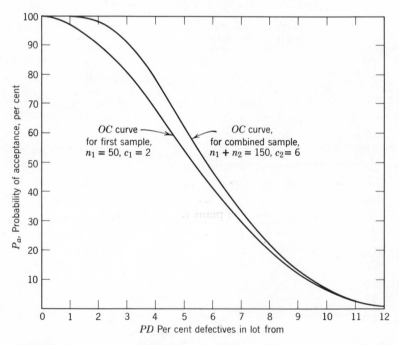

FIGURE 13. OC *curves for a double sampling plan:* n$_1$ = 50, n$_2$ = 100, c_1 = 2, c$_2$ = 6.

given process average percent defectives, $\overline{PD}$, with $LTPD$ specified and β at 10 percent. Separate tables are available for values of $LTPD$ of 0.5, 1.0, 2.0, 3.0, 4.0, 5.0, 7.0, and 10.0 percent. Dodge and Romig have also reduced to two charts the double sampling tables for $LTPD$ protection, which make it possible to design sampling plans for a wide range of conditions of $LTPD$, $\overline{PD}$, and N. Figures 14 and 15, which show these charts, make it possible to design a double sampling plan that yields minimum total average inspection, including the 100 percent inspection of rejected lots. Let us design a plan for a process averaging 0.3 percent defectives. $LTPD$ has been set at 5.0 percent, and $N = 1500$. The procedure for using the two charts is as follows:

1. Calculate $\overline{PD}/LTPD = 0.3/5.0 = 0.06$.
2. Calculate $LTPD \times N/100 = 5.0 \times 1500/100 = 75$.
3. Enter Figure 14 to find the applicable zones for c_1 and c_2. We find $c_1 = 0$ and $c_2 = 3$.
4. Enter Figure 15 with the data from 2 and 3 and find the sample sizes for n_1 and n_2:

For c_1, $LTPD \times n_1/100 = 2.8$
And $n_1 = 2.8 \times 100/5.0 = 56$
For c_2, $LTPD (n_1 + n_2)/100 = 7.4$
And $n_1 + n_2 = 7.4 \times 100/5.0 = 148$
Therefore, $n_2 = 148 - 56 = 92$

Double Sampling Plans with AOQL Protection. Paralleling single sampling plans, the Dodge-Romig tables give double sampling plans that minimize total inspection, including the 100 percent inspection of rejected lots, specifying the desired level of $AOQL$. As before, the tables are set for $\beta = 10$ percent and various given process averages, $\overline{PD}$. As before, the tables are given for a number of values of $AOQL$ ranging from 0.1 percent to 10.0 percent. The Dodge-Romig *Sampling Inspection Tables* also give OC curves for all the double sampling plans for $AOQL$ protection.

Sequential Sampling Plans

Double sampling has the advantage of lower inspection costs for a given level of protection, accomplished by taking a smaller sample initially from which the lot is either accepted or rejected, or the decision is indeterminate. Why not carry this basic idea further? This is essentially what happens with sequential sampling. Samples are drawn at random, as before, but after each sample has been inspected, the accumulated results are analyzed

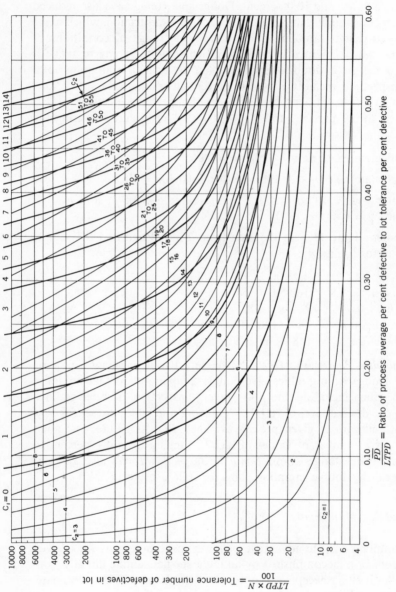

FIGURE 14. Chart for determining double sampling acceptance numbers c_1 and c_2; lot tolerance protection, Consumer's Risk, 10 percent. Figures 14 and 15 are adapted from H. F. Dodge and H. G. Romig, Sampling Inspection Tables, John Wiley & Sons, New York, 2nd ed., 1959.

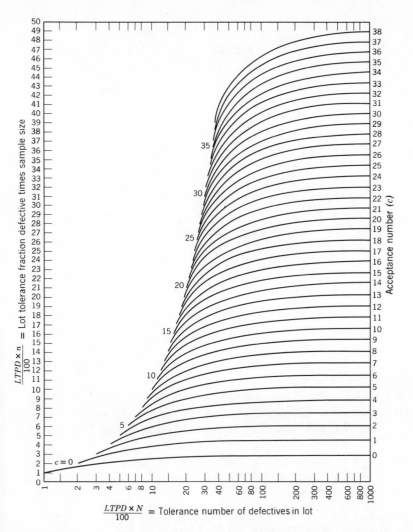

FIGURE 15. *Chart for determining double sampling sample sizes n_1 and n_2; lot tolerance protection Consumer's Risk, 10 percent.*

and a decision made to (*a*) accept the lot, (*b*) reject the lot, (*c*) take another sample. The sequential sample sizes can be as small as $n = 1$. Figure 16 shows the graphical structure of a sequential sampling plan. The main advantage of sequential sampling is a further reduction in the total amount inspection required to maintain a given level of protection as compared to double sampling. In the plan shown in Figure 16, a minimum of fifteen

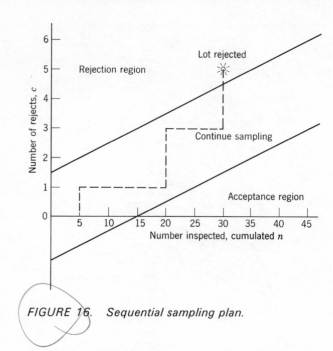

FIGURE 16. Sequential sampling plan.

items must be inspected in order to accept a lot. If the number of rejects on the graph rises such that the point falls on or above the upper line, the lot is rejected. If the point should fall on or below the lower line, the lot is accepted. Until one of these events happens, sampling is continued. As with single and double sampling plans, a sequential plan is specified by the four requirements AQL, α, LTPD, and β, which in turn determine OC curves of sequential plans which meet the functional requirements. Detailed procedures for the construction of sequential sampling plans are given in references [4, 10, 12].

Comparison of Single, Double, and Sequential Sampling Plans

As we have noted, the relative advantages and disadvantages of single, double, and sequential sampling plans do not rest on the protection that can be achieved. The risks of both the producer and consumer type are determined by the OC curve of the plan, and the risk levels can be preset as desired for any of the three types of plans. Table VI summarizes various factors which might influence the choice of the type of plan to use in a specific situation.

TABLE VI. Factors influencing choice of single-, double-, or sequential-sampling plan*

Factor	Type of Sampling Plan		
	Single	Double	Sequential
Protection against rejection of lots of high quality and acceptance of lots of low quality	Approximately equal		
Total cost of inspection	Most expensive	Intermediate	Least expensive
Variability of inspection load	Constant	Variable	Variable
Sampling costs when all samples can be taken as needed	Most expensive	Intermediate	Least expensive
Sampling costs when all samples must be drawn at once	Least expensive	Most expensive	Intermediate
Accurate estimation of lot quality†	Best	Intermediate	Worst
Sampling costs when dependent on the number of samples drawn	Least expensive	Intermediate	Most expensive
Amount of record keeping	Least	Intermediate	Most
Psychological: "give supplier more than one chance"	Worst	Intermediate	Best

*U.S. Navy, Standard Sampling Inspection Procedures, D4.03.02/14.
†If estimate is based on a large number of lots, differences from one type of sampling to another may not matter.

ACCEPTANCE SAMPLING BY VARIABLES /

In acceptance sampling by variables, we make and record actual measurements instead of simply classifying items as good or bad, as in attributes sampling. This difference in procedure changes many of the details of determining a plan that meets specifications for acceptable quality, producer's risk, minimum acceptable quality, and consumer's risk, since the appropriate statistical distribution is now the *normal* distribution instead of distributions for proportions. In addition, of course, inspection methods must change. Conceptually, however, the basic ideas on which the control of outgoing quality is maintained remain the same. The discriminating power of a plan is still represented by an *OC* curve, which shows the probability of acceptance for different levels of actual quality presented to the plan. To specify a plan which gives the desired protection requires procedures parallel to those in acceptance sampling by attributes.

Kinds of Variables Acceptance Sampling Plans

Variables acceptance sampling plans are divided into two main categories which depend on our knowledge of the population standard deviation, σ_x: where σ_x is known and constant and where it is unknown and may be variable. Furthermore, the classification of variables sampling plans may be extended to the kind of decision criterion, that is, where the criterion is the average of measurements, and where the criterion is the percent defectives which occur. To summarize, this classification is as follows:

1. Variables sampling plans where σ_x is known and constant.
   (a) The decision criterion is expressed as the acceptance average of measurements, $\bar{x}_a$.
   (b) The decision criterion is expressed as the percent defective items in the lot.
2. Variables sampling plans where σ_x is unknown and may be variable.
   (a) The decision criterion is expressed as the acceptance average of measurements, $\bar{x}_a$.
   (b) The decision criterion is expressed as the percent defective items in the lot.

To illustrate the concepts and procedures involved, we shall discuss variables sampling plans in which σ_x is known and constant, and refer the reader to other sources for procedures in which σ_x is unknown and may be variable [1].

Variables Sampling Plans in Which σ_x Is Known and Constant

Let us take as an example the case of the testing of a certain steel bar stock which is being received in batches from a vendor. Because of the use to which the material is put, it has been determined that a tensile strength of 90,000 pounds per square inch (psi) is required, and we wish the probability to be low, say 10 percent, that lots of this tensile strength would be accepted. In addition, it has been determined that an average tensile strength of 95,000 psi is representative of good quality, and we wish there to be a high probability, say 95 percent, that lots of this tensile strength would be accepted. We have a long history with this material and supplier so that σ_x is known to be 6000 psi, and the measurements normally distributed.

In summary, we know that $AQL = 95,000$ psi, $\bar{x}_t = 90,000$ psi (equivalent to $LTPD$ in attributes sampling), $\alpha = 5$ percent, and $\beta = 10$ percent. We wish to determine a sampling plan that will indicate an acceptance average for sample tests $\bar{x}_a$ and a sample size n that will accept lots according to the specifications given. The acceptance average for sample tests $\bar{x}_a$ is equivalent to c, acceptance number, in attributes sampling plans. In other words, when $\bar{x}_a$ is less than the value we determine as being critical, the lot from which the sample was drawn will be rejected and presumably returned to the supplier. If the average tensile strength is equal to or greater than $\bar{x}_a$, we will accept such lots.

The standard deviation of the sampling distribution of means for samples of size n will be $6000/\sqrt{n}$. To be accepted 95 percent of the time, $AQL = 95,000$ must be 1.645 σ units above the grand mean, $\bar{\bar{x}} = \bar{x}_a$, since 5 percent of the area under a normal curve is beyond $\mu + 1.645\,\sigma$ (see Table I, areas of the normal curve, Appendix). Therefore, $\bar{x}_a - 95,000$ is 1.645 σ_x units. To be accepted 95 percent of the time, then,

$$\frac{\bar{x}_a - 95,000}{6000/\sqrt{n}} = -1.645$$

Also, to ensure that lots of average tensile strength $\bar{x}_t = 90,000$ have only a 10 percent chance of acceptance.

$$\frac{\bar{x}_a - 90,000}{6000/\sqrt{n}} = +1.282$$

We now have two independent equations with two unknowns, $\bar{x}_a$ and n. They may be solved simultaneously to yield the following values:

$$\bar{x}_a = 92,200 \text{ psi}$$

$$n = 12$$

Figure 17 attempts to show the relationship of the various elements of the problem.

The OC curve for the plan just described is determined by simply cumulating the normal distribution curve for the sampling distribution of sample size n. The OC curve for this plan is shown in Figure 18.

Upper and lower tolerance levels are often specified on measurements of part dimensions, chemical content, etc., as a part of variables sampling plans specifications. In these instances, the variables sampling plan must provide two-sided protection from defectives occurring because the

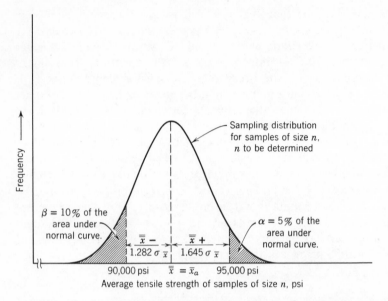

FIGURE 17. Question? What is the grand mean $\bar{\bar{x}}$, and the sample size, n, of a normal sampling distribution with the above characteristics, where $\sigma = 6000$ psi, and, therefore, $\sigma_x = 6000/\sqrt{n}$. The acceptance average, $\bar{x}_a$, of the plan we seek is the grand mean, $\bar{\bar{x}}$, of this sampling distribution, and the sample size of the plan is n.

measured characteristic may be too small or too large to be useful. A sampling plan would then specify a sample size and upper acceptance average and a lower acceptance average. Two equations must then be written for each limit. These equations would be solved for $\bar{x}_a$ (upper) and $\bar{x}_a$ (lower), and the integer value of n which most nearly satisfies α and β.

Criteria for acceptance can be expressed in percent defective, as with attributes sampling, even though actual measurements are made. This merely requires a conversion of units within the plan. Also, *double sampling* is as applicable to acceptance sampling by variables as to sampling by attributes.

Field of application of variables sampling. Obviously, inspection, recording, and computing costs per unit will normally be higher with variables sampling inspection plans than with attributes plans. Then why use variables plans? The most important reason is that for a given level of protection, variables plans will require smaller samples and less total inspection than do attributes plans. Table VII shows this contrast. The differences are smaller for small sample size levels, but if a plan required a sample size of 750 for attributes sampling, comparable protection could be

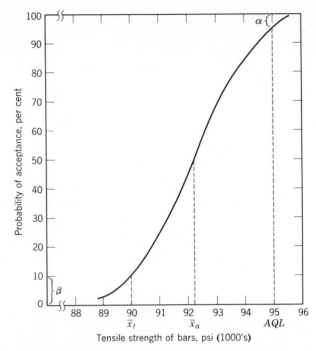

FIGURE 18. OC *curve for a variables acceptance sampling plan for the tensile strength of steel bars.*

obtained with a sample of only 125 with variables sampling. These smaller sample sizes can be very important where the inspection process destroys the part. From an economic point of view, then, variables inspection should be used where the smaller sample size tips the balance of costs of inspection, scrap, recording, and computing. In addition to the possible cost advantages, the data generated by variables inspection ($\bar{x}$ and s) provide more valuable diagnostic information in controlling production processes.

ECONOMICS OF DECISIONS
BASED ON ACCEPTANCE SAMPLING **|**

The bulk of the material presented here has had to do with the derivation of plans for acceptance sampling that meet specified values of risks for passing lots of specified quality. But what should these risks and quality levels be? Should the standard be tight or loose? The answer, of course, depends on relative

TABLE VII. Reductions in sample size by variables sampling plans as compared to attributes for comparable levels of protection

Attributes Sample Size	Variables Sample Size	Reduction in Sample Size	
		Number	Percentage
10	7	3	30
15	10	5	33
20	13	7	35
30	16	14	47
40	20	20	50
55	25	30	55
75	35	40	53
115	50	65	57
150	60	90	60
225	70	155	69
300	85	215	72
450	100	350	78
750	125	625	83
1500	200	1300	87

Adapted by permission from Sampling Inspection by Variables, by A. H. Bowker and H. P. Goode, copyright, 1952, McGraw-Hill Book Company, Table 3.1, p. 33.

values for costs of inspection and the costs or consequences of passing defective items. If, for example, we were searching for an economical single sampling plan, we could use the Dodge-Romig tables to find several plans at different $LTPD$ levels of protection, determining an I_{min}, the average minimum total inspection required, and AOQ. The balance of costs for a lot of size N for each plan would be

(Inspection cost per unit) $\times$ (I_{min} per lot)

$+$ (cost of passing a defective) $\times$ ($AOQ/100$) $\times$ (N).

The plan for which the sum of these two costs is minimum would in general satisfy requirements. More general economic models for sampling plans allow the α and β risks to vary [2]. Where the inspection process affects yield, the cost of production must also be accounted for.

The implications on managerial decision making of the principles of acceptance sampling are that the long-run effect of such a decision process will be decisions that are correct. The plain fact is that a manager is constantly faced with making decisions on the basis of incomplete or sampled data. When he can apply the principles of acceptance sampling, he can determine the risks involved, or conversely, he may assess the risks of a given decision.

REVIEW QUESTIONS

1. What is the function of acceptance sampling, and how is it distinguished from application areas of statistical control, discussed previously?

2. Summarize the conditions under which acceptance sampling is appropriate.

3. What are the general conditions under which a 100 percent sample is justified?

4. What information does the OC curve convey?

5. What is the effect on the OC curve of increasing sample size? Of increasing acceptance number?

6. For acceptance sampling by attributes, what is the statistical distribution which is most commonly appropriate? If pn is greater than 5, which distribution is used?

7. Outline the use of the Thorndike chart in determining OC curves for sampling by attributes.

8. Define AQL, α, $LTPD$, and β, and show their relationships on a typical OC curve.

9. Is it possible to specify exactly the levels of $LTPD$, AQL, α, and β, in determining an acceptance sampling plan for attributes?

10. What is the function of the AOQ curve? Can we specify $AOQL$ as one of the design specifications for a plan?

11. Describe the structure of a double sampling plan.

12. What are the advantages of double sampling over single sampling? What are the disadvantages?

13. Describe the structure of sequential sampling plans. What are their advantages and disadvantages?

14. Outline the general procedures necessary to construct an acceptance sampling plan for variables.

15. Under what conditions would a variables-sampling plan be used?

PROBLEMS

1. Referring to the V-belt pulley discussed in the problem section of Chapter 19, the bar stock from which the hubs are fabricated has the diameter specification of $0.875'' \pm 0.002''$. This specification is related to the problem of flange splitting and

"wobble" described in Problem 2 at the end of Chapter 19. It is felt that if 98 percent of the bars meet specifications, this would be excellent quality. Also, it has been decided that the company should not accept shipments in which as many as 10 percent of the bars do not meet specifications. If $\alpha = 5$ percent, and $\beta = 10$ percent, what single sampling plan will meet the stated requirements? Bars are ordered in lots of 400. Records indicate that the average number of bars which do not meet specifications in a lot is 12.

2. Determine the *OC* curve for the plan derived in Problem 1, and make a graph of it.

3. What is the *AOQL* of the plan derived in Problem 1?

4. What single sampling plan would hold the *LTPD* and β specifications given in Problem 1 and minimize total inspection?

5. What sampling plan would result if we determined that *AOQL* should be held to 2 percent, $\beta = 10$ percent?

6. What double sampling plan will provide the *LTPD* and β protections specified in Problem 1?

7. The flange material for the V-belt pulley must be relatively soft to carry out the press forming operations. Therefore, the material is specified with a Rockwell hardness of 55, and a hardness of 60 is regarded as unacceptable. The scrap rate goes up so fast when material with a hardness index above and beyond 60 is used that β has been set at 5 percent rather than the usual 10 percent. Alpha has been set at 5 percent. Determine the Rockwell hardness sample average for acceptance, $\bar{x}_a$, and the sample size needed for the requirements stated. The material is received in 100-feet rolls, $3\frac{1}{4}$ inches wide, 100 rolls per shipment. We have had considerable experience with the current supplier of the material so that the standard deviation of hardness for individual samples has been well established as $\sigma = 2$.

8. What plan would result if we set $\beta = 10$ percent for Problem 7?

9. Determine the *OC* curve for the plan in Problem 7.

REFERENCES

1. Bowker, A. H., and H. P. Goode, *Sampling Inspection by Variables*, McGraw-Hill Book Company, New York, 1952.

2. Bowman, E. H., and R. B. Fetter, *Analysis for Production and Operations Management*, Richard D. Irwin; Homewood, Ill., 3rd ed., 1967.

3. Dodge, H. F., and H. G. Romig, *Sampling Inspection Tables*, John Wiley & Sons, New York, 2nd ed., 1959.

4. Duncan, A. J., *Quality Control and Industrial Statistics*, Richard D. Irwin, Homewood, Ill., 3rd ed., 1965.

5. Enrick, N. L., *Quality Control and Reliability*, Industrial Press, New York, 5th ed., 1966.

6. Grant, E. L., *Statistical Quality Control*, McGraw-Hill Book Company, New York, 3rd ed., 1964.
7. Hoel, P. G., and R. J. Jessen, *Basic Statistics for Business and Economics*, John Wiley & Sons, Inc., New York, 1971.
8. Kirkpatrick, E. G., *Quality Control for Managers and Engineers*, John Wiley & Sons, Inc., 1970.
9. Statistical Research Group, Columbia University, *Sampling Inspection*, McGraw-Hill Book Company, New York, 1948.
10. Statistical Research Group, Columbia University, *Sequential Analysis of Statistical Data*, Columbia University Press, New York, 1945.
11. Tippett, L. H. C., *Technological Applications of Statistics*, John Wiley & Sons, New York, 1950.
12. Wald, A., *Sequential Analysis*, John Wiley & Sons, New York, 1947.
13. Vance, L. L., and J. Neter, *Statistical Sampling for Auditors and Accountants*, John Wiley & Sons, New York, 1956.

PART VI

SYNTHESIS

chapter 21

LARGE-SCALE
SYSTEM SIMULATION

Because large scale simulation can reach into virtually all phases of activity it serves as a vehicle for summation.

The distinction between the material in Chapter 16 and the material here is one of scale. The same general methods are applied in both the large- and small-scale simulations. A possible exception is that a high-speed computer is a necessity with large-scale simulations, whereas, in some instances, hand computation is feasible with simple problems. In addition, we will treat dynamic output simulation models which represent a fairly recent innovation of considerable interest to operations management.

The tremendous interest in large-scale system simulation represents a recognition of the need for a "systems" approach to the broad problems of the management of operations, indeed, the management of the entire enterprise. Past progress in operations management has of necessity focused on problems of limited dimensions, and these efforts have certainly produced rewards, both in terms of understanding the nature of the problems with which we deal, and in terms of the improvement of actual practice. But throughout these developments of models of work performance and measurement, allocation, waiting lines, facility design, inventories, and investment policy, the frontier thinkers have known that each compartmentalized problem that had been apparently solved had interactions with other compartmentalized problems. They were aware that the need was for a gigantic model where each area of past endeavor might represent a subsystem. Only with such a model could the complex interactions between subsystems be accounted for. Here, of course, mathematical analysis has not been effective. The answer to this call had to wait for the development first, of the large-scale high-speed electronic computer, and second, for the development of skill in simulation. Some of the outstanding work done in large-scale simulation has been in attempts to simulate an entire firm, in corporate modeling using interactive concepts, job shop simulation (discussed in Chapter 17), and dynamic output simulation models.

INTERACTIVE
SIMULATION SYSTEMS /

With the availability of time-shared computing, simulation can take on a new and conceptually important characteristic, that is, the decision maker can be included in the loop. Given the simulation model the decision maker can raise a host of "what if" questions about his operations and get back immediate answers showing the impact of the proposed operational change on the important indices of performance. Of course, through a series of computer runs one can assess the impact of these kinds of questions in batch mode computing also. The key difference, however, is the interactive capability of time-shared systems where the immediacy of results prompts new questions to be raised. Thus the decision maker takes on a mental set of problem solving, working in concert with the power of large-scale computing. The nature of questions to be raised depends on the particular situation, but with large corporate planning models typical "what if" questions might be:

1. If product prices are changed, what will the effect on cash flow? On profits?

2. If a proposed new item of equipment is purchased or leased, what will be the effects on profits and cash flow of alternate financing methods?

3. If a wage increase is granted, what will the the effect on production rates, use of overtime, risk of seasonal inventory, and so on, for a production program?

In Chapter 17 we discussed interactive simulation systems in the context of job shop scheduling and in this chapter we shall discuss such systems in the context of corporate planning.

General System Program

The heart of the interactive simulation system which we shall discuss depends on the availability of a set of interrelated subprograms which we shall call the general system program. Figure 1 shows the general system program in relation to basic data files and the logic for a specific corporate model. The economic series data file refers to general economic indices of interest for forecasting purposes, and the business series data file refers to data series specific to the organization being simulated, for example, product demand data. Internal to the general system program is a wide variety of subroutines which can be called to process data for later use in

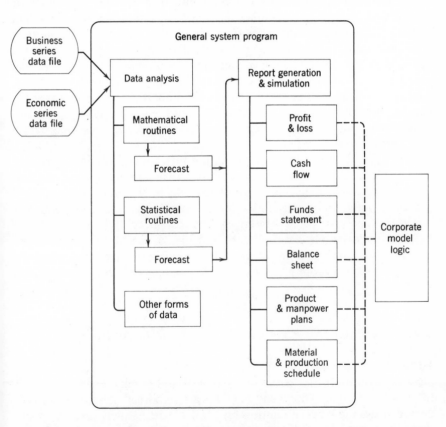

FIGURE 1. *Interrelationships within the general system program, and with files and model logic for a specific enterprise. Figures 1–10 are from J. B. Boulden and E. S. Buffa, "Corporate Models: On-Line, Real-Time Systems,"* Harvard Business Review, *July-August, 1970. Courtesy On-Line Decisions, Inc.*

simulation and report generation. The factor of key importance is that the general system program represents a set of subprograms which can be interrelated at will. The availability of specific subroutines in the general system program is greatly condensed in Figure 1.

The first step in using the system is to manipulate the raw data in the business and economic series files in meaningful ways so as to forecast future sales or other aspects of performance. The relationships are shown in a very general way in Figure 1, where we see that the result of processing by the mathematical and statistical routines is a forecast which is fed into the report generation and simulation phase.

With the standard subroutines available, an analyst might take raw sales data from the business file and smooth them by moving average or exponential smoothing techniques. He might then plot the smoothed data with a variety of economic indicators from the economic file or do multiple regression studies. The final result of his analysis is a forecast which is then an input to the report generation and simulation phase. Of course, he may wish to take more than one forecast into the simulation phase to see how they reflect on indices of performance. The important fact concerning the data analysis phase is the integrated nature of the general system program, which makes it possible to carry effects computed by one subprogram into another subprogram.

In the report generation and simulation phase, the decision maker uses his knowledge of the internal structure of the organization as represented by the corporate model logic to test the effects of a variety of different modes of operation. For example, he can obtain the results of parameter sensitivity analysis, profit objectives, changes in cost parameters, or of different forecasts. He can deal with fundamental structural changes in the enterprise by manipulating the corporate model. He can call for various kinds of standard profit and loss, cash flow, balance sheet statements, and so on.

Model Construction—Plywood Manufacturing As An Example

To demonstrate the nature of model construction used we shall examine a plywood operation. This situation is typical and is small enough in scope to show what is being done and how it is accomplished. Also, this example demonstrates the types of relationships which exist in many operations and shows how a model of the operations can be used.

The physical flow of materials for a plywood operation is shown in Figure 2. Company owned logs together with purchased logs (if required) are processed in the veneer manufacturing phase. This involves cutting a

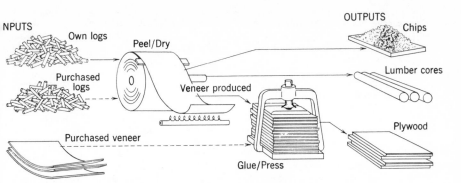

FIGURE 2.   Overall flow of plywood operations. Courtesy On-Line Decisions, Inc.

thin sheet of veneer from the surface of the log (peeling) and drying it to a specified moisture content. By-products of the peel/dry process are green lumber cores and chips, which are sold at transfer prices to other divisions of the company. Plywood is then glued and pressed with veneer produced in the previous operation and (if required) purchased veneer.

While this description of the process is simplified, it serves as an adequate basis for our discussion. The capacity of the glue/press operation in relation to the available company-produced veneer determines the amount of purchased veneer required. Similarly, the capacity of the peel/dry operation in relation to desired veneer output determines the amount of purchased logs required.

Plywood Profit and Loss.   The plywood model deals with profits and losses from plywood operations. The construction of the model is based on the simple algebraic relationships of sales and various costs. These relationships are based on a set of parameters which define the important factors in the model. Figure 3 shows a list of the parameters for the plywood model, identified by parameter number. At the end of the parameter list are "V-arrays," which involve important input data concerning prices and production.

Each line on the profit and loss statement then is computed according to a formula using the pertinent parameters. These formulas, or algebraic relationships, are shown in Figure 4. Each line numbered from .01 to 31.00 defines a corresponding line in the profit and loss statement. Following line 14.00, net profit before tax, is a list of computed ratios and other items of data of particular interest to management. These lines can be varied at will to provide other computed measures if desired.

The great flexibility built into the model is related to the parameter list.

Parameters (written as P1, P2, and so forth)

Parameter number	Description
1	Labor growth rate
2	Operating supplies growth rate
3	Raw materials growth rate
4	Initial pressing capacity (millions of square feet per month)
5	Month number (1-72) of pressing capacity increase
6	Increase in P4 as a fraction of P4
7	Initial veneer capacity (millions of square feet per month)
8	Month number (1-72) of veneer capacity increase
9	Increase in P7 as a fraction of P7
10	Price of own logs (dollars per log MBF)
11	Price of forest service logs (dollars per log MBF)
12	Fraction of logs from own supply
13	Discounts and allowances for plywood as a fraction of sales
14	Selling commission for plywood as a fraction of sales
15	Freight-out for plywood (dollars per MBF)
16	Yield MSF veneer per log MBF
17	Yield MSF 3/8-inch plywood per MSF veneer
18	Yield MBF lumber per MSF veneer produced
19	Yield chip units per MSF veneer produced
20	Operating supplies (dollars per MSF veneer produced)

Parameters (written as P1, P2, and so forth)

Parameter number	Description
21	Operating supplies (dollars per MSF plywood produced)
22	Labor hours per MSF veneer produced
23	Labor hours per MSF plywood produced
24	Labor cost (dollars per hour)
25	Sales eliminations of chips and lumber (percent as decimal)
26	Cost eliminations of own logs (percent as decimal)

V-arrays (written as V1, V2, and so forth)

Array number	Description
1	Desired plywood sales-production (millions of square feet per month)
2	Plywood prices (dollars per MSF)
3	Lumber transfer price (dollars per MBF)
4	Chip transfer price (dollars per unit)
5	Veneer purchase price (dollars per MSF)
6	Fixed costs ($1000 per year)
7	Selling expenses ($1000 per year)
8	General and administrative expenses ($1000 per year)
9	Other expenses ($1000 per year)

Read: MBF = thousands of board feet; MSF = thousands of square feet.

FIGURE 3. List of parameters and variable arrays for the plywood case. Courtesy On-Line Decisions, Inc.

The value of any parameter can be changed at will and the simulated effects of the change determined very quickly.

Results and "What if" Questions. An example of the profit and loss report for the plywood model is shown in the upper part of Figure 5. The report is for 1969 by quarters, based on actual data for quarters one and two, and on forecast data for quarters three and four. Following the profit and loss

Preliminary calculations

Desired plywood production	$DPP = V1$
Pressing capacity	$PC = P4$ if time $\quad P5$
	$\qquad P4 \times (1 + P6)$ if time $\quad P5$
Actual plywood production	$APP = Min\ (DPP, PC)$
Required veneer	$RV = APP/P17$
Veneer capacity	$VC = P7$ if time $\quad P8$
	$\qquad P7 \times (1 + P9)$ if time $\quad P8$
Veneer produced	$VP = Min\ (RV, VC)$
Purchased veneer	$PV = RV - VP$
Required logs	$RL = VP/P16$
Lumber produced	$FLP = VP/P18$
Chips produced	$CP = VP/P19$
Own logs	$FOL = P12 \times RL$
Forest service logs	$FSL = RL - FOL$

Line number	Description	Logic
.01	Plywood sales	$APP \times V2$
.02	Chips sales	$V4 \times CP$
.03	Lumber sales	$V3 \times FLP$
.04	Sales eliminations	$-(.02 + .03) \times P25$
1.00	Total sales	$.01 + .02 + .03 + .04$
1.01	Discounts and allowances (plywood)	$(.01) \times P13$
1.02	Commissions on plywood	$(.01) \times P14$
1.03	Freight-out for plywood	$APP \times P15$
2.00	Total allowances	$1.01 + 1.02 + 1.03$
3.00	Net sales	$1.00 - 2.00$
3.01	Raw materials	$[P10 \times P12 \times RL + P11 \times (1 - P12) \times RL] \times GROWTH\ (P2,0)$
3.02	Veneer purchase	$PV \times V5$
3.03	Operating supplies, manufacturing overhead	$[VP \times P20 + APP \times P21] \times GROWTH\ (P2,0)$
3.04	Labor	$[VP \times P22 + APP \times P23] \times P24 \times GROWTH\ (P1,0)$
3.05	Raw material cost eliminations	$-P12 \times VP \times GROWTH\ (P3,0) \times P26 \times P10/P16$
7.00	Total direct expenses	$3.01 + 3.02 + \cdots + 3.05$
8.00	Gross profit	$3.00 - 7.00$
9.00	Fixed costs	$V6$
10.00	Selling expenses	$V7$
11.00	General and administrative expenses	$V8$
12.00	Other expenses	$V9$
13.00	Total indirect expenses	$9.00 + 10.00 + 11.00 + 12.00$
14.00	Net profit before tax	$8.00 - 13.00$
22.00	Gross profit/net sales	$8.00/3.00$
23.00	Indirect expenses/net sales	$13.00/3.00$
24.00	Net profit/net sales	$14.00/3.00$
25.00	Plywood production (MM square feet)	APP
26.00	Veneer production (MM square feet)	VP
27.00	Lumber production (MM board feet)	FLP
28.00	Chip productions (units)	CP
29.00	Percent of new veneer capacity needed	$[RV - VC]/VC$
30.00	Percent of new pressing capacity needed	$[DPP - PC]/PC$
31.00	Labor (1,000 man-hours)	$VP \times P22 + APP \times P23$

FIGURE 4. Algebraic relationships for the profit and loss model for the plywood case. Courtesy On-Line Decisions, Inc.

YEAR 69

LINE ITEMS	QR1	QR2	QR3	QR4	YRT
SALES PLY	35800.0	37950.0	31200.0	33600.0	138550.0
SALES CHIPS	1350.0	1953.0	1827.0	1921.5	7051.5
SALES LUMBER	843.8	1260.0	1181.3	1260.0	4545.0
SALES ELIM					
TOTAL SALES	37993.8	41163.0	34208.3	36781.5	150146.5
D&A PLYWOOD	716.0	759.0	624.0	672.0	2771.0
COM PLY PLY	2148.2	2277.0	1872.0	2016.0	8313.0
FREIGHT PLY	-242.2	267.7	306.0	306.0	1122.0
TOT COM	3106.2	3302.7	2802.0	2994.0	12206.0
NET SALES	34887.2	37859.7	31406.3	33787.5	137940.5
RAW MATERIAL	4824.2	6831.2	6914.9	6999.7	25570.0
VENEER PURCH	8375.2	5694.1	9034.8	9252.4	32356.5
OP SUPPLIES	2860.8	3504.4	3844.5	3891.6	14101.2
LABOR	6544.8	8840.6	9181.2	9293.8	33860.4
COST ELIMIN					
COST OF SALE	22605.0	24870.2	28975.4	29437.6	105888.1
GROSS PROFIT	12282.5	12989.5	2430.9	4349.9	32052.4
FIXED COSTS	1250.00	1250.00	1250.00	1250.00	5000.00
SELLING EXP	750.00	750.00	750.00	750.00	3000.00
G&A EXPENSE	750.00	750.00	750.00	750.00	3000.00
OTHER EXPENSE	-125.00	-125.00	-125.00	-125.00	-500.00
TOT IND EXP	2875.00	2875.00	2875.00	2875.00	11500.00
NET PROFIT	9407.5	10114.0	-444.1	1474.9	20552.4
GP/NS	.35	.34	-.08	.13	.23
TIE/NS	.08	.08	.09	.09	.08
NP/NS	.27	.27	-.01	.04	.15

P-L MODE = 7/
ITERATION
DESIRED YEARLY PROFIT = 0/

TOT SALES	PROFIT	FRAC 1
150146.50	20552.36	1.0000
120117.20	14141.89	.8000
53870.76		.3588

FIGURE 5. Example of a profit and loss report for the plywood case, where quarters 1 and 2 represent actual experience and quarters 3 and 4 represent projections based on forecasts and simulation. Courtesy On-Line Decisions, Inc.

report, the typewriter terminal has printed "P-L MODE=," asking whether any further manipulation of the profit and loss statement is desired.

The analyst responded in this instance by typing "7/." This number called for an iteration on a desired profit level, and the diagonal called for the execution of the command. The program responded by printing "ITERATION" and "DESIRED YEARLY PROFIT=." At this point the analyst responded by inserting the desired profit figure. He inserted "0" to indicate that he wished a calculation of sales required for break even or zero profit. The typewriter terminal then printed out the sales, profit, and fraction of sales to forecasted total sales for three levels of sales volume including the break-even level. As we see in Figure 5, break even takes place at yearly sales of $53,870.76, or 36 percent of the forecasted sales level.

The interactive nature of the system is indicated by the conversational language employed.

Now suppose that the manager wants to assess the impact of a labor cost increase on net profit. For instance, he could vary the value of the parameter for labor cost per hour, denoted by the symbol "P24" in Figure 6. He calls for parameter sensitivity by specifying "P-L MODE=8/." The program responds by asking which parameter is to be varied, the range of

```
P-L MODE = 8/
PARAMETER SENSITIVITY
P#/MIN/MAX/INCREMENT/ = 24/5/6/.25/

    YEAR 69                 P/L

P24 = 5.000

LINE ITEMS                 YRT
NET PROFIT                 20552.4

P24 = 5.250

LINE ITEMS                 YRT
NET PROFIT                 18859.3

P24 = 5.500

LINE ITEMS                 YRT
NET PROFIT                 17166.3

P24 = 5.750

LINE ITEMS                 YRT
NET PROFIT                 15473.3

P24 = 6.000

LINE ITEMS                 YRT
NET PROFIT                 13781.0
```

FIGURE 6. *Sensitivity of net profit to the parameter P24, labor cost per hour, for the plywood case. Courtesy On-Line Decisions, Inc.*

variation, and the steps in which it is to be varied. The analyst types the parameter number, the minimum and maximum values of the parameter, and the increment of step size of the variation. If he wishes to see a plot of the sensitivity of net profit to labor cost, he can call for this from the standard programs available as well.

The Plywood Model as a Component of a Corporate Model. Let us pause for a moment to reflect upon the general nature of the input-output structure represented by the plywood model. The upper half of Figure 7

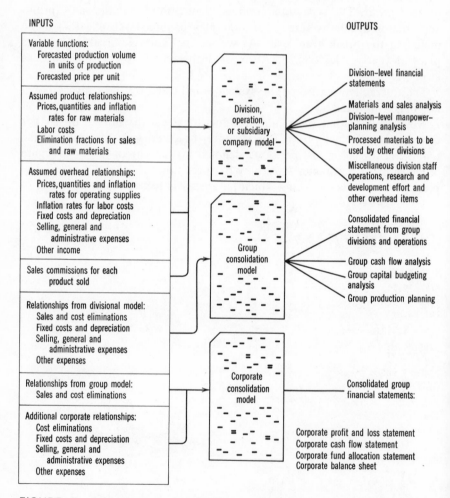

FIGURE 7. Input-output relationships for division or subsidiaries, group consolidation, and corporate consolidation. Courtesy On-Line Decisions, Inc.

summarizes the nature of the input-output relationships for a divisional type of operation such as that in the plywood model. A number of such models may be consolidated to form groups of models with the general input-output relationships shown in the middle section of Figure 7; or the process of consolidation can be carried still further so that a model of the whole corporation is formed, as in the lower part of Figure 7.

What top executives are likely to be most interested in, of course, are the group and corporate models. Yet by using the kind of structure illustrated by the plywood model as a basic building block, together with the successive layers of aggregation indicated in Figure 7, management can ask for the effects of proposed changes in prices, costs, equipment, financing, and so on, at *any* level; it can estimate the net effects on the total corporation quickly and accurately.

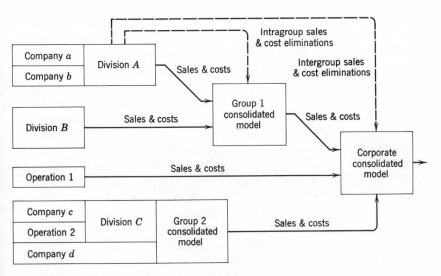

FIGURE 8. *Flows of sales and costs for consolidation of various levels in a corporate model. Courtesy On-Line Decisions, Inc.*

The revenue and cost flows involved in the input-output relationships appear in Figure 8 in generalized form for a large integrated corporate operation where a complex of subsidiary companies and divisions are consolidated in group models and a corporate model. The flows of revenues and costs take into account sales between groups and divisions, as the dashed lines indicate.

Potlatch Forests—An Example of A Corporate Model [4]

Potlatch Forests, Inc., is a large integrated forest products company having annual sales in the range of about $335 million, and it employs over 12,000 individuals in 44 plants and 36 sales offices spread over the entire country.

The company developed 22 models to describe its various operations, groups, and subsidiaries. The plywood model previously discussed is a good example of the type of models used by Potlatch, although the company's models are actually more sophisticated and involve more relationships. By interrelating these models, management can obtain a model for the entire corporation and thus see the end result of changes made at the operational or group levels.

The structure of the input-output relationships of the various divisions, groups, and subsidiaries is shown in Figure 9. Prior to the existence of the corporate models, management's assessment of the financial effects of the interactions of interplant buying and selling and changing product mixes involved long-time lags. The interactive system, however, greatly reduced the effort needed to evaluate alternate plans because the logic of the 22 models takes into account the complex financial flows between divisions and groups.

Since the model development phase, the Company has learned to use the models extensively and has developed a wide range of additional models. Potlatch's Director of Corporate Planning, states that the entire corporate planning process is highly interrelated with their on-line computer models. Major capital expenditure decisions are made only after testing a variety of alternative effects via the models. The existence of the modeling system has made possible a much more thorough exploration of "what if" questions both because answers can be computed in shorter turn-around times, and because the known existence of the models and the system encourages the asking of "what if" questions throughout the organization.

The biggest increase in model development and use in the first six months of 1971 has been in the project planning category, using special-purpose models. Potlatch used a total of 741 terminal hours in 1970, 452 of which were used in primary corporate planning and 289 hours used for special project planning. During the first six months of 1971 the usage rate increased to 816 terminal hours with 61 percent of this usage being in the project planning category. The cost of using the system has approximated $60.00 per hour.

Potlatch Forests now has 47 different models in use, 25 for primary corporate planning and 22 special purpose project models. Potlatch is highly decentralized in a geographic sense and corporate planners go directly into

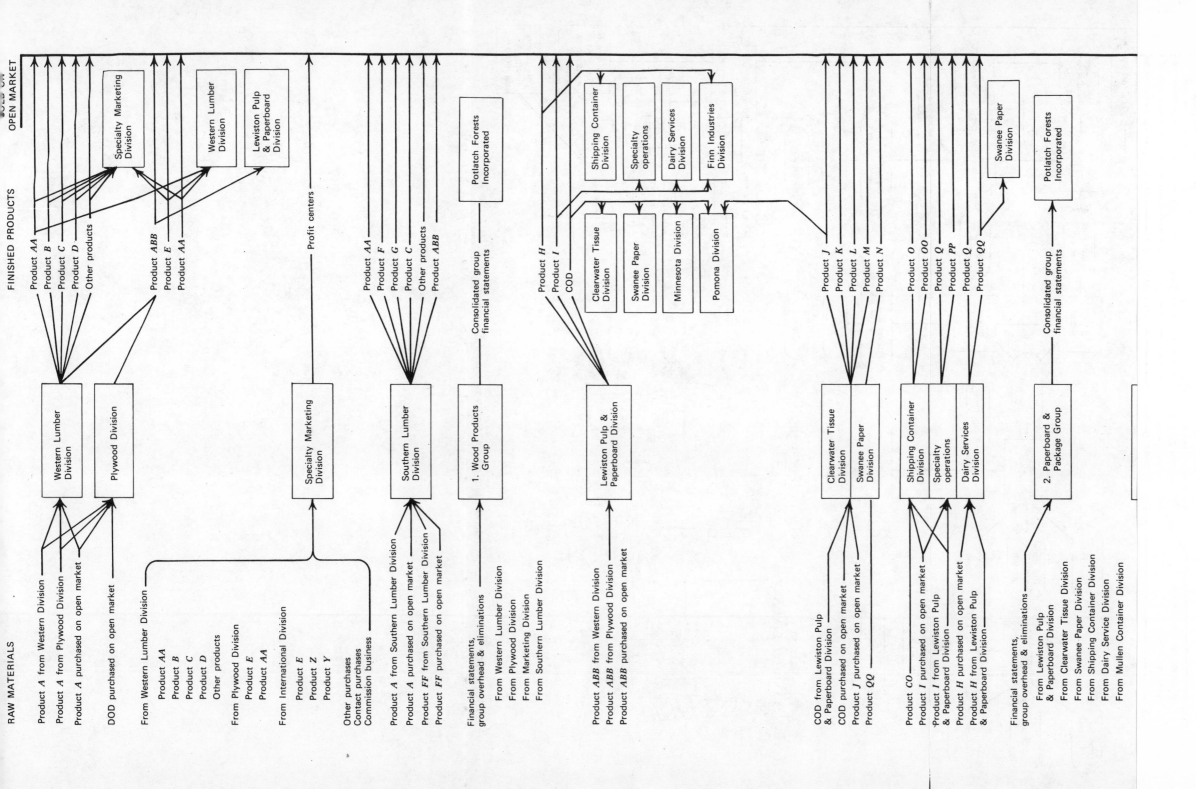

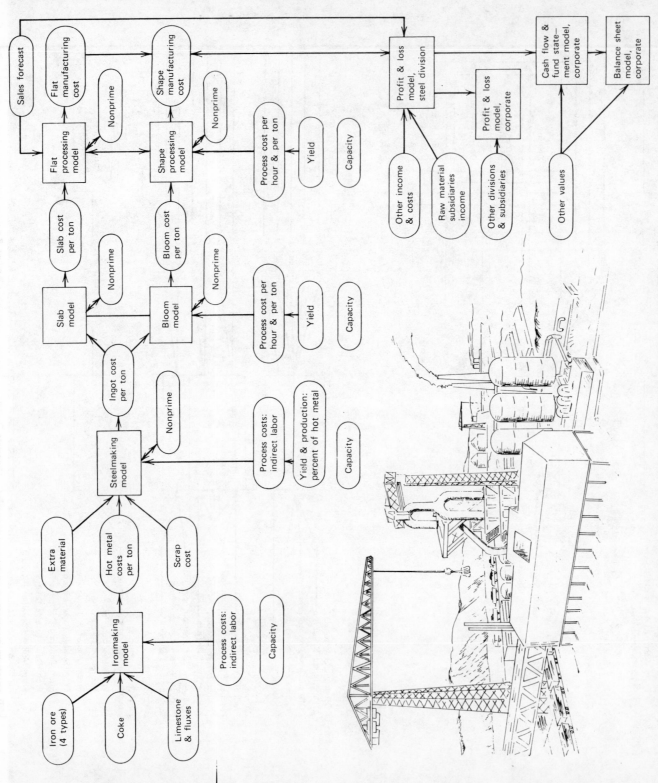

FIGURE 10. Relationships in Inland Steel model. *Courtesy Inland Steel and On-Line Decisions, Inc.*

the field with portable terminals to develop and test alternate plans with field managers. In addition, field managers are now beginning to develop their own models.

Inland Steel—Another Example of Interactive Simulation [2, 4]

While the Potlatch Forests case emphasizes the successive aggregation and consolidation of financial statements, the Inland Steel Company example focuses on the production process. The models which have been developed and their relationships are shown in Figure 10. Using the models, corporate planners can simulate very quickly the effects of a wide variety of planning assumptions. Each model deals with a basic process in the sequence from raw materials to finished products. The models simulate the various costs incurred in:

1. Conversion of ores to molten iron.
2. Conversion of molten iron to steel ingots.
3. Processing of ingots.
4. Finishing the steel to various end products.

The types of questions asked by Inland Steel management via the interactive models are typified by the following:

1. How much raw material is required to meet production forecasts?
2. What are the cost effects of various hot metal-to-scrap ratios and the resulting yields under various assumptions of raw material costs?
3. What are the capacity requirements for proposed levels of operation?

Interactive simulation models appear to hold great promise as being very practical vehicles for management to use in the development of corporate plans and to assess the impact of a wide variety of proposed modes of operation.

Use of Inland's Models. The Inland financial models were installed in the 4th quarter of 1969, too late for use in the 1970 annual profit plan. However, the models were used to test alternative strategies, changes in key variables, parameters and assumptions on a test basis by the corporate planning staffs during the first half of 1970 as part of a training and experimentation program.

The first live test of the models was in the preparation of the 1971 profit plan and the related five-year profit and cash projection. For the first time, alternate strategies and assumptions were used during the planning process and during the executive review of the total corporate formal plan.

In approaching the profit planning cycle for 1971, the company management was faced with unusual uncertainties. This lead to the use of the models to simulate four major alternative sets of conditions. All four were based on a basic premise that a strike in the automotive industry was a near certainty during the 4th quarter of 1970, and that if this should occur there would be a significant impact on 4th quarter shipments of the Inland Steel Company. However, the sales forecast for 1971 indicated a very strong sales demand for the first 7 months of that planning period, ending with the August 1st deadline date for negotiations with the steel workers union.

The first assumption of this basic premise was that the sales forecast for 1971 would follow a normal seasonal dispersion of shipments, much like what would happen in any normal year, with no impact from the actions of customers through hedge buying of steel inventories in anticipation of a possible strike. This gave a base condition for planning.

The second assumption was made that the historic pattern of prestrike hedge buying would occur in the first 7 months of 1971, as it had in all similar periods in the postwar period, and that there would be no strike, since agreement would be reached late on July 31st. In this condition, sales demand would decline sharply in August, September and October, with some recovery in the later months of the 4th quarter of 1971.

The third assumption involved the previous basic premise, but assumed a 30-day strike in the industry, with resumption of production in shipments after 30 days.

The fourth assumption assumed a 90-day strike, with the same prestrike hedge buying sales pattern occurring, as stated in the basic premise.

The financial model was used to simulate these four basic assumptions, all assuming the basic premise that there would be an auto strike in the 4th quarter of 1970. Management selected assumption number two, which was a prestrike buildup of inventories, but no strike occurring in the industry. This was used as the basis for the formal profit plan for 1971, but the other options were maintained in the profit planning manual as alternate strategies in the event conditions should change as they approached the August 1st strike deadline.

A major decision was made in September 1970 by top management to build semifinished and finished inventories to the largest level in the company's history to capitalize on the strong demand forecast indicated for the first half of 1971. The reason for this was that if the forecast was correct, and inventories were not accumulated, the mills would not be able to produce the steel fast enough to meet the customer delivery requirements, and there would be loss of sales revenue. This plan was followed, the excess inventory was liquidated on schedule by June 1, 1971, and the company achieved an all-time record industry market share of 6.8 percent versus a normal rate of 4.8 percent to 5.2 percent.

In late June 1971, it became apparent that the sales demand would not hold up through July 31st as anticipated, and that the odds on a strike on August 1st were growing. The company also evaluated similar inventory build-up strategies for either the poststrike period, should a strike occur, or for production over the last five months of 1971 should there not be a strike, as the preliminary sales forecast from market research for 1972 indicated a very strong market.

In early July 1971, the management requested an accelerated up-dating of the annual cash forecast for 1971, and the five-year cash projection for the years 1972 through 1976. Management recognized that rigorous planning of capital expenditures and long-term financing was required to meet the conditions confronting them.

Some of the reasons for this situation were:

1. Heavy normal expansion and replacement requirements for the steel division and the steel related subsidiaries of the company.

2. Burgeoning requirements for cash expenditures for pollution control equipment required by state and federal environmental agencies.

3. The need to meet long term bond issues that were scheduled for retirement over the next five-year period.

4. Very large requirements and opportunities for investments in real estate and housing projects for their new shelter company, the Inland Steel Urban Development Company.

There is growing interest at the steel works level of management to build tactical models to deal with the problem of selecting from many alternative production scheduling schemes the most promising schedule in relation to costs. A project was started in June 1971 to develop more models which interlock with the basic Inland Steel Financial Models to deal with this question. It is too early to assess the results or the possible success or failure of this project.

In June of 1971 a financial model was developed for a raw materials division to deal with alternative plans for the development of mines or for alternative ways of developing a single mine. It represents a modification of the capital budget model, in which the time horizon is extended 60 years, and the ability to handle depletion allowances and other special features, such as foreign tax credits, is built into the modeling system. Personnel in the raw materials division are now using the model in their day to day evaluations of the replacement alternatives for their largest iron ore mine, scheduled to phase out of production in the mid-1970's.

The Container Division of Inland Steel recently completed a model of the entire standard cost and budget system of its largest plant in Chicago. It is intended to be used for developing the annual budgets, for handling changes in the budgets and to test alternative production schedules and product mix effects, on a daily or weekly basis.

Two other subsidiaries of Inland Steel are presently studying the feasibility of modeling parts of their planning processes: INRYCO (Inland-Ryerson Construction Products Company) is working on a model to test the cost and profit effects of large bid-type projects on the profitability of the entire subsidiary. Their housing subsidiary, which uses the acronym INSTUD, is considering the feasibility of modeling long term construction ventures.

Van Den Berghs & Jurgens Ltd. (VdB & J) *

Van den Bergh & Jurgens Ltd., a subsidiary of Unilever Ltd., U. K. is a major producer of white and yellow fats in the United Kingdom. The margarine brands account for 65 percent of the total annual company's sales which approximate $200,000,000.

The company's organization structure as shown in Figure 11, is devised to allow the firm to approach three distinct segments of the market in the most appropriate manner. The retail sales of package margarines and white fats is controlled by Van den Berghs. Yellow and white fats of a similar nature that are required by the bakery and catering industry are supplied in commercial sized packages by Craig-Millar, while the industrial demand for refined and processed oils from manufactured and other food products is accomplished by the Loders and Nucoline Division. A fourth division has recently been added to handle diversified products other than those falling within the edible oils and fats market.

The process of manufacture of edible oils and fats is, in itself, extremely complex. Figure 12 is a schematic diagram with the principal flows and the basic stages in the operation. Up to 25 different crude edible oils are used in combinations of up to four or five oils per product for some 60 products manufactured by VdB & J. Any or all of these oils are passed through some or all of the processes indicated in the oil refining section of the flow diagram. The characteristics of the end product must remain constant and yet the qualities of the input oil vary from batch to batch and will certainly vary across a total range of edible oils in use. In consequence, the refining capacity of the company, while fixed in physical terms, is directly related

*From J. B. Boulden, and E. S. Buffa, "New Developments in On-Line Corporate Models," On-Line Decisions, Inc., 1972.

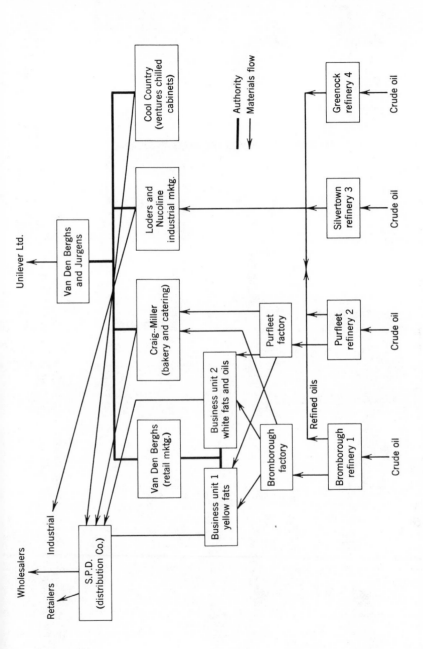

FIGURE 11. *Organization Structure and Materials flow at VdB & J. Courtesy of VdB & J Division of Unilever, Ltd. and On-Line Decisions, Inc.*

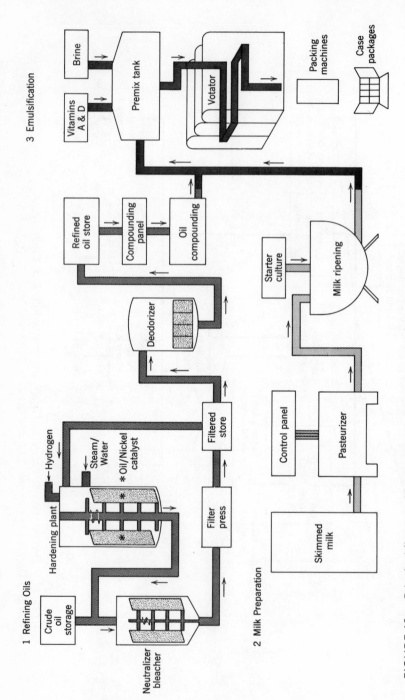

3 Emulsification

1 Refining Oils

2 Milk Preparation

FIGURE 12. Principal flows and basic stages of the process of manufacture of edible oils and fat. Courtesy of VdB & J Division of Unilever, Ltd. and On-Line Decisions, Inc.

to the oils that are being processed at a given time and to the end formulation of the individual products.

At a further level of complexity to this problem, variations may be made in individual product formulations to be able to optimize the use of lower cost raw materials. In the day to day operational sense, these formulations are calculated using a least cost linear program based on the prices of the individual batches of oils against the demand that is required. Mandatory changes in formulation occur between the summer and winter months, so that the final characteristics of the product remain the same despite significant changes in temperatures.

With no fixed capacity or formulation, but with all factors linked to the raw material price forecast of the crude oils, a more than usually complex model was necessary to provide the ability to determine profit margins and to ensure that the anticipated volume did not exceed the total capacity.

Organization and Planning at VdB & J. The annual and the five-year planning activity occur somewhat independently at VdB & J and at different times in the year, although similar procedures are followed in their preparation. The general planning processes are shown in Figure 13. The Policy Committee at the Board level of VdB & J establish general guide lines for the operating divisions. The business units establish basic product lines strategy and refer the matter to brand managers for their forecast of tonnages. These tonnage forecasts are then referred to the factories who use them in estimating costs of manufacture. The same forecasts are also used in establishing marketing cost and the estimation of other expenses.

This information all flows to the management accountants who prepare the forecasts which are submitted to the business units for consolidation and hence for reconsolidation into their division plans and subsequently into the plan for VdB & J for final approval.

This planning practice has been in existence for a number of years with significant drawbacks. First the time devoted to the creation of the plan, both from the revenue and cost aspects, was enormous and occupied the accountancy staff of the company full time for approximately six months of the year on the annual plan alone. Over 7,000 values were computed as input for the annual plan to generate 125 reports in 12 primary formats. Data was manipulated in a number of ways by various classifications, i.e. all brands sold to bakeries, all yellow fats, etc. When an assumption was changed in one area, thousands of recalculations were necessary.

With the tremendous amount of effort necessary to undertake the creation of a plan, it was impossible for the staff to submit several alternatives to the Board for consideration and, in the event of a plan being disapproved, it was extremely difficult to generate a new one. Further, the ability to update the plan was restricted to annual or biannual exercises because of the time

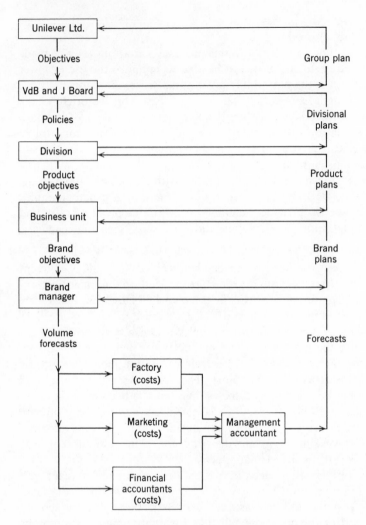

FIGURE 13. VdB & J Planning Process. Courtesy of VdB & J Division of Unilever, Ltd. and On-Line Decisions, Inc.

involved. This was clearly unacceptable in an environment where the raw material costs were rapidly fluctuating, a variation of over 100 percent having been experienced in the past two years in some costs. The ability to maintain the level of profits in the face of changing cost factors was critical. The need to merge the short and medium term plans to a continuous planning process was recognized and the search for a tool capable of providing this was undertaken by a group of internal and external consultants under the guidance of the Head of Planning for VdB & J.

The Modeling System (VANGUARD)*

VANGUARD is designed as a computerized tool for formulating Long Range Plans within Van den Berghs & Jurgens Limited. The system operates entirely in time sharing mode, and is thus available for the use of management via remote terminals. It is a corporate simulator which allows the user to explore the effect on the company trading position of changes in the whole range of variables applicable to the operation of the company: for example, (a) total market sizes and market shares, (b) brand sales values, (c) raw material prices, (d) product formulations, (e) refinery capacities, (f) personnel costs, (g) taxation rates, (h) working capital requirements, etc.

The system consists of a set of fifteen interrelated programs, or models, each relevant to a separate aspect of the company operation. These models work within the framework of a General System Program similar to the one discussed earlier. The overall system structure is shown in Figure 14.

The simulation can be carried out over a ten year period, currently 1967–1976, on a year by year basis. The only exception is the Raw Material/ Formulation and Capacity areas, which operate on a quarterly basis to allow for seasonal changes in Raw Material prices and formulations.

The system is accessed from a remote terminal and basic program with which the user is in communication is a General System Program. The various models are then called in by the user, who has at his disposal a range of system commands. Certain commands are used to set up the output format required by the user, who may request specified lines of output and specified years. Other commands allow the user to enter new data, to modify existing data as necessary, or to examine values of the data.

Finally, the user selects an appropriate command to execute the selected model in one of a variety of modes. The model may be simply executed and the output printed. Alternatively, the model may be set up to run a number of times, with a given data item being incremented by a determined amount on each run; this is used to examine the sensitivity of certain lines of output to changes in various inputs.

Finally, the user can enter a required value of an output line, and cause the model to search iteratively for the value of a selected variable which would be necessary to generate the output. For example, a desired brand profit may be entered, and the system instructed to seek the variable cost figure needed to generate this profit; as a more complex example, a target budgeted divisional expenses figure may be entered for 1976, and the sys-

---

*The description of the VANGUARD modeling system was contributed by Messrs. Cooper and Jones of VdB & J.

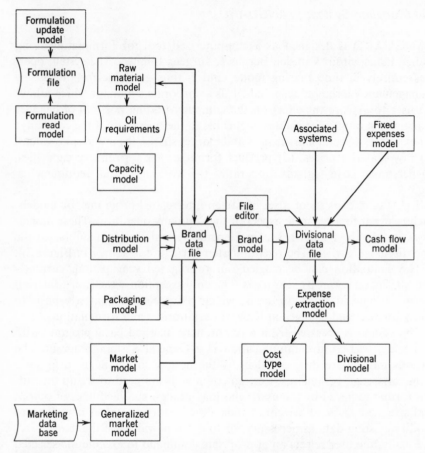

FIGURE 14. Vanguard system flowchart. Courtesy of VdB & J Division of Unilever, Ltd. and On-Line Decisions, Inc.

tem instructed to calculate the highest growth rate in personnel costs which would be permissible if this budget figure is to be attained.

The brand Model may be regarded as the heart of the system. Basically, it is used to examine the margin statement for any brand up to the level of profit before fixed expenses. All necessary data is stored on the Brand Data File, but any element of this may be changed by direct input from the terminal: this change may be either to provide a new value, or alternatively the current values may be inflated from a given year by a desired percentage.

Apart from looking at an individual brand, the model is used to aggregate brand data to the level of the company divisions. Very powerful data handling capabilities are provided within the model to allow for this. The fixed aggregations of brands, corresponding to the company profit reporting hierarchy, are stored within the model and any desired aggregation may be selected by the user who is also free to generate new hierarchies online; a new aggregation created in this way may be needed only once, but if desired can be stored for future use. The system allows an unlimited number of hierarchies.

A maximum of five complete sets of data corresponding to alternative possible strategies may be stored for each brand. The aggregation facility allows the users to specify for each brand the strategy selected when aggregating.

Any given aggregation can be passed to the Divisional Data file as the basis for a given divisional strategy. Each division may have as many as five individually specified strategies.

The Fixed Expenses model is then used to enter appropriate divisional expenses for each strategy, and to aggregate divisions to company subtotals and finally the company total, with the same degree of flexibility as at the Brand level. Thus the five-year company forward plan may be generated adaptively, with as many changes of values as desired, simulating the effects of combining various strategies for each operating division, and each business unit or product group within the division.

The total company source and use of funds is examined in the Financial Reporting Model, which is based on selected divisional strategies projected to the level of trading profit, and leading to the calculation of operational cash flow.

The actual costs and expenses forming any version of the plan may be examined in greater detail using the Cost Type and Divisional Models to break each expense down into categories (personnel, accomodation, etc.); any cost type may be changed to new values or by compound inflation rates (e.g. inflate at personnel expenditure by 10 percent compound from 1972). The model then applies the desired change to the expenses, and recalculates and prints the divisional or company statement.

Referring again to Figure 14, the Brand Data needed by the Brand Model may be input directly using the File Editor. The scope of the system is vastly increased by using the various available models (Packaging, Distribution, etc.) to generate each element of brand data.

In generating Sales Volume (SV) forecasts, and setting SV/ton for each brand, we should take into account the environment in which the company is operating. This is one of the functions of the Market Model. Apart from dealing with individual brands in terms of tonnage, marketing appropriation, SV and profitability, this model checks the total estimates for volume in various market sectors (yellow fats, oils, white fats, etc.) against predetermined estimates of the market size in this area.

Powerful analysis facilities are offered to the user in the Generalized Marketing Model. A marketing data base dealing with total markets, market splits, individual brand prices, volumes, advertising appropriations, etc. has been drawn from historical market research and company data. Significant relationships between any of these variables may be sought on-line using single or multiple linear regression analysis. Complex relationships may be developed by appropriate transformation, using analysis of variance to test improvements in fit derived from the introduction of successive terms in the relationship. In this way we can explore interbrand sensitivity, price-volume elasticity, advertising appropriation/volume correlations, overall market trends, etc. Any relationship found to have a satisfactory degree of significance may be used to generate forecasts which may then be passed forward into the Market Model.

All models in the system are linked and can be run in concert or individually according to the instructions of the planner. The system is on-line and interactive with conversational capability between the planner and the computer. The models can be run backward from objectives, or forward from market assumptions. That is, the user can specify objectives such as profitability and have the system search backward to determine appropriate strategies, such as pricing, to achieve these objectives within the organizational constraints.

Individual operations can be simulated down to the brand level (up to 60 brands) or various product groupings analyzed. Company output can be formulated by operating units or by time periods. Historical comparisons can be made and marginal or total analyses outputted. Costs can be analyzed by alternative classifications. The user can override the data files and input selected values or operating constraints, such as forcing capacity to a specified level. It is impossible to discuss the detail of the total system within the space limitations here. Therefore, we have selected the raw materials, capacity and brand models for more detailed elaboration in order to indicate the nature of some of the detailed relationships within these three models and some of the interrelationships between models.

Raw Materials Model. The purpose of the materials model is to provide two outputs to the master file, the oil requirements to the capacity model and the cost per ton of every product. In order to do this, the model's logic has the capability to convert the crude oil costs to refined oil costs and to assign a suitable formulation to each product. The final output value of cost per ton includes all the physical ingredients of the product, direct oil refining costs and an allowance for wastage loss in both factory and refinery.

Approximations in the computations of direct costs are made in order to produce a compact and efficient model. The model will handle 60 products or product groups and 24 oils. Products may have up to 12 formulations assigned to them. A product group has an "average" formulation assigned to it which takes account of the formulations of the individual products within the group together with an estimate of the sales of each product relative to the group total.

Crude oil costs are converted to refined oil costs by adding refinery costs and dividing by the yield factor. The formulation for each of the product groups is then chosen on the basis of refined oil costs. If a choice of formulation is possible, it is made on the basis of the ranking of oil costs, that is, on which refined oil groups is cheapest and which is second cheapest; the groups are palm, lard, fish and vegetable. The formulations themselves are generated by an offline linear programming model, and inputted to the system as necessary via a Formulations Model. Any of them can be updated as required.

Multiplying the formulation by the refined oil costs gives the oil blend costs for each product. The oil blend cost is multiplied by the fat factor, the cost of other ingredients is added, and this is multiplied by the factory waste factor. These three operations convert blend costs to finished product costs, which are stored on the master file.

To calculate oil requirements, the estimated demands for each product are multiplied by the factory waste factor and the fat factor. This gives the tonnage or refined oil needed to make the estimated quantity of finished product.

Using the formulation, the total refined oil tonnage is split up into the basic refined oils. These are converted to crude oil tonnages by dividing by the refinery yield. If at any time a subtotal of oil requirements exceeds an oil availability, the program recycles to the oil prices. At this point the price of the critical oil is set to a high figure, precluding its further use in that quarter. It is for this reason that a product can be assigned a priority in the use of source oils. If the priority is set to 1, that product has first call on any oil which may be in limited supply.

The facility exists to feed in separate formulations and override the model's logic. The Raw Materials Model need not be run in isolation. Indeed, its usefulness is vastly increased if run in conjunction with the Capacity Model and the Marketing Model. A typical sequence of events is illustrated in the flow chart of Figure 15.

Capacity Model. The Capacity Model is used to examine the oil requirements in tons of refined oils as outputted from the Raw Materials Model, and must examine them in the light of available refinery capacity. The

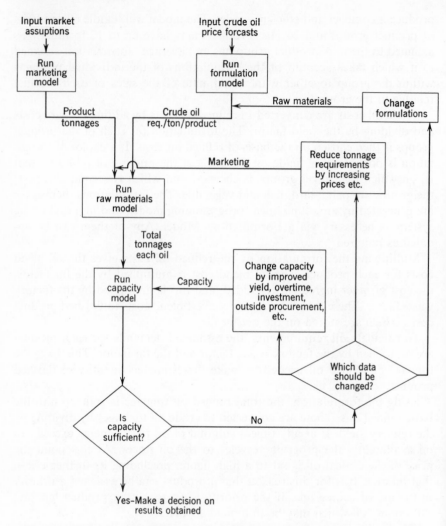

FIGURE 15. Flow chart showing interrelationships between Marketing, Raw Materials, Formulations, and Capacity Models for VdB & J. Courtesy of VdB & J Division of Unilever, Ltd. and On-Line Decisions, Inc.

Capacity Model calculates to what extent any given set of brand tonnages will utilize any set of production resources, and indicates when a capacity constraint has been reached.

Assumptions. Refining capacity is the bottleneck at present, and is likely to be so in the future. No other capacities have therefore been considered.

The available refinery capacities can also be grouped and treated as one set of resources.

Model Description. The model fits into the framework of a linear program with the following general description. A refinery can be divided into stages, where a stage is defined as follows:

It is a part of the refining process which can be considered independently of the parts immediately before and after. This implies that adequate buffering exists between stages—if it does not, then the buffering process itself could become a stage.

It must contain real alternatives. That is, when an oil enters a stage, it must be possible to process it on more than one type of "machine", where each type has a different throughput.

With the above definition, all stages are mathematically equivalent and the model is a model of a stage. The whole refinery can be dealt with by running the model once for each stage and merely altering the data. The stages to be considered initially are neutralizing and deodorizing. Other stages, such as filtering, can be considered at will whenever necessary and the data is available.

The input to the model is a list of oil tonnages, derived from the Raw Materials Model. Since the refineries are used as a common resource by all of the business units other than "Cool Country," it follows that this list must cover *all* products.

The list should preferably be of oil groups rather than individual oils to reduce the size of the data files. Semipermanent data is required concerning available hours for each machine group and process time for each oil group on each machine group.

The output from the model is a single index number from each stage. If each oil tonnage on the input list were multiplied by this number, then the resulting tonnages would occupy all the resources of that stage for all their available time, and they would be the largest tonnages possible with that property.

It follows that:

a. the stage with the smallest (or critical) index number is a bottleneck

b. any stage with an index number less than one is unable to process the current requirements

c. the critical index number can be applied to brand tonnages as well as oil tonnages

It should be noted that the index answers the question—if all the brand tonnages remain in the same proportion, by how much can production be increased? It is desired to investigate the consequences of increasing production on some, but not all, brands, and the amount of the largest increase is less than that indicated by the current value of the critical index number, then the increase can certainly be coped with and it is unnecessary to rerun the model. If any of the increases exceed the critical index, then because the relative tonnages of the brands have changed, the model should rerun to determine the new critical index.

Brand Model. The Brand Model is designed to offer the following facilities:

1. Examination of the margin statement for any single brand up to the level of profit before fixed expenses. Two alternative output formats are provided.

2. Examination of any combination of brands, up to the same level. Again both output formats are available. Certain fixed options may be generated automatically by the program by the input of a single parameter. Generalized options may be created by inputting the specific brands required.

3. Data may be picked up from the computer files, or alternatively, new values may be inputted direct from the teletype for Net Sales Value, tonnage or any cost of any brand. If new values are input at an aggregation level (e.g. Total Fluctuating Costs), then the system will automatically disregard the contributory items down from the data files (e.g. RM cost, Distribution Cost) for that brand.

   If a group of brands are being examined, then new data may be entered for an individual brand or brands, or for the whole group treated as one, at any level.

   Equally, when dealing with a group of brands, the model may be run backwards from a desired output value to determine either the total group value of a given cost, or specific brand contribution to that cost.

4. The model will automatically generate all the Business Unit and divisional margin statements on setting of the appropriate parameters. In addition, the model may be used to create data files at these levels for use by other models. Since these data files will represent the definitive five-year plan at these levels, use of this facility will be restricted to one account. This does not, of course, restrict in any way the ability of other models to manipulate data at the higher levels.

5. Historic data for the last five years may be taken in from appropriate files and manipulated in the same way as above, to give comparative figures. In addition, using the advanced aggregation commands, projected figures may be compared with historic on a percentage or wider basis.

"What if?" capability for the VANGUARD system. The general capability
to answer What If? type questions is indicated by the following specific
questions:

1. If the price of Brand X is reduced by 10 percent how does this
   affect sales, profits, cash flow and return on capital, and do we
   have the production capacity available?

2. If palm oil ceases to be available for product Z, what would be the
   best substitute and how is profitability affected?

3. What would be the effect on profitability of cutting out Brands A
   and B and replacing tonnage by Brand C; how much additional
   refining capacity would be created?

4. If labor costs were to rise by 15 percent per annum over three
   years, and 20 percent the following two years, by how much would
   we have to increase prices to maintain margins?

5. Where brands are highly interactive in one market, what is the
   most profitable mix of brand strategies?

6. What would be the effect of the closure of a major production unit
   for a long period due to a natural disaster or strikes?

7. What would be the effect of a totally new diversification project
   upon company resources and profits? This simulation will include
   the acquisition of another company versus direct diversification.

8. What is the minimum necessary increase in a brand sale volume
   to justify a price decrease?

9. When and how should brand selling prices be changed in a competitive market to offset forecasted changes in cost?

10. What utilization of existing production capacity is likely to service
    alternative marketing strategies from each sales division? Will a
    particular combination of strategies require additional capacity
    for processes and if so, how much?

11. Which particular combination of alternative divisional strategies
    is preferable for the company in each time period, with particular
    references to risk?

12. What would be the best response to a competitor's action in
    lowering prices?

13. If the price of a particular raw material were to increase, which
    products would be affected and what price adjustment is necessary?

14. If a particular raw material were to be in short supply, which

products would have priority call upon the limited quantities available?

15. What would the effect upon company resources and profits for the acquisition of a competitor in the same business?

16. If the share of a particular market changes, what would be the effect upon short and long term profits?

17. What is the effect of alternative forecasts of market size upon sales volume and production capacity available?

Summary Comments on Van den Berghs & Jurgens Limited. The VAN-GUARD modeling system is obviously not simply a system for generating reports, but rather contains the complex algebraic logic representing the cost functions and the materials flow of the total organization. The input data requirements to the planning process have been greatly reduced because the system itself internally generates many specific values such as product material cost from general inputs of key variables. Using this system, the planner has immediate response to his "What If?" questions.

The planning process itself was greatly streamlined during modeling and a number of reports with redundant information were eliminated. An evolutionary process was adopted with regard to modeling and expansion of the system, in fact preliminary specifications for a Mark 3 system were already in existence in the fall of 1971. These expansions are planned to accommodate problems of increasing complexity while ensuring that the flexibility of the system is not jeopardized. New models will be introduced and existing models expanded without reprogramming.

VdB & J is perhaps the first firm to combine the complementary capability of both batch and time share interactive systems, in a mutually compatible system. The interactive model is used for instant response and user interaction allowing a wide range of options to be experimented within a short period of time, while a compatible batch version is being developed for expanded outputs, and a greater degree of detail. Specifically, the examination of alternatives will be accomplished by the use of interactive simulation for revenue and costs over a five year period in broad detail and then refined to an annual operating plan with extensive detail for control and examination.

Job Shop Simulation of Real Systems

For some time there has been a great deal of interest in the simulation of intermittent production systems, the most complex of which is commonly termed the job shop. The job shop probably represents the most complex of production systems, because in the most extreme situation, the open job shop, the same product is never made twice so that the flow of parts and products through the system may follow any one of an extremely large number of possible paths. As we have noted previously, the characteristics of such a system demand a high degree of flexibility. We might state the overall problem of the operation of a job shop as one of balancing the costs of carrying in-process inventory, labor, the capital costs of capacity and the costs associated with meeting specified order completion dates. To have a high degree of labor and machine utilization it would be necessary to have a large number of orders waiting so that labor and equipment are very seldom idle. The result is relatively high in-process inventory carrying costs and poor schedule performance.

If we strive to meet order completion dates without fail, however, we need a very large equipment and labor capacity so that ordinarily, orders would not have to wait. This would result in relatively low in-process inventory costs but poor machine and labor utilization. The problem of balancing these costs in a complex system is at best a difficult one. Thus there has been a focus on system simulation as a technique for testing alternate decision rules as discussed in Chapter 17.

Hughes Aircraft Company's application of the IBM job shop simulator represents an adaptation of the program to the company's El Segundo plant operations. The adaptation made it possible to take order input data directly from random access files, transposed to the form required for simulation, and supplied with other input data to the simulator. Earl Le-Grande [6] made an initial study testing various dispatch decision rules with the El Segundo job shop simulation process and this study provided the basis for the decision rule used in the Hughes Job Shop Planning and Control System discussed in Chapter 17.

MODELS WITH
DYNAMIC OUTPUT /

It is often revealing in the simulation of something as complex as a business firm to show dynamically the impact of changes in environmental factors, such as market demand, and changes in alternate policies. By dynamic we mean simply in relation to time. Although other simulation models could obtain such data by printing out intermediate results and plotting them on a time scale, Jay Forrester [5] has developed simulation models which do this in a unique way, so that much of the computer output is in the form of graphs of important measures of effectiveness in relation to time. The particular advantage of this type of output is in its usefulness in the demonstration and analysis of the effects of time lags in the information system. As we shall see, average results of comparative policies often mask important dynamic effects. Forrester's approach provides insight into the inner workings of complex systems, particularly in the application of control theory to the business system.

Example of a Production-Distribution System

Figure 16 shows the gross structure of a production-distribution system in a typical hard goods industry like household appliances, for which Forrester developed a dynamic simulation model. Note that three levels of inventory exist—factory warehouse, distributor, and retailer. The circled lines show the flow of orders for goods from customers to retailers, retailers to distributors, distributors to the factory warehouse, and finally from the warehouse as orders for the factory to produce. The solid lines

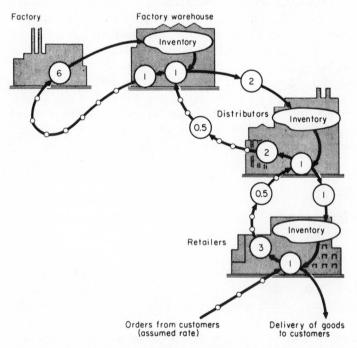

FIGURE 16. Organization of production-distribution system. Figures 16–19 are adapted from J. Forrester, Industrial Dynamics, MIT Press, 1961.

show the flow of the physical goods between each level of the structure in response to the orders. The circled numbers represent the time delays in weeks for each of the activities to take place. "Delivery of goods to the customer averages a week after the customer places an order. At the retail level, the accounting and purchasing delays average 3 weeks between time of sale and the time when the sale is reflected in an order sent out to obtain a replacement. Mailing delay for the order is half a week. The distributor takes a week to process the order, and shipment of goods to the retailer takes another week. Similar delays exist between the distributor and the factory warehouse. The factory lead time averages 6 weeks between the decision to change production rate and the time that factory output approaches the new level. Figure 16 is, of course, greatly simplified and the actual flow diagram for the simulation model is very complex.

"Policy on Orders and Inventories. To complete the initial description of the example, we need to know the policies that govern the placing of orders and the maintaining of inventory at each distribution level. We shall consider three principal components of orders: (*a*) Orders to replace goods sold, (*b*) orders to adjust inventories upwards or downwards as the level of business activity changes, and (*c*) orders to fill the supply pipelines with in-process orders and shipments. Orders are treated in the following ways:

"1. After a sales analysis and purchasing delay (3, 2, and 1 weeks for the three levels), orders to the next higher level of the system include replacement for the actual sales made by the ordering level.

"2. After sufficient time for averaging out short term sales fluctuations (8 weeks), a gradual upward or downward adjustment is made in inventories as the rate of sales increases or decreases.

"3. One component of orders in process (orders in the mail, unfilled orders at the supplier, and goods in transit) is necessarily proportional to the average level of business activity and to the length of time required to fill an order. Both an increased sales volume and an increased delivery lead time necessarily result in increased total orders in the supply pipeline. These 'pipeline' orders are unavoidable. They are a part of the 'basic physics' of the system structure. If not ordered explicitly for the purpose of pipeline filling (and often they will not be), the pipeline demand will come from a depletion of inventories, and the pipeline orders will be placed unknowingly in the name of inventory adjustments.

"The ordering rate will also depend on some assumption about future sales. Prediction methods that amount to extending forward (extrapolating) the present sales trend will in general produce a more unstable and fluctuating system. For our example, however, we shall use the usually conservative practice of basing the ordering rate on the assumption that sales are more likely to continue at their present level." [5]

Effect of 10 Percent Increase in Retail Sales. What happens when the system has previously been stable with retail orders flowing in at a constant rate followed by a simple 10 percent increase in retail sales, retail sales remaining constant at the new level? Figure 17 shows the effects of this simple change on distributor orders from retailers, inventories at the retail, distributor, and factory warehouse levels, and on factory production output. Instead of a smooth and orderly adjustment to the new level of retail sales demand, we see that there are wild fluctuations in some of these measures. The reasons are related to the lags in the system and to the inventory and ordering procedures used.

Because of delays in accounting, purchasing, and mailing, the increase in distributors' orders from retailers lags about a month in reaching the new 10 percent level. The surprise is, of course, that it does not stop at 10 percent, but reaches a peak of 18 percent at the eleventh week because of new orders added at the retail level (*a*) to increase inventories somewhat and (*b*) to raise the level of orders and goods in transit in the supply pipeline by 10 percent to correspond to the increase in the sales rate. "These inventory and pipeline increments occur as 'transient' or nonrepeating additions to the order rate, and when they have been satisfied, the retailers' orders to the distributors drop back to the enduring 10 percent increase."

The fluctuation in factory warehouse orders from distributors (not shown) is amplified beyond the 18 percent increase in distributor orders from retailers to a peak of 34 percent above the previous December. This occurs because the incoming order level at the distributors remains above retail sales for more than 4 months and is mistaken for a continuing increase in retail sales demand. Distributors' orders to the factory, therefore, include not only the 18 percent increase in orders which they have received but also a corresponding increase for the distributor inventories and for orders and goods in transit between distributors and the factory.

Finally, manufacturing orders to the factory are amplified even more because they are placed on the basis of the increasing factory warehouse orders and the falling warehouse inventories which we note is reduced to 15 percent below the previous December level. The result is that manufacturing orders to the factory increase to a maximum of 51 percent during the fifteenth week. Factory output which is delayed by a factory lead time of 6 weeks reaches a maximum of 45 percent during the 21st week. Meanwhile retail sales remain at 10 percent above the previous December level.

As retailers satisfy their inventory requirements with the increased

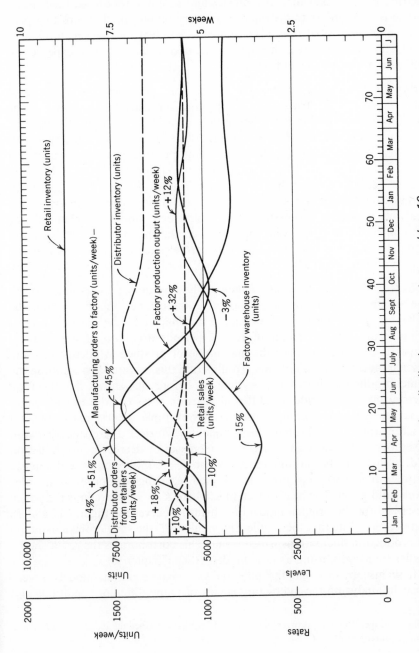

FIGURE 17. Response of production-distribution system to a sudden 10 percent increase in retail sales.

shipments they receive, they reduce their orders to distributors. The distributors find that their inventories and supply rates exceed their needs and so reduce orders to the factory. Factory output finally drops to 3 percent below the initial rate in December. The great fluctuations in factory production output have, of course, occurred at considerable expense, as well as both heartache and headache.

Effect of Eliminating Distributor Level. Let us consider the effects of changing the basic structure of the production distribution system. If the distributor level is eliminated and retailers' orders placed directly with the factory warehouse, some of the normal delays in the system are removed. This results in a dramatic reduction in the production fluctuations which result when a simple 10 percent step input is introduced as is shown in Figure 18. The comparable curve from Figure 17 based on the original production-distribution system structure is included for comparison. We are not, of course, suggesting that middlemen should automatically be eliminated, because the total arguments on that point are somewhat more complex than we have presented. Nevertheless, the dynamic model has shown an important advantage of simple, more direct distribution systems.

Effects of Changing Inventory Policy. The inventory policies described in the original model are of considerable importance in determining the behavior of the system. As we noted in Chapter 9, the reaction rate of adjustment and the length of review periods are both of considerable importance in determining the magnitude of production fluctuations and reserve inventory requirements. To illustrate this, Figure 19 is based on the same production-distribution system as before but shows the effect on factory production rate for different reaction rates of adjustment (length of review period remaining constant). For example, a curve marked with a reaction rate $K = 100$ indicates a policy in which a discrepancy between inventory and orders are reflected in increases or decreases in production orders equal to the full difference. When $K = 50$, only half the difference between inventory and orders is reflected in changes in production order levels, and so on. The heavy black line, where $K = 25$, represents the policy described for the original model on which the curves for Figures 17 and 18 were based. Note that the smaller the value of K, the smaller the magnitude of production fluctuations which result. This corroborates the result shown earlier by Magee, using a static model.* (See Chapter 9.)

It seems obvious that the potential of dynamic output models is very great in analyzing the interacting effects of many different conditions and

---

*John F. Magee, "Guides to Inventory Policy, II Problems of Uncertainty," *Harvard Business Review*, March–April 1956.

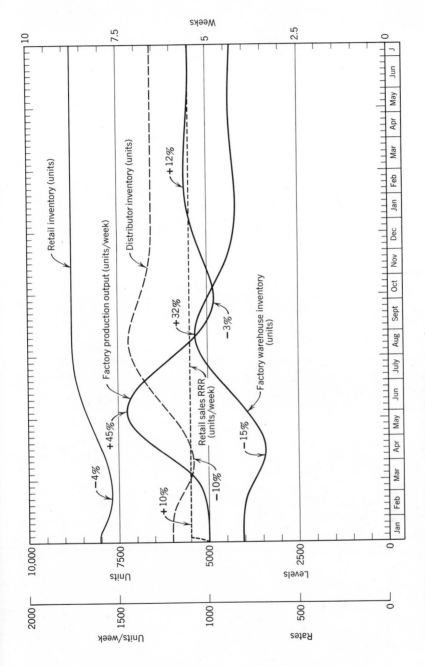

FIGURE 18.   Effect of eliminating the distributor level.

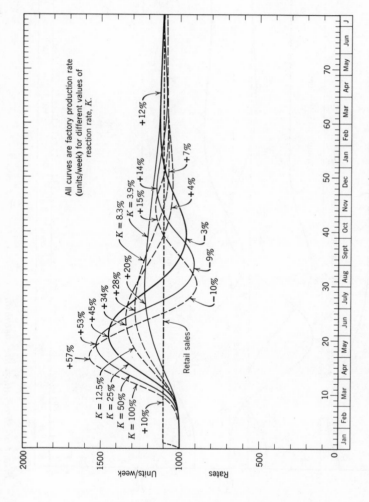

FIGURE 19. *Effect of different reaction rates on the magnitude of production fluctuations.*

management policies. Nevertheless, we should note that simply using well known managerial techniques, the wild oscillations shown in Forrester's models would be damped considerably. For example, a forecast coupled with sound aggregate planning as discussed in Chapter 13 would stabilize the very expensive production level fluctuations.

SUMMARY

The power of the large-scale systems simulation technique is actually only beginning to show itself. We should expect to learn a great deal about the interaction of the many variables in large-scale systems, and test out management policies and decision rules similar to the testing of dispatch decision rules at Hughes Aircraft Company and the General Electric Company as discussed in Chapter 17. Dynamic output simulation models promise to teach us a great deal about the effect of time lags in the information system of large-scale enterprises. Finally management is beginning to use large scale simulations of operations for corporate planning such as in the Potlatch Forest, Inland Steel, and VdB & J examples. This use of simulation is developing rapidly and indicates the great future promise of interactive simulation systems.

REVIEW QUESTIONS

1. Discuss the advantages and possible applications of large-scale system simulation in business and industry.

2. Contrast the simulation methodologies of the interactive systems using time-shared computing with systems which used batch made computing.

3. What difference results in simulation when the decision maker becomes a part of the loop with a computer model?

4. Describe the general characteristics of the "Job Shop Simulator."

5. Discuss the characteristics of the "El Segundo Job Shop Process."

6. Using the Hughes Aircraft Company simulation as a basis for your answer, is there any reason to use any dispatch decision rule other than random selection of orders?

7. What are the general characteristics of the dynamic output models developed by Jay Forrester?

8. Describe the general effects of a 10 percent increase in retail sales as shown by Forrester's dynamic output models. What are the basic characteristics of the production-distribution model which cause the kinds of effects noted?

9. What are the effects of eliminating the distributor level from the production-distribution model? Of tightening time lags due to clerical delays?

10. What are the effects of changing the reaction rate of factory production?

11. Discuss some of the probable future applications of dynamic output models similar to those developed by Jay Forrester.

REFERENCES

1. Baker, C. T., and B. P. Dzielinski, "Simulation of a Simplified Job Shop," *Management Science*, Vol. 6, No. 3, pp. 311–323, 1960.
2. Barkdoll, G., "Models—New Management Decision Aid," *Industrial Engineering*, December, 1970, pp. 32–40.
3. Bonini, C. P., *Simulation of Information and Decision Systems in the Firm*, Prentice-Hall, Inc., Englewood Cliffs, N.J., 1963.
4. Boulden, J. B., and E. S. Buffa, "Corporate Models: On-Line, Real-Time Systems," *Harvard Business Review*, July–August, 1970, pp. 65–83.
5. Forrester, J., *Industrial Dynamics*, MIT Press, Cambridge, Mass., 1961.
6. Le Grande, E., "Development of a Factory Simulation Using Actual Operating Data," *Management Technology*, May, 1963. Also reprinted as Chapter 9 in, *Readings in Production and Operations Management*, E. S. Buffa, editor, John Wiley & Sons, New York, 1966.
7. Jackson, J. R., "Simulation Research on Job-Shop Production," *Naval Research Logistics Quarterly*, Vol. 4, No. 4, December 1957.
8. Markowitz, H. M., B. Hausner, and H. W. Karr, *SIMSCRIPT: A Simulation Programming Language*, Memorandum RM-3310-PR, The RAND Corp., Santa Monica, Calif., November, 1962.
9. McMillan, C., and R. F. Gonzales, *Systems Analysis*, Richard D. Irwin, Inc., Homewood, Ill., Rev. ed., 1968.
10. Naylor, T. H., J. L. Balintfy, D. S. Burdick, and K. Chu, *Computer Similation Techniques*, John Wiley & Sons, New York, 1966.
11. Rowe, A. J., "Toward a Theory of Scheduling," *The Journal of Industrial Engineering*, Vol. XI, No. 2, March–April, 1960.
12. Sprowls, R. C., and M. Asimow, "A Computer Simulated Business Firm," in *Management Controls Systems*, Editors D. G. Malcolm, A. J. Rowe, and L. F. McConnell, John Wiley & Sons, New York, 1959.
13. *The Job Shop Simulator*, International Business Machines Corp., Data Systems Division, New York, revised, 1960.
14. Thierauf, R. J., and R. A. Grosse, *Decision Making Through Operations Research*, John Wiley & Sons, Inc., New York, 1970.
15. Toscano, F. C., *A Generalized Methodology for the Simulation of Transportation Systems*, Unpublished Ph.D. Dissertation, UCLA, 1965.
16. Wyman, F. P., *Simulation Modeling: A Guide To Using Simscript*, John Wiley & Sons, Inc., New York, 1970.

chapter 22

SUMMARY
AND CONCLUSION

We have studied the nature of problems and the major kinds of graphic, mathematical, and simulation models which have been applied in operations management. What have we learned? How do the materials tie together and relate to other areas of knowledge about formal organizations? Are these models significant in the study of production and operations management?

What we have learned may seem at first to be some detailed knowledge about models of flow and man-machine systems, statistical methods, waiting-line models, programming models, models of investment, and inventory and simulation models. But it should have been more than that. Formal models should also teach us something about the basic structure of certain kinds of important problems. For example, in studying linear programming we learn not only the structure and application of this important model, but we learn something fundamental about allocation problems in general. We learn to handle the effects of interacting and competing demands for limited resources and, perhaps more important, we learn the general nature of optimum solutions. This is important, for these general concepts should carry over into situations where the formal model is not applicable. In the practical operating situation, allocations of limited resources must often be made on an intuitive basis either because there is not time for formal analysis, or because the most important variables are not quantifiable. I believe that one can do this best if he understands the basic nature of the formal problem and the probable nature of good solutions. Another excellent example is the general waiting-line model. The individual who understands formal waiting-line models should be able to make a good snap judgment about the level of service to provide in a practical situation, because he realizes the great value of idle time of the server. The value of idle time, of course, is a concept which runs contrary to our fundamental training to conserve time, yet in the design of many systems provision of apparent overcapacity is the key to success.

Another important concept that the study of formal models fosters is the broader view of any problem, the "systems" view. This was perhaps best demonstrated by our study of inventory models where we discovered progressively that apparent advantages in inventory costs might be counterbalanced by large costs of production fluctuations. In general, we should learn that there is a substitution rate for everything. Sometimes it is better to substitute high labor rates for low time requirements, setup time for run time, scrap costs for direct labor, indirect labor for direct labor, delivery time for labor cost, and so on. The result is that in a production-distribution system we should produce some scrap and some late orders, incur some stock shortages, and have some idle labor. If we have none of these "wastes" we are undoubtedly overcontrolling some factors at extremely high cost to obtain advantages of little relative value. In short, we are suboptimizing.

The newer analytical techniques also involve a philosophy worth considering. These new methods are broadly applicable to operational systems, not just the manufacturing case. We need to broaden our thinking and develop the most general cases of the problems with which we deal. Then, a systematic analysis of the special cases puts both the broad problem and the special cases in context. The general model for investment analysis, *CERBS*, is a good example of this. We need to develop generalized models of production-distribution systems which apply to any special situation when the characteristics of that special case are inserted.

There are many things, however, which qualify as models of production or operations systems which we have not studied in this book. Many of these are important areas of specific interest which we could pursue. Plant location analysis has been studied carefully and today is represented by well-developed analytical models. Game theory represents a fascinating analysis of competitive models. The principles of automation and process control are also important to production systems and to the general theory of managerial control. Time availability has been our master in eliminating these important and interesting subjects. It was felt that the models selected for study were the ones of central interest and importance for a basic course.

We should state further that even for the subjects studied we have only scratched the surface. For example, in our study of programming, we did not recognize that there is considerable literature in the subjects of dynamic, quadratic, and integer programming. It would not be difficult to spend an entire semester on linear programming itself. Our coverage of waiting-line theory dealt with only the most basic models and considered only the steady-state conditions. There is also considerable literature that deals with transient conditions and with other assumptions for arrival and service distributions as well as other queue disciplines. Statistical analysis is a vast field, especially for the research worker. The new field of system simulation is moving so rapidly that it is difficult to say what will have been accomplished and what its position will be among the tools of production and operations analysis only a year hence.

Relationship to Other Fields

Production and operations analysis by the formal models we have discussed is a part of the broader study of formal organizations. Formal organizations do, of course, occur in a wide variety of situations including business, industry, government, religion, and so on. We have discussed the occurrence of production and operations systems in a similar context. The development of the study of formal organizations has at least two main branches:

1. *Decision theory*, which focuses on how decisions should be made. Decision theory develops formal models of rational behavior.

2. *Organizational behavior*, which studies how decisions are actually made. This branch is more empirical and observational in nature and studies individuals and small and large groups, focusing on actual human behavior in many of the decision-making situations. It has its roots in individual and social psychology, and sociology.

As might be expected, representatives of the two lines of thought are often critical of each other. Since the material that we have studied is more closely allied with decision theory, we will attempt to deal with some of the main criticisms leveled against it and to place the ideas of "how decisions are actually made" in context with formal decision-making models as an approach. Critics imply that the formal decision-making models are irrelevant, or nearly so, because people and their psychosociological characteristics are ignored in these models. Recent observations in the human relations area often show that a work group, when left to its own devices to plan and organize its efforts, will develop methods of operation which are superior to those specified by some technically oriented person.

The picture usually developed is one of the technically oriented person, usually an engineer (who apparently understands things but not people), who has designed a work system. It is assumed that the work system is ideal from the engineer's point of view. The behavioral science researcher enters the picture at this point to experiment with different organizational structures of the group, which ordinarily involve relaxing controls, giving workers greater flexibility in designing and organizing their own work situation. When left to their own devices, the workers reorganize activities to suit themselves, and productivity as well as other measures of effectiveness improve, often considerably. The implied conclusion is, then, that expertise is ineffective since workers can organize a superior system anyway; the important things are the psychological and sociological aspects of the situation, and structure, or formal analysis, are of secondary importance. There are several things wrong with these kinds of obvervations which make it difficult to draw firm conclusions of any kind.

1. The experimental design of the situation is loose so that we cannot appraise the independent effects of the real variables of the system. Indeed the variables are seldom defined. For example, in such experimental situations, what is the Hawthorne effect? (The Hawthorne effect is simply that an experimental group of employees may tend to produce spurious experimental results.)

2. Was the engineer's solution necessarily an optimal one to be used for comparison? If it was not, all we can say is that an existing design can often be improved. It might have been possible to improve it even more than was accomplished by the work group through careful analysis.

3. Who left the work group as a result of the reorganizations? If productivity went up, the size of the work group was probably reduced. Were the individuals who left the work group the high producers or the low producers? The selections were probably made by the work group itself, and the ones who did not fit into the group's standards may have been the poor producers. The result is that the combination of the Hawthorne effect plus the selection of workers could easily mask the effects of what could actually be poorer basic work methods.

The feeling of the behavioral scientist is apparently that the system designer is at home with rigidity, with everything neatly in its place, whereas work groups perform best when they have flexibility. This is pointed up by the "case of the speeding assembly line" reported by Bavelas*

---

*William F. Whyte, et al., *Money and Motivation*, Harper and Brothers, New York, 1955, Chapter X.

and quoted by Clark.† The setting is a paced line conveyor in a toy factory. "There, a group of girls were allowed to control the speed of the conveyor on which they were working. They sped it up when they felt like working, and they slowed it down when they didn't. Productivity and earnings soared, and soared higher by far than that which the engineers had believed to be normal output. Consequently, the engineers took the control of the lines' speed away from the workers, and restored it to a steadily predictable pace. The girls, apparently, had established an equilibrium of their own, for they all quit in protest."

The interesting thing about this case is that, based on research knowledge about the effective design of production lines, neither the engineer's solution nor the work group's solution represents ideal design. Here, formal analysis using a waiting-line model‡ and experimental research§ indicates that rigid pacing at any speed represents a relatively poor solution to serialized operations.

The best design that we know about would eliminate rigid conveyor pacing completely, replacing it with a system where the conveyor provided only transportation between the several operations, but allowing queues of material to build up between each of the operations in the sequence. The rationale is simply that the greater flexibility allowed when queues can build up makes it possible for operators to average their slow cycles against their fast cycles in their work-time distribution pattern. The result is more effective utilization of labor on the line. Here is a situation where formal analysis demands flexibility in the design, even more flexiblity than the workers themselves had thought desirable. Solutions specified by formal analysis are not necessarily rigid ones. We should recognize that the thing which work groups constructing their own methods and procedures contributes is not the most effective systems and procedures possible, but a high level of morale and this is certainly not to be minimized.

At the level of local methods and procedures, it may well be that psychosociological factors may be the most important. The evidence to date indicates that this is a sound hypothesis which should be tested by a really well-designed experimental research program. If the conclusion is that letting work groups design their own methods and procedures is the most effective approach, on balance, this means that business and industry

---

†James V. Clark, "A Healthy Organization," *California Management Review*, Vol. IV, No. 4, 1962.

‡G. C. Hunt, "Sequential Arrays of Waiting Lines," *Operations Research*, Vol. IV, p. 674, 1956.

§R. Conrad, *Setting the Pace*, Medical Research Council, APU232-55, Applied Psychology Research Units, London, 1955; R. Conrad and B. A. Hille, "Comparison of Paced and Unpaced Performance at a Packing Task," *Occupational Psychology*, Vol. XXIX, No. 1, 1955, pp. 15–28; E. S. Buffa, "Pacing Effects in Production Lines." *Journal of Industrial Engineering*, Vol. XII, No. 6, 1961.

should include as a part of worker training an attempt to transmit some of the principles of effective work design. This has been done to an extent in work simplification training programs offered to workers by a few forward-looking companies.

But what about the broader problems of programming, facilities design, and inventory systems, all of which cut across work group lines? Here we are dealing with problems of incredible complexity which transcend the knowledge and capability of the work group. Does the work group understand linear programming, investment policy and theory, statistical theory, and waiting-line theory? Can it do as well as a computer simulation program in evaluating the best dispatch decision rule, or in generating alternate production programs? The point is that there seems to be a realm where the work group might operate effectively, but it is generally at the local level. We soon outrun its capability to make rational decisions when we are talking about problems on a broader level. Here even the local supervisor or a technically oriented person with a local point of view is likely to be inadequate.

Can Formal Models Account for Human Factors?

If we mean that the model directly accounts for human values, the answer is no; however, in many instances we can account for restrictions imposed by management which are intended to reflect the needs of people and work groups. For example, let us consider the nature of the solutions to the problem of relative location of physical facilities exemplified by the CRAFT computer program described in Chapter 6. For a problem involving twenty departments there are many excellent solutions and perhaps hundreds of good solutions; that is, where the total annual material-handling cost is not more than 5 percent different from the best solution. If there is good reason for keeping two departments adjacent because of factors related to the social structures of the work groups involved, let this be stated as a requirement. The computer program can accept such a restriction. Also, it can evaluate the economic effect of such a restriction in 0.5 minute of computer time.

Although such flexibility in optimal solutions of formal models is not always present, it is true for a surprising number of cases. Recall the nature of linear programming solutions where alternate optima exist. We can generate an infinite number of optimal solutions, and there are always solutions which are not optimum, but which are near the optimum, as in the case of the relative location program just discussed. The dish-shaped total incremental cost curve is usually relatively flat near the minimum point. The practical effect of this is that we are not confronted with rigidity in problem solutions, but with great flexibility. As a practical matter, we should always recognize this fact. It can often be used to satisfy other nonquantifiable needs such as those imposed by psychosociological values. One of the great traps of formal models is preoccupation with optimal solutions.

Is It Significant?

Is the material we have studied significant? The production and operations phases of any organization ordinarily account for the largest expenditures for capital, materials, and labor and represent the vital function of the creation of goods and services in our economy. From a sociological point of view, such systems are of tremendous importance, for they employ the bulk of our labor force, and these people spend a large fraction of their lives working in such systems. Whether or not production systems are effectively designed and operated determines in an important way the real wages and salaries of these people. From an academic point of view, the formal models we have discussed represent the development of a theory of operational systems where none existed only a few years ago. We are witnessing the healthy growth of an applied science. From a practical point of view, the models we have discussed provide insight into the nature of many kinds of operational problems. The manager who has a basic understanding of the models and, therefore, the problems, can be expected to make better and more effective decisions. It is significant!

APPENDIX

TABLE I. Areas under the normal curve

Areas under the normal curve to the left of x for decimal units of σ' from the mean, $\bar{x}'$.

x	Area	x	Area	x	Area	x	Area
$\bar{x}' - 3.0\sigma'$	.0013	$\bar{x}' - 1.5\sigma'$	.0668	$\bar{x}' + .1\sigma'$	.5398	$\bar{x}' + 1.6\sigma'$	.9452
$\bar{x}' - 2.9\sigma'$	.0019	$\bar{x}' - 1.4\sigma'$	.0808	$\bar{x}' + .2\sigma'$	.5793	$\bar{x}' + 1.7\sigma'$	.9554
$\bar{x}' - 2.8\sigma'$	.0026	$\bar{x}' - 1.3\sigma'$	.0968	$\bar{x}' + .3\sigma'$	.6179	$\bar{x}' + 1.8\sigma'$	.9641
$\bar{x}' - 2.7\sigma'$	.0035	$\bar{x}' - 1.2\sigma'$	.1151	$\bar{x}' + .4\sigma'$	.6554	$\bar{x}' + 1.9\sigma'$	.9713
$\bar{x}' - 2.6\sigma'$	.0047	$\bar{x}' - 1.1\sigma'$	.1357	$\bar{x}' + .5\sigma'$	.6915	$\bar{x}' + 2.0\sigma'$	.9772
$\bar{x}' - 2.5\sigma'$	.0062	$\bar{x}' - 1.0\sigma'$	.1587	$\bar{x}' + .6\sigma'$	.7257	$\bar{x}' + 2.1\sigma'$	.9821
$\bar{x}' - 2.4\sigma'$	.0082	$\bar{x}' - .9\sigma'$	.1841	$\bar{x}' + .7\sigma'$	.7580	$\bar{x}' + 2.2\sigma'$	.9861
$\bar{x}' - 2.3\sigma'$	.0107	$\bar{x}' - .8\sigma'$	.2119	$\bar{x}' + .8\sigma'$	.7881	$\bar{x}' + 2.3\sigma'$	.9893
$\bar{x}' - 2.2\sigma'$	.0139	$\bar{x}' - .7\sigma'$	.2420	$\bar{x}' + .9\sigma'$	.8159	$\bar{x}' + 2.4\sigma'$	.9918
$\bar{x}' - 2.1\sigma'$	.0179	$\bar{x}' - .6\sigma'$	.2741	$\bar{x}' + 1.0\sigma'$	.8413	$\bar{x}' + 2.5\sigma'$	.9938
$\bar{x}' - 2.0\sigma'$	.0228	$\bar{x}' - .5\sigma'$	.3085	$\bar{x}' + 1.1\sigma'$	.8643	$\bar{x}' + 2.6\sigma'$	.9953
$\bar{x}' - 1.9\sigma'$	.0287	$\bar{x}' - .4\sigma'$	.3446	$\bar{x}' + 1.2\sigma'$	.8849	$\bar{x}' + 2.7\sigma'$	.9965
$\bar{x}' - 1.8\sigma'$	.0359	$\bar{x}' - .3\sigma'$	.3821	$\bar{x}' + 1.3\sigma'$	.9032	$\bar{x}' + 2.8\sigma'$	.9974
$\bar{x}' - 1.7\sigma'$	.0446	$\bar{x}' - .2\sigma'$	.4207	$\bar{x}' + 1.4\sigma'$	.9192	$\bar{x}' + 2.9\sigma'$	.9981
$\bar{x}' - 1.6\sigma'$	.0548	$\bar{x}' - .1\sigma'$	.4602	$\bar{x}' + 1.5\sigma'$	.9332	$\bar{x}' + 3.0\sigma'$	.9987
		$\bar{x}'$	.5000				

σ' units from the mean, $\bar{x}'$, associated with given values of the area under the normal curve to the left of x.

x	Area	x	Area
$\bar{x}' - 3.090\sigma'$	.001	$\bar{x}' + 3.090\sigma'$	.999
$\bar{x}' - 2.576\sigma'$	.005	$\bar{x}' + 2.576\sigma'$	.995
$\bar{x}' - 2.326\sigma'$	.010	$\bar{x}' + 2.326\sigma'$	.990
$\bar{x}' - 1.960\sigma'$	.025	$\bar{x}' + 1.960\sigma'$	.975
$\bar{x}' - 1.645\sigma'$	.050	$\bar{x}' + 1.645\sigma'$	.950
$\bar{x}' - 1.282\sigma'$	.100	$\bar{x}' + 1.282\sigma'$	.900
$\bar{x}' - 1.036\sigma'$	.150	$\bar{x}' + 1.036\sigma'$	.850
$\bar{x}' - .842\sigma'$	.200	$\bar{x}' + .842\sigma'$	.800
$\bar{x}' - .674\sigma'$	.250	$\bar{x}' + .674\sigma'$	.750
$\bar{x}' - .524\sigma'$	.300	$\bar{x}' + .524\sigma'$	.700
$\bar{x}' - .385\sigma'$	.350	$\bar{x}' + .385\sigma'$	.650
$\bar{x}' - .253\sigma'$	.400	$\bar{x}' + .253\sigma'$	.600
$\bar{x}' - .126\sigma'$	.450	$\bar{x}' + .126\sigma'$	.550
$\bar{x}'$	.500		

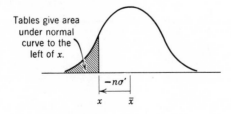

Tables give area under normal curve to the left of x.

$-n\sigma'$

x $\bar{x}$

TABLE II.   Factors useful in the construction of control charts*

Number of Observations in Sample, n	Chart for Averages Factors for Control Limits			Chart for Standard Deviations						Chart for Ranges						
				Factors for Central Line		Factors for Control Limits				Factors for Central Line		Factors for Control Limit				
	A	A_1	A_2	c_2	$1/c_2$	B_1	B_2	B_3	B_4	d_2	$1/d_2$	d_3	D_1	D_2	D_3	D
2	2.121	3.760	1.880	0.5642	1.7725	0	1.843	0	3.267	1.128	0.8865	0.853	0	3.686	0	3.2
3	1.732	2.394	1.023	0.7236	1.3820	0	1.858	0	2.568	1.693	0.5907	0.888	0	4.358	0	2.5
4	1.500	1.880	0.729	0.7979	1.2533	0	1.808	0	2.266	2.059	0.4857	0.880	0	4.698	0	2.2
5	1.342	1.596	0.577	0.8407	1.1894	0	1.756	0	2.089	2.326	0.4299	0.864	0	4.918	0	2.1
6	1.225	1.410	0.483	0.8686	1.1512	0.026	1.711	0.030	1.970	2.534	0.3946	0.848	0	5.078	0	2.0
7	1.134	1.277	0.419	0.8882	1.1259	0.105	1.672	0.118	1.882	2.704	0.3698	0.833	0.205	5.203	0.076	1.9
8	1.061	1.175	0.373	0.9027	1.1078	0.167	1.638	0.185	1.815	2.847	0.3512	0.820	0.387	5.307	0.136	1.8
9	1.000	1.094	0.337	0.9139	1.0942	0.219	1.609	0.239	1.761	2.970	0.3367	0.808	0.546	5.394	0.184	1.8
10	0.949	1.028	0.308	0.9227	1.0837	0.262	1.584	0.284	1.716	3.078	0.3249	0.797	0.687	5.469	0.223	1.7
11	0.905	0.973	0.285	0.9300	1.0753	0.299	1.561	0.321	1.679	3.173	0.3152	0.787	0.812	5.534	0.256	1.74
12	0.866	0.925	0.266	0.9359	1.0684	0.331	1.541	0.354	1.646	3.258	0.3069	0.778	0.924	5.592	0.284	1.71
13	0.832	0.884	0.249	0.9410	1.0627	0.359	1.523	0.382	1.618	3.336	0.2998	0.770	1.026	5.646	0.308	1.69
14	0.802	0.848	0.235	0.9453	1.0579	0.384	1.507	0.406	1.594	3.407	0.2935	0.762	1.121	5.693	0.329	1.67
15	0.775	0.816	0.223	0.9490	1.0537	0.406	1.492	0.428	1.572	3.472	0.2880	0.755	1.207	5.737	0.348	1.65
16	0.750	0.788	0.212	0.9523	1.0501	0.427	1.478	0.448	1.552	3.532	0.2831	0.749	1.285	5.779	0.364	1.65
17	0.728	0.762	0.203	0.9551	1.0470	0.445	1.465	0.466	1.534	3.588	0.2787	0.743	1.359	5.817	0.379	1.62
18	0.707	0.738	0.194	0.9576	1.0442	0.461	1.454	0.482	1.518	3.640	0.2747	0.738	1.426	5.854	0.392	1.60
19	0.688	0.717	0.187	0.9599	1.0418	0.477	1.443	0.497	1.503	3.689	0.2711	0.733	1.490	5.888	0.404	1.59
20	0.671	0.697	0.180	0.9619	1.0396	0.491	1.433	0.510	1.490	3.735	0.2677	0.729	1.548	5.922	0.414	1.58
21	0.655	0.679	0.173	0.9638	1.0376	0.504	1.424	0.523	1.477	3.778	0.2647	0.724	1.606	5.950	0.425	1.57
22	0.640	0.662	0.167	0.9655	1.0358	0.516	1.415	0.534	1.466	3.819	0.2618	0.720	1.659	5.979	0.434	1.56
23	0.626	0.647	0.162	0.9670	1.0342	0.527	1.407	0.545	1.455	3.858	0.2592	0.716	1.710	6.006	0.443	1.55
24	0.612	0.632	0.157	0.9684	1.0327	0.538	1.399	0.555	1.445	3.895	0.2567	0.712	1.759	6.031	0.452	1.54
25	0.600	0.619	0.153	0.9696	1.0313	0.548	1.392	0.565	1.435	3.931	0.2544	0.709	1.804	6.058	0.459	1.54
Over 25	$\dfrac{3}{\sqrt{n}}$	$\dfrac{3}{\sqrt{n}}$	—	—	—	†	‡	†	‡	—	—	—	—	—	—	—

$$† \; 1 - \frac{3}{\sqrt{2n}} \qquad ‡ \; 1 + \frac{3}{\sqrt{2n}}$$

Chart	Central Line	3σ Control Limits
$\bar{X}$	$\bar{\bar{x}}$	$\bar{\bar{x}} \pm A_1 s_x$ or $\bar{\bar{x}} \pm A_2 \bar{R}$
	μ_x	$\mu_x \pm A\sigma_x$
R	$\bar{R}$	$D_3\bar{R}$ and $D_4\bar{R}$
	$d_2\sigma_x$	$D_1\sigma_x$ and $D_2\sigma_x$
σ_x	s_x	$B_3 s_x$ and $B_4 s_x$
	σ_x	$B_1\sigma_x$ and $B_2\sigma_x$

Definitions: $A = 3/\sqrt{n}$, $A_1 = \dfrac{3}{c_2 \sqrt{n}}$, $A_2 = \dfrac{3}{d_2 \sqrt{n}}$, $B_1 = c_2 - K$,

$B_2 = c_2 + K$, $B_3 = 1 - \dfrac{K}{c_2}$, $B_4 = 1 + \dfrac{K}{c_2}$, $D_1 = d_2 - 3d_3$, $D_2 = d_2 + 3d_3$,

$D_3 = 1 - 3\dfrac{d_3}{d_2}$, and $D_4 = 1 + 3\dfrac{d_3}{d_2}$, where $K = 3\sqrt{\dfrac{(n-1)}{n}} - c_2{}^2$.

Warning: The fourth significant figures for D_1, D_2, D_3, and D_4 are in doubt for n greater than 5.

* Reproduced with permission from Table B2 of the *A.S.T.M. Manual on Quality Control of Material* p. 115. The c_2 factor is also given in Table 29 of W. A. Shewhart, *Economic Control of Quality of Manufacture Product*, D. Van Nostrand   Princeton, N.J., 1931, p. 185.

TABLE III. Finite queuing tables*

POPULATION 5

X	M	D	F	X	M	D	F	X	M	D	F
POPULATION			5	.100	1	.386	.950	.200	2	.194	.976
				.105	2	.059	.997		1	.689	.801
.012	1	.048	.999		1	.404	.945	.210	3	.032	.998
.019	1	.076	.998	.110	2	.065	.996		2	.211	.973
.025	1	.100	.997		1	.421	.939		1	.713	.783
.030	1	.120	.996	.115	2	.071	.995	.220	3	.036	.997
.034	1	.135	.995		1	.439	.933		2	.229	.969
.036	1	.143	.994	.120	2	.076	.995		1	.735	.765
.040	1	.159	.993		1	.456	.927	.230	3	.041	.997
.042	1	.167	.992	.125	2	.082	.994		2	.247	.965
.044	1	.175	.991		1	.473	.920		1	.756	.747
.046	1	.183	.990	.130	2	.089	.993	.240	3	.046	.996
.050	1	.198	.989		1	.489	.914		2	.265	.960
.052	1	.206	.988	.135	2	.095	.993		1	.775	.730
.054	1	.214	.987		1	.505	.907	.250	3	.052	.995
.056	2	.018	.999	.140	2	.102	.992		2	.284	.955
	1	.222	.985		1	.521	.900		1	.794	.712
.058	2	.019	.999	.145	3	.011	.999	.260	3	.058	.994
	1	.229	.984		2	.109	.991		2	.303	.950
.060	2	.020	.999		1	.537	.892		1	.811	.695
	1	.237	.983	.150	3	.012	.999	.270	3	.064	.994
.062	2	.022	.999		2	.115	.990		2	.323	.944
	1	.245	.982		1	.553	.885		1	.827	.677
.064	2	.023	.999	.155	3	.013	.999	.280	3	.071	.993
	1	.253	.981		2	.123	.989		2	.342	.938
.066	2	.024	.999		1	.568	.877		1	.842	.661
	1	.260	.979	.160	3	.015	.999	.290	4	.007	.999
.068	2	.026	.999		2	.130	.988		3	.079	.992
	1	.268	.978		1	.582	.869		2	.362	.932
.070	2	.027	.999	.165	3	.016	.999		1	.856	.644
	1	.275	.977		2	.137	.987	.300	4	.008	.999
.075	2	.031	.999		1	.597	.861		3	.086	.990
	1	.294	.973	.170	3	.017	.999		2	.382	.926
.080	2	.035	.998		2	.145	.985		1	.869	.628
	1	.313	.969		1	.611	.853	.310	4	.009	.999
.085	2	.040	.998	.180	3	.021	.999		3	.094	.989
	1	.332	.965		2	.161	.983		2	.402	.919
.090	2	.044	.998		1	.638	.836		1	.881	.613
	1	.350	.960	.190	3	.024	.998	.320	4	.010	.999
.095	2	.049	.997		2	.177	.980		3	.103	.988
	1	.368	.955		1	.665	.819		2	.422	.912
.100	2	.054	.997	.200	3	.028	.998		1	.892	.597

* From L. G. Peck and R. N. Hazelwood, *Finite Queuing Tables*, John Wiley and Sons, New York, 1958.

TABLE III (Continued).   Finite queuing tables

POPULATION 5–10

X	M	D	F	X	M	D	F	X	M	D	F
.330	4	.012	.999	.520	2	.779	.728	POPULATION			10
	3	.112	.986		1	.988	.384				
	2	.442	.904	.540	4	.085	.989	.016	1	.144	.997
	1	.902	.583		3	.392	.917	.019	1	.170	.996
.340	4	.013	.999		2	.806	.708	.021	1	.188	.995
	3	.121	.985		1	.991	.370	.023	1	.206	.994
	2	.462	.896	.560	4	.098	.986	.025	1	.224	.993
	1	.911	.569		3	.426	.906	.026	1	.232	.992
.360	4	.017	.998		2	.831	.689	.028	1	.250	.991
	3	.141	.981		1	.993	.357	.030	1	.268	.990
	2	.501	.880	.580	4	.113	.984	.032	2	.033	.999
	1	.927	.542		3	.461	.895		1	.285	.988
.380	4	.021	.998		2	.854	.670	.034	2	.037	.999
	3	.163	.976		1	.994	.345		1	.302	.986
	2	.540	.863	.600	4	.130	.981	.036	2	.041	.999
	1	.941	.516		3	.497	.883		1	.320	.984
.400	4	.026	.997		2	.875	.652	.038	2	.046	.999
	3	.186	.972		1	.996	.333		1	.337	.982
	2	.579	.845	.650	4	.179	.972	.040	2	.050	.999
	1	.952	.493		3	.588	.850		1	.354	.980
.420	4	.031	.997		2	.918	.608	.042	2	.055	.999
.420	3	.211	.966		1	.998	.308		1	.371	.978
	2	.616	.826	.700	4	.240	.960	.044	2	.060	.998
	1	.961	.471		3	.678	.815		1	.388	.975
.440	4	.037	.996		2	.950	.568	.046	2	.065	.998
	3	.238	.960		1	.999	.286		1	.404	.973
	2	.652	.807	.750	4	.316	.944	.048	2	.071	.998
	1	.969	.451		3	.763	.777		1	.421	.970
.460	4	.045	.995		2	.972	.532	.050	2	.076	.998
	3	.266	.953	.800	4	.410	.924		1	.437	.967
	2	.686	.787		3	.841	.739	.052	2	.082	.997
	1	.975	.432		2	.987	.500		1	.454	.963
.480	4	.053	.994	.850	4	.522	.900	.054	2	.088	.997
	3	.296	.945		3	.907	.702		1	.470	.960
	2	.719	.767		2	.995	.470	.056	2	.094	.997
	1	.980	.415	.900	4	.656	.871		1	.486	.956
.500	4	.063	.992		3	.957	.666	.058	2	.100	.996
	3	.327	.936		2	.998	.444		1	.501	.953
	2	.750	.748	.950	4	.815	.838	.060	2	.106	.996
	1	.985	.399		3	.989	.631		1	.517	.949
.520	4	.073	.991					.062	2	.113	.996
	3	.359	.927						1	.532	.945

TABLE III (Continued)

POPULATION 10

X	M	D	F	X	M	D	F	X	M	D	F
.064	2	.119	.995	.125	3	.100	.994	.180	2	.614	.890
	1	.547	.940		2	.369	.962		1	.975	.549
.066	2	.126	.995		1	.878	.737	.190	5	.016	.999
	1	.562	.936	.130	4	.022	.999		4	.078	.995
.068	3	.020	.999		3	.110	.994		3	.269	.973
	2	.133	.994		2	.392	.958		2	.654	.873
	1	.577	.931		1	.893	.718		1	.982	.522
.070	3	.022	.999	.135	4	.025	.999	.200	5	.020	.999
	2	.140	.994		3	.121	.993		4	.092	.994
	1	.591	.926		2	.415	.952		3	.300	.968
.075	3	.026	.999		1	.907	.699		2	.692	.854
	2	.158	.992	.140	4	.028	.999		1	.987	.497
	1	.627	.913		3	.132	.991	.210	5	.025	.999
.080	3	.031	.999		2	.437	.947		4	.108	.992
	2	.177	.990		1	.919	.680		3	.333	.961
	1	.660	.899	.145	4	.032	.999		2	.728	.835
.085	3	.037	.999		3	.144	.990		1	.990	.474
	2	.196	.988		2	.460	.941	.220	5	.030	.998
	1	.692	.883		1	.929	.662		4	.124	.990
.090	3	.043	.998	.150	4	.036	.998		3	.366	.954
	2	.216	.986		3	.156	.989		2	.761	.815
.090	1	.722	.867		2	.483	.935		1	.993	.453
.095	3	.049	.998		1	.939	.644	.230	5	.037	.998
	2	.237	.984	.155	4	.040	.998		4	.142	.988
	1	.750	.850		3	.169	.987		3	.400	.947
.100	3	.056	.998		2	.505	.928		2	.791	.794
	2	.258	.981		1	.947	.627		1	.995	.434
	1	.776	.832	.160	4	.044	.998	.240	5	.044	.997
.105	3	.064	.997		3	.182	.986		4	.162	.986
	2	.279	.978		2	.528	.921		3	.434	.938
	1	.800	.814		1	.954	.610		2	.819	.774
.110	3	.072	.997	.165	4	.049	.997		1	.996	.416
	2	.301	.974		3	.195	.984	.250	6	.010	.999
	1	.822	.795		2	.550	.914		5	.052	.997
.115	3	.081	.996		1	.961	.594		4	.183	.983
	2	.324	.971	.170	4	.054	.997		3	.469	.929
	1	.843	.776		3	.209	.982		2	.844	.753
.120	4	.016	.999		2	.571	.906		1	.997	.400
	3	.090	.995		1	.966	.579	.260	6	.013	.999
	2	.346	.967	.180	5	.013	.999		5	.060	.996
	1	.861	.756		4	.066	.996		4	.205	.980
.125	4	.019	.999		3	.238	.978		3	.503	.919

TABLE III (Continued). Finite queuing tables

POPULATION 10

X	M	D	F	X	M	D	F	X	M	D	F
.260	2	.866	.732	.340	6	.049	.997	.480	8	.015	.999
	1	.998	.384		5	.168	.983		7	.074	.994
.270	6	.015	.999		4	.416	.938		6	.230	.973
	5	.070	.995		3	.750	.816		5	.499	.916
	4	.228	.976		2	.968	.584		4	.791	.799
	3	.537	.908	.360	7	.014	.999		3	.961	.621
	2	.886	.712		6	.064	.995		2	.998	.417
	1	.999	.370		5	.205	.978	.500	8	.020	.999
.280	6	.018	.999		4	.474	.923		7	.093	.992
	5	.081	.994		3	.798	.787		6	.271	.966
	4	.252	.972		2	.978	.553		5	.553	.901
	3	.571	.896	.380	7	.019	.999		4	.830	.775
	2	.903	.692		6	.083	.993		3	.972	.598
	1	.999	.357		5	.247	.971		2	.999	.400
.290	6	.022	.999		4	.533	.906	.520	8	.026	.998
	5	.093	.993		3	.840	.758		7	.115	.989
	4	.278	.968		2	.986	.525		6	.316	.958
	3	.603	.884	.400	7	.026	.998		5	.606	.884
	2	.918	.672		6	.105	.991		4	.864	.752
	1	.999	.345		5	.292	.963		3	.980	.575
.300	6	.026	.998		4	.591	.887		2	.999	.385
.300	5	.106	.991		3	.875	.728	.540	8	.034	.997
	4	.304	.963		2	.991	.499		7	.141	.986
	3	.635	.872	.420	7	.034	.993		6	.363	.949
	2	.932	.653		6	.130	.987		5	.658	.867
	1	.999	.333		5	.341	.954		4	.893	.729
.310	6	.031	.998		4	.646	.866		3	.986	.555
	5	.120	.990		3	.905	.700	.560	8	.044	.996
	4	.331	.957		2	.994	.476		7	.171	.982
	3	.666	.858	.440	7	.045	.997		6	.413	.939
	2	.943	.635		6	.160	.984		5	.707	.848
.320	6	.036	.998		5	.392	.943		4	.917	.706
	5	.135	.988		4	.698	.845		3	.991	.535
	4	.359	.952		3	.928	.672	.580	8	.057	.995
	3	.695	.845		2	.996	.454		7	.204	.977
	2	.952	.617	.460	8	.011	.999		6	.465	.927
.330	6	.042	.997		7	.058	.995		5	.753	.829
	5	.151	.986		6	.193	.979		4	.937	.684
	4	.387	.945		5	.445	.930		3	.994	.517
	3	.723	.831		4	.747	.822	.600	9	.010	.999
	2	.961	.600		3	.947	.646		8	.072	.994
.340	7	.010	.999		2	.998	.435		7	.242	.972

TABLE III (Continued)

POPULATION 10-20

X	M	D	F
.600	6	.518	.915
	5	.795	.809
	4	.953	.663
	3	.996	.500
.650	9	.021	.999
	8	.123	.988
	7	.353	.954
	6	.651	.878
	5	.882	.759
	4	.980	.614
	3	.999	.461
.700	9	.040	.997
	8	.200	.979
	7	.484	.929
	6	.772	.836
	5	.940	.711
	4	.992	.571
.750	9	.075	.994
	8	.307	.965
	7	.626	.897
	6	.870	.792
.750	5	.975	.666
	4	.998	.533
.800	9	.134	.988
	8	.446	.944
	7	.763	.859
	6	.939	.747
	5	.991	.625
	4	.999	.500
.850	9	.232	.979
	8	.611	.916
	7	.879	.818
	6	.978	.705
	5	.998	.588
.900	9	.387	.963
	8	.785	.881
	7	.957	.777
	6	.995	.667
.950	9	.630	.938
	8	.934	.841
	7	.994	.737

POPULATION 20

X	M	D	F
.005	1	.095	.999
.009	1	.171	.998
.011	1	.208	.997
.013	1	.246	.996
.014	1	.265	.995
.015	1	.283	.994
.016	1	.302	.993
.017	1	.321	.992
.018	2	.048	.999
	1	.339	.991
.019	2	.053	.999
	1	.358	.990
.020	2	.058	.999
	1	.376	.989
.021	2	.064	.999
	1	.394	.987
.022	2	.070	.999
	1	.412	.986
.023	2	.075	.999
	1	.431	.984
.024	2	.082	.999
	1	.449	.982
.025	2	.088	.999
	1	.466	.980
.026	2	.094	.998
	1	.484	.978
.028	2	.108	.998
	1	.519	.973
.030	2	.122	.998
	1	.553	.968
.032	2	.137	.997
	1	.587	.962
.034	2	.152	.996
	1	.620	.955
.036	2	.168	.996
	1	.651	.947
.038	3	.036	.999
	2	.185	.995
	1	.682	.938
.040	3	.041	.999

X	M	D	F
.040	2	.202	.994
	1	.712	.929
.042	3	.047	.999
	2	.219	.993
	1	.740	.918
.044	3	.053	.999
	2	.237	.992
	1	.767	.906
.046	3	.059	.999
	2	.255	.991
	1	.792	.894
.048	3	.066	.999
	2	.274	.989
	1	.815	.881
.050	3	.073	.998
	2	.293	.988
	1	.837	.866
.052	3	.080	.998
	2	.312	.986
	1	.858	.851
.054	3	.088	.998
	2	.332	.984
	1	.876	.835
.056	3	.097	.997
	2	.352	.982
	1	.893	.819
.058	3	.105	.997
	2	.372	.980
	1	.908	.802
.060	4	.026	.999
	3	.115	.997
	2	.392	.978
	1	.922	.785
.062	4	.029	.999
	3	.124	.996
	2	.413	.975
	1	.934	.768
.064	4	.032	.999
	3	.134	.996
	2	.433	.972
	1	.944	.751
.066	4	.036	.999

TABLE III (Continued).   Finite queuing tables

POPULATION 20

X	M	D	F	X	M	D	F	X	M	D	F
.066	3	.144	.995	.105	1	.999	.476	.150	4	.388	.968
	2	.454	.969	.110	5	.055	.998		3	.728	.887
	1	.953	.733		4	.172	.992		2	.976	.661
.068	4	.039	.999		3	.438	.964	.155	7	.021	.999
	3	.155	.995		2	.842	.837		6	.068	.997
	2	.474	.966	.115	5	.065	.998		5	.185	.990
	1	.961	.716		4	.195	.990		4	.419	.963
.070	4	.043	.999		3	.476	.958		3	.758	.874
	3	.165	.994		2	.870	.816		2	.982	.641
	2	.495	.962	.120	6	.022	.999	.160	7	.024	.999
	1	.967	.699		5	.076	.997		6	.077	.997
.075	4	.054	.999		4	.219	.988		5	.205	.988
	3	.194	.992		3	.514	.950		4	.450	.957
	2	.545	.953		2	.895	.793		3	.787	.860
	1	.980	.659	.125	6	.026	.999		2	.987	.622
.080	4	.066	.998		5	.088	.997	.165	7	.029	.999
	3	.225	.990		4	.245	.986		6	.088	.996
.080	2	.595	.941		3	.552	.942		5	.226	.986
	1	.988	.621		2	.916	.770		4	.482	.951
.085	4	.080	.997	.130	6	.031	.999		3	.813	.845
	3	.257	.987		5	.101	.996		2	.990	.604
	2	.643	.928		4	.271	.983	.170	7	.033	.999
	1	.993	.586		3	.589	.933		6	.099	.995
.090	5	.025	.999		2	.934	.748		5	.248	.983
	4	.095	.997	.135	6	.037	.999		4	.513	.945
	3	.291	.984		5	.116	.995		3	.838	.830
	2	.689	.913		4	.299	.980		2	.993	.587
	1	.996	.554		3	.626	.923	.180	7	.044	.998
.095	5	.031	.999		2	.948	.725		6	.125	.994
	4	.112	.996	.140	6	.043	.998		5	.295	.978
	3	.326	.980		5	.131	.994		4	.575	.930
	2	.733	.896		4	.328	.976		3	.879	.799
	1	.998	.526		3	.661	.912		2	.996	.555
.100	5	.038	.999		2	.960	.703	.190	8	.018	.999
	4	.131	.995	.145	6	.051	.998		7	.058	.998
	3	.363	.975		5	.148	.993		6	.154	.991
	2	.773	.878		4	.358	.972		5	.345	.971
	1	.999	.500		3	.695	.900		4	.636	.914
.105	5	.046	.999		2	.969	.682		3	.913	.768
	4	.151	.993	.150	7	.017	.999		2	.998	.526
	3	.400	.970		6	.059	.998	.200	8	.025	.999
	2	.809	.858		5	.166	.991		7	.074	.997

TABLE III (Continued)

POPULATION 20

X	M	D	F	X	M	D	F	X	M	D	F
.200	6	.187	.988	.260	6	.446	.953	.310	5	.892	.788
	5	.397	.963		5	.712	.884		4	.985	.643
	4	.693	.895		4	.924	.755	.320	11	.018	.999
	3	.938	.736		3	.995	.576		10	.053	.997
	2	.999	.500	.270	10	.016	.999		9	.130	.992
.210	8	.033	.999		9	.049	.998		8	.272	.977
	7	.093	.995		8	.125	.992		7	.483	.944
	6	.223	.985		7	.270	.978		6	.727	.878
	5	.451	.954		6	.495	.943		5	.915	.768
	4	.745	.874		5	.757	.867		4	.989	.624
	3	.958	.706		4	.943	.731	.330	11	.023	.999
	2	.999	.476		3	.997	.555		10	.065	.997
.220	8	.043	.998	.280	10	.021	.999		9	.154	.990
	7	.115	.994		9	.061	.997		8	.309	.973
	6	.263	.980		8	.149	.990		7	.529	.935
	5	.505	.943		7	.309	.973		6	.766	.862
	4	.793	.852		6	.544	.932		5	.933	.748
	3	.971	.677		5	.797	.848		4	.993	.605
.230	9	.018	.999		4	.958	.708	.340	11	.029	.999
	8	.054	.998		3	.998	.536		10	.079	.996
	7	.140	.992	.290	10	.027	.999		9	.179	.987
.230	6	.306	.975		9	.075	.996		8	.347	.967
	5	.560	.931		8	.176	.988		7	.573	.924
	4	.834	.828		7	.351	.967		6	.802	.846
	3	.981	.649		6	.592	.920		5	.949	.729
.240	9	.024	.999		5	.833	.828		4	.995	.588
	8	.068	.997		4	.970	.685	.360	12	.015	.999
	7	.168	.989		3	.999	.517		11	.045	.998
	6	.351	.969	.300	10	.034	.998		10	.112	.993
	5	.613	.917		9	.091	.995		9	.237	.981
	4	.870	.804		8	.205	.985		8	.429	.954
	3	.988	.623		7	.394	.961		7	.660	.901
.250	9	.031	.999		6	.639	.907		6	.863	.812
	8	.085	.996		5	.865	.808		5	.971	.691
	7	.199	.986		4	.978	.664		4	.998	.555
	6	.398	.961		3	.999	.500	.380	12	.024	.999
	5	.664	.901	.310	11	.014	.999		11	.067	.996
	4	.900	.780		10	.043	.998		10	.154	.989
	3	.992	.599		9	.110	.993		9	.305	.973
.260	9	.039	.998		8	.237	.981		8	.513	.938
	8	.104	.994		7	.438	.953		7	.739	.874
	7	.233	.983		6	.684	.893		6	.909	.777

TABLE III (Continued). Finite queuing tables

POPULATION 20

X	M	D	F	X	M	D	F	X	M	D	F
.380	5	.984	.656	.480	11	.289	.974	.560	8	.976	.713
	4	.999	.526		10	.484	.944		7	.996	.625
.400	13	.012	.999		9	.695	.893	.580	16	.015	.999
	12	.037	.998		8	.867	.819		15	.051	.997
	11	.095	.994		7	.962	.726		14	.129	.991
	10	.205	.984		6	.994	.625		13	.266	.978
	9	.379	.962	.500	14	.033	.998		12	.455	.952
	8	.598	.918		13	.088	.995		11	.662	.908
	7	.807	.845		12	.194	.985		10	.835	.847
	6	.942	.744		11	.358	.965		9	.941	.772
	5	.992	.624		10	.563	.929		8	.986	.689
.420	13	.019	.999		9	.764	.870		7	.998	.603
	12	.055	.997		8	.908	.791	.600	16	.023	.999
	11	.131	.991		7	.977	.698		15	.072	.996
	10	.265	.977		6	.997	.600		14	.171	.988
	9	.458	.949	.520	15	.015	.999		13	.331	.970
	8	.678	.896		14	.048	.997		12	.532	.938
	7	.863	.815		13	.120	.992		11	.732	.889
	6	.965	.711		12	.248	.979		10	.882	.824
	5	.996	.595		11	.432	.954		9	.962	.748
.440	13	.029	.999		10	.641	.911		8	.992	.666
.440	12	.078	.995		9	.824	.846		7	.999	.583
	11	.175	.987		8	.939	.764	.650	17	.017	.999
	10	.333	.969		7	.987	.672		16	.061	.997
	9	.540	.933		6	.998	.577		15	.156	.989
	8	.751	.872	.540	15	.023	.999		14	.314	.973
	7	.907	.785		14	.069	.996		13	.518	.943
	6	.980	.680		13	.161	.988		12	.720	.898
	5	.998	.568		12	.311	.972		11	.872	.837
.460	14	.014	.999		11	.509	.941		10	.957	.767
	13	.043	.998		10	.713	.891		9	.990	.692
	12	.109	.993		9	.873	.821		8	.998	.615
	11	.228	.982		8	.961	.738	.700	17	.047	.998
	10	.407	.958		7	.993	.648		16	.137	.991
	9	.620	.914		6	.999	.556		15	.295	.976
	8	.815	.846	.560	15	.035	.998		14	.503	.948
	7	.939	.755		14	.095	.994		13	.710	.905
	6	.989	.651		13	.209	.984		12	.866	.849
	5	.999	.543		12	.381	.963		11	.953	.783
.480	14	.022	.999		11	.586	.926		10	.988	.714
	13	.063	.996		10	.778	.869		9	.998	.643
	12	.147	.990		9	.912	.796	.750	18	.031	.999

TABLE III (Continued)

POPULATION 20-30

X	M	D	F	X	M	D	F	X	M	D	F
.750	17	.113	.993	POPULATION			30	.032	2	.286	.992
	16	.272	.980						1	.843	.899
	15	.487	.954	.004	1	.116	.999	.034	3	.083	.999
	14	.703	.913	.007	1	.203	.998		2	.316	.990
	13	.864	.859	.009	1	.260	.997		1	.876	.877
	12	.952	.798	.010	1	.289	.996	.036	3	.095	.998
	11	.988	.733	.011	1	.317	.995		2	.347	.988
	10	.998	.667	.012	1	.346	.994		1	.905	.853
.800	19	.014	.999	.013	1	.374	.993	.038	3	.109	.998
	18	.084	.996	.014	2	.067	.999		·2	.378	.986
	17	.242	.984		1	.403	.991		1	.929	.827
	16	.470	.959	.015	2	.076	.999	.040	3	.123	.997
	15	.700	.920		1	.431	.989		2	.410	.983
	14	.867	.869	.016	2	.085	.999		1	.948	.800
	13	.955	.811		1	.458	.987	.042	3	.138	.997
	12	.989	.750	.017	2	.095	.999		2	.442	.980
	11	.998	.687		1	.486	.985		1	.963	.772
.850	19	.046	.998	.018	2	.105	.999	.044	4	.040	.999
	18	.201	.988		1	.513	.983		3	.154	.996
	17	.451	.965	.019	2	.116	.999		2	.474	.977
	16	.703	.927		1	.541	.980		1	.974	.744
.850	15	.877	.878	.020	2	.127	.998	.046	4	.046	.999
	14	.962	.823		1	.567	.976		3	.171	.996
	13	.991	.765	.021	2	.139	.998		2	.506	.972
	12	.998	.706		1	.594	.973		1	.982	.716
.900	19	.135	.994	.022	2	.151	.998	.048	4	.053	.999
	18	.425	.972		1	.620	.969		3	.189	.995
	17	.717	.935	.023	2	.163	.997		2	.539	.968
	16	.898	.886	.023	1	.645	.965		1	.988	.689
	15	.973	.833	.024	2	.175	.997	.050	4	.060	.999
	14	.995	.778		1	.670	.960		3	.208	.994
	13	.999	.722	.025	2	.188	.996		2	.571	.963
.950	19	.377	.981		1	.694	.954		1	.992	.663
	18	.760	.943	.026	2	.201	.996	.052	4	.068	.999
	17	.939	.894		1	.718	.948		3	.227	.993
	16	.989	.842	.028	3	.051	.999		2	.603	.957
	15	.999	.789		2	.229	.995		1	.995	.639
					1	.763	.935	.054	4	.077	.998
				.030	3	.060	.999		3	.247	.992
					2	.257	.994		2	.634	.951
					1	.805	.918		1	.997	.616
				.032	3	.071	.999	.056	4	.086	.998

TABLE III (Continued). *Finite queuing tables*

POPULATION 30

X	M	D	F	X	M	D	F	X	M	D	F
.056	3	.267	.991	.085	5	.108	.997	.120	2	.999	.555
	2	.665	.944		4	.282	.987	.125	8	.024	.999
	1	.998	.595		3	.607	.948		7	.069	.998
.058	4	.096	.998		2	.955	.768		6	.171	.993
	3	.288	.989	.090	6	.046	.999		5	.367	.977
	2	.695	.936		5	.132	.996		4	.666	.927
	1	.999	.574		4	.326	.984		3	.940	.783
.060	5	.030	.999		3	.665	.934	.130	8	.030	.999
	4	.106	.997		2	.972	.732		7	.083	.997
	3	.310	.987	.095	6	.057	.999		6	.197	.991
	2	.723	.927		5	.158	.994		5	.409	.972
	1	.999	.555		4	.372	.979		4	.712	.914
.062	5	.034	.999		3	.720	.918		3	.957	.758
	4	.117	.997		2	.984	.697	.135	8	.037	.999
	3	.332	.986	.100	6	.071	.998		7	.098	.997
	2	.751	.918		5	.187	.993		6	.226	.989
.064	5	.038	.999		4	.421	.973		5	.451	.966
	4	.128	.997		3	.771	.899		4	.754	.899
	3	.355	.984		2	.991	.664		3	.970	.734
	2	.777	.908	.105	7	.030	.999	.140	8	.045	.999
.066	5	.043	.999		6	.087	.997		7	.115	.996
	4	.140	.996		5	.219	.991		6	.256	.987
	3	.378	.982		4	.470	.967		5	.494	.960
	2	.802	.897		3	.816	.879		4	.793	.884
.068	5	.048	.999		2	.995	.634		3	.979	.710
	4	.153	.995	.110	7	.038	.999	.145	8	.055	.998
	3	.402	.979		6	.105	.997		7	.134	.995
	2	.825	.885		5	.253	.988		6	.288	.984
.070	5	.054	.999	.110	4	.520	.959		5	.537	.952
	4	.166	.995		3	.856	.857		4	.828	.867
	3	.426	.976		2	.997	.605		3	.986	.687
	2	.847	.873	.115	7	.047	.999	.150	9	.024	.999
.075	5	.069	.998		6	.125	.996		8	.065	.998
	4	.201	.993		5	.289	.985		7	.155	.993
	3	.486	.969		4	.570	.950		6	.322	.980
	2	.893	.840		3	.890	.833		5	.580	.944
.080	6	.027	.999		2	.998	.579		4	.860	.849
	5	.088	.998	.120	7	.057	.998		3	.991	.665
	4	.240	.990		6	.147	.994	.155	9	.029	.999
	3	.547	.959		5	.327	.981		8	.077	.997
	2	.929	.805		4	.619	.939		7	.177	.992
.085	6	.036	.999		3	.918	.808		6	.357	.976

TABLE III (Continued)

POPULATION 30

X	M	D	F	X	M	D	F	X	M	D	F
.155	5	.622	.935	.200	9	.123	.995	.250	11	.095	.996
	4	.887	.830		8	.249	.985		10	.192	.989
	3	.994	.644		7	.446	.963		9	.345	.975
.160	9	.036	.999		6	.693	.913		8	.552	.944
	8	.090	.997		5	.905	.814		7	.773	.885
	7	.201	.990		4	.991	.665		6	.932	.789
	6	.394	.972	.210	11	.030	.999		5	.992	.666
.160	5	.663	.924		10	.073	.997	.260	13	.023	.999
	4	.910	.811		9	.157	.992		12	.056	.998
	3	.996	.624		8	.303	.980		11	.121	.994
.165	9	.043	.999		7	.515	.952		10	.233	.986
	8	.105	.996		6	.758	.892		9	.402	.967
	7	.227	.988		5	.938	.782		8	.616	.930
	6	.431	.967		4	.995	.634		7	.823	.864
	5	.702	.913	.220	11	.041	.999		6	.954	.763
	4	.930	.792		10	.095	.996		5	.995	.641
	3	.997	.606		9	.197	.989	.270	13	.032	.999
.170	10	.019	.999		8	.361	.974		12	.073	.997
	9	.051	.998		7	.585	.938		11	.151	.992
	8	.121	.995		6	.816	.868		10	.279	.981
	7	.254	.986		5	.961	.751		9	.462	.959
	6	.469	.961		4	.998	.606		8	.676	.915
	5	.739	.901	.230	12	.023	.999		7	.866	.841
	4	.946	.773		11	.056	.998		6	.970	.737
	3	.998	.588		10	.123	.994		5	.997	.617
.180	10	.028	.999		9	.242	.985	.280	14	.017	.999
	9	.070	.997		8	.423	.965		13	.042	.998
	8	.158	.993		7	.652	.923		12	.093	.996
	7	.313	.980	.230	6	.864	.842		11	.185	.989
	6	.546	.948		5	.976	.721		10	.329	.976
	5	.806	.874		4	.999	.580		9	.522	.949
	4	.969	.735	.240	12	.031	.999		8	.733	.898
	3	.999	.555		11	.074	.997		7	.901	.818
.190	10	.039	.999		10	.155	.992		6	.981	.712
	9	.094	.996		9	.291	.981		5	.999	.595
	8	.200	.990		8	.487	.955	.290	14	.023	.999
	7	.378	.973		7	.715	.905		13	.055	.998
	6	.621	.932		6	.902	.816		12	.117	.994
	5	.862	.845		5	.986	.693		11	.223	.986
	4	.983	.699		4	.999	.556		10	.382	.969
.200	11	.021	.999	.250	13	.017	.999		9	.582	.937
	10	.054	.998		12	.042	.998		8	.785	.880

TABLE III (Continued).   Finite queuing tables

POPULATION 30

X	M	D	F	X	M	D	F	X	M	D	F
.290	7	.929	.795	.340	16	.016	.999	.420	18	.024	.999
	6	.988	.688		15	.040	.998		17	.056	.997
	5	.999	.575		14	.086	.996		16	.116	.994
.300	14	.031	.999		13	.169	.990		15	.212	.986
	13	.071	.997		12	.296	.979		14	.350	.972
	12	.145	.992		11	.468	.957		13	.521	.948
	11	.266	.982		10	.663	.918		12	.700	.910
.300	10	.437	.962		9	.836	.858		11	.850	.856
	9	.641	.924		8	.947	.778		10	.945	.789
	8	.830	.861		7	.990	.685		9	.986	.713
	7	.950	.771		6	.999	.588		8	.998	.635
	6	.993	.666	.360	16	.029	.999	.440	19	.017	.999
.310	15	.017	.999		15	.065	.997		18	.041	.998
	14	.041	.998		14	.132	.993		17	.087	.996
	13	.090	.996		13	.240	.984		16	.167	.990
	12	.177	.990		12	.392	.967		15	.288	.979
	11	.312	.977		11	.578	.937		14	.446	.960
	10	.494	.953		10	.762	.889		13	.623	.929
	9	.697	.909		9	.902	.821		12	.787	.883
	8	.869	.840		8	.974	.738		11	.906	.824
	7	.966	.749		7	.996	.648		10	.970	.755
	6	.996	.645	.380	17	.020	.999		9	.994	.681
.320	15	.023	.999		16	.048	.998		8	.999	.606
	14	.054	.998		15	.101	.995	.460	19	.028	.999
	13	.113	.994		14	.191	.988		18	.064	.997
	12	.213	.987		13	.324	.975		17	.129	.993
	11	.362	.971		12	.496	.952		16	.232	.985
	10	.552	.943		11	.682	.914		15	.375	.970
	9	.748	.893	.380	10	.843	.857		14	.545	.944
	8	.901	.820		9	.945	.784		13	.717	.906
	7	.977	.727		8	.988	.701		12	.857	.855
	6	.997	.625		7	.999	.614		11	.945	.793
.330	15	.030	.999	.400	17	.035	.999		10	.985	.724
	14	.068	.997		16	.076	.996		9	.997	.652
	13	.139	.993		15	.150	.992	.480	20	.019	.999
	12	.253	.983		14	.264	.982		19	.046	.998
	11	.414	.965		13	.420	.964		18	.098	.995
	10	.608	.931		12	.601	.933		17	.184	.989
	9	.795	.876		11	.775	.886		16	.310	.977
	8	.927	.799		10	.903	.823		15	.470	.957
	7	.985	.706		9	.972	.748		14	.643	.926
	6	.999	.606		8	.995	.666		13	.799	.881

TABLE III (Continued)

POPULATION 30

X	M	D	F	X	M	D	F	X	M	D	F
.480	12	.910	.826	.560	19	.215	.986	.650	16	.949	.818
	11	.970	.762		18	.352	.973		15	.983	.769
	10	.993	.694		17	.516	.952		14	.996	.718
	9	.999	.625		16	.683	.920		13	.999	.667
.500	20	.032	.999		15	.824	.878	.700	25	.039	.998
	19	.072	.997		14	.920	.828		24	.096	.995
	18	.143	.992		13	.972	.772		23	.196	.989
.500	17	.252	.983		12	.993	.714		22	.339	.977
	16	.398	.967		11	.999	.655		21	.511	.958
	15	.568	.941	.580	23	.014	.999		20	.681	.930
	14	.733	.904		22	.038	.998		19	.821	.894
	13	.865	.854		21	.085	.996		18	.916	.853
	12	.947	.796		20	.167	.990		17	.967	.808
	11	.985	.732		19	.288	.980		16	.990	.762
	10	.997	.667		18	.443	.963		15	.997	.714
.520	21	.021	.999		17	.612	.936	.750	26	.046	.998
	20	.051	.998		16	.766	.899		25	.118	.994
	19	.108	.994		15	.883	.854		24	.240	.986
	18	.200	.988		14	.953	.802		23	.405	.972
	17	.331	.975		13	.985	.746		22	.587	.950
	16	.493	.954		12	.997	.690		21	.752	.920
	15	.663	.923		11	.999	.632		20	.873	.883
	14	.811	.880	.600	23	.024	.999		19	.946	.842
	13	.915	.827		22	.059	.997		18	.981	.799
	12	.971	.767		21	.125	.993		17	.995	.755
	11	.993	.705		20	.230	.986		16	.999	.711
	10	.999	.641		19	.372	.972	.800	27	.053	.998
.540	21	.035	.999		18	.538	.949		26	.143	.993
	20	.079	.996	.600	17	.702	.918		25	.292	.984
	19	.155	.991		16	.837	.877		24	.481	.966
	18	.270	.981		15	.927	.829		23	.670	.941
	17	.421	.965		14	.974	.776		22	.822	.909
	16	.590	.938		13	.993	.722		21	.919	.872
	15	.750	.901		12	.999	.667		20	.970	.832
	14	.874	.854	.650	24	.031	.999		19	.991	.791
	13	.949	.799		23	.076	.996		18	.998	.750
	12	.985	.740		22	.158	.991	.850	28	.055	.998
	11	.997	.679		21	.281	.982		27	.171	.993
	10	.999	.617		20	.439	.965		26	.356	.981
.560	22	.023	.999		19	.610	.940		25	.571	.960
	21	.056	.997		18	.764	.906		24	.760	.932
	20	.117	.994		17	.879	.865		23	.888	.899

TABLE III (Continued).   Finite queuing tables

POPULATION 30

X	M	D	F	X	M	D	F	X	M	D	F
.850	22	.957	.862	.900	26	.683	.953	.950	28	.574	.973
	21	.987	.823		25	.856	.923		27	.831	.945
	20	.997	.784		24	.947	.888		26	.951	.912
	19	.999	.745		23	.985	.852		25	.989	.877
.900	29	.047	.999		22	.996	.815		24	.998	.842
	28	.200	.992		21	.999	.778				
	27	.441	.977	.950	29	.226	.993				

TABLE IV.   Table of random digits*

78466	83326	96589	88727	72655	49682	82338	28583	01522	11248
78722	47603	03477	29528	63956	01255	29840	32370	18032	82051
06401	87397	72898	32441	88861	71803	55626	77847	29925	76106
04754	14489	39420	94211	58042	43184	60977	74801	05931	73822
97118	06774	87743	60156	38037	16201	35137	54513	68023	34380
71923	49313	59713	95710	05975	64982	79253	93876	33707	84956
78870	77328	09637	67080	49168	75290	50175	34312	82593	76606
61208	17172	33187	92523	69895	28284	77956	45877	08044	58292
05033	24214	74232	33769	06304	54676	70026	41957	40112	66451
95983	13391	30369	51035	17042	11729	88647	70541	36026	23113
19946	55448	75049	24541	43007	11975	31797	05373	45893	25665
03580	67206	09635	84612	62611	86724	77411	99415	58901	86160
56823	49819	20283	22272	00114	92007	24369	00543	05417	92251
87633	31761	99865	31488	49947	06060	32083	47944	00449	06550
95152	10133	52693	22480	50336	49502	06296	76414	18358	05313
05639	24175	79438	92151	57602	03590	25465	54780	79098	73594
65927	55525	67270	22907	55097	63177	34119	94216	84861	10457
59005	29000	38395	80367	34112	41866	30170	84658	84441	03926
06626	42682	91522	45955	23263	09764	26824	82936	16813	13878
11306	02732	34189	04228	58541	72573	89071	58066	67159	29633
45143	56545	94617	42752	31209	14380	81477	36952	44934	97435
97612	87175	22613	84175	96413	83336	12408	89318	41713	90669
97035	62442	06940	45719	39918	60274	54353	54497	29789	82928
62498	00257	19179	06313	07900	46733	21413	63627	48734	92174
80306	19257	18690	54653	07263	19894	89909	76415	57246	02621
84114	84884	50129	68942	93264	72344	98794	16791	83861	32007
58437	88807	92141	88677	02864	02052	62843	21692	21373	29408
15702	53457	54258	47485	23399	71692	56806	70801	41548	94809
59966	41287	87001	26462	94000	28457	09469	80416	05897	87970
43641	05920	81346	02507	25349	93370	02064	62719	45740	62080
25501	50113	44600	87433	00683	79107	22315	42162	25516	98434
98294	08491	25251	26737	00071	45090	68628	64390	42684	94956
52582	89985	37863	60788	27412	47502	71577	13542	31077	13353
26510	83622	12546	00489	89304	15550	09482	07504	64588	92562
24755	71543	31667	83624	27085	65905	32386	30775	19689	41437
38399	88796	58856	18220	51016	04976	54062	49109	95563	48244
18889	87814	52232	58244	95206	05947	26622	01381	28744	38374
51774	89694	02654	63161	54622	31113	51160	29015	64730	07750
88375	37710	61619	69820	13131	90406	45206	06386	06398	68652
10416	70345	93307	87360	53452	61179	46845	91521	32430	74795
99258	03778	54674	51499	13659	36434	84760	76446	64026	97534
58923	18319	95092	11840	87646	85330	58143	42023	28972	30657
39407	41126	44469	78889	54462	38609	58555	69793	27258	11296
29372	70781	19554	95559	63088	35845	60162	21228	48296	05006
07287	76846	92658	21985	00872	11513	24443	44320	37737	97360
07089	02948	03699	71255	13944	86597	89052	88899	03553	42145
35757	37447	29860	04546	28742	27773	10215	09774	43426	22961
58797	70878	78167	91942	15108	37441	99254	27121	92358	94254
32281	97860	23029	61409	81887	02050	63060	45246	46312	30378
93531	08514	30244	34641	29820	72126	62419	93233	26537	21179

TABLE IV (Continued).   Table of random digits

03689	33090	43465	96789	56688	32389	88206	06534	10558	14478
43367	46409	44751	73410	35138	24910	70748	57336	56043	68550
45357	52080	62670	73877	20604	40408	98060	96733	65094	80335
62683	03171	77195	92515	78041	27590	42651	00254	73179	10159
04841	40918	69047	68986	08150	87984	08887	76083	37702	28523
85963	06992	65321	43521	46393	40491	06028	43865	58190	28142
03720	78942	61990	90812	98452	74098	69738	83272	39212	42817
10159	85560	35619	58248	65498	77977	02896	45198	10655	13973
80162	35686	57877	19552	63931	44171	40879	94532	17828	31848
74388	92906	65829	24572	79417	38460	96294	79201	47755	90980
12660	09571	29743	45447	64063	46295	44191	53957	62393	42229
81852	60620	87757	72165	23875	87844	84038	04994	93466	27418
03068	61317	65305	64944	27319	55263	84514	38374	11657	67723
29623	58530	17274	16908	39253	37595	57497	74780	88624	93333
30520	50588	51231	83816	01075	33098	81308	59036	49152	86262
93694	02984	91350	33929	41724	32403	42566	14232	55085	65628
86736	40641	37958	25415	19922	65966	98044	39583	26828	50919
28141	15630	37675	52545	24813	22075	05142	15374	84533	12933
79804	05165	21620	98400	55290	71877	60052	46320	79055	45913
63763	49985	88853	70681	52762	17670	62337	12199	44123	37993
49618	47068	63331	62675	51788	58283	04295	72904	05378	98085
26502	68980	26545	14204	34304	50284	47730	57299	73966	02566
13549	86048	27912	56733	14987	09850	78217	85168	09538	92347
89221	78076	40306	34045	52557	52383	67796	41382	50490	30117
97809	34056	76778	60417	05153	83827	67369	08602	56163	28793
65668	44694	34151	51741	11484	13226	49516	17391	39956	34839
53653	59804	59051	95074	38307	99546	32962	26962	86252	50704
34922	95041	17398	32789	26860	55536	82415	82911	42208	62725
74880	65198	61357	90209	71543	71114	94868	05645	44154	72254
66036	48794	30021	92601	21615	16952	18433	44903	51322	90379
39044	99503	11442	81344	57068	74662	90382	59433	48440	38146
87756	71151	68543	08358	10183	06432	97482	90301	76114	83778
47117	45575	29524	02522	08041	70698	80260	73588	86415	72523
71572	02109	96722	21684	64331	71644	18933	32801	11644	12364
35609	58072	63209	48429	53108	59173	55337	22445	85940	43707
81703	70069	74981	12197	48426	77365	26769	65078	27849	41311
88979	88161	56531	46443	47148	42773	18601	38532	22594	12395
90279	42308	00380	17181	38757	09071	89804	15232	99007	39495
49266	18921	06498	88005	72736	81848	92716	96279	94582	22792
50897	22569	48402	80376	65470	19157	49729	19615	79087	47039
20950	65643	52280	37103	66977	65141	18522	39333	59824	73084
32686	51645	11382	75341	03189	94128	06275	22345	86856	77394
72525	65092	65086	47094	14781	61486	61895	85698	53028	61682
70502	57550	29699	36797	35862	90894	93217	96158	94321	12012
63087	03802	03142	72582	44267	56028	01576	69840	67727	77419
16418	07903	74344	89861	62952	49362	86210	65676	96617	38081
67730	17532	39489	28035	13415	83494	26750	01440	01161	16346
27274	98848	59506	28124	33596	89623	21006	94898	03550	88629
44250	52829	22614	21323	28597	66402	15425	39845	01823	19639
57476	33687	81784	05811	66625	17690	46170	93914	82346	82851

TABLE V. Cumulative Poisson distribution for selected values of the mean, m*

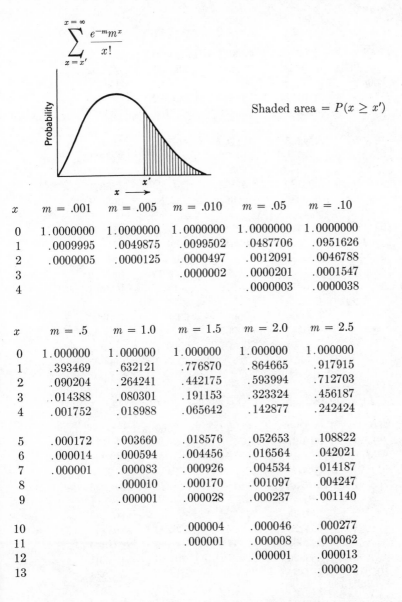

$$\sum_{x=x'}^{x=\infty} \frac{e^{-m}m^x}{x!}$$

Shaded area $= P(x \geq x')$

x	$m = .001$	$m = .005$	$m = .010$	$m = .05$	$m = .10$
0	1.0000000	1.0000000	1.0000000	1.0000000	1.0000000
1	.0009995	.0049875	.0099502	.0487706	.0951626
2	.0000005	.0000125	.0000497	.0012091	.0046788
3			.0000002	.0000201	.0001547
4				.0000003	.0000038

x	$m = .5$	$m = 1.0$	$m = 1.5$	$m = 2.0$	$m = 2.5$
0	1.000000	1.000000	1.000000	1.000000	1.000000
1	.393469	.632121	.776870	.864665	.917915
2	.090204	.264241	.442175	.593994	.712703
3	.014388	.080301	.191153	.323324	.456187
4	.001752	.018988	.065642	.142877	.242424
5	.000172	.003660	.018576	.052653	.108822
6	.000014	.000594	.004456	.016564	.042021
7	.000001	.000083	.000926	.004534	.014187
8		.000010	.000170	.001097	.004247
9		.000001	.000028	.000237	.001140
10			.000004	.000046	.000277
11			.000001	.000008	.000062
12				.000001	.000013
13					.000002

*Extracted from E. C. Molina, *Poisson's Exponential Binomial Limit*, D. Van Nostrand, Inc., New York, 1942, with the permission of the Bell Laboratories.

TABLE V (Continued). Cumulative Poisson distribution for selected values of the mean, m

x	m = 3.0	m = 3.5	m = 4.0	m = 4.5	m = 5.0
0	1.000000	1.000000	1.000000	1.000000	1.000000
1	.950213	.969803	.981684	.988891	.993262
2	.800852	.864112	.908422	.938901	.959572
3	.576810	.679153	.761897	.826422	.875348
4	.352768	.463367	.566530	.657704	.734974
5	.184737	.274555	.371163	.467896	.559507
6	.083918	.142386	.214870	.297070	.384039
7	.033509	.065288	.110674	.168949	.237817
8	.011905	.026739	.051134	.086586	.133372
9	.003803	.009874	.021363	.040257	.068094
10	.001102	.003315	.008132	.017093	.031828
11	.000292	.001019	.002840	.006669	.013695
12	.000071	.000289	.000915	.002404	.005453
13	.000016	.000076	.000274	.000805	.002019
14	.000003	.000019	.000076	.000252	.000698
15	.000001	.000004	.000020	.000074	.000226
16		.000001	.000005	.000020	.000069
17			.000001	.000005	.000020
18				.000001	.000005
19					.000001

x	m = 5.5	m = 6.0	m = 6.5	m = 7.0	m = 7.5
0	1.000000	1.000000	1.000000	1.000000	1.000000
1	.995913	.997521	.998497	.999088	.999447
2	.973436	.982649	.988724	.992705	.995299
3	.911624	.938031	.956964	.970364	.979743
4	.798301	.848796	.888150	.918235	.940855
5	.642482	.714943	.776328	.827008	.867938
6	.471081	.554320	.630959	.699292	.758564
7	.313964	.393697	.473476	.550289	.621845
8	.190515	.256020	.327242	.401286	.475361
9	.105643	.152763	.208427	.270909	.338033
10	.053777	.083924	.122616	.169504	.223592
11	.025251	.042621	.066839	.098521	.137762
12	.010988	.020092	.033880	.053350	.079241
13	.004451	.008827	.016027	.027000	.042666
14	.001685	.003628	.007100	.012811	.021565

TABLE V (Continued)

x	$m = 5.5$	$m = 6.0$	$m = 6.5$	$m = 7.0$	$m = 7.5$
15	.000599	.001400	.002956	.005717	.010260
16	.000200	.000509	.001160	.002407	.004608
17	.000063	.000175	.000430	.000958	.001959
18	.000019	.000057	.000151	.000362	.000790
19	.000005	.000018	.000051	.000130	.000303
20	.000001	.000005	.000016	.000044	.000111
21		.000001	.000005	.000014	.000039
22			.000001	.000005	.000013
23				.000001	.000004
24					.000001

x	$m = 8.0$	$m = 9.0$	$m = 10.0$	$m = 11.0$	$m = 12.0$
0	1.000000	1.000000	1.000000	1.000000	1.000000
1	.999665	.999877	.999955	.999983	.999994
2	.996981	.998766	.999501	.999800	.999920
3	.986246	.993768	.997231	.998789	.999478
4	.957620	.978774	.989664	.995084	.997708
5	.900368	.945036	.970747	.984895	.992400
6	.808764	.884309	.932914	.962480	.979659
7	.686626	.793819	.869859	.921386	.954178
8	.547039	.676103	.779779	.856808	.910496
9	.407453	.544347	.667180	.768015	.844972
10	.283376	.412592	.542070	.659489	.757608
11	.184114	.294012	.416960	.540111	.652771
12	.111924	.196992	.303224	.420733	.538403
13	.063797	.124227	.208444	.311303	.424035
14	.034181	.073851	.135536	.218709	.318464
15	.017257	.041466	.083458	.145956	.227975
16	.008231	.022036	.048740	.092604	.155584
17	.003718	.011106	.027042	.055924	.101291
18	.001594	.005320	.014278	.032191	.062966
19	.000650	.002426	.007187	.017687	.037417
20	.000253	.001056	.003454	.009289	.021280
21	.000094	.000439	.001588	.004671	.011598
22	.000033	.000175	.000700	.002252	.006065
23	.000011	.000067	.000296	.001042	.003047
24	.000004	.000025	.000120	.000464	.001473

TABLE V (Continued). Cumulative Poisson distribution for selected values of the mean, m

x	m = 8.0	m = 9.0	m = 10.0	m = 11.0	m = 12.0
25	.000001	.000009	.000047	.000199	.000686
26		.000003	.000018	.000082	.000308
27		.000001	.000006	.000033	.000133
28			.000002	.000013	.000056
29			.000001	.000005	.000023
30				.000002	.000009
31				.000001	.000003
32					.000001

x	m = 13.0	m = 14.0	m = 15.0	m = 16	m = 17
0	1.000000	1.000000	—	—	—
1	.999998	.999999	1.000000	1.000000	1.000000
2	.999968	.999988	.999995	.999998	.999999
3	.999777	.999906	.999961	.999984	.999993
4	.998950	.999526	.999789	.999907	.999959
5	.996260	.998195	.999143	.999600	.999815
6	.989266	.994468	.997208	.998616	.999325
7	.974113	.985772	.992368	.995994	.997938
8	.945972	.968380	.981998	.990000	.994567
9	.900242	.937945	.962554	.978013	.987404
10	.834188	.890601	.930146	.956702	.973875
11	.748318	.824319	.881536	.922604	.950876
12	.646835	.739960	.815248	.873007	.915331
13	.536895	.641542	.732389	.806878	.864976
14	.426955	.535552	.636782	.725489	.799127
15	.324868	.429563	.534346	.632473	.719167
16	.236393	.330640	.431910	.533255	.628546
17	.164507	.244082	.335877	.434038	.532262
18	.109535	.172799	.251141	.340656	.435977
19	.069833	.117357	.180528	.257651	.345042
20	.042669	076505	.124781	.187751	.263678
21	.025012	.047908	.082971	.131832	.194519
22	.014081	.028844	.053106	.089227	.138534
23	.007622	.016712	.032744	.058241	.095272
24	.003972	.009328	.019465	.036686	.063296

TABLE V (Continued)

x	m = 13.0	m = 14.0	m = 15.0	m = 16	m = 17
25	.001994	.005020	.011165	.022315	.040646
26	.000966	.002608	.006185	.013119	.025245
27	.000452	.001309	.003312	.007459	.015174
28	.000204	.000635	.001716	.004105	.008834
29	.000089	.000298	.000861	.002189	.004984
30	.000038	.000136	.000418	.001131	.002727
31	.000016	.000060	.000197	.000567	.001448
32	.000006	.000026	.000090	.000276	.000747
33	.000002	.000011	.000040	.000131	.000375
34	.000001	.000004	.000017	.000060	.000183
35		.000002	.000007	.000027	.000087
36		.000001	.000003	.000012	.000040
37			.000001	.000005	.000018
38				.000002	.000008
39				.000001	.000003
40					.000001
41					.000001

x	m = 18	m = 19	m = 20	m = 21	m = 22
2	1.000000	1.000000	—	—	—
3	.999997	.999999	1.000000	1.000000	1.000000
4	.999982	.999992	.999997	.999999	.999999
5	.999916	.999962	.999983	.999993	.999997
6	.999676	.999846	.999928	.999967	.999985
7	.998957	.999480	.999745	.999876	.999941
8	.997107	.998487	.999221	.999605	.999803
9	.992944	.996127	.997913	.998894	.999423
10	.984619	.991144	.995005	.997234	.998495
11	.969634	.981678	.989188	.993749	.996453
12	.945113	.965327	.978613	.987095	.992370
13	.908331	.939439	.960988	.975451	.984884
14	.857402	.901601	.933872	.956641	.972215
15	.791923	.850250	.895136	.928426	.952307
16	.713347	.785206	.843487	.888925	.923108
17	.624950	.707966	.778926	.837081	.882960
18	.531352	.621639	.702972	.773037	.831004
19	.437755	.530516	.618578	.698320	.767502

TABLE V (Continued).   Cumulative Poisson distribution for selected values of the mean, m

x	$m = 18$	$m = 19$	$m = 20$	$m = 21$	$m = 22$
20	.349084	.439393	.529743	.615737	.693973
21	.269280	.352826	.440907	.529026	.613091
22	.200876	.274503	.356302	.442314	.528358
23	.144910	.206861	.279389	.359544	.443625
24	.101110	.150983	.212507	.283971	.362576
25	.068260	.106746	.156773	.217845	.288281
26	.044608	.073126	.112185	.162299	.222901
27	.028234	.048557	.077887	.117435	.167580
28	.017318	.031268	.052481	.082541	.122503
29	.010300	.019536	.034334	.056370	.087086
30	.005944	.011850	.021818	.037419	.060217
31	.003331	.006982	.013475	.024153	.040514
32	.001813	.003998	.008092	.015166	.026531
33	.000960	.002227	.004727	.009269	.016918
34	.000494	.001207	.002688	.005516	.010509
35	.000248	.000637	.001489	.003198	.006362
36	.000121	.000327	.000804	.001807	.003755
37	.000058	.000164	.000423	.000996	.002162
38	.000027	.000080	.000217	.000536	.001215
39	.000012	.000038	.000109	.000281	.000667
40	.000005	.000018	.000053	.000144	.000357
41	.000002	.000008	.000025	.000072	.000187
42	.000001	.000004	.000012	.000035	.000096
43		.000002	.000005	.000017	.000048
44		.000001	.000002	.000008	.000024
45			.000001	.000004	.000011
46				.000002	.000005
47				.000001	.000002
48					.000001

TABLE VI.   The negative exponential distribution

Unitized negative exponential distribution where the mean and standard deviation are equal to one ($\mu = \sigma = 1$). Table values indicate the probability that a given value of x, x', will be exceeded. Alternately, in the context of continuous discount functions, the table values indicate the continuous discount factor for given values of rt, where r is the rate of discount and t is the number of periods.

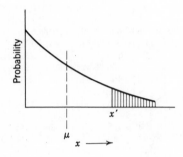

x'/μ or rt	Value of e^{-x} or e^{-rt}	x'/μ or rt	Value of e^{-x} or e^{-rt}	x'/μ or rt	Value of e^{-x} or e^{-rt}	x'/μ or rt	Value of e^{-x} or e^{-rt}
.00	1.000	.20	.819	.80	.449	2.30	.100
.01	.990	.21	.811	.85	.427	2.40	.091
.02	.980	.22	.803	.90	.407	2.50	.082
.03	.970	.23	.795	.95	.387	2.60	.074
.04	.961	.24	.787	1.00	.368	2.70	.067
.05	.951	.25	.779	1.05	.350	2.80	.061
.06	.942	.26	.771	1.10	.333	2.90	.055
.07	.932	.27	.763	1.15	.317	3.00	.050
.08	.923	.28	.756	1.20	.301	3.10	.045
.09	.914	.29	.748	1.25	.287	3.20	.041
.10	.905	.30	.741	1.30	.273	3.40	.033
.11	.896	.35	.705	1.40	.247	3.60	.027
.12	.887	.40	.670	1.50	.223	3.80	.022
.13	.878	.45	.638	1.60	.202	4.00	.018
.14	.869	.50	.607	1.70	.183	4.20	.015
.15	.861	.55	.577	1.80	.165	4.40	.012
.16	.852	.60	.549	1.90	.150	4.60	.010
.17	.844	.65	.522	2.00	.135	4.80	.008
.18	.835	.70	.497	2.10	.122	5.00	.007
.19	.827	.75	.472	2.20	.111	5.50	.004
						6.00	.002

TABLE VII. PV$_{sp}$, present value factors for future single payments

(Years, ← Periods
Months,
¼'s, etc)

Years Hence	1%	2%	4%	6%	8%	10%	12%	14%	15%	16%	18%	20%
1	0.990	0.980	0.962	0.943	0.926	0.909	0.893	0.877	0.870	0.862	0.847	0.833
2	0.980	0.961	0.925	0.890	0.857	0.826	0.797	0.769	0.756	0.743	0.718	0.694
3	0.971	0.942	0.889	0.840	0.794	0.751	0.712	0.675	0.658	0.641	0.609	0.579
4	0.961	0.924	0.855	0.792	0.735	0.683	0.636	0.592	0.572	0.552	0.516	0.482
5	0.951	0.906	0.822	0.747	0.681	0.621	0.567	0.519	0.497	0.476	0.437	0.402
6	0.942	0.888	0.790	0.705	0.630	0.564	0.507	0.456	0.432	0.410	0.370	0.335
7	0.933	0.871	0.760	0.665	0.583	0.513	0.452	0.400	0.376	0.354	0.314	0.279
8	0.923	0.853	0.731	0.627	0.540	0.467	0.404	0.351	0.327	0.305	0.266	0.233
9	0.914	0.837	0.703	0.592	0.500	0.424	0.361	0.308	0.284	0.263	0.225	0.194
10	0.905	0.820	0.676	0.558	0.463	0.386	0.322	0.270	0.247	0.227	0.191	0.162
11	0.896	0.804	0.650	0.527	0.429	0.350	0.287	0.237	0.215	0.195	0.162	0.135
12	0.887	0.788	0.625	0.497	0.397	0.319	0.257	0.208	0.187	0.168	0.137	0.112
13	0.879	0.773	0.601	0.469	0.368	0.290	0.229	0.182	0.163	0.145	0.116	0.093
14	0.870	0.758	0.577	0.442	0.340	0.263	0.205	0.160	0.141	0.125	0.099	0.078
15	0.861	0.743	0.555	0.417	0.315	0.239	0.183	0.140	0.123	0.108	0.084	0.065
16	0.853	0.728	0.534	0.394	0.292	0.218	0.163	0.123	0.107	0.093	0.071	0.054
17	0.844	0.714	0.513	0.371	0.270	0.198	0.146	0.108	0.093	0.080	0.060	0.045
18	0.836	0.700	0.494	0.350	0.250	0.180	0.130	0.095	0.081	0.069	0.051	0.038
19	0.828	0.686	0.475	0.331	0.232	0.164	0.116	0.083	0.070	0.060	0.043	0.031
20	0.820	0.673	0.456	0.312	0.215	0.149	0.104	0.073	0.061	0.051	0.037	0.026
21	0.811	0.660	0.439	0.294	0.199	0.135	0.093	0.064	0.053	0.044	0.031	0.022
22	0.803	0.647	0.422	0.278	0.184	0.123	0.083	0.056	0.046	0.038	0.026	0.018
23	0.795	0.634	0.406	0.262	0.170	0.112	0.074	0.049	0.040	0.033	0.022	0.015
24	0.788	0.622	0.390	0.247	0.158	0.102	0.066	0.043	0.035	0.028	0.019	0.013
25	0.780	0.610	0.375	0.233	0.146	0.092	0.059	0.038	0.030	0.024	0.016	0.010

TABLE VIII. PV$_a$, *present value factors for annuities*

Years (n)	1%	2%	4%	6%	8%	10%	12%	14%	15%	16%	18%	20%
1	0.990	0.980	0.962	0.943	0.926	0.909	0.893	0.877	0.870	0.862	0.847	0.833
2	1.970	1.942	1.886	1.833	1.783	1.736	1.690	1.647	1.626	1.605	1.566	1.528
3	2.941	2.884	2.775	2.673	2.577	2.487	2.402	2.322	2.283	2.246	2.174	2.106
4	3.902	3.808	3.630	3.465	3.312	3.170	3.037	2.914	2.855	2.798	2.690	2.589
5	4.853	4.713	4.452	4.212	3.993	3.791	3.605	3.433	3.352	3.274	3.127	2.991
6	5.795	5.601	5.242	4.917	4.623	4.355	4.111	3.889	3.784	3.685	3.498	3.326
7	6.728	6.472	6.002	5.582	5.206	4.868	4.564	4.288	4.160	4.039	3.812	3.605
8	7.652	7.325	6.733	6.210	5.747	5.335	4.968	4.639	4.487	4.344	4.078	3.837
9	8.566	8.162	7.435	6.802	6.247	5.759	5.328	4.946	4.772	4.607	4.303	4.031
10	9.471	8.983	8.111	7.360	6.710	6.145	5.650	5.216	5.019	4.833	4.494	4.192
11	10.368	9.787	8.760	7.887	7.139	6.495	5.988	5.453	5.234	5.029	4.656	4.327
12	11.255	10.575	9.385	8.384	7.536	6.814	6.194	5.660	5.421	5.197	4.793	4.439
13	12.134	11.343	9.986	8.853	7.904	7.103	6.424	5.842	5.583	5.342	4.910	4.533
14	13.004	12.106	10.563	9.295	8.244	7.367	6.628	6.002	5.724	5.468	5.008	4.611
15	13.865	12.849	11.118	9.712	8.559	7.606	6.811	6.142	5.847	5.575	5.092	4.675
16	14.718	13.578	11.652	10.106	8.851	7.824	6.974	6.265	5.954	5.669	5.162	4.730
17	15.562	14.292	12.166	10.477	9.122	8.022	7.120	6.373	6.047	5.749	5.222	4.775
18	16.398	14.992	12.659	10.828	9.372	8.201	7.250	6.467	6.128	5.818	5.273	4.812
19	17.226	15.678	13.134	11.158	9.604	8.365	7.366	6.550	6.198	5.877	5.316	4.844
20	18.046	16.351	13.590	11.470	9.818	8.514	7.469	6.623	6.259	5.929	5.353	4.870
21	18.857	17.011	14.029	11.764	10.017	8.649	7.562	6.687	6.312	5.973	5.384	4.891
22	19.660	17.658	14.451	12.042	10.201	8.772	7.645	6.743	6.359	6.011	5.410	4.909
23	20.456	18.292	14.857	12.303	10.371	8.883	7.718	6.792	6.399	6.044	5.432	4.925
24	21.243	18.914	15.247	12.550	10.529	8.985	7.784	6.835	6.434	6.073	5.451	4.937
25	22.023	19.523	15.622	12.783	10.675	9.077	7.843	6.873	6.464	6.097	5.467	4.948

· INDEX